Shore Establishments of the Royal Navy

Shore Establishments of the Royal Navy

Being a list of the Static Ships and Establishments of the Royal Navy

Compiled by
Lt. Cdr. B. Warlow, R.N.

Maritime Books

Published by Maritime Books,
Lodge Hill, Liskeard, Cornwall

First edition 1992
Second edition 2000

ISBN 0 907771 73 4

Typeset and printed in Great Britain by
Penwell Limited, Callington, Cornwall

Contents

Author's Preface

My initial interest in shore establishments came about whilst I was compiling lists of seagoing ships, and found some names which did not seem to fit. Further research usually revealed these to be shore establishments - or, as they are known in the Service - "Stone Frigates". The traditional names were straightforward (DRAKE, CAMBRIDGE etc), but not all were so simple. The main difficulty was that many shore establishments were originally ships that were hulked to become training or accommodation centres (GANGES etc). A further complication was that, prior to 1 January 1959, the Naval Discipline Act only applied to those officers and men who were borne on the books of one of His/Her Majesty's Ships of war. Thus all personnel were allocated to a nominal ship when not actually serving in a proper seagoing warship. At the turn of the century these shore establishments were mainly old hulks and the original ship names were taken into use. When other ships/hulks were added to increase the capacity, the newly joined ship was given the first ship's name, but with an additional suffix (e.g. PERSEUS became DEFIANCE II) In some cases the original hulk was given the suffix 'II' when another hulk replaced it but the original hulk was retained in use (e.g. GANGES II). Indeed, GANGES II continued alone after her replacement as GANGES had departed.

In some instances, especially Air Stations, the suffix was used to indicate a satellite establishment at another location - e.g. HERON II. Similarly with PEMBROKE X which was many miles from PEMBROKE. Sometimes the suffix just indicated a separate ledger section contained within the main establishment (DRAKE X, VICTORY III - although at times these sections were sometimes moved out of the main establishment). Sometimes the suffix indicated a shore establishment which came under a flagship afloat, so that when the flagship changed, the shore establishment name changed too (i.e. at Aden, EFFINGHAM III became HAWKINS III and then NORFOLK III. Occasionally there appear to be gaps, as DRAKE X would indicate there was a DRAKE IX, but this does not always seem to follow.

At one stage - April 1941 - a policy was laid down that Coastal Forces Bases would bear the name of the parent establishment of the port with a suffix - i.e. MINOS II, but bases already extant would retain the names they already held (HORNET).

Later, when proper shore accommodation was provided, a ship was nominated to carry the establishment name, and later, even small craft were used for this purpose. Thus a 27 feet long Montagu whaler was notionally crewed by hundreds of officers and men. This nominal ship would sometimes have to alter, for example, when the nominal ship itself had to be broken up, or was sunk. At other times it had to change for practical reasons. The trawler bearing the depot ship name PEMBROKE was sent to mine-sweep off Swansea in 1939, so another vessel nearer Chatham was found to take the name, whilst the trawler reverted to her original name of STOUR.

The provision of a nominal depot ship also created other anomalies. The DOLPHIN was lost whilst under tow; the ST ANGELO was mined; the MANTIS became a constructive total loss, and the FOLIOT was lost by collision. Other losses were the CABOT and HORNET. Even the enemy were confused as they claimed to have sunk the ST ANGELO, and in a way, they were right.

Establishments formed after 1959 (PALATINE, SHERWOOD etc) did not run this risk, having no need for a nominal depot ship, and the Navy List ceased to record these nominal depot ships from 1962.

Not all establishments were named for disciplinary purposes, the ATLANTIC ISLE being named in 1943 so that births and deaths there could be registered.

Perhaps the first real shore establishment was the DIAMOND ROCK. She was on an island - Roche du Diamant - that was taken on 8 January 1804 and was commissioned to guard a stretch of water. Their Lordships actually named it FORT DIAMOND, but the formal notification arrived after the commissioning. She survived 18 months before being captured. It is, perhaps, to this establishment that we owe the term "Stone Frigate" when talking of shore establishments, but the term could well have been more general and coined by the ever resourceful and witty sailor. In World War II the Royal Canadian Navy even commissioned HMCS STONE FRIGATE.

The real problem comes in defining a shore establishment. Queen's Regulations state that the title "Her Majesty's Ship" is confined strictly to commissioned ships flying the White Ensign. There are also definitions of Naval Establishments (paid for out of Navy Votes and therefore coming under the Ministry of Defence (Navy)'s control); Fleet Establishments (Naval Establishments manned by the Royal Navy, Royal Marines, Women's Royal Naval Service or by civilians engaged for Fleet services); Civil Establishments (Naval establishments manned on a civilian basis, e.g. Dockyards, Victualling Yards, Naval Armament Depots etc); Medical establishments (Naval Hospitals and Sick Quarters). However, none of these definitions really clarifies the position of a shore establishment, especially in the days when it has to use the name of a seagoing ship. Thus, in my researches, I have taken the most catholic and broadest definition and have included many names that would appear to be on the fringes of any definition. This includes many depot and repair ships, and some ships that were hulked and used as accommodation ships. Indeed, in this I am going back to the origins of many of the more well known establishments, for EXCELLENT started in that way, a ship employed statically that took over some real estate nearby and then gradually transferred its ''centre' until it was totally above the high water mark. DEFIANCE was another such establishment, for when the last hulks were towed away, both from the Torpedo School in the 1950s, and from the Maintenance Base in the 1970s, shore bases remained. Some were never afloat, like the majority of Naval Air Stations, but were moved from one place to another. Some Depot Ships never seemed to move -"aground on their own pile of tin cans" - but suddenly, when they had become features of the local landscape, did up anchor and confounded their critics. In the case of the battleship IRON DUKE, which was used as base ship at Scapa Flow, she was afloat, but was sunk by enemy air attack, but continued to operate as a base whilst lying on the bottom with her upperworks above water.

Names were selected with the usual care, often reflecting the tasks of the establishment - BEE - a Coastal Forces Base. Sometimes the names were traditional - CAMBRIDGE at Wembury commissioned 100 years to the day after its predecessor. Sometimes the name was selected just because of the original hulk's name (GANGES). Sometimes the first vessel attached to that unit gave it its name (DRYAD). On occasions a local name was used (VECTIS), or a local landmark commemorated (SPHINX), or the name of a vessel with local connections (GALETEA, MALABAR). Sometimes fate took a hand. When the Flower class sloop MARJORAM was selected to become the Drill Ship of the London Reserves on the Thames, she was sent for refit and was lost on the way there. As a result another vessel was nominated for the task, this time the SAXIFRAGE, the common name of that flower being, co-incidentally, London Pride. It is not true to say that names traditionally associated with places continued to be used at that same place. TERROR was at Bermuda in 1857-1918, but nowadays that name is remembered as being at Singapore.

Bird names were used for Air Stations (HERON) - some with local connotations (CHOUGH for Cornwall), and some with other connections (FLEDGLING for a Naval Air Training Establishment). However, the Manx Eagle is called Urley and the Air Station there took that name, but it could also refer to the bird that caught the worm! Other subtle signs of a sense of humour appear, MONSTER in Loch Ness, TORMENTOR as a Training establishment. Confusion could sometimes occur when names were used in more than one place at once (PROTECTOR, RN Netlayer and RCN Base); QUEEN CHARLOTTE - RN Gunnery Range and RCN Depot; COLLINGWOOD - RN Training Establishment and RCN corvette. By 1942 there were three INDEFATIGABLES in the Royal Navy, which led to two being renamed. To add to research difficulties, names would sometimes change their spelling over the years (and between references) (VENDERUTHY/VENDERUTHIE).

There have also been unofficial names - SHEATHBILL in the Falklands, and some clever puns. When the destroyer PORCUPINE was torpedoed and broke in half, each half was taken into use as static accommodation. The sailors dubbed the forward section HMS PORK, and the after section HMS PINE. Names have also been given to training simulators within establishments, some examples are:

ACQUIRED	A workshop replacing harbour training ship at SULTAN July 89
AMETHYST	Bridge simulator DRYAD 96
BOADICEA	Damage Control - PHOENIX February 96
DAMOCLES	Submarine Trainer NEPTUNE to 85, then DRAKE 85-95
HAZARD	Damage Control PHOENIX
HAVOC	Damage Control - RALEIGH
ONPHYR	Submarine Fire Fighting - DOLPHIN
PUGNACIOUS	Submarine Trainer - NEPTUNE 70-11.93
STORM	Submarine Simulator
TACTICIAN	Submarine Trainer NEPTUNE
THRASHER	Submarine Trainer DRAKE 01.96-
TRIUMPH	Damage Control RALEIGH 97
UNIQUE	U Class simulator DOLPHIN
VERACITY	Vanguard Class Submarine Command Team Trainer NEPTUNE 11.93-
VOYAGER	Vanguard Class SSBN Control Room Simulator NEPTUNE

Simulator and Trainer names and names of blocks in establishments have not been included, although unofficial names of establishments have been where known to aid researchers.

Some establishments changes their names (VIVID/DRAKE) and some units started as 'numbers' - usually Naval Parties, but were later named, particularly the MONABs and Port Parties. Naval Parties were, and still are, groups of officers and men formed to fulfil a special task in a location or during an operation, and they could be mobile because of their task (i.e. in a merchant ship) or static. Those parties that were commissioned with a ship name are included. Sometimes they reverted to their Naval Party number when their 'commissioned ship' paid off.

Sometimes a name was selected for a location and was not then used (THISTLE - Bute) (RINALDO - Barry) (RANGER - Middlesbrough). Some names are included to clarify an obscure situation, or just to question whether the name referred to a shore establishment or something else. Unfortunately it has often been the case that the deeper the research, the more questions are raised. Precise dates of commissioning and paying off (decommissioning) have been given where known, but some references are so tenuous/tentative that I have sometimes included a ship name where no other data is available. Often official records are at variance with each other, and with memory, and where options exist, I have again included them for completeness. Regrettably it has not been commercially viable to include all references in the published work, although I have noted them in my manuscript. I have also included Nominal Depot Ships, those vessels bearing the name for the purposes of the Naval Discipline Act, where known. Although it is logical that the shore barracks at Devonport, say, should have such a vessel, it seems strange that the Reserve Fleets when commissioned required one. For example, in 1956 the Reserve Fleet at Portsmouth was called collectively BELLEROPHON, with the Flag borne in the (capable of going to sea) battleship VANGUARD, using as a nominal depot ship the Fast Motor Boat 42407!

Because time has passed and traces of many establishments have disappeared, a gazetteer has been included listing the establishments that were in a town, port or city. Some establishments were in the country, and nearby locations have been used - though several towns could claim allegiance to some Air Stations. In the case of the principal ports, a broad sweep of the establishments in the locality has been made rather than try to differentiate between, say, St Budeaux and Devonport in the Plymouth area - though many could argue that Devonport has been separate since its founding on 1 January 1824. Others could argue that Torpoint, also included in the Plymouth port, being in Cornwall, should be treated separately. However, when, in the case of DEFIANCE, the establishment was in the River Tamar betwixt and between and later was located on both banks of the river, suitable division is hard to arrange. The rationale has been to sweep such establishments in the port area into 'conurbations', which are listed at the front of the gazetteer. The gazetteer has also been used to include notes on unnamed shore establishments, airfields etc.

Abroad, boundaries have changed, countries have altered their names, divided, etc.. India and its subsequent division have been particularly difficult for gazetteer entries. Similarly some counties in the UK have been renamed (Dyfed/Pembrokeshire). Commonwealth Navies ceased to appear in the Navy List in 1980. India, Pakistan and South Africa vanished earlier, whilst the Canadian Forces unified on 1 February 1968 with consequent effects on the naming of their shore bases. Some locations have been difficult to define - there are 14 Newports in the UK - letters addressed to Newport without a county are a headache for the Post Office. To try to simplify the gazetteer, locations have taken the name in use at the time when the establishment existed. It is hoped that no offence will be taken with the result, for no offence is intended, and certainly no disrespect. The gazetteer is included only in the hope that it may be of use and of interest.

In both lists and gazetteer the order is alphabetical, and where 'nothing' comes before 'something' - i.e. SEA EAGLE will come before SEABORN. 'ST.' appears in the position due to its full title of SAINT. Where different spellings exist, there is one master entry, with the others showing cross-references. i.e. 'SEREPTA - see SAREPTA'.

This second edition has taken into account the further researches I have carried out, and the correspondence from readers who have spotted possible omissions or errors. It also includes developments that have occurred over the past few years, often sadly reflecting the dwindling size of the Royal Navy. Doubtless there is yet more research to be carried out, but this list now comprises over 3,100 entries, and I believe contains the majority of the information available. I am grateful to all who have contributed by word of mouth or by letter, both with advice and guidance. My particular thanks go to the staff of the Naval Historical Branch. However, I must assure readers that any errors in fact or interpretation are mine, and mine alone.

Ben Warlow
Burnham-on-Crouch
1999

Abbreviations

Basic abbreviations are not included

Accom Sh	Accommodation Ship
Acs	Accounts
Adty	Admiralty
AES	Admiralty Experimental Station- Note: AMES-Air Ministry Experimental Station - was a cover name for early RDF Stations
AMC	Armed Merchant Cruiser
Ammo	Ammunition
Ann	Announced
ANCXF	Allied Naval C-in-C of the Expeditionary Force
A/P	Auxiliary Patrol
Apps	Appointments
Aux	Auxiliary
BB	Battleship
BCr	Battlecruiser
BD	Boom Defence
BU	Broken Up
C & M	Care and Maintenance
Capt	Captured
Cd	Commissioned
CF	Coastal Forces
CG	Coast Guard (Ship)
Chat	Chatham
CO	Combined Operations
Comb	Combined
Comml	Commercial
Conv	Converted
Cr	Cruiser
Ct	Court
DD(s)	Destroyer(s)
Dev	Devonport
DF	Destroyer Flotilla
DG	Degaussing
Div	Division
Dk	Dock
Drl Sh	Drill Ship
DS	Depot Ship
Estab	Establishment
EVT	Educational & Vocational Training
FAA	Fleet Air Arm
FF	Frigate
Flag	Flagship
Flot	Flotilla
FOBAA	Flag Officer British Assault Area - Op Neptune
Fr	French
Ft	Fort
Gib	Gibraltar
Hbr (Serv)	Harbour (Service)
HK	Hong Kong
HL(D)	Harbour Launch (Diesel)
HL(P)	Harbour Launch (Petrol)
HMCNRS	His/Her Majesty's Canadian Naval Radio Station
Hosp Sh	Hospital Ship
HQ	Headquarters
IN	Indian Navy
LC	Landing Craft
Lch	Launch
Lpool	Liverpool
Maint	Maintenance
MB	Motor Boat
Med	Mediterranean
Ment	Mentioned
ML	Motor Launch
M/L	Minelayer
MNBDO	Mobile Naval Base Defence Organisation Ex Fortress Unit
MOLCAB	Mobile Landing Craft Advanced Base
MONAB	Mobile Naval Air Base
M/S	Mine-sweeper
MWSS	Minor War Signal Station (Run by RM, later by WRNS)
NAB	Naval Auxiliary Boat - vessels under 100 ft long
Nav	Navigation
NAY	Naval Auxiliary Yacht - vessels over 100 ft long
NCSO	Naval Control of Shipping Officer
NL	Navy List
NOIC	Naval Officer in Charge
Nom DS	Nominal Depot Ship
NP	Naval Party
Org	Organisation
PLUTO	Pipe Line Under The Ocean (Op Neptune)

Plym	Plymouth
PN	Pakistan Navy
PO	Paid Off
Ports	Portsmouth
Poss	Possibly
Prob	Probably
Pt	Port
Purch	Purchased
PWSS	Port War Signal Station (RN)
Qtn Sh	Quarantine Ship
RAN	Royal Australian Navy
Rb	Relieved by
RCN	Royal Canadian Navy
Ref	Refers/Reference
Req	Requisitioned
Res	Reserve
RESTO	Restored to Owner
RF	Reserve Fleet
RIN	Royal Indian Navy
RMBPD	Royal Marine Boom Patrol Detachment (ex RHSD)
RNAS	Royal Naval Air Station/Section/Service
RNATE	Royal Naval Apprentice Training Establishment
RNR	Royal Naval Reserve
RPN	Royal Pakistan Navy
Rx Sh	Receiving Ship
SAN	South African Navy
Sch	School
Sel	Selected
SM	Submarine (3 SM is Third Submarine Flotilla/ Squadron)
SO	Senior Officer
Soton	Southampton
Spore	Singapore
Sqn	Squadron
Sta	Station
TAMY	Transportable Aircraft Maintenance Yard
TBD	Torpedo Boat Destroyer(s)
TE	Training Establishment
Temp	Temporary/temporarily
Tlr	Trawler
Torp	Torpedo
Tng	Training
Trinco	Trincomalee
TS	Training Ship
Tx	Transfer/transferred
V	Vice
Yd	Yard
Yt	Yacht

Ship Names

Ships' names in alphabetical order - a date in brackets after a ship's name is its launch date.

Years are expressed in four figures only where clarification of the century is required.

A

ABASTOR Tilbury, PLUTO TE
Cd 01.11.1943, PO 17.10.45
Nom DS: NAB INTERLUDE 01.11.43 - 07.45
HL(P) 43627 07.45-

ABATOS Norfolk House/Rex House, Woolston, PLUTO TE & SNO
Cd 21.09.1943 At Woolston, tender to SHRAPNEL. HQ from Norfolk House to To Rex House 26.11.45, PO 03.46 - some acs say closed 45, no Apps in NL 10.45
Nom DS: NAB GONDOLIER PRINCE 21.09.43-
Ref NP 1678 01.12.45 Norfolk House, 09.12.45-12.46 Rex House.

ABERCROMBIE (1942) Chat/Sheerness, Drl Sh/RF
Monitor, RF Accom Sh Sheerness - 03.06.46, Turret Drl Sh v. EREBUS 02.46-49, SO RF Chat v. AUSONIA 29.06.49-52, BU 12.54

ABERDARE (1918) Malta GC, TS
M/S, hulk as Gunnery Sch for Patrol Service Malta 30.09.44-, sold 13.03.47

ABERDONIAN (1909) Ft William/ Dartmouth, CF DS
Req 26.04.1940. Cd 22.07.40, Temp Maint Ship for A/P MBs Chat 08.40, at Ft William 10.40 - 11.41, at Dartmouth 01.42 - 45, tender to BRITANNIA II, motor craft DS by 07.43, non-mobile status 01.09.44, PO 27.03.45 and tx to DST

ABERFOYLE - see DOLPHIN

ABOUKIR (1807) Chat, Rx Sh
3rd Rate, Rx Sh 06.1824-16.08.1838

ABOUKIR (1848) Jamaica, Rx Sh
2nd Rate, Rx Sh 1861-1877

ABOUKIR Alexandria, Naval Accom Camp
To have been Cd 20.04.1941, but named SPHINX instead.

ACADIA RCN SCC TE
At Point Edward NS, ex PROTECTOR - summer 1956-63, and at Cornwallis NS summer 1964-86 (at least)

ACCRINGTON (1910) Ports, 'Accom Sh'
Hired 12.1915 - 11.18, Demonstration ship for C-in-C Ports 17.04.17-29.11.18, was a rescue ship WW II

ACHERON (1866) Nore, TS for Stokers
NORTHUMBERLAND(qv) was TS for Stokers at Chat and Cd as ACHERON 01.06.1904 - became a hulk in 1909 - task to RNB when space in basin was required for other ships.

ACHILLES (1863).Weymouth/Lpool, CG
Iron Ship, CG ship Portland 01.07.1869-01.04.1875, Lpool 01.04.1875-17.05.77, renamed HIBERNIA 1902 (qv), EGMONT 03.1904 (qv), EGREMONT 06.16 (qv), PEMBROKE 06.19 (qv), sold 26.01.23

ACHILLES (1905) Chat/Ports, Stokers' TS/RF Parent
Cr, TS Chat 1918-19, RF Parent Ports 01.02.19-06.19, then Stokers' TS Ports v. DIADEM 06.19-20 (at least), sold 05.21

ACQUISITION Dundee, Mobile Degaussing Wiping Unit
Drifter (1913) hired as tender 03.1940 and was degaussing vessel 03.41-10.43

ACTAEON (1831) Cork/Ports, Hbr Serv
6th Rate, survey vessel 1856, lent Cork Hbr Board 02.1870 as hulk, tx to Ports 1880, sold there 02.1889

ACTAEON (1832) Ports, Torp Sch Sh
VERNON 4th Rate became Torp Sch Ship 26.04.1876, when replaced by DONEGAL 14.01.1886 renamed ACTAEON and retained Ports till sold 14.09.1923

ACTAEON Sheerness, Torp Sch/A/P Base
– ARIADNE (1859)(qv) to Hbr Serv 1884, renamed ACTAEON 06.06.1905 and Cd as Torp Sch Sheerness, also DS for TBD Sheerness 1910, PO 31.03.1922, sold 11.12.22. When first naval flying sch was established at Eastchurch in 12.1911, all officers and men were borne on the books of ACTAEON. First course started 02.03.1912. Officers and men were tx to books of PEMBROKE II by 06.13.
SHANNON (1906)(qv) attached for a period
Was an A/P Base in WW I

ACTAEON II Sheerness, Torp Sch
DIDO (1869)(qv) renamed ACTAEON II 1906 as Torp Sch, Sheerness, hulk 1921, sold 17.07.22

ACTIVE (1799) Dev, Rx Sh
5th Rate, Rx Sh 02.1826, renamed ARGO 11.1833(qv), BU 10.1860

ACTIVE (1845) Sunderland, Res Drl Sh
5th Rate, Drl Sh Sunderland 1863, renamed TYNE - TS 30.07.1867 (qv), renamed DURHAM 18.11.1867 - Drl Sh Sunderland (qv),1868, then to Leith, sold 12.05.1908

ACTUA Sheerness, Powder Hulk
Floating Battery, powder hulk at Sheerness 1870

ADALVIK Iceland, W/T Sta
Known by that name 10.1942 - not a ship name.

ADAMANT (1911) SM DS
Cd 04.1912, 5 SM Ports 1912, 8 SM Ports Cd 27.04.12, 7 SM Chat 01.14, 8 SM Harwich 07.14, to Med 03.15 (Dardanelles & Brindisi), left Med 09.19 - to Dev PO 22.10.19 to C & M, 2 SM Dev Cd 21.11.19-20, 2 SM Rosyth 01.20, Dev 03.20-21, Portland 03.22-03.23, Ports 24, Med (Malta) 08.25-26, Dev 11.26 - replaced by STUART and sold 09.32

ADAMANT II (1915) SM DS
LILY (1915) renamed VULCAN II 15.10.1923 as Periscope Sch, and then ADAMANT II 1929, Dev till sold 25.06.30

ADAMANT (1940) SM DS
Cd 04.02.1942 - to Colombo - on arrival to be 4 SM but diverted Kilindini as DS surface ships. Later 42 to Trinco but recalled when HECLA lost 11.42. 4SM from ADAMANT to WUCHANG 29.05.43. By 07.43 to Trinco, to Fremantle 4SM 04.45-48. SORF Ports 15.04.48-11.53 (rb MAURITIUS), 3 SM Rothesay/Faslane 05.10.54 v MONTCLARE - 62 - rb MAIDSTONE. 2 SM Dev v FORTH 06.62 - PO 14.02.66 - 2 SM disbanded. Sold 11.09.70

ADMIRABLE Taranto, A/P Parent
Drifter (1914) re 1914, DS Net Drifters by 08.01.17-01.03.17 rb QUEEN (qv) and sunk 15.05.17 in Adriatic. Listed as Trawler DS Adriatic, Taranto 03.18-12.18

ADRIA (1914) Persian Gulf, Base Ship
Taken up for service 02.09.1942, Cd 29.01.43 as Base Ship - renamed GOMBROON (qv) 12.43, laid up 12.45, sold 04.47

ADRIATICO Taranto, A/P DS
05.1916-06.17 - Vessel lent by Italian Government

ADVAR Madras, CF Base WWII
Poss mis-spell of ADYAR (qv)

ADVENTURE (1809) Dev, Storeship
AID, Transport, renamed 05.1821, storeship 1849 - sold 1853

ADVENTURE (1904) SM DS
Cr, conv to seagoing SM DS 1910, sold 03.20

ADVENTURE (1924) Beach Repair Ship
M/L, conv to repair ship 02.44 - 03.44 Lpool, Gold Beach Normandy 06.44-10.44, Ports 10.44-05.45, Cuxhaven 05.45-06.45, then res Ports/Falmouth, BU 06.47
Flag ANXCF 09.09.44 - see ROYAL HENRY

ADYAR Madras, India, RIN Local Naval Defence & CF Base
By 03.10.1943-46

ADYAR Madras, India
In NL 1955 as Naval Base and Pink List from 12.59-76 as Resident Naval Officer

AEGUSA Taranto, Base
12.1943 - one of 6 names sel for bases in Italy, considered for Taranto but not sel

AEOLUS (1825) Ports/ Motherbank, Storeship/Hosp Sh
5th Rate, Storeship Ports 1855, temp Hosp Sh Motherbank 1880, BU 03.1886

AEOLUS (1891) Queenstown, Flag/Guard/Drl Sh
Cr, Flag and Port Guard Queenstown v EMPRESS OF INDIA 1902-03, seagoing RNR Drl Sh Queenstown Cd 19.06.03-05, sold 05.14

AEOLUS Tring, Herts, Kite and Balloon Depot
Cd 01.12.1942, PO 01.03.46
Nom DS: Hbr Lch WINGS OF MORNING 01.12.42-11.45

AEROLITE Brightlingsea, Accom Sh
Yt, taken up for service as Accom Sh 02.04.41, to be RESTO 06.41, released 01.07.41

AETON Normandy, Accom Barge for shore working parties PLUTO
LBV(M) 51, named 04.05.44, conv and Cd 22.06.1944, to DST 12.07.46

AFRICA (1905) Ports, Accom Sh/TS
BB, PO 07.11.1918, Cd as overflow ship 02.12.18 - PO by 09.19. Stokers' TS 01.20-03.20, sold 06.20

AFRIKANDER Simonstown, S Africa, Base
Cd 20.08.1914, Tx to S Africa 15.06.23-04.11.32 (RN Base then FLORA (qv)), returned to RN, 02.04.57 tx to Youngsfield - see entry below - and finally PO 13.02.76
Note entry re AFRIKANDER I - becoming AFRIKANDER 1942
Nom DS
Tug LUDWIG WIENER Cd 16.08.1914-19.03.15
German Whaler BISMARCK seized 1914, Cd 01.07.18-sold 19
Iron Screw Gunboat TICKLER (1879) 26.02.19-12.32(became AFRIKANDER II) - BU 1937 though in NL as AFRIKANDER to 1948

Iron Screw Gunboat GRIPER (1879), was FLORA, became AFRIKANDER 04.11.32-sold 37
YC 229, ex steam lighter TICKLER, cooking lighter 07.04.14 - 08.43 (BU hull beyond repair)
HL(D) 3942 08.43-09.44 (though in Red List 47-12.49 and Pink List 50-58)
GENERAL BOTHA (ex THAMES) (qv) 09.44-
In WW I was the base for southern and Eastern Africa. In WW II included S African Air Station at Wingfield (later MALAGAS (qv) and Wynberg, which section moved to Wingfield 18.05.42
Simonstown Dockyard handed over 02.04.57

AFRIKANDER I Simonstown, S Africa, Accounting Base
Listed 01.1941 - personnel at RNAS Wynberg tx from AFRIKANDER III to AFRIKANDER I 02.06.41, Listed as becoming AFRIKANDER 01.11.42

AFRIKANDER II Simonstown, S Africa, Base
TICKLER (1879) Iron Screw Gunboat, was AFRIKANDER and became AFRIKANDER II 12.1932, sold 1937
Was S African Div RNVR 1936-40, PO 01.06.43 and was SAN Service HQ 1941-46

AFRIKANDER III Capetown, S Africa, Base
Base for RNAS Wynberg 1940-02.06.41 - though remained as address for stores. S African RNVR Base 1941. Renamed GNU 01.11.42(qv)

AFRIKANDER IV Durban, S Africa, Base
Durban Base re-established 01.01.41 as independent of AFRIKANDER I (but in NL 1940 and apps from 08.39). renamed KONGONI 01.11.42 (qv)

AFRIKANDER V Freetown, Sierra Leone, Base
Cd 10.1939, PO 15.03.40 when acs tx to EDINBURGH CASTLE (qv)

AFRIKANDER V Diego Suarez, Base
Name sel for base, Tlr GENERAL FOCH allocated as Nom DS 21.05.42, but base Cd as IRONCLAD 24.05.42 (qv)

AFRIKANDER VI
In NL 1940, apps from 09.39

AFRIKANDER VII
In NL 1940, apps from 08.39

AFRIKANDER Youngsfield, Wynberg, S Africa, RN Base
Tx from Simonstown 02.04.57 (see entry above) - PO 13.02.76
Nom DS - FMB 42424 1957-62 (at least) (although HL(D) 3942 still listed 01.58 - see previous entry)
S Atlantic Station closed 12.04.67

AGAMEMNON (1929) Hbr Serv as Amenity Ship
Blue Funnel Liner, conv to M/L 10.40, PO 02.11.43, Cd 08.11.44 for pass to Canada for conv, but conv cancelled, PO Vancouver 22.01.45, released 22.11.45

AGGRESSIVE Newhaven, CF Base
Was named FORWARD II (qv), renamed 04.11.42 - though name appears in a list of 05.40. Independent command, acs FORWARD 11.41. In Paris Hotel and E Quay (06.44), PO 16.04.45
Nom DS - WHITE SPRAY to 16.04.45

AGINCOURT (1817) Dev, DS/ Rx Sh
3rd Rate, DS 1848, Rx Sh 1865, renamed VIGO 04.1865(qv), sold 10.1884

AGINCOURT (1865) Chat/ Portland, TS
BB, Chat 1895-03.1897, Boys' TS Chat 06.97-99, Portland TS attached BOSCAWEN 1899-06.1904, BOSCAWEN III 06.04-10.05, then to Harwich - see BOSCAWEN III

AGNIBAHU Bombay, India, IN OSA Missile Boat Base
For Pink List 06.73, in NL 1974-76

AGRANI Coimbatore, India, IN Petty Officers' TE
In NL 1967-76

AGRIPPA Naples, RN Element NATO HQ Allied Forces S Europe
Cd 26.06.1997-extant 99

AIGLE (1801) Woolwich/Sheerness, coal hulk
5th Rate, coal hulk at Woolwich 1853, sunk during torp trials 1870 and sold 24.11.1870

AIK LAM (1941) Colombo/Mandapam, M/S Repair Ship
Repair ship 1944, Colombo 04.44-07.44, Mandapam 04.45-, wrecked 22.03.46

AISNE (1945) Chatham, Living Ship
DD, Living ship Chat RF 12.1950, BU 06.70

AJAX (1809) Kingstown, CG
3rd Rate, CG 01.02.1858-31.03.1864, BU 1864

AJAX (1880) Clyde, CG
BB, Clyde 15.08.1885-14.04.1891, sold 03.1904

AJAX (1912) Nore, SO RF
BB, SO RF v CALLIOPE 14.05.24 - PO 24.10.26 rb MARSHAL SOULT, sold 11.26

AJAX (1962) Dev, Hbr TS
FF, Hbr TS v Salisbury 11.07.1985 - 87, BU 15.02.88

AKBAR (1801) Milford/Lpool, Qtn Sh
4th Rate CORNWALLIS renamed AKBAR 13.08.1806, troopship, Qtn Sh Milford 09.1824, at Lpool 1835 till sold 1862

AKBAR (1816) TS
3rd Rate HERO renamed WELLINGTON 04.11.1816, renamed AKBAR 10.05.1862. TS - reformatory ship Lpool, BU 08.04.1908

AKBAR (1876) Lpool/Invergordon, Reformatory Ship/DS
Iron Screw Ship TEMERAIRE renamed INDUS II 04.1904 as TS, renamed AKBAR 14.10.1914, reformatory ship Lpool, 01.15 to Invergordon with ALGIERS (qv) - 20, sold 26.05.21

AKBAR Kolshit, Bombay, RIN TE
Direct entry TE Cd 01.1944, task tx to CIRCARS 12.44, PO late 50.

AKLAVIT Aklavit, North West Territories, RCN Radio Sta
Estab by 08.1949, HMCNRS 1953-12.03.61, to new site as INUVIK

AKRAM Gwadar, Pakistan, PN Naval Base
1999

AL RAWDAH (1911) Clyde/Rothesay, SM Accom Sh
Tx from War Dept as accom sh 09.06.1941, allocated SM DS Holy Loch 17.03.41, to Clyde 3 SM 06.41, alloc 7 SM 11.43 as aux DS but retained 3 SM, 3 SM v WOLFE 16.03.44, to Min of War Transport 06.10.45

ALACRITY Azores, Fixed A/S Defences (NP 911)
08.10.1943-02.11.43
Alacrity was codeword for Azores, prob not a ship name

ALAMEIN (1945) Dev, Accom Sh
DD, RF Living ship 03.50-11.51 (at least), BU 12.64

ALARM (1845) Pembroke/ Queenstown, Coal Hulk
6th Rate, coal hulk 1860, at Pembroke 1865-75, Queenstown 1880-95, sold 07.07.1904

ALASTOR (1874) Burnham-on-Crouch, Store Depot
Finnish sailing barge on R Crouch 1942, taken up as store depot 07.01.44, PO 27.07.45. Reported as moored Bradwell as base for Army river patrols at some time. For disposal 22.09.45

ALAUNIA (1925) Repair Ship
Cd as AMC 29.08.39, conv to repair ship 42-45, purch 08.12.44, Cd 16.08.45 for Far East. Res Gareloch 12.46-47, TS for engine room ratings Dev 06.06.47-10.56 - task to SULTAN, tow to BU 03.09.57

ALAUNIA II (1915) Dev, Nominal Base and TE
Monitor MARSHALL NEY ex M13 renamed VIVID 06.22 (qv), became DRAKE 01.01.34 (qv), renamed ALAUNIA II 47, for disposal 10.56, BU 10.57.

ALBATROSS (1928) Bombay/Dev/Ports/Normandy, Base/Repair Ship
RAN aircraft tender, tx to RN 1938, conv to repair ship 42. A/S seaplane repair base ship Freetown 39-42, temporarily to CO HQS Bombay 03.43-07.43, LC Accountant and Maintenance Base Plym 10.43-05.44 rb FOLIOT I, Cd 06.05.44, Normandy 08.06.44-11.08.44 (torpedoed), to Portsmouth/ Falmouth repairs, PO 08.08.45, sold 12.10.46 (PRIDE OF TORQUAY)

ALBATROSS Nowra, NSW, Australia, Naval Air Station
Nowra used by NABBINGTON and NABSWICK (qv) to 18.03.1946 - ceased ops 31.01.46, then to RAAF control. Ann 28.04.48 to be Cd as ALBATROSS, Cd 31.08.48, extant 99

ALBATROSS II Scholfields, NSW, Australia
Name alloc RNAS Scholfields NSW 1953 prior to becoming NIRIMBA (qv)

ALBEMARLE (1901) Dev, Accom Sh
BB, PO 18.04.1917, then accom sh Dev Cd 01.01.18, PO by 09.19, sold 11.19

ALBION (1802) Ports, Rx Sh
3rd Rate, Rx Sh 1831, BU 1836

ALBION (1898) Dev, Accom Sh
BB, at Humber from 08.1916-01.11.18, Accom Sh Dev for VIVID v ESSEX Cd 05.11.18, PO by 09.19, sold 12.19

ALBRIGHTON (1941) Normandy, Temp Ferry Craft HQ Ship
Hunt class DD, Normandy 06.44, sold 57

ALBRO LAKE Dartmouth NS, RCN Radio Sta
Established 1942, NRS 1953-01.07.56, HMCNRS 01.07.56-18.09.67, moved to MILL COVE (qv)

ALCA (1927) Base Mining DS
Hired as M/L 02.1940, Cd 26.11.40 as Base Mining DS under COCHRANE, From 01.01.41 under ORLANDO, 05.41 ann to be Base Ship for MNBDO (qv). Independent command, own acs 29.01.42, At Freetown 42, then Home Waters. PO 16.10.45

ALDEBARAN Archangel, N Russia, Nom DS NOIC Archangel (NP 200)
British Naval Mission Archangel - SBNO Archangel to be appointed, acs PRESIDENT I 08.10.41. SBNO Murmansk was 16 miles away and a separate organisation.
Cd 01.07.44 (NP in Post Office circulars by 06.42), PO 05.10.45 (NP returned UK 20.10.45)
Nom DS: MB 9571 01.07. 44-
Had a steam lch named ALDEBARAN 01.45-05.45

ALDEGROVE Aldegrove, BC, RCN Radio Sta
Late 1943 - 01.06.55, HMCNRS 01.06.55-01.07.56, HMCS 01.07.56-10.08.67, became CFS ALDEGROVE

ALECTO (1911) SM DS
Cd 20.06.1912. Gt Yarmouth 14-18, 8 SM 16-01.19 (Dover), 4 SM Blyth 05.19-09.19, 3 SM Ports 09.19-21, Gib 04.22, Dev 22-26, 5 SM Ports 26-34, 6 SM v TITANIA 09.35, Res 6 SM Portland 09.35-39, 5 SM DOLPHIN 39-40, 7 SM Rothesay 40-04.45 - to res, Accom Sh Rothesay 05.45, BD Accom Sh Greenock v ST COLOMBA 13.04.46, PO 01.07.46, Tow to BU 26.07.49.

ALERT (1894) Persian Gulf, DS
Sloop, lent Basra civil authority 1906, used as DS in Gulf, Mesopotamia, 08.15-, sold 12.01.26 at Basra, pilot vessel, BU 10.49.

ALERT Sydney, NSW, Special Repair Ratings (Dockyard) Camp
Cd 01.09.1945, tender to WOOLLOOMOOLOO, PO 05.03.46
Nom DS: TANAC Tug 155 01.09.45-

ALERT (1945) Sasebo, Japan, HQ ship
Despatch vessel, temp HQ ship till rb LADYBIRD 08.50, BU 10.71

ALEXANDER Plym, Powder Hulk
Fr, 2nd Rate, capt 1806, powder hulk 1811, sold 1822

ALEXANDRA (1875) Weymouth, CG
BB, CG Weymouth 08.03.1891 - 18.04.1901, sold 06.10.1908

ALEXANDRA (1891?) Ports/ Soton, Accom Sh
Yt, acquired 29.05.1941, use as accom sh by Capt ML Ports, re-alloc as accom sh CO 21.09.42, refitted and engines removed 09.42, at Soton classed unfit and for disposal 06.43, in use till 44.

ALEXANDRIA (1875) Isle of Wight, TS
BB, off Osborne as Cadets' TS 1904, sold 10.1908

ALFROESSA Freetown, Provisioning hulk for escort forces
10.1943, ex Dakar, renamed WOOLWORTH (qv) 28.02.44

ALGERINE (1895) Esquimalt, BC, Canada, DS
Sloop, to Canada 1914, at Esquimalt PO 08.14, DS for SM 06.15-, To Canadian Govt for Training A/P 08.17, DS 17-19, sold 11.04.19, BU 1924

ALGERINE Cardiff, Base Ship
Name sel 01.09.1939, NOIC ordered 27.08.39, believed not used

ALGIERS (1860) Chart, Base Ship
ANSON, screw ship, renamed ALGIERS 11.01.1883, Flag of Admiral Superintendent Chat 01.08.1891 - BU 04.1904

ALGIERS (1870) Invergordon, Floating Store
TRIUMPH was TENEDOS, then INDUS IV, renamed ALGIERS 14.10.1914, floating store Invergordon, sold 07.01.1921.

ALGOMA (1913) Scapa Flow? DS
Ex Belgian SS LONDON ISTANBUL taken up for service as M/S DS 15.09.41, fitted out Glasgow 09.41 and renamed AMBITIOUS (qv) 11.11.41

ALICE (1930) Base & Accom Sh
Req 09.39. Armed Yt. accom Sh 1941, re-alloc as mobile accom sh for TLC crews - complement for day passage only whilst enroute Troon 26.03.42, sold 47

ALISDAIR (1937) Ipswich, Accom Sh
Yt, hired as HDPC 10.1939, PO 20.01.43 and alloc as temp accom sh Ipswich 03.43, rb EMPEROR OF INDIA 06.43 and conv to D/F calibration task 08.43. Was to be allocated to the Hydrographer 06.45 but cancelled and to C & M 17.07.45. RESTO 06.03.46

ALLENBY Folkestone, CO Base
Named 01.12.42, Cd 14.03.44, PO 10.04.45 - accom to War Office
Poss called BLUEBIRD III before this date
Nom DS: BLUEBIRD III to 10.04.45

ALLIANCE (1945) Gosport, SM Museum SM
Visit SM DOLPHIN 11.73 v TABARD - 12.76 rb GRAMPUS. To SM Museum 28.02.78, brought ashore, extant 1999.

ALLIGATOR (1821), HK, Hosp Sh
6th Rate, Hosp Sh HK 1846, sold there 30.10.1865

ALMANZORA (1914), Accom Sh
Hired as AMC 23.08.1915-20.12.19 and as accom sh 08.04.40-40

ALONZO Woolwich/Ports/Leith, Convict Hosp Sh/Chapel
Sloop, convict hosp sh Woolwich 1817, Ports by 1831, chapel at Leith by 1840, scuttled 1842

ALVISTA Exmouth
NAB, HQ Ship for Cdr Y Sqn LBV, Cd 20.03.44 off TENNYSON

AMBITIOUS Shetlands, Base Ship
Cd 26.01.1918 v BRILLIANT, PO 13.12.19 - acs to VICTORIOUS
– AMBITIOUS (1907), drifter, hired 1914, renamed AMBITIOUS II 31.07.19 till RESTO - note in NL 12.19 AMBITIOUS II with Admiral as SNO
– AIR POCKET (1918) Adty Drifter, renamed AMBITIOUS 01.08.19 - sold 10.20 and re-named CINERARIA

AMBITIOUS M/S DS
ALGOMA (1913), Belgian, hired 1940, renamed AMBITIOUS 11.11.41, Cd 16.01.42, mainly operated Scapa Flow with short spells elsewhere including Altbea, Humber (refit 12.42-08.43), Rosyth, Methil, Temp CF DS Lerwick 01.44, fit out as M/S HQ Ship 44, Southend M/S DS 17.05.44, Normandy 12.06.44, Ports 07.44-10.44, Le Havre 24.10.44, Sheerness 21.12.44, Terneuzen 05.45 - 21.06.45 (when base closed) then to Antwerp to RESTO, PO 16.07.45.

AMBROSE (1903) SM DS/Accom Sh
Merchant Cr hired and Cd 10.12.1914, purch 20.10.15 and conv to SM DS Glasgow 11.15-06.17, to C & M 06.17, Cd 01.12.17, Berehaven 17-18, Ports 03.18-08.18, Falmouth 12.18, Dev 12.18-01.03.19, 4 SM China 01.03.19-06.28, Rosyth accom sh 04.12.28 (Cd 23.10.28), renamed

COCHRANE (qv) 01.06.38 as DS Rosyth, BU 08.46

AMBROSE Dundee, 9 SM Base
Approved to construct at Carolina Pt, Dundee 30.01.1940. Cd 18.04.40, Estab PO 31.01.46 (movements record states ship PO 01.03.46), Base closed 03.03.46, Acs closed 31.03.46.
Nom DS: CARMANIA III(Drifter) 18.04.40-05.12.45
MFV 18 05.12.45-31.01.46

AMBROSE II Lerwick, SM Base
Cd 16.11.42, PO 31.12.44
Combined SM/CF Base, acs for SM from AMBROSE to FOX 01.03.44
Nom DS: NAB TEAL 16.11.42-

AMBROSE Halifax, NS, Canada, SM Base
Cd 03.01.1956, PO 12.05.67
Base for 6 SM. 6 SM formed 15.05.55 to 22.04.66, when became 1 RCN SM Sqn
Nom DS: HL(D) 43678 03.01.56-
HL(D) 5232 15.05.57-62 (at least)

AMENARTUS (1918) Shoreham, Accom Sh
Yt, allocated 14.08.42 - originally mis-spelt ANENARTUS, purch 10.02.42, laid up Shoreham (spelt ARMENARTUS) 24.08.44, to ST for disposal 14.09.44

AMETHYST III (1877) Holyhead, A/P Parent
Yt, 01.08.1915 v BOADICEA II, PO 08.02.17 rb MERSE (was to have been SAPPER)

AMIABLE (1910) Ports, Workshop
Drifter, hired WWI and as DGV 05.1940. Floating workshop for minor repairs in Op Neptune Western Area anchorage 05.44, resto 46

AMIENS (1919) Mechanicians' TS
Fr ship used as Free Fr Mech TS 29.03.41 to 43 (at least)

AMPHITRITE (1816) Milford Haven, CG
5th Rate, CG 05.03.1857-11.06.1860, BU 1875

AMPHITRITE (1898), Ports, Accom Sh
Cr, accom sh 22.06.1915-PO 18.06.15, Re-Cd for Rear Admiral M/L 09.04.18, sold 1920.

AMZARI Vizagapatam, India, RN LC Base
Cd 01.03.1945 (Acs BRAGANZA), PO 46
Originally ann as name for Mandapam Base 29.08.44
Nom DS: TANAC Tug V157 01.03.45-

ANANSA Calabar, Nigeria, Nigerian Naval Base
Listed 1966-78

ANDELLE (1922) M/S Maintenance ship
Cd as M/S 10.1940, conv to maintenance ship for Far East 11.43, BU 11.04.45

ANDERSON Colombo, Ceylon, Barracks and Radio Sta
Cd 10.02.1945, Independent command, acs UKUSSA, ex Anderson Secure W/T Sta, PO 31.07.46 - became civil estab and functioned to 55
Nom DS: Passenger lch 421234

ANDROMACHE (1832) Pembroke, Powder Hulk
6th Rate, powder hulk 1854 - BU 1875

ANDROMACHE (1890) N Shields/Harwich/Gib, Drl/Accom sh
Cr, RNR Drl Sh N Shields 01.07.1901-02.11.03, Harwich 04-05 rb SCYLLA late 04, DS in Med 15, accom sh Gib 14.06.16 (Cd 26.05.16 at Chat for passage to Gib)-(DS by 01.03.18-12.18) - 31.08.19 (sail Gib), PO at Dev 13.09.19, to C & M, sold 1920

ANDROMEDA (1897) Dev TS
Cr, Boys' TS Dev 1913-29 as POWERFUL II 1913-11.19, renamed IMPREGNABLE II 11.19-20.01.31, renamed DEFIANCE - Torp Sch, BU 08.56

ANENARTIUS - see AMENARTUS

ANENOME (1940) Harwich, Accom Sh
Corvette, accom sh 12.46-47 rb NIZAM 11.46, sold 1950

ANGRE Mint Rd, Bombay, India, IN Barracks
Ex DALHOUSIE (qv) 09.1951 - 11.76

ANGRE II Bombay
In NL 1955

ANHOLT Island off Denmark
Cd as HM Ship 1811, attacked by Danes 27.03.1811

ANKING (1824) Singapore/Netherlands E Indies, Base Ship
Hired as a Base Ship at Singapore 11.10.1941 (Charter Pty T98A), fitted out HK, Cd 08.01.42 for duty as Base Wireless Ship Batavia, Cd as Base Ship Batavia 08.02.42 and used as Base & Accom Sh. Sunk 03.03.42 by Japanese surface forces S of Java, formally PO 04.03.42

ANNA CAPANO (1897) Med, DS for Fixed A/S Defences
Italian ship, Med 05.44 - v. BLAIR ESK, visited Algiers & Italy - "Useful but recognised by no one". Tx to Italians as a fleet auxiliary.

ANNAPOLIS (1918) Halifax NS, RCN TS
DD (ex USS MACKENZIE), tx to RCN 09.40, became TS attached to CORNWALLIS (qv) 08.04.44-04.06.45, BU 06.45

ANONYMA Southampton, Accom Sh
07.1943-10.44 (at least)
Statement 12.04.43 that ML 237 not named ANONYMA but was SEASERPENT (qv)

ANSON (1812) Standgate Creek/Hobart, Tasmania, Qtn/Convict hulk
3rd Rate, Qtn Sh Standgate Creek 1831, convict hulk Tasmania 1844 - BU 1851

ANSON (1886) Queensferry, CG

BB, CG 01.03.1901-mid 03, sold 13.07.1909

ANSON (1940) Portland/Dev, Hbr TS
BB, Hbr TS v NELSON from 05.46 - rb VANGUARD 10.11.49, RF living ship Dev 03-05.50 then to Gareloch res 03.08.50. BU start 12.57

ANTELOPE (1802) Bermuda, Convict Hosp Sh
4th Rate, Convict Hosp Sh 1824, BU 1845

ANTELOPE (1893) Portishead/Ports, Drl Sh/SM DS
Torp Gun Boat, Drl Sh Portishead to 1905 rb HUSSAR, Hbr Serv for SM 25.06.10-12, conv to DS 1915, sold 27.05.19

ANTHORN - Prob a misquote for NUTHATCH(qv) which was at Anthorn

ANTONIA (1921) Repair Ship
Hired 09.1939, conv to Auxiliary Fleet Repair Ship Ports 1940, purch 04.42, allocated to Kilidini on completion, estimated 07.42. Cd 19.08.42 but renamed WAYLAND (qv) 17.08.42, released 18.05.46, BU 01.48

ANTRIM Belfast, Tlr Base
Name ann 28.02.41, Cd 06.03.41, closed down 05.08.43, name lapsed, base closed though reports of it being renamed CAROLINE II 01.01.44.
Nom DS: Hbr Lch WHITE HEATHER 06.03.41-31.12.43 (became GADWALL) (qv)

AORANGI (1924) Trinco/HK, SM Accom Sh
DS for Tug Control Organisation Op Neptune. At Lee-on-Solent 05.05.44, Spithead 01.06.44, Soton to 12.07.44, rb EMPRESS OF RUSSIA (qv), arrive Clyde 13.07.44, Glasgow 25.07.44, hired as accom sh 07.44 and conv for SM crew accom Fairfields, sail Greenock 06.08.44, used as SM DS - 4 SM Trinco 07.44 - 06.45, then as Fleet Train Accom Ship Far East - 08.45. Transit Barracks HK 12.45, PO 22.09.46

APHRODITE Episcopi, Cyprus, FOME HQ & Base
Cd 01.12.1954 v OSIRIS, HQ close 18.05.62, PO 30.06.62
Nom DS: Dinghy 91/52 01.12.54-62

APHRODITE II Famagusta, Cyprus, Naval Base, Maritime HQ Nicosia
Cd 01.12.1958 (command assumed 05.59) - 61
Nom DS: Dinghy 92/52 58-61

APOLLO (1891) Soton/Dev, Drl Sh/DS
Cr, RNR Drl Sh Soton 01.07.1901-13.12.1904 rb BRILLIANT, DS 4DF Dev Cd 01.09.17-19, DS Local DD Flot Dev 1920, BU 08.20

APPIAN Codeword covering tx of CO personnel to Eastern Theatre 04.1944 - see OPPIDAN

APPLEDORE Appledore, Naval Base and CO TE
Cd 01.08.1942. Estab apart from CO Experimental Base to USN 24.07.43, became USN Advance Amphibious Base Cd 29.07.43-PO 25.05.44 and returned to RN, PO 23.04.48
Included Fremlingham and Appledore camps
Nom DS: MFV ANNIE VESTA 01.08.42-
MFV THE -01.46
MFV 91 01.46-05.46 (at least)
HL(P) 42588 47

APPLEDORE II Ilfracombe, CO Base
Cd 17.09.1943, PO 30.11.46
Previously EXCELLENT II (qv) - 2nd MNBDO MENACE, 17.09.43, tx to Collingwood Hotel, Ilfracombe 10.43 as APPLEDORE II
Nom DS: NAB GLORIA 17.09.43-11.45

AQUARIUS (1900) DS
HAMPSTEAD, purch 1902 and renamed, distilling ship, conv to DS 06.1907, Home Fleet 1907-, 8 DF Chat 01.07.13 - DD DS Forth 1914-15, then SM DS Med 1915, repair ship Adriatic (Corfu) 03.18-mid 01.19, Black Sea DD DS 1919-, PO Nore by 1920 and sold.

AQUARIUS Spore
Ex RAF vessel for general duties transport at Spore 14.12.41-13.02.42, sunk off Tjibea Is 14/15/02.42

ARAGON (1905) Base Ship
Listed as Base Ship in one record but used as Expeditionary Force Transport 01.09.14 till sunk 30.12.17

ARARAT Castle Toward, Dunoon, Argyll, CO Tng Centre
Cd 01.06.1942, acs DINOSAUR, renamed BRONTOSAURUS (qv) 03.08.42
Nom DS: Drifter YOUNG MUN 06.42-08.42

ARBELLA Boston, Lincs, CO Base for LCT
Cd 21.01.43, To C & M 02.1944, PO 09.08.45, task to MYLODEN
Also included Kings Lynn
Nom DS: was to be NAB WINGCLIFFE but cancelled
MB BRITANNIA - 21.01.43-09.08.45

ARCHAIS Syracuse, Sicily
Name sel for Syracuse for convening Courts Martial and reported Cd 05.44, but not required by 08.44 - prob never actually Cd
Port Party Syracuse was NP 840

ARCHANGEL White Sea, RN Base
06.1941-

ARETHUSA (1817) Lpool, Qtn Sh
5th Rate, Qtn Sh 06.1836, renamed BACCHUS 12.03.1844 (qv), BU 08.1883

ARETHUSA (1849) Greenhithe, TS
4th Rate, TS 1874 at Greenhithe till BU 1934

ARETHUSA Medway TS
2nd Rate, TS at Upnor, Medway 1933-73, hired as accom sh v CORNWALL and named PEKIN 06.40-07.45 (qv)

ARGO (1799) Dev, Rx Sh

ACTIVE, 5th Rate, Rx Sh 02.1826, renamed ARGO 11.1833, BU 10.1860

ARGONAUT (1898), Ports, Hosp/Accom Sh
Cr, TS Special Entry Cadets v HIGHFLYER 10.10.13, Hosp Sh Ports 1915-17, accom sh for stokers Cd 01.01.18 - 03.20 (supplemented by TERRIBLE 12.18), sold 1920

ARGONAUT (1941) Ports, Accom Sh
Cr, accom sh 02.48, sold 11.55

ARGUS (1917) Nore, Base & Accom Sh
Italian CONTE ROSSO purch 1916, conv to aircraft carrier, PO 06.12.44 and used as Base & Accom Sh Nore (conv Belfast), -12.46, sold 05.12.46

ARIADNE (1816) Alexandria, Coal Hulk
6th Rate, coal hulk 1837, sold 1841

ARIADNE (1859) Ports TS
FF, Hbr Serv 1884 - attached VERNON (qv) Ports 1880-1905, renamed ACTAEON 06.06.1905(qv) as TS Sheerness, sold 11.12.1922

ARIADNE (1898) Ports/Dev, TS
Cr, used as stokers' TS Ports 10.1913-15, at Dev under IMPREGNABLE 07.07.1915-and overflow ship for VIVID 09.09.15-16, lost 26.07.17

ARIADNE (1943) Dev, Accom Sh
M/L, accom sh 02.48, BU 06.65

ARIEL Warrington, Lancs, Air Radio & Air Mechanics TE
Cd 08.10.1942 at Risley, also called Culcheth, moved to Worthy Down 01.07.52 (Equipment and Trials Section 15.07.52) - see below
Nom DS: Naval Control Tender VIGIA 08.10.42-07.45
DG Hbr Lch RAGLAN II 07.45-
TRSB 43779 by 04.48-52 (became KESTREL, then ARIEL)

ARIEL II Warrington, Lancs, RNAS
South camp of old ARIEL after main sch moved to Worthy Down, from 01.07.1952-12.52

ARIEL Worthy Down, Nr Winchester, RNAS/RN Air Electrical Sch
01.07.52 (location ex KESTREL, personnel ex Warrington) - PO by 1959, estab tx to War Dept 01.11.60
Nom DS: TRSB 43779 01.07.52 (ex Nom DS KESTREL/prev ARIEL)-53
TRSB 43782 1954-59

ARIEL II South Camp, Worthy Down, Nr Winchester, RNAS/RN Air Electrical Sch
Cd 01.07.52-31.10.59 when became absorbed into new ARIEL II - see next entry

ARIEL II Worthy Down, Air Electrical Sch
31.10.59 - PO 01.12.60 (tx to Army)
Name given to remnants of Sch when majority tx to Lee-on-Solent

ARIEL Lee-on-Solent, RNAS
DAEDALUS renamed ARIEL when ground tng moved there 31.10.1959. Renamed DAEDALUS 05.10.56 (qv)
Nom DS: TRSB 4424 1959-62
TRSB 43782 1962-65

ARIGUANI (1926) Gib, Accom Sh
Ex catapult ship, alloc Gib as accom sh 19.02.1942

ARK ROYAL (1914) DS
Ex merchant ship, purch 1914 for use a seaplane carrier, temp SO RF Nore v AJAX 03.25-, used as DS Res M/S Sheerness v BLENHEIM 12.25-12.27, ReCd 01.04.28 in RF as carrier, renamed PEGASUS 21.12.34 (qv)

ARMADILLO Glenfinnart, Loch Long, CO Camp (Naval Beach Cdo Sch)
Camp tx ex War Office 12.10.42, Cd 25.11.42, PO 30.09.45, destore to 15.10.45, closed 11.12.45.
Nom DS: 16ft tlr boat 1757 25.11.42-

ARMENARTUS - aee AMENARTUS

ARO (1898) Rosyth, Torp Sub DS
Purch 19.10.1914, Allocated to Loch Ewe but sent to Rosyth 01.1915, DS there 12.02.15-PO 04.18. Troopship 14.08.18, Victualling Supply Ship Archangel 09.19, sold 1920.

ARON Iceland, Service Base Vessel
Req for service at Iceland Service Base 07.41 - 10.05.42 (at least)

ARRAS (1918) Accom Sh
Fr patrol vessel, used as accom sh alongside AMIENS (qv) 04.03.1941 - 04.43 (at least)

ARROGANT Trinco, Store hulk
ADASIER, purch 1810, store hulk, sold 1842

ARROGANT (1848) Newhaven, CG
FF, CG 01.03.1858-22.08.59, sold 03.1867

ARROGANT (1896) DS
Cr, conv at Dev to SM DS, Cd 01.07.1911, 4 SM DS Ports 11-14, 1914-16 (was A/P DS 09.14 - rb ATTENTIVE 10.10.14 at Dover and rb HARRIER 02.12.14 at Ramsgate) 5 SM and Base Flag Dover 1916-18, was parent for RNAS Dover, Guston and Capel by 03.18, ML DS Dover by 27.10.17-03.19, PO 15.03.19, 3 SM Harwich 03.19-09.19, Accom Sh for SM Sch Ports & 3 SM 01.10.19 - 09.22, sold 11.10.23

ARTHUR - Skegness, believed to refer to ROYAL ARTHUR (qv)

ARTIFEX (1924) Repair Sh/TS
AMC AURANIA, nominated as DD DS 31.10.41, start fit out Dev 11.41 after being torpedoed that month. To C & M 22.04.42, allocated Kilindini 04.42, renamed 12.11.42 and purch, Cd 10.05.44, East Indies 44-45, HK 12.45, to res Gareloch 46-48,

at Rosyth by 05.48 for artificer tng - sold 28.12.60

ASAKO Pt Harcourt, Nigerian Naval Base
1975-78

ASBURY Asbury Park, New Jersey, Accom Barracks
US Navy Sta on Rhode Is (Quonset Pt) used by FAA Sqns forming in USA, was in SAKER II to 01.10.42, then Cd 01.10.1942 as extension of SAKER II (qv), independent command, PO 29.02.44, signal sch continued as BritNavSigSch and accounting staff to 31.03.44, when became SAKER II again..

ASCANIA (1925) Repair Sh
Hired as AMC 1939-42, ann to be conv to repair sh 02.03.42 but PO 21.10.42, re-conv for trade

ASCANIUS Normandy, DS (see also MATADOR - NP 1658)
Merchant ship assigned DS duties Normandy, arrived there from LochEwe 08.06.44, carried Cdre DS (NP 1657) till HAWKINS completed bombardment duties. Left beaches 13.07.44 for Newport. When returned to beaches was mined. To Soton 30.07.44, poss repairs Falmouth. NP 1658 PO 07.08.44.

ASCENSION Ascension Is, Naval Base
From 1816, run as a ship with CO and First Lt. On 01.11.1922 administration of island tx from Admiralty to the Colonial Office and the RM garrison left. Base ship was FLORA (qv) 19th Century & CORMORANT (qv) 1910-1922. (Name used by FF 1943-46)

ASHANTI (1959) Ports, Hbr TS
FF, Hbr TS for SULTAN v DIAMOND 1981-86, sunk as target 09.88

ASIA (1824) Ports, Flag
2nd Rate, was guardship 1858, Flag Admiral Superintendent from 01.04.1862 to 1905 (at least) - sold 07.04.1908. Living ship in Ports till RNB opened 1903.

ASSAULT Nelson's Bay, Pt Stephens, NSW, Australia, RAN CO Base
Cd 01.09.1942, PO 07.04.45

ASSEGAI Nr Durban, S Africa, TE
Estab approved 08.1942, Cd 01.10.42, to C & M 02.44, PO 15.05.44 and Re-Cd 16.05.44 (C & M Party) but Drafting Office tx there 01.06.44 and PO 30.11.45. Established as a CO TE, transit pool and Central Drafting Office for Eastern and Med Fleets and S Atlantic Station. Believed to include Mechanical Training Centre Pietermaritzburg - an RN camp under canvas in a field called "Hay-Paddock" 1943, and which was placed in C & M 18.02.44. Torp Sch ex Alexandria (PHAROS) at ASSEGAI by 01.44
Nom DS: Hulk CORSICA 01.10.42-

ASSINIBOINE (1954) Halifax NS, Canada, TS
FF, static TS 14.12.1988-94 (at least)

ASSISTANCE (1900) Repair Ship
Purch 1900, TS for boy artificers, conv to repair ship 1906, Cd 28.11.06, Home Fleet 06-10, Scapa Flow 14-18, Rosyth 08.18-12.18, Atlantic Fleet 20-23, to Med 03.23. Cd 15.09.24-(refit Ports 13.10.26-01.04.27) - 1929 rb RESOURCE, Res Ports, handed over to BU in part payment for MAJESTIC (CALEDONIA)) 11.03.37

ASSISTANCE (1944) Aux Fleet Repair Ship
Cd 21.01.1945. Spore 11.45, returned USN 15.08.46

ASTRAEA (1893) Cameroons
Cr, held acs of Expeditionary Force 01.01.16-31.03.16, sold 07.20

ASTRAEA Lagos, Nigeria, Base
Cd 11.1941, PO 08.08.45

ASTRAVEL (1944) Repair Sh
Ex Fleet Tender 7, from USA 1944, conv to A/S repair ship, to Peterhead for sheathing prior to service in Far East, but Far East duty cancelled 09.45, reverted to FT 7 22.09.45, PO 28.09.46 and returned USA 47

ASTREIOD Shoreham, Accom Sh
1942, acquired 28.01.43, laid up Shoreham 08.44, for disposal 14.09.44.
Also spelt ASTROID and ASTEROID

ASVINI Colaba, Bombay, India, IN Hospital
Cd 0800, 01.09.1951 (ex Comb Military Hosp) - 1976

ATALANTA (1844) TS
JUNO, 6th Rate, renamed MARINER 10.01.1878, ATALANTA (TS) 22.01.1878, foundered in Atlantic 12.02.1880

ATLANTIC ISLE Tristan da Cunha, Naval Estab
Cd 01.01.1944, PO 10.05.46
Was manned when Napoleon was a prisoner at St Helena to prevent Fr using it as a base for his rescue.
10.03.42 the S Africans set up a secret Met Sta there (RN and SAAF manned) - known as "Job Nine". Cd to allow registration of births and deaths of personnel and dependents. Met & W/T Sta . Tender to AFRIKANDER.

ATLAS (1782) Ports, Powder hulk
2nd Rate/3rd Rate 1802, powder hulk 1814, BU 1821

ATMAH (1898) Grangemouth, Base & Accom Sh
Target Yt, 07.1940, PO 17.01.44 to become accom sh Grangemouth for personnel in ships refitting, in C & M 09.44, laid up 14.10.46

ATREUS (1911) East Indies, Base Ship
Req 1940, controlled M/L Base Ship, Cd 02.11.40, East Indies 43, lent RAN - RESTO 44

ATTACK Portland, CF Base
Approved to construct 15.09.1939. Cd 15.01.1941, tender to BOSCAWEN, own acs 01.09.41, PO 31.12.45 (Barracks and office space lent US Forces 28.04.44)
Nom DS: Hbr Lch 248 (ex OSPREY)-01.41 - reverted to Nom DS OSPREY 31.12.45

ATTACKER (1944) Gareloch, Living Ship
LST 3010, named ATTACKER 1947, living ship Gareloch Res v MESSINA 09.47. To MOWT as EMPIRE CYMRIC 54, BU 10.63

ATTENTION Coal Hulk, Ascension Is
INDEPENCIA (qv), renamed 1846, sold 1847

ATTENTIVE (1904) Dover, Base Ship
By 10.10.1914 v ARROGANT and 15.01.15 v PEMBROKE - 01.16 (became ATTENTIVE II/III(qv))
Cr was Flag of Admiral of Dover Patrol 1914 and hence Base took her name

ATTENTIVE II Dover, Base (Office of ATTENTIVE ashore at Dover)
Parent for Aux small craft, Dover WW I - by 12.1914 - PO 31.10.19 - became PEMBROKE V (qv)
ATTENTIVE II and III amalgamated as ATTENTIVE II 01.05.1919
Acs of MLs from ARROGANT 15.03.19. Flag of Rear Admiral Controlled Minefields from SURF 03.19,
Parent for DD by 1918/19, then all small craft when II and III amalgamated 05.19.
Nom DS: SEARCHER II (1908) Drifter to 25.05.19
FAIRWIND (1918) Drifter 25.05.19-07.19
ADDER (ex War Dept BURGOYNE) 07.19 - (sold 23)

ATTENTIVE III Dover, A/P Parent
01.1916 ex ATTENTIVE (qv) - 01.05.1919 (amalgamated into ATTENTIVE II)
Nom DS: SEAWARD HO (1915) Tlr 01.04.18-01.05.19

ATTENTIVE Portland, Base
Name allocated to Base at the Comml Pt of Portland 01.09.39, NOIC there by 29.08.39, but name not used.

ATTOCK Pakistan, PN RF
Listed 1952 as Commanding RF, was Fleet Replenishment Ship, sold 1956

AUDACIOUS (1869) Kingstown/Hull/ Chat, CG/DS
BB, CG Kingstown 10.1870-07.71, Hull 07.71-07.75, 01.8.79-14.08.81 and 01.04.90-07.02.94, used as DD DS Chat 1902, renamed FISGARD (qv) 04.1904, TS 01.01.1906, renamed IMPERIEUSE (qv)1914 - 19, VICTORIOUS (qv) 1919-27, sold 13.03.27

AURANIA - see ARTIFEX

AURORA Falmouth/Dev, Coal ship
Ex Fr CLORINDE, capt 1814, coal hulk Falmouth 1835-50, Dev 1851 - BU 05.1851

AURORA (1861) Clyde, CG
FF, CG Clyde 08.05.1874-20.07.1877, BU 12.1881

AURORA (1887) Bantry, CG
Cr, CG Bantry 03.05.1893-30.03.1895, sold 1907

AUSONIA (1921) Repair Ship
Ex Liner, AMC, PO 07.05.1942, purch 06.42, conv to Heavy Repair Ship Ports, Cd 02.05.44, Kilindini 12.07.44-09.44, Aden 09.44-05.45, Bombay, Trinco 06.45-14.06.46, Greenock 02.08.46, to res Gareloch 12.46-07.47, Chat RF attached to Mechanical TE, FO Commanding RF Chat v KENT 14.07.47 -15.06.49 rb DUKE OF YORK (at Ports), SORF Chat to ABERCROMBIE 29.06.49, to Sheerness 07.49 - SORF to 07.50, Rosyth 07.50-07.54, at Millwall Docks 07.54-11.55, then res there to 06.57, refit Dev 09.07.57-15.09.58, Cd 16.09.58, to Malta GC 10.58 v RANPURA - 09.64 (5 SM 02.06.62-07.64 when disbanded), Ports PO 18.08.64, Tow to BU 13.09.65

AUSTRALIA (1886) Newhaven/ Southampton, CG
Cr, CG Newhaven/Southampton 08.06.1893-07.02.1903 rb VENUS, sold 04.1905

AVALON St John's, Newfoundland, RCN Base, HQ FO St John's
Cd 31.05.1941, PO 31.07.46
Capt D Newfoundland 09.41
Known as AVALON I 17.09.41-10.44 "never fully cd"
Nom DS: Hbr craft ALBERTA 1941-42
GEORGIAN (1910) hired as base ship for RCN 1941, renamed AVALON, renamed AVALON II 09.09.41(qv), purch 05.42, laid up and later sold

AVALON II St John's, Newfoundland, Accom Sh
27.09.41-10.43 (still in NL 02.44 and Red List 07.44-05.45)
Acs of RNAS Argentia 12.43
SS GEORGIAN (see AVALON above) taken up as accom sh AVALON 2 (not II) 17.09.41-10.44

AVALON III Argentia, Newfoundland, RN Base & RNAS (but HMCS)
Ann to be set up 11.1941, Cd 01.01.42 as independent accounting base for RN personnel in Newfoundland, PO 31.03.46.
RN estab Newfoundland ceased 06.05.46 - acs to VICTORY X, RNO Newfoundland closed 31.03.51
Acs DD and corvettes based on Halifax and Argentia were borne on books AVALON III
Term "Fort William" was used for RN Officers' Quarters
Nom DS: NAB ZIG ZAG (Hbr Craft 31) 01.01.42-

AVALON IV Argentia, Newfoundland, RNAS at USN Air Sta
11.1943 - personnel were on books AVALON III

under Captain D - PO 05.07.44 - though in one list 10.47

AVALON St John's, Newfoundland, RCN Base
01.05.1951-PO 09.04.64
Moved from Buckmaster's Field to Pepperell 10.12.62

AVALON Long Pond St John's, Newfoundland, RCN SCC TE
Summer Camp 1985-86 (at least)

AVALON Petone, Wellington, New Zealand, RNZN TE
04.1944-07.44 (at least)
Electrical Sch

AVEREST Shoreham, Accom Sh
Taken up 07.1942, - re-allocated to Shoreham for NFS 12.06.43, laid up in C & M 23.03.46, sold to former owner 05.03.47

B

B 11 (1906) Med, DS
SM, DS to 01.11.1916, task to EGMONT, independent command 31.12.1916, work in Italian Cr MARCO POLO (qv), sold 1919

BACCHANTE (1811) Standgate Creek/Deptford, Rx/Qtn Sh
5th Rate, Qtn Sh Standgate creek 1837, Rx Sh/Cholera Ship Deptford by 1857, BU 1857

BACCHANTE (1901) Nore, Parent RF Group
Cr, SNO Dakar WWI, Parent Gp IV RF 04.19-rb SUPERB 05.19, sold 01.07.20

BACCHANTE Sta Hotel, Aberdeen, Base
NOIC ordered to post 27.08.1939, name sel 01.09.39, Cd 11.09.39, PO 31.12.45, acs to COCHRANE
M/S and A/S Base, covered Peterhead and Aberdeen
Nom DS: ML IRIS 11.09.39-12.43
HL(P) 42921 12.43-10.44
MFV CONCORD 10.44-

BACCHUS (1817) Lpool/Dev, Qtn Sh
ARETHUSA, 5th Rate, while Qtn Sh renamed BACCHUS 12.03.1844, to Dev 1865 till BU 08.1883

BACCHUS (1915) Cordu/Ismid, Repair Ship/Stores Carrier
By 05.1918-at Corfu, 12.18 Ismid, 01.03.19 Ports, 09.19 Archangel, renamed BACCHUS II 05.36, sunk as target 15.11.38

BACHEQUERO (1937) Normandy, DS
Oiler conv to LST used as Rhine DS Normandy 08.06.44-28.06.44, PO 06.08.45, Resto 02.46
Name spelt BACHACHERO in Normandy Operation Order.

BACOS Nile, Radio/Radar Sta
Ment

BADGER Parkestone Quay, Harwich, M/S Base
NOIC ordered to post 27.08.1939, name sel 01.09.39, Cd 13.09.39, PO 21.10.46
Overflow became BUNTING (qv) 02.40. Also used by 4th MTB Flot pre 06.40 (became BEEHIVE (qv))
RF Accounting Base 01.04.46.
Nom DS: MB EPPING ex LNER 13.09.39-12.01.40
Yt WESTWARD 12.01.40-10.46

BAHADUR Monara, Karachi, India/Pakistan, RIN/RPN/PN Boys' TE
Cd 05.1940, quoted as PO 05.09.48, but tx to RPN, still in lists to 1973.
Hulk DALHOUSIE attached 1944-45

BAKHTYAR Chittagong, Bengal, PN Base
Cd 01.12.1948 - previously HMS PATUNGA - to 10.12.71, when became Bangladesh Navy's ISSA KHAN.
Spellings vary and include BAKHTIYAR and BAKHTAAR

BALDAHUR Monara, Karachi, India/Pakistan
Ment 05.09.1945, poss same as BAHADUR (qv)

BALDUR Iceland, Base
06.1940 (Base ment at Reykjavik, poss not Cd till 23.10.40). 04.06.45 BALDUR II became BALDUR, RN Camp Reykjavik, when NEMESIS left (see Nom DS), PO 03.46
Included RNAS at Kaldarnes, formed 25.06.43 for damaged aircraft Hvitanes (to be withdrawn 02.11.43) .
Hvalfjord reduced to a fuelling Base 11.44. Naval Estab Akureyri closed 12.07.45
Nom DS: ST CLAIR (1937) 23.10.40-06.10.43(to convoy rescue ship)
SOUTHERN ISLES ex PRINCESS MARIE JOSE, renamed NEMESIS 03.41
was BALDUR 06.10.43-04.06.45

BALDUR II Reykjavik, Iceland, RN W/T Sta and Transit Camp
Cd 29.06.1942. became BALDUR 04.06.45 (qv)

BALDUR III Hvitanes, Iceland, RN Base
Cd 20.11.42, to C & M and closed 04.08.45
Nom DS: Dumb Barge OTTER 20.11.42-08.45

BALFURA Bombay, RIN Torp Sch
07.1944-12.44 (at least)

BALLINDERRY (1942) Barrow, RF HQ
FF, SO RF 1957-10.10.60 rb PLUTO, BU 07.07.61

BALTYK Okehampton, Devon, Polish Naval TE
Cd 01.01.1945

BALMORAL (1900) Clyde Base & Accom Sh
Paddle Ship hired as M/S WWI and as AA Ship

1940. Hbr Serv as accom sh for AFD IV, Clyde, 07.1943 - released 13.04.46

BAMBARA Trinco, Ceylon, RNAS
Cd 01.01.1944, PO to C & M 31.12.47, Tx to RAF 05.51.
RNAS operated as lodger unit on RAF Sta under LANKA, then HIGHFLYER until Cd. Comprised RNAS China Bay and tx to RN ex RAF 15.11.44 when Cd and became known as RNAS Trinco. Also RN Aircraft Maintenance Yard Clappenburg Bay and Naval Accom Camp Nachchikunda. 18.03.46 took over transit and holding camp task from MAYINA (qv)
Nom DS: TRV 421029 01.01.44-

BANGALOW (1939) RAN Repair Ship
Coaster, hired 1942-46, Cd as Loop Laying vessel 23.06.42

BARACUDA India, CF Base
Alternate spelling of BARRACUDA (qv)-

BARBROOK West Africa, Base
Cd 01.04.1941 as independent command and all BD vessels on W African coast were tenders to her. Acs in ELAND, Freetown. (qv)
This was prob an entry meant for BARBROOK II (qv), and the ""II" has been omitted. BARBROOK (1938) was a BDV in W Africa 1938-12.45 - sold 1958

BARBROOK II Freetown, Sierra Leone, BD Depot & Base
Cd 01.04.1943 independent command, acs ELAND. PO 01.10.49 and became TAGARIN (qv)
RNAS Hastings (SPURWING) was under BARBROOK II 1946-47. Also carried personnel ex ELAND from 30.04.46

BARPETA Bombay, India, TS
Steam ship allocated for CO Tng 03.06.1943-45

BARRACUDA RIN CF Base and Repair Ship
HEINRICH JESSEN (1940) (qv) hired as RIN Base Ship 26.07.1942, renamed BARRACUDA (BARACUDA in some records) listed at Bombay 09.42, Chittagong, Bengal 42-21.07.43 and Trinco 22.07.43-13.10.45. Also left Madras for Trinco 09.02.44 and covered Arakan Coast 1944-45 (replaced by BLINJOE and returned Calcutta). Calcutta 05.45, to Rangoon 10.05.45. PO to C & M at Calcutta 19.02.46, RESTO 1946

BARROSA (1812) Ports, Slop Depot
5th Rate, Slop Depot 1823, sold 1841

BARROSA (1945) Ports, Stores Hulk/ Refit Support
DD, Ports RF living ship 1950, stores hulk 1971 - DLG refit support v CORUNNA 1973-76, sold 08.78

BASILISK Pt Moresby, New Guinea, Base
31.12.1942-17.12.1945
Nom DS: ML BARETO

BASILISK Pt Moresby
Cd 14.11.1974 - PO 31.01.83

BASTIG Malta GC
Ment as being at ST ANGELO

BATAVIER Woolwich, Hosp Sh
Dutch 4th Rate, capt 1799, Hosp Sh 1819, BU 1823

BATAVIER II (1920) Lough Foyle, Accom Sh
Dutch MV taken up by RAF as accom sh, Lough Foyle 11.03.1941. Hired 1940-46

BATAVIER IV (1903) Tobermory, TS
Dutch vessel, hired 05.1940, taken up 24.09.40, known as TRAINING III in 09.40 when nominated to replace WESTERN ISLES (qv) for A/S Tng, Dunoon. Renamed EASTERN ISLES 01.11.40 (qv) then WESTERN ISLES 04.41-46 (qv)

BEACHY HEAD (1944) Escort Main Ship
Cd 27.03.45, East Indies 1945 - returned UK 01.47, renamed VULKAAN (Dutch)26.03.47, handed over 15.04.47. returned RN 01.50 (arrived Chatham 31.01.50), to RCN 06.10.51 renamed CAPE SCOTT (qv) 1953 and BU 1978

BEACONSFIELD Seaman's Mission, Pt Melbourne, Australia, Base of Vice Admiral (Q) (NP 480)
Cd 15.02.1945 (though Flag BPF(Admin) 11.44 and NP 480 there by 11.10.44), PO 30.11.45 (Flag BPF(Admin) to GOLDEN HIND 01.12.45)
Nom DS: TANAC Tug 135 15.02.45-

BEAULY FIRTH (1944) Maint Sh
Cd 11.06.1945, Pacific Fleet 45, Spore 12.45, to MoT 12.08.46

BEAVER Hull, RN Base Grimsby
NOIC arrive 23.08.1939, name sel 01.09.39, Cd 26.12.39 (apps from 22.08.39 and vessels alloc as tenders from 20.09.39) PO 12.03.46
M/S and A/P vessels became tenders when ROYAL CHARTER (qv) PO 18.08.41
Nom DS: MB CORONIA 26.12.39-22.01.41
Drifter ENERGY 23.01.41-19.06.44
MFV ROYAL CHARTER 19.06.44-21.12.45
MFV 967 21.12.45-

BEAVER I Grimsby, Base
1939-45

BEAVER II Immingham, RN Base
Cd 12.1939, PO 11.03.46
Apps from 01.11.39. depot for 20th DF and Rescue Tugs in Humber, and CF vessels and 5 DF 06.40. Took over CF Base from BEAVER III 01.04.42. CF Section closed 01.07.45 - closure party cont to poss 08.46.

BEAVER III Immingham, CF Base
Name alloc 30.04.1941. Cd 01.05.41, PO 01.04.42. CF tx to BEAVER II when BEAVER III abolished 04.42 - CO BEAVER III became Cdr (CF) in BEAVER II.

Nom DS: Base Hbr Duty MB BRITANNIA 01.05.41-

BEE (1915) Yangtze, HQ ship
River Gunboat, Flag Yangtze 01.1922-08.28 (at least), sold 22.03.39 at Shanghai

BEE Weymouth, CF Base
Named 04.08.1942, Cd 01.09.42, using old Contraband Control Base HQ, Hotel Edward & Alexander Gardens and Theatre, PO 17.10.43 -tx to Holyhead when South Coast overcrowded with build up for Op Overlord - see next entry - site used by GRASSHOPPER (qv)
CF "Finishing Sch"
Nom DS: Danish MFV MARY II 01.09.42-17.10.43

BEE Holyhead, Combined CF and M/S Base
Cd 0001Z on 18.10.43 CF ex Weymouth(see previous entry), M/S Base closure - ann 03.04.44, PO 21.07.45 - Holyhead reduced to RNO Status
Used location ex TORCH (qv). CF Tng tx from ST CHRISTOPHER 03.44.
Nom DS: Hbr Lch 3980 18.10.43-

BEECROFT Apapa, Nigeria, Nigerian Naval Base
Listed 1960-78

BEEHIVE Boomer Hall, Felixstowe, CF Base
Cd 01.07.1940, PO 18.10.45
Was operating 01.40 with 1st MTB Flot (ex Med) using Air Sta hangar as part of BADGER with VULCAN as DS, known as RN Depot Felixstowe Dock 04.40
Nom DS: MB 37241 01.07.40-

BEEHIVE II Felixstowe, CF Base
Incorrectly allocated 04.1941 and cancelled 10.07.41 when it was clarified that Base name was BEEHIVE

BELFAST (1938) Dev/Ports/ London, RF/Museum Ship
Cr, RF Accom Sh Dev 07.1964, HQ Ship Cdre RF Ports v SHEFFIELD 23/24.05.66, then accom sh with Cdre Res Ships 1966-71. Became Museum Ship in London 10.71 - extant 99

BELFORT (1919) Fowey/Dartmouth, MGB & MA/SB Base and Accom Sh
Allocated Dutch at Holyhead 16.07.40 but not taken up. Cd in RN 07.09.1940, in use to 05.45, return to Fr 1946
Fr Patrol Vessel seized 03.07.40, left Plym 08.09.40 for Fowey, arrived 11.09.40 - MGB & MA/SB Base. Tx to Dartmouth 02.10.41 under BRITANNIA III (qv) - CF DS and still there 05.45

BELLATRIX Murmansk, Russia, Base, SBNO Murmansk
Cd 01.07.1944 - 05.10.45
Personnel for North Russia on books PRESIDENT I 01.1942 - NOIC extant 02.42
Part of NP 100 - at Murmansk by 08.41, see also SPICA

Nom DS: NAB GRYLSE 01.07.44-03.45

BELLEISLE (1819) Chat/Sheerness, Hosp Sh
3rd Rate, Troopship 1841, Hbr Serv 1854, Hosp Sh Chat 1865, at Sheerness 1870, BU 10.1872 at Chat

BELLEISLE (1876) Kingstown, CG
Coastal Defence Ship, purch while building, Cd at Kingstown 02.07.1878, there to 30.04.1893, target 1903, sold 1904

BELLEROPHON (1786) Sheerness/Plym, Convict Ship
Prison ship Sheerness 10.1815, at Plym by 1820, renamed CAPTIVITY (qv) 05.10.24, sold 21.01.1836

BELLEROPHON (1818) Ports, Convict Sh/Rx Sh
TALAVARA, renamed WATERLOO 23.07.1817, renamed BELLEROPHON 05.10.24, to Hbr serv 1848, Rx Sh Ports 1856-90, sold 12.01.1892

BELLEROPHON (1865) Pembroke, Pt Guard Ship
BB, Pt Guard 30.04.1892-05.07.1893, became INDUS III (qv) 1904, sold 1922

BELLEROPHON (1907) Chat, TS
BB, turret Drl Sh Chat 01.1919 - sold 11.21

BELLEROPHON Ports, RF
Cd 01.07.1950, PO 01.02.1971
SO RF in ADAMANT 1950-52, MAURITIUS 53, CLEOPATRA 54-55, VANGUARD 56-60, RAME HEAD 65-66, on 28.12.56 VANGUARD became both FOCRF (ex DIDO & CLEOPATRA) and SORF Ports (ex LIVERPOOL & BOXER)
Note: Sailor's name for this ship "Billy Ruffian"
Nom DS: FMB 43111 07.50-06.12.56
FMB 42407 06.12.56-70 (at least)

BELLONA (1812) Dev, Rx Sh
INDUS, 3rd Rate, renamed BELLONA 03.11.1818, Rx Sh 1840 - BU 27.06.1868

BELLONA (1909) Ports, Stokers' TS
Cr, Stokers' TS 10.1920, sold 05.1921

BELVIDERA (1809) Ports, Rx Sh
5th rate, Hbr Serv 10.1846, Rx Sh 1856 - sold 10.07.1906

BEN LOMOND (1945) Clyde, Accom Sh
LST 3013, named 1947. Res Amphib Force 02.48, living ship Gareloch 12.50, allocated Op Hesperus 04.53. Allocated as temp CF DS 01.09.55 (Cd 31.08.55)-07.10.55, Temp CF DS Danish Waters 28.05.56(Cd 01.05.56)-03.07.56, HQ Chat RF v., DIADEM 25.07.56-08.57 rb MULL OF GALLOWAY, then to res, BU 03.65

BEN NEVIS (1945) Clyde, Accom Sh
LST 3012, named 1947, res Clyde 08.50-, SO SM Clyde and 3 SM accom sh 56-02.65 rb NARVIK, BU 12.03.65

BEN TABERT (1915) Solent/Normandy, M/S DS
Tlr, M/S gear removed Humber 11.1943, allocat-

ed Ports temp for towing duties 04.03.44, used as DS Normandy (Omaha) 11.06.44 -, resto 1946.

BENBOW (1813) Hbr Serv
3rd Rate, to Hbr Serv 02.1848, Marine Book Ship 1848, Russian Prisoner of War ship 1854, coal hulk Sheerness 08.1859 till sold 23.11.1894

BENBOW (1885) Greenock, CG
BB, CG Clyde 23.05.1894 - mid 1903, sold 1909

BENBOW Trinidad, Base
Cd 22.01.1941, PO 21.05.47
22.01.41 part of GOSHAWK accom camp was renamed BENBOW, though GOSHAWK (qv) which was to be Base and RNAS continued as RNAS - separate accounting organisation established in BENBOW 02.42
Nom DS: Skid Towing Ship CORTICELLI(ex GOSHAWK) 22.01.41 - (RESTO 15.07.46)

BENBOW II
In Post Office circular 22.04.1944, Apps in NL from 05.07.45 - not listed 1946

BERMUDA Ireland Island, Bermuda, RCN Radio Sta 03.07.1963-10.07.66

BERRY HEAD (1944) Escort Maint ship
Accepted 02.06.1945, HK 10.45-02.46, RF Sheerness Cd as accom sh 30.05.46, then SO RF there 04.06.46-53 (RF closed 01.04.53, BERRY HEAD remained temp under SORF Chat), Dev 54 - (SO Res Ships 26.01.54-12.03.56) (rb EURYALUS as living ship when to refit 10.56) - 58, modernised Chat 60-31.07.64, Res Dev 14.08.64-65, living ship RF Ports 67-68, modernised Ports 68, Cd 01.11.68, Far East 02.69-70 rb TRIUMPH, Dev refit 71, Chat res & preservation 13.09.71-01.72, SO Res Ships Chat v HARTLAND POINT 72-75, PO 03.76 for return to Canadian authorities under Mutual Aid Agreement 1948. Accom Sh Dev 76-, Ports de-equip 88, BU 03.90

BERYL (1898) Buncrana, SM DS
Yt, hired 01.1915-19, Cd 01.15 - resto 10.03.19
DS Northern Patrol while GIBRALTAR (qv) in refit 08.03.18-22.08.18

BESSIER Weymouth, Accom Sh
NAB, allocated 04.09.1942, allocated to Weymouth v PAULINE 03.44, laid up C & M Weymouth 07.10.44

BHATIARY Nucox's Bazar, Chittagong, Bangladesh NB
1996 - extant 1999

BHAWALPUR Pakistan, PN RF
Cd 01.02.1955, not listed 1960
BAHAWALPUR (1941) ex BARODA, ex LUCKNOW, Tlr, sold 1959 prob same ship

BHERUNDA Colombo, Ceylon, RNAS
Cd 01.10.1943, PO 30.11.45 (retard party to 31.12.45)
Was Colombo Racecourse, RAF Sta taken over by RN 01.09.43. Included RNAD Colombo (Rowlands Garage)
Nom DS: TRV 421028 01.10.43-

BIRMINGHAM (1913) Nore, Flag RF
Cr, Rear Admiral RF Nore (and Parent Gp B) 01.1922-06.22 rb CALLIOPE, Flag Africa v LOWESTOFT Cd 15.11.23-08.28 (at least), sold 02.31

BIRNBECK Birnbeck Pier and Island, Weston-Super-Mare, Experimental Sta (Weapon development)
Named 20.06.1942, Cd 02.10.1942, PO 31.01.46
Nom DS: Ferry MV PRINCESS IDA 02.10.42-04.44
NAB PERSIL nominated 04.44 but cancelled
NAB SOUTHERN MAID 04.44-

BITER (1855) Ports, Coal Hulk
Gunboat, conv to coal hulk 24.01.1865, at Ports 1870-1900 (at least), retitled C16, sold 03.1904

BLACK ARROW (1934) RNAS
Yt hired as Hbr defence Patrol Craft 01.1940-45, but a list has this name as an RNAS - poss a Nom DS with name changed.

BLACK BAT No 13 Wharf, Dev, CF Base
Approved 13.03.1943, Named with acs DRAKE IV 26.12.43 (not an independent command so no Nom DS), Cd 14.02.44 as tender to DEFIANCE, and Cd 01.05.44 tender to DEFIANCE, acs DRAKE IV, PO 16.07.45 (some reports indicate 11.07.45)
Nom DS: MB 42668 14.02.44 -

BLACK DRAGON Gib, Hulk
Ex Danish TS KOBENHAVN (1914) - oil hulk, purch while building, sold 1922 (also known as C600)

BLACK EMELLE Chichester, Accom Sh
08.1942 - acquired 16.02.43,-1945 (when attached SEASERPENT (qv)), to be laid up 20.06.45
Ex ML, EMELLE, known as BLACK EMELLE

BLACK PRINCE (1861) Queenstown/Clyde, TS/CG
Ironclad, was Flag Queenstown 1866-67, CG Clyde 09.1868-08.05.1874, became Boys' TS Queenstown 1898, renamed EMERALD (qv) TS Queenstown 03.1904, renamed IMPREGNABLE III (qv) TS Dev 06.1910, renamed BLACK PRINCE 12.10.22, sold 1923

BLACKCAP Stretton, Warrington, Lancs, RNAS
Cd with one third complement 01.06.1942, then Cd 15.06.42, closed for flying 01.08.58, to C & M 31.03.58, PO 04.11.58, closed 31.12.58 (under SANDERLING)
First arrangements made for RN there ("Stretton, Chesshire") 09.03.42, expanded to 2 Sqns, in exchange for RAF facilities LANDRAIL. Operational 05.42. Exchange of facilities no longer required by RAF and tx to RN outright 21.12.42

Also included RNAS Ollerton; Market Drayton (tx to RN 13.08.42 - name change to Hinstock shortly after, Cd 14.06.43 under BLACKCAP, became GODWIT (qv) ; Inskip (1942 - before Cd as NIGHTJAR 1943 (qv); Speke (1944-07.04.45 - tx to Woodvale/RINGTAIL II(qv); and Burscough (when PO as RINGTAIL 15.06.46(qv); see also URLEY.

Nom DS: Small MB OS2 01.06.42-07.08.43 - became BRITANNIA, Eaton Hall (qv)
Diesel lifeboat 40146 (ex BRITANNIA) 08.08.43-11.45 (damaged by fire 21.11.45, laid up 02.46 and sold
TRSB 4424 04.48(at least)-56
MFV 1023 09.56-58

BLACKHAWK USS, Inverness/Portland, M/L DS
Inverness 08.1918, Portland 12.18, Inverness 03.19

BLACKWOOD (1955) Ports/Rosyth, TS/Accom Sh
FF, Hbr TS Ports 1967-68, Accom Sh Rosyth 04.68-70, attached SULTAN as Hbr TS 07.1970-74, rb RUSSELL, BU 11.76

BLAIRESK Med, DS for Fixed A/S Defences
11.1943-05.44, assessed as useless, rb ANNA CAPANO (qv)

BLAKE (1808) Ports, Rx Sh
BOMBAY, renamed BLAKE 1819, Rx Sh 1828, BU 12.1855
Reputed to have been a Rx Sh at Ports for 40 years

BLAKE (1889) DS
Cr, conv to DD DS 1907, Nore 1908-09, Home Fleet 09-14, Grand Fleet (Scapa) 14-19 (2DF 12.14, 11 DF 08.16-19, to Harwich 5 DF 01.03.19 and v GANGES II as M/S DS 01.12.19-09.20, rb BLENHEIM, then to Sheerness 21-12.22 again rb BLENHEIM, sold 22

BLANCHE (1819) Ports, Rx Sh
5th Rate, Rx Sh 1852 to BU 10.1865

BLANDFORD Lunenburg Co NS, RCN Radio Sta
HMCNRS 1965-11.07.66, became CFS MILL COVE (qv)

BLANKNEY (1940) Sheerness, RF Living Ship
DD, living ship 1950, BU 03.59

BLAZER Bembridge, Isle of Wight, TE/Gunnery Range
There by 28.12.1943 with acs OSBORNE, To be Cd 04.44, Cd 01.01.45 tender to EXCELLENT, PO 01.04.46 - Not in NL till 01.45 with apps 12.44
Nom DS: NAB ALARIC 24.01.44-(allocated)-31.12.44
Diesel Lch 1853 01.01.45-

BLENHEIM (1813) Standgate Creek/Ports/Weymouth/Milford, Qtn Sh/CG
3rd Rate, Qtn Sh Standgate Creek 1831-, Guardship Ports 1850, CG Weymouth 01.02.1858-11.06.1860, CG Milford 12.06.1860-01.09.1865, BU 1865

BLENHEIM (1890) DS
Cr, conv to DD DS 1905-06, Home Fleet 06-13, Med 14-19 (including Dardanelles 14-15) (Tlr task to OSIRIS 07.15) (5DF Brindisi 10.18, Ismid 12.18) C & M Malta 12.02.19, 6 DF 01.03.19 - PO and Re-Cd 28.06.19, DS for Reserve M/S Harwich v BLAKE 09.20-22, Sheerness v BLAKE 12.22-07.25 rb ARK ROYAL, Dockyard control Nore 06.02.26, sold 26

BLENHEIM (1919) DD DS
SS ACHILLES purch 07.08.1940, renamed BLENHEIM 24.09.40, Cd 05.01.42 as DD DS Iceland v HECLA, Med 1944-45 (at Alexandria 05.45), Released 18.05.46, to Dof ST 18.11.46, BU 22.01.48

BLINJOE (1929) Bombay, RIN Base Ship/Accom Sh
Dutch vessel, nominated as alternative choice of ML DS to MELCHIOR TREUB/WUSUEH 10.42, hired as RIN CF Base Ship 12.1943-45, allocated Bengal Auxiliary Flot v GENERAL MICHIELS 07.44, Arakan v. BARRACUDA (qv), Calcutta 07.45

BLOEMFONTEIN (1944) Simons Bay, SAN Moored TS
M/S ex ROSALIND, moored TS 04.1961-07.63, sunk as target 05.06.67

BLONDE (1819) Ports, Rx Sh
5th Rate, Rx Sh 11.1850 and renamed CALYPSO 09.03.1870, sold 28.02.1895

BLOSSOM (1806) Standgate Creek, Qtn Sh
Sloop, Qtn Sh 1833 till BU 1848

BLUE JACKET Bombay, India, RN Nom DS
Cd 01.01.1948 - in NL to 1959
Nom DS: Cdre Bombay's 35 ft barge 43802 01.01.48-
MB 39661 1951

BLUEBIRD Glasgow, Accom Sh
Ex Nom DS SPARTIATE (qv) reverted to name BLUEBIRD 01.12.1944 as accom sh DSVP ship-keepers

BLUEBIRD III Folkestone, RNAS
Poss renamed ALLENBY (qv) 10.03.1944
BLUEBIRD II ex BLUEBIRD - Air Sea Rescue Folkestone 03.42. Reference to RNAS could be as Nom DS but doubtful

BLUFF Durban, S Africa, SAN TE
Listed 1957-61
For Radar Plotters

BOADICEA II Kingstown, Co Dublin/Holyhead, A/P Parent
A/P DS Kingstown 01.07.1915 v ILEX (qv) - PO 16.05.1919
A/P DS Holyhead - 01.07.1915 - 31.07.15 rb AMETHYST III(qv)

Retard party to EAGLET 31.03.1919
Nom DS: Yt BOADICEA (1882) hired and renamed when Cd (also used WW II) 17.05.1915 - 06.03.19
Tlr HENRY FORD (1917) - 06.03.19-16.05.19 (sold 1921)

BOADICEA (1908) Nore/Dartmouth, RF/TS
Cr, Nore Res Parent Gp 3 by 02.1919-20 and Gp IV 04.1919-24.05.19 rb SUPERB. Hbr Serv Dartmouth 01.21 v POMONE(qv) (was to have been renamed POMONE but kept own name), sold 13.07.26

BOADICEA Soton, Accom Sh
By 08.1942, acquired 31.12.42-07.44, to Dof ST/ C & M in Hamble 25.07.44, to DofST no longer required 21.10.44

BOMBARDIER (1915) White Sea, A/P DS
06.1915-08.1915 rb IPHIGENIA (qv)
Tlr purch 1914 while building, sold 1920

BOMBAY Bombay
In a list of 1944 as "NCS and LL whalers" with apps back to 1939

BONAVENTURE (1892) Haulbowline/ Harwich/Humber/Tyne, SM DS
Cr, conv to SM DS, Cd 02.04.1907, Haulbowline, Section of 2 SM Home Fleet 1907-12, 6 SM Harwich 15.10.12-14, Humber 1914, Tyne 1914-18 (also in charge Patrols 11.15) (6 SM then 2 SM 06.16), 2 SM Gib 08.1918-01.19, PO & ReCd Ports 02.19, alloc 5 SM Blyth but refit Ports 03.19-17.10.19, 4 SM for China 09.19 but rb TITANIA and PO 17.10.19 and sold 1920.

BONAVENTURE Tyne
MV BONAVENTURE was offered to Adty 29.07.1940 as Auxiliary Ammo Guard Ship

BONAVENTURE (1942) Loch Striven, SM DS
CLAN CAMPBELL conv to DS for midget SM 1942, Cd 26.01.43, served Home Waters including Loch Striven.14 SM 07.12.44-10.09.45 (14 SM PO and BONAVENTURE became independent command), Pacific from 07.45, res 47, sold to Clan Line 23.03.48
BONAVENTURE Duncan Dock, Capetown, S Africa, SAN Estab
HQ SAN Forces and SAN Res, listed 1943 - 12.58

BORDE (1921) N Africa/Gib, Repair Ship
Req 18.10.1939 as M/S, conv to repair ship 11.41, Cd 14.07.42, N Africa, Gib 04.44, C & M 05.44, handed over to BU 11.04.45 and sank on way to breakers. Not PO till 19.07.45

BORODINO (1911) Scapa Flow/Archangel, Stores Ship/ DS
Hired 01.12.1914-28.04.19, Junior Army & Navy Stores Ship Scapa Flow, Cd 29.05.19 Archangel - SNO shallow draught river craft. Used as blockship WW II

BOSCAWEN Chat/Soton/Portland, Guard Ship/TS
– BOSCAWEN (1844) Guardship Chat 1851, TS Soton 1862, to Portland 13.10.1866 - Cd as TS for boys 01.01.1867 at Portland, renamed WELLESLEY (qv) TS 21.03.1874
– TRAFALGAR (1841) renamed BOSCAWEN 1873 as TS Portland - also included camp on hillside by 1882, not listed 06.1904, sold 10.07.1906
– MINOTAUR ex ELEPHANT (1863), renamed BOSCAWEN 03.1904 (see also BOSCAWEN II), to Harwich 09.1905, arrived by 10.1905, renamed GANGES (qv) 21.06.1906, renamed GANGES II (qv) 25.04.1908, sold 30.01.22

BOSCAWEN II Portland, TS
MINOTAUR ex ELEPHANT (1863), Portland as TS 1893, renamed BOSCAWEN II 1893-1904 (NL shows her under old name to 06.1904), renamed BOSCAWEN 03.1904 (qv)

BOSCAWEN III Portland, TS
AGINCOURT (1865)(qv), at Portland 1899, renamed BOSCAWEN III 03.1904, left Portland 09.1905, arrived Harwich by 10.1905, renamed GANGES II (qv) 21.06.1906
Some reports state she was BOSCAWEN III 1899-1905, NL shows her under old name till 06.1904 (also listed as Boys' TS Chat 1879-1904)

BOSCAWEN Portland, Base
Cd 01.07.1932 ex VICTORY XI (qv), PO 31.12.47 (OSPREY became Base)
A/S and M/S Base. Rear Admiral CF on her books 1940.
Nom DS: Barge No 114 1934
MB 3632 1940-18.01.41(but still in NL 1941-47)
Steam Lch 251 19.01.41 - (aold 01.49)?
MB 761 25.07.47-

BOSCAWEN II Portland
Address for personal correspondence 10.1944

BOXER (1942) Ports
LST(1), Living Ship RF, SORF to 06.11.1956 rb VANGUARD, tx completed by 17.12.56, BU 12.58

BOUCLIER (1937) TS and DS-Accom Sh
Fr Torp Boat, allocated to Dutch, Holyhead 07.1940, Cd as Fr DS at Dev 12.01.41-09.45, used for A/S Tng and Accom Sh for corvette ACONITE (1941 - Free Fr ACONIT 07.41) 06.06.41.

BOURNEMOUTH QUEEN (1908) - Ft William/ Lamlash, Base & Accom Sh
Also called BOURNEMOUTH BELLE in some books
Paddle Steamer, hired as M/S WWI (BOURNE) and as AA ship 04.1941. Guard ship Harwich 26.09.42, accom sh Ft William Cd 19.10.43, PO 16.02.44. Alloc trials ship DMWD Trials Lamlash 24.03.45, Resto 08.11.45

BRADFORD (1918) Dev, Accom Sh

DD, Ex USN, reduced to C & M 02.06.1943. Cd 02.06.43 as tender to FOLIOT (qv). Accom sh and accounting base for CO personnel to 10.44 (at least). BU 08.46

BRAGANZA Bombay, India, RN Base
Cd 01.01.1943 and also 01.09.43, PO 30.06.46
Originally carried RN Personnel in Bombay excluding CO. Incorporated SALSETTE (qv) 01.04.44 when became CO Base
Nom DS: 30ft ML ex RNO Bombay 01.01.43-

BRAGANZA II Bombay, India
01.09.1943, independent command. Ceased to exist 30.06.44
Carried Administrative and Maint Staff of CO and Dockyard Bombay
Incorporated SALSETTE II (qv) 01.04.44

BRAGANZA III Bombay, India, LC Signal & Navigation TE
1944-PO 31.10.45
Incorporated SALSETTE III (qv) 01.04.44

BRAMBLE (1945) Pt Edgar, Accom Sh
M/S, Cd 01.12.1948 as living ship - 49, BU 08.61

BRANTFORD (1941) Digby, RCN Hbr TS
Corvette, moored TS Digby 10.44, sold 1950

BRAZEN (1808) Deptford, Floating Chapel
6th Rate, Deptford 1827 - BU 1848

BRECON (1942) Ports, Accom Sh
DD, accom sh 03.05.50-12.50 (at least), BU 09.62

BREDA (1912) Rothesay, SM Tender
Yt, purch 1939 as convoy leader, SM tender 1940, 7 SM Rothesay 1941, sunk 18.02.44 in collision, Campbeltown Loch

BREVDRAGEREN Deptford, Army DS
Danish Sloop, capt 1807, prison ship 1818, Army DS 1820, sold 1825

BRIES Poole, Accom Sh
NAB, allocated 18.08.1942, acquired 11.03.43, laid up C & M /DST 14.06.45

BRIGHTON Brighton, RN W/T Unit
Address for RN W/T units BRIGHTON I and II was Training Sch, 29 Queen's Rd, Brighton from 27.04.1942. Not Cd as such

BRILLIANT (1814) Dundee/Inverness, RNR Drl Sh
5th Rate, RNR TS 1859, Dundee Drl Sh 01.04.1862-01.01.1874, then Drl Sh Inverness (Kessock Ferry) v. NETLEY till renamed BRITON (qv) 08.11.1889, sold 1908

BRILLIANT (1891) Soton/Tyne/ Shetlands, RNR Drl Sh/DS
Cr, RNR Drl Sh Soton v APOLLO 13.12.1904-1905, Stokers' TS Chat v CHAMPION 09.13, DS Tyne 1914-15, A/P DS Shetlands v ZARIA (qv) 01.11.15-26.01.18 rb AMBITIOUS (qv), PO 16.02.18, blockship 23.04.18

BRISBANE Alicia St., Brisbane, Australia, RANVR Depot
Ex PENGUIN IV(qv) RANVR Depot, Cd as BRISBANE 01.08.1940, renamed MORETON qv) 30.09.42
Included Pt Moresby & Thursday Is

BRISTOL Ashley Down, Bristol, TE
Cd 10.1942, independent command, acs BRITANNIA, own acs 11.42, PO 01.01.43
First 7 terms of Dartmouth College tx 17.10.42 - see also BRITANNIA IV.
Closed when main college tx to Eaton Hall

BRISTOL Muller's Orphanage, Bristol, TE
Cd 15.02.1943, PO 28.12.43
Muller's Orphanage returned to War Office 01.01.44

BRISTOL (1969) Whale Island, Ports, Hbr TS
DD, TS Ports 22.03.1993 v KENT, Cd 06.05.93, extant 99

BRITANNIA Ports/ Dartmouth/ Eaton Hall, Chester, TS
Cd 01.01.1859 - PO 01.07.1953, renamed DARTMOUTH (qv) to release name for Royal Yt. Title Britannia Royal Naval College used from 1953.
– BRITANNIA (1820) 1st Rate, Flag Ports 1840, Guardship Ports 1851, Cadets' TS Ports 01.01.1859, to Portland 02.1862, to Dartmouth 09.1863, BU 1869
– PRINCE OF WALES (1860), renamed BRITANNIA 03.03.1869, hulk 09.1909, sold 13.11.1914
– HINDOSTAN (1841) joined BRITANNIA 1860 as accom sh(qv), renamed FISGARD III (qv) 12.10.1905
College opened ashore 09.1905 - foundation stone laid 17.03.1902. College closed 08.1914, cadets sent to sea. At this time there was a BRITANNIA (1904) BB, lost 09.11.1918 and the College was known as BRITANNIA (Hulk) - Officers being borne in ESPIEGLE and POMONE (qv). In WW II, Cadets were sent to Eaton Hall, Eaton, Chester 09.1942-21.09.46. Junior terms also accom at Howstrake Camp, Isle of Man to 07.1941, and also in BRISTOL (qv). College closed 31.03.43 and was then used as CO TE (DARTMOUTH III/EFFINGHAM (qv)), and tx to USN 01.01.44. Eaton Hall Cd as BRITANNIA 01.02.42
Nom DS: OSBORNE 01.06.22-37 refers to steam Lch BETA ex RN College Osborne Nom DS (qv)
Steam Lch 227 04.05.1937-18.06.43
34 ft Twin Screw Diesel Lifeboat 40146 01.03.43-07.08.43 (became BLACKCAP) (qv)
Small MB OS2 08.08.43-
Steam Lch 227 12.46-03.48
FMB 37132 03.48-52

BRITANNIA II Dartmouth, Tlr Base

06.1940-23.12.42, renamed DARTMOUTH (qv)

BRITANNIA III Dartmouth, CF Base,
Name alloc 30.04.1941, Cd 01.05.41, independent command, acs BRITANNIA II 10.41, PO 23.12.42, renamed DARTMOUTH II (qv)
Poss at Royal Dart Hotel, Kingswear. BELFORT (qv) attached 1941
Nom DS: Hbr Lch SILVER STAR 01.05.41-12.11.41
NAB SUNBEAM 13.11.41 -23.12.42 (became DARTMOUTH II) - reverted to BRITANNIA III ex CICALA (qv) 12.44

BRITANNIA IV Bristol, TE
Ann RN College to tx temp to Ashley Down, Bristol as BRITANNIA IV 03.10.42, but cancelled. Later tx as BRISTOL (qv)

BRITANNIA (1953) Royal Yt, Museum Sh
PO 10.12.1997 and to Leith as Museum Sh

BRITON (1812) Ports, Convict Ship
5th Rate, convict ship 1841 - target 1860, BU 1860

BRITON (1814) Inverness, RNR Drl Sh
BRILLIANT (qv) renamed BRITON 08.11.1889 while at Inverness Drl Sh, there till sold 12.05.1908

BRITON (1883) Newfoundland, RNR Drl Sh
CALYPSO Cd 03.09.1902 at Dev as Drl Sh Newfoundland RNR, renamed BRITON 15.02.1916, sold 07.04.22

BRONINGTON (1953) Manchester, Museum Sh
M/S, Museum sh 1989, extant 1999

BRONTOSAURUS Castle Toward, Dunoon, Argyll, CO Base
Cd 07.08.1942 ex ARARAT, PO 10.07.46, retard party to 31.07.46, base facilities for 130 LCT Flot at Hopper's Pier remain
Nom DS: YOUNG MUN(1911) Drifter 08.08.42-07.46

BROWN Cocos Islands
Codeword in use 29.04.44 v. JAMES (qv) to 18.07.45
Base established & RAF airfield 21.04.45-, base closed 20.05.46

BRUCE (1910) TS
CAESAREA, later MANXMAID, later BRUCE, hired as radar TS 10.1941, renamed MANXMAID 23.06.42 TS (qv), conv to local escort vessel, RESTO 1945

BRUCE Crail, Fife, RNAS/ Boys' TE
Cd 29.04.47, ex JACKDAW. PO 25.10.49 but listed as Reserve Air Sta till at least 1960 (see JACKDAW)
Nom DS: HL(P) 451020 29.04.47-52 (No apps in NL then)

BRUCE Rosyth, Res Ships
RS Div Rosyth was to be renamed BRUCE 26.07.1960, but not used. RF became COCHRANE via DUNCANSBY HEAD (1962) - see also notes on DUNDONALD/NEPTUNE

BRUNSWICK (1790) Chat, Powder Hulk
3rd Rate, powder hulk 1812, BU 1826

BRUNSWICKER Saint John, New Brunswick, Canada, RCN Base & Res Div
221-223 Prince William St
01.09.1939, Cd 01.11.41, tender to CAPTOR II, independent command 01.09.42, - 1986 (at least) - extant 1998

BRYONY (1941) Dartmouth, Accom Sh
Corvette, accom sh 01.1947, sold to Norway 1948

BUCHAN NESS (1945) Gareloch, LC Maint Ship
Cd 26.07.1945, Res Amphibious Force Gareloch 02.48, PO 1950, living ship Gareloch 12.50, res in Gareloch 1952-SORF Gareloch 12.54-, To extended res 04.58, BU Faslane 1959

BUFFALO Standgate Creek, Qtn Sh
Ex East Indiaman, purch 1813, qtn sh 1831, timber carrier 1831, wrecked 1841

BUFFALO East London, S Africa, SAN Estab
Listed 1944, (in PO Circular 22.03.44)

BULL Massawa, Eritrea, RN Base
Cd 01.07.1942, acs to SHEBA 01.02.46, to C & M 06.03.46, PO 01.10.46.
Later became Ethiopian Naval Academy

BULLFROG Fixed A/S Defences
Codename for Operations in Arakan, left UK 12.08.1943 for Ceylon, Parties 30 and 31 (NP 1030/1031)

BULWARK (1860) TS
HOWE, 1st Rate, renamed BULWARK, Hbr Serv 03.12.1885, renamed IMPREGNABLE (qv) 27.09.1886, reverted to BULWARK 12.1919, sold 18.02.1921

BUNTING Harwich/Ipswich, A/P Base
Cd 25.02.1940, independent command 14.06.40, PO 10.11.44, M/S and A/P Tlrs to EPPING (Harwich), absorbed by WOOLVERSTONE (qv). Reported as at Ipswich 07.43-09.44
Nom DS: BUNTING (ex MERLIN)(1896) - hired as Danlayer 01.40,
02.40 - 22.10.40, renamed FREELANCE, renamed BUNTING 11.44-46
FREELANCE (1908) Yt, hired as A/P Yt 28.09.40
22.10.40 - 03.44 renamed FREEWILL accom sh (qv)
EMPERIOR OF INDIA (1906) Paddle, hired as A/P vessel WI, as M/S 12.39, AA ship 11.40, accom sh 43-46(qv), was Nom DS 03.44-10.11.44
became WOOLVERSTONE (qv)

BURDEKIN (1943) Corio Bay, Geelong, Australia, RAN SO RF

FF, res 18.04.46 - sold 1961

BURLINGTON (1921) M/S DS
Ex CHARTERED, hired as M/S 17.05.1940, renamed SOOTHSAYER 1940 (MoD record shows her as renamed FAIRFAX direct from BURLINGTON), renamed FAIRFAX 1941, repair ship (qv), BU 1945

BURONG (1921) Mandapam, India, RN M/S Base
Cd 15.01.1944 acs LANKA, PO 11.46
Coaster hired as M/S Base Ship 01.44-46
Nom DS: MB 39288 15.10.44-

BURRARD Vancouver, BC, Canada, RCN Base
Estab 01.09.1939, Cd 05.1942 - 15.08.42 (as NOIC) and 15.08.42-28.02.46 (as NOIC and DS)
Separate entries in NL for BURRARD (Base) and BURRARD (DS)
In 1942 became HQ Pacific Fleet v NADEN

BUSHNELL (1915) Buncrana/ Berehaven/Portland, USS SM DS
Arrived Queenstown 27.01.18, Berehaven 03.1918-08.1918, Buncrana 05.18-11.18(poss 2 separate sections), Portland 12.18-01.19

BUSHWOOD (1930)
Purch as M/S 1940, DG Vessel 1942, Store carrier 44-11.46, RESTO 11.46
Listed as support ship Far East 1944

BUXTON (1918) Halifax/Digby, NS, Canada, TS
DD (ex USS EDWARDS), tx RN 10.1940, tx RCN 08.43, Static TS Halifax (CORNWALLIS) 04.11.43, Pictou 10.44 and later Digby, PO at Sydney NS 02.06.45, BU 03.46

BUZZARD (1887) London, RNR Drl Sh
Sloop, RNR Drl Sh 1904, renamed PRESIDENT (qv) 01.04.1911, Lent temp to Marine Society Greenhithe 30.01.1918 (see under WARSPITE), reverted to BUZZARD 10.02.1921 when SAXIFRAGE renamed PRESIDENT, sold 1921

BUZZARD Lympne, Kent, RNAS
Cd 01.07.1939 (ex 22 Gp RAF), PO 25.09.39 (temp - civilian caretakers - to allow manning of SPARROWHAWK (qv). Appd to re-open temp as FAA TE 03.11.39, renamed DAEDALUS II (qv) 03.04.1940 and handed over to RAF 22.05.40
Nom DS: Steam Lch 216 01.07.39 -

BUZZARD Palisadoes, Kingston, Jamaica, RNAS
Cd 21.12.1940 ex MALABAR III (qv) to handle all services when RNAS opened, but base named MORGAN instead. RNAS remained BUZZARD 21.01.41. Independent command 16.08.41, PO 15.07.1943. Cd 16.07.43 in C & M at 3 mths notice, acs MORGAN. Listed as an active base 03.09.44, PO 31.12.44, admin to War Office with C & M Party - PO 30.06.45(?)
Nom DS: DOUGLAS ALEXANDER (A/P Vessel) 21.12.40-01.08.41
- became Nom DS MORGAN
NAB NANIN 01.08.41 -

BYRSA Bougie, Algeria, RN Base (NP 656)
Cd 01.01.1943, tx to Castellamare 10.43
Pt Pty had mainly tx Castellamare by 10.43 when name tx and remaining personnel came under HAMILCAR (qv)
Nom DS: Small MB ex POZARICA 08.43-

BYRSA Castellamare/ Naples, Italy, RN Base (Pt Party Naples - NP 864)
Tx ex Bougie by 10.1943, then to Naples 12.43. Acs closed and to ST ANGELO 31.12.45. PO at Naples 01.04.46
C-in-C Med's Flag hoisted 09.07.44 ex HANNIBAL, carried FO Naples by 10.45

BYTOWN Ottawa, Ontario, Canada, RCN HQ/Res
Named 31.07.41, quoting order of 14.06.41, for personnel in Naval Service HQ and Res.
Cd 31.07.41 - 21.05.42 BYTOWN was DS for HQ Res Section was named CARLETON (qv) 01.11.41 - PO 21.05.42
21.05.42-23.11.42 BYTOWN was DS for HQ and Res. Res then named CARLETON again (qv)
23.11.42 - 07.01.64 BYTOWN was DS for HQ.
Became Canadian Forces HQ 1964, name still in use by Officers' Mess. Lisgar, Ottawa 1997.
Nom DS: HC 128 ex ORACLE 06.42-13.10.45

BYTOWN II Galt, Ontaria, RCN (WRCNS) TE
10.1942 - 01.06.43 - became CONESTOGA (qv)
Not Cd

C

CABBALA Tortworth Court, Falfield, Gloucestershire, Coding Sch
Cd 01.03.41, 25.09.42 tx to Lowton
Took over Higham Court (C & M) ex GANGES 31.01.42. Tng tx to Risley (target 01.09.42) and to re-site Tortworth Camp at Gt Malvern (22.07.42). Tortworth Camp tx to War Office 25.09.42 and vacated 17.11.42. Higham Court Camp vacated 09.11.42 and tx to Brox Fare, Nr Nottingham.
Nom DS: 52.5ft Diesel Lch 3708 (THALIA) 01.03.41-08.42 (tx - see below)

CABBALA Lowton, Warrington, Lancs, Coding Sch
25.09.42 - 11.46 (became SCOTIA(qv)) - see also entry below
EVT task from GOSLING 05.46
Nom DS: Diesel Lch 3708 09.42(see CABBALA above)-05.46

CABBALA Millmeece, Eccleshall, Nr Stafford, EVT Centre
Cd 11.46 (ex FLEDGLING (qv) PO 02.48 (to Min of Supply)

CABOT Bristol/Thorpe Arch, Wetherby, TE
Cd 13.07.1940 at Bristol, estab to No 2 Hostel,

Thorpe Arch 15.09.42, PO 15.07.44 (then Cd as DEMETRIUS (qv))
In list of bases as at Avonmouth 29.10.44
Overflow estab for DRAKE at Muller's Orphanage (RNTE Ashley Down) Bristol 02.05.40. Tng to Risley (target 01.09.42) and to Wetherby (target 15.09.42). Muller's Orphanage vacated and handed over to War Office 15.09.42 (but see also BRISTOL)
Nom DS: BOUNTIFUL (1911) Drifter 13.07.40-11.41 (sunk - when raised renamed BOUNTEOUS to avoid confusion)
Motor Barge MINNIE FLOSSIE 24.11.41-

CABOT St John's, Newfoundland, RCN Res Naval Div
Cd 20.09.1949 - listed 1976, extant 1987.
Moved from Buckmaster's Field to Pleasantville 06.43

CADMUS Avonmouth, Bristol, Base
Name sel for Base at Comml port of Avonmouth 01.09.1939. NOIC ordered 27.08.39, name not used - Base reduced to RNO status 28.07.45, base ceased 28.09.45, and closed 15.10.45

CAESAR (1896) Black Sea/Egypt, DS
BB, DS Black Sea/Sea of Marmara. Arrive Constantinople 02.12.1918. By 01.10.19 rb JULIUS (qv) and to Malta for crew change 10.19. To Pt Said v HANNIBAL as DS Egypt 04.12.19-01.03.20. To UK 01.03.20 PO at Dev 28.04.20, sold 1921
Alloc as DS Caspian Sea v MANTIS/MANTIS II 27.11.18-but task to THESEUS 12.18(qv)
DS Naval Brigade Belgrade to 01.04.19 (task to EGMONT)

CAESAR (1944) Dev, RF living ship
DD, living ship 12.1950-11.51 (at least), BU 01.67

CAGWAY Pt Royal, Jamaica, CG Base
HMJS, listed 1989, extant 1999

CAIRNS Cairns, Australia, RAN Minor Warship Base
Cd 01.02.1974 - extant 1999
Also supports RANR and Thursday Island RANR Sub Divs

CAIRO (1902), Gt Yarmouth, Tlr Base
Tlr, hired as Base Ship 10.1914-11.1914 rb WHITE EAR, M/S 1916-19
CALCUTTA Gib/Ports, DS/TS
1909-15
HERCULES (1868) conv to barracks for Dockyard employees Gib 1906, renamed CALCUTTA 1909. From Gib for Shotley as Boys' TS (05.04.1914), attached MTE Ports, renamed FISGARD II (qv) 04.15

CALCUTTA (1918) Dev/Hull, RF/RNVR Drl Sh
Cr, SO RF Dev 1938, Drl Sh 07.1939 (allocated 14.04.39 after trials) - 27.08.39. Lost 1941
Div formed 21.10.1938 - see GALATEA

CALEDON (1916) Dev/Nore, SO RF
Cr, SORF Dev 1935-36, Nore 1938-39, sold 22.01.48

CALEDONIA (1808) Greenwich, Hosp Sh
See DREADNOUGHT

CALEDONIA (1862) Rockferry, Birkenhead, CG
2nd Rate, CG Rockferry temp by 01.1873, permanent by 01.1874 - 01.04.1875, sold 30.09.1886

CALEDONIA (1810) Queensferry, Boys' TS
Cd 22.09.1891, closed 03.01.1906
IMPREGNABLE, TS 1862 (qv), renamed KENT (qv) 1888, renamed CALEDONIA 22.09.1891, sold 10.07.1906

CALEDONIA Rosyth, Boys' and Articifers' TS
Liner ex MAJESTIC, ex BISMARCK (1914), Cd 23.04.1937, destroyed by fire 29.09.39, wreck sold 03.43, raised 12.07.43
Boys evacuated to Isle of Man 04.09.39. Cunningham Camp taken over 05.09.39, named ST GEORGE (qv), acs COCHRANE.
Mechanical TE moved ashore by 09.09.39. Artificer tng continued ashore and estab was named CALEDONIA in 1946 (see below)

CALEDONIA Oban, Base
Cd 01.07.1943 (was ST ANDREW(qv), PO 30.09.45, closed 10.09.45
Nom DS: ST JOHN (ex ECILA) 01.07.45-

CALEDONIA Rosyth, RNATE
Cd 01.12.1946 - formal naming of old Mechanical TE - (see CALEDONIA above), ceased to operate as TE 14.12.1985, PO 17.12.1985, site retained as part of COCHRANE (qv)
Nom DS: Hbr Lch 134 12.46
MWB 45960 23.07.45-11.76 (at least)

CALEDONIA Rosyth, RN Support Estab
Cd 01.04.1996 in old CALEDONIA building as support base for ships in refit

CALLIOPE (1837) Dev, Chapel/Factory Ship
6th Rate, floating chapel 1860, factory ship at Dev 1865 - BU 11.1883

CALLIOPE Tyne, Res Drl Sh
1907 - (Division formed ashore 1905) - 1915 (gap 1915-31 for Cr CALLIOPE 1914-31), then 10.1931-extant 99
Name sel for shore base at comml pt Tyne 01.09.1939. CALLIOPE (base) Cd 04.09.39, NOIC ordered 27.08.39. CALLIOPE (ship) moved from Elswick 1939 to Albert Edward Dock N Shields. (By 04.1940 all RNVR Divs were closed). PO 23.02.46 - acs to PEMBROKE I and II., and ship returned up river 12.08.46 to resume RNVR task. Name was in use when Reserve re-established 10.46, and kept in 1951 when RNR Divs named. Moved ashore 06.67 (shore estab Cd 68 as CALLIOPE) at South Shore Rd, Gateshead
Nom DS: CALLIOPE (1884) screw corvette 29.10.07-06.15 renamed HELICON (qv)

10.31 renamed CALLIOPE-sold 04.10.51
FALMOUTH (1932) sloop - conv to Drl Sh 1948 v. CALLIOPE
26.04.51 - 01.68 (BU 04.68)

CALLIOPE (1914) Nore RF,
Cr, SORF Nore v BIURMINGHAM 01.22-12.24, rb AJAX, SORF Nore v SPENSER 12.27-, sold 08.31

CALPE Gib, HQ unit RNR
Cd 18.11.1965 - PO 31.03.93
Cd in Dockyard, moved to old USOC Club House 1983

CALSHOT (1930) Solent, DS
Ferry, hired 12.1940-09.45, used as LC Engineering & maint vessel 06.44

CALYPSO (1819) Ports, Rx Sh
5th Rate, BLONDE (qv), renamed CALYPSO 09.03.1870, Rx Sh till sold 28.01.1895

CALYPSO (1883) St John's, Newfoundland, Res Drl Sh
Cd 03.09.1902, renamed BRITON (qv) 15.02.16, sold 1922, store hulk, still at St John's WW II

CAMBRIA Cardiff/Penarth, RNR Drl Sh
Cd 30.06.1947 in Merchant Navy Centre, Cardiff. Name allocated 1951. By 1950 was at East Dock, Cardiff. Name allocated 1951. By 10.80 at Hayes Pt, Penarth - extant 1999
Nom DS: DERG (1943) FF, was WESSEX 1951(qv), then allocated CAMBRIA 10.04.54-01.04.59 - downgraded to hulk, allocated as permanent Drl Sh 30.12.54
BU 09.60

CAMBRIAN (1841) Dev, Factory
5th Rate, hulk 1872, floating factory 1880 - sold 12.01.1892

CAMBRIAN (1893) Dev, Stokers' TS
Cr, became Stokers' TS, renamed HARLECH (qv) 08.08.1916, renamed VIVID (qv) 09.21, sold 02.23

CAMBRIAN (1916) Nore, SORF
Cr, SORF Nore 1931-33, sold 07.34

CAMBRIAN (1943) Chat, Accom Sh
DD, RF lving ship 12.48-11.51, BU 09.71

CAMBRIDGE Plym, Gunnery TS
Cd 09.08.1856 as Gunnery TS, moved ashore into VIVID 1907
– CAMBRIDGE (1815) 3rd Rate - Gunnery Ship 08.1856-BU 22.03.1869
– WINDSOR CASTLE (ex VICTORIA (1857) - renamed CAMBRIDGE 1969, sold 24.06.1908

CAMBRIDGE Wembury, Nr Plym, Gunnery Range
Cd 09.08.1956 (100 yrs to day after previous CAMBRIDGE Gunnery Sch) - extant 1999 - though poss to close as live firing no longer required 1999
1939 - opened by Army, 1940 - established as a naval firing range

Nom DS: HL(D) 421044 10.08.57-sold 24.05.59 though still listed 1960

CAMILLA (1776) Sheerness, Rx Sh
6th Rate, Rx Sh 1814, sold 1831

CAMPANIA Scapa Flow
Purchased 1914 as aircraft carrier, Scapa Seaplane Base and Horton Bay RNAS WWI, sunk 05.11.1918

CAMPANIA (1943) Rosyth, Accom Sh
Aircraft carrier, accom sh 01.47. Festival of Britain Ship 30.03.51-01.11.51 (returned RN), BU 11.55

CAMPERDOWN (1820) Ports, Rx Sh/Coal Hulk
TRAFALGAR, 1st Rate, renamed CAMPERDOWN 22.02.1825, Rx Sh Ports 1854-57, coal hulk Ports 1857, renamed PITT 1882, sold 1906

CAMPERDOWN (1885) Lough Swilly/Harwich, CG/SM Berthing Ship
BB, CG Lough Swilly 05.07.1900-06.05.1903, SM Berthing Ship Harwich 10.1908-07.11, sold 11.07.11

CAMPERDOWN (1944) Dev, Accom Sh
DD, RF living ship 02.48-12.49, BU 09.70

CAMPERDOWN Marine Parade, Dundee, Tay RNR Drl Sh
Cd 08.1969 - PO 29.071994
UNICORN/CRESSY (qv) was Drl Sh to 1968

CANA - see CANNA

CANADA (1765) Chat, Convict Hosp Sh
3rd Rate, Chat 1810, BU 1834

CANADA Halifax, NS, Canada, RN Base
Cd 01.08.1942 v SAKER (qv)(poss v. SAKER II), PO 30.06.1944 (renamed SEABORN (qv)))
RNAS Dartmouth (from 01.08.42-10.43 - see SEABORN) and RNAS Yarmouth (from 01.01.43)
RN Tel Air Gunners' Sch came under CANADA

CANNA Spore, Res Drl Sh
06.1955-63, BU 09.63 was a beached hulk used for damage control and painting classes - approved for disposal by scrap 18.02.65 - also spelt CANA in Pink List
Service Craft ex MRC 1109

CANNAE Bone/Philippeville, Algeria, Base (NP 623)
Cd 01.01.1943, PO 01.12.44, Re-Cd 02.12.44 as tender to HANNIBAL - PO 07.05.45
At Bone, took on personnel remaining at Philippeville (ex ELISSA) 10.43.
Nom DS: Motor Cutter 4064 (ex ALARM) 26.08.43-

CANNING (1896) Orkney, Kite Balloon Ship/DS
Cd 29.06.1915 as Kite Balloon Ship, as DS 1917, sold 12.02.20

CANOPUS Dev, Rx Sh
FRANKLIN (Fr), capt 01.08.1798, renamed CANOPUS, Rx Sh Dev 1863 till sold 10.1887

CANOPUS (1897) Chat, Accom Sh
BB, Accom Sh 1916 - Cd 01.07.1917 in continuation as overflow ship, PO 09.1919, sold 02.1920

CANOPUS Ras El Tin Sch, Alexandria, Base/TE
Cd 18.12.1940, tender to NILE, PO 20.10.45
Nom DS: Sailing Cutter 4922 18.12.40-

CANOPUS II Alexandria, TE
1943-?
In PO Circular 22.03.43

CAP TOURAINE (1923) Normandy, DS
Ex Loch Ewe, arrived Sword Beach 08.06.44-to Gold 29.06.44, to Soton 10.07.44, to beaches 20.07.44 - end 08.44 -
See TOREADOR - also spelt CAP TOURANE in Red List/OpOrder

CAPE BRETON (1944) Halifax/Esquimalt, RCN Escort Maint Ship
FLAMBOROUGH HEAD, RCN 02.05.1951, Cd 31.01.1953, at Halifax and renamed CAPE BRETON - Repair Ship and TE. Conv to Escort Maint Ship and to West Coast 1958. Cd Esquimalt 16.11.59, PO 10.02.64, accom sh Esquimalt 64 - hulk 1972 - to Artificial Reef Soc BC 30.03.99 to be sunk off Gabriola Is

CAPE SCOTT (1944) Halifax, RCN Escort Maint Ship
BEACHY HEAD, renamed VULKAAN (Dutch) 1946-49, RCN 06.10.1951 and renamed CAPE SCOTT 1953. Halifax as workshops 1953, Cd 28.01.59 at Halifax, PO 01.07.70 Fleet Maint Gp Atlantic 72-75, BU 1978

CAPE WRATH (1945) CF Maint Ship
Cd 05.03.1946, Res Gareloch 01.06.46-05.50, to Ministry of War Transport 16.06.50, sold 03.51, BU 51

CAPETOWN (1919) Dev, Accom Sh
Cr, for CO Dev 02.1944, became Shuttle Control Ship Normandy 07.06.44, accom sh Dev 44-45, BU 46

CAPRICE (1943) Dev, TS
DD, attached THUNDERER v. MANXMAN 01.1971-72, BU 06.79

CAPTAIN (1783) Plym, Rx Sh
3rd Rate, CARNACTIC, renamed 1815 Rx Sh - BU 1825

CAPTAIN (1786) Plym, Rx Sh
1st Rate, ROYAL SOVEREIGN, renamed 1825, Rx Sh - BU 1841

CAPTIVITY (1786) Plym, Convict Ship
BELLEROPHON, prison ship 10.1815, renamed CAPTIVITY 05.10.1824, sold 01.1836

CAPTOR Saint John, New Brunswick, Canada, Base/NOIC
09.1939-07.45
Nom DS: RCMP Vessel HC73 (hired for Examination Service 05.09.39-43)
1943-

CAPTOR II Saint John, New Brunswick, Canada, DS and Accom Sh
Accom Sh ex DOT Vessel PWD Dredger No 1 10.1939-08.09.43
DS 01.04.41-30.09.44 (task to BRUNSWICKER 09.44-01.01.46) -
In Red List 05.45

CARADOC (1916) Colombo, Escort Base Ship
Cr, Base Ship Colombo 22.03.1944-24.10.45, BU 03.46
CARDIFF (1917) Nore, SORF
Cr, SORF Nore 1935-36, Vice Admiral (DDs) RF Flot, Dev 1939, sold 01.46

CARIBBEAN (1890) Accom Sh
Hired as AMC 19.11.1914, fitted out as accom sh for 600 artificers at Lpool 06.1915. Cd 09.15 but foundered on passage Scapa Flow 26.09.15

CARIBOU Corner Brook, Newfoundland, RCN Div
Cd 21.11.1952 - PO 31.03.58 but listed to 1961

CARINA London, Small Vessel Pool
20.06.1940 - C & M 20.04.44, re-allocated Nore Pool as DS at East India Dock 15.02.45
GOLDEN EAGLE (1899) hired as A/S Yt 01.40, renamed CARINA 08.04.40

CARLETON Dows Lake, Ottawa, RCN Base/RCNR Div
Established 15.09.1939 - Cd 01.11.41 (ex BYTOWN(qv)) - PO 21.05.42. Originally co-located with BYTOWN but moved to Rideau St 12.41. Re-opened 23.11.42 - listed to 1970, extant 1987 (at least)

CARLISLE (1918) Alexandria, Base Ship
Cr, constructive total loss 09.10.43, became Base Ship 1943-45, allocated to Aden but remained Alexandria, BU 49

CARMELA (1903) Pembroke Dk/Loch Tarbert, Accom Sh
12.08.1941-11.45
Yt, accom sh 764 Sqn RNAS Pembroke Dk 20.08.41, re-allocated to RNAS Machrihanish, Loch Tarbert 04.09.43, purch 43, sold 11.45

CARMENITA (1920) Soton, Accom Sh
Aux barge, hired as Barrage Balloon Vessel 12..1939, accom sh 1942-11.45

CARNACTIC (1823) Ports, Coal/Powder hulk
3rd Rate, coal hulk Ports 01.1860, lent War Department as powder hulk 08.1886-10.91, powder hulk Ports 1900 - sold 19.02.1914

CAROLINE (1882) Harwich, TS
11.1899-04.1908
Corvette, hbr serv 1897, arrived Harwich 11.1899 in preparation for arrival GANGES, 04.1908

renamed GANGES (qv), 09.13 renamed POWERFUL III (qv), 11.1919 renamed IMPREGNABLE Iv (qv), sold 31.08.29

CAROLINE (1914) Belfast, RNR/RNVR Drl Sh/Base
Cd 01.04.1924 - extant 1999
Cr, demilitarised 1923, 01.04.24 became Res Drl Sh Belfast. Name sel for base at comml port Belfast 01.09.1939. NOIC ordered 27.08.39, ship taken over by NOIC and conv to DEMS Drl Sh 19.10.39. Cd as a Base 19.10.39 at Milewater Basin. PO 31.01.46. RNVR Ulster re-instated 01.10.46 (CO nominated 10.01.46) in CAROLINE. Name allocated to RNVR Div 1951. Cr still there 1999 though plans extant 1992 to preserve her as Museum ship at Hartlepool if RN pay her off.

CAROLINE II Belfast, CF Base
Name allocated 30.04.1941 but base established at Larne instead of Belfast and named RACER II (qv).

CAROLINE II Belfast, Tlr Base
Cd 01.01.1944 ex ANTRIM (qv) - to be Escort Base, independent command, acs CAROLINE. PO 07.05.1946? (In NL 04.46)
Nom DS: NAB DAPHNE 01.01.44 - total loss 05.06.46 (under name CAROLINE II)

CARPENTARIA Thursday Is, Queensland, RAN Base
16.02.1945-30.06.46
Nom DS: ML SILVER LINING

CARPENTARIA London, RAN HQ
01.01.1946 (ex CERBERUS II (qv)) - 31.10.1981
Australian Naval Representative UK

CARRICK Greenock, RNR/RNVR Drl Sh/Base
05.1925-1947
CITY OF ADELAIDE, clipper ship, purch privately by RNVR Greenock as Drl Sh 27.03.1923 and renamed CARRICK. Cd 05.1925 and closed as Drl Sh 1940. By 04.40 was in use for DEMS Tng. Cd 28.10.1940 as tender to ORLANDO. Accom Sh Greenock by 01.12.40. 01.10.46 Reserve Div reconstituted in CARRICK. Presented to RNVR Club of Scotland 1947. Sank 1969, but plans for preservation in 1990.

CARRICK II (1883) Greenock, Accom Sh
05.02.1942-11.46
PHAETON, Cr, sold 1913, became TS INDEFATIGABLE 01.01.1914. Purch 1941 and allocated accom sh Greenock 15.11.41. 05.02.42 renamed CARRICK II to avoid confusion as three INDEFATIGABLEs existed then. Accom Sh for BD personnel ST COLOMBA 10.45-11.46, to DST, BU 20.01.47

CARRON (1827) Harwich, Coal Hulk/Breakwater
Wood Paddle Vessel, lent as coal hulk 1846, breakwater at Harwich 1848 - BU 01.1885

CARRON (1944) Chat, Living Ship
DD, living ship 12.1950,. BU 04.67

CARTIER 1475 Drummond St, Montreal, RCN Res and Div
Cd 01.11.1941 - 01.09.42 (tender to HOCHELAGA). 01.09.42-15.09.45 (independent command), 09.06.44 amalgamated with DONNACONNA (Fr speaking), listed to 1954
Original vessel named CARTIER renamed CHARNY 09.12.1941 to avoid confusion

CARYSFORT (1914) Dev, SORF
Cr, SORF v EREBUS 25.07.1927-08.28, BU 10.31

CARYSFORT (1944) Ports, Accom Sh
DD, accom sh 02.1948, BU 10.70

CASERNE BIR HACHEIM Emsworth, Hants, Fr Depot
08.1942 Free Fr Drafting Depot - extant 08.1943

CASERNE BIROT Greenock, Fr Naval Estab
08.1942 Free Fr Shore Estab - barracks closed 05.01.46, finally closed 08.03.46

CASERNE SURCOUF Clapham Common, Fr Naval Estab
08.1942 Free Fr Transit Company Estab

CASSANDRA (1943) Chat, Living Sh
DD, living ship 11.1951, BU 04.67

CASSIUS Bermuda, Diving Bell Vessel
Schooner, purch 1847, listed to 1852

CASTLEMAINE (1941) Melbourne, TS/ Museum Ship
M/S, Static TS at Flinders Naval Depot by 09.1957, to Maritime Trust 1973, Museum ship there from 06.74 - extant 99

CASTOR (1832) Capetown/ N Shields, Flag/ Drl Sh
Flag Capetown 1849-51, Res Drl Sh N Shields 01.04.1862 -12.11.1895 rb MEDUSA, sold 08.1902

CASTOR (1915) Nore, SORF
Cr, SORF v MARSHAL SOULT 01.04.1927-10.10.27 rb SPENSER, sold 30.07.36

CATANIA (1895) Taranto, ML DS
Yt, Cd 20.02.1917 v QUEEN - 01.04.18 rb OUR ALLIES

CATARAQUI 47 Wellington St, Kingston, Ontario, Canada, RCN Base & Res Div
20.09.1939 - Cd 01.11.41 - 01.09.42 (tender to STADACONA), 01.09.42-listed to 1970(independent command) - extant 1986

CAVALIER (1944) Soton/Brighton/ Hebburn/Chat, Museum Sh
DD, Museum Sh 1977, to Soton 21.10.77, to Brighton 11.83, to Hebburn 05.87, for sale to Penang 97 but cancelled, to Chat 15.05.99 - extant 99

CAVENDISH (1944) Dev/Harwich, Accom Sh
DD, RF living ship Dev 12.1949, Harwich 11.1951, Bu 08.1967

CELEBRITY Milford Haven, Tlr Base
20.11.1940 - PO 16.07.45 - acs to LUCIFER
DS for mine destructors 1941, for M/S 1942, later assumed duties of Base Ship for M/S and A/S vessels and for Minewatching Officers and Ratings (06.43).
Nom DS: MY RENOWN 20.11.43-17.02.44
Drifter PERILLA nominated but cancelled
Mining Tender GILBERT EUGENE 17.02.44-16.07.45

CELTIC Chichester Hbr/Oban, HQ of RMBPD
1943-10.44
Old Thames Barge, 1943 - HQ of RMBPD Chichester Hbr, to Oban 04.44

CENTAUR (1947) Dev/Ports, Accom Sh
Aircraft Carrier, accom sh Dev for EAGLE refit 10.1966-06.67, accom sh Ports 06.67-70, Dev by 01.71-72, BU 07.72

CENTURION (1911) Ports/Dev, RF/Base
BB. Flag RF Ports v COURAGEOUS 24.04.1924-06.04.26 rb WEYMOUTH, used as target ship, then Base for Tlrs and Aux vessels Dev 03.1940-23.04.41, rb PARIS (Fr), conv to dummy BB, scuttled 09.06.44 Normandy - PO 09.06.44

CENTURION Lythe Hill House, Haslemere, Central Drafting Depot
Established 1956, Cd 05.04.1957, ship name assumed 24.08.64, tx to Gosport 06.1970

CENTURION Grange Rd, Gosport, Hants, Drafting Depot/Pay and Accounting Centre
Cd 16.10.1970 - tx ex Haslemere - PO 31.03.94 - became CENTURION Building, tender to SULTAN

CERBERUS Williamstown (Flinders Naval Depot), Victoria, Australia, RAN TE/Base
1900 - Cd ashore at Hann's Inlet, Western Port Bay 01.04.21 - Williamstown Naval Depot closed 15.06.1921 - known as CERBERUS rather than Flinders Naval Dockyard from 14.12.62-extant 1999
Nom DS: CERBERUS (1868) built for Victoria, Hbr Serv 1900, to RAN 1911, Cd 01.07.1912 at Williamstown as Depot - 31.03.21 (to Geelong 15.06.1921). became PLATYPUS II (qv), sold 23.04.24 and used as breakwater Pt Philip Bay 1926
PROTECTOR (1884) Cr 01.04.1921 renamed CERBERUS when hulked as TS. Renamed PROTECTOR and sold 1924
KOORONGA, MB, 06.06.1924-sold 1948
Tug TB10 to 1958

CERBERUS II London/Washington, RAN Depot
1917-31.12.1965 - London Depot, NA Washington included from 1952 (at least) - see also CERBERUS III. Became CARPENTARIA (qv) at London, WARATAH at Washington (qv)

CERBERUS III Melbourne, RANVR Depot
01.09.1920-31.03.1921 - Flinders Naval Depot - later Cd as CERBERUS
01.04.1921-16.06.1921 - Naval TE Williamstown
RANVR Depot Melbourne, incl Williamstown, renamed LONSDALE (qv) 03.42
31.03.1964-31.12.65 - Naval Admin Centre Washington (see CERBERUS II)

CERBERUS IV Adelaide, RANVR Depot
Birkenhead Naval Depot named CERBERUS IV 03.09.1939, renamed TORRENS (qv) 01.08.40, renamed ENCOUNTER (qv) 03.66

CERBERUS V Fremantle, RANVR Depot
Renamed LEEUWIN (qv) 13.03.1942

CERBERUS VI Hobart, RANVR Depot
Renamed DERWENT (qv) 01.08.1940, HUON (qv) 13.03.1942

CERES (1917) Dev/Ports/Normandy, Accom Sh
Cr, PO and tender to FOLIOT (qv) 04.11.1943, DS Normandy 07.06.44-and v DESPATCH temp 02.09.44, became Base and Accom Sh Ports 01.45, sold 05.46

CERES Thorpe Arch, Wetherby, Yorks, TE
01.10.1946 ex DEMETRIUS-31.03.58
Renamed when Cr name became available. Was RN Supply & Secretariat Sch, moved to Chat Barracks(PEMBROKE) 01.04.58
Nom DS: HL(D) 3982 10.46-58

CERES Harrogate Rd, Yeadon, Leeds, Communications Tng Centre
Cd 01.10.1984 - PO 31.07.94

CETO Ramsgate, A/P Parent Ship
06.03.1915 v HARRIER - 30.09.1919, acs to PRESIDENT
Base closed 14.10.1919
Nom DS: Yt(1885) hired 08.09.14-19.03.19
Yt OMBRA(1902) 20.03.18-22.02.19
Tug CODFISH (1915) 22.02.19-Resto 08.19

CEYLON Malta GC, Flag/Rx Sh
5th Rate BOMBAY, purch 1805, renamed 1808, Rx Sh 1835 - sold 1857 at Malta, Flag 1849-50

CFMU 1 Europe, CF Mobile Unit (NP 1711)
06.1944-PO 06.09.1945
Formed at Chat, then to Newhaven for 3 weeks, started ops at Arromanches(Mulberry) 07.44, staff living ashore under canvas at Courseilles. To Ostend 'car ferry building' 10.44.-05.45 by road via Brussels. Also operated at Cuxhaven 06.45-07.45, to HORNET disbanding 08.45

CFMU 1 Den Helder, CF Mobile Unit
Cd 01.06.1950 - at Den Helder 10.06.50-26.06.50, PO 29.06.50

CFMU 1 Felixstowe, CF Mobile Unit
Cd 0900 05.02.1951 - at Felixstowe 11-28.02.51, PO at HORNET 07.03.51 (poss CFMU 2 (qv))

CFMU 2 Europe, CF Mobile Unit (NP 1712)
1944, named GADFLY (qv) 28.07.1945 - 10.46, reverted to NP Number till 10.47
Op at Lerwick 10.44, Felixstowe 03.45, Wilhelmshaven, Cuxhaven and Copenhagen 06.45, and from Nakskov to Flensburg 13.06.45-10.47

CFMU 2 Felixstowe, CF Mobile Unit
11.02.1951-07.03.51
This could be CFMU I (qv)

CFMU 3 Ports/Frederickshaven, CF Mobile Unit
Cd at HORNET 01.09.1951, at Frederickshaven 09.09.51-01.10.51, PO at HORNET 01.10.51

CHALEUR Quebec City, RCN DS/NOIC
Established 09.1939, Cd 27.04.40-21.10.45

CHALEUR I Quebec City, RCN DS
Name used for CHALEUR once CHALEUR formed

CHALEUR II Quebec City, RCN DS
01.04.1941-12.45

CHALKIS Aegean, Tlr DS
Steamer, Cd 12.1917 v WHITEHEAD as Tlr DS, tender to OSIRIS II/EGMONT, - PO 19.08.19, became Fleet Messenger

CHALLENGER (1858) Chat, Rx Sh/Accom Sh
Screw Corvette, survey ship 1872, Rx Sh Chat 1880 - by 1910 accom sh Chat for boats' crews for Captain of Dockyard. To be rb PRINCE RUPERT 03.1920, sold 06.01.1921

CHAMAK Manora, Karachi, RIN/RPN/PN Radar TE
08.1944 previously known as HIMALAYA II whilst still building, Cd 06.45, listed PN to 1947-62

CHAMPION (1878) Chat, Stokers' TS
1904-19
Screw Corvette, Hbr Serv 1904, rb BRILLIANT as Stokers' TS 09.1913, called CHAMPION (old) 1915, sold 23.06.19

CHAMPLAIN (1919) Halifax, Nova Scotia, RCN Res TS
DD, ex TORBAY, RCN and renamed 01.03.1928, Res TS Halifax 05.28-25.11.36, sold 37

CHANCELLOR (1904) Scapa Flow, Officers' Accom Sh
1915-19 - hired Tlr

CHANTICLEER (1942) Azores, Base
Sloop, damaged 18.11.1943, PO 22.11.43, renamed LUSITANIA II (qv) as DS Azores 31.12.43, BU 1945

CHAPLET (1944) Ports, Living Ship
DD, living ship RF 12.1950, Bu 11.65

CHAPMAN SAN Base
1980-81

CHARGER Medway/Woolwich, Coal Hulk
Packet, purch 1830 as COURIER, renamed HERMES 1831, renamed CHARGER 1835, coal hulk Medway 1835, Woolwich by 1840 - BU 1854

CHARLOTTETOWN (1943) Esquimalt, RCN TS
FF, New Entry TS 03.1946-25.03.47, sold 47

CHARNY Halifax, NS, RCN TS
CARTIER (qv), TS Halifax 18.09.1939, renamed CHARNY 09.12.41-12.12.45 - ment as shore estab in lists but was a TS at Halifax

CHASER (1945) Harwich/Portland, Accom Sh/SM Support Ship
LST 3029, named 1947, to res Gareloch 08.03.50, living ship Harwich for 4 M/S 10.54-05.56(HQ Ship temp while MULL OF GALLOWAY refit 15-22.06.55), tow to Portland 08.11.56, Support Ship 5 SM Portland Cd 17.11.56 - PO 1960 (when FORTH returned UK 09.60), sold 27.11.61

CHASSEUR (1855) Sheerness/Chat, Factory Ship
Iron Screw Floating Factory, purch 1855, at Sheerness 1870, at Chat 1875 - sold 25.05.1901

CHASSEUR 106 Cowes, Isle of Wight, Accom Sh
11.1941-01.42
Fr Chasseur (1918-21), C & M at Ports, to be used for spares 06.41, for use as accom for Free Fr crews & maint personnel of Fr VTBs at Cowes 16.11.41. Not required 01.42, became annex to Chasseur Base Cowes 04.42

CHATHAM (1813) Chat, Sheer Hulk
Sheer hulk, BU 1876

CHATHAM (1911) Chat RF
Cr, FO RF Chat/Sheerness 01.01.1919-, lent New Zealand 1920-24, sold 07.26

CHATHAM II Ceylon, Base
02.03.1923 v SOUTHAMPTON II(qv) - 07.25, rb EFFINGHAM II (qv) - Cr CHATHAM was Flag EI 03.03.1923-25

CHATHAM Prince Rupert, BC, RCN Base and RCNR Div
Res Div 01.09.1939-14.06.40. NOIC Prince Rupert estab 06.40-. Cd 01.04.42-07.45, Res Div 21.10.46-31.03.64, listed to 65

CHAUDIERE (1957) Esquimalt, BC, RCN Alongside TS
FF, TS 23.05.1974 - sunk as reef 08.12.1992

CHEERFUL (1944) Aden, Accom Sh
M/S, allocated as accom sh for M/S Aden 10.1958, but cancelled 11.1958. BU 09.63

CHEETAH Bombay Hbr (Trombay), RN/RIN CF Base
Ann as HMIS MTB Tng Base 21.05.1942.and there 05.42. Cd 01.10.42 at Trombay. In 1944 split into CHEETAH I and II (qv) to 31.12.45 (15.09.44 Admin tx from RIN to RN). CF in EI lapsed 01.01.46

CHEETAH I Bombay, RIN CF Accounting Section (Admin)
1944

CHEETAH II Bombay, RIN CF Accounting Section (Engineers & Torp Workshop, Mankurd)
1944

CHEETAH Bombay, RIN Ratings' Demobilisation Centre/Maint Base
Cd 31.12.1945, ReCd 13.09.48 as Fleet Maint Base/title SORF lapsed - PO by 04.56
CF Base that changed its task and tx to RIN

CHEMBUR Bombay, RM Camp
Cd 24.02.1945 independent command, acs BRAGANZA, PO 15.03.46
For transit RN/RM personnel, holding depot and base for accom and admin Flot personnel working from Bombay
Nom DS: LCM 118 24.02.45-

CHERWELL (1918) Boom Working & Maint Vessel
Ex Mersey, Tlr JAMES JONES, renamed 1920, ReCd as Boom Working & Maint Vessel 26.10.1943, sold 1946

CHEVIOT (1944) Rosyth, TS
DD, Hbr Serv attached CALEDONIA Spring 1960 v TALYBONT - 07.62 rb SAINTES, BU 22.10.62

CHEVRON (1944), Rosyth, Accom Ship
DD, accom sh for COCHRANE 1962 till sold 10.69

CHICHESTER (1843) Thames, TS
4th Rate, laid up 1843, lent as TS for boys on Thames 1866 - sold 05.1889

CHICOUTIMI (1940) Pictou, RCN Hbr TS
Corvette, 10.44 -08.44-04.45 Hbr TS attached to CORNWALLIS, BU 06.46

CHILDERS (1945) Malta GC/Gib, Accom Sh
DD, RF accom sh Malta GC 09.1950-05.51, tx to Gib as SO RF 05.51 - 16.01.53, BU 63

CHILKA Vishakapatmam, IN New Entry TE
1991 - extant 1999

CHILWA Calcutta, RN Base
Cd 01.10.1944 independent command. 01.04.45 own acs, PO 15.12.45
Nom DS: D Type Tug Boat DP 174 01.10.44-

CHINKARA Cochin, LC Base
Cd 01.10.1944, 01.04.45 independent command, own acs, PO 03.06.46. Retard Party to 31.07.46
MOLCAB Depot (Anson Camp) at Willingden Is.. RN Estab Calcutta closed 01.02.46 except for movement of hbr craft.
Nom DS: MTL 1124 01.10.44-

CHINTHE Rangoon, Major NP (NP 1031)
Cd 01.04.1945 PO 30.11.45 (RATANABON (qv) Cd 01.12.45) (NP disbanded 09.12.46)
Nom DS: Naval Servicing Boat RN1 (ex LCM(I) 118 - allocated - but see CHEMBUR
Hbr Serv Lch 43943 01.04.45-

CHIPPAWA Winnipeg, Manitoba, RCN Base & Res Div
01.09.1939 - Cd 01.11.41 - 01.09.42, tender to NADEN, and 01.09.42-87 (at least)

CHITTAGONG (1942) Karachi, Pakistan, PN RF
M/S HARTLEPOOL, RIN KATHIAWAR 1942, RPN CHITTAGONG 1948, RF HQ Ship 03.1950-52, sold 56

CHOUGH Culdrose, RNAS
Name alloc whilst under construction, land purch 02.1944, work started 06.44, but finally Cd as SEAHAWK (qv) 17.04.1947

CHRISTIAN VII Standgate Creek, Qtn Sh
Danish 3rd Rate, capt 1807, Qtn Sh 1814 - BU 1838

CHRISTOPHER - see ST CHRISTOPHER

CHRYSANTHEMUM (1917) London, RNR/RNVR Drl Sh
Sloop, arrived London 12.05.1939 as Res Drl Sh. By 04.40, Res Tng had ceased, in use for MN Defence Courses. 10.04.41 renamed CHRYSANTHEMUM II (to release name for corvette). Part of Res Div when reconstituted 01.10.46. Sold 1987, BU 09.95

CHRYSANTHEMUM II London TS
10.04.1941 - 1946 - see CHRYSANTHEMUM above

CHUNHSING HK, Accom Sh
07.1941-12.41
Customs Vessel, lent HK RNVR as accom sh for Chinese Ratings

CHURCHILL Churchill, Manitoba, RCN Radio Sta
Built 01.08.1943. Naval -01.12.1950. Cd 01.07.56, PO 11.07.66, became Canadian Forces Sta CHURCHILL

CICILA Royal Hotel, Kingswear,(Dartmouth), CF Base
01.08.1943 ex DARTMOUTH II (qv) - PO Noon 31.12.44
De-equipping base for CF craft for reserve from 09.44
Nom DS: BRITANNIA III 01.08.43-31.12.44

CICERO Braintree, Essex, TS and Rehabilitation Centre
Cd 23.10.1947 ex Wallington Camp Fareham 15.09.47 - PO 19.04.48 - tx to Worthy Down - KESTREL - acs PEMBROKE II.
Regulating Sch and RN Orthopaedic Rehabilitation Centre
Nom DS: HLD 3826 23.10.47-48

CINCERIA (1911) St Margaret's Hope, Scapa Flow, BD DS
Cd 01.07.1918 - 09.05.1919 - task to VICTORIOUS II

Nom DS: Drifter CINCERIA hired 1915-24.05.1919
Tug WICKSTEAD (1915) 24.04.19-PO 11.10.19

CIRCARS Vizagapatam, RIN Base
12.12.1939, Cd as CIRCARS 04.42, - 1976 (at least) - poss extant 1992 as 50th anniversary celebrated. Base & Boys' TE, CF Base WWII, named as Local Naval Defence and CF Base 11.43

CIRCE (1827) Dev, Hbr Serv
5th Rate, convict ship Dev attached IMPREGNABLE 1874, became IMPREGNABLE IV (qv) 18.10.1915, sold 1922

CIRCE (1942) Dundee, Drl Sh
M/S, Res Drl Sh by 09.1951 v JEWEL - 06.02.1963, sold 02.67

CITY OF LONDON (1927) Trinco, Accom Sh
Purch 1944, at Trinco 10.1944, sold 05.46

CITY OF PERTH Brightlingsea, Base
01.10.1916 v WILDFIRE - PO 31.10.1921
Nom DS: CITY OF PERTH, (1907) Drifter, hired 1915, Base Ship 1916-21.06.1919
EMBLEM (1907) Drifter, 21.06.19-02.09.19
WILLIAM ASHTON (1917) Tlr 02.09.19-sold 22

CITY OF YORK (1904) Kirkwall, Officers' Accom Sh
07.1917-09.1918 (at least)
Hired Tlr 1915-1919

CLARENCE (1826) Mersey, TS
2nd Rate, GOLIATH, renamed 1826, lent as TS Mersey 1865 till burnt out 17.01.1884

CLARENCE (1833) Mersey, TS
ROYAL WILLIAM, 1st Rate, renamed CLARENCE 1885 as RC Reformatory Ship, accidentally burnt out 26.07.1899

CLAVERHOUSE Leith/Edinburgh, Res Drl Sh/Base
Cd 16.12.1922, name chosen as compliment to Marquis of Graham, was to have been ST ANDREW. Name sel for shore base at comml port of Leith 01.09.1939. By 22.09.39 in use as Base for Leith and Granton. By 04.40 Res tng ceased and was in use for MN Defence Courses. Base PO 15.08.1945. Name re-allocated to Forth Res Div 01.10.46 - formally in use 1951. At Granton Sq. Edinburgh by 04.51. Cd ashore when ship PO 03.59 - PO 31.07.1994
Nom DS: M23 (1915) Monitor Cd 16.12.22 - tow to BU 24.04.59
SEAGULL (1937)M/S 1955-BU 05.56

CLAVERHOUSE II Granton, M/S Base
Cd 08.06.1941. PO 1945
Captain M/S in Op and Admin command M/S to Granton in CLAVERHOUSE II 08.06.41
Nom DS: 35 ft MB on fixture list CLAVERHOUSE 08.06.41-

CLEOPATRA (1878) Dev, Hbr Serv
Corvette, Hbr serv attached DEFIANCE (qv) 1905, renamed DEFIANCE III (qv), sold 07.1931

CLEOPATRA (1915) Nore, SORF
Cr, SO RF 1928, sold 06.1931

CLEOPATRA (1940) Ports, RF Living Sh
Cr, FO Commanding RF 05.11.1953 v JAMAICA - 17.12.56 rb VANGUARD. BU 12.58

CLINKER (1856) Ports, Coal Hulk
WAVE, Gunboat, coal hulk 1869, renamed CLINKER 30..12.1882, sold 1890

CLIO (1858) Bangor, TS
Corvette, TS for Boys, N Wales 1876-1914 (at least), sold 03.10.1919 - see also under WARSPITE

CLIO Barrow-in-Furness, Base
Cd 15.09.1939. PO 0900 05.04.45 (and in NL 10.46)
Name sel for comml port 01.09.1939, NOIC ordered 27.08.39, there by 29.08.39. Naval Base to NOIC status 04.45
Nom DS: MY MINIDO (1924) 15.09.39-02.09.42
MFV HARBINGER 02.09.42-05.04.45
MA/SB 4 1946 (poss a name allocated unofficially to this craft)

CLIVE (1919) Flag RIN/TS
Sloop, Flag of FO Commanding RIN struck in CLIVE 09.11.1938 on tx to new HQ Delhi. TS at Bombay for Res 1944, sold 1946.

CLOWN (1856) HK, Coal Depot
Gunboat, coal lighter 1867, later YC1 then YC 6, lost 1871

CLYDE (1828) Aberdeen, Res Drl Sh
5th Rate, RNR Drl Sh Aberdeen 01.09.1870, sold 05.07.1904

CLYDE (1876) Aberdeen, Res Drl Sh
WILD SWAN, sloop, renamed CLYDE 01.05.1904, as Drl Sh Aberdeen to 1910 (at least), renamed COLUMBINE (qv) 05.1912, Cd 01.07.1913 as Base Ship Forth, sold 04.05.1920

COCHRANE Rosyth,, Base
Cd 01.06.1938 as Rosyth Base v GREENWICH. PO 30.11.1947. Separate titles COCHRANE (shore) and COCRANE (ship) (ex COCHRANE II) lapsed 16.12.46. Became Base 01.01.1948 v LOCHINVAR. Accom Sh Rosyth Cd 01.10.47 was an independent command. Name continued in use through a series of Nom DS. Was RN Barracks Donibristle in NL 1955-62 . To close late 1961, task to LOCHINVAR - became COCHRANE II 01.12.62 when task tx to living ships and COCHRANE closed. From 1962 was Rosyth Naval Base ReCd ashore 11.12.1968 - Base closed 11.1995, COCHRANE closed 31.03.96 - new support facilities in CALEDONIA (qv)
Included SORF 1938-39. Assumed duties of SORF

Forth v QUEENSFERRY 01.08.1947. RFForth closed 31.05.50. RF Rosyth was to be DUNDONALD or NEPTUNE 1959.
Nom DS: AMBROSE (1903) renamed COCHRANE 01.06.1938 - sold 08.46
(By 01.11.45 Supply Department in premises occupied by COCHRANE II)
KILLARNEY (qv) - also accom sh to 02.46
DODMAN POINT(1945)/GIRDLE NESS(1945)(qv) 02.46-49
GIRDLENESS(1945)/ MILNE(1941)(qv) 11.51
MSPB 4729 13.07.55 - sold 21.11.58(listed to 1960)
DUNCANSBY HEAD(1944)/GIRDLE NESS(1945)(qv) 01.12.62-10.12.68

COCHRANE I Rosyth, Base
1940-05.45

COCHRANE II Rosyth, Supply & Accounting Base for Tenders
05.01.1940 (at least) - 01.11.45 (absorbed into COCHRANE(Ship))-premises continued in use
RF Forth Area from COCHRANE II to EMERALD 01.11.45

COCHRANE II Donibristle, Barracks
01.12.62 (ex COCHRANE) - 28.02.63

COCHRANE III Primrose Camp, Rosyth, EVT Centre
1942-43 and listed 07.44-05.45 as accom estab and in 1946 as EVT Centre
1942 was Quarry Office Qtrs, Rosyth, part of COCHANE - accom estab for FF and Minewatching personnel. Ment in lists 1945-47 but with no apps

COCHRANE V ledger for CO Personnel involved in Op Apostle (return to Norway)
05.1945

COCKATRICE (1886) Drl Sh
Gunboat BRAMBLE, renamed COCKATRICE 06.1896, conv to Drl Sh 1905 but sold 03.04.1906

COCKATRICE (1942) Hull, SORF
M/S, SORF Hull (Brigham & Cowans) 02.1957, BU 29.08.63

COCKFOSTERS London, Pt Party Transit Camp
Cd 12.06.1944, PO 12.09.1945
Transit camp/ holding depot for personnel going to and returning from Germany. Replaced by ST CLEMENT III(qv)
Nom DS: LILY OF LAGUNA 12.06.44-

CODFORD Ports, Accom Sh
Taken up 29.08.1942, allocated 04.10.1942-05.46 (at least). In C & M Bursledon 03.47, handed over to AOSD 21.03.47
Was also listed as ML 553 12.42

COEL MARA II Oban, Kite Balloon DS
05.03.1944

COLETTE (1926) M/S Repair Ship
Aux Barge, hired as Barrage Balloon Vessel 05.1940, M/S Repair Craft 1940-06.45

COLLEEN Queenstown, Rx Sh/A/P Depot/ C-in-C Western Approaches
Cd 01.12.1913 - PO 15.03.1922 (see VIVID IV)
A/P DS 1914 incl Belfast and Larne which became VALIANT II 03.1915, and Kingstown which became ILEX 03.15
Nom DS: ROYALIST (1883) corvette, at Queenstown 1900-1913 as hulk. - Rx Sh.
Cd as COLLEEN 1913-1922 and handed over to Irish Government 02.23, BU 1950

COLLEEN II 30 Canning Place, Lpool, CO Irish Sea
1921-22 (tx to VIVID IV)

COLLEEN III Pembroke Dk
1921

COLLINGWOOD (1882) Bantry, CG
BB, CG Bantry 09.03.1897-06.1903, sold 11.05.1909

COLLINGWOOD (1908) Dev/Portland, TS
BB, Gunnery Turret Drl Sh Dev by 02.1919(Res status)-10.1920 (at least) rb GLORIOUS, part of Boys' TS Portland, tender to COLOSSUS, 22.09.21-03.22, sold 12.12.22

COLLINGWOOD Fareham, Nr Ports, TE
Cd 10.01.1940 - extant 1999
Opened as TE for RN Special Reservists, became TE for Radar and Electrical Ratings when Electrical Branch formed 01.04.46. Became RN Weapon Engineering Sch when Branch changed its name in 1960s.
Nom DS: Diesel Lch 3545 10.01.40-still in NL 1951
Yt WAL by 1948 - 12.49 (at least)
MFV 41 05.50-04.56
MFV 53 04.56 - sold 10.59 but still listed to 62

COLLINGWOOD II Soton, Pay Centre
1941 at South Western Hotel, pay centre of Government Tng centres - by 29.05.41 had been renamed VICTORY V (qv)

COLOMBIA SM DS
Dutch MV conv to Dutch SM DS 20.11.1940. Torpedoed off S Africa 27.02.43

COLOMBO (1918) Dev/Zara, SORF /Base Ship
Cr, SORF Dev 04.11.36-39. C was SBNO Zara 16.12.44 and forward Base Supply Ship CF Zara. Became Base for Tlrs and small craft Dev v PARIS (qv), Cd 01.07.45 - closed ledgers 14.03.46 - to DRAKE IV, PO 15.03.46, sold 22.01.48

COLONSAY Grimsby, M/S Base
Cd 01.08.1940, PO 31.07.45
Nom DS: Duty MB MEGGIES 01.08.40-08.10.41(renamed COQUETTE-lost by fire 09.42)

COLOSSUS (1848) Portland, CG

3rd Rate, CG Portland 11.06.1860-30.06.1864, sold 03.1867

COLOSSUS (1882) Holyhead, CG
BB, CG Holyhead 16.11.1893-17.11.1901, sold 06.10.1908

COLOSSUS (1910) Portland/Dev, TS/Accom Sh
BB, Flag RF Dev Section I 31.01.1919-21 rb GLORIOUS, part of Boys' TE Portland 22.09.21, closed 11.05.22, to Dev as accom sh for IMPREGNABLE Cd 03.01.24, PO 03.01.28, sold 07.28

COLUMBIA (1918) Lpool, Nova Scotia, Ammo DS 07.1944-12.06.45
DD (ex USS HARADEN), tx to RCN 24.09.40, damaged 44, used as static fuel and ammo depot for ships in refit at Lpool NS 09.44-12.06.45, sold 07.08.45

COLUMBIA (1956) Halifax, NS, Canadian Hbr TS
Canadian DD used as Hbr TS 18.02.1974 - 93, later sunk as reef for divers -Campbell River, BC

COLUMBINE (1826) Sheerness, Coal Hulk
Sloop, coal hulk Sheerness 1854 - sold 12.01.1892

COLUMBINE Rosyth/Pt Edgar, DS
Cd 01.07.1913 - moved ashore to Pt Edgar 09.17, land purch 10.1920, to C & M 1927-38. Re-opened as LOCHINVAR (qv) 1938.
Included A/P Cromarty - task to STEPHEN FURNESS 18.01.1915, and Peterhead by 09.1914-15. Also A/P DS Lough Larne 04.15 and A/P DS Forth/Granton 08.14-01.05.16 rb GUNNER at Granton.
Relieved as DS Rosyth by CRESCENT (qv) 01.05.1916 - COLUMBINE remaining as her tender.
Tender to WOOLWICH as overflow accom 13 DF 06.11.1917 and Cd 01.12.1917 as DD DS v WOOLWICH, Cd 01.07.1918 as independent command as Nom DS Pt Edgar and 13 DF - 01.11.1919
Nom DS: CLYDE (ex WILD SWAN) (1876) renamed COLUMBINE 05.1912 - was to have been
ROMULUS, Cd 01.07.1913 - became COLUMBINE (Old) 01.11.19, sold 04.05.20
MERCURY (1878), SM DS 1906, was to have been COLUMBINE 1912, prob not renamed but some acs state renamed 1914 - sold 07.19
DARKNESS (1918), Drifter, renamed COLUMBINE 01.11.19 - sold 1923 (still listed as Nom DS 1925)
BLACK FROST (1918) Drifter, renamed COLUMBINE 1925, by 1929 was hulk attached GREENWICH, sold circa 1931

COMET (1944) Dev, Accom Sh
DD, Accom Sh 03.1950-11.51, BU 10.66

COMMONWEALTH Kure, Base (NP 2504)
Cd 01.06.1946 (RN), Cd 01.01.48 (RAN), PO 04.11.56
NP at Kure 02.46 onwards
Nom DS: Aux Yawl EVELINE (recapt from Japanese) 01.06.46-

COMUS (1914) Dev, RF
Cr, SORF 20.04.1931-12.33, sold 28.07.34

COMPTON CASTLE Dartmouth, Accom Sh
Req 07.08.1941 - 13.09.41

CONCORD (1945) Rosyth, Hbr TS
DD, ex CORSO (1946), Hbr TS attached CALEDONIA 10.09.58-BU 23.10.62

CONDOR Arbroath, RNAS
Cd 19.06.1940, advance offices opened 05.1940. Re Cd 01.12.1946. NE Tng from GAMECOCK 11.11.58. PO 01.04.1971, became RM Barracks from 04.09.1970 - extant 99
Included RNAS Dundee (Stannergate) (CONDOR II), which was also a RN Seaplane Site 1912 - WWI, and Easthaven (later PEEWIT(qv))
SANDERLING (qv) was a tender 01.10.63-31.10.63
Nom DS: Steam Pinnace 647 19.06.40-
Safety Boat 4194 12.44-
TRSB 421030 12.46 - 53
TRSB 43761 54-55
TRSB 421249 01.04.55-62

CONDOR II Dundee, RNAS
Cd 15.07.1941 - PO 15.06.44, to C & M 08.44
Easthaven, later PEEWIT (qv) also recorded under CONDOR II

CONESTOGA Galt, Ontario, RCN - WRNS TE
First class 10.1942, Cd 01.06.43 (ex BYTOWN II) - 31.03.45
Moved from Kingston, Ontario. At Galt by 29.08.42

CONGELLA Durban, SAN
1944 - in PO Circular 22.03.44

CONIDAW (1939) Le Havre, M/S HQ Ship
Cd 12.1944, PO and Resto 22.08.45
Yt hired as M/S 1939-45. British M/S Base to French on loan 17.07.45

CONQUEROR (1911) Ports, Boys' TE
BB, Flag VA RF Ports (temp) while KING GEORGE V in refit 01.11.1919-16.12.1919, FO Commanding RF Ports 1920 - by 06.22 rb COURAGEOUS. Boys' TS 1922, sold 19.12.22

CONQUEST (1915) Atlantic Fleet, SM DS
Cr, DS 1SM v INCONSTANT 1921-28, sold 08.30

CONQUESTADOR (1810) Dev, Powder Hulk
3rd Rate, 4th Rate 1831, powder hulk 1860 - sold 05.1897

CONSTANCE (1915) Ports, Flag RF
Cr, Flag RF v DARTMOUTH 01.01.28-09.12.30 rb FROBISHER, then Res till sold 06.36

CONWAY Mersey/Llanfair PG, Mercantile Marine

Services Assoc Sch Ship
02.1859-1953, moved ashore to Conway Building, Plas Newydd - opened 21.10.49 and to new buildings 05.64. Shore estab PO 10.07.74
1) CONWAY(1832) - 6th Rate, TS 02.1859 - renamed WINCHESTER 28.08.1861, BU 06.1871
2) WINCHESTER (1822) 4th Rate, renamed CONWAY 11.1861(lent) - renamed MOUNT EDGCUMBE (qv) 01.09.1876, sold 08.04.1921
3) NILE(1839) 2nd Rate, renamed CONWAY 24.07.1876(lent). She was originally on the Mersey at Rock Ferry, Birkenhead, and tx to anchor off Bangor Pier, Menai Str 1941. Stranded in Menai Str enr Lpool for docking 14.04.53 and wreck burnt 31.10.56

COOK Wellington, New Zealand, Depot & TE
Cd 01.01.1943, PO 18.06.46

COOK II Wellington, New Zealand, Depot (Advanced Base)
10.02.1943-46

COOK III Wellington, New Zealand, Depot
1947

COOK Halifax House, Strand, London, RNZN Depot
To 01.04.1949, renamed MAORI (qv)

COONAWARRA Nr Berrimah, Darwin, RAN Depot
Cd 16.03.1970 - extant 1999
Naval Radio Sta 1971, Patrol Boat & Communications Depot (Shoal Bay & Humpty Doo) 1984

COPRA Largs/Southend/London, CO Pay & Drafting Office
Cd 30.08.1943 acs ex QUEBEC and DINOSAUR - at Chelsea Ct SW7, vacated by 03.08.44. COPRA (Drafting) at Southend by 11.43, to Largs 05.10.45. COPRA (Pay) at Largs by 08.44. Medical History Sheets to ARBELLA 08.44. COPRA PO 30.06.46, Largs (main buildings, The Moorings) vacated 15.07.46, retard party closed 15.01.47.
Nom DS: THE SWAN 30.08.43-

COQUETTE Grimsby
COLONSAY (qv) was renamed COQUETTE 09.10.1941, but prob this referred to the Nom DS only. Destroyed by fire, constructive total loss 09.42

CORAL HARBOUR (HMBS) New Providence Is, Bahamas, Bahamas Base
1989 - extant 1999

CORBRAE (1912) M/S Maint Ship
Purch as mine destructor vessel 03.1940, PO for conv M/S DS Barry 30.11.43, Cd as M/S Store & Repair Ship 15.03.45, independent command, own acs, East Indies 06.45-02.46, for disposal 11.46

CORDELA (1930) Pt Said, Accom Sh
Tlr, C & M as tender to PROMETHEUS, acs of Anglo-Hellenic Schooner Flot 12.07.1944-ReCd as M/S 05.10.44

CORDELIA (1914) Dev, RF Parent
Cr, RF Parent Section III (temporary) 01.1919 - sold 07.23

COREOPSIS (1917) Mudros, DS
Sloop, sold 06.09.1922.
Post of SNO Mudros in COREOPSIS lapsed 14.02.1920 - poss indicates sloop acting as a Base.
Tlr JOHN BOWLER Cc as Nom DS Mudros 12.02.20

CORINTHIA Malta GC, Greek SM DS
Malta GC 10.1944, Piraeus 12.45, Crete 12.46

CORIOLANUS Algiers, CF Base
Ment 1943, poss a local name or associated with Tlr CORIOLANUS (1940), lost 05.05.45

CORMORANT (1877) Gib, Base
Sloop, Hbr Serv 04.11.1889, Cd 05.11.1889 as tender to GOSHAWK (Duty Guard Ship Gib), Cd 01.06.1900, renamed ROOKE 01.07.46 (Base moved ashore) - BU 1949
Included Ascension Is 1910-22

CORMORANT II Gib, RNAS
27.05.1943, to be independent command 05.43, PO 01.11.44
North Front, RAF Airstrip, tx to RN 26.09.40-01.08.41 as CORMORANT II?, but returned to RAF. Became CORMORANT II again later.
Small RNAS at Tafar Oui (Oran area) acted as parent for all disembarked FAA in N Africa from 03.06.43 - withdrawn 23.12.43

CORNCRAKE Ballyhalbert, Co Down, RNAS
Cd 17.07.1945, independent command, own acs, PO 13.11.45 (C & M) and tx RAF 24.01.46
Lodger facilities on loan from RAF to 10.46
Nom DS: 20 ft MB ex RFA SERBOL 17.07.45-

CORNCRAKE II Kirkistown, Co Down, RNAS
Ex RAF 14.07.1945. Cd 17.07.45, PO 15.01.46
On loan from RAF to 10.46

CORNET CF TE
Ment WW II, poss a play on HORNET (qv)?

CORNFLOWER HK, Res Drl Sh
1) Sloop (1916), lent HK Government as Res Drl Sh 31.03.1934. Sold for BU 1940 - TAI HING, bought back 09.40 and renamed CORNFLOWER, sunk 15.12.41 by bombing (still in NL 1948)
2) LYSANDER (1943) lent HK Government and renamed CORNFLOWER 03.1950 as HK RNVR Drl Sh to 11.04.51, found unsuitable, BU 23.11.57
3) Name continued on shore at Gloucester Rd to 06.67

CORNWALL Tilbury, Lent as Boys' TS
1) CORNWALL (1812) renamed WELLESLEY 18.06.1868 as TS, BU 1875
2) WELLESLEY (1815) renamed CORNWALL 18.06.1868 TS, sunk 24.09.1940 in air attack, due to be replaced by ARETHUSA 06.40

CORNWALLIS (1813) Hull/Sheerness, CG/Jetty
3rd Rate, CG Hull 01.01.1857 - 01.04.1864, part of jetty Sheerness by 1865, renamed WILDFIRE (qv) as Sheerness Sub Depot 01.04.1916, BU 1957

CORNWALLIS Halifax/Deepbrook, Nova Scotia, RCN TE
Started at Halifax (Nelson Barracks & Dy) Cd 01.05.1942 - 14.04.43. moved to Deepbrook /Digby 14.04.43. Cd 01.05.43, closed 28.02.45, still listed 04.45, re-opened 01.05.49, became CFS CORNWALLIS 01.04.66, title HMCS CORNWALLIS over gate 1968. In NL to 1970, Pink List to 1976. Replaced HMCS VENTURE(qv) and HMCS SAMBRO (qv), TE and responsible for admin control of all schools at Halifax, including Pictou.
In 1998 was peacekeeping force camp.

COROMANDEL Bermuda, Convict Ship
MALABAR, purch 1804, storeship 1805, renamed COROMANDEL 07.03.1815, convict ship Bermuda 10.1827-BU 12.1853

CORONIA Loch Ewe/Lamlash
NAB temp allocated as Kite Balloon DS Loch Ewe 09.07.1941, acquired 15.10.41, then to Lamlash for RM Beach Battalion 05.42. To DNST 03.43, reallocated as tender for convoy assembly 09.43

CORTICELLI Trinidad
Skid Towing Ship, said to have been Nom DS before GOSHAWK, was renamed GOSHAWK 06.11.1940 as Nom DS, renamed BENBOW 22.01.41 as Nom DS. This renaming could have led to confusion and she prob was not a base in her own name.

CORUNNA (1945) Ports, Refit Support Ship
DD, DLG (HAMPSHIRE) refit support 1971-73, sold 08.74

COUCY (1919) Ports, TS
Fr Patrol Vessel seized 03.07.1940 at Plym, allocated Dutch personnel at Holyhead 16.07.40, not used by Dutch and so used by A/P, and became Land Fighting TS Ports 24.09.1942. returned to Fr 1944

COURAGEOUS (1916) Rosyth/Ports, RF/TS
Cr, RF Parent Rosyth 30.01.1919-11.06.1919 rb HERCULES, Ports as Turret Drl Sh v ST VINCENT 10.19-06.24. Also SO RF & Group I Parent 01.22 -rb CENTURION by 12.24. Used as Boys' TS Ports in 1920s, Cd as aircraft carrier 1928 and sunk 17.09.39

COURAGEUX (1800) Chat, Lazaretto
3rd Rate, Lazaretto 1814, BU 1832

COURBET (1911) Ports, DS
Fr BB seized 03.07.40 at Ports, Free Fr DS from 07.40, C & M 19.03.41, Cd 22.03.43 (RN crew), sunk as breakwater Arromanches 09.06.44

COVERDALE Coverdale, New Brunswick, Canada, RCN Radio Sta
Established as HFDF Sta 1941, became RCN Radio Sta 01.12.1949-01.07.56, first RCN Radio Sta to be Cd, 01.07.56-19.07.66. Became CFS Coverdale.

CRAIL - Prob refers to JACKDAW at Crail (qv)

CRESCENT (1810) Rio de Janeiro, Negro DS
5th Rate, Rio de Janeiro as Negro DS 01.1840 - sold 1854

CRESCENT Oban/Scapa Flow/Rosyth, DS
1) CRESCENT (1892) Cr, sel as pt DS Rosyth 02.1916, fit out 25.03.16, 01.05.1916 v COLUMBINE as Flag and General DS Rosyth, A/P DS Oban 10.1916-06.17 rb NESMAR II(qv), SM DS 1917, Scapa Flow 1917-18, DS 13 SM 08.18-12.18, Rosyth DS 3 SM 1918-19, 09.05.19 DS Oban v NESMAR II, sold 22.09.21
2) GLORY (1899) BB, renamed CRESCENT 01.05.20, DS, PO 28.02.22, C-in-C West Coast Scotland to COLUMBINE. Sold 19.12.22
3) SUTLEJ (1899) Cr, overflow ship Rosyth 1917-18, included in estab CRESCENT 1918, sold 09.05.21

CRESCENT II Aberdeen & Peterhead
08.10.1919 (acs ex NAIRN - Aberdeen) - 1921

CRESCENT III Shandon, Dumbartonshire, Base
1921
Adty Experimental Sta Shandon closed 31.03.1920

CRESCENT IV North Scotland
1921

CRESCENT V Invergordon, CO North Coast Scotland Area and KHM Invergordon
1921-01.1922 (not listed 06.22)

CRESSY Dundee, Res Drl Sh
UNICORN (1824), 5th Rate, powder hulk 1860, RNR Drl Sh Dundee 11.1873. renamed UNICORN (qv) 02.1939, employed as Nom DS Dundee. Renamed CRESSY 01.01.1942 - Base. PO 31.08.1945. closed 31.03.46. Res Div re-established 01.10.46 and name used. Name allocated 1951. Renamed UNICORN 14.07.59. Handed over to UNICORN Preservation Soc 29.09.68

CRESWELL Jervis Bay, RAN College & Fleet Support
Cd 20.01.1958 (ex FRANKLIN(qv)) - extant 1999
Originally located Jervis Bay 1915. Tx to CERBERUS 1930. Returned Jervis Bay by 1958

CRICKET Burseldon, LC Base
Cd 15.07.1943. Independent command, acs SHRAPNEL 17.10.43, To close 01.03.46 - last arrivals 20.05.46. Poss PO 15.07.46
Nom DS: NAB HAPPY LASS 15.07.43-30.04.45
Hbr Lch 30445 30.04.45-05.45
HL(P) 436622 05.45-03.46

CROCODILE (1825) Cork, Rx Sh
6th Rate, Rx Sh 08.1850 - sold 11.1861

CROSSBOW (1945) Ports, Hbr TS
DD, attached SULTAN as Hbr TS 03.66 v SOLEBAY - 03.71 rb DIAMOND. BU 12.71

CRUISER Malta GC, Accom Sh
Ex LARK, accom sh 1910-1914

CRYSTAL PALACE Crystal Palace, Sydenham, RNVR Tng Div
12.1915-21.03.1919
Under VICTORY VI. An unofficial name. Formerly believed to be named VICTORY II, also called 'The Glasshouse'

CUCKOO
1) CUCKOO (1873), renamed VIVID (qv) 1912, renamed VIVID (old) 1920, YC 37 1923, sold 1958
2) AMELIA (ex HAWK) (1888) renamed COLLEEN (qv) 1905), COLLEEN (Old) 1916, renamed EMERALD 29.04.1918, renamed CUCKOO 29.04.1918 - PO 16.09.19, sold 08.22
Uncertain as to whether either of these vessels operated as a base under the name CUCKOO.

CUILLIN SOUND (1944) Harwich, Repair Ship
Cd 31.08.1945 & 04.09.45 (poss 1st date cancelled and replaced by second) res Cat B Harwich - accom sh for personnel in RF-10.09.45, SORF Harwich 15.02.46 (acs ex SCARBOROUGH and acs RF ex BADGER)-25.06.46 rb DUNCANSBY HEAD, to DST 15.10.46

CULGOA (1945) Sydney, NSW, Australia, RAN Accom Sh
FF, accomm sh for WATERHEN 12.1962-06.1971, sold 01.1972

CUMBERLAND (1807) Chat, Convict Ship
3rd Rate, convict ship 1830, renamed FORTITUDE (qv) 1833, sold 1870

CUMBERLAND (1842) Sheerness/Clyde, Guardship/TS
3rd Rate, guardship Sheerness 1862-63, lent Clyde TS Association 1870, burnt/wrecked 1899

CURACOA (1917) Cardiff, Res Drl Sh
Cr, allocated to Cardiff RNVR pre WW II (14.04.39), but did not arrive prior to mobilisation - conversion to AA Ship completed 04.40, sunk 02.10.42

CURLEW Dunoon, Hbr Defence Sect of OSPREY - TE
Cd 10.07.1943, independent command, acs OSPREY, PO 06.08.1946
EVT Estab 15.02.46
Nom DS: NAB ARACHNE 01.11.43-11.43
NAB TITLARK II 11.43-

CURLEW St Merryn, RNAS
01.01.1953 ex VULTURE, closed for flying 14.12.53, C & M 14.07.55, PO 10.01.56 - to Air Ministry 01.01.56
Became Sch of Aircraft Maint & Naval Air Ordnance Sch
Nom DS: TRSB 43780 01.01.53(ex Nom DS VULTURE) -1956

CURLEW (1954) - Hobart, Australia, Museum Ship
M/S, Ex CHEDISTON, to RAN 1961. PO 04.90 and purch at Sydney - to preservation Hobart Tasmania till 2003 - plans to return her to Montrose where built 2003 (50 yrs before)

CYCLOPS (1905) Repair Ship/ DS
Ex INDRABARAH, Cd 05.11.1907, Home Fleet/ Scapa Flow. Nom DS Northern Flotilla Tlrs v HANNIBAL at Scapa Flow 28.08.14, rb ZARIA 25.02.15 - remained Scapa Flow as A/P DS - Repair Ship. PO 01.04.19, Flag to VICTORIOUS II and Re-Cd for White Sea Duty (Archangel) as Repair Ship. Returned Chat 10.19, conv to SM DS 1920-22, RF Nore 1922, Atlantic Fleet 1 SM v PANDORA Chat 1922, Gib 03.23, Med 27-39.Flying Boat DS Arzeu (Nr Oran) 09.37. De-store Malta 01.02.38 - to Res 20.03.38 then refit. Cd 09.10.39 - to Harwich 3 SM 09.39. Cd 17.11.39 and refit Chat. 3 SM at Harwich till rb MAIDSTONE in 3 SM 27.05.40, to 7 SM Rothesay 7 SM 06.40. PO 12.45. Portland 7 SM 02.46 rb MAIDSTONE 17.09.46, BU 29.06.47
Known as 'Cycle Box'

CYCLOPS II Scapa Flow, Land Defences & M/S Craft, Kirkwall
11.1917-01.04.1919 - renamed VICTORIOUS II)
18.02.1919 - Acs ex ZARIA to CYCLOPS II, renamed VICTORIOUS II

CYCLOPS II White Sea, DS
To 11.07.1919 - task to LOBSTER (qv)
For men on Up River Transport Vessels N Russia

CYDYLLA Ports, Accom Sh
Ex ML, taken up 29.02.1942 - but failed survey 28.09.42

CYSNE II (1906) Barrow-in-Furness, Accom Sh
Yt, hired as Hbr Defence Patrol Craft 02.1940, allocated temp to Barrow as Accom Sh for lorry crews 02.09.1940. PO 14.10.40. To Greenock Pool 1942. In use till re-allocated to military service 31.05.44. To C & M 21.06.45

D

DACRES (1943) Normandy, LC HQ Ship
FF, temporarily HQ Ship conv Dundee 1943-44, full complement as HQ Ship 21.02.44, Normandy 06.44, returned USN 01.46

DAEDALUS (1826) Bristol, Res Drl Sh
5th Rate, Drl Sh Bristol 01.04.1862-1910, sold 14.09.1911. Bristol Res to Jamaica St HQ 1910, then to FLYING FOX (qv) 1924

DAEDALUS (1856) Chat, Nom DS

THUNDERBOLT, floating battery was floating pier at Chat 1873, as DAEDALUS (Cd 25.12.1915 - PO 10.03.1919) was Nom DS for the RNAS to 01.04.1918 and DS Flying Sch 08.1918. Sunk 1948 and raised and BU 1949.
Included RNAS Cranwell, Kingsnorth, Eastchurch, Grain (and Pt Victoria), Manston (including Westgate), Plym - Cattewater, Mullion, Tresco and Newlyn

DAEDALUS Lee-on-Solent, RNAS
Opened 1917 as Seaplane Sch, tx to RAF 01.04.1918. Handed over from RAF and Cd 24.05.1939 - RN Barracks with RNAS subsidiary. Cd 15.03.57 as DAEDALUS, renamed ARIEL (qv) 31.10.59 but name DAEDALUS retained for HQ at Wykeham Hall from 31.10.59. Renamed DAEDALUS 05.10.65. PO 29.03.96 - retard party to 31.07.96
Included various outstations, Cowdray Park for res aircraft (06.1941), Defford, Ford (1940 and 1950 when PO as PEREGRINE(qv)), Gosport (1947), Heston (1945-47), Manston (1974), Portland (till 1959 when Cd as part OSPREY (qv)), Tangmere (1942-50), Thorney Is.
Nom DS: Hbr Serv Lch 3710 24.05.39-(1951 in Motor Boat List)
TRSB 4423 by 04.48-60
TRSB 4422 54-12.56
TRSB 43780 01.12.56-01.10.57
TRSB 4424 01.10.57-58
TRSB 43775 09.60(FO Home HQ)-62 & 18.10.66-

DAEDALUS II Lympne, Kent, RNAS
Ex RAF 01.07.1939 when Cd as BUZZARD (qv) C & M 25.09.39. Separate acs as DAEDALUS II 01.01.40. Re-opened as DAEDALUS II 03.04.40. Tx to RAF 05.40 - task to Newcastle-under-Lyme - see DAEDALUS II below

DAEDALUS II Sandbanks, Dorset, RNAS (Seaplane Base/TE)
Established 26.04.1940, Cd 15.05.1940 as DAEDALUS II, to C & M 09.10.1943. Later became LC Base - see TURTLE

DAEDALUS II Lawrenny Ferry, Pembs, RNAS
Tx ex RAF - detached from Pembroke Dk as RNAS 01.02.1942 and Cd. To C & M 24.10.43.

DAEDALUS II Old Bank House, Penhill St, Newcastle-under-Lyme, RN Aircraft TE
05.1940 ex Lympne, see DAEDALUS II above - PO 31.01.1946

DAEDALUS III Lee-on-Solent/Bedhampton, RNAS Camp/Release Centre
Opened 09.1943. Named Bedhampton Camp 03.02.44 - accom and release centre, named DAEDALUS III 29.09.45, closed 01.02.47

DAHLIA (1915) Newport, Res Drl Sh
Sloop, allocated Newport RNVR 1923. There 02.01.24-05.26 (at least) rb MUTINE. To Red Sea, Cd 28.10.1926. BU 02.07.32
1932 ann Sub Div to close

DALHOUSIE (1886) Basra/Bombay, DS/Rx Sh
Troopship. RN Depot Basra 1918 - PO 12.07.1919 and tx to Royal India Marine. Rx Ship Bombay 1924
-09.51 - renamed ANGRE (qv).
Name given to Local Naval Defence Base and RIN Depot, Bombay 11.1943.
Moved to Karachi 1944 and attached to BAHADUR till sold 1945

DALHOUSIE II Bombay, NOIC and Naval Base
Cd 01.1944-1946

DALRIADA Navy Building, Eldon St., Glasgow, Res HQ unit
Name approved 02.10.1964, Cd 30.04.65 at Inverkip, to Navy Building 1968, took over task of GRAHAM(qv) and retitled Res Tng Centre 10.1994 - extant 1999

DANAE (1867) Mersey, SM Mining Hulk
Corvette, lent War dept 1886 as SM Mining Hulk, Mersey, sold 15.05.1906

DANAE (1918) Normandy, DS
Cr, DS Normandy 12.06.1944 - 15.08.44, to Polish Navy 04.10.44-46, Handed over for BU 24.03.48

DAPPER (1855) Dev, Cooking Depot
Gunboat, tng hulk 1885, cooking depot 1895, renamed YC37 1909, sold 10.05.22

DARTMOUTH (1813) Leith, Qtn Sh
5th Rate, qtn sh 1831 - BU by 1854

DARTMOUTH (1910) Ports, SO RF
Cr, Vice Admiral Commanding RF Cd 01.04.1927 v WEYMOUTH - 12.27 rb CONSTANCE, sold 13.12.30

DARTMOUTH Dartmouth, Base
Cd 01.02.1943 ex BRITANNIA II - PO 01.10.1945
NOIC Lapse 30.06.45 but DARTMOUTH continued as Base
Nom DS: Yt WHITE LADY 01.02.43-07.45
PL(D) 4308 07.45 - 07.46 (Nom DS next DARTMOUTH(qv))

DARTMOUTH II Dartmouth, CF Base
Cd 23.12.1942 ex BRITANNIA III (qv) (name ann 22.03.43), renamed CICALA (qv) 08.43
Nom DS: NAB BRITANNIA III (ex SUNBEAM) 23.12.42-08.43

DARTMOUTH III Dartmouth, CO TE
Cd 01.02.43 (established in RN College by 18.03.43), renamed EFFINGHAM (qv) 19.07.43
CO boat tng from Inveraray to Dartmouth 01.43 when College tx to Eaton Hall 01.43

DARTMOUTH Dartmouth, RF Parent Ship
Cd 01.10.1945, PO 02.12.46

Nom DS: PL(D) 4308 (ex Nom DS prev DARTMOUTH above) 01.10.45-15.07.46
MSPB 44321 15.07.46-

DARTMOUTH Dartmouth, Britannia Royal Naval College
Cd 01.07.53 - extant 1999 - though by 1998 title in NL was 'Dartmouth BRNC'
Ex BRITANNIA (qv) - to release name for Royal Yacht
Nom DS: FMB 37132 53-60
FMB 44463 30.07.55-1958
FMB 42419 59-65

DASHER (1797) Deptford/Woolwich, Army DS/Convict Ship
Sloop, Army DS Deptford 1820, convict ship Woolwich 1832, BU 1838

DAUNTLESS (1847) Newhaven/Hull, CG
FF, CG Newhaven 23.08.1859-31.03.1864, CG Hull 01.04.1864-31.12.1869, sold 01.05.1885

DAUNTLESS Burghfield, Nr Reading, TE
Cd 11.12.1953, PO 14.08.1981
WRNS TE. Advance Party arrived 23.07.45, main staff 31.07.45 from Westfield College NW3. Then called HMTE DUNTLESS. Tng to RALEIGH 15.08.81
Nom DS: HL(D) 3984 11.12.53-1962

DAWN Poole,, Accom Sh
Houseboat - 29.08.1942, acquired 16.02.1943 - 07.44 at least - for disposal 08.44

DAYDREAM Ports Command, Accom Sh
Acquired 28.09.1942 but failed survey 21.10.42

DAYSPRING Poole, Accom Sh
Aux Yt, 29.08.1942 - acquired 15.01.43 - 07.44 (at least) - for lay up Lymington 20.08.44 - to DST for disposal 14.09.44

DEDAIGNEUSE Deptford, Rx Sh
Fr 5th Rate, capt 1801, at Deptford by 1814, Rx Sh by 1819, sold 1823

DEER SOUND (1939) Repair Ship
PORT QUEBEC, hired as M/L 1940, renamed DEER SOUND 05.12.44, repair ship 01.01.45, purch, 02.45 Colombo, Sydney, 04.45 Manus, Leyte, 09.45 HK, 02.46 Melbourne, Fremantle, 03.46 Rosyth, PO 20.11.46, to DST and resto 20.12.47

DEFENCE (1815) Ports/Woolwich, Convict Ship
3rd Rate, Convict Ship Ports 1849-51, Woolwich 1852 - burnt 07.1857

DEFENCE (1861) Shannon/Mersey/Dev, CG/Workshop
Iron Screw Ship, CG Shannon 1874-76 (temp while VALIANT refitting), CG Mersey (Holyhead then Lpool) 15.06.1880-08.08.1885, floating workshop Dev 1890, renamed INDUS (qv) 06.1898, hulk 1922, BU 16.08.1935

DEFENDER Lpool, Ocean Escort Base
01.01.1944-, independent command, acs EAGLET, PO 16.08.45
Nom DS: Diving Boat 246 01.01.44-16.08.45

DEFIANCE Dev, TE
Cd 31.12.1884, PO 14.07.1954, then moved ashore and Cd as independent command, acs DRAKE till PO 20.04.1959.-TAS Tng to RN Barracks (Dev)
Also used as Base for M/S, A/S and A/P vessels in W II, and CF Base to 23.01.46
Combined A/S Fixed Defences and Controlled Mining Tng and Practical Development Centre in Morice Yd 12.45
Plan in 07.1946 for FROBISHER to relieve DEFIANCE and DEFIANCE II on completion of Cadet TS role cancelled
1) DEFIANCE (1861) Cd 13.12.1884 as Torp Sch Ship Dev, BU 26.06.1931
2) ANDROMEDA (1897) renamed POWERFUL II (qv) 23.09.1913, renamed IMPREGNABLE II (qv) 11.1919, renamed DEFIANCE 20.01.1931, BU 14.08.56
3) Nom DS: MSPB 41350 07.1956-1959

DEFIANCE II Dev, TS
1) PERSEUS (1861) Hbr Serv with DEFIANCE 1886, renamed DEFIANCE II 1904, sold 26.06.1931
2) SPARTAN (1891) Hbr Serv with DEFIANCE 1907, renamed DEFIANCE II 08.1921 (some records say DEFIANCE), sold 26.06.1931
3) INCONSTANT (1868), Hbr serv 1898, renamed IMPREGNABLE II (qv) 06.1906, attached DEFIANCE 10.1920, renamed DEFIANCE IV 01.1922, renamed DEFIANCE II 12.1930, BU 04.04.1956

DEFIANCE III Dev, TS
1) CLEOPATRA (1878) Corvette, Hbr Serv attached DEFIANCE renamed DEFIANCE III 01.1922, sold 07.1931
2) VULCAN (1889) DS (qv) renamed DEFIANCE III 17.02.1931, BU 12.1955

DEFIANCE IV Dev, TS
INCONSTANT (1868), Hbr Serv 1898, renamed IMPREGNABLE II (qv) 06.1906, attached DEFIANCE 10.1920, renamed DEFIANCE IV 01.1922, renamed DEFIANCE II 12.1930, BU 04.04.1956

DEFIANCE Dev, Fleet Maint Base & 2 SM DS
Cd 15.02.1972, PO 21.04.78, staff moved ashore to location known as Fleet Maint Base, Devonport, which Re-Cd as DEFIANCIE 12.03.1981. - PO 31.03.1994 (some acs state 25.03.1994) - incorporated into DRAKE
FORTH (1938) DS (qv) renamed DEFIANCE 15.02.72-21.04.78

DEGA Vizakhapatnam, IN Air Sta
Cd 1991 - extant 1999

DELAMARE Piraeus, Athens

Ment in a list

DELHI (1918) Belfast, Res Drl Sh
Cr, allocated as Res Drl Sh 05.1946-07.47 but not used, SPEY allocated in lieu 04.47, BU 03.48

DEMETER (1920) Scapa Flow, Stores Ship
BUENOS AIRES, Cargo Liner, mined 1940, hulk, purch as stores carrier (RFA), renamed 06.1941, Gutter Sound, Scapa Flow 1943. Ammo hulk 10.1945, sold 1949

DEMETRIUS Wetherby, Accountant Branch/Supply & Secretariat TE
Cd 15.07.1944, establishment ex CABOT (qv). Accountant Sch tx from Highgate Sch (PRESIDENT V(qv)), renamed CERES (qv) 01.10.1946
Accountant Branch renamed 26.10.44
Nom DS: NAB RUNNYMEDE 15.07.44-

DERBY HAVEN (1944) CF DS
Cd 25.07.1945, to East Indies, HQ Ship Malaysian personnel 01.46-02.01.47, PO 12.08.47. Accom Sh for M/S Queenborough v ESKIMO 11.47-01.48 (at least). Sold 30.07.49 - Persian BABR, PO 1969

DERG (1943) Soton/Cardiff/ Penarth, Res Drl Sh
FF, Soton from 09.04.1947 v ZETLAND, renamed WESSEX (qv)1951 as Drl Sh - when Res Div names allocated). 06.1952 tx to Cardiff as CAMBRIA(qv) - named 14.04.54. CO RF Cardiff v. WILTON and reverted to DERG 01.04.1959. CO RF Penarth 12.1959. RF closed 29.08.1960, BU 09.60

DERWENT Tasmania, RAN Base
01.08.1940 ex CERBERUS VI (qv) - 01.03.1942, renamed HUON(qv)
Base Staff

DERWENT (1941) Plym, DS
DD, DS for 23 ML Flot 1945, sold 11.1946

DESPATCH Bermuda, Sheer Hulk
Brig, ex Transport Office 1816, sheer hulk 1826 - 1865

DESPATCH (1919) Normandy/Ports, Accom Sh
Cr, under ODYSSEY 17.04.44, Normandy 07.06.44-08.44 rb CERES, Res 09.45, accom sh Ports 1945, BU 05.04.1946

DEVASTATION (1871) Queensferry/ Dev/Bantry/Gib, CG
Turret Ship, CG Queensferry 07.08.1885-09.05.1890, Pt Guard Dev 05.12.1893-01.1898, Temp CG Bantry 04.1898-06.1898, Pt Guard Gib 08.11.1898-04.1902, Torp Sch Ports 1904, sold 12.05.1908

DIADEM (1782) Plym, Rx Sh
3rd Rate, Rx Sh 1831, BU 1832

DIADEM (1896) Ports, TE
Cr, Stokers' TS 1914-18 (closed 10.15-01.18), Cd as accom sh Ports 01.01.1918, accom sh and TS by 08.18-03.19 rb ACHILLES 06.19, but still listed as accoms sh and TS 10.1920, sold 09.05.1921

DIADEM (1942) Sheerness/Ports/Dev/ Chat, SO RF
Cr, RF Sheerness 12.1950-05.51, to Ports RF - living ship 11.1951. SO RF Dev 06.10.52 - 01.54, SO RF Chat 01.54 v DUNCANSBY HEAD - 25.07.56 rb BEN LOMOND, sold to Pakistan 25.05.57, renamed BABUR, later Hbr TS JAHANGIR(qv)

DIAMANTINA (1944) Brisbane, RAN Museum Ship
FF, later survey ship, PO 02.1980, Queensland Maritime Museum as Exhibit 10.1980 - extant 1999

DIAMOND (1950) Ports, Hbr TS
DD, Hbr TS, attached SULTAN v CROSSBOW 06.1970 - 1981 rb ASHANTI, BU 11.1981

DIAMOND ROCK Diamond Rock, off Martinique, Fortress
Seized 07.01.1804, Cd as HM Sloop 08.01.1804, lost 02.06.1805
Poss to have been called FORT DIAMOND

DIANA (1822) Chat, DS
5th Rate, DS 1835, BU 1874

DIANA Halifax, Nova Scotia, RCN DS
DS 20.08.1914 - PO 1919
Shore barracks, Halifax 11.1914-1919, included staff at Quebec, Camperdown W/T Sta and RN College of Canada
Nom DS: Boom Gate Vessel No 2 20.08.1914-07.09.1915
2 tenders to RN College of Canada bore the name - ex schooners
ADVOCATE (08.1911-1914) and ARTHUR W (09.1915-03.1919)

D'IBERVILLE Quebec City, RCN New Entry TE
Established 02.1952, Cd 21.10.1952 in MONTCALM (qv) - 31.07.1961
See also HOCHELAGA

DIDO (1836) Sheerness, Coal Depot
Corvette, coal hulk 1860 - sold 03.1903

DIDO (1869) Forth/Sheerness, TS
Corvette, hulk 1886, Mine Depot Forth - 1905, then TS Sheerness, renamed ACTAEON II (qv) 1906, sold 07.1922

DIDO (1896) Hull/Harwich/Ports, CG/DS
Cr, CG Hull 11.02.1903 v GALATEA - mid 1903, conv to SM DS 1912, DS 6 SM 1912-14, 3 SM 1914, DS 3 DFand 10 DF Harwich 1914, rb DILIGENCE as 3 DF DS 09.1914, DS 10 DF Harwich 1914 - 01.03.1919 rb HECLA, Res DD DS Ports 1919-26, C & M 22.02.26, sold 16.12.26

DIDO (1939) Ports, RF Flag Group
Cr, FO RF 28.08.1951 v DUKE OF YORK - 07.07.1952 rb JAMAICA but retained as Flag for Coronation Review and was accom sh to 17.12.56 rb VANGUARD, BU 07.58

DIEPPE (1944) Dev, Accom Sh

LST 3016, named 1947, Res Malta GC 11.1949-19.06.1951, Gib 04.52 - and Malta GC from 08.08.53. Refit Malta GC 22.06.59-31.03.59, Cd 12.04.60, PO 16.09.60 and to res Malta GC. Accom Sh Dev 07.64-69, in use by dockyard in Dev 1970-76, sold 25.02.1980

DILAWAR China Creek, Karachi, RIN/RPN/PN TE
Cd 02.1942 - 1972 at least (Flag to HIMALAYA 1973), Barracks for RIN, then RPN/PN.
Listed as Boys' TE tender to BAHADUR in RIN History
Reference to DILAWAR as CO estab Bombay 10.41-43 - poss refers to DILWARRA (qv)

DILIGENCE (1814) Dev, Coal Hulk
Transport, coal hulk 08.1861, later C 72, sold 05.07.1904

DILIGENCE (1907) Scapa Flow/Sheerness, DS
TABARISTAN, purch 1913, completed as DS 10.1913, Allocated Ports v FISGARD 23.08.1914, DS 3 DF v DIDO 19.09.1914, Cd for 12 DF 09.12.1915 - Scapa Flow - 1919 (at Dundee 12.1918). Cd for 7 DF China 01.03.1919 but PO 04.1919 to C & M Chat 01.05.1919. Res Sheerness 05.19-04.21, CD for 7 DF Med 12.09.21. PO 11.24. Res Dev 12.24. Atlantic Fleet 11.25. PO Dockyard control Dev 16.01.26, BU 11.26

DILIGENCE (1944) Repair Ship
Cd 04.03.1945, HK 12.1945, returned to USN at Subic Bay 29.01.1946

DILIGENCE Hythe, Nr Soton, RF and Base
Cd 03.03.1953 - 1960, PO as independent estab 31.03.1960 and run by civiliian contractor. Closed 30.04.1963
For commissioning and equipping M/S. Naval Liaison Party remained when civilian manned.
Nom DS: MFV 174(ex RALEIGH) 03.53-09.59

DILIGENCE (1981) Falkland Is/ Persian Gulf, Forward Support Ship
STENA INSPECTOR - as such served in Falklands War 1982. Purch 10.83 and Cd 12.03.1984 as RFA. Falkland Is to 1987, Persian Gulf 08.87-89, Falklands 89, Gulf 90-92 Falklands 92,UK 12.92, Falklands 94-95, Far East 97, Gulf 01.98-, UK 12.98, Falklands 98-99, UK 08.99-

DILIGENTE (1916) Cowes, Isle of Wight, Base Ship
Fr Chasseur used as Base for Chasseurs from 06.1941 - towed to Marvins Yard Cowes to set up base 07.41 - closed 05.07.45

DILWARRA Manora, Bombay, RIN CO
SS DILWARRA, allocated to CO India 06.1943. There is a ref to DILAWAR (qv), Manora, CO Base 10.1941-1943 which poss refers to DILWARRA

DINOSAUR Troon, CO Base
Cd 01.04.1942 - Pay and Drafting Section to COPRA (qv) 07.09.43. PO 27.05.46
Tank LC HQ 13.03.42, TE for Major LC Officers and Major LC Gunnery Sch.
Used Troon Golf Club, Crosbie Towers Troon req approved as HQ and WRNS accom 07.02.42.
Aircraft Recognition Sch ex WARREN 02.06.45
Nom DS: MB POU POU FLEE(T23) 01.04.1942-01.43
NAB JOY 01.43-

DINOSAUR II Irvine, LC Base
01.11.1943 - 31.12.44, renamed FULLARTON (qv)
Major LC work up and repair base Troon and slipway Irvine. Independent command.

DIOMEDE (1919) Dev, Boys' TE
Cr. TS 1938-39, sold 05.04.46

DIPPER Henstridge, Somerset, RNAS
Construction started 08.1941. Cd part complement 01.04.1943. PO 11.11.1946, became tender to HERON. Re-opened as satellite to HERON(qv) 08.1949-09.52(flying ceased 19.11.52) & 1954 - 06.1957. Listed as in C & M 12.55-12.59.
CF Depot Henstridge closed 01.10.51
Nom DS: Hbr Lch 226 01.04.43-

DISCOVERY (1789) Woolwich/Deptford, Convict Ship
Sloop, convict ship Woolwich 1818, Deptford by 1831, BU 1834

DISCOVERY (1901) London, Res Flag
Survey vessel, tx from Scouts to RN for RNVR 06.54, became Flag Admiral Commanding Reserves and Cd on Thames 20.07.1955, post abolished 1976 and ship handed over to Maritime Trust 02.04.79

DISCOVERY Vancouver, BC, RCN Base and Res Div
01.09.1939 - Cd 01.11.1941 - tender to GIVENCHY 01.09.42. At Royal Vancouver Yacht Club, Stanley Pk. To Deadman's Is 26.01.44. Officially opened 21.10.44. Listed to 1976, extant 1995

DIXI (1913) Falmouth, Accom Sh
Fr merchant ship seized 1940, accom sh 11.1940, DG vessel 1941-45

DODMAN POINT (1945), Rosyth/Harwich/Sheerness/Dev, Repair Ship
Cd 05.10.1945. Home waters. Part of COCHRANE (qv) accom sh v KILLARNEY 02.1946-1950. To Harwich v WOOLWICH 05.51. Tx from RF Harwich to RF Sheerness late 1951. RF Dev accom sh 12.1953-62 (Repair organisation v ALAUNIA 09.1956)(SO Reserve Ships 13.03.56-12.03.57), BU 16.04.63

DOLPHIN Ft Blockhouse, Gosport, SM Depot and Sch
Taken over from Royal Engineers 1904. Cd 03.05.1905, became independent command 31.08.1912. 6 SM 1918-19, 5 SM 12.24-01.01.61, then 1 SM. TE only by 12.93. Sch tx to RALEIGH 17.09.97. PO 30.09.98. Closed 01.04.99 - task to

RALEIGH/DRYAD - became accom unit for Army Medical College.
Nom DS:
1) DOLPHIN (1882) sloop, hulk 1907, DS 2 SM 1912, sold 13.03.1925, foundered under tow 19.04.25,
raised and BU 1977
3) PANDORA ex Russian SM DS SETI, purch 11.1914, renamed DOLPHIN 03.10.24. Sunk 23.12.39 by mine while under tow to Blyth for conv to blockship (or DS at Blyth?)
4) ABERFOYLE, puch 04.11.1920, renamed DOLPHIN 03.38, for disposal 47
5) TRSB 43775 08.48 (at least) - 54 (also listed 01.58)
6) TRSB 43776 55-03.57
6) TRV 4(1943) 14.03.57-1960

DOLPHIN II Gosport, Accom for DOLPHIN
Part of HORNET - 1957-58

DOLPHIN III Gosport, Accom Unit
Name quoted in connection with a part of HORNET used by Joint Services Sail Tng Centre 1974-extant 99

DOMINION (1903) Chat, Accom Sh
BB, PO 05.04.1918, accom sh Chat 15.04.1918-04.19 (at least), PO by 08.19, sold 05.21

DOMINION Stoke Damerell Sch, 6 Havelock Tce, Dev, RCN DS
01.10.1940-01.03.1941, renamed NIOBE (qv)

DONDIN Pt Elizabeth, S Africa, SAN ACF Tng Base
In NL 1957-59, prob a mis-spelling of DONKIN(qv)

DONEGAL (1858) Lpool/Ports, CG
1st Rate, CG Rock Ferry 01.09.1864 - 01.07.1869, then became VERNON (qv) 14.01.1886, sold 1925

DONKIN Pt Elizabeth, S Africa, SAN ACF Tng Base
01.1944 - 1961 (mis-spelt DONDIN in NL & Pink List 1957-9). SAS DONKIN from 01.11.54 - extant 1968

DONNACONA Drummond St, Montreal, PQ, RCN Base & Res Div
01.09.1939 - Cd 26.10.43 (ex MONTREAL(qv)) - amalgamated with CARTIER (English speaking) 09.06.1944, listed to 19766, extant 1987

DONNACONA II
Tng Vessel Montreal 26.10.1943 - 07.46 (ex MONTREAL II)

DORDRECHT (1796) Sheerness, Rx Sh
Dutch 3rd Rate, capt 1796, Rx Sh 1800 - BU 1823

DORIS (1896) Aden, DS East Indies
Cr, DS 02.12.1917 v DUFFERIN. PO Bombay 04.12.1918 (see JUMNA), sold 02.1919

DORITA (1920) Soton, Accom Sh
Hired as BD vessel 1941 - accom sh Soton by 07.1943-11.45

DORLIN Dorlin House, Acharacle, Argyll, CO Base/Special Tng Estab
Cd 23.03.1942, C & M 06.04.44, closed 28.11.44
Dorlin House had been in use by the RN in 1940.
Nom DS: Prototype Coble Raiding Craft 23.03.42-

DOROTHY Soton, Accom Sh
Steam Yt hull, 08.1942 - acquired 31.12.42, - laid up Lymington 01.45, resto 30.08.45

DOROTHY Thames, Accom Sh
Sailing Barge, 23.03.1945 - accom sh Thames

DOTTEREL (1898) Bermuda, Rx Sh
Sloop, hulk 1827, Rx Sh Bermuda 1851-65, listed as sold at Bermuda 1848

DOTTEREL East Haven, Angus, RNAS
Cd 01.05.1943 as PEEWIT (qv), though DOTTEREL was the original name sel

DOUGLAS (1918) Hartlepool, Flag RF
DD leader, FO Commanding RF 02.07.1944 v MALAYA - 01.10.44 rb SCARBOROUGH, sold 20.03.45
DOVER Deptford, Rx Sh
Fr Troopship BELLONE, capt 1811, Rx Sh 1825, sold 1836

DOVEY (1943) Barrow-in-Furness, CO RF
FF, CO RF Barrow 04.1953 till BU 11.55

DRAGON (1798) Pembroke, Qtn/Marine Barracks Ship
3rd Rate, Qtn Sh 1824, Marine Barracks Ship by 1835, renamed FAME 1842, BU 1850

DRAGON Navy House, Cambrian Place, Swansea, Communications Tng Centre
Cd 01.10.1984. PO 30.06.1994

DRAGONFLY S Hayling Is, CO Base
Cd 07.06.1943, PO 15.01.1946
Was CO ' suspense base',acs VICTORY III, became MOLCAB Assembly Depot and Landing Barge Base, including NPs 2400 and 2401

DRAKE (1875) Clyde, Drl Sh
SHELDRAKE, Gunboat, renamed DRAKE 13.03.1888, Drl Sh RN Artillery Volunteers Clyde, renamed WV29 1893, renamed DRAKE 1906, sold 03.04.1906

DRAKE Dev, Barracks and Base
Was VIVID (qv), renamed DRAKE 01.01.1934 - extant 1999
Airport at Roborough used from 09.1939 as part of DRAKE. - tx to Air Ministry 01.05.1942.
Included overflow camps at Yealmpton, Cornwood and Roborough and Signal Sch Glenholt(1942).
Overflow estab at Bristol (Muller's Orphanage) see CABOT.
RN Signal Sch, St Budeaux (1958)and later inside

Barracks
RN Hydrographic Sch ex Chat 09/09.1959 - extant 99 and RN Laundry Sch (to 1972)
Title RN Barracks changed to HMS DRAKE 01.11.1961
Incorporated DEFIANCE from 01.04.1994 when Re-Cd to cover whole of Naval Base Devonport (incl 2 SM)
Known as "Jago's Mansions"
Nom DS: MARSHAL NEY (ex M13, ex VIVID) (1915) 01.01.34-47 (then ALAUNIA II and BU 10.57)
HL(D) 3960 (ex Nom DS PEEWIT) 01.48-01.08.56
HL(D) 3962 01.08.56-07.58
MSPB 5505 07.58-62

DRAKE I Dev, Accounting Base
1943 (at least), lapsed 01.11.1961

DRAKE II Dev, Accounting Base
By 25.02.1940 - 1958 (at least)
By 10.43 was at Stoke Damerell Sch, Dev. To RNB 05.45. Post WW II included Roborough Airport

DRAKE IV Dev, Accounting Base (Tenders)
Cd 08.1939 - PO 31.12.1946 - acs to DRAKE I (Officers), DRAKE II (Ratings), TARTAR (RF)
At RN Port Library 28.09.1939 - for DD at Plym. No 8 Hut, Parade Ground 20.06.45, Raglan Barracks 1946. Took acs from LUCIFER 31.03.46, from RF v COLOMBO 14.03.46. RF acs to UNICORN 01.07.46

DRAKE V Dev/Tavistock, Accounting Base
RAN Accounting Base 13.01.41 at Port Library. From 05.41 at Tavistock Golf Clubhouse. Closed 27.09.41 - acs to DRAKE IV/NAPIER

DRAKE X Pembroke Dock, SO RF
SO RF named DRAKE X 02.1948 - 1952
DRAKE X Dev, Accounting Base (Tenders)
1952 (at least), lapsed 01.11.1961

DREADNOUGHT (1801) Greenwich, Hosp Sh
2nd Rate, Hosp Ship 1827, BU 03.1857

DREADNOUGHT (1808) Greenwich, Hosp Sh
1st Rate, CALEDONIA, renamed DREADNOUGHT 21.06.1856 as Hosp Sh (but in NL 1857 as CALEDONIA), BU 1875

DREADNOUGHT (1875) Bantry, CG
BB, CG Bantry 30.03.1895-08.03.1897, Torp Sch Dev 1904, sold 14.07.1908

DREEL CASTLE Falmouth, A/P Base
Drifter Cd 02.02.1915. Nom DS A/P Falmouth, Penzance and Scillies v VIVID 01.10.1915 - 16.09.1919 (acs to VIVID IV)
Flag of Rear Admiral Falmouth struck 15.08.1919
Nom DS: DREEL CASTLE (1908) Drifter 01.10.1915 - 01.02.1918 renamed MARIA SMITH
MARIA SMITH, Drifter 01.02.1918 - 09.1919

DRIVER (1875) Deptford, Convict Ship
Sloop, convict ship 1825, BU 1834

DROMEDARY Bermuda, Convict Ship
HOWE, purch 1805, renamed DROMEDARY 06.08.1806, convict ship 08.1819, sold 08.1864 in Bermuda

DROMMEDARIS Saldanha Bay, S Africa, SAN Gymnasium
01.11.1954 - 1958

DROMMEDARIS Simons Town, SAN SM Facility
Cd 01.10.1971 - renamed HVCO BIERMANN (qv) 08.76

DRONACHARYA Cochin, IN Trials Estab
1990 - extant 1999

DRUDGE (1882) Ports, Workshop
Gunboat, purch 1901, renamed EXCELLENT (qv) 01.12.1916, renamed DRYAD (qv) 01.02.1919, renamed DRUDGE 1919. Armourers' workshop, sold 27.03.1920

DRUID (1825) Lpool, Qtn Sh
5th Rate, Qtn Sh 1850 - sold 1863

DRYAD (1795) Ports, Rx Sh
5th Rate, Rx Sh 1832 - BU 1860

DRYAD Ports/Southwick Park, Navigation & Direction Sch
Cd 01.01.1906 in Naval Academy Building, Ports Dockyard, using gunboat DRYAD as a tender. Cd 01.02.1919 using DRYAD as Nom DS. Moved to Southwick Park, move complete and Cd there 27.09.1941 - extant 1999
Allied C-in-C HQ for D Day 26.04.1944. Tactical Sch opened 02.06.1970. Seamanship Tng to PHOENIX 01.01.1971
Nom DS:
Gunboat DRYAD (1893) 01.01.1906 - 01.18 renamed HAMADRYAD, sold 24.09.1920
DRUDGE (1882) (qv) 01.02.1919 - 08.1919
RATTLER (1886) - gunboat 09.1919 - sold 10.24
CARSTAIRS ex CAWSAND (1919) 04.01.24 - 15.08.24 - renamed CARSTAIRS - sold 1935
Steam Pinnace 54 24-28
Steam Pinnace 191 28-32
MB 240 34-47 (but note next 2 entries)
30' MB 1687 to 02.42
30' FMB 3642 02.42 - 07.46
MFV 628 07.46 - 12.48
MFV 110 12.48 - 1962

DUBLIN (1812) Dev, Rx Sh/Fitting Out Hulk
3rd Rate, Hbr Serv Dev 1845, Rx Sh 1865-70, fitting out hulk for res 1875 - sold 07.1885

DUCHESS OF ROTHESAY (1894) Brightlingsea, Base/Accom Sh
Hired as M/S in WWI and 11.1939. Laid up 08.1940. Alloc accom sh Brightlingsea 04.42-1945 -

to DST 02.11.45.
Used as Base for LCT Flotilla.

DUFFERIN (1904) Bombay, RIN TS
Troopship RIM. AMC 1914. Nom DS for shore personnel East Indies at Aden v EURYALUS 11.1917-02.12.1917 rb DORIS. Flag East Indies 10.1918. TS 1927. At Bombay 1943-44. For sale 1955

DUIKER Toulon, SAN Admin Base
For SM building 1967-72

DUKE (1777) Standgate Creek, Qtn Sh
2nd Rate, Hbr serv 1799, Qtn Sh 1835, BU 1843

DUKE (1896) Pt Said, DS
Cd as Nom DS 01.07.1918 - previously known as RN Depot Pt Said, tenders acs v EGMONT II ex EURYALUS. PO 08.04.1919 - task to HANNIBAL
1) DUKE OF DEVONSHIRE, hired as A/P paddler 25.03.1916 - renamed DUKE 05.06.1916, at Pt Said by 02.1917. RN Depot Pt Said 1917-19, renamed DUKE II 27.02.1919. - also req WWII
2) POLLY, tug(1916), was DUKE 27.02.1919-08.1919 (sold)

DUKE Great Malvern, TE
Cd 27.05.1941. 05.43 Provided tented accom for New Entry Stokers. PO 31.03.1946 - became Royal Signals and Radar Estab
Nom DS: Chat 27' whaler 190 27.05.41-

DUKE OF WELLINGTON (1852) Ports, DS
Ex WINDSOR CASTLE, 1st Rate, Hbr serv 05.1863, Rx Sh Ports 1865, became Flag v VICTORY 1869 until VICTORY ReCd as Flag 01.08.1891, and was also the general depot from 1869 until the men marched to the new barracks from her in 1903. Sold 12.04.1904

DUKE OF YORK (1940) Ports, Flag RF
BB, Flag of RF v AUSONIA 15.06.49 - 28.08.51 rb DIDO, BU 02.58
DULLISK COVE (1944) Hull Repair Ship
Ex EMPIRE PERAK, allocated BPF v MULLION COVE 05.45, Cd 07.06.45, Colombo 08.45, Darwin, Sydney 09.45, Brisbane 10.45, HK 12.45, Spore, Aden 02.46, Rosyth, 25.03.46, to DST 05.06.46, sold 30.07.47

DUMANA Alexandria/Bathurst, DS/Accom Sh
Taken up as DS Alexandria 09.1940, released 11.40.
Base Ship at Bathurst for Sunderland aircraft - poss not the same ship

DUNCAN (1811) Standgate Creek, Qtn Sh
3rd Rate, Qtn Sh 1826 - BU 10.1863

DUNCAN (1859) Queensferry/ Sheerness/Chat, CG/Barracks
1st Rate, CG Queensferry 16.06.1867-01.03.1870, the to Sheerness as Flag, Cd 01.04.1873. DUNCAN and RN Barracks amalgamated 01.01.1882. PO 31.03.1889, renamed PEMBROKE (qv) at Chat 1890. Renamed TENEDOS II(qv) 09.1905, sold 11.10.1910

DUNCAN (1901) Chat, Accom Sh
BB, overflow ship RN Barracks Cd 10.04.1917 - 04.19(at least), PO by 09.1919. Sold 02.1920

DUNCAN (1957) Rosyth, Hbr TS
FF, Hbr TS attached CALEDONIA v SAINTES 1972-1984. BU 02.1985

DUNCANSBY HEAD (1944) Escort Vessel Maint Ship
Cd 09.08.1945, SO RF Harwich - accom sh v CUILLIN SOUND 25.06.46 - 21.01.47 rb TYNE. To res 07.07.47, Living Ship Sheerness RF by 12.1950-52, to Chat RF as SO RF16.10.52-01.54 rb DIADEM. RF Chat to 18.05.60, then Rosyth SO Res Ships Cd 18.05.60 (was to have been RF ship name but BRUCE chosen later(qv)) - SORF V BRUCE 1962. Cd as part of COCHRANE (qv) 01.12.62. Sold 12.69

DUNDONALD Auchengate, Comb Tng Centre
Cd 01.04.1942. PO 16.09.46 - retard party in FULLARTON
Holding and Tng Base for Naval Beach Cdo. Holding Base for CO personnel, Comb Tng Centre (Middle East) stayed in DUNDONALD - Gailes Camp - 03.45 on return from Middle East. Absorbed ARMADILLO(qv) 07.45
Nom DS: NAB ELSHIN 01.04.42-11.42
NAB SHELAGH 11.42-

DUNDONALD II Auchengate, Comb Signal Sch
Cd 01.04.1942, closed 30.06.46 - task to Fremington House, Barnstaple
Naval Wings of Comb Tng Centre and Comb Signal Sch
Nom DS: NAB ELSHIN nominated but cancelled
Ketch ALBYN(1934) 01.04.42 - laid up 11.45, NDS to 13.03.46
Skiff 926 13.03.46-06.46

DUNDONNALD Rosyth, RF
Name sel 1959 instead of NEPTUNE. BRUCE/COCHRANE used instead (qv)

DUNGENESS (1945) LC Maint Ship
Cd RCN 02.10.1945. Home Waters, PO & to MOWT 03.06.1946 - sold 1947

DUNINO
Name in NL 1946 - poss refers to location - see JACKDAW II

DUNLUCE CASTLE (1904) Base Ship/Accom Sh
Liner, req 29.08.1939. Accom sh for Scapa Flow v VOLTAIRE - was to be Cd as PROSPERPINE 03.11.39 and sailed Elderslea Wharf 04.11.39, but was Cd 07.11.39 as DUNLUCE CASTLE and as Base Ship Immingham. 01.04.40 was DS for M/S and A/S vessels Scapa Flow (Lyness). Task (Base Mail and Accom Sh) tx to PROSERPINE 16.06.45. C & M Rosyth 03.07.45. PO 17.07.45. To MOWT

17.07.45, BU 07.45

DURBAN (1919) Normandy, Block - ship
Cr, Cd 07.04.44 as independent command, acs ODYSSEY and expended as breakwater Normandy 09.06.44 . PO 09.06.44

DURBAN (1957) Durban, Natal, SAN Maritime Museum Ship
M/S, Museum Ship 05.05.88-

DURHAM (1845) Sunderland/Leith, Res Drl Sh
ACTIVE, 5th Rate, was Drl Sh Sunderland 1867, renamed DURHAM 18.11.1867, at Leith 1888-1906 - sold 12.05.1908

DURHAM CASTLE (1904) Store Ship
Req 1939, mined and sunk 26.01.1940 enroute Scapa Flow

DWARF (1936) Ports/Clyde, SM Tender
Cd 26.03.1937, with 5 SM Portsmouth to 06.1941, then 3 SM Clyde 07.41 till sold 03.62

DWARKA Okha, Gulf of Kutch, India, IN Estab/Base
By 01.1974-1979
In a list 07.06.73

E

EAGLE (1804) Falmouth/Milford/Soton/Lpool, CG/Res Drl Sh/A/P Parent
3rd Rate. CG Falmouth 1831. CG Milford 01.01.1857-05.03.1857, Drl Sh Soton 1860, Drl Sh Mersey RNR from 1862 (at Birkenhead to at least 1872)(plus RNAV 1872)(RNVR - formed 1904 in Customs House, to EAGLE 1911-26). A/P Parent ship WWI - Cd 30.09.1914 under PRESIDENT.(included Lough Foyle from 11.14 and Kingstown (later COLLEEN) from 01.15). Independent command 16.10.1914. Renamed EAGLET(qv) 23.03.1918. PO 08.1926, lost by fire 04.27

EAGLESCLIFFE HALL (1928) Accom Sh
08.1942-46 - used as Military Storeship 05.44-07.44/24.10.44-06.45/08.07.45-09.08.45

EAGLET Lpool, Res Drl Sh/Base
1) EAGLE(1804)(qv) 3rd Rate, renamed EAGLET 23.03.1918 while serving as Res Drl Ship Lpool and A/P Parent - PO 08.26, lost by fire 04.27
2) SIR BEVIS (1918) Sloop, renamed IRWELL(qv) 09.1923, renamed EAGLET 1926, Bu 1971
09.39 name sel for use by Shore Base in comml port of Lpool, NOIC detailed and arrived 23.08.39. EAGLET Cd as Base 04.12.39 - By 04.1940 the Res Div has been closed and was in use for Merchant Navy Defence Courses - PO and NOIC lapse 28.02.46.
Ship used for Res when reconstituted 01.10.46 and name allocated to Mersey Div of Res in 1951.
At Salthouse Dock 1922-66. Ashore at Princes Dock Cd 1971 - extant 1999.

EAGLET II Birkenhead, Base for A/S and M/S Tlrs
Opened 20.09.1939, name changed from IRWELL(qv), closed 15.08.42, renamed IRWELL(qv)

EAGLET III David Lewis Northern Hosp, Lpool, T124X Central Depot and Accom Estab
20.09.1939-24.12.1940 renamed MERSEY (qv)

EASTBOURNE (1955) Rosyth, Hbr TS
FF, Hbr TS for CALEDONIA v RAPID 08.1973 - 01.1984, Bu 07.03.1985

EASTERN ISLES (1891) Lpool, Accom Sh
Yt WESTERN ISLES (qv) hired as A/S TS 04.1940. Renamed EASTERN ISLES 22.04.41. Allocated Londonderry for Instructional duties 07.41, but released from A/S Tng and PO 26.11.41. To Lpool and Cd as accom sh for EAGLET II 01.12.41-45. Resto 20.04.46 - see also WESTERN ISLES

EASTON (1942) Rosyth, Hbr TS
Hunt Class DD, attached CALEDONIA as Hbr TS 11.1949 - BU 01.1953

ECLIPSE (1867) Plym, depot for Naval Mines & Ordnance
Corvette, ex SAPPHO, lent to War dept as hulk for mine storage at Dev 1888-1914. Mine Depot WWI. For sale 1921

ECLIPSE (1894) Dev, DS
Cr, Accom Sh for SM Flot 1915. Accom sh 2 DF Dev 08.1916, then attached 4 DF Dev 11.1917-03.1919 rb ESSEX. Still accom shipDev 04.19. Sold 1921

ECONOMUS Taranto, Italy, RN Base
One of 6 names allocated for RN Bases in Italy and considered for Taranto but not sel 12.1943

EDEN (1918) Plym, Base Repair ship
Tlr ex THOMAS JOHNS, ex EDEN, ex SAN IMMORTELLE, allocated as hulk to Capt D Plym as Base Repair Ship and for pierhead facilities 01.06.1946. BU 10.1947

EDGAR (1858) Motherbank, Spithead, Customs Hulk
2nd Rate, lent as Custom's Hulk (Qtn Sh Motherbank) 02.1870-sold 1904

EDGAR (1890) Holyhead, CG
Cr, CG Holyhead 09.04.1903-mid 1903, Boys' TS (seagoing) 1905-06, sold 1921

EDINBURGH (1811) Ports/Leith, Guardship/CG
3rd Rate, Guardship Ports 1850-51, CG Leith 01.03.1858-01.03.1864, sold 11.1865

EDINBURGH (1882) Hull/Queensferry, CG
Ex MAJESTIC, renamed 1882, Turret ship, CG Hull 07.02.1894-12.1894, then CG Queensferry 12.1894 - 22.09.1897. Sold 11.10.1910

EDINBURGH CASTLE (1910), Freetown, Sierra Leone, Base
Hired as AMC 1914-1919, fitted out Dev as Base Wireless Ship Sierra Leone 08.1939. Plans to use her as accom sh Scapa Flow cancelled. Cd 12.10.1939, replaced AFRIKANDER V (qv) at Freetown 15.03.1940. A/P to ST MINVER but acs retained in EDINBURGH CASTLE 01.04.41. Acquired 24.06.41. PO 15.05.44. Laid up at Freetown 05.44 as in such a poor state. Scuttled by 'gunfire' 60 miles off Freetown 25.09.45.
Included RNAS Hastings 01.04.1941-22.03.43 - became SPURWING (qv)

EDINBURGH CASTLE II Freetown
Ment 11.1944

EDWARD VII (1906) Thames, Cable Repair Ship
Tlr, hired 1914. Cable Repair Vessel 1917-19. Repair cable Thames Estuary WWI

EFFINGHAM (1921) Ports, SO RF
Cr, SO RF Ports 30.09.1932-39 (post lapsed 09.39). Wrecked 18.05.1940

EFFINGHAM II Ceylon, Base
Cd 02.07.1925 ex CHATHAM II(qv) - 21.09.32(became HAWKINS II(qv))
Name taken from Flagship of East Indies Sta at the time

EFFINGHAM Dartmouth, CO Base
19.07.1943 ex DARTMOUTH III (qv) - 31.12.1943. Task tx to WESTCLIFF (qv) - training to WESTCLIFF III/ST MATHEW (qv), when RN College tx to USN 01.01.44.
Nom DS: NAB WATER GYPSY 19.07.43 - 31.12.43

EGERIA (1807) Dev, Rx Sh
6th Rate, Rx Sh 1825 - BU 1865

EGMONT (18110) Rio de Janeiro, Rx Sh
3rd Rate, storeship 12.1862, Rx Sh at Rio de Janeiro 1865 - sold at Rio 01.1875

EGMONT Malta GC, Base Ship
03.1904-30.06.1933
1) ACHILLES (1863) renamed HIBERNIA 1902 (Base Ship Malta(qv)) - renamed EGMONT 03.1904, still as Base Ship Malta - to release name for new Battleship under construction, PO 04.05.1914 - allocated as TS v ACTAEON 05.04.1914, altered to be TS and join ACTAEON 10.07.1914, renamed EGREMONT (qv) 01.11.1916, then PEMBROKE (qv) 06.1919 and sold 26.01.1923.
2) FIREFFLY (1877), renamed EGMONT as Base Ship Malta 03.04.1914 - new base ashore in Ft St Angelo Cd 05.05.1914, also carried acs A/P Taranto 1915. Renamed FIREFLY 01.03.1923, sold 05.1931
3) BULLFROG (1881), renamed EGMONT 03.1923, renamed ST ANGELO - new name for Base Ship Malta 01.07.1933. Sold 1933

EGMONT II Malta GC, Accounting Base for vessels at Pt Said
To 06.1918 (at least) - rb DUKE(qv)

EGMONT II Malta GC, Accounting Base for DD in Med
01.11.1925-1932

EGMONT Malta GC, Accounting Base
For personnel ex HANNIBAL 23.12.1943

EGREMONT Chat, Base Ship
ACHILLES (1863), later HIBERNIA/ EGMONT (qv), renamed EGREMONT 01.11.1916. Hulk Cd as accom sh Chat 07.01.1918, renamed PEMBROKE (qv) 06.06.1919, sold 01.1923

EILEEN (1910) Cromarty/West Indies, A/P Base/ML Base
Yt, hired 04.11.1914 v EVENING STAR(qv) as A/P Parent Cromarty - rb STEPHEN FURNESS 18.01.1915. Rear Admiral appointed Cdre in Charge EILEEN and Patrol West Indies (appointment 08.01.1917) v LEVIATHAN 01.04.1917 - 03.1919. PO Ports 30.04.1919 - left 12 MLs with C & M Party at Trinidad - see EILEEN II.

EILEEN II Trinidad, Nom DS
04.1919 - 07.1919
Pay Acs of Officers and men of MLs, (even though EILEEN PO). Under MALABAR for discipline and acs

EL HIND (1938) Bombay, RIN CO TS
Hired 1943 - CO TS Bombay 06.1943. Cd 21.12.1943, lost by fire in Bombay Docks 14.04.44

ELAND Freetown, Sierra Leone, Base
Cd 01.10.1941 - PO 30.04.1946 - acs to BARBROOK II
Nom DS: Dockyard 52.5 ft Hbr Lch 220 01.10.41-

ELAND II Freetown, Sierra Leone,
1945 - closed 12.04.46

ELARA Karainagar, Ceylon, R Ceylon N Base
Listed 09.1957 - 1973 at Kayts and also at Karainagar 21.05.1962 and 1971-79

ELENA Pembroke Dock, Accom Sh
Yt, presented free 11.1942. Conv to accom sh 1943. To RAF for accom sh Pembroke Dock 05.43

ELFIN (1905) Ports, SM DS
Tender to BONAVENTURE (Humber/Tyne) 1914-15. Ports (DOLPHIN) by 10.1920-21, sold 02.1928

ELFIN Blyth, SM Base
Cd 22.12.1939 v TITANIA - PO 21.09.1945
6 SM - on closure amalgamated into 5 SM at DOLPHIN
NOIC Blyth abolished 15.08.45
Nom DS: ELFIN(1933) tender renamed NETTLE 20.08.1941 & to Rothesay as transport
Motor Drifter ROTHA 20.08.40 - 21.09.45

ELFIN II Blyth, CF Base
Ann Base to be established 06.40, named, 30.04.41 and Cd 01.12.41 - acs in ELFIN. To 26.10.42, abolished and turned over to ELFIN
Nom DS: MFV ROZEL 01.12.41-26.10.42

ELISSA Philippeville, Base - NP 634
Cd 01.01.1943 - 01.11.43, name tx to Messina
When majority of Port Party had tx to Messina, remainder came under CANNAE (qv)
Nom DS: Tug BALLOTIN 1943

ELISSA Messina, CO Base - NP 870
01.11.19453, name tx from Philippeville. - PO 31.10.45 acs to HAMILCAR
Also covered Augusta, Catania and Syracuse

ELIZABETHVILLE Soton, DS - (NP 1729)
Allocated as DS v CAP TOURANE (qv). At Soton to store 30.08.1944. NP joined 01.09.44. No longer required 17.09.44 - still at Soton - destored.

ELSIE Chichester, Accom Sh
08.1942 - acquired 09.01.43, laid up Hamble 08.44, DST for disposal 14.09.44

ELTRICH Inveraray, Accom Sh
07.1943

EMELLE Ports, Accom Sh
08.1942, ex ML, known as 'Black Emelle'(qv)

EMERALD (1876) Chat, Powder Hulk
Corvette, powder hulk Chat 1898, sold 10.07.1906

EMERALD (1861) Queenstown, Flag
BLACK PRINCE, TS Cd 21.01.1899, renamed EMERALD 03.1904, Flag Queenstown, rb HOOD 14.07.1910, renamed IMPREGNABLE III(qv) 06.1910, sold 02.1923

EMERALD (1888) Dev, TS
AMELIA, ex HAWK, Gunboat, renamed COLLEEN 1905, became COLLEEN (Old) 1916, renamed EMERALD 01.02.1918, attached Gunnery Sch Dev. Cd 29.04.1918 as gunnery tender to VIVID and renamed CUCKOO, sold 10.08.1922.

EMERALD (1920) Forth, RF Parent
Cr, RF Parent 01.11.1945 v COCHRANE II. PO 18.12.1945 to Res, RF became QUEENSFERRY (qv) 19.12.45. Sold 23.07.48

EMERALD STAR Fishguard, Experimental Base
Base under general direction ISRE, administered by RNO Fishguard and "run as a shore establishment" (14.10.1943) - listed 10.44 and in Red List 06.05.45(though this could refer to Nom DS)
NAB req for special service Fishguard 25.11.43 - acquired 13.03.44

EMMA Shoreham, Accom Sh
07.42 - acquired 30.01.43, to be laid up Shoreham/DST 08.44 and no longer required/DST for disposal 14.09.44

EMPEROR OF INDIA (1906) Ipswich, Base & Accom Sh
Hired as A/P vessel 1916, renamed MAHRATTA 1918, resto 1920. Hired as M/S 12.1939 and as AA ship 11.1940. Accom Sh Ipswich v ALISDAIR & TITAN 04.06.43. Was Nom DS BUNTING (qv) 03.44-11.44, then WOOLVERSTONE (qv) 04.45 - 02.46. Resto 1946

EMPIRE COMFORT (1944) Holy Loch, Accom Sh
Ex Corvette YORK CASTLE, Rescue Ship, SM Accom Sh 12.1945-01.03.46. To MOWT as troopship 1946, sold 1955

EMPIRE SHELTER (1944) Holy Loch, Accom Sh
Ex corvette BARNARD CASTLE, Rescue Ship, SM Accom Sh 12.1945-01.03.46. To MOWT as troopship 1946, BU 1955

EMPRESS (1859) Clyde, TS
REVENGE, 2nd Rate, CG Pembroke Dk 1859, Base Ship Queenstown 08.1872, renamed EMPRESS 03.1890, lent Clyde Industrial TS Association, sold 31.12.1923

EMPRESS OF INDIA (1891) Queenstown, Flag
BB, Flag 10.1901-02 rb AEOLUS, sunk as target 1913

EMPRESS OF RUSSIA Ports, DD DS
08.1944 - PO 13.10.1944 and to MOWT
Capt D17 - admin of Fleet and Hunt class DDs - see also AORANGI

ENCHANTRESS Soton/Ports, MB Patrol Depot/Accom Sh
WWI
There was a Yt ENCHANTRESS 1903-35, but reports of this TS for Officers and motor mechanics at Soton say it was burnt out in 1916 and replaced by HERMIONE (qv) - but see also RESOURCE II
The Yt was Cd 04.03.1918 as tender to EXCELLENT as Officers' overflow ship

ENCOUNTER (1902) Sydney, RAN Rx Sh
Cr, to RAN 12.1919, Rx Sh Sydney 1919-23, renamed PENGUIN 1923 (qv)

ENCOUNTER Adelaide, Admin Support & Res TE
Cd 01.03.1965 ex TORRENS(qv) - PO 21.03.1994 (29.04.1994 in some acs)

ENDEAVOUR (1912) Spore/Suez/ DS/Accom Sh
Survey vessel, DS for BDV Spore, acs SULTAN II 02.1941. To Colombo and Red Sea, manned by survivors of PRINCE OF WALES and REPULSE, then surveying. PO 01.06.1943, tender to STAG, accom sh Suez 06.43 - 10.45, when no longer required and for disposal. Sold 09.46

ENDYMION (1797) Dev, Rx Sh
4th Rate, Rx Sh 1860-BU 18.08.1868

ENDYMION (1865) Hull, CG
FF, CG Hull 01.10.1875 - 31.07.1879, sold 1885 as

hulk, BU 1905

ENDYMION (1891) Queenstown, Flag
Cr, Flag and Guard Ship Queenstown 1913-14, sold 16.03.1920

ENTERPRISE (1843) Oban, Coal Vessel
Sloop, coal hulk for Northern Lights, Oban, 1860 - sold 15.09.1903

ENTERPRISE (1919) Normandy, DS
Cr, alloc as DS Normandy 30.08.44, but res Ports 09.44, sold 04.46

EPINAL (1919) Ports, Accom Sh
Fr Patrol Vessel seized 1940, accom sh and berthing for FS PRESIDENT THEODORE TISSIER Cd 29.07.1940, returned to Fr 1945

EPPING Harwich, M/S Base
Cd 01.07.1940, PO 21.07.1945 - aux M/S to BADGER
1) LNER Tender EPPING(1914) hired as Nom DS 30.08.1939, renamed BADGER (qv) 13.09.39, renamed EPPING 12.01.40, renamed FERRY PRINCE 12.42, resto 1945
2) Yt LEXA hired as M/S 01.12.1939, purch 11.42, Nom DS 12.1942-06.43, sold 1946
3) Yt SOUTHWESTER accom sh Harwich 06.43 - to C & M 08.45

EREBUS (1869) Sheerness/Portland, TB DS
INVINCIBLE DS 1901, renamed EREBUS 04.1904 - TBD DS Sheerness, though NL shows her at Portland. 07.04.-01.15 then Ports preparing for FISGARD II, renamed FISGARD II (qv) 01.1906

EREBUS (1916) Plym/Chat/ Ports, Flag/Turret Drl Sh
Monitor, Gunnery Sch Nore 12.01.1919 - & Turret Drl Sh 12.19 till brought forward for sea service Med 25.09.22 - but then sea service cancelled, remained Turret Drl Sh Chat/Sheerness to 01.26. Turret Drl Sh Dev v MARSHAL SOULT 01.03.26-, SO RF Dev and Cadets' TS v THUNDERER 01.09.26-25.07.27 rb CARYSFORT as SO RF. Gunnery Sch & Cadets' TS Dev 25.07.27 - 19.12.31(Cadets' TS cease) - attached Gunnery Sch till 1933. Flag Plym v IMPREGNABLE 25.07.27 - Flag to Mt Wise (VIVID) 19.12.31. Turret Drl Sh Ports & Cadets' Hbr TS 10.33-05.01.39 rb FROBISHER. Prep for sale to S Africa 12.38, tow to Soton for refit 01.39. Retained in RN 09.39. Res Chat as Turret Drl Sh & accom sh 07.45-13.07.46 rb ABERCROMBIE, To C & M 03.09.46, BU 01.47

ERIDGE (1940) Alexandria, Base
DD, damaged 08.1942 and used as Base Ship, sold Cairo 13.02.47

ERIN (1913) Nore, TS/RF
BB, Turret Drl Sh and Flag Nore RF Group A Parent 18.12.1919 - PO 05.05.1922. BU 1923

ERNE (1940) Soton, Res Drl Sh
Sloop, allocated as Res Drl Sh 05.46 - ZETLAND allocated till ERNE ready 10.46. Conv to Drl Sh 06.50-, Soton v DERG 1952, Cd as WESSEX(qv) 04.06.1952, sold 27.10.65

ESA Invergordon, Target Repair Depot
Lifeboat. 07.1943-05.46 (at least) - not for disposal, retained for service 07.47

ESAMBARA Ceylon:? - Poss an erroneous entry in a list for BAMBARA(qv)

ESKIMO (1937) Chat/Queenborough, Accom Sh/Base Sh
DD, accom sh Chat v ST TUDNO 01.46, base ship for M/S Queenborough 12.02.46-11.47 rb DERBY HAVEN, BU 06.49

ESPIEGLE (1900) Dartmouth, Nom DS
Sloop, Nom DS for RNC (BRITANNIA - as new BB BRITANNIA launched 12.1904) 09.1904-1910 rb POMONE. Rx Sh Pt Said WW I, SNO Persian Gulf 03.1923-, sold 07.09.1923

ESQUIMALT Esquimalt, RCN Base
Listed 1968-70 (vice NADEN?) (in Pink List 09.1975 on - extant 1995 though name NADEN still in use

ESSEX (1901) Dev, DS
Cr, DD DS 1916-19, accom sh Dev Cd 01.01.1918 - 12.18 rb ALBION, allocated to be part POWERFUL TS 12.18, to be DD accom sh 03.19 v ECLIPSE (attached APOLLO) - 1920, to join IMPREGNABLE 03.21 though sold 11.1921

ESSEX Ness Rd, Shoeburyness, Communications Tng Centre
Cd 01.10.1984. PO 31.01.1992

ESTON
Name proposed for Fixed A/S Defences S Italy, - was codeword for South Giovanni - Op Baytown. Arrived Algiers 21.08.1943

ETHALION (1802) Harwich, Breakwater
5th Rate, Hbr Serv 09.1823. Lent Harwich Corporation as breakwater 05.1835 - listed to 1877

ETOILE POLAIRE (Fr) Birkenhead, Net Defence DS 07.1943

EUPHRATES Basra, Iraq, Naval Base
Cd 01.09.1941, Reduced to tender JUFAIR 21.06.1945, PO 06.01.1946
See also SEABELLE and SHOREHAM
Base Ship for Shatt-el-Arab 03.45
Nom DS: NAIF - motor dhow 01.09.41-M/S Dhow 9 13.07.44
Wooden Hull ex IVY,RIN accom vessel 07.44-

EUROCLYDON Verdala, Malta GC, Transit Barracks
Cd 04.1945 independent command, start closing 21.01.47, PO 31.01.47
Ex PoW Camp, was used as a Store Depot when

closed
Nom DS: MFV 23 04.45-

EUROPA (1897) Mudros/Smyrna, Greece, DS
Cr, Flag Mudros & DS TBD Aegean 07.15-20, with A/P Tlrs & MBs. Pt Said tenders to Pt Said 14.03.1916. DS Lighters from 05.1916. VALHALLA II and tenders became tenders to EUROPA 01.08.1918. Cdre Aegean Sqn 01.01.1919-.From Mudros to Smyrna 29.10.1919-03.1930. To Malta 03.20 and PO. Sold 15.09.1920

EUROPA II Accounting Base
Stavres Beach Party to 31.12.1916 rb ST GEORGE.

EUROPA Sparrow's Nest, Lowestoft, Patrol Service Central Depot
Site req 23.08.1939. Staff arrived 25.08.39, 1st recruits arrive 26.08.39, 1st Draft out 27.08.39.
Was PEMBROKE X to15.02.1940, then ROMOLA (see note below), then EUROPA 14.04.40. PO 01.06.46. ReCd as tender to PEMBROKE IV 01.06.46 - closed down 27.08.46.
ROMOLA was Lowestoft Base, and name ceased use 14.03.40. EUROPA first listed as Lowestoft Base but was used solely for RN Patrol Service Depot.
There was a plan to move the depot to the Lion Hotel at Shrewsbury 06.40, then to the Barge Hotel, Shrewsbury, but both plans were cancelled.
Nom DS: MB 39663 to 05.44
Hbr Lch 42752 05.44-06.46

EUROPA II Bungay, Overflow Camp
Cd 25.09.1945 independent command, acs EUROPA, PO 31.05.46, tx to Air Ministry 01.06.46
Also known as Flixton, tx from RAF, intended as satellite for HORNBILL II(qv).

EURYALUS (1803) Chatham/Gib, Convict Ship
5th Rate, convict ship Chat 1826-40 (at least), Gib 1847 - renamed AFRICA 1859, sold 1860

EURYALUS (1901) Pt Said, DS
Cr, Tlr DS Pt Said 10.1915-01.1916. Also Flag East Indies and DS Aden to 11.1917 rb DUFFERIN. PO at HK 08.1918, sold 07.1920

EURYALUS (1939) Dev, SO RF
Cr, RF accom sh v BERRY HEAD & RAME HEAD 10.56, SO RF 12.03.57-02.12.57, BU 1959

EVENING STAR (1894) Cromarty, A/P DS - Area 4 1914 - rb EILEEN (qv) 11.1914

EVEREST Ports, Accom Sh
07.1942-

EVOLUTION Chelsea Ct, London/Ports, Ops Base
Named as special base for bases, acs EXCELLENT II 26.08.1942. Cd 17.09.1942, when it was a section of EXCELLENT II acs. Reverted to EXCELLENT II (qv) 04.10.43 and was renamed ODYSSEY (qv) 01.11.43. Still listed 10.44 as a base at Ports.
Nom DS: Power Boat 37252 30.10.42-

EXCALIBUR The Brunds, Alsager, Stoke on Trent, New Entry Seaman TE
Cd 22.12.1942 ex TIGER'S WHELP (qv), C & M 01.12.44, Used by RM for Motor Transport Driver Tng 03.45, ReCd 05.46, PO 31.12.47 - retard part acs BLACKCAP
Nom DS: HL(D) 52.5 ft 3944 22.12.42-01.12.44
10ft Sailing Dinghy 263 12.46-

EXCELLENT Whale Island, Ports, TE
Land purch 26.11.1853, used for tng, first occupied 01.12.1866. Cd 01.01.1869, Cd on shore 01.05.1891. Closed 01.10.1985 as independent command and became part of NELSON (qv).
Also included Fraser Gunnery Range, which incorporated ST GEORGE (qv) at one period.
1) EXCELLENT (1797) 3rd Rate, Gunnery TS 1830. Bu 1835
2) BOYNE (1810) 2nd Rate, renamed EXCELLENT 01.12.1834, Gunnery Sch to 1859. Renamed QUEEN CHARLOTTE 22.11.1859, BU 06.1861.
3) QUEEN CHARLOTTE (1810) 1st Rate, renamed EXCELLENT 31.12.1859 Gunnery TS. Sch moved ashore 1891, BU 01.1892
4) HANDY ((1882) gunboat, renamed EXCELLENT 01.05.1891, renamed CALCUTTA 01.12.1916, SNAPPER 08.1917, sold 04.1922
5) DRUDGE(1887) gunboat, renamed EXCELLENT 01.12.1916-12.02.1918 reverted to DRUDGE - became DRYAD, sold 03.1920
6) JACKDAW (1903) Tlr, renamed EXCELLENT 12.02.1918-14.04.1919, sold 1919
7) WILLIAM LEACH (1918)Tlr, renamed EXCELLENT 14.04.1919-1920, sold 1920 - still listed as Nom DS 1922
8) ANDREW JEWER (1918) Tlr, renamed NITH 1920, renamed EXCELLENT 06.22 - sold 1948
9) HAINNEVILLE (Fr Tug seized 07.1940), Cd as EXCELLENT 15.01.1942 - while Tlr EXCELLENT in refit - renamed EXPONENT 04.42
10) HL(D) 3711 11.1945-1962

EXCELLENT II Ports/ Bournemouth/ Chelsea, Accounting Base
to 01.1941, was a separate set of ledgers at EXCELLENT for naval staff of First MNBDO (MARTIAL(qv)). Moved to Westcliffe Gardens, Bournemouth 01.05.1942. Also included second MNBDO (MENACE) and later EVOLUTION(Combined Ops).
Renamed APPLEDORE II 17.09.1943 - tx to Ilfracombe 10.43.
The Section renamed EVOLUTION 17.09.43 ReCd at Chelsea Ct SW3 01.10.43 as EXCELLENT II and renamed ODYSSEY 01.11.43

EXCELLENT Whale Island, Ports, TE
Cd 01.04.1994, - ceremony 18.03.94 - extant 1999
Mooted to re-open 1993, and officer app in command with date to be reported, but cancelled.
RN Sch of Management & Leadership (ROYAL

ARTHUR section), PHOENIX NBCD Sch, RN Regulating Sch, RN Military Tng Sch also Solent RNR Tng Centre by end 1994 - see KING ALFRED.

EXMOUTH (1854) Thames, TS
2nd Rate, lent Metropolitan Asylum's Board as TS 1877, sold 04.1905

EXMOUTH (1901) Dev, Accom Sh
BB, Overflow Ship Dev 1917. Accom sh Dev Cd 01.01.1918-04.1919(at least) PO by 09.1919. Sold 01.1920

EXMOUTH (1905) Scapa Flow, Accom Sh
TS, evacuated 1939. HQ River Thames Fire Floats 1942. Purch from LGC - Tng Sch to Lydney, Glos 04.42 - fitted out as accom sh for Close Protection Craft personnel at Tilbury 04.42, and tow to Scapa Flow. Cd 08.08.1942 v ST SUNNIVA - independent command, acs IRON DUKE - 06.45. Was M/S DS 1943.
Renamed WORCESTER (qv)09.08.45 as Thames Nautical Tng College.

EXPERIMENT (1784) Lpool, Qtn Sh
5th Rate, Qtn Sh 1805, sold 1836

EXWEY (1888) Weymouth, Accom Sh
MONARCH, Paddle M/S WWI, hired 27.08.1939. Accom Sh 1944-08.46

F

BASE F (For Freddy)
Formed for Op Bonus - (proposed assault on Madagascar) 03.01.1942 - but no longer required 18.01.42

FABIUS Taranto, Base
01.01.1944 - 31.12.1945, acs to ST ANGELO, PO 01.04.46
One of 6 names proposed for Italy 12.1943 and included Pt Parties at Bari, Brindisi and Eastern Italy
Nom DS: LCM 1149 01.01.1944-

FAIRFAX (1940) Repair Ship
BURLINGTON, req 1940, renamed FAIRFAX (not SOOTHSAYER) 1941. To be conv to LL Repair and Store Ship for Far East 11.1943. To C & M 24.01.44. Handed over to BU 11.04.45

FAIRFAX Pt Moresby, RAN Mobile Base Organisation 1943

FAIR LADY II Soton, Accom Sh
08.1942 - acquired 19.12.42, laid up in C & M Lymington 11.01.45

FALCON (1877) Dev
Gunvessel, Hbr Serv 1890, for new torp range Dev 1905, quoted as DEFIANCE II at one stage, but see PERSEUS, sold 28.06.1920

FALCON Hal Far, Malta GC, RNAS
Cd 15.04.1946, tx from RAF, C & M by 03.65, PO 31.08.65, tx to RAF 01.09.65
Built as a shore base for aircraft of Med Fleet, opened 16.01.1923. used by RN WW II
Nom DS: HL(D) 4497 15.04.46-(65)
MFV 283 to 11.54
HL(S) 320 11.54 on

FALKLANDS Ottawa, Canada, Res Div
Ment in Magazine 1999-(? ex BYTOWN)

FALMOUTH (1932) Dev/Tyne, Res Drl Sh
Sloop, RF living ship Dev 02.1948 - allocated as Drl Sh 1948 (Engines to RALEIGH) v CALLIOPE (qv) 26.04.1951 - renamed CALLIOPE 05.10.51-01.68, BU 04.68

FALMOUTH (1959) Ports, Hbr TS
FF, Hbr TS attached SULTAN 1984-88, BU 04.05.89

FALSETTE Bombay
Prob an erroneous entry in a list for SALSETTE(qv)

FAME (1798) Pembroke, Marine Barracks Ship
3rd Rate, DRAGON(qv), renamed 1842 at Pembroke - BU 1850

FANN Dakar, Senegal, Base
Cd 01.03.1944, PO 30.06.45
From 15.09.44 pay acs in MELAMPUS, remained an independent command
Nom DS: ML TINA 01.03.44 -30.06.45

FARADAY (1923) Dartmouth, DCO Base Ship
Cable ship, hired as Base Ship 10.40, was to be Cd as DCO Base Ship Dartmouth 12.40 where she was fitting out, but was released for cable ship duties18.03.41 as Non Cd MFA, sunk 26.03.41, raised and to MOWT

FARAWAY Greenock, TE and HQ of FO Carrier Tng
Cd 01.06.1944, PO 05.46
Nom DS: NAB FARAWAY

FAREHAM (1918) Malta GC, Accom Sh
Sloop, v ST ANGELO III as M/S Base St Paul's Bay, Cd 13.02.1945 - . Included RNPS Pool Malta 10.45 on. PO 16.12.46 - amalgamated with PHOENICIA as accom sh, handed over to BU 04.10.48
Capt Hunt Class DD to FAREHAM 03.45

FAVORITE (1864) Queensferry, CG
Corvette, CG Queensferry 29.07.1872 - 20.12.1876, sold 30.03.1886

FAVOUR (1908) Scapa Flow, Officers' Accom Sh
07.1917-09.1918
Drifter, hired 05.1915 - 1919 and WW II

FAVOURITE (1829) Dev, Coal Hulk
Sloop, coal hulk 08.1859 till sold 17.05.1905

FEARLESS (1912) Rosyth, SM DS
Cr, K Class SM Leader 05.1916, 12 SM 1918-19, 1 SM Rosyth 01.03.1919 - PO 27.10.1919 rb INCONSTANT, sold 11.1921

FENTONIAN (1912) Thames, Accom Sh
Tlr, hired WW I and as A/P 11.1939. M/S 1940, Fuel carrier 03.44. PO 17.01.1945 and Re Cd 17.01.45 as accom sh C-in-C Nore's Special Service Pool - tender to YEOMAN. To Tyne for re-conv to fishing and resto 05.45

FERMOY (1919) Portland/Malta GC, SM DS
Sloop, SM DS 12.07.1919 for Campbeltown Periscope Sch, Portland Periscope Sch 09.1919 v HARVESTER & Cd 12.07.1919-1934. Damaged beyond repair at Malta 30.04.41, PO 01.06.41

FERMOY II Navy House, Pt Said, Accounting Base
03.09.1939-08.02.1940
Name discontinued when STAG(qv) opened as DS Suez Canal Zone

FEROZE Bombay and Malabar Hill, RIN Officers TE/Demobilisation Centre
Cd 01.11.1943 as Res Officers' TE. Post War Demobilisation Centre to 12.1950

FERRET Londonderry, Base
Cd 09.12.1940, PO 21.06.47 - was to have become PHOENIX as Joint A/S Sch but became SEA EAGLE (qv)
Separate accounting org for Tlrs and craft from 01.02.41. In 42 FERRET held the acs of HM Ships at St John's Newfoundland and Argentia
Nom DS: MY ALOHA MOANA 17.01.41-03.44
WAGTAIL 03.44-31.03.44
POLECAT 31.03.44-04.45
Yt ONORA(1923) 05.45-09.45 (at least) - poss to 03.46
MB 3629 03.46-05.46
MB 441338 06.46-

FERRET II, Londonderry, CF Base
Ann 04.1941-

FERRET III Beach Hill Camp, Londonderry
1942-10.46

FERRET IV Lisahally, Londonderry, Capt SM surrendered U-boats
05.1945 - PO 19.07.46 - to C & M
Ex US Operating Base 05.02.42 - 02.09.44. Tx to RN 31.08.44

FERRET Templer Barracks, Ashford, Kent, HQ Unit RNR
Cd 09.10.1982 - moved to Chicksands 1997 - site required for railway

FERRET Chicksands, Bedfordshire, HQ Unit RNR
Tx from Ashford 1997-extant 1999

FERRY PRINCE (1914) Harwich
EPPING (qv) was BADGER(qv) then EPPING, renamed FERRY PRINCE 1943 and resto 1945

FERVENT Royal Temple Yt Club, Ramsgate,Base
Cd 10.10.1939 - apps from 25.08.39. PO 17.09.45
Name sel for comml pt 01.09.39 - NOIC ordered 27.08.39, arrived by 29.08.39
CF Base established 01.03.44 (tx from Dover - WASP)
Nom DS: MB WHITE MARLIN 10.10.39-11.40
MB ABERDONIA cancelled
MB WALKER II 11.40-06.44
HL(P) 42884 06.44 - 17.09.45

FERVENT II Ramsgate?
04.1941-10.45

FFOLIOTT Dev
Name quoted as used by BRADFORD when a Base - see FOLIOT

FIELD MARSHAL SMUTS Saldanha Bay, S Africa, S African TE
1946-52 (at least)
New Entry TE and Depot

FIELDFARE Evanton, Ross-shire, RNAS
Allocated as RN Aircraft Repair Yard B 06.1943. Cd 09.10.1944 - to C & M 24.03.48, PO 05.48 - listed to 1959 (at least)
Used by the FAA pre WWII, known as Novar/Navar to 1937, and FAA were lodgers from 01.40. Under MERLIN before Cd - used for ship inspections 09.39. Tx on loan 01.09.44-an attached unit, acs OWL - to be an independent command when personnel available, -30.11.46, tx to RN 01.12.46
OWL(Fearn) was under FIELDFARE when in C & M 07.1946
Nom DS: TRSB 421249 09.10.44-
TRSB 43780 09.47-

FIELDGATE (1902)
COLLINGWOOD, Tlr - BDV, renamed FIELDGATE 10.1940 - listed as a shore estab in one list - prob in error for COLLINGWOOD

FIERCE (1945) M/S HQ Ship
M/S, allocated to E Indies late 1945, Cd 03.01.46-to Med 04.45-46, Ports refit 47, then Med 48 - BU 08.59 - though in 53 to Coronation review Spithead

FIFE NESS (1945) LC DS
Cd 29.11.1945, operated in Home Waters, PO and to MOT 25.07.46(as RCL 920), to RAF as ADASTRAL 1947-48, mercantile 1949, BU 1960

FINWHALE (1959) Ports, Hbr TS
SM, Hbr TS v GRAMPUS - 10.87 rb ORPHEUS, BU 03.88

FIREBRAND Stranraer, Base
Cd 16.09.1939 - PO 23.09.39
Name sel for comml pt 01.09.39 - NOIC ordered (temp) 27.08.39. Poss its opening was only notional. NOIC Stranraer closed 31.07.45

FIREFLY Poole, Accom Sh
08.1942 - acquired 13.02.43 - laid up Lymington/DST 08.44 - no longer required - for disposal 14.09.44

FIREQUEEN Ports, Depot
Ex CANDANCE, Yt, purch 1882, General Depot Ports Cd 01.12.1899 -1914 (at least). PO 28.05.1919, sold 05.07.20

FIREWORK Barrow-in-Furness/London/ Dartmouth, Base for P Parties (NP 1571-1575 & 3006)
08.1943 teams were at Vintry House, then to 81 Ashley Gdns, SW1 - teams at Forest Gate - then teams to Barrow-in-Furness when London came under flying bomb attack. Cd 01.04.1944. Task to Brixham - Tx to VERNON (D)(qv) 27.10.44. Practical diving aspects at Dartmouth.
Nom DS: HM Tug ALCIS 01.04.44 - 27.10.44

FISGARD (1819) Woolwich, TS/Nom DS
5th Rate, by 1848-72 was Flag at Woolwich, used to train engineers and Nom DS for personnel ashore. BU 10 1879

FISGARD Ports, TS
1) AUDACIOUS (1869) DS 1902, renamed FISGARD 04.1904. Cd 01.01.1906 as Boy Artificer TE, rb DILIGENCE and RELIANCE 08.1914, renamed IMPERIEUSE (qv) 14.10.1914 - repair ship - tow to Scapa Flow 16.09.14, sold 03.27
2) SPARTIATE (1898), renamed FISGARD 17.07.1915, - new Mech TE at Chat took over tng 01.01.32, PO 14.01.1932. Sold 07.32

FISGARD II Ports, TS
1) INVINCIBLE (1869), renamed EREBUS(qv) 04.1904, renamed FISGARD II 01.1906 - lost enroute Scapa Flow where she was to be a workshop 16.09.1914
2) HERCULES (1868) renamed CALCUTTA (qv) 1909, renamed FISGARD II 17.07.1915, sold 07.1932

FISGARD III Ports, TS
1) HINDOSTAN (1841) (qv) renamed FISGARD III 12.10.1905, renamed HINDOSTAN 08.1920, sold 10.05.1921
2) TERRIBLE (1895), joined estab v ARGONAUT 25.11.1919, renamed FISGARD III 08.1920, sold 07.1932

FISGARD IV Ports, TS
SULTAN (1870), renamed FISGARD IV 1906, renamed SULTAN (qv) 1931 - was DS 1940-45, sold 13.08.1946

FISGARD Torpoint, Cornwall, TE
10.1940 Artificer Tng moved from Chat to RN Artificer TE, Torpoint. Estab Cd with name 01.12.1946. Tng ceased 21.12.1983 - to PSA though land retained as part of RALEIGH(qv)
Nom DS: 52ft HL 39456 01.12.46-
MSPB 41350 06.48-03.50 and 1956 (also in NL 01.58)
MSPB 43101 by 12.1950-55 and 57-59
MC 5645 09.60 - 11.76 (at least)

FLAMBOROUGH HEAD (1944) Maint Ship
Cd 02.05.1945, 09.45 HK, 12.45 Brisbane, 01.46 Spore, Penang, Colombo, 02.46 Aden, Pt Said, 10.03.46 Chat, PO 20.06.46. To DST /MOWT 13.06.46-05.03.48, Accom Sh Target Trials 04.48-07.49, to RCN 1500, 02.05.1951, renamed CAPE BRETON (qv) 31.12.1953, hulk 1972, to be sunk as a reef 1999

FLAMER (1804) Gravesend/Greenhithe, Alien Service/CG
Brig, Alien Service Gravesend 1815-45, CG Greenhithe by 1853 till sold 1858.

FLAMER (1856) HK, Hosp Sh
Gunboat, hosp sh 1868, blown ashore in typhoon 1874 and wreck sold

FLAMINGO (1876) Plym, Coal and Water Depot
Gun vessel, attached DEFIANCE 1892-1907 - local coal and water depot. Lent to Plym Pt Sanitary Authority and sold 25.05.1923

FLAMINGO Langebaan, Nr Saldanha, S Africa, SAN Air Sea Rescue Base
01.11.1969-03.1987

FLEDGLING Millmeece, Eccleshall, Staffs, TE
Cd 15.04.1943, PO to C & M 31.01.1946 - became CABBALA (qv) 11.1946
Ministry of Supply camp taken over for tng of WRNS Air Mechanics - independent command,acs DAEDALUS II
Nom DS: HL(D) 3982 15.04.43-

FLINDERS (1919) Poole, Accom Sh
RADLEY (ex survey ship, ex M/S) - to be conv to accom sh Portland 04.1940. Was accom sh 08.1940-05.46, sold 08.45

FLIRT (1867) Stornoway, Drl Sh
Gun vessel, RNR Drl Sh 1876, sold 11.1888

FLORA (1844) Capetown, S Africa, DS
5th Rate, Hbr Serv 1851, at Cape as Rx Sh from at least 01.04.1869, rb PENELOPE 02.1889 and remained as her tender. Sold 09.01.1891
Ascension was a tender to FLORA in 19th Century - closed by Fisher

FLORA Simonstown, S Africa, Base
GRIPER (1879) Gunboat, hbr serv 1905, renamed YC373, renamed FLORA, Cd 15.06.1923 as Base Ship, renamed AFRIKANDER 04.11.1932 (qv), sold 1937

FLORA Invergordon/Aultbea, Loch Ewe, Base
Cd 01.10.1939. PO 16.07.45
Name sel for base at comml pt Invergordon 01.09.39. NOIC ordered 27.08.39. Name also used for Base at Aultbea - Port A - tender to FLORA 10.39. Acs tx to Greenock 10.39. Ann base at

Invergordon to close 08.56, and oil fuel depot there to close 1986
Nom DS: Hbr Steamboat 225 01.10.39 - 10.07.45

FLORA II Invergordon, CF Base
Cd 01.09.1942, independent command, acs FLORA. Closed 04.11.1943 - amalgamated with FLORA.
Nom DS: MB GOOD CHEER 05.11.42-04.11.43

FLORINDA (1873) Portland/Poole, Accom Sh
Yt, purch 06.1940. accom sh NOIC Poole 07.40, acquired 02.04.42, allocated as accom sh 2nd MGB Flot 10.43, Portland 12.43 on, laid up Weymouth/DST 04.45

FLOWERDOWN Flowerdown, Nr Winchester, Radio Sta
Built for Army 1916, RN (RNAS non flying) 1918-19, RAF 1922 on. RN 30.09.29, named 15.12.42, Cd 10.01.1943. PO 06.05.60 - task to FOREST MOOR - tx to GCHQ 1965
Nom DS: HLD 3504 10.01.43 - (still in MB List 01.51)
MFV 106 12.48-11.08.57
MFV 124 12.08.57 - sold 10.59 -still listed 1960

FLY (1831) Dev, Coal Hulk
Sloop, coal hulk Dev 1855 till BU 1903

FLY (1863) Plym, Accom Sh for Pilots
CG Cutter, hulk for accom duties Dev 1904 till BU 1928

FLYCATCHER Ludham, Norfolk, RNAS
Cd 04.09.1944, ex RAF Sta on loan to RN. 16.02.45 returned to RAF in exchange for Middle Wallop(see FLYCATCHER below).
HQ MONAB org
Nom DS: RUMMY III 04.09.1944 -16.02.45

FLYCATCHER II Ludham, Norfolk
Ment

FLYCATCHER III Ludham, Norfolk
Ment

FLYCATCHER Middle Wallop, Hants, NAS/ HQ MONAB Org
16.02.45-independent command, own acs - from RAF v Ludham. PO 10.04.1946 - to RAF
Nom DS: NAB OLOMA 16.02.45-

FLYCATCHER Kai Tak, HK, RNAS
Cd 01.04.1947 ex NABCATCHER (qv) - PO 31.12.47
Nom DS: ASR Lch(RAF)1629 04.47-

FLYING FOX Bristol, Res Drl Sh
1) M/S (1918) allocated as Res Drl Sh 24.03.1920, conv Pembroke Dk 1923, in use 1924 - Res Div previously at 37 Jamaica Rd from 1909 ex DAEDALUS. By 04.1940 was closed and FLYING FOX in use for MN Defence Courses. DEMS Tng Centre closed by 04.07.1945. Res reconstituted 01.10.1946, name in use. Name re-sel for Severn Div Res Drl Sh 1951. Berthed Mardyke Wharf. Ship sold 26.01.1973
2) Shore HQ at Winterstoke Rd opened 18.11.1972 using this name - extant 1999

FOINAVON (1919) Ports, Accom Sh
Yt, hired as accom sh 04.10.1939. Examination Service accom sh Cd 14.06.1940 - earmarked for service abroad - PO for refit Soton 20.01.1942. Allocated as Mobile Gunnery Sch, Pt Tewfik 02.42 and Cd as DEMS TS Pt Tewfik 10.04.43 acs STAG - used by Force G - STAG(A) 04.43-06.43. PO and reduced to C & M 19.12.45 - to AOSD for disposal 23.07.46

FOLIOT Tamerton Foliot, Plym, Accom Camp
Cd 27.07.1942 - PO 31.03.46 - became FOLIOT IV Camp for personnel on special service' there was also a Foliot Keyham Office (FKO) in North Yd, Dev
See also BRADFORD (FOLIOT)
Nom DS: MAY QUEEN(1902) passenger lch 27.07.42-lost in collision 17.11.43
Passenger Lch 421187 17.11.43 -03.46

FOLIOT I Plym, LC accounting Base and Special Service HQ Camp
By 03.1944. On 06.05.44 LC accounting and maint org tx from ALBATROSS. Hutted camp PO 15.03.46. Estab PO 31.03.46 - camp became over-flow for RN Barracks
At Tamerton Foliot (hutted accom) and Calstock. Prob same as FOLIOT above and new name used when other parts FOLIOT formed

FOLIOT II Efford, Plym, Repair Base
Listed 07.1943 - not listed by 12.44

FOLIOT III Bickleigh, Plym, LC Base
07.1943-10.46
Holding Base for CO personnel

FOLIOT IV Granby Barracks, Plym,
02.04.1946 ex FOLIOT/FOLIOT I. PO 12.08.46
Also Foliot Keyham Office(FKO) in N Yd, Dev
In one list as CF Base

FORAL Southwold (NP 1667)
Ment - on 29.02.44 HQ Force L moved to St Felix Sch, Southwold. Force L HQ disbanded 06.44. Poss a corruption of 'Force L'

FORCE PROFIT Iceland, RNAS
06.1940 - comprised aircraft at Iceland, on books DAEDALUS

FOREST MOOR Darley, Nr Harrogate, Radio Sta
Cd 1700, 03.10.1960, ex Army camp tx 1958, v FLOWERDOWN (qv) - extant 1996, not listed 1997
Staff victualled from 10.1959 whilst fitting out

FORESTER (1877) Ports, Coal Hulk
Gunboat, coal hulk 1894, sold 1904

FORMIDABLE (1825) Sherness/Bristol, Flag/TS

2nd Rate, Flag Sheerness 1862, lent as TS 16.07.1869 till sold 10.07.1906

FORT DIAMOND Off Martinique, Fortress
See DIAMOND ROCK

FORT RAMSAY Gaspe, Quebec, RCN Base/NOIC
12.1941 - (Cd 01.05.42) - 31.07.1945

FORT WILLIAM see AVALON III

FORTE (1858) Chat, Rx Sh
FF, Rx Sh Chat 18809-85, coal hulk Sheerness - burnt by accident 23.11.1905

FORTE (1812) Chat, Base/Rx Sh
PEMBROKE, 3rd Rate(qv), Base Ship Chat 04.1873, renamed FORTE 1890, Rx Sh, sold 1905

FORTE (1896) Ports, TS
FURIOUS, Cr, renamed FORTE 06.1915 - attached VERNON (qv) - hulk, sold 05.1923

FORTE Falmouth, Base
Cd 24.08.1939 - PO 31.01.1946 - CO remained as SO RF Falmouth. Naval Base Falmouth closed, RNO and Base Staff withdrawn 08.06.1950
FOIC lapse 30.06.45 - FORTE continued as Base
Nom DS: MV GALLANT 24.08.39 -01.12.41 - renamed GALLANT III
MINIDO (qv) - ment as FORTE 01.40-but she was Nom DS CLIO (qv)
Lugger BLACK PEARL 01.12.41 -24.10.45
MFV 1203 24.10.45 but cancelled
MFV 773 24.10.45 - 04.46

FORTE I Falmouth, Naval HQ Tregwynt
Block named FORTE I to avoid confusion (10.05.1941)

FORTE II Imperial Hotel, Falmouth
Listed 05.1940
CF Base quoted as FORTE II (30.04.1941) - but corrected to FORTE IV (10.05.1941)

FORTE III Falmouth
Taylor's Garage (10.05.1941)

FORTE IV Falmouth, CF Base
07.08.1941-06.11.1944
Was ment as early as 04.1941.
Nom DS: MB METEOR 08.07.41 -01.12.41 (renamed METEOR II)
Lugger INTERNOS 01.12.41 - 30.10.42 (renamed NESTORIN)
Quay Punt JOE RAT (PRATT) 30.10.42 - 06.11.44

FORTH (1833) Dev, Guard Ship
5th Rate, Guard Ship 1850-51, renamed JUPITER (qv) 1869, sold 1883

FORTH (1886) SM DS
Cr, conv to SM DS 1904, Dev 1904-1914, Humber 10 SM 1914-06.1916 rb VULCAN, Harwich addl to MAIDSTONE 9 SM 1916, 7 SM Harwich 08.16 — refit Ports 20.02.19-PO 08.04.19 & Re Cd Ports 09.04.19-for VERNON SM and Mining Sch for experimental and instructional work-PO 20.11.19, sold 11.1921

FORTH (1938) SM DS
Cd 12.03.1939 - 08.39 Dev v LUCIA - Dundee 08.39, Rosyth 10.39-2 SM formed 11.39. Holy Loch v CYCLOPS 09.40-41, Halifax Nova Scotia 02.41-06.41, St John's Newfoundland 06.41-09.41 (escort maint, rb GREENWICH), Clyde 01.42 - 3SM v TITANIA Holy Loch 03.42-20.05.47 rb MONTCLARE - refit Dev to 11.47, then Malta GC v WOOLWICH Cd 01.01.48 - (FO Flot DD Med 19.03.48) - DD to TYNE 1951 - Suez 1956. 1 SM 1952-26.09.60 - tx to NARVIK, Dev 2 SM 01.11.60-06.62, Chat (refit) 11.62-03.66, Spore 7SM 01.06.66-31.03.71. To UK 07.06.71 (7 SM ashore Spore), arrive Dev 14.01.72. renamed DEFIANCE (qv) 15.02.72, BU 1985

FORTITUDE (1807) Chat/Sheerness, Convict/Coal Hulk
CUMBERLAND, 3rd Rate (qv), convict ship Chat 03.1830, renamed FORTITUDE 15.11.1833, coal hulk Chat 1850-60, Sheerness by 1865 till for sale 1870

FORTITUDE Ardrossan, Base
Cd 20.04.1940, PO 30.09.45 - retard party remained
Name sel for base at comml pt Ardrossan 01.09.39, NOIC ordered 27.08.39, listed as FORTITUDE 25.02.40.
Nom DS: MB ENGLYN 20.04.40-04.42
Danish MFV FANO (seized 1940) 04.42-30.09.45

FORTITUDE II Ardrossan, CF Base
Cd 07.05.1941, in NL 02.44, not in NL 08.42
Nom DS: Hbr Lch AELDA II (15 ft small boat previously carried by AELDA) - 07.05.41-02.42

FORTUNA Soton, Accom Sh
08.1942, acquired 24.12.42 - 07.44 . To DST C & M on Hamble 07.44, no longer required 21.10.44
Ex ML - a hull, poss spelt FORTUNE

FORWARD (1877) Bermuda, Coal Hulk
Gunboat, coal hulk 1892 at Bermuda till sold 1904

FORWARD Newhaven, Base
Cd 13.09.1939, PO 07.07.45
Name sel for comml pt Newhaven 01.09.39, NOIC ordered 27.08.,39
RNVR Sussex Div closed 12.10.39 and Drill Hall in Bridge St taken into use as Base - HQ RNVR became KING ALFRED(qv)
Nom DS: SS SETON 13.09.39-20.06.41
MB SPITFIRE 20.06.41-11.11.41
WHITE ORCHID 11.11.41-07.07.45

FORWARD II Newhaven, CG Base
Cd 04.03.1941 - 04.11.42, renamed AGGRESSIVE(qv)

In London and Paris Hotel 05.41
Nom DS: WHITE SPRAY 04.03.41-04.11.42

FORWARD Birmingham, Communications Tng Centre
Cd 01.10.1984, extant 1999
At Broad St 1984, and at Sampson Rd North from 1986

FOSSBECK (1930) DS
Hired 11.1939 as aircraft transport, fitted out as Boom DS at Cardiff 12.41, Cd 14.05.42, resto 05.46

FOUDROYANT (1798) Dev, TS
2nd Rate, guardship 1820, TS at Dev 1862, attached CAMBRIDGE (qv) - sold as TS 12.1892, wrecked 1897

FOUDROYANT (1817) Ports/Hartlepool, TS
TRINCOMALEE, 5th Rate, Res Drl Sh 01.1861 - 19.05.1897, sold, renamed FOUDROYANT, TS. Taken over from IMPLACABLE Committee 01.03.1941 as stores ship. In use as TS with IMPLACABLE under title FOUDROYANT Cd 03.07.43. resto 08.05.47 - tow to Hartlepool 24.07.1987 for preservation & there 1999.

FOX (1893) Archangel, DS
Cr, DS for Archangel River Expeditionary Force, Cd 01.04.1919 in UK, left UK by 15.04.1919 - to 09.1919, sold 07.1920

FOX Lerwick, Shetlands, Base
Cd 25.08.1939, PO 30.09.45
Nom DS: MFV FRIENDLY GIRLS to resto 31.10.445

FOX II Lerwick, Shetlands, CF Base
Cd 20.07.1942 - 31.03.44 to be comb with AMBROSE II but cancelled. Commanding Officer CF lapse, CF under NOIC 31.03.44. Approved to re-open 08.44-1945
Nom DS: MFV LEA RIG (1939) 20.07.42 - nominated but not Cd as FOX II

FOX III - address used by CO Northern Force letters 23.06.43

FOXEARTH Pacific, Base
02.1945 - codeword for intermediate base in Pacific - see PEPYS, but project abandoned 09.45

FOXGLOVE (1915) Londonderry, Accom Sh
Sloop, damaged 09.07.1940, accom sh Londonderry - Advance Base Ship and Guardship - Re-Cd 02.01.43, full complement 12.05.43 - Guardship Meville from 08.07.43. BU 10.1946

FRANCES Ports, Accom Sh
08.1942, acquired 10.02.1943, laid up Swanwick/DST 08.44, no longer required 28.06.45

FRANKLIN Jervis Bay, NSW, RAN College
Yt ex ADELE purch 1912, Cd 14.09.1915 - tender to RAN College - staff borne on her books - sold 1924, but still listed as the college Nom DS when College tx to CERBERUS 1930. College renamed CRESWELL (qv) by 1958 when returned Jervis Bay. Yt hired as ADELE WWII.

FRASER (1953) Kingston, Ontario/ Bridgewater NS, RCN Museum Ship
FF, to Canadian Heritage Foundation for preservation 1995, at Bridgewater by 1998

FRATTON (1925) Normandy, Accom Sh
Hired as Barrage Balloon Vessel 08.1940, accom sh 04.44, sunk 18.08.44 Seine Bay

FREDERICK WILLIAM (1860) Weymouth/ Queenstown/ Limerick, CG
Ex ROYAL FREDERICK 1860, 1st Rate, CG Weymouth 01.07.1864-06.03.1865, Queenstown 06.03.1865-31.01.1866, Limerick 31.01.1866 - 09.1868, renamed WORCESTER (qv) 1876, sold 07.1948

FREELANCE (1908) Ipswich, Accom Sh
1) Yt, hired for A/P work 28.09.1940, accom sh 10.40, renamed BUNTING(qv) 11.40, renamed FREEWILL(qv) 03.44 - accom sh, disposed of 1945
2) BUNTING (ex MERLIN) (1896) Yt, renamed FREELANCE 11.1940, to Ports pool 03.44, to Plym Special Service 04.44, laid up Cremyll, Dev, C & M no longer required 06.44, reverted to BUNTING 11.44-1946

FREEWILL Great Yarmouth, Accom Sh for Capt M/S
By 03.44 - listed to C & M/DST 07.44 but in use 03.09.44, C & M DSVP shipkeepers Kings Lynn 12.44

FROBISHER (1920), Ports/Normandy, TS/DS
Cr, Hbr Serv as Cadets' TS Ports Cd 07.01.39 v EREBUS. DS Mulberry B, Normandy after Bombardment Task 06.44 - hit by torp Courseilles 09.08.44 - return UK 15.08.44. Allocated to be Cadets' TS v DIOMEDE 08.44, and on completion of Cadets' TS role (rb DEVONSHIRE) to join DEFIANCE 07.46 v INCONSTANT and VULCAN. But to Res and BU 1949

FROLIC (1872) Thames, RN Artillery Volunteers' Drl Sh
Gun vessel, Drl Sh v RAINBOW 1888-1892 - RNAV disbanded 01.04.1892, renamed WV30 (CG) 1893, renamed WV41 1897, sold 04.1908

FT 7 (1944) Peterhead, A/S Repair ship
Fleet tender, ex ASTRAVEL (qv) 1944-45, A/S Repair Ship 1944-47. To C & M 12.10.45, returned USA 22.01.47

FT 14 (1944) Chittagong/Burma, CF Supply & Advanced HQ Ship
Fleet Tender, Chittagong 08.1944, Akyab Peninsula 01.45, returned USA 1946

FULLARTON Irvine, Ayrshire, LC Base
Cd 01.01.1945 ex DINOSAUR II, PO 30.11.1946,

finally closed 16.02.1947
FULLARTON(Troon) closed and dockyard work ceased 18.04.46

FULMAR Lossiemouth, Morayshire, RNAS
Cd 02.07.1946 ex RAF, - 29.09.1972 - to RAF
RNAS at Twatt (see TERN) PO 09.1946 but was under FULMAR whilst in C & M. Also RNAS Skeabrae & Dunreay (ex TERN II) by 1948. Closed for flying 02.04.51 for runway repairs. Used by RN detachment to 1979
Nom DS: MFV 283 02.07.46-08.54
TRSB 43777 By 04.48 - in MB List 01.51
HL(S) 320 08.54-
TRSB 421030 11.07.55-10.12.55
MFV 278 10.12.55-1960
MFV 237 09.60-1962

FULMAR II Milltown, Morayshire, RNAS
02.07.1946 ex RAF - 29.09.72 to RAF
Satellite of FULMAR

FURIOUS (1850), Ports, Coal Hulk
Paddle FF, coal hulk 03.1867 till sold 1884

FURIOUS (1896) Ports, Hbr Serv
Cr, hbr serv 1912, renamed FORTE 06.1915 - part of VERNON (qv), sold 05.1923

FURNEAUX Brisbane, RN Depot
Cd 01.04.1945 - 29.10.1945

FURNEAUX II Brisbane, Accounting Base
To be Cd 01.09.1945 as a section of FURNEAUX holding acs of British Pacific Fleet escorts, but task given to GOLDEN HIND (qv). In NL 10.1945 with apps 07.1945

FUSTIAN Catania, Sicily (NP 842)
Code name for Catania 09.1943 - Fixed A/S Defences allocated Catania 1943 using this code name as ship name. NP there 09.43 - Op Baytown

G

GADFLY (1879) Cape, S Africa, Coal Hulk
Gunboat, coal hulk 1905, sold 1918

GADFLY Flensburg, Germany, CF Maint Base (NP 1712)
Cd 28.07.1945 ex CFMU 2(qv) acs PEMBROKE IV - 09.1946 reverted to CFMU 2
Nom DS: Ex German TRV No 21 28.07.45-08.45
Ex German Vessel TANGA 08.45-31.10.45
Ex German OTTO WUNSCHE (ex ROYAL ALEXANDRA) 01.11.45-29.11.45
TRV 27 29.11.45-

GADWALL Sydenham, Belfast, RNAS
Cd 21.06.1943 ex RAF, acs CAROLINE, 01.04.44 self accounting, PO 30.04.46 - became GANNET III(qv)
Also Tlr Base ship 1943

Nom DS: MB WHITE HEATHER - ex Nom DS ANTRIM 21.10.43-46

GALATEA (1810) Jamaica, Coal hulk
5th Rate, coal hulk 08.1836 - Bu 1849

GALATEA (1887) Queensferry/Hull, CG
Cr, CG Queensferry 03.05.1893-12.1894, at Hull 12.1894 - 10.02.1903, rb DIDO, sold 1905

GALATEA Earles Rd, Hedon Rd, Hull, Res Drl Sh
Res formed 21.10.1938. Cr CALCUTTA (qv) allocated. Mobilised 1939, re-formed 1951 - PO 31.03.1958

GALLIPOLI Taranto, A/P DS
01.1916-06.1917
Vessel lent by Italian Government

GAMANU Colombo, Ceylon
In PO Circular 09.05.1945 et al - prob alternative spelling of GAMUNU(qv)

GAMUNU Ceylon, Res HQ
Ceylon Naval Volunteer Force handed over to Admiralty, Cd 01.10.1943 - 1944 (at least). Victualling and Pay Ceylon VR from GAMUNU to LANKA 01.10.1944.
Post War refs are to GEMUNU and GANUNU(qv)

GAMECOCK Bramcote, Nuneaton, Warwickshire, RNAS
03.12.1943 ex RAF. Cd 12.12.1946 independent command, Naval Air Mechanic Tng. New Entry Tng ceased 01.11.58 - tx to Arbroath. Closed to flying from 06.11.58. PO 25.03.59 - tx to Army - (Royal Artillery, Gamecock Barracks extant 1990)
Nom DS: HL(D) 3983 03.12.46-1959

GANDER Gander, Newfoundland, RCN Radio Sta
Established 1938, tx from DOT 1941, 1941-1957, HMCNRS 05.1957-10.07.1966

GANGES Falmouth/Harwich/Shotley, TS/TE
1) GANGES (1821) 2nd Rate, TS 05.1865, at Falmouth 30.01.1866, to Dev for refit 08.1899, arr Harwich 11.11.1899, to Shotley 1903, renamed TENEDOS III (qv) 21.06.06 - left Shotley 05.07.06, renamed INDUS V (qv) 13.08.1910, renamed IMPREGNABLE III(qv) 12.10.1922, sold 31.08.29
2) MINOTAUR (1863), ex ELEPHANT, renamed BOSCAWEN 03.1904, renamed GANGES 21.06.1906, renamed GANGES II 25.04.1908, Prob renamed GANGES when ex CAROLINE departed (see below). Base Ship WWI 10.1919 rb BLAKE and 01.12.1919 old GANGES renamed GANGES II - Hbr Lch as Nom DS - see below, BU 30.01.22
3) CAROLINE (1882) Corvette, Hbr Serv 1897, renamed GANGES 04.1908, renamed POWERFUL III (qv) 09.1913, renamed IMPREGNABLE IV (qv) 11.1919, sold 31.08.1929
4) RN TE Barracks, Cd 04.10.1905 ashore at Shotley, took name GANGES 1927. Was an A/P Base WWI - see GANGES II - reported GANGES

PO and renamed GANGES II 01.12.1919. Boy's Tng ended there 16.05.1940 - tx to ST GEORGE (qv) and Hostilities Only New Entry Tng started 04.1940. Highnam Court Camp Gloucester used as overflow 28.04.1941 - 31.01.42-tx to CABB-BALA(qv). Re-opened as Boys' TE 07.1945. Tng ceased 07.06.1976, estab closed 10.76
Nom DS: Hbr Lch 50 01.12.1919-1924
Hbr Lch 40 by 12.24-1925
Steam Lch 218 01.01.25 - 10.49
HL(S) 352 10.49-08.06.57
MFV 1257 08.06.57-1962

GANGES II Shotley, TE - also Base WW I and shortly after
1) AGINCOURT (1865) renamed BOSCAWEN III 03.1904, renamed GANGES II 21.06.1906, coal hulk C109 09.1908 - conv at Chat to 1910. BU 1960
2) MINOTAUR (1863) renamed BOSCAWEN 03.1904, renamed GANGES 21.06.1906, renamed GANGES II 25.04.1908, Base Ship WWI 10.1919rb BLAKE, and 01.12.1919 Old GANGES renamed GANGES II, BU 30.01.22. NL shows her as GANGES II in 1912 and as GANGES 10.1915-04.1919, and GANGES II 01.1920 on - prob a naming as Nom DS when ex-CAROLINE departed.

GANNET (1888) Chatham?
NYMPHE, sloop, renamed WILDFIRE (qv) 12.1906 - Base Ship, renamed GANNET 11.02.1916 - Gunnery tender, renamed PEMBROKE (qv) 01.06.1917, sold 10.02.1920

GANNET (1877) Chat/Scapa Flow, Diving Tender
TRENT, gunboat, renamed PEMBOKE (qv) 09.1905, renamed GANNET 01.06.1917 - diving tender Scapa Flow, then diving tender to Gunnery Sch Chat 03.1919 - sold 21.02.1923

GANNET Eglinton, Co Londonderry, RNAS
Cd 15.05.1943, lent by RAF from 01.05.43 - 03.03.47. 04.03.47 tx to RN. Flying ceased 29.04.59. PO 31.05.59, closed 30.09.59 - re-opened as SEA EAGLE (qv).
Included Cluntoe - lent by RAF 1947 - 58; Maydown 1943 - Cd as SHRIKE (qv); Toome ex RAF, 1947 - 1954 - lent to RAF 17.10.1951 - 25.12.54, returned and to res.
Nom DS: NAB SCHALINE II by 23.03.44-31.03.44
NAB ADERYN 31.03.44-11.45
MB 36131 06.46-03.47
TRSB 4422 03.47-21.10.48
ASL 7 21.10.48 - 1956 and NL 01.58
TRSB 421030 28.09.56-59

GANNET II Maydown, N Ireland, RNAS
01.10.1945 ex SHRIKE (qv) - C & M 1947, closed 1953

GANNET III Sydenham, Belfast, RNAS
01.05.1946 ex GADWALL (qv) - 02.07.1973 - to RAF

GANNET Capetown, S Africa,
In PO Circular 22.03.1944

GANNET Halifax, Nova Scotia
Was to be the name of ML Base Cd 06.05.1943, but name VENTURE (qv) chosen instead. Actually open 06.05.43 - 12.05.43 but renamed retrospectively.

GANNET Prestwick, Ayrshire, RNAS
Cd 23.11.1971 - extant 1999
Airfield used 1940-41 on lodger basis
Retitled HMS GANNET, RNAS Prestwick 01.01.1994

GANUM Colombo, Ceylon, Naval Volunteer Force
Ment - prob an alternate spelling of GANUNU (qv)

GANUNU Colombo, Ceylon, Naval Volunteer Force Base
1947-1957 and Royal Ceylon Naval Base 1951-53 (at least)
Poss a later way of spelling GAMUNU (qv) - also spelt GEMUMU(?)

GANNYMEDE Woolwich, Convict ship
6th Rate, ex Fr HEBE, capt 1809, convict ship 1819, BU 1838

GARTH (1940) Chat, Accom Sh
Hunt Class DD, accom sh for M/S personnel Queenborough 1945 v ST TUDNO - 1947, BU 08.58

GARUDA Coimbatore, India, RN Aircraft Repair Yard
Cd 01.10.1942 - PO 01.04.1946
RNAS at Cochin - see KALUGA, under GARUDA until 01.04.1946.
RNAS at Sulur - see VAIRI - under GARUDA 1945-46
Nom DS: 32ft Lch LANDSEND 01.10.42-

GARUDA Wellington Is, Cochin, RIN Air Sta
1954 - extant 1994
Poss VENDERUTHI II 1952-53

GATESHEAD (1942) Mother ship for Midget SM
Tlr, Dev 1951-tx from 5 SM to 2 SM 20.11.52-1953 (to res after Op HESPERUS), BU 1959

GAYUNDAH (1884) RAN TS
Gun vessel, sold 1921

GELO Catania, Italy, Base
05.1944, name sel for Base at Catania for covening courts martial and disciplinary courts - to be Cd, but cancelled

GEMUNU Trincomalee/Colombo/ Welisara, Ceylon, Royal Ceylon Naval HQ
1952-1959 Trincomalee, 1957-1971 Colombo, 1971-1979 Welisara
See also GAMUNU and GANUNU (name used to 1957).
HQ replaced by RANGALLA 1974

GEMUNU II Colombo, Ceylon,

R Ceylon Navy BD Depot and Workshops 1957-58

GENERAL BOTHA (1885) Capetown, S Africa TS/RN Accom Sh
THAMES, Cr, SM DS 1903-1919(qv), sold to S Africa 1920, renamed TS GENERAL BOTHA - taken over as accom sh and Base by RN at Simonstown 10.42. Known locally as THAMES 1944 to avoid confusion with S African TE ashore at Simonstown. Renamed AFRIKANDER (qv) 09.44 as Nom DS, sunk by gunfire, Simons Bay 13.05.1947

GENERAL BOTHA Simonstown, S African Nautical College
1944 (at least)-1961

GENERAL GORDON Gravesend, TE
Ex GORDON (qv), opened 27.01.1941, renamed GENERAL GORDON 01.12.1943, PO 30.01.44, became civil TE, Nautical Sea Tng College, Gravesend
Nom DS: GAMEBIRD 01.41-01.44

GENERAL MICHIELE Base & Accom Ship
Dutch Vessel, re-allocated as Base & Accom Sh Bengal Aux Flot 05.1944. rb BLINJOE. (Released from salvage duty 04.44 and returned to trade 09.44.)

GENOA Plym, Rx Sh
3rd Rate, Fr BRILLIANT, capt 1814, Rx Sh 1835, BU 1838

GEORGE D IRVIN (1911) Solent/ Normandy/Chat, M/S DS/Store Ship
Tlr, hired 1914-1919 and 1940-07.45. To Humber after removal of M/S Gear 11.43. 03.44 temp duty at Ports - towing, DS Solent and Normandy 23.06.44 - Sword Beach. Transport Duty under Cdre Belgium 12.44, to Dover M/S Force 02.45, store ship Chat 05.45, to be released 08.06.45

GEORGE II Algiers, Gunnery TE
Ref in Gun Log at Winchester

GERBERDINE JOHANNA Ipswich, M/S DS 04.1944-
Dutch Tlr, M/S 04.1940, to be fitted as M/S DS Ipswich 04.1944

GIBEL DERSA Gibraltar, Accom Sh
1943 - resto 31.12.1943

GIBRALTAR Milford, Powder/Qtn Sh
2nd Rate, ex Spanish FELIX, capt 1780, powder hulk 1813, qtn sh 1824, Bu 1836

GIBRALTAR (1860) Belfast, TS
1st Rate, lent as TS Belfast Committee 1872, renamed GRAMPIAN 1889, sold 1899

GIBRALTAR (1892) Shetlands/Portland, DS/TS
Cr, DS for armed tlrs of Northern Patrol 1914 - Longhope/Swarbacks Minn, Shetlands 06.1915-12.1918 (rb BERYL 08.03.1918-05.1918 while refitting Chat). Left Swarbacks Minn 31.01.1918 rb SANDRINGHAM. At Kirkaldy for A/P 12.1918-02.1919, then DS A/S Flot Portland 03.1919-1920 and also as A/S Sch v SAREPTA (qv) 22.11.1919 - task tx to HEATHER 15.03.1923, then OSPREY, PO 24.04.1923, sold 09.1923.

GILOLO Morotai, Moloccas, Halmaheras Is, Netherlands East Indies, RAN Base
Cd 15.10.1945 - PO 10.02.1946
HMS GILOLO PO 10.02.46 - in NL as RAN Base Staff Morotai - administrative org known as 'RAN Base'set up in the USN Base at Morotai prior to being Cd HMAS GILOLO
Nom DS: AWB 402. 40ft wooden workboat

GIMLI Hnasusa, Manitoba, RCN SCC Summer Camp
1985-86 at least

GIPSY London, Accom Sh/A/P DS
Stated in official records as House Boat from Essex Yt Club - wrongly called CARLOTTA - though unofficial records state she was a Yt - spelt GYPSY ex CARLOTTA. Hired as A/P Depot 01.02.1941. Sunk at Tower Pier in air raid 10.05.1941

GIPSY Swansea, M/S Base
Cd 25.04.1942 - acs LUCIFER - 03.46
Nom DS: NAB LITTLE GIPSY 25.04.42-05.42
MFV FORGET ME NOT 30.05.42-
Kite Balloon Vessel 07.44-10.44 (at least)

GIRDLE NESS (1945) Rosyth, Repair Ship/DS
Ex PENLEE POINT, Repair Ship Cd 06.09.1945, Ports repairs 12.45, Rosyth accom sh 09.46-02.52 (rb NIGERIA 08.51 and to RF as accom sh), to Dev for refit conv to guided missile trials ship 02.1953-56, PO 12.61, Rosyth accom sh 03.62-Cd as part of COCHRANE (qv) 01.12.62, sold 10.07.70

GIVENCHY (1918) Esquimalt, BC, RCN Dockyard & Base
RCN DS 12.41, NOIC 12.42-07.45, HQ and Base 1944-45.
Tlr, ex Fisheries dept 15.04.1939, accom sh Cd 25.06.40-21.10.40, became GIVENCHY (Hulk) 21.10.40-18.04.43 and then GIVENCHY II 18.04.43(see below). Barracks name from 04.43 - PO 03.03.47
For RF and Aux vessels administration, building in dockyard built for GIVENCHY became VENTURE (qv)

GIVENCHY II Equimalt, BC, Barracks for Fishermen's Reserve
Res Base 08.42, used GIVENCHY (Hulk) (see above) as GIVENCHY II 18.04.43-17.10.45. Appears to have a PO date 07.12.1943 and a name change date 07.44. Sold 19.09.1946

GIVENCHY III Como Spit, BC, RCN Seamanship TE and Co Estab.
01.10.1943 ex NADEN III - 01.03.1946, became

NADEN II

GLASGOW (1909) Ports, TS
Cr, RF Flag v ST VINCENT 28.11.1919 - Stokers' TS Ports 1921-PO 06.22, sold 1927

GLEN FORBES Addu Atoll, MNBDO
24.11.42 rb MATIANNA

GLEN USK (1914) Accom Sh
Paddle steamer, hired as M/S WWI, & 09.1939, AA Ship 1942, PO 28.02.45 Antwerp as accom sh-10.45

GLENDOWER Pwllheli, Seamanship TE
Cd 01.10.1940, independent command, tng ceased 25.07.46, PO 01.09.46
Used as overflow by ROYAL ARTHUR 06.40 (named GLENDOWER RNTE)
Nom DS: Cutter 4263 01.10.40-

GLENMAY Kingstown, DS
Was to relieve PATROL (qv) as DS Kingstown 11.18, but cancelled.

GLENMORE (1922) Scheldt Estuary, Accom Sh
GLEN GOWER, paddle steamer, hired as M/S 15.09.1939, renamed GLENMORE 01.42, AA Ship 07.1942, rb QUEEN OF KENT in Scheldt Estuary 01.45, accom sh Balloon Barrage Scheldt 01.45-05.47

GLOGOR Penang, R Malayan Navy VR
In list of Res Divs pre WW II

GLORIOUS (1916) Dev, TS
Cr, Turret drl Sh 12.1919 v COLLINGWOOD - 1924 (to be rb TERROR 04.22 but cancelled), SO RF v COLOSSUS 1921-12.24 rb THUNDERER. Conv to aircraft carrier 1930, sunk 08.06.40

GLORIOUS II
Ment 1939-40

GLORY (1899) Murmansk/Rosyth, DS
BB, A/P DS Cd 01.08.1916, Pt Murman 01.10.16 - White Sea v ALBEMARLE - 12.10.1919 arrived Rosyth to PO 01.11.19 and then refitted and Re-Cd as DS Rosyth v CRESCENT and SUTLEJ 16.03.20. renamed CRESCENT (qv) 01.05.20 and sold 12.1922

GLORY I Murmansk, A/P DS/Accounting Section for men onboard GLORY
06.1918-03.1919
Anti-Bolshevik Operations started 02.08.1918, completed 27.09.1919 - GLORY II ledgers merged into GLORY I 1918/1919 - see below

GLORY II Murmansk, A/P DS/ accounting section GLORY for White Sea A/P Tlrs
06.1918 - 02.1919
GLORY I and II ledgers merged as GLORY I - victualling 31.12.1918 and cash on 13.01.1919

GLORY III Murmansk, Accounting section GLORY for Special Marine Detachment
03.05.1918

GLORY IV White Sea, DS
Cr, ex Russian ASKOLD, Cd 03.08.1918 Murmansk, Archangel 19.08.1918-31.10.1918, then Murmansk. PO on Clyde 16.04.1919 - returned to Russian Navy 1920

GLOUCESTER (1832) Chat, Rx Sh
3rd Rate, Rx Sh 1861 till sold 03.1884

GLOUCESTER II Colombo/Trinco, Ceylon, Base
10.1938 (ex NORFOLK II(qv)). 01.04.1940 renamed LANKA(qv)
Cr GLOUCESTER Flag East Indies at that time

GLOUCESTER III Aden, Base
27.01.1939 ex NORFOLK III(qv). 01.04.1940 renamed SHEBA (qv)
Cr GLOUCESTER was Flag East Indies at this time

GLOUCESTER Ottawa, Ontario, RCN Radio Sta
Established as HFDF Sta 1943. Sch for Radiomen 1948. Naval Radio Sta 01.12.1950 - 01.04.1953. HMCS 01.04.53 - 11.07.1966, became Canadian Forces Ship GLOUCESTER.
Included Radio Sta Gander, Aklavik, Massett.

GLOWWORM (1916) Danube, SNO Gunboats & MLs
Gunboat, SNO 1920-25, PO at Malta 14.09.25 and sold 09.1928

GLUTTON Augusta, Sicily (NP 841)
Code name for pt of Augusta 09.1943 - Fixed A/S Defences and Mobile Radar used this as name 07.43. NP 841 was Party Table Glutton 03.43 to 02.45

GNU Capetown, Base
Cd 01.11.1942 ex AFRIKANDER III (qv), PO 15.01.1946
Nom DS: Hbr Lch HINEMOA 01.11.42-1946

GOATFELL (1934) Antwerp, Accom Sh
Ex CALEDONIA, hired as M/S 11.1939, AA ship 06.1941, accom sh Antwerp 05.44, left Ports for Nore 23.06.44, PO 24.05.45, laid up on Clyde, no longer required

GOATHLAND (1942) Normandy, Temporary LS HQ Ship
DD, 05.06.44 sail for Normandy, damaged by mine 24.07.44, BU 08.45

GODWIT Ollerton/Hinstock, Salop, RNAS
Ex Ministry of Aircraft Production/RAF 13.08.1942. Sch of Blind Flying Cd 14.06.1943 independent command, acs BLACKCAP. Cd 01.04.44 own accounts. PO 28.02.47
Known as Ollerton till 21.10.1943, then as Hinstock
Included Bramcote 1946 until Cd as GAME-COCK(qv). Also Bratton - RAF airfield used for Tng 1943-44.
There is a ref to GODWIT moving to Peplow

03.45, and another to its being at Weston Park, Shropshire from 30.06.45-02.47 (see GODWIT II). 1945 report that all flying was at Peplow

GODWIT II Peplow/Weston Park, RNAS
28.02.1945 ex RAF. PO 1949 at Peplow (1.5 miles from Hinstock)
Satellite landing ground at Weston Park 1945

GOHANTAK see GOMANTAK

GOLD Normandy, Beach Sub Area (NP 1567)
Cd 09.06.1944 - staff returned UK by 19.07.44

GOLDCREST Angle, Pembs, RNAS
01.05.1943 ex RAF, Cd as GOLDCREST 15.05.43 acs VULTURE, tx to Dale 05.09. 43, Angle to RAF 07.09.43
Nom DS: HL(P) 42570 15.05.43 -05.09.43

GOLDCREST Dale, Pembs, RNAS
Tx from Angle to ex RAF Sta Cd 05.09.43, own acs. C & M 31.03.48. PO 31.10.1948, became HARRIER (qv) 01.02.48
Nom DS: HL(P) 42750 05.09.43-05.46 (at least)

GOLDCREST II Brawdy, Pembs, RNAS
01.01.46 ex RAF as satellite to GOLDCREST (Dale). C & M 31.03.48. became GOLDCREST 04.09.1952 (qv)
Included relief airfield at St Davids lent by RAF 1947-1961 (ceased flying 30.09.58-)

GOLDCREST Brawdy, Pembs, RNAS
Cd 04.09.1952 ex GOLDCREST II, in res post 1960 for runway extension - re-opened 01.04.63, PO 01.04.71, tx to RAF
Nom DS: TRSB 421249 04.09.52-
MB 421134 04.05.54-
MSPB 44314 1954-12.56
TRSB 4422 01.12.56-1960

GOLDEN EAGLE (1909) Thames, Accom Sh
Paddle Steamer, hired WWI, accom sh Thames (Balloon vessels) 01.40 and as AA Ship 1941. Accom Sh 1945, resto 06.45

GOLDEN FLEECE (1944) Dev, Accom Sh
M/S, accom sh 02.1948. BU 08.60

GOLDEN HIND Sydney, NSW, RN Manning Depot
Cd 20.11.1944 (ex GREAT BRITAIN, which name was not used). Held acs of escorts in British Pacific Fleet. Flag Admiral Admin British Pacific Fleet ex BEACONSFIELD 01.12.45. Became GOLDEN HIND I and II, when these merged, GOLDEN HIND III formed to avoid confusion, then renamed GOLDEN HIND. Cd 07.06.46 ex GOLDEN HIND III, PO 31.01.47
At Woolloomooloo 21.04.46, then York St, Sydney
Nom DS: Tug 230 20.11.44-

GOLDEN HIND I Sydney, NSW, Accounting Base, Barracks & Drafting Pool
Held acs GOULD 01.04.46-15.04.46
Closed 19.04.46 - Drafting Pool to Colombo

GOLDEN HIND II Woolloomooloo, Sydney, NSW, RN Repair Base
Named 05.1945 but renamed WOOLLOOMOOLOO (qv) 01.07.45 - however, records report-
Acs to TAMAR 12.45. Acs of personnel in Tokyo to GOLDEN HIND II 01.01.46.
Accounting base for personnel in estabs in Sydney, WRNS Quarters Sydney and seagoing tenders closed 31.03.46 (see GOLDEN HIND III)

GOLDEN HIND III Sydney, NSW
Formed 31.03.1946 - all acs personnel remaining Sydney and Base Ship Sydney became GOLDEN HIND. PO 06.06.46 - became GOLDEN HIND
Address to 21.04.46 was Carrier Buildings, Bourke St Woolloomooloo, from 22.04.46 was 10th Floor, Grace Building, York St, Sydney

GOLDEN HIND (1931) Grangemouth, Accom Sh
Yt, hired 09.1940, laid up 11.44, when used as DSVP shipkeepers' accom sh Grangemouth, sold 1946

GOLDFINCH Takali, Malta GC, RNAS
Civil airport pre WWII, used by RAF from 30.10.1940. RN lodger unit 1943. Fleet Requirements Unit(FRU) to 01.44. To RN on loan 02.44. (FRU 11.1944-12.45). Cd 01.04.45 acs FALCON. C & M 1947-50. PO 09.06.53 and to RAF in C & M, re-opened 01.08.55
Nom DS: HL(D) 43357 01.04.45-13.01.47
MFV 72 14.01.47-05.53 (later Nom DS ST ANGELO)

GOLIATH (1842) Grays, Essex, TS
2nd Rate, lent as TS Forest Gate Sch District 1870 at Grays, burnt 22.12.1875

GOMANTAK Vasco de Gama, Goa, Indian Base
1965-1976, listed as GOHANTAK 1975-76

GOMBROON (1914) Hormuz, Persian Gulf, Rangoon, Base
ADRIA(qv), Bombay 03.43, renamed GOMBROON 31.12.43. At Hormuz 12.43 and NOIC Basra 12.04.44. Approved to release as Base Ship Persian Gulf Escorts 11.44. Bombay 04.45, Colombo/Trinco 05.45, Rangoon 05.45. At Rangoon 18.07.45-11.45 (Burma Coast Escort Force). PO 31.12.45 and to DST

GONDOLIER QUEEN Poole, Accom Sh
08.1942 - 10.44 (at least). Laid up 03.45, to C & M for disposal 09.46

GOOD HOPE Pt Elizabeth, S Africa, TE
Cd 01.08.1942, to C & M 02.44, PO 30.06.44
For CW candidates and included Mechanical TE Pietermaritzburg
Nom DS: YC221 01.08.42-

GOODWIN (1917)
SS - req as guardship, Downs Base - fitted out London 29.08.39 - AA Ship 1941

GORDON Gravesend, TE
GAMEBIRD, Nautical Sea Tng College, Gravesend renamed GORDON and Cd 27.01.1941. renamed GENERAL GORDON 01.12.1943 (qv). Reverted to original name GAMEBIRD when finally PO 30.11.44.
For tng RNR ratings who were to go into the Merchant Navy on completion.

GOSHAWK (1872) Gib, Base
Gunboat, was SO Gib 1890 rb CORMORANT (qv) 1894. Hulk 1902, sold circa 1906

GOSHAWK Piarco, Trinidad, RNAS
Cd 06.11.1940, to C & M 1945, PO 28.02.46
Was originally known as MALABAR II - RNAS for tng. Advance party 10.10.1940. Was Base Ship until BENBOW (qv) Cd - then incorporated RNAS - Base became BENBOW and RNAS continued as GOSHAWK
Nom DS: Skid Towing Ship CORTICELLI 06.11.40 - 22.01.41 (became BENBOW)
Large Chriscraft Crash Boat 22.01.41-

GOSLING Risley, Nr Warrington, Lancs, New Entry TE
Cd 01.07.1942, PO 21.10.1947
TE for Air Fitters and Mechanics and Radio Mechanics and RM Trainees of RNAS Defence Force.
EVT task to CABBALA 03.1946.
Became General Service TE (Pt I Stokers) 01.03.1946.
Included RM Tng Camp, Lowton. Additional accom for GOSLING Cd as ARIEL (qv) 08.10.1942
Nom DS: Tender CAMORET 01.07.1942-
Naval Control Tender 10.44
32ft cutter 5982 12.46-

GOSLING III - ment in a book 1942

GOULD Chatham Barracks, Ceylon
Cd 01.04.1946 on site of MAYINA (qv) - acs GOLDEN HIND I to 15.04.46, then self accounting. PO 30.09.46 (staff tx to SULTAN in RAJAH (8-14.09.46) and FORMIDABLE (14-18.09.46)
Barracks for British Pacific Fleet

GOURKO (GHURKA) (1911) Scapa Flow, Floating Theatre
Purch 07.08.1914 as Canteen ship, sold 1919. Purch as Blockship 1940 and scuttled off Dunkirk 04.06.1940

GRAFTON (1892) Egypt/Black Sea, DS
Cr, Rear Admiral Egypt in GRAFTON, staff ashore in Ismalia 05.1918. DS for British ships supporting White Russians 1919. Sold 07.1920

GRAHAM Glasgow, Res Drl Sh
In 1926 Scottish Res divided into East Scotland and Clyde Divs. Marquis of Graham was the first Commanding Officer of the Clyde Div. Name used by Div's tender MMS 1048 (1948-50). Name allocated to Clyde Res Div 04.1951 - had been at Whitefield Rd, Govan since 10.1906 when HQ formed. PO 30.09.1993 - task to DALRIADA

GRAMPIAN (1860) Belfast, TS
GIBRALTAR, lent as TS Belfast Committee 1872, renamed GRAMPIAN 1889, sold 1899

GRAMPUS (1802) Deptford, Seamen's Hosp Sh
4th Rate, ex LION, Hosp Sh 1820, sold 1832

GRAMPUS (1874) Ports, Powder Hulk
TREMENDOUS, 3rd Rate, renamed GRAMPUS 23.05.1845, powder hulk 1852-1870, laid up Ports till sold 10.05.1897

GRAMPUS (1957) Ports, Hbr TS
SM, at DOLPHIN v ALLIANCE 02.1976 - 1979 rb FINWHALE, target 1980

GRANBY (1941) Halifax, Nova Scotia, RCN Diving DS
M/S, diving tender Cd 23.05.1953-15.12.1966, sold 1975

GRANBY (1944) Halifax, Nova Scotia, RCN Diving DS
FF ex VICTORIAVILLE 1966, DS 21.12.1966-PO 31.12.1973. Sold 1974

GRASSHOPPER Weymouth, CO Base
Cd 15.10.1943, On site vacated by BEE(qv) - included Alexandria Hotel. HQ Assault Group G2 03.1944 (NP 1682). PO 28.04.1944 - personnel to BOSCAWEN, site to USNAAB 29.04.44
Nom DS: Steam Pinnace 766 15.10.43 - 28.04.44

GREAT BRITAIN Sydney, NSW, RN Barracks
10.1944, name proposed for barracks, but Cd as GOLDEN HIND (qv)

GREAT NORE Thames Fort, AA Tower
Built 1941-42 - Cd 08.1943 - Army control, not HM Ship. Post war to C & M

GREBE Dekheila, Nr Alexandria, RNAS
Cd 16.09.1940 acs NILE - ex NILE II(qv). 01.04.41 Self accounting. PO 31.01.46 - returned to Egyptian control 18.03.46
Nom DS: Hbr Lch 20 01.11.40-
HL(D) 3962 03.46-05.46

GREENWICH (1915) DD DS
Purch while building, Cd 10.06.1916. Scapa Flow 14 DF v HECLA 11.07.1916-1919. 1 DF Atlantic Fleet 01.03.1919 - (09.19.rb SANDHURST at Copenhagen). - 23. Med 12.1924 - PO 21.09.25. res Ports - 04.26-27 (FO RF temp v CENTURION 04.26, rb WEYMOUTH). Became Base at Rosyth Cd 16.08.1927 and arrived there 03.09.27-01.06.38 then Res DD DS Rosyth. Scapa Flow 1939-41. Clyde v HECLA 06.41. St John's, Newfoundland v. FORTH 09.41. Capt D Newfoundland 15.09.41. Iceland 1942-44 (Home Fleet 1943-45). Res 07.45.

For BU on rb RESOURCE in Ports RF 03.46, PO27.05.46. Sold 11.07.46

GREGALE Malta GC, CF Base
Construction approved 15.09.1939. MTB Flot arrived 09.12.42 and to SM Base Manoel Is before tx to Tax Biex. Cd 05.03.1943, independent command, acs ST ANGELO, PO 31.08.1946
Nom DS: Diesel Lch 3973 05.03.1943 - 08.46

GREYHOUND (1859) Dev, Breakwater
Sloop, Hbr Serv Dev 09.1869, breakwater by 1880, sold 03.04.1906

GRIFFON (1832) Ports, Coal Hulk
Sloop, Hbr Serv 1854, coal hulk 1857, BU 1869
Listed as GRIFFIN from 1858 - prob to release name for GRIFFON(1860)

GRIFFON Pt Arthur, Ontario, RCN Base & Res Div
01.09.1939 (02.04.40), Cd 01.11.41 as tender to NADEN, independent command 01.09.42. Listed to 1977, extant 1987

GRUNO Harwich, Accom Sh
10.1944

GUELPH Halifax, Nova Scotia, RCN DS
A/P DS 01.05.1918 ex STADACONA I. To 31.01.1919.. DS 03.05.1920 v NIOBE - 01.07.1923 - became STADACONA. Included a shore estab and HQ staff Ottawa
Patrol boat GUELPH (ex CD 20) taken up and Cd 10.11.1917

GUISCARD Bari, Base
05.1944, name sel for Base for convening Courts Martial and disciplinary courts but not commissioned.

GUNMETAL Messina, Italy (NP 870)
Code name for port of Messina 09.1943. Fixed A/S Defences allocated it as ship name 07.43. NP 870 - (Party Gunmetal) also in Pantellaria 06.1943-07.1943 prior to entering Messina

GUNNER (1915) Granton, A/P DS
01.05.1916 v COLUMBINE. Base closed 30.11.1919
Staff at Granton by 11.1914 - Cd 15.03.1915 - Flag down 15.07.1919
Tlr purch 1914 (while building), sold 10.1919

GWEN MARG Falmouth, Repair Ship
09.1943 Quay Punt used for servicing LC

GYPSY London, Accom Sh
See GIPSY

GYPSY M/S Base
Hired as M/S base ship 1942 - 1946
This may be a ref to GIPSY at Swansea (qv)

H

H 2 (1915) Med, DS
SM, Cd 10.11.1916 with SM tenders - with ships attached Italian Fleet, Venice 1916-17, sold 03.21

HAIG Rye, CO Base
Named 01.12.1942, Cd 20.08.1943, PO 15.09.1943. Re-Cd 22.02.44 independent command, acs LYNX, PO 10.01.1945
Nom DS: NAB MAVIS 22.02.44-10.01.45

HAIDA (1942) Halifax, NS/ Toronto, RCN Accom Sh/Memorial
DD, accom sh Halifax 03.1950-07.1950, to Toronto as Memorial 25.08.64 - extant 99

HAIDER Pakistan, Fleet HQ
1999

HAITAN (1909) Addu Atoll/Calcutta/Bombay/Akyab, Base Ship
Taken up as Base Ship E Indies, Charter Party T98 10.1941. Cd 11.1941, Cd at Addu Atoll 26.01.42 - base was to have been called HIGHFLYER but name HAITAN retained. To Bombay 02.44 - 03.45. Calcutta/Akyab as A/S Base Ship 04.45-08.45, PO at Bombay 08.45. To C & M 05.10.45,to DST at Bombay 07.01.46
Base at Addu Atoll included RNAS 11.42, and became MARAGA 01.02.44 (qv)

HAJI MOHSIN Dhaka, Bangladesh, Base
1984 - extant 1999

HALCYON (1894) Lowestoft, A/S and A/P DS
Gunboat, DS A/P Lowestoft 08.1914 - PO 14.03.1919 rb HALCYON II, sold 11.19

HALCYON II Lowestoft, A/P DS
Cd 15.03.1919 v HALCYON - 08.1919
Nom DS: MB SALMON 15.03.1919-

HALIGONIAN Halifax, NS, RCN Res Div
05.09.1939 - Cd? 01.10.1943 - 31.08.1946 - in NL 06.44 (apps from 01.03.44)-10.46
Originally in STADACONA, To King Edward Hotel 12.43, to Gottingen St 10.44 - see also SCOTIAN

HALIFAX Halifax, NS, RCN HQ
1966-1970 (CFS v HMCS STADACONA)

HALLAM Claremont Cres, Sheffield, Communications Tng Centre
Cd 01.10.1984 - PO 31.01.1992

HALO Pictou, NS, RCN Work Up Base
WWII - poss a corruption of HALIGONIAN - ment in one book

HAMADRYAD (1823) Cardiff, Hospital
5th Rate, lent 03.1866 as Seamen's Hospital, Cardiff, sold 11.07.1905

HAMILCAR Djedjelli, Algeria/Messina, CO Base

Name sel for N African Base 23.12.43, Cd 06.02.43 - at Djedjelli. Base for CO personnel in Central and Western Med and LC Base. Tx to Messina 23.06.44. PO 31.03.46 - remaining personnel acs ST ANGELO - NB Messina closed 13.04.46. Carried acs personnel at Bougie (see BYRSA) 44-03.46.
Ex NP 645 Pt Pty Bizerta - Algiers 11.42 - though Bizerta was HASDRUBAL
Nom DS: LCP 723 01.01.43-
HAMILCAR II Bougie, Algeria/ Messina, CO Base
01.09.1943 - 02.44 at Bougie. Still listed 07.44 and in PO circular 09.05.45

HAMILTON (1918) Nova Scotia, RCN TS
DD, ex USS KALK, Cd RCN 23.09.1940, TS at CORNWALLIS (qv) 08.19433-08.06.45, BU 07.45

HAMLA Marve, Mandapam/Bombay, RIN as LC Base/later IN Supply & Secretariat Sch
01.12.1942 - formed at Mandapam by 04.43. Tx to Versova, Bombay into old TE KHANJAR 04.44, and part to HAMLAWAR(qv), later tx to Mazir Camp. Extant Bombay 1999

HAMLA II Mandapam, CF TE
1945-46

HAMLAWAR Marve, Bombay, RIN Component No 1 Coastal Tng Centre
Ex No 1 Comb Tng Centre Madh Is
1944-46 tx to RM later

HANDY (1812) Chat, Floating Chapel
5th Rate, ex NYMPHE (qv) ex NEREIDE, Hbr Serv 03.1836, renamed HANDY 07.09.1871, floating chapel & police ship - BU 03.1875

HANNIBAL (1810) Milford, Qtn Sh
3rd Rate, Lazaretto, Milford, 08.1825 till BU 12.1833

HANNIBAL (1854) Ports, Hulk
2nd Rate, Guardship Ports 12.1858-59, tender to ASIA 02.1863 - hulk 1891 - part of DUKE OF WELLINGTON (qv), sold 12.04.1904

HANNIBAL (1896) Scapa Flow/Egypt, A/P Base
BB, DS Scapa Flow for Northern Flot Tlrs 08.1914-28.08.1914 rb CYCLOPS. A/P Base Alexandria (Egypt & E Indies) 29.11.1915. Rear Admiral Egypt from 10.03.1919 (SNO Alexandria ceased). Moved to Alexandria from Pt Said 04.19. rb CAESAR 10.19 (crew change at Malta). PO Malta 25.10.1919, sold Malta 28.01.20

HANNIBAL Algiers/Taranto, Base
01.01.1943. Self accounting till PO 14.05.45. ReCd 15.04.45 independent command, acs ST ANGELO - British personnel Algiers, Oran & Bone, PO 31.01.46
Formed from NPs 601,612 and 645. By 11.43 carried acs FO Taranto Area
C-in-C Med from HANNIBAL to BYRSA 09.07.44. By 10.44 incl Bari, Brindisi, Naples & Maddalena acs
Nom DS: Fr ML - 12.75 m 08.43-03.44
MFV 77 15.03.44-08.44
MFV 105 08.44-04.45
MFV 623 04.45-

HANNO Base
Name sel for Base in N Africa 12.1943 and to be Cd 01.01.43 - prob not used

HANSA Marma, Goa, Indian Air Base
05.09.1961-(in Pink List from 01.1974) - extant 1999

HANTONIA (1911) Appledore, Accom Sh
Hired as LS 03.04.1942, allocated as accom sh Appledore - fit out at Dev 04.42. To be named MARATHON, but cancelled 08.42. Rb PRESIDENT WARFIELD (qv) 11.1942. remained in service to 07.1945

HAPPY LASS Soton, Accom Sh
08.1942, accom sh for WRNS boats' crews CRICKET (qv), became Nom DS CRICKET 10.43. Laid up 04.45

HARBINGER (1905) Fairlie, Ayrshire/Portland, TS
Paddle Steamer ex PIONEER. Hired for examination Service 06.1940. TS 1941 - experimental vessel? - Fairlie. Listed to 05.46 (at least) as A/S Experimental Estab (ex OSPREY Portland, tx to Fairlie 28.11.1940) - to Portland 1946. BU 11.1957

HARDY (1804) Ports,Convict Hosp Sh
Brig, storship 1818, hosp sh 11.1823, sold 06.08.1835

HARDY (1953) Ports, Stores & Accom Sh
FF, Ports by 10.1979, sunk as target 07.1984

HAREBELL (1918) Portland, Captain A/P
Sloop, Captain A/P 04.1922-10.05.37 rb HASTINGS, then Dev Res till sold 23.12.38

HARLECH (1893) Dev, Stokers' TS
Cr, CAMBRIAN, renamed HARLECH as Stokers' TS 08.08.1916, renamed VIVID (qv) 09.21, sold 21.07.1923

HARLEQUIN (1836) Dev, Coal Hulk
Sloop, coal hulk 1860 till sold 1889

HARLEQUIN (1897) Accom Sh
Paddle Ferry, used as M/S WWI, accom sh 09.1942 but wrecked on passage Chat to Clyde 09.42

HARMAN Canberra (12 miles SE), ACT, RAN Radio Sta
In use by 04.1941, Cd 01.07.1943 - extant 1999
Nom DS: ML HARMAN(NAB 296)

HARMONY (1910) Hbr Serv
UNISON, Drifter, hired WWI, to hbr serv 01.1940, renamed HARMONY 1943-44 (at Scapa Flow)

HARMONY Batavia/Tandjong Priok, Netherlands E

Indies
Name used by NP 2481 1946-47

HAROLD E HOLT New Cape, RAN Communications Sta
1991 - extant 1999, prob not a 'ship' name

HARRIER (1894) Ramsgate, A/P DS Dover/Downs
Torp Gunboat, Ramsgate 14.08.1914 as A/P DS v ARROGANT, 06.03.1915 rb CETO, sold 02.1920

HARRIER Kete, Pembs, RN Sch of Air Direction
Cd 01.02.1948 ex GOLDCREST(qv). Tng to DRYAD 07.1960 (part to HERON 04.1961). PO 02.01.1961
Name VECTOR proposed 1947
Nom DS: HL(D) 39449 1947-1960 (though sold 24.11.1958)

HART (1883) Gib, Accom Hulk
RAPID, corvette, hulk 1906, coal hulk C7 1912, renamed HART 09.06.1915, accom sh Gib and SM DS, sold 1948

HARTLAND POINT (1944) Clyde/Belfast, Repair Ship
Cd 12.07.1945. For lay up in C & M 06.1946, Gareloch by 02.48 (res Amphibious Force). Living Ship Gareloch 28.07.1950 - to dockyard control 01.12.56, modernised Nore 10.59-04.60, Far East 18.05.60-05.65, to UK and Res Rosyth 1966-67. Res Ports 1968-69, SO Res Ships Chat 01.71-72 rb BERRY HEAD. Accom Sh Belfast 1972-73, Chat 1973-74, sold 1974, BU 1979

HASDRUBAL Bizerta (Sousse, Sfax, Ferryville,Tunis) /Salerno/Taranto, Base (NP 645/875)
Cd 20.05.1943 & Cd 01.07.1943 (Pt Parties Sousse and Sfax). 04.45 PO and Re-Cd acs ST ANGELO personnel at Bizerta and Ferryville. PO 22.12.45
CF Advanced Base at Bizerta 09.43-. In 02.44 covered Bizerta, Tunis, and FO Western Italy
By 03.44 included Salerno and Taranto
Nom DS: 32ft cutter RND1 05.43-07.44
NAB QUESTOR 07.44-

HASLEMERE (1925) Normandy, Accom Sh
Hired as Barrage Balloon vessel 10.1940, accom sh 04.44-06.45, was a Mulberry Control Ship at Normandy 07.06.44

HASTINGS (1819) Lpool/Dev, CG/Hulk
3rd Rate, purch 1819, CG Lpool 03.04.1857-01.02.1860, coal hulk 1870 Dev - sold 09.1885

HATHI Delhi/Kandy, Ceylon, RN depot
At Delhi Cd 01.01.1944 independent command, acs of naval personnel in Delhi. PO 31.12.45
Also included Kandy, Ceylon, SO Eastern Fleet
Nom DS: MFV 501 (ex BIWAKO) 02.44-04.45

HAVANNAH (1811) Cardiff, TS
5th Rate, lent as TS (Ragged Sch Ship Cardiff) 19.03.1860-sold 1905

HAWK (1869) Queenstown, RNR Drl Sh
CG Vessel, Drl Sh 1876, renamed AMELIA 1888, COLLEEN 1905, COLLEEN (Old) 1916, EMERALD (qv) 1918, CUCKOO 1918 and sold 08.1922

HAWK (purch 1888) Lough Swilly, CG
Ex OBERON ex LADY ALINE, CG steam yt - Lough Swilly 1903-renamed UNDINE 1904, sold 04.06

HAWKE (1855) Queenstown, CG
3rd Rate, CG Queenstown 01.01.1857 - 06.03.1865, BU 1865

HAWKE (1891) Lough Swilly, CG
Cr, CG Lough Swilly 06.05.1903 - mid 1903, sunk 15.10.1914

HAWKE Exbury House, Exbury, Soton, Upper Yardmen TE
Cd 10.08.1946 ex KING ALFRED II, PO 28.09.1950 - task to Dartmouth (see next entry)
Nom DS: HDML 74 11.48-11.49
MSPB 42475 11.49-09.50

HAWKE Dartmouth, Upper Yardmen TE
28.09.1950 from Exbury, see entry above - 01.05.1955 - to Pt Edgar as TEMERAIRE(qv)
Nom DS: MSPB 42475 09.50-1955

HAWKINS (1917) Spore/Normandy, DS
Cr, Captain-in-Charge Spore 02.07.1925-08.28 whilst Flag China Sta, Cdre DS Flag v ASCANIUS - Normandy/Juno 15.06.44 - Flag ashore 29.07.44 and ship to UK. PO to Res 14.09.44. Sold 08.47

HAWKINS II Ceylon, Base
21.09.1932 ex EFFINGHAM II (qv) - 22.01.35, became NORFOLK II (qv)
Cr HAWKINS was Flag E Indies at this time

HAYDON (1942) Sheerness, Living Ship
DD, RF 11.1951, Bu 05.58

HAZARD (1894) Barrow/Ports/Dover, SM DS
Gunboat, SM DS (the first) at Barrow 1901, Ports 1902-14, Dover 1914 - PO 18.02.1918, lost in collision SS WESTERN AUSTRALIA 28.01.1918

HEADINGLEY Wesley College, Headingley, Leeds, W Yorks, WRNS TE
Cd 27.01.1944 acs PEMBROKE III, 01.07.44 acs BEAVER, PO 14.01.1946, trainees to DEMETRIUS (qv) 15.01.1946
Nom DS: Drifter DIAMANT 27.01.44-

HEATHER (1916) Portland, A/S Sch & A/P DS
Sloop, Cd 15.03.1923 v GIBRALTAR until OSPREY (qv) opened 01.04.1924, and remained DS A/S Flot. PO when rb WOOLSTON 11.09.31, sold 1932

HEBE (1826) Woolwich, Convict/Rx Sh
5th Rate, Rx Sh 1839, Connvict Ship 1845-60, hulk 1861, Rx Sh 1865 till BU 1873

HEBE (1892) SM DS
Gunboat, M/S 1909, conv to DS 1909, Harwich

1910, Chat 6 SM 1914 then Tyne 1914-16, 7SM v VULCAN Leith 06.1916-17, 3 SM Humber 1917 - PO 23.01.1919 and remained Humber, sold 10.1919

HECLA (1878) Chat/Buncrana, DS
Ex BRITISH CROWN, purch 1878, DS Chat 1905, 4 DF Home Fleet 1908-16, 14 DF to 11.07.1916 rb GREENWICH. DS 7 SM 06.1916. To Buncrana 09.1917 - 12.18 (2 DF and A/P DS) - rb HECLA II for A/P acs by 10.1917. Chat 12.1918-03.1919, Cd DS 4 DF Harwich v DIDO 01.03.1919, PO 21.10.1919. Re-Cd 22.10.1919 as DD DS RF Sheerness - 1920. Res Chat 1922 - PO dockyard control Nore 11.02.26 - sold 07.26

HECLA II Buncrana, A/P DS
By 10.1917 (from HECLA) - PO 21.07.1919, task to COLLEEN
Nom DS: Drifter WHEAT STALK (1910) to 06.1919
Steam Lch 226 07.06.1919-PO 21.07.1919 (13.09.1919 in MB Book)

HECLA (1940) Clyde/Iceland, DD DS
Cd 27.12.1940, allocated Clyde. Then allocated to Iceland but cancelled. Re-allocated Hvalfjord when rb GREENWICH 06.41. rb BLENHEIM then to UK 11.41. Mined 15.05.42 off Cape Agulhas - repairs Simonstown 05.42-10.42, and torp and sunk 12.11.42 off Gib while enroute Eastern Fleet

HECTOR (1862) Soton, CG
Iron Screw Ship, CG Newhaven (but at Soton) 01.05.1868 - 22.04.1886, sold 11.07.1905

HEIMDAL (1892) Burntisland, Pt Edgar/Leith
Norwegian HQ Ship
07.1943 - 05.45 (at least)

HEINRICH JESSEN (1940) Rangoon/Akyab, Burma VR HQ Ship
Danish MV used as HQ Ship Burma RNVR to 1942 - last ship to leave Rangoon 07.03.42 - to Akyab. To Calcutta 03.05.42. Became HMIS BARRACUDA (qv) 26.07.42

HELDER Brightlingsea, CO Base
Cd 05.04.1942 (moved from NEMO where had been since at least 23.09.1940) acs QUEBEC. 11.1942 independent command, acs NEMO. PO 30.09.44 - absorbed by NEMO
Parent ship for Raiding Craft Flot. NP camp at St Osyth Stone & in Martello Tower, Point Clear (S Side of creek - NEMO on N Side), After PO was used as accom for NPs enroute Netherlands - known as 'RN Camp St Osyth'
Nom DS: NAB MOSS ROSE 05.04.42-30.09.44

HELENA (1843) Ports/Ipswich/Chat, Chapel/Hbr Police Ship
Brig, coal depot for gunboats Ports 1861-65. Floating Chapel Ipswich 12.1868 then Police Hulk Chat 1883 - rb PRINCE RUPERT after conv 03.20. Sold 06.01.1921

HELENE St Osyth, Brightlingsea, Essex
In one list as in Martello Tower (note HELDER above) - there was a HELENE Yt, lease lend at Georgetown -offered to USN 06.44 - but this name is prob a corruption of HELDER

HELICON (1884) Tyne, Res Drl Sh
CALLIOPE - screw corvette, lent to Tyneside res 29.10.1907, renamed HELICON 17.05.1915 to release original name for Cr to be lch 01.1914 and sold 08.1931. renamed CALLIOPE 10.1931, sold 04.10.1951

HELICON Aultbea, Base
Cd 14.06.1941, Loch Ewe to C & M 13.02.45, reduced to Mine Clearance Base 07.08.45. PO 06.08.45
Listed as independent command, but acs ORLANDO from 01.01.46
L Ewe to be Fleet Base, alternative to Scapa; convoy assembly anchorage alternative to Oban; refuelling base 01.1941
Accounting org at Aultbea under name HELICON ann 05.41
Nom DS: MB RELIANCE 14.06.41-19.12.43 (lost from moorings in gale)
NAB T4 19.12.43-06.45
HL(S) 335 06.45-still listed in Red List 19.02.47

HELIOPOLIS (1903) Persian Gulf
Yt, allocated to Persian Gulf v SHOREHAM (qv) 02.1940, but SHOREHAM was rb Yt SEABELLE (qv). HELIOPOLIS attached FAA 1945-46

HELVIG (1937) Base Depot Mining DS
Danish Vessel, seized 1940, fitted out at Hull 09.40. Cd 28.11.40 acs CARRICK and in COCHRANE II from 01.1941. For use as long range radio ship with MNBDO 05.41. Self accounting 03.42. Nucleus complement 20.07.44 and conv to seaward defence ship. Cd 17.04.45 as Seaward Defence Ship, (Greenock/ Londonderry) PO 14.03.46 and to DST, Resto 04.46

HEPATICA (1914) Ports, Accom Sh
Yt, hired as accom sh 21.08.40, renamed OUTLAW 24.04.41, tx to War Department 02.1942

HEPHAESTOS see HIFAISTOS

HERALD (1973) Persian Gulf, DS
Survey Ship, used as M/S DS 1988-90

HERCULES (1815) HK, Military Stationary Ship
3rd Rate, HK 1853 till sold 08.1865

HERCULES (1868) Greenock/Weymouth/Ports/Gib, CG/Accom Sh
BB, CG Greenock 09.05.1878-01.05.1881, CG Weymouth 01.05.1881-13.05.1890, offices of C-in-C Ports 1905, fitted out as floating barracks 1906 and was such at Gib for dockyard employees 1906-

09, renamed CALCUTTA while at Gib 09.99 (prob to release name for new BB), renamed FISGARD II (qv) 04.1915 at Ports. Sold 07.32

HERCULES (1910) Harwich/Rosyth, RF
BB, carried SNO at Harwich 1919, Rosyth RF Parent 12.06.1919-10.20 (at least), sold 11.21

HERISLE Ammo/Coal Hulk
Ammo hulk 06.1942-01.11, then coal hulk 01.44-30.12.44

HERMES (1916) Chat, Rx Sh
MINOTAUR, 3rd Rate, Hbr Serv 11.1842, renamed HERMES 27.07.1866 Rx Sh, BU 1869

HERMES (1898) Parent Ship
Cr, fitted for seaplanes 1913, reported as seagoing parent ship for Naval Wing of RFC from 08.1913, sunk 31.10.1914

HERMIONE (1893) Lough Larne/Soton, DS
Cr, Guardship Soton and A/P Cd 08.08.1914 - (Hamble River 1914-01.15, Cowes 03.15), PO 03.1915 rb MAGPIE - to C & M. Cd 10.05.15 Lough Larne v VALIANT II(01.06.15) - 01.01.1916 rb THETIS. Cd Soton DS MB Res 11.01.1916 v ex RESOURCE II/RESOURCEFUL (qv). - 03.21 (at least). Sold 1921, became TS WARSPITE (qv)

HEROINE (1758) Sheerness/Deptford, Hbr Serv/Rx Sh
VENUS, 5th Rate, renamed HEROINE 1809, Hbr Serv 1817, Rx Sh Sheerness by 1819-21, Rx Sh Deptford 1826 till sold 09.1828

HEROINE (1841) Dev, Blacksmith's Shop
Packet Brig, Blacksmith's Shop 1865, BU 12.1878

HERON Yeovilton, RNAS
Cd 18.06.1940 - extant 1999
Closed to Flying 30.11.56-03.02.58 - work on runway - RAF Merrifield used (see under)
Included RNAS at:
Charlton Horthorne, Somerset - see HERON II
Duxford 1941-43
Haldon, Nr Bishopsteignton 1941-46 see HERON II
Henstridge, Som, DIPPER (qv) 1943-46 - see also HERON II
RAF Merrifield, Som 21.11.56-31.01.58/ 01.01.1960 - 31.12.60/ 1972 - in use 1990
Sigwells, Nr Sherborne
Tangmere 1942-1950
Wittering 1943-45 - Naval Air Fighter Development Unit
Nom DS: HL(D) 3509 18.06.40-01.08.56
HL(D) 3506 01.08.56 (ex Nom DS VULTURE) - 1962

HERON II Haldon, RNAS
18.08.1941 ex RAF - 05.43 - to C & M, C & M Party withdrawn 17.02.46

HERON II Charlton Horthorne, RNAS
Operated from 26.05.1942. Cd 01.01.43 as RNAS Charlton Horthorne. PO 01.04.1945 - to RAF 17.04.45 in exchange for Zeals - see HUMMINGBIRD

HERON II Henstridge Marsh, Som, RNAS
8 miles E of Sherborne. Ann to be developed 08.1941. Developed 1941-43 - Cd as DIPPER(qv) 01.04.1943-46. 11.11.46 became tender to HERON. Satellite 08.49-09.52 (flying ceased 11.52) & 10.54-06.57

HESPERIDES Fayal, Azores, Base (NP 912)
Cd 08.10.1944 ex LUSITANIA II (qv), PO 26.11.45
Nom DS for LUSITANIA II was CHANTICLEER (1942) sloop - prob continued in use ass such

HIBERNIA (1804) Malta GC, DS
1st Rate, Base at Malta from 1855, sold 10.1902

HIBERNIA (1863) Malta GC, DS
ACHILLES, renamed HIBERNIA 1902 as Base, Malta, renamed EGMONT (qv) 03.1904, returned UK 1914, renamed EGREMONT (qv) 06.16, renamed PEMBROKE (qv) 06.19, sold 01.23

HIBERNIA (1905) Chat, Accom Sh
BB, PO 15.10.1917 for refit and to be overflow ship Chat, rb QUEEN as accom sh 30.06.1919 and sold 11.1921

HIFAISTOS (1920) Alexandria/Greece/ Italy, Greek Naval DS
Alexandria 12.04.1944-07.44, left Naples 23.09.44, Piraeus 12.04.45-47

HIGHFLYER (1898) East Indies, Flagship
Cr, Flagship E Indies Cd 01.08.1919-04.21, sold Bombay 06.21

HIGHFLYER Dartmouth, Base
Name sel for shore base at comml pt Dartmouth 01.09.1939, but not used. NOIC ordered 27.08.39

HIGHFLYER Addu Atoll, Base
Name of Base ann 27.03.1942, but cancelled 04.06.42

HIGHFLYER Trinco, Base
Cd 01.07.1943 - 15.10.1957 - 30.09.58 (see entry below)
Included China Bay RNAS - see BAMBARA.
C-in-C from Colombo to Trinco 15.07.46. By 29.09.47 in 3 parts, RNO Colombo/SPDC - ships Veyangoda/Ceylon West W/T Sta. Included RN Radio Sta Welisara & Kotugoda - Sta closed 07.09.58
Nom DS: MB ABERDANE BOAR 01.07.43-06.48
MFV 648 06.48-08.50
MFV 866 08.50-57
FMB 44453 15.01.58 - (1959) (sold 21.08.58)

HIGHFLYER Welisara & Kotugoda, Ceylon West Group of Radio Sta
01.10.1958 - PO 01.03.1962 (to Ceylon

Government) - some acs report closed 31.03.62
East Indies Sta closed 07.09.1958
Nom DS: FMB 44453 1958 (sold 21.08.58) - 1959
MFV 866 1960-62

HILDA (1895) London, Accom Sh
Yt, hired as accom sh 01.09.1939, described as HQ Barge. Renamed TOWER (qv) and Cd 01.01.41 as A/P Depot London. Renamed HILDA 08.45, to C & M 03.09.45 and laid up 11.45

HILSA Mandapam, India, Indian CF Base
By 1943. Tx to RN 15.09.44 (in Post Office Circular 09.05.45)in NL 01.1945, not by 07.45

HIMALAYA (1853) Dev, Coal Hulk
Troopship, purch 1854, coal hulk 12.1895 (C60) - sold 28.02.1920. Sunk in air attack Portland 1940.

HIMALAYA Manora, Karachi, RIN/RPN/PN Gunnery TE
Cd 26.11.1943 - 1973

HIMALAYA II Karachi, RIN TE
08.1944 Radar Sch being completed - known as HIMALAYA II. Renamed CHAMAK(qv) 08.44

HIMERA N Africa, Base
Name sel for Base 23.12.43, to be Cd 01.01.43. Prob not used

HINDOSTAN (1841) Dartmouth, TS
2nd Rate, joined BRITANNIA at Dartmouth 1868. To Ports and renamed FISGARD III 12.10.1905, reverted to HINDOSTAN 08.1920. sold 10.05.1921

HINDOSTAN Dartmouth, TS
Ex RN Air Lighter No 54, conv to tng hulk 1990 and to Dartmouth

HINDU KUSH Mudros, SM DS
Ex Merchant ship, Cd 11.1914 - 1915

HINDUSTAN (1903) Chat, Accom Sh
BB. overflow accom ship Cd 11.02.1918, rb QUEEN 30.06.1919, sold 05.1921, BU 1923

HIRON POINT Khulna, Bangladesh, Naval Base
1998-extant 1999

HOCHELAGA Montreal, Quebec, RCN DS
NOIC 28.09.1939-05.03.42 & 20.09.43-30.09.45
DS 12.05.41-30.09.45
Nom DS: Cabin Cr MARGO V

HOCHELAGA II Montreal, Quebec, RCN DS
Cd 21.04.1941 - listed to 12.45
Manning Depot 1939-20.12.41 & 20.12.41-20.09.43
NOIC 1940-05.03.42
Pay Div 20.09.43-30.09.45
Nom DS: Hbr Craft 49 -PO 06.45

HOCHELAGA La Salle, Quebec, RCN Supply Sch & Depot
Cd 01.10.1955 - listed to 01.04.1966, part of CFB MONTREAL, then closed (see D'IBERVILLE)

HOGUE (1811) Clyde, CG
3rd Rate, CG Clyde 01.03.1858-30.06.1864, BU 1865

HOLDFAST (1921) Downs/Portland, Guardship
LONDON, hired as guardship 28.08.1939, allocated Downs Base - fit out Dundee 26.08.39 - Cd 16.09.39 as HOLDFAST. To Ministry of Shipping after rb SURPRISE and PO 06.40. Store carrier 01.42. To be resto 03.42. Reverted to LONDON 21.07.42 - fitted out as Cable ship at London and renamed HOLDFAST 12.10.42 - PO 18.06.46, C & M and to DST 06.46

HOLM SOUND (1944) Repair Ship
Cd 15.08.1945 - Cochin, Trinco, Colombo, Cocos 01.46, Fremantle 02.46, Trinco, Aden, Suez 03.46, Ports 22.04.46-, Res Forth as living ship 09.46 - PO 05.02.48 - to DST, laid up Clyde, sold 04.48

HONNINGSVAAG (1940) Rosyth, Norwegian DS
Tlr, taken up as DS 09.1940 - ex German MALANGEN - capt 04.40 Iceland 1941, Rosyth. Greenock Aultbea 42, Leith, Oban 44, listed as A/S Tlr 44

HOOD (1859) Chat, Accom Sh
Ex EDGAR, 2nd Rate, lent War department as barracks at Chat 1872 till sold 1888

HOOD (1891) Pembroke/Queenstown, Pt Guard/Rx Sh
BB, Pt Guard Pembroke 12.12.1900-1901, Flag Queenstown v EMERALD 14.07.1910 - Rx Sh by 04.1913 rb COLLEEN (qv), blockship Portland 04.11.1914 where wreck remains 1999

HOOGHLY Calcutta, RIN/IN base - also Gunnery Sch
01.12.1942 - listed to 10.46 (poss PO 01.02.46) not listed 1947-53 but listed again 1954-76
RN Barracks Calcutta closed 31.03.46

HOPE (1824) Pembroke, Qtn/Rx Sh
Brig, qtn sh 1852 - Rx Sh 1875 - BU 10.1882

HOPE Chat, Convict Sh
Cutter, convict ship 1857

HOPETOUN Pt Edgar, LC and M/S Base
Cd 25.10.1943 independent command, acs CLAVERHOUSE, PO 28.02.46
Name of Base while LOCINVAR (qv) at Granton
Also CO Stokers' Driving TE
Subsidiary Bases as Bo'ness, Grangemouth, Alloa, Innellan and ROYAL SOVEREIGN.
Included VERNON M/S department (from Kimmerghame House to Pt Edgar 05.44, Engineering tng section to Rosneath 10.45)
Nom DS: Hbr Lch 137 25.10.1943-

HOPETOUN II Pt Edgar, Nom de Plume
Name approved as Nom de Plume of BB ROYAL SOVEREIGN(1915) 11.1943 - as overflow accom sh. Lent to Russian Navy 30.05.1944. Though one list dates estab from 06.44-07.45

HORMURG Persian Gulf
Ment

HORMUZ opposite Jarashi, narrows of Khor Kuwai
Barracks, radio masts, relic of Curzons's gunboat diplomacy - empty by late 1950s with Arab caretakers.(Hammond Innes)
Naval Base Khor Kuwai tx to RAF 01.09.45 (see GOMBROON)

HORNBILL Culham, Abingdon, RN Aircraft Receipt & Despatch Centre
Cd 01.11.1944, independent command, PO to Res 30.09.53, In C & M 1954-59
Nom DS: NAB SILVER VANITY 01.11.44-11.45
TRSB 43761 04.48(at least) - 1952

HORNBILL II Beccles/Halesworth, RNAS
Beccles, lodger facilities ex RAF 01.07.1945-18.07.53
Halesworth, tx 01.08.45, Cd as SPARROWHAWK(qv) 05.08.45
Bungay, satellite of Halesworth - see EUROPA II

HORNET Gosport, CF Base
There was a CF Base on the site in WWI - ann to close and be under DOLPHIN 26.11.1918
Opened by 19.04.1921 when CF tx from OSEA (qv) - CMBs under VERNON 01.1922-06.1923 and DOLPHIN 12.1924-12.26. Named 04.07.25. Cd 13.01.26 - PO 31.03.26. Re-Cd as annex of VERNON. Closed 11.05.34.(MTB 01 and 02 Cd 30.06.36 under VERNON). Re-Cd 20.12.39 - tender to VERNON(Victualling) but independent command. Occupied 10.04.40. Independent command 01.10.40. PO 30.09.57 - closed and evacuated 31.10.58. Temporary use as workshops 1963-64 (see DOLPHIN II), centre for Joint Service Adventurous Tng centre (Yts) 23.05.64 - extant 1999
Nom DS: CMB 102 04.07.25-31.03.26 & 13.11.26-1928 (at least)
25 ft MB 3623 20.12.39-12.41 (lost)
HL(D) 3947 12.41-1948 (at least)
TRSB 43773 26.06.52-56
HL(D) 3817 to 57

HOTSPUR (1828) Dev, Chapel Hulk
5th Rate, RC Chapel Hulk 1859, renamed MONMOUTH 1868, sold 1902

HOTSPUR (1990) Holyhead/Harwich/ Bermuda, CG
Turret ship, CG Holyhead 08.08.1885-21.05.1887, Harwich 21.05.1887 - 09.05.1893, Guard Bermuda 1897 - 1903, sold 02.08.1904

HOUND (1942) Dev, RF Living Ship
M/S, RF living ship 09.47-rb PADSTOW BAY 24.01.1949, BU 09.62

HOWARD Halifax, Nova Scotia/ Ottawa, Ontario, RN Depot
Cd 12.06.1948 - 1988
Cd as visiting vessel for the administration of offenders imprisoned or in detention in America/West Indies. At Halifax to 05.51, then to Ottawa, Truro Building, Albert St (1950), Laurier Ave West (1953-57), Elgin St (1970). BDLS Ottawa was NP 1010 (1979 on)
Nom DS: 25 ft Motor Cutter 1948
MC 431041 12.48-1962

HOWE (1885) Queenstown, CG
BB, CG Queenstown 01.01.1897 - 1901, sold 11.10.1910

HOWE (1940) Dev, SO RF
BB, Hbr Tng Home Fleet (Portland) v QUEEN ELIZABETH 01.46-06.48 rb KING GEORGE V. SO RF Dev v UNICORN 17.05.49-05.10.52, BU 05.58

HUGO BIERMANN Simonstown, SAN SM Facility
Ex DROMMEDARIS (qv) 08.1976-

HUMBER (1876) Med, Storeship
Ex HARAR, purch 1878, Med 1889-95, sold 1907

HUMMING BIRD Zeals, RNAS
Cd 18.05.1945 independent command, acs HERON, PO 15.02.46, C & M Party withdrawn 07.06.46
Ex RAF, lent 14.04.45 v Charlton Horthorne, originally satellite to HERON (qv)
Nom DS: HL(D) 3824 18.05.45 - (in Red List 05.46)

HUNTER Windsor, Ontario, RCN Base & Res Div
21.12.1939, Cd 01.11.41 - tender to STADACONA - 01.09.1942, then indepndent command, listed to 1977, extant 1987

HUNTER (LST 3042) (1945) Clyde, SO RF
SO RF Gareloch and accom sh (Sea Cadets) 1947 - 12.1949. EMPIRE CURLEW (MOT) 1956, BU 08.1962

HUON Hobart, Tasmania, RAN Depot & Res TE
Cd 01.03.1942 ex CERBERUS VI, ex DERWENT. - PO 1994
Originally manned in 1911 as District Naval Depot
Nom DS: ML ARCADIA 1945-1953
HDML 1374 12.02.53 -

HUSSAR (1807) Chat, Rx Sh
5th Rate, Rx Sh 09.1833-52 (at least), target 1861, burnt 1861

HUSSAR (1894) Portishead, Drl Sh
Torp Gunboat, Drl Sh v ANTELOPE Cd 18.11.1905 - 09.06, sold 12.1920

HYACINTH (1829) Ports, Coal Hulk
Sloop, coal hulk 1860 till BU 1871

HYACINTH (1898) Capetown, A/P DS
Cr, Flag Cape 1913-1919 and A/P DS Cape 06.1918-10.1918, sold 10.1923
Included Zanzibar Depot, Rufigi Transport

HYAENA Deptford, Storeship
6th Rate, ex HOPE, purch 1804, storeship 1813 till sold 1822

HYDERABAD (1917) River Dwina, Upriver DS
Purch 1917, DS 1918-19, sold 1920

HYDROGRAAF Harwich, Accom Sh
08.1943 - 09.44 at least
Netherlands vessel, accom sh for Dutch personnel in Motor M/S

HYPERION (1807) Newhaven, CG
5th Rate, CG 1825 - BU 1833

I

ICARUS Houton Bay and Caldale, Scapa Flow, RNAS
Cd 01.10.1917 - 03.1918
ICARUS ex TRENT - Central Depot for Air Services, Orkney

IDAHO (1910) Milford Haven, A/P Depot
16.08.1916 v SABRINA II (qv) - 01.10.1919 - books to VIVID V (qv)
Flag struck 31.07.1919, Base closed 07.10.1920
Nom DS: Yt hired 04.1915-02.02.1919 and WWII
Tlr GIOVANNI GUINTI (1918) 19.01.19 - sold 1919

ILEX (1896) Kingstown & Holyhead, A/P DS
Cd 12.03.1915 v EAGLE/COLLEEN - 01.07.1915 rb BOADICEA II (qv), PO 20.07.1915
Yt hired 06.09.1914-20.07.1915

ILLUSTRIOUS (1803) Ports, DS/TS/ Guardship
3rd Rate, DS 1848, Boys'/Cadets' TS 04.1854-59 rb BRITANNIA 01.01.1859, Guardship 1859, BU 12.1868

ILLUSTRIOUS (1896) Tyne/Grimsby/ Chat/Ports, Storeship/Accom Sh
BB, Guardship Tyne 1914 rb ST GEORGE 10.1914, Tlr DS Loch Ewe 10.1914-12.1914, rb VANESSA. 01.15 Grimsby and PO by 01.16 and laid up Immingham to 09.16. Cd Chat 16.08.16 and in C & M 28.08.16 as tender to PEMBROKE as accom sh. Cd 08.11.1917 at Chat for voyage Rosyth to fit out as ammo ship. Fit out as Ammo Ship Tyne 1917-1918, (continue to ..)Fit out as ammo ship Ports 03.18-09.19. Ammo ship Ports 09.1919-20, sold 06.20

ILTON CASTLE Dartmouth, Fuel Supply Vessel
Hulk, req 10.1943 - total loss 06.08.1945

IMAUM (1826) Jamaica, Rx Sh
3rd Rate, ex E Indiaman LIVERPOOL, Rx Sh 07.1842 till BU 1863

IMMINGHAM (1907) Ports, Rx Sh
Hired as accom sh 10.1914, store carrier 04.1915, sunk in collision 06.06.1915

IMMORTALITE Ports, Rx Sh
5th Rate, Ex Fr ALCEMENE capt 1814, Rx Sh 1835, sold 1837

IMMORTELLE S African HQ unit
Late 1950s

IMPERIEUSE Sheerness/Standgate Creek, Qtn Sh
5th Rate, ex Spanish MEDEA, capt 1804, renamed IPHEGENIA, renamed IMPERIEUSE 1805, qtn sh Sheerness 1818-31 (at least), at Standgate Creek by 1835 till sold 1838

IMPERIEUSE (1883) Portland, DS
Cr, renamed SAPPHIRE II as Torp boat DD DS Portland 02.1905. renamed IMPERIEUSE 06.1909 - listed at Portland as IMPERIEUSE 06.1909 - sold 09.1913

IMPERIEUSE Scapa Flow/Rosyth, Repair/Store Ship
AUDACIOUS (1869) BB, renamed FISGARD 04.1904, tow to Scapa Flow 16.09.1914, arrived 01.10.1914. renamed IMPERIEUSE Repair Ship 14.10.1914. DS Tlrs Scapa Flow 11.1914 - task to ZARIA, DS for Tugs 15.02.1919 when ZARIA left Scapa Flow. Was to be v VICTORIOUS (Pt Office and Post Office) 21.07.1919 and to be renamed VICTORIOUS 10.1919 - but cancelled. PO 21.07.1919 - tasks to VICTORIOUS. Left Scapa Flow 31.03.1920 to Rosyth for Naval Stores. Sold 03.1927

IMPERIEUSE I Gareloch, NOIC and Stokers' TE
Cd 12.05.1944 as NOIC at Gareloch as IMPERIEUSE I covering IMPERIEUSE II(qv). NOIC post abolished 17.11.44.
Nom DS: MELORA 12.05.44-07.45

IMPERIEUSE II Gareloch/ Dev, Stokers' TE
Cd 12.05.1944 - at Gareloch, REVENGE and RESOLUTION which had been SHRAPNEL II at Soton (qv). Ships reverted to own names for tow to Dev. Arrived 11.12.44

IMPERIEUSE Dev, Stokers' TE
Was set up as Stokers' TE Dev when REVENGE - arrived first - and RESOLUTION arrived from Gareloch. Cd 11.12.1944 - Later included RENOWN (1916)(also turret drl sh 11.45), UNICORN (1941), VALIANT (1914) and NEWFOUNDLAND (1941) - Cd as IMPERIEUSE 21.06.1946. Ships reduced to res 10.47 or tx (NEWFOUNDLAND) when task tx to RALEIGH(qv) 10.03.48. PO 01.06.48

IMPLACABLE Dev/Falmouth/Ports, TS
Fr DUGUAY-TROUIN capt 1805, became a TS for Cadets 07.1855 at Dev, but task to ILLUSTRIOUS, then became boys' TS 1860. Merged into LION TE 1871 (qv). Lent for preservation 1912, at Falmouth 1922-28, later to Ports, taken over 01.03.41 for stores. By 06.43 joined FOUDROYANT and was part of FOUDROYANT TE at Ports (qv). Scuttled 02.12.1949

IMPLACABLE (1899) Ports/Scapa/ Buncrana/ Shetlands, DS
BB, PO 23.08.1917, then accom sh Ports. Cd

01.01.1918 as accom sh Ports, then Northern Patrol DS Shetlands, Kirkwall 14.03.18, Lerwick 29.05.18, Buncrana by 09.08.18-09.18, Kirkwall 09.18,Portland 09.12.1918-02.05.1919, tenders tx to RESEARCH. PO at Portland 22.07.1919, to res & C & M. Sold 08.11.21

IMPREGNABLE (IMPREGNABLE I) Dev, Flag/Boys' TS/ Rx Sh
1862-1929 - last boys drafted 01.01.1929 - then closed.
DS 1 SM 01.10.1915. POWERFUL(qv) & IMPREGNABLE merged into one TS 1919.
Also Flag Dev (19th Century & 03.1903-24.07.1927 - Flag to EREBUS. Flag in ROYAL ADELAIDE 1860-89)
1) IMPREGNABLE (1810), Dev by 1828, Flag by 1839, TS/Rx Sh 01.01.1862, renamed KENT (qv) 09.11.1888, renamed CALEDONIA (qv) 22.09.1891, sold 10.07.1906
2) HOWE (1860) renamed BULWARK (qv) 03.12.1885, renamed IMPREGNABLE 27.09.1885, became IMPREGNABLE I 27.06.1911, renamed BULWARK 01.12.1919, sold 02.21
3) POWERFUL (1895) renamed IMPREGNABLE 01.12.1919, sold 31.08.1929

IMPREGNABLE II Dev, Boys' TS
1) INCONSTANT (1868), renamed IMPREGNABLE II 27.06.1911, renamed IMPREGNABLE (Old) 01.12.19, renamed DEFIANCE IV (qv) 01.22, renamed DEFIANCE II 12.30, BU 04.56
2) ANDROMEDA (1897), renamed POWERFUL II (qv) 23.09.1913, renamed IMPREGNABLE II 01.12.1919, renamed DEFIANCE (qv) 20.01.31, BU 08.56

IMPREGNABLE III Dev, Boys' TS
1) BLACK PRINCE (1861) renamed EMERALD (qv) 03.1904, renamed IMPREGNABLE III 06.1910, reverted to BLACK PRINCE 12.10.22, sold 21.02.23
2) GANGES (1821) renamed TENEDOS III (qv) 21.06.1906, renamed INDUS V (qv) 13.08.1910, renamed IMPREGNABLE III 12.10.1922, BU 31.08.29

IMPREGNABLE IV Dev, Boys' TS
1) CIRCE (1827) Hbr serv 1866 - attached IMPREGNABLE from 1874, renamed IMPREGNABLE IV 18.10.1915, sold 07.1922
2) CAROLINE (1882) renamed GANGES (qv) 04.1908, renamed POWERFUL III (qv) 09.1913, renamed IMPREGNABLE IV 01.12.1919, sold 08.29

IMPREGNABLE St Budeaux, Plym, Boys' TE/Hostilities Only Communications Ratings
Cd 11.11.1935 - opened in old detention barracks - 1947
In 02.45 it was proposed to merge IMPREGNABLE and RN Camp St Budeaux as MOUNT EDGCUMBE, but cancelled 03.45. Relationship between this and next entry in 1946-47 unclear - poss tng ceased during war and communicators only, then when tng restarted it was treated as a separate section.
Nom DS: Steam Lch 209 11.11.35 - 1947
HL(P) 45737 by 11.47

IMPREGNABLE St Budeaux, Plym, TE and Overflow Camp for DRAKE
02.12.1946 - PO 25.05.1948 - to C & M
Took one entry of Boys, joined 14.05.47 - final parade 09.05.48, tng ceased next day
Nom DS: Steam Lch 209 1947-48
HL(P) 45737 By 11.47-05.48

INCISOR Fixed A/S Defences
For Southern Italy, proposed 21.08.1943. INCISOR was the codeword for Reggio Calabria - Operation Baytown

INCONSTANT (1868) Dev, Accom Sh
FF, accom sh 1898, renamed IMPREGNABLE II (qv) 27.07.1911, renamed DEFIANCE IV (qv) 01.22, and DEFIANCE II (qv) 12.30. BU 04.04.56

INCONSTANT (1914) SM DS
Cr, DS 1 SM v FEARLESS Cd 27.10.1919 - 21 rb CONQUEST, sold 06.22

INDEFATIGABLE Mersey, TS
1) INDEFATIGABLE (1848) 4th Rate, lent as TS on Mersey 03.01.1865, sold 26.03.1914
2) PHAETON (1883) Cr, sold 1913, renamed TS INDEFATIGABLE 01.01.1914, acquired as accom sh Greenock 18.10.1941, renamed CARRICK II (qv) 05.02.42 (renamed as there were then 3 INDEFATIGABLEs in the RN), BU 20.01.47

INDEPENCIA Ascension Island, Coal Hulk
Ex slaver, purch 1843, coal hulk, renamed ATTENTION 1846, sold 1847

INDIA New Delhi, RIN/IN HQ
Named by 1945 - extant 1996
RIN HQ to Delhi/Simla 03.41

INDOMITABLE (1907) Nore, RF Parent
BCr, Nore Res Parent Group 2 02.1919-1920, sold 01.12.1921

INDUS (1839) Dev, Guardship & Flag Admiral Superintendent
1860-1905 (this and subsequent ships using the name)
1) 2nd Rate(1839), Guardship Dev 14.07.1860, sold 11.11.1898
2) VALIANT (1863) relieved INDUS as Guardship 1898 and took the name - see INDUS IV - for a few months only

INDUS (INDUS I) Dev, Mech TE and Workshop
01.01.1906-15.08.22
DEFENCE (1861) floating workshop 1890, renamed INDUS 06.1898 at Dev,, Cd as workshop and Mech TE 01.01.1906 (Mech Te to Chat 1910).

Renamed INDUS I 08.09.1910.PO 15.08.1922 and became hulk, sold 16.08.1935 (still in NL 1946)

INDUS II Dev, DS for Fleet Res
1) TEMERAIRE (1876) renamed INDUS II 08.09.1910. renamed AKBAR (qv) 14.10.1914, BU 26.05.21
2) FLORA (1893) Cr, renamed INDUS II 10.1915, for sale 1918, BU 12.12.22
3) VICTORIOUS (1895) BB, repair ship Scapa Flow 03.1916, to Dev 20.03.20, renamed INDUS II 03.20, BU 19.12.22

INDUS III Dev, TS
BELLEROPHON (1865) BB, renamed INDUS III 09.09.1910, BU 12.12.22

INDUS IV Dev, TS
1) VALIANT (1863) (qv) bore name INDUS as guardship 1898 (qv), renamed INDUS IV 1904, DS for Torp Boat DD, renamed VALIANT (old) DS 1916, renamed VALIANT III 1919, oil hulk 1924, BU 12.1956
2) TRIUMPH (1870) (qv) renamed TENEDOS No 1 (qv)04.1904, renamed INDUS IV 08.09.1910, renamed ALGIERS (qv) 14.10.1914, sold 07.01.1921

INDUS V Dev, TS
GANGES (1821)(qv) renamed TENEDOS III 21.06.1906, renamed INDUS V 08.09.1910, renamed IMPREGNABLE III (qv) 12.10.22, sold 31.08.1929

INDUSTRY (1814) Isle of Man, Chapel
Transport, Chapel, Isle of Man 1820 till BU 1846

INDUSTRY (1854) Cape/Dev/Soton, Storeship
Cape 1870, Dev 1875, Soton 1900, BDV 1901, sold 1911

INFLEXIBLE (1780) Halifax, Nova Scotia, DS
3rd Rate, DS 1820, BU 1820

INFLEXIBLE (1876) Ports, Guardship
BB, guardship 26.11.1893 -97, sold 15.09.1903

INFLEXIBLE (1907) Nore, RF Parent
BCr, Nore Res Parent Group 1 02.1919-1920, sold 01.12.21

INGENIEUR CACHIN (1923) Lpool/Soton, DS
Fr M/L seized at Soton 03.07.1940, Cd 01.08.40, allocated to Lpool v MINARD. Renamed VOLONTAIRE 1941. Free Fr DS, Resto 1945

INGENIEUR MINARD (1911) Ports, Accom Sh
Fr ferry seized 13.07.1940 at Soton. Accom Sh Tlr Base Ports VERNON II 08.40 - rb MARSHAL SOULT 12.40. Laid up Ports C & M 03.41, re-allocated as accom sh Ports 09.42. Passenger tender Cherbourg 09.44, to DST 09.44, Resto 27.06.45

INKONKONI Durban, S Africa, SAN TE
01.11.1954 (ment 1948) - listed to 1961

INSKIP Inskip, Preston, Lancs, Radio Sta
Opened 01.09.1958 (ex NIGHTJAR (qv)) - operational 12.01.59. Cd 21.03.1966. PO 09.03.95 - became civilian manned RN W/T Sta Inskip

INSPECTOR GENERAL TWENT Falmouth, DS for 'G' Torp Boats
Dutch ship, DS 1940

INTREPID (1770) Plym, Rx Sh
3rd Rate, Rx Sh 1810 till sold 1828

INTREPID (1891) Ports/Russia, DS
Cr, Hbr serv Ports 1904-09, conv to M/L, DS North Russia 1915-16, DS White Sea Cd 02.04.1917-12.17, sunk as blockship 23.04.1918

INUVIK Inuvik, North West Territories, Canada, RCN Radio Sta
HMCNRS 12.03.1961 - 10.09.1963, HMCS 10.09.1963 - 19.07.66, became CFS INUVIK

INVERNESS Inverness, LC Base
09.1944 - Prob ref to location of MONSTER (qv)

INVESTIGATOR (1811) Thames, Police Ship
Brig, Thames 03.1837 till BU 10.1857

INVICTA (1940) Accom Sh
Hired as Landing ship 1940, allocated as emergency accom sh 11.1941, no longer required as accom sh 04.42. Cd as ALC Carrier 06.42 - to MOWT 10.45

INVINCIBLE (1808) Dev, Coal Ship
3rd Rate, coal hulk 1853 till BU 01.1861

INVINCIBLE (1869) Hull/Soton, CG
Iron Screw Ship, CG Hull 13.10.1870-07.1871, CG Soton (Newhaven) 23.11.1886 - 07.06.93, Torp Boat DD DS 1901-06, renamed EREBUS (qv) 1904, FISGARD II (qv) 1906, foundered 17.09.1914

IOLAIRE Stornoway, A/P Base
26.09.1915 v MANCO - PO and Base Closed 19.05.1919 task to PRESIDENT I
In Charge Naval Patrol Dundee & Southern Force at Granton . Also 14 SM and 21 DF(11.1918)
(Southern and Northern Patrol to Portland 24.11.1918)
1) Yt IOLAIRE (1902) hired 03.15, renamed AMALTHAEA 06.11.18 - resto 1919, hired WWII - see next entry
2) Yt AMALTHAEA, hired 03.15, named IOLAIRE 06.11.18, lost by stranding & PO 01.01.19 - heavy loss of life.
3) Tug LADY WINDSOR hired 07.14-1919, renamed IOLAIRE 01.01.19-PO 19.05.19

IOLAIRE Ports/Aultbea/Greenock, Base & Accom Sh
Yt (1902) hired WWI - see last entry - hired as accom sh 09.1939 with MINERVA (qv). Formed base for M/S and A/S Tlrs at Ports 01.01.40, replaced by MARSHAL SOULT (qv) 10.12.40. Acquired 27.01.43, accom sh Aultbea by 03.44, Accom Sh Greenock 05.45, renamed PERSE-

PHONE (qv) 07.06.45, sold 46

IONA Pt Said, Greek DS
04.1944-06.05.45 (at least)

IPHIGENIA (1808) Woolwich, TS, Lent Marine Society
5th Rate. Lent 07.1833 - 1848, Bu 05.1851 - see also under WARSPITE

IPHIGENIA (1891) White Sea/ Archangel, M/S DS
Cr, DS White Sea 10.1915 v BOMBARDIER - PO 01.12.1916 (rb VINDICTIVE 10.16).Cd 24..03.17, Murmansk 03.17-07.17, Yukanski 06.17-10.17, Archangel 10.17-12.17, Murmansk 12.17-01.18, PO Chat 17.01.18 - sunk as blockship 23.04.18

IQBAL Karachi, RPN Depot
14.08.1948 ex MONZE - renamed on establishment of RPN - by 1999 Commando Base

IRIRANGI Waiouru, New Zealand, RNZN Radio Sta
Opened 1942. Cd 30.10.1951 - Tri Service 1966, extant 1994. Known as Waiouru W/T Sta
Nom DS: ML 3554 1959-65

IRMA Scapa Flow, Repair Unit
Danish MFV, seized 1940, conv to floating mobile ASDIC & echo sounding maint and repair unit for Fleet and DD escorts 12.42 - 45

IRON DUKE (1870) Hull/Kingstown/Leith, CG
BB, CG Hull 07.1875-01.10.1875, Kingstown 01.10.1875 - 17.07.1877, Leith 09.05.1890 - 03.05.1893, sold 1906

IRON DUKE (1912) Ports/Scapa Flow, TS/Base
BB, Boys' TS Ports 09.1932-38, to Scapa Flow 1939 - bombed, sunk and grounded 17.10.1939. PO and Re-Cd as Base 26.10.39 - independent command. PO 06.08.1945, handed over for BU 02.03.46

IRONCLAD Diego Suarez, Madagascar, Base
Cd 24.05.1942 - was to be AFRIKANDER V (qv) but name changed before Cd, PO 13.02.1945 (control of port to Fr).
Included airfield at Andrakaka (lodger facilities) - to RAF 16.09.44
Nom DS: Fr Tlr GENERAL FOCH 24.05.42-12.42
LCM 117 12.42-

IROQUOIS (1941) Halifax, Accounting Base
DD, took acs of Atlantic vessels when SCOTIAN PO 28.02.47, BU 09.66

IRRESISTIBLE (1859) Newhaven/Bermuda, CG/DS
2nd Rate, CG Newhaven 01.04.1864 - 30.04.1868, DS Bermuda 09.1868. Sold 1894 at Bermuda

IRWELL Manchester/Mersey, Res Drl Sh/Tlr Base
1) SIR BEVIS (1918) sloop, refit Sheerness 1922, renamed IRWELL 09.19233 as Drl Sh Manchester Sub Div of Mersey Res, renamed EAGLET (qv) 1926, BU 1971
2) GOOLE (1919) ex BRIDLINGTON, M/S, completed 04.1926 as drl sh, renamed IRWELL 09.1926. renamed EAGLET II 20.09.1939. Base for Tlrs and DS Lpool, by 04.40 all Res Divs were closed. Renamed IRWELL and Cd 15.08.42 as Tlr Base, Birkenhead - independent command, acs EAGLET, PO 16.07.45 - buildings to ONSET. Res Div reconstituted 01.10.46 - IRWELL ex GOOLE at Morpeth Dk, Birkenhead 1955-58 (at least). Last listed 1962 at Salthouse Dk. BU 27.11.62

ISIS (1819) Sierra Leone, Coal Hulk
4th Rate, coal hulk 03.1861 till sold 03.1867

ISKRA Gib, DS/CF Base
Polish TS used as SM DS under name PIGMY (qv) 1940. Accom sh as ISKRA 31.03.41. Cd as ISKRA 11.08.1941 as CF Base, tender to CORMORANT. PO 19.01.45. Returned to Polish Government 04.48

ISLA Poole, Accom Sh
08.1942 - no longer required - to DST 25.07.45, laid up 08.45

ISLAND PRINCE (1911) North Shields, A/S Parent
01.10.1914, Cd independent command 01.11.14 - PO and Pt M/S Base closed 15.04.1919 - task to SATELLITE
1) Tlr No 62, hired 1914-1919 - PO 16.03.19
2) Tlr GENERAL BOTHA (1916) 16.03.1919-PO 08.19 (hired 1916-19 & WWII)

ISLE OF THANET (1925) Normandy, Ferry Control Ship
Passenger vessel/Landing Ship, ferry control vessel 30.06.44

ISSA KHAN Chittagong, Bangladesh, Dockyard, Stores Depot & Armament Inspection & Supply Depot and Naval Academy
10.12.1971 ex PN Base BAKHTIYAR (qv) - extant 1999

ITHURIEL (1915) Rosyth, SM DS
DD, DS 13 SM Rosyth 06.18, DS 2 SM Rosyth, 01.03.1919 - DS 1SM Rosyth 01.09.1919, sold 11.21

ITHURIEL Newport, Mon, Base
Name sel for shore base at comml pt Newport 01.09.39. NOIC ordered 27.08.39. Post filled by 29.08.39 - name prob never used
Newport Naval Base closed 18.06.45

ITHURIEL (1941) Gib, Base
DD, damaged beyond repair Bone 28.11.1942, tow to Gib 18.08.43 - became base and A/S TS for two years. In C & M Gib 04.45 as base for Italian A/S Tng SMs - from Gib 01.08.45 for Inverkeithing - BU 08.45

IVERNIA Salcombe, Accom Sh for USN
Houseboat, req 01.1944, resto 25.02.44

IXION Glasgow, Rescue Ship Accom Sh
07.1943, ex VIGILANT, no longer required and fitted out for survey duties 11.43 - to target towing service Larne 05.44 but cancelled - re-allocated

Ports pool 08.44, then Examination Vessel Arromanches 11.44, to Nore, special service 12.44, to be resto 12.01.46, to DST 05.04.46

J

JACKDAW (1855) Dev, Cooking Depot
Gunboat, cooking depot 1886 till sold 11.1888

JACKDAW Crail, Fife, RNAS
Cd 01.10.1940, PO 28.04.47 - re-opened as BRUCE (qv)
Listed under JACKDAW in C & M 1952-60 - used by University Flying Sqn, storage depot and Joint Service Linguistic Sch
Nom DS: MFV FRANCOLIN ex SPEEDWELL 01.10.40-18.03.43
Dinghy HANDY 18.03.43-
Safety Boat 4108 12.44-

JACKDAW II Dunino, Fife, RNAS
01.12.1942 ex RAF & Cd 15.12.42. C & M 02.04.46
Became MERLIN III (qv) 01.10.45

JAHANARA Ahmednagar, RIN Women's New Entry TE
Opened 11.1944

JAHANGER Pt Quasim, Karachi, PN Naval Base
1999

JAHANGIR (1942) Karachi, TS
Cr, Ex DIADEM, renamed BABUR on tx to Pakistan, renamed JAHANGIR 1982 as TS - deleted 1985

JALA PADMA Bombay, CO TS
03.06.1943-, Tng MT Ship

JAMAICA (1940) Ports, FO Commanding RF
Cr, living ship RF Ports 11.51, Flag 07.07.52 and 05.53 v DIDO (DIDO was Flag for Coronation Review) - 05.11.53 rb CLEOPATRA, Bu 12.60

JAMES Cocos Island
06.1943, codeword for Cocos island, changed to BROWN 04.44

JAMES CHAPMAN (1917) Sierra Leone, DS
Tlr, 08.11.1919 - in charge BD Party Sierra Leone - sold 1922

JAMES COOK Caladh Castle, Glen Caladh, Nr Tignabruich, Bute, CO TE
Cd 11.11.1942, attached MONCK for pay, stores and victualling. PO 30.09.45 - de-store to mid 10.45
Naval Beach Pilotage TE - Originally ann to be spelt JAMES COOKE - later corrected
Nom DS: MB RN 218 11.11.42-
HL(P) 42531 08.45-30.09.45

JARAWA (also spelt JAWARA) Pt Blair, Andaman Is, IN Base
04.1964 - first entry in Pink List 01.74 - listed to 1976, extant 1999

JAWARHALAL NEHRU E Zhimala, IN Academy
Planned for 1992, extant 1996, from Goa to E Zhimala 1997

JEANNE ET GENEVIEVE (1917) Aultbea, Accom Sh
Fr vessel, seized Plym 03.07.1940, laid up until allocated as accom sh Balloon Servicing, Aultbea 08.41 - 09.44 (at least), resto to Fr 07.11.44
JEEVANTI Vasco De Gama, IN Base
Listed 1969-76

JEHANGIR Cocancada (Colonda), India, RIN Coastal TE Component No 2
Cd RIN 04.1944 (originally to have been RN) - 04.1946
Ex No 2 Combined Tng Centre

JEWEL (1944) Dundee, Res Drl Sh
M/S, Drl Sh Tay Div Res 01.1948 - rb CIRCE 09.51, to RF Clyde 10.51-later part of Dartmouth Tng Sqn, BU 04.67

JINNA Pt Ormara, Pakistan, PN Base
1999

JOHN BOWLER (1918) Mudros, Base
Tlr, Cd 12.02.1920 as Nom Parent Ship Mudros, sold 1922

JOSEPH STRAKER (1848) North Shields, Mission Ship
Ex DIAMOND, 6th Rate, lent TS 04.1866, renamed JOSEPH STRAKER 13.01.1868, Mission Sch, N Shields, sold 09.1885

JUFAIR Bahrein, Persian Gulf, Base
Cd 01.04.1943, independent command, acs EUPHRATES. 06.45 EUPHRATES reduced to tender of JUFAIR. PO 31.08.46 - SNO Persian Gulf then afloat in WILD GOOSE - but to new base ashore 30.08.50.
Nom DS: Motor Dhow SINBAD 01.04.43-

JUFAIR Bahrein, Persian Gulf, Base
Cd 07.11.1955 - 15.12.1971
SNO Persian Gulf to new base ashore 30.08.1950.
By 08.61 was base for Amphibious Warfare Sqn
Nom DS: 63ft ML 45785 Dhow JUFAIR - sold 24.12.55
ML 42460 1955-62

JULES VERNE (1931) Harwich/Rosyth, DS
Fr DS serving with RN, Harwich 23.03.1940, Rosyth 05.40, 10 SM, to operate from Dundee 05.40 but Fr SM to France 06.40.

JULIUS Constantinople, Base for Hbr Craft
Cd 01.10.1919 v CAESAR - 23.09.23
Nom DS: PHINGASK Drifter (1908)Hired 01.15 - 01.10.19-1920
NIXA 05.20-22
IMOGENE Hbr Craft 03.23

JUMBO
Ment in a list. In 06.44 there was a DG Tender JUMBO at Harwich and then Gt Yarmouth rb SEAGULL

JUMNA (1866) Medway, Powder Hulk/Coal Hulk
Troopship, coal hulk 1893, powder hulk Friendly Pt Medway 1900, 1995-99 at Ports awaiting conv to TS, coal hulk Chat 1905, sold 07.1922

JUMNA Bombay/E Indies, Base Ship
Cd 26.04.1919 - see DORIS, to 1921, became SOUTHAMPTON II (qv) - but still listed 06.22. Ex PEARL. Ex steam lch 87, was at Naval ordnance depot Bombay, Cd for disciplinary purposes, all personnel on E Indies Sta not in seagoing ships, including Stores and Wireless Sta Staff

JUNO (1844) Ports, Police Ship
6th Rate, Police Ship 1865 - renamed MARINER (qv) 1878, renamed ATALANTA TS 1878, lost 12.02.1880

JUNO Normandy, HQ Beach Area (NP 1568)
Cd 06.06.1944 - at Courseilles ceased to operate 0800, 12.09.44
Nom DS: Yt LETNER(1936) 06.06.44-09.44 (revert to LETNER)

JUPITER (1813) Dev, Troopship/Coal Hulk
4th Rate, troopship Plym 1819 - coal hulk Dev 04.1846 till BU 1870

JUPITER (1833) Dev, Coal Hulk
FORTH, 5th Rate, renamed JUPITER coal hulk 12.1869, sold 04.08.1883

JUPITER (1895) Tyne/Dev, DS
BB, Tlr DS Tyne v ST GEORGE 12.1914 - 02.15 rb ST GEORGE. To Archangel 02.15. Accom sh Dev 22.12.1916, was to go to Scapa Flow v ZARIA but cancelled. A/P Stores ship Dev 03.18-05.18, refit Dev 05.18, was to replace ESSEX 08.18 but cancelled. Accom sh Dev 11.18-05.19. Sold 01.20

JUPITER Gareloch, RF
Cd 01.07.1950 - previously known as RF Clyde. PO 06.09.57 at Faslane (in lists to 1959)
SO RF in BUCHAN NESS 1954-, WOOLWICH 1955-
Nom DS: MSPB 44317 1950-59

JUSTITIA Woolwich, Prison Ship
1) ZEALAND, Dutch 3rd Rate, seized 1796, hbr serv 05.1803, renamed JUSTITIA 19.08.1812, sold 02.11.1830
2) HINDOSTAN (1804) 4th Rate, renamed DOLPHIN 22.09.1819, renamed JUSTITIA 1830 convict ship, sold 24.10.1855

JUTLAND (1946) Chat, Living Ship
DD, living ship 12.1950, BU 05.65

K

KAHU Russell Is, Solomon Is, RNZN Base
Cd 01.04.1944 - 04.47
Nom DS: ML 400 01.04.44-

KAI (1926) Store Carrier & Repair Ship
Whaler, hired as M/S 08.07.1940, to be M/S Store Carrier & Repair ship v. BORDE 12.1943. Naples 04.45 - resto 05.46

KALUGU - spelt KALUGA in some lists, Cochin, India, RNAS
Cd 01.02.1945, independent command, acs GARUDA, Under GARUDA until 01.04.46. PO 01.08.46 - retard party in BAMBARA to 09.09.46
Aircraft erection depot
Nom DS: EUREKA MB J944 01.02.44-

KALYANI Vishakhapatnam, IN Hospital
Listed 1971-76

KAPTAI Kaptai, Bengal, Bangladesh Naval Base
1989 - this is place name entered in error -see SHAHEED MOAZAAM

KARAKARA (1926) Sydney, New South Wales, RAN Base Ship
Taken up 27.02.1941, purch 07.41, Cd 14.10.41, to Darwin 11.41, Aux BD Vessel, Sydney 1950-02.72, sunk as target 1973

KARDIP Andaman Is, Nicobar, NOIC - IN
12.1974(at least)-1976

KARONGO see KORONGO

KARSAZ (1930) Karachi, RPN TS
HINDUSTAN, RIN Sloop, renamed KARSAZ RPN 14.08.1948 and hulked as Mechanical TE, BU 1951. Called KARSAZ II in one ref.

KARSAZ Karachi, PN Electrical & Mechanical TE
1958-73

KATE LEWIS (1916) Alexandria, Flag
Tlr, purch as M/L 08.1916, wore Flag Rear Admiral Alexandria when hauled down 01.08.1936. Sold 1939

KATHIWAR Nairobi, Kenya
In several lists including one of WRNS abroad KATHIAWAR was RIN M/S 1942

KATHIWAR Okha, India
Listed 1974

KEDAH (1927) CF Base/Accom Sh/HQ (NP 2442)
Spore, Cd 25.05.1940 as Aux A/S and AA vessel - Local Defence Flot. C & M 07.01.42-03.42. Arrive Trinco 16.03.42 - to be temp mobile DS pending UK refit 06.43. retained Eastern Fleet as overflow accom sh Trinco 09.43, and as CF Base to 12.04.44. Chittagong 04.44-. Cd 08.45 as W/T Base Ship for E Indies and as accom sh for NOIC of captured port before suitable accom available ashore. Spore

as Flag FO Malaya - Flag hoisted 05.09.45 (NP 2442). To be released on completion of task (10.45), Arrive UK 02.12.45 - conv to trade at Barrow, PO 11.02.46, to DST 14.02.46

KELANTAN (1921) M/S DS
Hired as A/P vessel 18.12.1941 Spore. Arrived Ceylon 16.03.42, PO 22.12.42. Conv to A/S and M/S Maint & Instructional Ship Woolwich. Cd as M/S Store & Repair Ship 17.01.44. Solent 06.44, Ports 07.44-09.44, HK 12.45, PO and to DST 24.09.46

KEMPENFELT (1943) Chat/Simonstown, SO RF
DD, SO RF Chat to 12.46 rb KENT, SO RF Simonstown 11.51. Sold to Yugoslavia 10.56

KENT (1798) Dev, Sheer Hulk
3rd Rate, Sheer Hulk 1856 till BU 1881

KENT (1810) Dev, Accom Sh
IMPREGNABLE (qv) TS 1862, renamed KENT 09.11.1888, for use in epidemics, renamed CALEDONIA (qv) 22.09.1891, sold 1906

KENT (1926) RF Flag
Cr, Flag FOCRF 21.10.1945 v SCARBOROUGH - in Gareloch 1945 - 13.10.46 (offices FOCRF in Vintry House, Queen St Place, E4 10.45) rb MULL OF GALLOWAY as SO RF Clyde - temp relief as FOCRF 04.09.46-11.46 was LONDON. At Chat 04.11.46-13.07.47 rb AUSONIA, also SO RF Chat v KEMPENFELT 12.46, sold 01.48

KENT (1961) Ports, TS
DD, facilities ship Ports 1971 v VOLAGE, alongside TS at Whale Is v DIAMOND 07.80, rb BRISTOL (qv) 22.03.1993, sold for BU 09.1997

KENYA (1939) Rosyth, Accom Sh
Cr, accom sh CO RF 12.1953-55, BU 10.62

KESTREL Worthy Down, Nr Winchester, RNAS/ General Serv Estab
Cd 24.05.1939 ex RAF. C & M 31.03.48, Cd 01.04.48 as General Service Estab (CICERO (qv) to KESTEL 19.04.48), PO to C & M 09.01.50, PO 01.07.52 - became ARIEL (qv)
Included airfields at: Bush Barn 01.08.44-45; Haslemere; Jersey (03.40-31.05.40); Somerford; Thorney Is (1940-48).
Nom DS: Hbr Serv Lch 3546 24.05.39-06.52
TRSB 43779(ex ARIEL) to 07.52 (became ARIEL)

KESTREL II
Listed 06.1944 - prob one of airfields under KESTREL - there was a small vessel KESTREL III

KHANJAR Varvosa, Bombay, RIN New Entry TE
By 06.44, tng ceased 1944, buildings occupied by HAMLA (qv) on tx from Mandapam 04.44. Still listed 12.04.45 - In Post Office circulars 22.03.44 and 09.05.45

KILELE Tanga, Tanganyika, RNAS
Cd 01.10.1942, 01.01.44 to C & M, PO 31.05.44 C & M parties to barracks, PO 30.06.45
See also TANA.
Nom DS: MB SWAN 01.10.42-

KILLARNEY (1893) Rosyth, Accom Sh
Hired as accom sh & to Rosyth 13.06.1940 - 13.08.46 when PO and to DST.
Part of COCHRANE to 02.46, rb DODMAN POINT/GIRDLE NESS

KILLINGHOLME (1912) Kite Balloon DS
Paddle Steamer, hired as Fleet messenger WWI, and as Kite Balloon Servicing Vessel 05.1941. PO 20.07.44. by 12.44 in C & M and released to DST 04.12.44

KILORAN (1930) Dartmouth. Accom Sh
Yt, hired on examination serv 11.1939, laid up 1941. CF accom sh 12.08.41-44 (for 15th MGB Flot & Inshore Patrol Flot) rb WESTWARD HO (qv). Lent USN 12.44-06.45, then laid up in C & M

KING ALFRED Hove Battery, Hove, Sussex/Exbury, TE
Ex RNVR HQ 14.09.39 - Res closed 10.39. Drill Hall became FORWARD (qv). South Victoria Tce in use as TE by 04.1940 - 07.01.46 (tx to Exbury House)
07.01.1946-08.46 at Exbury, poss called KING ALFRED II (qv) - became HAWKE (qv)
TE for temp RNVR Officers, over 48,000 passed through.
By 03.1943 there were various sections:
KING ALFRED (H) - Main Building, Kingsway, Hove
KING ALFRED (L) - Lancing College, Shoreham by Sea
KING ALFRED (M) - Mowden Sch,The Droveway, Hove
Nom DS: MB 1649 (Sussex Div RNVR) 14.09.39-11.45
Vessel named D'SEL by 11.1941-24.11.45(prob same as above)
HL(P) 42581 11.45-05.46

KING ALFRED II Mowden Sch, TE
1940-1944 (and in NL 10.45)
By 03.43 name KING ALFRED (M) was used instead of KING ALFRED II

KING ALFRED Exbury, Nr Southampton, TE
07.01.46 - tng moved from KING ALFRED, Hove, to 06.46, then closed, PO 05.08.46 and re-opened 10.08.46 as HAWKE (qv)

KING ALFRED Whale Is, Ports, RNR Tng Centre
Opened 01.04.1994, Cd 08.06.94. extant 1999
Opened on closure of SUSSEX and WESSEX (qv)

KING ALFRED II Hove,
When KING ALFRED moved from Hove to Exbury 07.01.46, Hove became KING ALFRED II, PO 06.46

KING ARTHUR Oslo, Norway, RN Base (NP 2030)
Cd 21.05.1945 - 07.06.1945 (to RNoN) - revert to NP 2030
NP 1736 was FO Norway - HQ left 82 Ashley Gdns 07.06.45,
Nom DS: Ex German ML 54249

KING BORS Kristiansand, Norway, RN Base (NP 2031)
Cd 14.05.1945, PO 19.07.45 - reverted to NP 2031
Nom DS: Ex German Patrol Boat

KING GEORGE V (1911) Ports/Dev, RF
BB, Vice Admiral RF 1919-20 rb CONQUEROR temp 01.11.1919-16.12.19, seagoing TS Portland 1923, turret drl Sh & tender to IMPREGNABLE 26.11.23-26, sold 12.26

KING GEORGE V (1939) Portland, TS
BB, TS v HOWE 11.1947 - 06.09.49, BU 1958

KING MARK Stavanger, Norway, RN Base (NP 2032)
14.05.45 - PO 31.07.45, reverted to NP 2032

KING MELIODAS Bergen, Norway, RN Base, (NP 2033)
Cd 24.05.1945, PO 26.07.45, To RNoN, reverted to NP 2033
RNO Bergen closed 30.08.45
Nom DS: Ex German Hbr craft

KING PELLINORE Trondheim, Norway, RN Base (NP 2034)
Cd 01.06.1945 - 31.07.45, to RNoN, reverted to NP 2034
Nom DS: Ex Luftwaffe Lch

KINGFISHER (1845) Dev, Hbr serv
Brig, laid up 1852, attached IMPREGNABLE at Dev 1875 till sold 26.04.1890

KINGFISHER (Great) Yarmouth, A/P Base
Cd 23.08.1915 v MUIRA, base amalgamated with Lowestoft 20.09.1919 and closed 30.11.1919 - acs to PEMBROKE IV.
Nom DS: Tlr KINGFISHER(1915) ex ALCYON - purch 1915 - renamed ADELE 15.06.1918
Drifter ADELE (1915) 15.06.18-07.02.19
Tlr DOROTHY F 08.02.19-04.19
Hbr Lch 186 04.19-

KINGS Halifax, Nova Scotia, RCN Officers' TE
Cd 01.10.1941, on move of Officers' TE from STADACONA ex STADACONA III to university of Kings' College Halifax, to 19.05.45 (final parade). PO 31.05.45

KINGSCLIFFE Rosyth, Accom Sh
1990

KINGSMILL (1943) Normandy, Temp HQ Ship
DD Escort, Normandy 06.44, returned USN 07.45

KINGSTON Kingston, Jamaica, Bathing Place
Ex Slaver CORTES capt 1858, sunk as bathing place at Kingston, BU 03.1867

KINGSWEAR CASTLE Dartmouth, Accom Sh
Req 07.08.1941 - released 13.09.1941

KINNARD HEAD (1944) see MULL OF GALLOWAY

KIPANGA Killindini, Kenya, RNAS
Cd 01.06.1942, PO 31.03.1944
Depot for RN Air Personnel ashore in E Africa/RN Aircraft Yard. Included Voi, Pt Reitz, Mackinnon Rd .
Nom SL: NAB GLOSSINA 01.06.42-

KIPANGA II Voi., Pt Reitz, Mackinnon Rd, RNAS
Voi (in C & M 11.44), Pt Reitz (RAF Airfield - to C & M 1945), and Mackinnon Rd (to C & M 15.05.44) were developed 09.1942.

KISSY Freetown, Sierra Leone?
Ment - poss a place name rather than a ship name

KNOCK JOHN FORT Thames Estuary, Fort No 4
Cd 16.07.1942, tender to BADGER, 01.08.42 tender to WILDFIRE. Poss to C & M 06.45, in NL 1947 with no apps

KONGONI Durban, Base
Cd 01.11.1942 ex AFRIKANDER IV (qv). PO 31.01.1946. Re-Cd 01.02.46 independent command, acs AFRIKANDER, PO 31.05.46
Also included section at SAAF Air Sta Stamford Hill - reported Cd 31.03.44-PO 31.01.46 (see KONGONI II)
Nom DS: Sullage Lighter No 382 01.11.42-

KONGONI II Durban, S Africa
07.45
Was this the Stamford Hill Airfield - see KONGONI above ?

KOOLUNGA Gorleston, Gt Yarmouth
Ment

KOOMPARTOO (1922) Sydney, New South Wales, RAN Base Ship
Purch 1942, PO Darwin 1945, Sudney 1950 - sold 08.06.62, BU 1966

KOOPA Melbourne, RAN Mobile DS
12.04.1945-12.45

KORONGO Nairobi, Kenya, RN Aircraft Repair Yd
Cd 01.09.1942, PO to C & M 01.10.1944 - but in NL to 1947
Spelt KARONGO in some lists
Known locally as Eastleigh, but name altered to avoid confusion with Eastleigh, England.
Nom DS: 28ft MB TEWA (HC3) 01.09.42-03.44
MFV ANGEL (No HC 12) 03.44-

KOSMOS (1916) Le Havre, A./P DS
Tlr, hired 1916-19, A/P DS 01.07.1917 when Le Havre became independent of VICTORY - 08.1919 (at least)

KREDEMNON Weymouth College, Weymouth, Degaussing Estab
Cd 01.06.1940, PO 12.07.40

Cdr and 400 men. Name came from Greek for Magic Circle
Nom DS: Hbr Lch 251 to 11.07.40

KUDAT (1914) Pt Swettenham, Base Ship
Aux vessel 06.1941, sunk 30.12.41 by air attacks while fitting out as Base Ship for coastal force (Roseforce)

KUNJALI Bombay, IN Estab (Detention Quarters & Regulating Sch)
Listed 1969-76

KUPARU (1940-4) New Zealand, Museum Ship
Ex PEGASUS, Ex P3563, Ex HDML 1348, Museum Ship 1988 on

KURANDA Cairns, Queensland, RAN Base
08.05.1944 - 02.01.45
Nom DFS: ALC 15, Tlr LUCY STAR 08.05.44-02.01.45

KUTCHING BASE Kutching, Sarawak, RMN Base
By 10.1969 - 1971 (at least)

KUTTABUL (1922) Sydney, New South Wales, DS
Ferry, RAN DS Cd 26.02.1941, tender to PENGUIN, sunk by midget SM Sydney 31.05.42. Wheelhouse on parade ground of next KUTTABUL 1994

KUTTABUL Potts Pt, Garden Island, Sydney, New South Wales, Depot
Cd 01.01.1943 ex PENGUIN, renamed when Balmoral Naval Barracks Cd as PENGUIN (qv). Shore base for dockyard personnel and staff of Rear Admiral in Charge Sydney. Extant 1999
Main barracks and admin block opened 1966
Nom DS: OTTER

KUTTABUL II Sydney, New South Wales, RAN, Captain of the Port
21.03.1960-01.04.71

L

LA FLORE (1935) A/S TS
Fr DD at Ports till 1941 then used for Tng. A/S TS 08.43. In res Hartlepool 05.44, to Fr 1945

LA HULLOISE (1943) Halifax, Nova Scotia, RCN Depot & Accom Sh
FF, depot and accom sh 12.1949, re-Cd 1949, BU 1966

LABUAN East Malaysia, Base
1978

LABURNAM Spore, Drl Sh
1) Sloop (1915) res drl Sh - Straits settlement 1935, arrived 30.03.35, lost 02.42 at Spore - PO 28.02.42
2) Ex Japanese WAKATAKA, M/L seized, renamed LABURNAM as drl Sh 09.1948 - 51
3) Malay RNVR Spore 1952-63 renamed SINGAPURA (qv) 22.09.1963

LACHLAN (1944) Devonport, New Zealand/Guam, RNZN Accom Sh
FF, RAN, lent RNZN as survey ship, tx 05.10.49. Accom Sh Devonport New Zealand 1974-09.93, Guam 09.93 - 03.94, then BU

LADAS (1918) Gosport, SM DS
Sloop, sold 1920, re-purch as mooring vessel Gosport 1920, DS 5 SM Gosport 1930 till sold 08.36

LADAS Poole, Accom Sh
01.1943, LEDA, Motor cruiser, accom sh (qv), renamed LADAS 01.43 at Poole. Acquired 30.04.43, laid up Lymington/DST 08.44, no longer required and for disposal 14.09.44

LADAVA Milne Bay, New Guinea, RAN Base
Cd 01.10.1943 - 30.10.45
Nom S: ML D Boat 111

LADBROKE Syracuse, Italy (NP 840)
09.1943. Codename for Sicilian port of Syracuse - Operation Husky. NP 840 - Party Ladbroke landed there 07.43. Fixed A/S Defences and Mobile Radar for the port used that name 06.43

LADY BLANCHE (1907) Tobermory, Accom Sh
Yt, hired WWI and 09.1939, accom sh 07.42-11.45

LADY GAY Chichester, Accom Sh
08.1942, acquired 24.12.42, laid up Lymington 05.45, no longer required/DST 28.06.45
Named as LADYE GAYE in some lists

LADYBIRD Sasebo, Japan, Base
Ex MV WUSUEH (China Nav Co) purch 08.1950, Base Ship Cd 23.08.1950 at HK for Sasebo v ALERT (which had been temp HQ ship) - PO 2400 10.04.53 rb TYNE 11.04.53. resto 13.05.53. HQ of Flag Officer Second in Command Far East Sta

LAGUNA BELLE (1896) Soton/Ryde, Isle of Wight, Accom Sh
Paddle steamer, hired 09.1939 - M/S then AA ship. To DST and as Accom Sh Soton 27.01.1944 for MN CO personnel. HQ ship Mulberry Whale Section Solent 06.44, Ryde 10.44-06.45.

LAIRDS ISLE (1911) Torp Sch Ship
Hired as Armed Boarding Vessel 28.08.1939 for the Downs - fitted out Lpool. Sch ship 1940 - LSI(H) 12.43-06.46

LANCASHIRE (1917) Accom Sh for Dockyard Labour
Conv to dockyard accom sh 06.1944 - 08.45 Fleet Train accom Sh Far East, 09.12.45 Colombo enroute Hong Kong, 01.46 no longer required

LANDBREEZE MOLCAB 6
Cd 1945, PO 1946

Name allocated 11.44 - had not been authorised by 08.45 (no longer required). One account reports name not used - Book of reference on MOLCABs indicates it was a "spare name"

LANDGUARD (1930) Colombo, Ceylon, Base
Ex US Coast Guard cutter SHOSHONE, lent RN 1941. Accom sh Colombo 04.45 (machinery in poor condition). DS Colombo 07.45. Flag E Indies 1946. Sold 09.49 - tow to Spore then Manilla 10.49.

LANDLINE MOLCAB 4
Name allocated 11.44. Formed in DRAGONFLY. By 08.45 was NP 2403 - not Cd but assembling in UK for Spore. By 24.09.45 listed as disbanded.

LANDLOCK Cochin/Spore, MOLCAB 2
Formed in DRAGONFLY, Cd 01.06.1945 from NPs 2401 and 4288. Enroute Cochin 03.45. At Cochin 08.45, then to Spore - Blakang Mati Island. PO 15.12.45
Nom DS: Tug TANAC 112 01.06.45-

LANDMARK MOLCAB 5
Name allocated 11.44. Formed in DRAGONFLY as NP 2404, Cd 1945-46. Date of Assembly reported as not yet know (08.45). No longer required 23.08.45. One account says it was not used

LANDRAIL Campbeltown, RNAS
Civil airport Campbeltown req by Air Ministry for Admiralty for TSR spring/summer 1940 under MERLIN. Named 18.12.1940, Cd 01.04.41, renamed LANDRAIL II (qv) when Machrihanish became parent 15.06.41

LANDRAIL Strabane/Machrihanish, Argyllshire, RNAS
Name approved 18.12.1940, but temp allocated to site at Campbeltown (see previous entry). Cd 15.06.1941 - Campbeltown then became LANDRAIL II as satellite. 08.41 name Strabane was replaced by Machrihanish (known by sailors as "Bag 'n 'ammick). 12.1942 RAF no longer required facilities. PO to C & M 16.04.46 (3 mths notice). Re Cd 17.04.46 as tender to SANDERLING Re Cd 01.12.51. Closed to flying 10.09.52, to C & M 01.12.52 - under SANDERLING. Used by Fleet Requirements Unit 1958, PO and tx to Air Ministry 27.05.63
Nom DS: MB SILVER MOON 15.06.41-08.02.42
MB 40212 09.02.42-
TRSB 43782 01.12.51-

LANDRAIL II Campbeltown, RNAS
15.06.1941 - 1945 ex LANDRAIL (qv)

LANDSEER Antwerp/Hayling Is, MOLCAB 3
Formed in DRAGONFLY, Cd 25.,.02.1945, PO 10.08.45 - disbanded at DRAGONFLY by 11.08.45
NP 2402 - at Borehem, Nr Antwerp by 04.45
Nom DS: MSPB RN 2690

LANDSWELL Trinco, Ceylon, Cochin/Spore. MOLCAB 1
Formed in DRAGONFLY, Cd 25.03.1945, PO 01.04.1946
Trinco location could refer to Nom DS only. NP 2400 at Cochin by 03.45. Later to Spore at Naval Base Sick Quarters and Leyang, Spore by 11.45
Nom DS: Tug TANAC 150 25.03.45-

LANKA Colombo/Trinco, Ceylon, Base
01.04.1940 ex GLOUCESTER II (qv), PO 31.10.1946 - acs to HIGHFLYER
Included RNAS China Bay (from 01.08.1940) and Puttalam (from 11.42 - see RAJALIYA). Flag Ceylon 1945
Nom DS: MB 1160 01.04.40-
45 ft Service Lch 37273 10.08.46-31.10.46

LANKA I Ceylon, Accounting Base (Personnel ashore & RMs)
02.1945 - 02.46 (at least)

LANKA II Ceylon, Accounting Bas
02.1945 - 15.02.46 (acs to LANKA I 31.01.46)
Accs of Escort Forces and other seagoing vessels, East Indies. RN Personnel Rangoon from 12.45.

LANKA III Ceylon, Accounting Base
02.1945 - 04.1946
General Service transit personnel and Fleet Pool

LANKA HQ Volunteer Naval Forces Royal Ceylon Navy
1955-1967

LANSDOWNE Sydney, Nova Scotia, RCN A/P DS
16.05.1917 - 30.11.1917 and 01.05.1918-10.12.1918 (APV ex Coast Guard Ship LANSDOWNE)

LAOMEDON (1912) Aden, DS
Chartered as Boom DS 03.08.1939, req 19.03.40, Cd 01.08.40. reported as acting as DS Aden 07.41. Own acs by 01.01.42. For resto 27.08.45, to DST 02.11.45

LAPWING (1785) Milford, Rx Sh
6th Rate, Rx Sh 1813 till BU 1828

LARGS (1938) Bizerta, Tunisia, HQ
Fr AMC CHARLES PLUMIER, seized 22.11.1940 and renamed LARGS as LS 1941. 09.1943 C-in-C Med set up operational HQ onboard in Bizerta - Administrative HQ at Algiers - 10.1945 allocated for C & M, PO 09.12.1945 at Le Havre.

LATONA (1890) Kingstown/Salonika/ Corfu/Malta GC, Drl Sh/M/L-SM DS/ Accom Sh
Cr, SM DS 1902-03 (Home Waters), Res Drl Sh Kingstown 1905, M/L 05.1907, A/P DS Salonika 01.1918-07.1918 rb ST GEORGE, Corfu 05.1918 - PO at Malta 23.12.1918 (Corfu base closed). Overflow ship Malta 1919-20, sold 12.1920

LAURUS Loop Repair Ship
Cd 19.12.1944

LAVATERA (1913) Inverness, A/P Base
Cd 01.06.1917 v THALIA, Base closed 15.10.1919

1) LAVATERA, Drifter, hired 03.1915, Cd 15.05.1915-20 and WWII
2) EFFORT (1907) Drifter. - PO 12.08.1919
3) MB DART from 12.08.1919

LAVINIA (1806) Lpool/Dev, Qtn/Coal hulk
5th Rate, Qtn Sh Lpool 1836-1845, coal hulk Dev by 1852 - sunk by collision 1868

LAVINIA (1847) Dev, Coal Hulk
SEAHORSE, 5th Rate, coal hulk Dev by 1857, renamed LAVINIA 05.05.1870 - sold 1902

LAWFORD (1943) Normandy, Temp LS HQ Ship
DD escort, sunk by air attack 08.06.1944 at Normandy

LAWSON Tilbury, Accom Tender
07.1943-

LE VOLONTAIRE see INGENIEUR CACHIN

LEANDER (1882), DS
Cr/Despatch Vessel, DS 1904, Med 1904-05, Atlantic 1905, Nore 1906, Dev 1907-14. Tlr DS Humber/Flamborough Head 09.1914 - 12.14 rb PEKIN, Grand Fleet (Scapa Flow) 1914-1919 -DS 3 DF Granton 01.1918-30.06.1918 rb WOOLWICH, Immingham DS 20 DF 30.06.18-03.19. For C & M 09.1919, PO Dev 18.12.1919 for disposal, sold 1920

LEDA (1828) Dev, Police Hulk
5th Rate, police hulk 05.1864 till sold 05.1906

LEDA Ports, Accom Sh
By 08.1942, motor cr, accom sh Ports, renamed LADAS (qv) 01.1943

LEDSHAM (1954) Clyde, Res Accom Sh
M/S, Clyde RNR Accom Sh 1967, sold 1971

LEEUWIN Fremantle, RAN Base
01.08.1940 ex CERBERUS V (qv) - RANVR depot. PO 11.11.1986 (tx to Army)
Nom DS: MB 179 04.43-
Aux Schooner 06.45-11.45

LEIGH Southend-on-Sea, Base
Cd 01.10.1941 acs PEMBROKE IV - had been under PEMBROKE IV from 09.1939. PO 31.10.1945, acs to WILDFIRE and PEMBROKE IV Southend Pier was used as assembly point for convoys from 09.1939. Also included WRNS Signals Unit, Hampton, Beehive Lane, Gt Baddow, Chelmsford (09.43) and NP Holehaven Creek (1944). Used Palace Hotel and later 3 houses in Royal Terrace
Nom DS: Tug WEMO 01.10.41-31.08.45

LEIGH II Southend-on-Sea, Base
Prob an accounting section

LEONIDAS (1807) Upnor, Gun Cotton Ship
5th Rate, became gun cotton ship Upnor 1872, sold 04.08.1907

LEONIDAS Corfu, United States Navy DS
08.1918

LEONIDAS Takoradi, Gold Coast, Base
Cd 26.01.1942. PO 20.07.45

LETNA (1936) - also spelt LETNER
Purch as Hbr Defence Patrol Craft 25.10.1939, was Nom DS JUNO (qv) 06.06.1944. 01.45 allocated NP 1731 - FO Holland and then Nore Pool, sold 07.46

LEVEN (1813) Chat/Woolwich/ Limehouse, London, Convict/Rx Sh
6th Rate, Hbr Serv 1827, convict ship Chat 1831-, Woolwich by 1840, Limehouse by 1845, Rx Sh 1848, BU 07.1848

LEVIATHAN (1790) Ports, Convict Sh
3rd Rate, Convict Ship 1816, target 1846, sold 1848

LEVIATHAN (1901) West Indies, A/P Parent (MLs)
Cr, Flag North America & W Indies 10.03.,1916-19, as such acted as A/P Parent rb EILEEN (qv) by 06.1917. Bu 1920

LEYDENE - ment in a list, but prob name of location - see MERCURY

LIFFEY (1856) Coquimbo, Chile, Store & DS
FF, store hulk Coquimbo 1877, sold 04.1903 - stores to Esquimalt

LILY (1837) Ports, Coal Hulk
Brig, coal hulk 1860, later C29, later C15, sold 07.04.1908

LIMOSA Loop Repair Vessel
Cd 03.11.1944-

LION (1777) Sheerness, Sheer Hulk
3rd Rate, sheer hulk 1816, sold 1837

LION (1847) Clyde/Dev, CG/Boys' TS
2nd Rate, CG Clyde 01.07.1864 - 08.1868, Boys' TS Dev 1871. Sold 11.07.1905. Joined by IMPLACABLE (qv) 1871

LION (1910) Rosyth, SO RF
BCr, SO RF 1921 v NEW ZEALAND - PO 30.05.1922, sold 01.24

LIVELY (1813) Dev, Rx Sh
5th Rate, Rx h 1831 till sold 04.1862

LIVERPOOL (1937) Ports, Accom Sh
Cr, RF living ship 12.1953 - SORF, task to VANGUARD 17.12.56, BU 07.58

LIZARD Shoreham, CO (LC) Base
Cd 07.10..1942 independent command, C & M 21.10.1945, closed completely 31.12.1945
Haslemere Hotel, Hove and others. Accom & LCP Maint Base John Brown's Wharf & LCT Hard Shoreham.
Nom DS: Yt MINERVA III (1935) 07.10.42-03.45
NAB BRITISHER 03.45-09.07.45

27ft whaler No 826 09.07.45-

LLANDUDNO (1940) Lowestoft, TS
M/S Cd as TS for Engineer Officers based on Lowestoft 11.45, for disposal 03.46, sold 08.05.47

LOBSTER (1915) White Sea, DS for Up River Transport Vessels
07.1919 v CYCLOPS II/PRESIDENT VI - PO 15.10.1919 - acs to Ministry of Shipping Lighter/oil Barge

LOCH ARKAIG (1945) Hartlepool, RF HQ
FF, RF HQ on setting up 22.09.1952-1955 rb WEAR, sold 1960

LOCH GORM (1944) Dev RF Living Ship
FF, Living Ship 11.1951, sold 09.1961

LOCH TRALAIG (1945) Jackson Dock, West Hartlepool, RF HQ
FF, RF HQ W Hartlepool v WEAR 09.1956-06.62, BU 08.63

LOCHAILORT Inverailort Castle, Nr Inverness, CO Sch for Boat Oficers
Cd 24.08.1942, PO 31.01.45
Nom DS: 15ft Tlr skiff 24.08.42-

LOCHINVAR Pt Edgar/Granton, DD-M/S Base
DD depot, moved ashore from COLUMBINE (qv) 09.1917. Land purch 10.1920. To C & M 1929-30. M/S Tng Base from Portland Cd 21.11.1939. Operational M/S Base 01.41. Moved to Granton & Cd 25.10.43. returned Pt Edgar 01.03.46. During 10.43-03.46 Pt Edgar was renamed HOPETOUN (qv). Relieved as Base by COCHRANE 01.01.48. PO 29.02.48. Re-Cd as M/S Trials estab 29.02.48. Cd 01.09.51 as independent command. M/S task to VERNON 03.1956. In 1958 absorbed buildings ex TEMERAIRE and v COCHRANE as accom for ships refitting at Rosyth. From 19.03.63 was base for Fishery Protection Vessels. PO 01.09.75, became tender to COOCHRANE. 16.11.75 ceased as independent command - closed by mid 12.75
Nom DS: Hbr Lch 230 21.11.39-
MSPB 43917 03.53-62

LOCHINVAR II Granton/Pt Edgar, Accounting Base
1946 Granton. 1946-57 Pt Edgar

LOCUST (1939) Normandy/Holland/ Bristol, HQ ship/ Res Drl Sh
Gunboat, temp LS HQ Ship Normandy 1944, Harwich 05.45, Holland 05.45-07.06.45, Res 07.45, additional Drl Sh Bristol 20.09.1951 - sold 05.06.68, BU Newport

LOFOTEN (1945) Malta GC/Portland/ Rosyth, Support Ship
LST 3027, named 1947. PO to Res 11.12.1947 Res Malta 1949. Living Ship & SO RF to 11.51. Accom Sh Malta 1958-61. RF Ports 1962. Conv to Helicopter Support Ship Dev and Cd for Portland 23.06.1964 - 30.06.67, then RF Dev. To Rosyth 03.70 for conv to refit Support Ship - in use 1970-76. Support for Nuclear SM refit Rosyth 1982-, tow to Belgium for BU 10.1993

LONDON (1840) Zanzibar, Storeship
2nd Rate, storeship Zanzibar 04.1874 till sold 1884

LONDON (1899) Dev, RF Parent
BB, accom sh Dev Cd 01.01.1918 - C & M by 03.18, RF Gp 2 Parent Dev 01.1919 - sold 04.06.1920

LONDON (1921) Weymouth, Guardship
See HOLDFAST

LONDON (1927) Nore, FO Commanding RF
Cr, temp Flag v KENT at Chat 04.09.1946-11.46 rb KENT, BU 01.50.
LONDON ISTANBUL - see ALGOMA

LONDONDERRY (1958) Ports, Hbr Ts
FF, Hbr TS for SULTAN 1985-88, sunk as target 25.06.89

LONGSET Swansea, A/P Parent Bristol Channel
01.1916 v OMBRA - 06.02.1917 rb SHIKARI, formally PO 16.02.1917
Tlr (1914) hired 1915 and lost 06.02.1917

LONSDALE Melbourne, RAN Depot
1941 ex CERBERUS III (qv). Included Williamstown - PO 13.11.92 (as Res Depot)
Nom DS: Water Lighter MWL 256 1960s

LONSDALE II Melbourne?
1945-53 (at least)
Poss an accounting section

LORD LANSDOWNE (1913) Oban, Parent-W Coast Scotland & Hebrides Armed Yts for Special Service
19.09.1917 v GIBRALTAR - 12.1917 rb NESMAR II
Tlr hired 1916-1919

LORD WARDEN (1865) Queensferry, CG
BB, CG Queensferry 21.12.1876-07.09.1885, sold 02.1889

LORMONT (1927) Guardship
SS, req for contraband control, guardship The Downs Base 25.08.1939 - fitted out London 09.39, sunk in collision 07.12.40

LORNA DOONE (1891) Clyde, Accom Sh
Paddle steamer, hired WWI and as M/S 07.12.1939. AA Ship 05.42, accom sh 09.43 - allocated AFD IV, Clyde - released 13.04.1946

LOTUS Cowes, Isle of Wight/Hamble, Base Ship
Motor vessel, allocated as Base Ship at Cowes 28.09.1939. ML LOTUS replaced as DS Inner Patrol, Hamble by Yt MELISANDE (qv) 11.39 - prob same vessel

LOUISBURG Rosneath, Dunbartonshire, CO Base
Cd 15.04.1942. PO 03.08.1942 - renamed ROSENEATH (qv)

LOWENA Soton, Accom Sh

House Boat, by 08.1942, acquired 04.12.1942 - 10.44 (at least) - laid up Lymington/DST 11.01.45, for disposal 1946.

LOWESTOFT (1913) S Africa, Flag
Cr, Flag 01.1922, by 11.23 rb BIRMINGHAM, sold 01.1931
Tenders included Ascension Island

LOYAL (1941) Malta GC, Base Ship
DD, constructive total loss 12.10.1944, approved as accom sh Malta 05.01.1946, Base ship 01.46 - to C & M 14.08.1947, to BU 31.07.48

LUCIA (1907) SM DS
Capt 1914, conv to SM DS 1916, Cd 22.07.1916, Tees 10 SM 22.07.1916-12.18, Tees 7 SM 01.03.1919 - to Dev on return from Baltic 10.19. 2 SM Dev 07.12.19 - ready to sail for Med 19.09.22. Sail for Med from Ports 23/25.09.22-23. Portland 03.23. Ports 1923-25. Malta 02.25-10.26. PO Nore 12.26-06.27. 2 SM Dev 08.27-29, SM 1 Malta 1929, 2 SM Atlantic Fleet 1931, Home Fleet 1932-34, Malta 1935, Home Fleet 36-39 rb FORTH 05.39. 8 SM E Indies Cd 26.08.39 with balance of crew Merchant Navy. Left Bombay for Mesirah 30.08.39. To Colombo 04.40, SO Red Sea Force 29.06.40. Repair ship and accom sh Aden 08.40. Damaged Colombo Hbr 05.04.42. Durban to Kilindini 01.44. left Colombo for UK 11.45. Bombay 12.45. Dev 02.46 de-store. C & M 12.07.46, sold 09.46

LUCIFER Swansea, Base
Cd 01.11.1939. PO 31.03.46 - acs to DRAKE IV. Base closed 12.07.46
Name sel for comml pt 01.09.39, NOIC to arrive 23.08.39 with apps from 24..09.39. M/S Base Milford Haven tx to Swansea 16.07.45 (acs tx SKIRMISHER to LUCIFER 01.09.45). Base also included Cardiff (1944-45 at least), Avonmouth, Barry and Newport
Nom DS: NAB ZEPHYRA 01.11.39-20.11.41
NAB MERIDIES 21.11.41-09.10.42
Hbr Steam lch 311 10.42-02.46

LUPIN (1916) Ports, Accom Sh
Sloop, used as accom sh for boys 1939, dockyard riggers 1944, sold 22.03.46

LUSAIR Torokina, Solomon Is, RAN Base Staff
05.03.1945-20.10.1945

LUSITANIA Terceira, Azores, Base (NP 911)
Cd 08.10.1943, PO/close down complete by 01.09.1945
RNAS to be established at Lagens, Terceira 1944 but not progressed
Nom DS: SBNO Azores' Base Barge 08.12.43-

LUSITANIA II Fayal/Horta, Azores, base (NP 912)
Cd 08.10.1943, renamed HESPERIDES (qv) 08.10.1944
Nom DS: Sloop CHANTICLEER (1942) damaged 18.11.1943 and renamed 31.12.43 (LUSITANIA). BU 1945

LUSITANIA III Azores
1944 - prob an accounting section

LYNX Dover, Base
Cd 17.09.1939. Flag struck 10.07.1945, PO 30.11.1946
Name sel for comml pt 01.09.1939, Apps from 24.08.39
Included Dover College.
Nom DS: Picket Boat MB 332 17.09.39-

LYNX II Dover, LC Base
Cd 01.01.1945, PO as LC Base 09.08.1945

M

MACAW Wellbank, Cumberland, TE
Cd 17.11.1943 acs NIGHTJAR, 01.01.44 self accounting, PO 13.09.46 (to Ministry of Supply by 31.08.46)
Also described as RNAS Bootle Sta
Transit camp for FAA pilots enroute from Canada
Nom DS: Hbr Lch WAYFARER II
17.11.43-03.45
LUPIN II 08.03.45-13.09.46

MACHLIMAR Venduruthi/Versova, N of Bombay, RIN Torp & A/S Sch
Cd 28.12.1942, Cd 04.43, PO 30.11.46
Tng combined with RIN Signal Sch - see TALWAR.
Mechanical TE to 1944 then to SHIVAJI 01.44.
Also included Cooks' TE, Varsova, Bambay

MADANG Madang, New Guinea, RAN Base
01.10.1944 - 07.02.46

MADAGASCAR (1822) Dev/Rio de Janeiro, Storeship
5th Rate, store ship Dev 1850, Rio by 1862 - sold 05.05.1863

MADDALENA Sardinia, Out Station
Prob WWII - there was a CF Advanced base there 1943-44 - see Gazetteer - Mediterranean

MADH Madh, RIN No 1 Comb Tng Centre
02.1944 (was RN but tx to RIN by 02.44)-1945
Unclear in records whether name refers to ship/place/or both - prob place name

MADRAS (1942) Bombay, RIN SO RF
M/S, SO RF 02.1948, sold 1960

MAEANDER (1840) Weymouth/ Ascension Is, CG/Store ship
5th Rate, CG Weymouth 01.01.1857 - 31.01.1858, coal hulk 11.1859, store ship Ascension Is 1862, wrecked 07.1870

MAGA LIESBERG Transvaal, SAN Citizen Force Unit

MAGIC CIRCLE (1927) Scapa Flow, Mobile

Deperming Unit
Yt CREOLE, renamed 04.1941, at Scapa Flow 05.1941, resto 1946

MAGNETIC Townsville, Queensland, RAN Base
Cd 01.09.1942, PO 26.07.48 (in Pink List to 1956 - deleted 09.57)

MAGNIFICENT (1806) Ports/Jamaica, Hosp/Rx Sh
3rd Rate, Hbr Serv Ports 1819, Hosp & Store Sh Jamaica 1825 - Rx Sh Jamaica by 1828 - sold 1843

MAGNIFICENT (1894) Rosyth/Dev, Storeship/ Accom Sh
BB, Tlr DS 10.1914-12.14, Accom Sh Dev 03.03.16 - PO 08.08.17, then conv to ammo storeship at Belfast, Cd 12.11.18 at Rosyth, arrived Methil 17.11.18 as ammo hulk to 1920, sold 09.05.21

MAGPIE (1889) Ports/Soton, Yarmouth, Isle of Wight, DS
Gunboat, BD 1902, DS and Repair Ship Soton 03.1915 v HERMIONE (at Yarmouth, Isle of Wight) - PO 29.01.1919 to dockyard control R Hamble. Sold 29.12.21

MAGO N Africa, Base
Name approved for base in N Africa 23.12.1942 - to be Cd 01.01.43. Prob not used

MAH JONGG Poole, Accom Sh
08.1942 - laid up Lymington/DST 08.44, no longer required & for disposal 14.09.44

MAHELAH (1898) Gt Yarmouth, Accom Sh (see MIRANDA)
Yt, hired 03.1940 as accom sh v TARANSAY, laid up 09.45, sold 46

MAID MARION (1938) Bengal, A/P DS
Yt, hired 09.1939 for A/S Duties, SM tender 03.44, A/P DS 1945-46, HQ ship Bengal Aux Flot 06.45, for disposal 01.47

MAIDSTONE (1811) Ports, Rx Sh/Coal Hulk
5th Rate, Rx Sh 1832, coal hulk 1839-65, BU 1865

MAIDSTONE (1912) SM DS
8 SM Ports Cd 15.10.1912-14, Harwich 07.14 - 8SM & 9 SM Yarmouth/Harwich 06.16-12.18, Chat, 3 SM Harwich 01.03.19-30.06.19, Dev 01.07.19 - Ports 09.19-21. 3 SM Gib 22, Dev 1922-26, 2 SM Dev 11.26-PO 02.02.28, sold 31.08.29

MAIDSTONE (1937) SM DS/Accom - Prison Sh
Completed 1938. To Med 3 SM, 7 SM Freetown 10.1939, 3 SM Scapa Flow 03.40 v CYCLOPS 27.05.40 - DD DS rb TYNE 12.40, 3 SM v TITANIA 01.41, 8 SM Gib 16.03.41, Algiers 11.42, Alexandria 43, Trinco 03.44, Fremantle 16.09.44, Sydney, Subic Bay 20.05.45, HK 08.45, 8 SM lapsed 11.12.45. 7 SM Portland v CYCLOPS 17.09.46 & 2 SM 1946-58. Flag Home Fleet 20.08.56-31.03.58. Dockyard control 25.07.58 - Home Fleet and 2 SM to TYNE 11.04.58. Rebuilt Ports to 1962. Faslane 3 SM v ADAMANT Cd 01.05.62 - 01.68. 3 SM to shore 31.12.67 - see NEPTUNE. 24.01.68 to Rosyth then Belfast as accom sh/prison sh 1969-28.01.77. Sold 04.05.78

MAIDSTONE II Alexandria, Accounting Base
Med DDs acs opened as MAIDSTONE II 31.08.1939, acs of all personnel in Alexandria and Cairo, office in No 46 Shed, Madmoudiyeh Quay, Alexandria. Acs of TAMAR II to MAIDSTONE II 21.10.39. Name ship for personnel on her books became NILE 01.11.39 (qv). Still listed NL 1944

MAITLAND Newcastle, New South Wales, RAN Base
RANVR depot named 13.03.1942 (but Cd 01.08.1940) - 21.09.46
Nom DS: MOONGLO 04.43-
ML LORNE 19.03.45-08.45

MAJESTA (1899) Campbeltown, Accom Sh
Yt, purch 1940, Hbr defence, PO and laid up Inverness 07.1942. Accom sh for rescue tugs personnel Campbeltown 04.43-09.45, sold 1946

MAJESTIC (1853) Lpool, CG
2nd Rate, CG 01.02.1860 - 31.08.1864, BU 1868

MALABAR (1818) Ports, Coal Hulk
3rd Rate, coal hulk 10.1848, renamed MYRTLE (qv) 30.10.1883, sold 11.07.1905

MALABAR (1866) Bermuda, Rx Sh
Indian Troopship, at Bermuda as Rx Sh 1897, renamed TERROR (qv) as Base Ship 01.05.1901, sold 1918

MALABAR Bermuda/Palisadoes, Jamaica, Base
Cd 14.02.1919 v MUTINE at Commissioner's House (09.02.1914 by NL record) - 31.03.1951
ReCd 01.06.1965 at Moresby House, Ireland Island - tender to PRESIDENT, PO 31.03.1995
Included RAF Bermuda, tx to RN 24.05.1939, RNAS to C & M 01.02.1944; and Palisadoes, Jamaica - see BUZZARD. Absorbed Work Up Base SOMERS ISLES (qv) 04.43.
Nom DS: Steam Pinnace 19 14.02.1919-
Steam Pinnace 1921 - poss same vessel as above
Steam Lch/Pinnace 211 1932 - 01.39 (at least)
Steam Lch/Pinnace 211 12.10.45 -26.01.46
MB 44781 26.01.46-11.46
Motor M/S 223 (later 1723) 11.46-12.47
Hbr Lch 3510 by 02.48-51

MALABAR II Bermuda
Name used by pre WW II seaplane sta, discontinued 1940

MALABAR II Port of Spain, Trinidad, Base
Cd 01.08.1940
SNO Appointed to organise Port Patrol 08.1939. Base at Trinidad became GOSHAWK v MALABAR II 26.09.1940. When RNAS Cd as GOSHAWK, it absorbed the Base task.
ML Base Trinidad closed 24.07.1945

MALABAR III Bermuda
Name used by pre - WWII seaplane sta, discontinued 1940

MALABAR III Jamaica, Base
Base at Jamaica to 09.1940, when became BUZZARD (qv). BUZZARD became name of new RNAS Jamaica 21.12.40, which also absorbed the Base task

MALAGAS Wingfield/Wynberg, Nr Capetown, RNAS & RN Aircraft Repair Yard
Cd 01.07.1942 - ex Union Government Airfield.which was developed To C & M & PO 31.05.1946
Came under AFRIKANDER prior to 07.42. Absorbed RNAS Wynberg 18.05.1942.
Nom DS: Scott Payne Power Boat 38246 01.07.41-

MALAHAT Equimalt, British Columbia, RCN Res Div Victoria
15.01.1944 - 15.01.1946
23.04.1947-1986 (at least) - extant 05.97
Div to SAULT STE MARIE 05.53-01.55

MALAYA (1915) Ports. Accom Sh
BB, to C & M 30.12.1943, FO RF Clyde (new post) 15.01.1944-05.44, then ReCd for bombardment duties 06.44. With RAMILLES became tender to VERNON 15.05.45, both called VERNON (RAMILLES) (qv), later 05.45 both renamed VERNON II(qv). To C & M and Dockyard control by 12.47, sold 20.02.48

MALAYA Spore/Lumut Perak, Malay(si)a, RMN/Malaysian Base
RMN Barracks Woodlands became MALAYA 09.1958-1971, tx from Woodlands, Johore Str, Spore to Lumut 1981 - extant 1999

MALINES (1922) Kabret, TS
Hired as escort 11.1940, sunk 19.07.1942, salved 01.43. 02.44 in use as temp CO TS Kabret, resto 1944

MALLOW (1915) Melbourne, RAN Res Drl Sh
Sloop, to RAN 07.1919, Drl Sh 1925, dismantled 07.1932

MALTA Plym, DS
2nd Rate, capt 1800, DS 1836, BU 1840

MAMARI (1911) DS
Hired 10.09.1939 as DS and refitted Belfast, but became dummy carrier HERMES and sunk 04.06.1941

MANATEE Yarmouth, Isle of Wight, LC Base
Cd 15.11.1942, independent command, acs OSBORNE, approved to PO 09.1944
Norton & Savoy Camps
Nom DS: NAB WHITE HEATHER 15.11.42-07.45

MANCHESTER CITY (1937) Home Waters/E Indies, Controlled Mining Base Ship (also MNBDO)
Hired as Minelaying Base Ship 1939, req for service with MNBDO 09.39, Cd as Controlled Mining Base Ship 20.12.1940. Repairs 1941. To E Indies as independent command 27.12.1941, at Kilindini 05.42, PO and de-store Glasgow 28.07.45, resto 07.03.46

MANCO (1908) Stornoway, A/P DS
Hired as supply Ship 10.12.1914, Cd 12.14, refit Lpool then A/P DS 01.01.15 v VANESSA - 26.09.1915 rb IOLAIRE. PO 04.10.1915

MANDOVI Goa, IN Seaman's TE
12.1974-01.1975-(at least)

MANELA (1921) Iceland, Accom Sh/Base Ship
Hired as seaplane DS 1939 - independent command. DS Floatplanes under DAEDALUS 05.40. To RAF Coastal Command 17.06.40 as accom sh, Base Ship iceland for Sunderlands 1941

MANILLA Yokohama, Japan, Stores Depot
Ex INGEBURG, taken over 28.02.1870, store and victualling depot Yokohama, sold 14.08.1872

MANIPUR DD DS
Fitted out 1916 - see SANDHURST

MANORBIER CASTLE (1898) Scapa Flow, Officers' Accom Sh
Tlr, accom sh by 07-1917-09.1918, for resto Grimsby 07.1919

MANTIS/MANTIS II Caspian Sea, DS
To 31.12.1918 rb THESEUS
MANTIS (1915) River Gunboat, sold 20.01.1940

MANTIS Lowestoft, CF Base
Cd 26.07.1942 ex MINOS II (qv), PO 30.06.1945
Nom DS: NAB ELVIN 28.08.42-30.06.45

MANXMAID (1910) TS
Hired as radar TS 10.1941, but not conv. Ex CAESAREA, ex MANXMAID, ex BRUCE (qv) - renamed MANXMAID by 12.41 as TS . Conv to ALC carrier 07.42, resto 1945

MANXMAN (1940) Spore, M/S DS
M/L, RF living ship Sheerness 1948-to 12.1950, conv at Chat to DS for M/S 17.07.61-02.63. Spore 1963-68, Ports 12.12.68. Conv as TS for Engineer Officers 02.69-05.69, TS at Dev 1968-09.70 rb CAPRICE, BU 06.10.72

MANZANITTA (1911) Taranto/Brindisi, Base for Net Drifters
10.1915 v EGMONT - 09.1916
Drifter, wrecked 06.09.1916

MAORI London, RNZN HQ in UK
01.04.1949 ex COOK, listed to 1967, then staff under WAKEFIELD
Nom DS: ML 35701959

MARAGA Addu Atoll, Base/RNAS
Cd 01.02.1944, 10.12.45 to C & M. Base closed 21.02.46 and estab PO 28.02.46
RNAS there in 1942 under HAITAN (qv), PO

20.03.45
Nom DS: MFV 509 (ex HOWE SOUND II) 01.09.44-05.45

MARATHON Appledore, Accom Sh
See HANTONIA

MARAZION (1919) HK, SM DS
M/S, parent ship 4 SM, Cd 08.07.19.Sailed for China 09.1919, rb FALMOUTH 09.32, sold HK 1933

MARCO POLO Venice
Italian Cr. SNO Venice had address RN MARCO POLO 12.1916

MARGARET Falmouth, LC Support vessel
09.1943 - quay punt vessel for LC

MARGARET WETHERLEY (1911) Scapa Flow, Officers' Accom Sh
07.1917-09.1918(at least)
Tlr hired as BD vessel 1915-19

MARIANNE Kingston, Jamaica, Rx Sh/Lazaretto
Ex slaver, purch 1858, BU 1867

MARINER (1844) Ports, Police Ship
JUNO,6th Rate (qv), police ship 1865, renamed MARINER 10.01.1878, renamed ATALANTA TS 22.01.1878, foundered in Atlantic 12.02.1880

MARLBOROUGH (1855) Ports, TS for Engineers/General Depot
1st Rate, TS Ports 12.1878 - 07.1888, Rx Sh 12.1888, part of Depot 03.1892 till men moved to new RN Barracks 1903. Renamed VERNON II (qv) 03.1904, sold 10.1924.

MARLBOROUGH Eastbourne, TE - Torp Sch
Name ann 21.06.1942, Cd 24.09.1942 (with apps from 16.06.42), tng ceased 29.03.47, PO 21.04.47, closed 30.06.47
At Eastbourne College, Old Wish Rd. Provisionally sel in 12.41 lest DEFIANCE or VERNON (Roedean Sch) were put out of action
Nom DS: Steam Pinnace 686 24.09.42-

MARRYAT Glasgow, Admiralty Signal Estab Extension
18.02.1946 ex SHERBROOKE, closed 30.06.46
Nom DS: MFV 1177

MARS (1794) Ports, Hbr Serv
3rd Rate, Hbr Serv 1820 - BU 1823

MARS (1848) Dunbee, TS
2nd Rate, lent as TS on the Tay 13.05.1869, sold 10.06.1929

MARS (1896) Invergordon, DS
BB, DS Invergordon 01.09.1916 v PRINCETOWN - 04.1920 (at least), sold 09.05.1921 - see also THALIA
Acs of Cromarty were tx from THALIA to MARS 31.05.1919

MARS Harwich, RF
Cd 01.07.1950 - PO 31.03.1954 task to MULL OF GALLOWAY
RF closed 28.03.54
Nom DS: MSPB 44317 to 1950 (this entry poss just a proposed Nom DS)
MFV 436 06.07.1950-31.03.54

MARSHAL NEY (1915) Chat/Ports/ Dev, Base Ship
Ex M13, monitor, accom sh for ACTAEON Chat Cd 01.02.1919, PO at Sheerness 01.08.1919. Ports SM Sch (DOLPHIN) DS 31.07.1920-04.22, renamed VIVID (qv) 06.22. renamed DRAKE (qv) 01.01.34. renamed ALAUNIA II (qv) 1947, BU 06.10.57

MARSHAL SOULT (1915) Dev/Ports/ Nore, DS/TS
Ex M14, monitor, for Gunnery Sch Ports Cd 26.11.1918 - 01.01.19 rb TERROR. For Gunnery Sch Dev by 04.19-06.23. Turret Drl Sh Ports 12.24. Turret Drl Sh Dev Cd 19.03.25 - 01.03.26 rb EREBUS. Turret Drl Sh Chat Cd 19.02.26-28. Also SO RF Nore v AJAX. Cd 01.04.27-08.38. Tlr Base Ports Cd 10.12.40 v VERNON II (MINERVA, INGINIEUR MINARD & IOLAIRE (qv)). PO 31.03.46 (Cdr M/S to PORCUPINE), BU 08.46

MARTELLO Lowestoft, A/P Base
Cd 31.05.1940 - Became Officer-in-Charge Lowestoft 01.10.45, PO 22.10.46
Nom DS: ML ORCOMA 31.05.40-08.05.41
Yt ARONIA (1929) 08.05.41-30.09.45
Tug NESS POINT (1937) 30.09.45-1946
Tug TID 172 07.05.46-11.07.46
Hbr Lch 43597(ex NABBERLEY) 11.07.45-22.10.46

MARTIAL MNBDO DS
Cd 27.01.1941, PO 31.12.43 at Alexandria
See MNBDO 1. Acs EXCELLENT II

MARVE Marve, Bombay, RM Camp/CO Experimental Estab
Cd 24.01.1945 - 09.45
Nom DS: LCM 66 24.01.45 - (11.45)

MARY Ports, Accom Sh for Capt ML
Houseboat, accom sh 01.1941

MARYLOU Soton, Accom Sh
Ex ML, 08.1942 - acquired 08.12.42, sold 28.07.44

MARYLYN Boom DS
28.08.1939-05.01.40

MASHOBRA (1920) Narvik, MNBDO Ship
Steam Ship, hired as Base Ship 02.10.1939, Cd 04.05.40, bombed and beached at Narvik 25.05.40 - PO 23.05.40

MASSET Queen Charlotte Is, British Columbia, RCN Radio Sta
NRS 1943-45, ex RCAF. HF DF 1949-57, HMCNRS 1957-11.07.66, CFS MASSET 1966 on

MASTODON Exbury House, Exbury (Beaulieu) Nr Soton, CO Base (TLC Base)

Cd 06.05.1942. To C & M (14 days'notice) 04.45. Closed 06.07.45
Nom DS: MB PETA 06.05.42-21.05.43 (destroyed by fire)
NAB HEADLAND BELLE 11.43-

MATADOR Nom DS (NP 1658)
Cd for Ferry Service Personnel in Red Ensign ships, 06.05.1944 - to Normandy beaches 08.06.44-13.07.44, to Newport, returned to beaches but damaged, to Soton 30.07.44, repairs Falmouth, PO 07.08.44
Admin Unit in ASCANIUS (qv)

MATAPAN (1945) Dev, Living Ship
DD, RF Living Ship 03.1950-12.50 (at least), BU 08.1979

MATIANA Accom Sh
For MNBDO at Addu Atoll v GLEN FORBES 24.11.1942 - 04.44

MATSQUI Sumas, British Columbia, RCN Naval Transmitter Site
1942-12.45 ex SUMAS, separated 12.1945-01.06.55, then under ALDERGROVE - see also SUMAS which became MATSQUI 1959-

MATTHEW TOWN INAGUA Gt Inagua Is, Bahamas, Bahamian Base
1999

MAURITIUS (1939) Ports, Accom Sh
Cr, living ship RF 11.1953 v ADAMANT, SO RF 12.53, BU 1965

MAURITIUS Mauritius, Radio Sta
Opened 15.02.1962 (apps from 1961). Cd 19.03.62. Ceased operating 30.11.75, closed 16.01.76, PO 30.03.76, handed over 31.03.76.
The Cr MAURITIUS (1939) was not BU till 27.03.65 and was known as MAURITIUS (Ship) to avoid confusion.
Radio Sta at Mauritius had operated in WW I and closed 15.07.1921, and was also opened in WWII. NP 1212 there 04.1960-04.1961 and NP 4321 from 04.64-03.75

MAYFLY Soton, ML Accom Sh
08.1942, acquired 08.12.42 - 10.44 (at least). To DST for disposal 08.46

MAYINA Chatham Camp, Colombo, Ceylon, Transit & Holding Camp
Cd 01.01.1945. PO 31.03.1946 - replaced on site by GOULD (qv)
Nom DS: Ex MB 43992

MEAMSKIRK RN Hospital
In one list, prob ref to place and not to ship name

MECKLENBURGH (1922) Ports/Clyde, Accom Sh
Dutch Motor Vessel, used by Dutch Navy 09.09.1940-16.01.41. Ex RNLN accom sh at Ports, hired as RN accom sh 02.41. Alloc as accom sh AFD IV, Clyde 04.42, rb VIKING, MECKLENBURGH to be LSI(H) 04.43

MEDEA (1883) Soton, Res Drl Sh
Cr, Res Drl Sh Soton Cd 12.11.1895 - 30.06.1901. Sold 04.1914

MEDEA (19104) Peterhead, Accom Sh
Yt, hired as Barrage Balloon Vessel 04.1941. Accom sh 09.42. Sold 11.45

MEDEA (1915) Ports, TS
Ex M22, monitor, M/L 1919, renamed MEDEA 01.12.1925.Mechanical TE 1938, sold 12.1938

MEDINA (1916) Ports, TS
DD, attached FISGARD as TS 01.05.1919. Sold 05.1921

MEDINA Puckpool, Nr Ryde, Isle of Wight, FAA Camp/LC Base
FAA camp, overflow from Naval Aircraft Depots, Cd 15.11.1939 tender to DAEDALUS. PO 31.07.1942
Once GOSLING and WAXWING had opened, camp tx to C-in-C Ports 07.42
Cd 31.07.42. 01.10.42 acs OSBORNE as LC Base, PO 28.03.45
Nom DS: Steam Lch 237 15.11.39-

MEDUSA (1888) N Shields/ Queenstown, Res Drl Sh/Hbr Serv
Cr, Res Drl Sh N Shields 12.11.1895 - 30.06.1901. Bantry Bay as calibrating vessel 1910. Tender to COLLEEN 1915. Hbr Serv Queenstown 1917-18, sold 1920

MEDUSA (1915) DS
Ex M 29, monitor, renamed MEDUSA 01.12.1925. PO 31.10.41. renamed TALBOT (qv) as DS 01.09.1941. renamed MEDWAY II (qv) 01.06.44. renamed MEDUSA 01.04.45. Sold 09.09.46

MEDWAY (1812) Bermuda, Convict Ship
3rd Rate, convict ship 10.1847 - sold 11.1865

MEDWAY (1928) SM DS
Cd 03.07.1929 at Dev. To China Sta 4 SM v TITANIA (Wei Hai Wei summer, HK winter) 10.1929-11.39. To Med 1 SM 01.05.40. Lost 30.06.1942 whilst moving from Alexandria to Beirut

MEDWAY Alexandria, Accounting Base
Listed 1942-45

MEDWAY II Beirut/Malta GC, SM Base
Cd 01.07.1942 independent command, acs in Haifa but at Beirut. 1 SM at Beirut 1942-02.44 Acs MEDWAY II to MORETA (qv) 16.02.44-. 1 SM to ST ANGELO., amalgamating with 10 SM as TALBOT (PO 21.09.44). MEDWAY II PO 28.02.46 - incorporated into PHOENICEA
Nom DS: Unnamed Ml 01.07.42-
M29 (1915) Monitor ex MEDUSA/ TALBOT was 01.06.44-01.04.45
BAGSHOT (1918) M/S 01.04.45-28.02.46

MEDWAY III Malta GC,
1944-45
One account locates this at Bagshot Surrey 1945-02.46 - but this is prob a confusion with BAGSHOT (1918) - see MEDWAY II above

MEDWAY Spore, SM DS
Ex LCT 1110, redesignated MRC 1110, renamed MEDWAY, Cd 30.11.1959 for 10 SM (7 SM from 1962). At Spore 1959-68 rb FORTH. Sold 1970 at Spore
Nom DS: MRC 1110

MEDWAY QUEEN (1924) Granton, Accom Sh
Hired as M/S 09.1939. Cd as M/S TS Granton 29.04.44-01.46. PO and to DST 11.04.46

MEEANEE (1843) HK, Hosp Sh
Ex MADRAS, 2nd Rate, to War Department as Hosp Sh 05.03.1867 at HK - BU 1906

MEHRAN Karachi, NAS, Pakistan Navy
1996-extant 1999

MELAMPUS (1820) Newhaven/Ports/Chat, CG/RC Chapel/Magazine
5th Rate, Hbr Serv 1854, CG Newhaven 01.01.1857 - 01.03.1858, RC Chapel Ports 1870-, lent War Department 08.1886 - 10.1891, floating magazine Ports 1895, ordnance Chat 1900 - sold 03.04.1906

MELAMPUS (1890) Kingstown/Harwich, CG/Res Drl Sh/DS
Cr, CG/Res Drl Sh Kingstown 01.05.1893 - mid 1903-task to LATONA 1905. Res Drl Sh Harwich 1905-1910. Sold 1910

MELAMPUS Bathurst, The Gambia, Base
Cd 03.1942, PO 30.06.1945
Nom DS: THE PRINCE OF WALES (1922) ex Colonial River Steamer 06.41-01.10.42
NAB PAMELA 01.10.42-
NAB MISCHIEF 01.44

MELAMPUS II Dakar, Senegal, Base
Opened 01.11.1943 - 8.45

MELCHIOR TRIUB (1913)Persian Gulf, Base/DS
Personnel ship taken up 21.10.1942 - released 17.12.1942 - later an Army hosp sh. - alternative spelling MELCHICK TREVIS

MELISANDE (1883) Hamble, DS
20.10.1939 - 06.09.1945
Yt, hired WWI and req 20.10.39 to replace LOTUS (qv) at Hamble as DS Inner Patrol. Purch 08.1941, sold 1945.
Original HQ of Combined Ops 15.06.40 which moved to TORMENTOR (qv) 08.40.

MELISSA (1916) A/P Repair Vessel
Yt, hired 09.1939, purch 09.41, re-alloc accom vessel Ports 10.452, laid up 05.43, sold 1945

MELITA (1942) see SATELLITE

MELVILLE (1817) HK, Hosp Sh
3rd Rate, hosp sh 03.1857 - sold 1873

MELVILLE (1915) Queenstown, US Naval DD DS
Arrived Queenstown 22.05.1917. - 12.1918, left Soton for USA 07.01.19
Poss operated at Rosneath/Weymouth 1944-45 - see Gazetteer - US Forces

MELVILLE Darwin, N Territory, RAN Base
01.08.1940 ex PENGUIN V -21.08.1975
Nom DS: DB1
MB 196/PICTON 04.43-47

MENACE Ports, MNBDO II
MENACE Cd 03.12.1941 as Operational Base Ship, not as Base Ship for MNBDO II. PO 12.12.41. Name held in abeyance for MNBDO II. Cd 27.01.43, acs EXCELLENT (this may be explanation for location as Ports), PO 1943 (acs to APPLEDORE II)
Nom DS: Hbr Steam Lch 171 27.01.43-

MENAI (1814) Ports, Rx Sh
6th Rate, Rx Sh 1831 - target 1851, BU 04.1853

MENELAUS (1810) Chat/Motherbank, Spithead, Marine Hosp/Qtn Sh
5th Rate, Marine Hosp Sh Chat 1832, Motherbank Qtn Sh 1840 to sold 10.05.1897

MENESTHEUS (1929) Amenity Ship
Hired as M/L 14.12.1939. PO Lochalsh to C & M 10.43. Allocated as Amenity Ship (Red Ensign) to be conv in Canada 10.44. Cd under White Ensign 08.11.44 for passage to Canada, PO Vancouver 22.01.45. To Far East 02.45-(only such ship used) - return UK 07.46. Resto 06.01.48

MENTOR Stornoway, M/S Base
Cd 16.09.1939, PO 15.11.44. Stornoway Base closed 27.06.45
Name sel for comml pt 01.09.39, NOIC ordered 27.08.39. Included operating base for Walrus aircraft at Lewis Castle 11.40 -called MENTOR II in one account. To C & M (temp) 07.41.
Also included work up base for M/S at Mull 10.43 (see WESTERN ISLES)
Nom DS: MB MARJORIE 16.09.39-02.05.41
Yt SULAIRE 02.05.41-27.06.45

MENTOR II Stornoway, CF Base
Cd 24.06.1941, closed down 09.43
Name also ment for Seaplane Base - see MENTOR above
Nom DS: Yt BRINMARIC 24.06.41 - hull sold 1943

MEON (1943) DS
FF, LSHQ (small) 1945, earmarked as relief for DERBY HAVEN as DS 32 M/S 08.1949. Re-Cd for Amphibious Warfare Sqn Med 01.05.53. To Sheerness 20.10.59, refit and to Med 04.60 - 65. BU 05.66

MERASHEEN (1941) LL Maint & Repair Ship

Ex MMS 122 - 05.1945, for sale 1946

MERCATOR (1931) Freetown, Sierra Leone, SM Accom Sh
Belgian TS taken over by Adty as SM Accom Sh Freetown 09.1942, Cd 05.01.43 for passage and PO 15.02.43 on arrival and became part of PHILOCTETES (qv). Returned to Belgians at Freetown 07.45

MERCIA Smith St, Coventry, Communication Tng Centre
Cd 01.10.1984, PO 29.07.1994

MERCURY (1826) Woolwich/Sheerness, Coal Hulk
5th Rate, coal hulk Woolwich 1861, at Sheerness 1870 till sold 03.04.1906

MERCURY (1878) Ports/Harwich/Chat, SM DS
Despatch Vessel, Navigation Sch Ship 1903, SM DS Ports 1906-13, Harwich 1913, hulked 1914 for service at Rosyth with COLUMBINE (qv). Accom sh Chat Cd 07.01.1918 - PO 03.1919, sold 09.07.1919

MERCURY Leydene House, East Meon, Nr Petersfield, TE
Cd 16.08.1941 independent command. Last trainee left 08.1993, PO 08.93
HM Signal Sch, ex HM Barracks Ports 1904-41. In 1941 there were extensions at Bristol, Cambridge, Liss etc. In 11.43 RN W/T Sch St Bedes, Eastbourne and WRNS TE Soberton Towers. Later Sch of Maritime Operations, Communications & Navigation Faculty. Had Experimental Section at Lythe Hill House, Haslemere and Production and Development Section at Whitwell Hose, Haslemere (see MERCURY II). SCU Leydene independent establishment 01.09.1995 - see Gazetteer.
Nom DS: MB 3520 16.08.41-
HL(D) 1854 1948-06.50 (still listed to 12.50)
HL(D) 42473 06.50 - 62 (but sold 18.06.59)

MERCURY II Haslemere, Experimental Signal Estab /Adty Signal Estab
Cd 25.08.1941 - opened as independent command from 27.08.41 - mid 1952
Set up as experimental section of Signal Sch 1917 when task from VERNON to Signal Sch. To Eastney (apps from 30.12.1935 - apparatus from 14.07.36) - to study RDF (Radar). When Signal Sch moved, ASE also moved 04.41 (HQ to Lythe Hill House, Haslemere, Production Departtment to Whitwell Hatch Hotel end 05.41, small part remained in Signal Sch Ports (13.05.41) and became independent 08.41. Labs and Workshops to King Edward Sch, Whitley, Valves to Waterlooville, Aerials to Nutbourne, Trials to Tantallon, Nr N Berwick.
Nom DS: FMB 3521 27.08.41-07.46
MFV 1016 07.46-(sold 05.47)

MERCURY II Portsdown, Ports, Admiral Signal & Radar Estab
Mid 1952 - listed to 1969

MERGANSER Crimmond/Rattery, Aberdeenshire, RNAS
Naval Observer Sch approved 12.1942, land purch 1943, work started 03.43. Cd as Torp Bomber Recce Aircrew TE 03.10.1944 - own accounts, independent command. Known as Crimmond till 01.07.45, then Rattray to clarify postal address. PO 30.09.1946 - land owned by Adty but managed by Dept of Agriculture for Scotland till 1958. Major part of site sold 05.1963, but in 1973 484 acres bought back for use as W/T Sta.
Nom DS: TRV 421251 10.44-

MERLIN Ports, Rx Sh
Sloop, purch 180-3, Rx Sh 1819 till sold 1836

MERLIN Donibristle, Fife, RNAS
Cd 24.05.1939 ex RAF Sta - PO 23.10.1959
Has been RNAS 1917-01.04.1918 (to RAF on formation).
Included Sta at Campbeltown 1940-41 (see LANDRAIL), Evanton 1940-44 (see FIELDFARE), Fearn 1942 (see OWL), Drem 1945 (see NIGHTHAWK). Also RN Aircraft Repair & Storage Yard Donisbristle (closed 28.08.59); RN Ancillary Repair Depot, Dunfermline; RN Component Recovery Depot, Forthbank,, Alloa; RN Aircraft Propeller Works, Dundee; Engine Storage Depot, Alloa. (1945)
Nom DS: Steam Lch 213 04.05.39 - (listed to 1948)
Safety Boat A566 12.44-21.05.46
Type B Lighter 39 by 04.48-01.11.48
24 ft Marine Tender 4405 01.11.48-54

MERLIN II Donibristle,
10.1946-47

MERLIN III Dunino, Fife, RNAS
01.10.1945 ex JACKDAW II (qv)

MERLIN III Donibristle
10.1946-1947

MERMAID (1825) Dublin, Powder Hulk
5th Rate, powder hulk 1850,lent War department 08.05.1863, at Dublin 1865-Bu 1875

MERSE (1914) Holyhead, A/P DS
Tlr, Cd 29.01.1917, DS 08.02.1917 v AMETHYST III - 22.05.1917 - lost by mining, rb VANESSA II

MERSEY (1814) Ports, Rx Sh
6th Rate, Rx Sh 1832 - BU 07.1852

MERSEY (1858) Queenstown, Flag
FF, Flag Queenstown 01.04.1867 - 16.08.1872, sold 1875

MERSEY (1885) Harwich, CG
Cr, CG Harwich 09.05.1893 - 22.05.1898 & 11.02.1903 v SEVERN - mid 1903, sold 04.1905

MERSEY Lpool/Neston, T124X Depot
Cd 25.12.1940 ex EAGLET II (qv), PO 31.12.1946

In David Lewis Northern Hosp 12.40, to Neston Camp, Wiral 02.12.45. To Royal Liver Buildings 08.07.46
Nom DS: Hbr Lch SCOUT 25.12.40-

MESSENGER Woolwich, Coal Hulk
Paddle steamer, purch 1830, coal hulk 1845 - sold 11.1861

MESSINA (1945) Gareloch/Dev, Accom Sh
LST 3043, named 1947. Living Ship Gareloch to 09.47. Accom Sh Dev 02.69-70, Dockyard use Dev 1970-76, sold 09.80

METELLUS Italy, Base
One of 6 names sel for bases in Italy, considered for Taranto but not used (12.1943)

MICHAEL (1944) Spore, Accom Sh
M/S, accom sh 05.1950, BU 11.56

MIDGE HK Hosp Sh
Ex Gun vessel, hosp sh 1890-1905

MIDGE Gt Yarmouth, CF Base
Name ann 15.11.40, Cd 01.01.1941, PO 21.07.45
Nom DS: ML MINERVA 01.01.41-

MIDGE II Gt Yarmouth
1944

MILDURA (1941) Brisbane, RAN Static TS
M/S, Static TS Brisbane by 09.1957 - sold 09.65

MILFORD (1809) Milford, Qtn Sh
3rd Rate, Qtn Sh 06.1825 - BU 07.1846

MILFORD (1932) Dev, Accom Sh
Sloop, allocated RNVR DS 08.46 but not required 05.49, accom sh 02.48, BU 06.49

MILLCOVE Mill Cove, Nova Scotia, RCN Radio Sta
Ex NRS BLANDFORD 11.07.1966, open 19.12.67, never Cd as HMCS or HMCNRS - see also ALBRO LAKE

MILNE (1941) Harwich, Accom Sh
DD, RF living ship 12.1949-03.50, part of COCHRANE (qv) 11.51, sold to Turkey 1958

MINDARI Woolloomoolloo, Sydney, New South Wales, RAN Gunnery & Aircraft Recognition Sch
01.07.1945 - PO 04.48 (though listed to 09.1957)

MINDEN (1810) HK, Hosp Sh/Store ship
3rd Rate, hosp sh 1842, store ship 1850, sold 04.07.1861

MINERVA (1820) Ports, Workshop
5th Rate, hbr serv 1861, workshop 1865 - sold 28.02.1895

MINERVA (1895) DS
Cr, temp DS 6 DF 1912-13, sold 10.1920

MINERVA (1915) Ports/Clyde/Soton, DS/Workshop
M33, monitor, conv to M/L 1919, renamed MINERVA 12.25, was attached VERNON at Ports. Established as Tlr Base Ports v VERNON 12.39 with Yt IOLAIRE as accom sh - known as VERNON II by 04.40 and became part of MARSHAL SOULT (qv) 10.12.40 when MINERVA, INGINEUR MINARD and IOLAIRE were replaced by that ship. Became a floating BD workshop Clyde, Ports and Soton 09.44-10.44, to Hartlepool 24.07.1987 for preservation - to Ports by 1992 - extant 1999

MINERVA Sheerness, RF
Cd 01.07.1950 - 1953, RF closed 01.04.53. Dockyard sold 26.06.59
SO RF in BERRY HEAD 01.51, MULL OF GALLOWAY 12.52
Nom DS: MFV 951 07.50-03.53

MINIDO (1924) Falmouth/Barrow-in-Furness, Base
Yt, hired 09.1939, became Base Ship CLIO (qv) at Barrow 15.09.39 - 02.09.42 - returned 1946.
FORTE (qv) at Falmouth Cd 24.08..39 ex MINIDO - poss same vessel as by 10.10.39 Nom DS FORTE was GALLANT

MINNA (1939) Med/Lunna Voe, Shetlands, Mother Ship
Scottish Fishery Protection Vessel, hired 08.1940, Special Service African Coast Flat Med 04.42. UK Mid 43. Target and mother ship for motor submersible canoes, Lunna Voe 10.44 - resto 46

MINONA (1906) Campbeltown, Argyllshire, Rescue Tug Base Ship
26.11.1940-05.45
Yt, hired A/P WWI, examination serv 11.39, purch 09.41, DS 1940-25.01.46, resto 47

MINONA Harwich, T124X Depot/Rescue Tug Base
25.01.46 - closed PM 31.01.47
Yt above in subsequent role
Nom DS: Yt MINONA to 24.01.46
HL(P) 441609 25.01.46-05.46 (at least)

MINOS Waveney Rd, Lowestoft, Naval Base
Cd 01.,07.1940, PO 30.09.45
Nom DS: MV MINOS 01.07.40 - alloc but not taken up
NAB RITA 01.07.40-10.44
SYLVIA 10.44-08.45

MINOS II Lowestoft, CF Base
Name ann 30.04.41, opened 01.05.40, renamed MANTIS (qv) 26.07.42
Nom DS: MB LADY RITA 01.05.41 - constructive total loss 12.07.42

MINOTAUR (1816) Chat/Sheerness, Rx Sh
3rd Rate, Standgate creek 11.1842-, Rx Sh Sheerness by 1856, Guard ship there 1860, hulk 1863, Rx Sh Chat by 1866, renamed HERMES 27.07.1866, BU 1869

MINOTAUR (1863) Portland, TS
Ex ELEPHANT, Iron Screw Sh, temp attached BOSCAWEN Portland 1895, renamed BOSCAWEN (qv) 03.1904, GANGES (qv) 21.06.1906, GANGES II (qv) 25.04.08, sold

30.01.1922

MINSTREL (1865) Bermuda, Coal Hulk
Gunboat, coal hulk 1874 0 sold 1906 (?)

MIRAGLIA (1923) Brindisi/Genoa/Malta GC, CF DS
Ex Italian seaplane carrier GIUSEPPE MIRAGLIA surrendered at Malta GC 10.09.1943. used as CF DS Brindisi 09.43-05.45, at Malta GC 05.45-07.45, at Genoa 12.45 as aircraft tender (Allied control).

MIRANDA Gt Yarmouth, M/S Base
Cd 16.10.1940, PO 21.07.1945 (WATCHFUL (qv) remained 10 further days)
Nom DS: NAY MAHELAH (1898) (qv) 16.10.40-07.45

MIRTLE Mine Investigation Range
1940 - Secret location, name from initials of task

MISOA (1937) Normandy, CF DS
Oiler hired and conv to LST 12.1940. Rhino DS Normandy 06.44-01.07.44. CF DS British Assault Area 08.44, C & M Inveraray 06.04.45, released to DST 04.45

MIURA (1911) Gt Yarmouth, A/P DS
04.1915 - 23.08.1915 rb KINGFISHER, PO 23.08.15
Tlr, hired 1914, mined 23.08.1915

MGB 16 Solent/Spithead, Mobile Radar Workshop
Ex MA/SB (1939/40) - allocated 21.07.1944

ML 291 Rhine, A/P DS
Cd about 12.1918 - Rhine Flot withdrawn 01.1926 - still listed 06.1926

ML Ports, Accom Ships
08.1942, various MLs used as accom sh Ports - including - ML 124 - unsatisfactory survey/ ML 237 - acquired 01.03.43 - later SEA SERPENT (qv)/ ML 553 - known as CODFORD (qv)

MNBDO
Embarked in SS BELLEROPHON, NEURALIA & NUDDEA 28.08.1935 to strengthen air defences, Malta - under PRESIDENT III

MNBDO I Gosport/Scapa Flow/Narvik/ SE Coast/Suda Bay/Egypt/Palestine
Formed 01.1940 at Ft Cumberland, Fixed A/S Defences by 08.01.1940. At Scapa 02.40, in MASHOBRA (qv) lost at Narvik, to Iceland 10.05.40 (Op Fork), then defended Kingsdown to Sandwich section of SE Coast to 01.41. Part arrived Suda Bay before loss 05.41. rest to Indian Ocean/Palestine - 1941 guard duties Morscar Barracks, Egypt, - 1942 Haifa guarding refineries. - see also MANCHESTER CITY,MARTIAL, MASHOBRA. Acs EXCELLENT II

MNBDO II Ports/Alton/Hayling
Fixed A/S Defences kitted up 07.40. Approved to assemble 06.41 - acs EXCELLENT II (later APPLEDORE II). Formed 15.07.41 - ALCA and HELVIG Base Ships. Assembled at Eastney, Ports, Cd in MENACE (qv), accom at Alton & Hayling Is (S Hayling & Sunshine camps). Camps set up 5 locations mid Wales (Ynysy Maengwyn (HQ), Arthog, Llanegryn, Llwyngwril & Barmoyuth 07.42) - extant at Yns-Maengwyn & Towyn 08.43). In UK 05.03.42-22.01.43/ then Middle East to 31.07.43/ then Sicily & Italy to 25.01.44/ then UK to 30.04.44

MOA New Zealand, Coal Depot
Brig, purch 01.1861, coal depot New Zealand 1865 - sold 12.1876

MODESTE (1944) Ports, Hbr TS
Sloop, part of VERNON II (qv) 12.1947, attached VERNON 12.49, BU 03.61

MOGA Jamaica, RNAS
1943-44
Admin of BUZZARD (qv) when PO to C & M 15.07.43 until finally PO 31.12.44

MOIRA (1933) Freetown, A/P DS
HDP vessel, Cd 01.10.1941, independent command v ST MINVER - 10.07.42
MFV hired on hbr serv 01.40-purrch 03.42, laid up 01.46

MONAB XI
Was to be formed 29.05.1945 - for other MONABs - see ship names starting NAB-

MONARRA Maharagama, Ceylon, RN Aircraft Repair Yard/Transit Camp
Cd 01.12.1944 independent command, acs BHERUNDA. Tx to FO Ceylon as transit camp 01.10.1945, acs MAYINA. 04.45 Nom DS for personnel in Ceylon. 30.9.46 acs from GOULD to LANKA, PO 29.10.46
Also described as Aircraft TE for Singalese recruits to FAA - one list describes it as Amphib Craft TE.
Nom DS: MB EUREKA J992 01.12.44-

MONARCH (1868) Simon's Bay, S Africa, Guardship
Guardship 1897-1902, renamed SIMOON (qv) as DS 1904, sold 1905

MONARCH (1911) Ports, Boys' TS
BB, TS 1920s, RF Parent Gp II 01.1922-PO 05.05.1922, sunk as target 20.01.25

MONARCH London/Pin Mill, Accom Sh
Barge Yt, hired as M/L DS 06.1941. Allocated London Officers' Accom A/P London 02.07.41, laid up Teddington 01.42. Allocated Pin Mill ML Base as accom sh 26.05.42, sold 1945

MONA'S ISLE (1905) Base/Accom Sh
Hired as Armed Boarding vessel 27.08.1939, fitted out Lpool. AA Guardship Methil 10.40 - Tyne 05.41. Accom Sh 03.42, PO 29.11.43, resto and became personnel ship under Red Ensign

MONCK Largs/ Pt Glasgow/Rosneath, HQ Comb Tng

Cd 01.04.1942, (QUEBEC II (qv) at Largs PO 31.03.42) - PO 30.09.46 - retard party for 1 month HQ of SO Assault Ships & Craft. Was HQ Comb Tng at Largs, Vice Admiral Comb Tng & Staff Largs to London 27.07.42. Approved to expand 19.11.42. Included FO Carrier Tng, RN Barracks, LC Base Pt Glasgow and ICE Sch Rosneath by 1944.
Nom DS: MB MOJA (T26) 01.04.42-01.43
RAF Lch 412 01.43-02.44
EUREKA PB 357 02.44-

MONCK II Greenock, HQ FO Unallocated LC/FOSLU
Cd 01.01.1944 acs MONCK - PO 01.10.44
Nom DS: Yt MELITA(1930) 01.01.44-02.44
Barge of FOLSU(RAF Lch 412) 01.02.44-01.10.44 - Became MB 441845

MONGE Karachi, RIN Base
See MONZE

MONGLA Khulna, Bangladesh, Bangladeshi Shore Estab
1989-extant 1997 (Nu Mongla by 1999 - qv)

MONMOUTH (1796) Deptford/Woolwich, Sheer Hulk
3rd Rate, sheer hulk Deptford 1815, Woolwich by 1831, BU 1834

MONMOUTH (1828) Dev, Chapel Hulk
HOTSPUR, 5th Rate (qv), Chapel Hulk 1859, RC Chapel Dev 1865-renamed MONMOUTH 1868, sold 1902

MONSTER Fortrose, Nr Inverness, CO Base
Cd 15.11.1943. PO 15.08.44
Nom DS: Fire Float INGEBORG II 15.11.43-

MONTCALM Laurier Ave, Quebec, PQ, RCN Base & Res Div
01.09.1939 - Cd 01.11.41 - 01.09.42, tender to CHALEUR II.
01.09.42-1986 (at least) - independent command. See also D'IBERVILLE

MONTCLARE (1921) DD-SM DS
Ex METAPEDIA, req 29.08.1939 as AMC. Purch 06.42 as SM DS & PO 15.04.42 for conv at Soton. Cd as DD DS 08.44, on Clyde 10.44, then to British Pacific Fleet - Fleet Train, conv for Rear Admiral Fleet Train to 01.45. - Sydney 04.45, Manus 05.45, Brisbane 24.06.45, Manus 30.06.45-20.08.45, HK 03.01.46, arrive Ports 20.02.46. Conv to SM DS 1946, allocated 7 SM Portland v CYCLOPS 01.46. 3 SM Holyhead. Rothesay v FORTH 20.05.47 - 05.10.54 rb ADAMANT. Res Ports 12.02.55, tow to BU 28.01.58

MONTREAL Montreal, Quebec, RCN Res Div
21.11.1941 - 01.09.42 - tender to HOCHELAGA II. 01.09.42 - 26.10.43 - independent command. Renamed DONNACONA (qv).
There was a RCN FF MONNTREAL launched 12.06.43 - BU 47

MONTREAL II
Hbr Craft MONTREAL 20.07.42 - 26.10.43, renamed DONNACONA II

MONTREAL CIRCLE Prince Rupert, British Columbia, RCN Radio Sta
07.1953-07.1960

MONZE (also spelt MONGE) Karachi, RIN Base
01.12.1942 - 14.08.1948 - renamed IQBAL (qv) on tx RPN
Name of Local Naval Defence Base 11.43

MORAGA - see MARAGA

MORAY FIRTH (1944) Maint Ship
Cd 02.10.1945. Pacific Fleet 01.46. To MOT 13.05.46, sold 1947

MORETA Haifa, Base
Cd 01.09.1942 independent command, own acs. PO 31.07.1946, acs to STAG
Nom DS: Patrol Vessel MORETA 01.09.42-

MORETON Brisbane, RAN Base & Res Div
Cd 01.10.1942 at Alice St (ex BRISBANE (qv) - closed 1946
Re-activated for RANR 1949 at Kangaroo Pt, Cd as MORETON at New Farm 1960 - PO 11.05.1994
Nom DS: ML MILGA 04.43-45
ML MB 180 1945-

MORGAN Kingston, Jamaica, Base
Cd 01.08.1941, independent command, acs BUZZARD. PO 31.03.45 (one ac says 01.04.46)
Name of Naval Base as distinct from RNAS, v BUZZARD. ML Base at Pt Royal, Jamaica Cd as tender to MORGAN 20.07.1943, closed 24.07.45
Nom DS: Tug DOUGLAS ALEXANDER (ex BUZZARD) 01.08.41-

MOSQUITO Mahroussa Jetty, Alexandria, CF Base
Cd 15.02.1942 acs NILE, independent command, PO 01.12.45 to C & M
Nom DS: 16ft Dinghy No 1955 15.02.42-

MOSQUITO I Haifa, CF Base
10.1943 (in PO Circular 22.03.44 & 09.05.45)

MOSQUITO II Beirut, Lebanon, CF Base
1942 (In PO Circular 22.03.44 & 09.05.45)

MOSQUITO III Benghazi, Cyrenaica, CF Base
WW II - CF at Benghazi 1942 - see Gazetteer - Med

MOSQUITO III Pt Said, CF Base
WWII (In PO Circular 22.03.44 & 09.05.45)

MOTI Bombay, RIN CF Base
Listed 02.1944 - 10.45 (In PO Circular 09.05.45 as MOT I) - poss ref to Iranian Gunboat KARKAS capt 1941 and returned 1946

MOUNT EDGCUMBE (1822) Dev, TS
WINCHESTER, 4th Rate, renamed CONWAY II (qv)1861 TS, renamed MOUNT EDGCUMBE

01.09.1876. Lent to Devon & Cornwall Industrial Tng Committee as TS and sold 08.04.1921

MOUNT EDGCUMBE Plym, Barracks
Approved to amalgamate IMPREGNABLE (qv) and RN Camp St Budeaux as one Estab named MOUNT EDGCUMBE 02.1945 - but cancelled 03.45

MOUNT STEWART Teignmouth, Mobile Flotation Unit Base
Cd 28.08.1944, tender to DARTMOUTH. PO 28.02.46 - organisation to APPLEDORE
Special Service Estab, but ment 10.46. MFU also termed Motor Fuelling Unit, but cover for small submersibles for use in Pacific War. 07.42-10.42 MFU at Dartford, then Crayford. 09.42 to Scotland, Nr Erith. 02.44 task tx from DMDW to DDOI. Later to Teignmouth
Nom DS: 42 ft Motor Pinnace 28.08.44-

MRC 1097 Bahrein, M/S Support
1965-66

MTB 685 (1943) Poole, Accom Vessel
PO 28.10.44, conv to accom vessel Poole 11.44-25.12.44. allocated as Accom sh Poole 19.01.45 - 05.45 (at least). For disposal 04.49, sold 1950

MTONGWE Kenyan Naval Base
Listed 1969 - 1979
Kenya Navy inaugurated 12.12.64

MULGRAVE (1812) Milford, Lazaretto/Powder Hulk
3rd Rate, Lazaretto 09.1836 - powder hulk by 1853 - BU 12.1854

MULGRAVE Mulgrave, Nova Scotia, RCN Chief Examination Officer
Listed 12.1941
Note: RCN M/S launched 05.1942

MULL OF GALLOWAY (1944) CF - M/S Maint Ship
Ex KINNARD HEAD. Cd 15.05.1945. East Indies 1945, Ceylon 08.45, Penang 09.45, sail Colombo 01.02.46 for Ports then res Gareloch 27.06.46-52 (living ship 12.50 at least). SO RF Clyde 13.10.46 v KENT - 1951. DS Target Trials under C-in-C Ports 02.48-49. Refit as M/S HQ Ship 01.53. Cd as HQ Ship of Maint & Base Ship Harwich 01.04.54. (MARS PO 31.03.54) - 57 (Inshore Sqn tx to Med 01.09.56). Chat refit 04.12.56-, RF Chat 17.04.57 - (living ship v BEN LOMOND). Ports 05.05.60 (SORF v VANGUARD 08.06.60 - rb RAME HEAD 10.63). To Canadian Authorities 11.02.65. BU 16.02.65

MULL OF KINTYRE (1945) Motor Craft - M/S Maint Ship
Cd 15.11.1945, to Far East (Okinawa & Kure, Japan) 1945-46. HQ Ship Target Trials under C-in-C Ports 09.46-49, SO RF Harwich 01.05.1950-10.53, then RF - repair & accom sh Rosyth 17.11.53 - 55, conv to M/S Maint Ship Ports 1959 (to dockyard control to wait conv 09.56)-61. Cd 02.08.61, Spore 18.10.61-03.68 (res from 62). Tow to UK, arrive 05.05.68, sold 12.69

MULL OF OA (1945) CF Repair Ship
Ex TREVOSE HEAD, cancelled 1945

MULLION COVE (1944) Maint Ship for Hull Repairs
Cd 09.07.1945, Trincomalee 09.45-02.46, Greenock 22.03.46, PO 18.06.46 to DST - sold 1948

MUNSHI Lagos, Accom Sh
Train ferry steamer, taken up as DS for Tlrs and M/S, Lagos 29.08.41. Allocation cancelled 01.42. Resto 05.44

MURAENA (1907) Ports/Poole, Accom Sh
Yt, req as accom sh for Fr immobilised ships and re-allocated accom sh for Group and Unit Officers M/S & A/S Flot Ports 07.08.1940. Overflow ship for MARSHAL SOULT to 10.44 (at least). To Poole as accom sh under DSCD 09.45-05.46. To War Office 17.12.46 - for disposal 03.04.48

MUTINE (1900) Bermuda/Jamaica/ Newport, Mon, DS/Res Drl Sh
Sloop, survey vessel 1907, DS Bermuda 12.1917 - 03.19 rb MALABAR, carried SNO Jamaica 01.19-03.19. Re-Cd for survey work 01.06.1919. Res Drl Sh Newport v DAHLIA 09.25. Sold 16.08.32 - RNVR Sub Div Newport closed 1932

MVITA Kilindini, Mombasa, E Africa, DS
01.07.1950 - TANA (qv) ceased (E African Force formed 01.07.1950 - absorbed Kenya VR) - listed to 1962
Nom DS: MFV 206 1957-61

MYCTEA Accom Barge - see NYCTEA

MYLAE Italy, Base
One of 6 names sel for bases in Italy, considered for Taranto but not used (12.1943)

MYLODON Lowestoft, CO Base/LCT Base
19.01.1943 - PO 28.06.46 - administered by Nore from 31.07.45
Some lists include Gt Yarmouth. Took over from ARBELLA 01.07.45
Nom DS: NAB SYLVIA IV 19.01.43-07.45
NAB ELVIN 07.45-11.45
HL(P) 441155 11.45-05.46 (at least)

MYRTLE (1818) Ports, Coal Hulk
Ex MALABAR (qv), 3rd Rate, coal hulk from 1848, renamed MYRTLE 30.10.1883 - sold 11.07.1905

N

NABARON Ludham/Manus, Admiralty Is, MONAB IV
Formed 15.11.1944, Cd 01.01.45 at Ludham (FLYCATCHER), completed tng 10.01.45, sail mid

01.45, Cd 02.04.45 at Ponam Is, Manus (there by 02.45), PO 10.11.45 - retard party under PEPYS/GOLDEN HIND
Nom DS: NAB PRIMROSE 01.01.45-07.45

NABBERLEY Ludham/ Bankstown, Nr Sydney, NSW, MONAB II
Formed 27.09.1944, Cd 18.11.44 at FLYCATCHER, completed tng 29.11.44. Cd 29.01.45 at RAAF Bankstown (lent RN 29.01.45), PO 31.03.46
Included Component MR 2 from 21.05.45
Nom DS: Hbr Lch 43597 18.11.45-07.45 (became MARTELLO)

NABBINGTON Ludham/Nowra, NSW, MONAB I
Formed 06.09.1944, Cd 28.10.44 at FLYCATCHER, completed tng 15.10.44, sail early 11.44, 02.01.45 RAAF Nowra (lent RN from 02.01.45), Cd 02.02.45 at Nowra, - acs of all miscellaneous personnel at Jervis Bay on books NABBINGTON 07.45, PO 15.11.45
Replaced at Nowra by MONAB V (NABSWICK)
Nom DS: Hbr Lch 42755 28.10.45-

NABCATCHER Middle Wallop/Kai Tak, HK, MONAB VIII
Formed 28.02.45 as NABSTEAD (qv), Cd 01.07.45 at FLYCATCHER as NABCATCHER, completed tng 24.04.45. 07.45 advance party left UK to join MONAB II (NABBERLEY) at Bankstown till rest arrive. .09.45 to HK (re-occupied 03.09.45), 01.04.47 renamed FLYCATCHER (qv)
Nom DS: MB 1646 01.07.45-

NABHURST Middle Wallop, MONAB X
Formed 01.05.1945, Cd 01.09.45 at FLYCATCHER, independent command, own acs, retained in UK, PO 12.10.45
Nom DS: MB 39431(FMB 3941) - (07.46)

NABREEKIE Middle Wallop/Meeandah, Queensland, MONAB VII
Formed 31.01.1945 as NABSFIELD (qv), completed tng 27.03.45, Cd 01.06.45 at FLYCATCHER as NABREEKIE, Cd 09.08.45 at Meeandah, shared airfield at Archerfield with NABSFORD (qv), PO 05.11.45.

NABROCK Middle Wallop/Sembawang, Spore, MONAB IX
Formed 27.03.1945 as NABSMERE, completed tng 22.05.45, Cd 01.08.45 at FLYCATCHER as NABROCK, Cd 05.10.45 at Sembawang, PO 15.12.45, Re-Cd as SIMBANG (qv)

NABSFIELD MONAB VII
Formed 31.01.1945, completed tng 27.03.45 as NABSFIELD, renamed NABREEKIE (qv) when Cd 01.06.45

NABSFORD Ludham/Archerfield, Queensland, TAMY No 1
Cd 01.02.1945 independent command, own acs, at FLYCATCHER, Cd 27.03.45 at Archerfield (shared with NABREEKIE), PO 31.03.46
Nom DS: MB VERONY II 01.02.45-07.45

NABSMERE MONAB IX
Formed 27.03.1945, completed tng 22.05.45 - to sail for Australia 05.45 as NABSMERE but Cd 01.08.45 as NABROCK (qv)

NABSTEAD MONAB VIII
Formed 28.002.1945, completed tng 24.04.45, to sail end 04.45 for Australia as NABSTEAD, but Cd 01.07.45 as NABCATCHER (qv)

NABSTOCK Middle Wallop/ Maryborough, Queensland/ Schofields, MONAB VI
Formed 03.01.1945, completed tng 28.01.45, to sail for Australia end 02.45. Cd 01.04.45 at FLYCATCHER, independent command, own acs, Cd 01.06.45 at Maryborough, 15.11.45 replaced MONAB III (NABTHORPE) at RAAF Schofields. PO 09.06.46 - to RAAF - became RAN NIRIMBA (qv) 1953
Nom DS: MB VIXEN 01.04.45-07.45
HL(P) 42583 07.45-

NABSWICK Ludham/Jervis Bay/ Nowra, MONAB V
Formed 06.12.1944, completed tng 31.01.45. Cd 01.02.45 at FLYCATCHER. Cd 28.04.45 at Jervis Bay. 15.11.45 replaced MONAB I (NABBINGTON) at RAAF Nowra, PO 18.03.46 - became RAN ALBATROSS (qv)
Nom DS: MV SAILOR PRINCE 01.02.45-07.45

NABTHORPE Ludham/ Schofields, NSW, MONAB III
Formed 28.10.1944, completed tng 13.12.44, Cd 04.12.44 at FLYCATCHER, Cd 18.02.45 at RAAF Schofields NSW (lent RN), PO 15.11.45, replaced by NABSTOCK (qv)
Nom DS: NAB YARE 04.12.44-06.45
NAB BROOKE 06.45-

NADEN Esquimalt, British Columbia, RCN DS
DS 01.06.1920 v RAINBOW - 31.07.22 (books tx to GUELPH). ReCd 01.11.1922 (ceremony 03.09.22) - 07.25
Barracks & TE 01.06.20-31.07.26 - (Barracks ex Army 1858-1862, ex RN 1862-1906) and listed as DS
01.11.22-01.04.66 - became CFS ESQUIMALT - but name still in use 1997
Pacific HQ to BURRARD 1942. RN Section closed 08.03.46
Noted as Schooner (1913) in 1922 and as Motor Vessel 1925-39

NADEN II Esquimalt, RCN Mechanical TE/Barracks
12.1941 - 12.43 - part of GIVENCHY
In PO Circular 03.44

NADEN II Como Spit, Comox, British Columbia, RCN Seamanship TE
01.04.46 ex GIVENCHY III - 1949 became QUANDRA

NADEN III Como Spit, Comox, British Columbia, RCN TE
12.1941 - 01.10.43 - became GIVENCHY III

NADEN III Esquimalt, British Columbia, RCN
1944-12.45 (in NL 1944 most apps Nursing Staff)

NADIA Pt Said, DS for ZZ Craft (M/S Force)
Ex PRINCESS ELIZABETH, tug, hired as DS 10.1944-46

NAIAD (1797) Valparaiso/Callao, Peru, Storeship
5th Rate, coal depot 01.1847, storeship Valparaiso 1950-51, Callao 1862, sold 02.02.1866

NAIAD (1890) Tyne, DS
Cr, M/L 1910, Tyne 1916-04.1920 (at least), sold 1922

NAIRN Aberdeen, A/P DS Peterhead & Aberdeen
Cd 01.03.1918 and v THALIA 06.18. PO 08.09.1919, men to books CRESCENT II (qv)
Office at Peterhead to Aberdeen 11.08.1919 - Peterhead Base closed 12.05.19
Nom DS: Yt NAIRN (1913) hired 15.04.15-27.02.19
Drifter CLOVER (1911) 27.02.19-08.06.19
Tlr DRIVER (1910) 09.06.19 - (1920)

NALINI Calcutta, RIN TE for Women's service
Opened 01.1945

NAMUR (1756) Chat, Rx Sh
2nd Rate, 3rd Rate 1805, Rx Sh 1807, BU 1833

NANKIN (1850) Pembroke Dk, Rx Sh/Hosp Sh
4th Rate, hosp hulk 1866, sold 28.02.1885, but Rx Sh Pembroke Dk 1884-09.05.1895 - bore Superintendent Pembroke Dk 1870-1895 - see SATURN. BU 1905

NAPIER Alexandria/ Far East, RAN Shore Base
RAN 7 DF acs ex DRAKE V (DRAKE V closed 27.09.41) to Alexandria 09.41-, Far East by 02.07.44 - 26.08.45.
Was linked to DD (1940), Capt D7 (RAN) Cd 12.1940, PO 25.10.45 and Re Cd RN - BU 1956

NARCISSUS (1801) Woolwich, Convict Hosp Sh
5th Rate, Woolwich 1823, sold 1837

NARCISSUS (1859) Clyde, CG
FF, CG Clyde, 20.07.1877-09.05.1878, sold 1883

NARIMBA - see NIRIMBA

NARVIK (1945) Med/ Faslane/ Rosyth, DS
Ex LST 3044, named 1947. Res Amphibious Force Gareloch 02.48, Atomic Research 1948-49, res Gareloch 05.49, then Monte Bello Cd 18.01.52, res Clyde 07.06.54, Res Chat 05.07.55, Cd 25.10.55 & 07.01.58 (Grapple Sqn), Res Chat 07.04.59. DS for 5 SM and M/S Med v FORTH Cd 19.07.60-SM1 19.08.60 -02.06.62 (SM to AUSONIA). Accom sh Dev 03.08.62-22.06.65, Cd at Dev 20.02.65. 3 SM Faslane 22.06.65 v BEN NEVIS - set up Base (see NEPTUNE) - 03.68. Rosyth Storeship 03.68-, dockyard offices Rosyth 1970 - sold 12.1971

NASAR Sembawang, Spore, RNAS
Construction started 04.1941, Name alloc 09.09.41, to 16.02.42

NAUTILUS (1913) MNBDO
In 05.1941 controlled M/L Tlr NAUTILUS earmarked for MNBDO II from 08.41 - for disposal 09.44
Also Tlr, hired as M/S (RIN) 1941-46

NAUTILUS Hamble, Accom Sh
12.1942 - 07.44 to DST/ C & M Lymington, 14.09.44 no longer required. PO 16.09.45

NELSON (1814) Melbourne, Store/Coal Hulk
1st Rate, 02.1867 Government of Australia at Melbourne. Floating Battery & TS 1868. The first ship to fly what became the Australian National Flag 1870. Stricken 1892, sold 28.04.1898. Coal hulk (after stripping) at Sydney, named NELSON (not in Naval service), then Tasmania. Finally BU 09.1928 at Launceston, Tasmania

NELSON (1876) Ports, Guard/TS
FF, guardship Ports 10.1891-1893, TS for stokers Cd 01.06.1904 - sold 12.07.1910 (tng tx to RN Baracks & RENOWN)

NELSON (1925) Portland, Hbr TS
BB, Hbr TS end WWII - 1946 rb ANSON and then FO Training v ANSON 27.02.47.BU 03.49

NELSON Ports, RN Barracks
01.08.1974 (Barracks ex VICTORY) - extant 1999
Included VERNON site from 1986-known as NELSON (Gunwharf) - closed 01.04.96
Also EXCELLENT site 1985-94 (when Re-Cd as EXCELLENT)
To be merged with Naval Base 2000 (poss name retained)

NEMESIS Iceland, Accom Sh
SOUTHERN ISLES ex PRINCESS MARIE JOSE, Belgian, hired 19.07.1940 as A/S TS - renamed NEMESIS 03.41 and allocated Iceland as accom sh 07.43. Renamed BALDUR 06.10.43 as Base Ship Iceland - renamed NEMESIS 04.06.45, PO 12.07.46. Resto at Antwerp 08.45

NEMO Brightlingsea, A/P Base
Opened 11.06.1940, Cd 01.07.40, PO 16.05.45 (from NOIC to RNO). Base closed 09.45
CO Base 1940-05.04.42 - then to HELDER - NEMO absorbed HELDER when PO 09.44.
In North/main part of town
Nom DS: Orig req as NEMO II

NEPAL (1941) Dev, Living Ship RF
DD, arrived RF Dev 08.11.1950 - living ship, BU 01.1956

NEPTUNE (1874) Holyhead, CG
BB, CG Holyhead 21.05.1887-16.11.1893, sold 15.09.1903

NEPTUNE Chat, RF
01.07.1950-11.05.1960
SO RF ABERCROMBIE 50-52, DUNCANSBY HEAD 1952-53, DIADEM 54-56, DUNCANSBY HEAD 1957-
Nom DS: Motor M/S 1775 (ex 275) 01.07.50-54
Motor M/S 1075 - 01.55
LCM(7) 7020 01.55-13.05.56
MSPB 41354 14.05.56-60

NEPTUNE Rosyth, RF
Name proposed for RF 1959 but rejected in favour of DUNDONALD

NEPTUNE Faslane/Helensburgh, SM Base/Naval Base
Cd 10.08.1967 - independent command - extant 1999
Base opened 30.06.1966, tx ashore from MAIDSTONE 31.12.67, formal opening 05.68.
Base of 3 SM (67-), 10 SM (67-93), Captain SM Tng (1974-93), 1 SM (01.01.94-extant 99).
Became Naval Base Faslane 01.04.95 (Flag from Rosyth.)

NEREUS (1821) Valparaiso/Coquimbo, Chile, Store ship
5th Rate, storeship Valparaiso 1843-75, sold 22.01.1879 At Coquimbo, Chile

NESMAR II (1911) Oban, A/P Base - Armed Yt/Special Service
01.1918 v CRESCENT and LORD LANSDOWNE - PO 09.05.1919. Then tender to CRESCENT 09.05.1919-till base closed 11.11.1919
Drifter

NETAJI SUBHAS Calcutta, IN estab (NOIC)
12.1974-76 (at least)

NETLEY (1866) Inverness (Kessock Ferry), RNR Drl Sh
Gunboat, Drl Sh - 1876 rb BRILLIANT, sold 09.1885

NETTLE Portland, DS
Ex PENNAR (War department), RN 1906, Periscope Sch 1921, then 6 SM Portland by 1924 - sold 1934

NETTLE (1933) Blyth/Clyde, SM Tender
ELFIN, DS 6 SM Blyth 1941, renamed NETTLE 28.08.1941 when rb Drifter ROTHA, tx to Clyde, for sale 1957

NEW ZEALAND (1911) Rosyth, SO RF
BCr, FO RF 1920-, sold 12.1922

NEWCASTLE (1813) Lpool, Qtn Sh
4th Rate, qtn sh 1824, sold 1850

NEWCASTLE (1860) Hull/Plym, CG/Powder Hulk
FF, CG Hull 1870-74, powder hulk Plym 1889 - sold 1929

NEWFOUNDLAND (1941) Dev, TS and SO RF
Cr, Hbr TS Dev 11.09.1947 - 01.07.50 rb WARRIOR. Also SO RF v TARTAR 11.07.47-10.03.48 rb UNICORN. Then Stokers' TS 10.03.48 tender to RALEIGH on tx IMPERIEUSE to RALEIGH. Sold to Peru 11.59

NEWPORT CORNER Newport Corner, Nova Scotia, RCN Radio Sta
Established 1940, operational 05.1943-, HMCS 1957-11.07.66

NEWT West Quay, Newhaven, CO Base
Cd 15.10.1942, independent command accounts FORWARD - under C & M party, to be used for CO personnel from time to time. 03.45 no longer required as LC Base, became accom for Eclipse Parties (NPs into Europe), PO 22.06.45
LCT Hards at Sleeper's Hole & Seaford & accom in Fort Rd.
Nom DS: NAB KARINA 15.10.42-22.06.45

NGAPONA Fanshawe St, Auckland, New Zealand, RNZN Res Div
1948 - extant1999
Nom DS: SDML 3561 1957
SDML 3555 1964-67

NIAGARA (1918) Sydney, Nova Scotia, RCN TS
DD, ex USN, moored TS 03.44 - BU 12.47

NIAGARA Massachusetts Ave, Washington, RCN Staff
02.09.1951 - 01.04.1966 (PO back-dated to 01.09.65)

NICHOLAS Tripoli, Lebanon, Syria, Base Depot Ship
In PO Circular 09.05.45 - -in Red List 07.44 -06.45 - misc duties and NOIC
Anglo Hellenic Schooner Force NICHOLAS II Cd 20.08.43 - no longer fit 01.08.44
Party Nicholas (NP 868) was in Op Avalanche 1943

NIGER (1945) M/S HQ Ship
M/S, Cd 21.09.45 to East Indies, Penang/Spore 03.46, 02.47 -48 refit Dev then res Dev, BU 02.66

NIGERIA (1901) DS
Hired as store carrier (RFA) 11.1916, DS 1917-18

NIGERIA (1939) Dev/Rosyth, Accom Sh
Cr, Dev RF living ship 12.1950, Rosyth v GIRDLE NESS 08.51-54, then refitted for tx India 08.57

NIGHTHAWK Drem/MacMerry, E Lothian, RNAS
Cd 21.04.1945, tender to MERLIN, Cd 01.06.45 as NIGHTHAWK, independent command, own acs, PO 15.03.46 (both returned to RAF)
Drem on indefinite loan from RAF. MacMerry Cd as satellite to Drem 01.06.45
Nom DS: 50 ton Steam Pinnace 672 01.06.45-(01.51)

NIGHTINGALE
1952-57 - Mining tender (1931) to 07.1957, allocation of Nom DS indicates was a shore estab - hence inclusion - but poss ref to own boat number in reg-

ister as it was small craft
Nom DS: MB 37282

NIGHTJAR Inskip,Lancs, RNAS
Cd 15.05.1943, independent command, PO 02.07.46 - to C & M under BLACKCAP
Originally called RNAS Elswick to 04.43, became Radio Sta 1958 and INSKIP (qv) 1966
Included Burscough - see RINGTAIL
Nom DS: Belge MFV ANNIE II 15.05.43-12.43
Patrol Vessel KISMET 12.43 -
MFV NIGHTJAR foundered under tow 12.03.46

NIGHTSWICK Firth of Forth
Ment in two lists - no dates

NILE (1888) Dev, Guard
BB, guardship Cd 13.01.1898 - 02.1903, sold 09.07.1912

NILE Ras el Tin Point, Alexandria, Base
Cd 24.04.1939, PO 30.06.46
For personnel on books MAIDSTONE II - & also most personnel in E Med during WWII. Also included RNAS Aboukir 1941 and RNAS Dekhelia 1943 (see NILE II and GREBE), Tobruk, Mersa Mutruh, Pt Tewfik and Cyprus (1942)
Nom DS: Steam Barge No 7 01.11.39-

NILE II Alexandria, Base
Pre-WW II airport at Alexandria taken over by Egyptian Air Force 1939 and used by FAA as NILE II. Cd as GREBE(qv) 1940. NL 1941 shows both GREBE and NILE II. Also in one list name in use 10.1943 on.

NIMBLE (1860) Hull, Res Drl Sh
Gunboat, CG tender at Hull 1879-1885, res drl sh Hull 1889 - 1900, sold 10.07.1906

NIMROD (1828) Dev, Coal Depot
Ex ANDROMEDA, 6th Rate, renamed before launching, coal hulk 02.1853, became C1, then C76, sold 07.1907

NIMROD, Campbeltown, TE and A/S Base Ship
Cd 01.03.1940 as tender to OSPREY. Cd 10.05.1940 independent command, PO 28.02.1946 - NOIC to lapse and retard party in LANDRAIL
TE at Dunoon and Experimental Section at Fairlie (see OSPREY) to train in conjunction with NIMROD 10.1940.
Nom DS: MB of Yt LADY BLANCHE 01.03.40-

NIOBE (1897) Halifax, Nova Scotia, RCN DS
Cr, tx to RCN 06.09.1910, arrived Halifax 21.10.10 and became DS 06.09.1915-31.05.1920. Badly damaged in explosion 06.12.1917 but continued in service with no funnels, masts nor ventillators. PO 1920 - see GUELPH. Sold 1922

NIOBE Plym/ London/Greenock/ London, RCN Depot
Cd 01.03.1941 ex DOMINION (qv) - at Albert Rd, Dev. PO 30.06.1941 - acs to Canada House, then VICTORY 31.07.41. Recommended tx to St Johns, Newfoundland. Accom in Canada House 01.07.41. At Smithston Institute, Nr Greenock, Re-Cd 15.12.41 - 01.04.46. Sub Office in Londonderry 08.03.43 for RCN ships there. Also RCN camp Greenock 11.43.
Re-Cd 09.02.1946 at Haymarket, London SW1. At W1 by 1950, at SW7 by 1952-61, W1 in 1962 - PO 31.08.65 acs to CDLS, London.

NIOBE II Belfast, RCN DS
Cd 09.04.1956 - 17.01.57
Temp self accounting shore estab for RCN personnel standing by BONAVENTURE in refit

NIRIMBA Schofields, Nr Sydney, NSW, RAN Air Sta, TE
09.06.1946 ex NABSTOCK (qv) to RAAF, reopened 1952 as Aircraft Repair Yard known as ALBATROSS II. Cd 01.04.53, PO 28.02.55, Cd 05.01.56 as TE, PO 25.02.94
Used as TE for all technical apprentices tng, and some general entry technical tng from 1956. - called "Quakers Hill", spelt NARIMBA in some lists

NITH (1942) Normandy, Temp HQ Ship
FF, conv to Brigade HQ Ship 10.43.LS HQ Ship Normandy 1944, sold to Egypt 11.1948

NIZAM (1940) Harwich, Accom Sh
DD, accom sh 11.1945 and also v ANENOME 11.46-03.47. BU 11.55

NONSUCH Soton, Accom Sh
Houseboat, 08.1942 - laid up Swanwick/DST 04.44, resto 11.01.45

NONSUCH 102nd St, Edmonton, Alberta, RCN Base & Res Div
Estab 01.09.1939 - Cd 01.11.41 - 01.09.42 - tender to NADEN. 01.09.42-30.11.64. Independent command In Pink List to 01.66, then back into Pink List 08.75 -86 (at least)

NORFOLK II Ceylon, Base
22.01.1935 ex HAWKINS II (qv) - 01.39? - became GLOUCESTER II (qv)
NORFOLK(1928) Cr, Cd 26.10.37 for E Indies

NORFOLK III Aden, Base
22.01.1935 (ex HAWKINS III?) - 27.01.39 - became GLOUCESTER III(qv)
NORFOLK (1928) Cr, Cd 26.10.37 for E Indies

NORTHAMPTON (1876) Newhaven/Sheerness, CG/TS
FF, CG Newhaven 22.04.1886 - 23.08.1886, Seagoing TS for Boys 06.1894-11.1904 (Sheerness by 1902), sold 04.04.1905

NORTHAMPTON (1888) Thames, Hbr Serv
SHARPSHOOTER, gunboat, seagoing TS 1895-

1900, renamed NORTHAMPTON 1912 Hbr Serv, Boy Scouts Association 1921, sold 27.03.22

NORTHLAND (1911) Inveraray, Accom Sh
American ship on lease lend, accom sh Inveraray 01.43 - 44. Returned to War shipping Administration of America 06.44

NORTHMAN Faroes, Base
Cd 01.04.1941, independent command, acs PYRAMUS (Ex POLE STAR, name not used (qv)). PO 26.03.43 - renamed POLAR BEAR (qv)
Tlr NORTHMAN (1911) hired WWI and as A/P Tlr 07.40, allocated Faroes Patrol 07.41 and became Base Ship 01.42-06.45, resto 03.46

NORTHNEY Hayling Is, TE for LC/ CO Camp
Cd 15.06.1940 without name under VICTORY III. 01.41 independent command - known as NORTHNEY from 26.01.41. Cd 03.02.41, PO 01.01.46
Hayling Is Camp 1 - LC Base, LC Maint 08.45
Nom DS: Small LC Infantry 03.02.41-

NORTHNEY I Hayling Is, LC Base
By 01.10.1942. PO 21.03.46
Poss refers to NORTHNEY whilst NORTHNEY II - IV extant

NORTHNEY II Hayling Is, LC Base
In list 06.04.1942
01.10.42 - reduced to 50% personnel & in C & M Normandy Ops 06.44 - PO 21.01.46
Camp 2 - Assembly Base for LC Base Mobile Units for foreign service 08.45. TE for Engine Room Ratings.

NORTHNEY III Hayling Is, LC Base
In list 06.04.1942
01.10.42 - reduced to 50% personnel & in C & M for Normandy Ops 06.44. PO 22.12.45
Camp 3 - Holding Base for CO Personnel 08.45

NORTHNEY IV Sunshine Camp, Hayling Is, LC Base
Ex MNBDO camp, Cd 25.11.1942, C & M 03.12.45, PO 10.12.45
Camp 4 - for receipt of ratings returning UK ex France 06.44 on, also Holding Base for CO personnel 08.45

NORTHUMBERLAND (1798) Standgate Creek, Qtn Sh
3rd Rate, qtn sh 1827 - BU 1850

NORTHUMBERLAND (1866) Weymouth/Chat, CG/DS
Iron Armoured FF, CG 13.05.1890 - 08.03.1891, Stokers' DS Chat 1898, renamed ACHERON (qv) 03.1904, hulk C8 1909, hulk C68 1926, sold 06.1927

NORTHUMBRIA Tyne, Res Drl Sh
Alternative name to CALLIOPE sel 1951 for Res Div Tyne, CALLIOPE sel later

NORTHWOOD Northwood, Middlesex, HQ Unit RNR
Formed 06.05.1957, Cd and named 10.04.59. Tx from WARRIOR (qv) to Brackenhill House 28.03.88 and ReCd 13.07.88, extant 1999

NSB 51 Ex LCT(I) 13, E Med, CF Mobile Workshop
Allocated 30.08.1944

NUMONGLA Khulna, Bangladesh, Bangladeshi Naval Base
1998-extant 1999 (see also MONGLA)

NUBIAN (1871) Simonstown, Coal Depot
Ex PROCIDA, coal depot, purch 1901, in NL 02.1902-01.1905, became C370 1904, sold 15.07.1912

NUTHATCH Anthorn, Cumberland, RNAS
RN Lodger Unit Spring 1940 - 2 sqdn Skua & Swordfish & 1 Albacores. Ann to be opened as RN Receipt & Despatch Unit 06.43.
Cd 07.09.44, part complement, independent command, own acs as Receipt & Despatch Unit, closed to flying 12.57, PO 28.02.58 and to C & M 1600, 31.03.58 - tender to SANDERLING. For disposal 03.11.59
Under Civil Engineer Manager Scotland 30.11.59-27.06.60 - became NATO Radio Sta 27.11.64
Nom DS: MSPB 44320 by 10.46-59

NYCTEA Normandy, Accom Barge for shore end working party PLUTO
LBV (M)(I) 381, fitted out and name as accom barge 05.1944. Cd 11.06.44 - destore and release from Op Pluto 06.45, to DST 15.01.46 (spelt MYCTEA in some acs)

NYMPH Chat, Nom DS
In a list as 1919, prob ref to NYMPHE (qv)

NYMPHE (1812) Woolwich/Sheerness, Rx Sh/Chapel & Police Ship
Ex NEREIDE 1811, Hbr serv 03.1836. Rx Sh Sheerness 1840-, Rx Sh Woolwich 1865-56, Rx Sh Sheerness 1857-, RC Chapel & Police Ship Sheerness 1865, renamed HANDY 07.09.1871, BU Chat 03.1875

NYMPHE (1888) Chat, Base Ship
Sloop, renamed WILDFIRE (qv) as Base Ship 12.1906, renamed GANNET (qv) 1916, renamed PEMBROKE(qv) 07.1917, sold 10.02.20

O

OCEAN (1805) Sheerness, DS - Coal Hulk
2nd Rate, DS 1841-52, coal hulk 1853 - BU 12.1875

OCEAN FISHER (1919) Orkneys, DS
Tlr, Armed Patrol DS Orkneys 09.1939-

OCELOT (1962) Chat, Museum SM
SM, to Chat Historic Dockyard Trust 05.05.92 - extant 1999

ODIN Plym, Rx Sh
Danish 3rd Rate, capt 1807, Rx Sh 1811 - BU 1825

ODYSSEY Collingwood Hotel, Ilfracombe/ London, NP Accounting Base
01.11.1943 ex EXCELLENT II ex EVOLUTION (qv) - PO 31.05.46
To Chelsea Court SW 3 on 12.06.45 - C & M Party under EXCELLENT - also quoted as ex APPLEDORE II (qv) - but that was a different section of EXCELLENT II.
Nom DS: FMB 37352 -08.03.46
HL(D) 3712 08.03.46-31.05.46

OLIVIA Soton, Accom Sh
A hull, 08.1942 - acquired 24.12.42 - to DST in C & M at Lymington 07.44

OLPHERT Wellington, New Zealand, RNZN Res Div
1948 - extant 1999
Nom DS: SDML 3562 1957-64

OLYMPUS (1961) Halifax, Nova Scotia, Hbr TS
SM, tx from RN to Canada 08.1989 as Hbr TS, extant 1993

OMAN Khorkuwai, Persian Gulf, Poss Khor Kuwait - Hannah creek
By 03.1945 (at least), 01.05.45 reduced to tender to JUFAIR, 01.09.45 Base tx to RAF

OMBRA (1902) Swansea, A/P DS Bristol Channel
12.09.1915 - 11.15 rb LONGSET
Yt, hired 09.1914-03.19 (became CETO (qv) 20.03.18) & WWII

OMEGA Gt Yarmouth, Accom Sh
NAB allocated 24.05.1944

ONSET Birkenhead, CO Base
Cd 31.05.1945, independent command, acs EAGLET, PO 04.03.1946 - to C & M 15.03.46
Tx to IRWELL (qv) accom 19.07.45. CO Base LC Receipt & Despatch/Storage and Ferry Units
Nom DS: NAB 96 31.05.45-

ONSLOW (1968) Sydney, Museum SM
SM, PO 31.03.1999 - to National Maritime Museum, Sydney - opened to public 22.06.99-

ONTARIO Kingston, Ontario, RCN SCC TE
Summer Camps 1982-86 (at least)

ONYX (1892) SM DS
Sloop, SM DS 1907, Section VI SM Dev 1910, 1 SM Dev 1914-16 (under IMPREGNABLE 10.1915), Torbay 1917-18, W/T TS Dev 01.18-09.18. A/P DS Torbay 01.09.1918 - 01.02.1919 - tow to Dev.(Naval Base Torquay closed 24.04.1919). Portland for SAREPTA SM 05.19, renamed VULAN II (qv) 06.19, sold 1924

ONYX (1966) Birkenhead, Museum SM
SM, for preservation and display, tow from Ports to Birkenhead 11.1991 - extant 1999

OP HOOP VAN ZEGER (ZEGEN) (ZEEMAN) Poole, Accom Sh
Dutch Yt, 08.1942 - acquired 08.02.1943, - 29.06.45, laid up/DST 06.45

OPPIDAN SW Pacific
Codeword for tx of Amphibious Forces from UK to SW Pacific 06.44 (see also APPIAN)

OPOSSUM (1856) HK, Hosp Sh/Mooring Hulk
Gunboat, hosp hulk 1875, mooring vessel 1891, renamed SIREN 1895, sold 1896

ORANJE NASSAU Holyhead, Netherlands DS
Netherlands DS Holyhead v STUYVESANT 08.1941 - there by 09.09.40 - by 10.44 listed as at London (poss ref to personnel only) - 13.12.45 arrived Rotterdam

ORARA (1907) Melbourne, RAN DS
Cd as RAN M/S 09.10.1939, DS A/S Instructional Sch Newcastle 12.45-46 (In PO Circular 09.05.45)

ORCA (1935) Ardrishaig/Tarbert, Accom Sh
Ex CACHALOT, Yt, hired as A/P Yt 09.1940, accom sh for SEAHAWK (Ardrishaig) 02.43, allocated accom sh Tarbert with JAMES COOK (qv) 11.44, laid up 10.45

ORCADIA (1944) Dev, Accom Sh
M/S, Accom Sh 05.1948 - 03.50, BU 12.58

ORESTES (1824) Ports, Coal Depot
Sloop, coal hulk 11.1852 (known as C28) - sold about 1905

ORFORD NESS (1945) Maint Ship
Completed as a merchant ship

ORIFLAMME (1890) Prob Grimsby, Base Ship
ST GERGE, Yt, hired 03.03.1915, renamed ORIFLAMME 06.18, Capt D Ship 7 DF 06.18-10.18 (independent command Cd 06.07.18), renamed WALLINGTON (qv) 01.10.18, Base ship Humber 01.10.18-03.19.

ORIOLE (1910) Ft William/Dieppe, Accom Sh
EAGLE III, paddle steamer, hired as M/S WWI and again 11.1939. Experimental M/L 1941-43, accom sh 1943 -08.45 (Ft William from 09.43-07.44 (at least), at Terneuzen rb SANDOWN to 04.45), To DST 29.08.45 and at Dieppe 09.45.

ORION (1879) Malta GC, Res Drl Sh/DS
Armoured corvette, ex Turkish BOORDJI ZAFFER, Torp Boat DD DS Malta 1902, was Res Drl Sh Malta 1904-09, renamed ORONTES (qv) 12.09, stores ship/Torp Boat DD DS, sold 06.13

ORION (1910) Portland, RF Parent
BB, RF Parent Portland 1920, Ports RF 03.21, sold 19.12.22

ORION Dev, RF
01.07.1950 - 31.12.66 task to TYNE
SO RF HOWE 1950-, DIADEM 52-53, BERRY HEAD 54-55, EURYALUS 57, WOOLWICH 57-61, TYNE (q) was SO's ship 61 and took on RF HQ

01.01.67.
Nom DS: FMB 45502 07.50-52
MSPB 41343 12.52-05.55
FMB 42514 26.05.55-61
FMB 39402 65-

ORLANDO (1811) Trinco, Hosp Sh
5th Rate, Hosp Sh 1819 - sold 1824

ORLANDO (1886) Australia
Cr, Flag Australia 25.05.1888 - 1898, sold 1905
Bore acs of shore based personnel whilst Flag

ORLANDO Greenock, Base Acs Staff
Cd 01.04.1940, PO 01.08.46
Nom DS: MB PENGUIN 01.04.40-07.01.43 (became ROLAND)
NAB ENGLYN 01.43-laid up 10.45
PB(D) 41337 10.45-

ORONTES (1870) Ports, Offices and Workshops
SWIFTSURE, renamed ORONTES 03.1904, Fleet Res Offices and workshop for civilians, sold 04.07.1908

ORONTES (1879) Malta GC, DS
ORION, renamed ORONTES 12.1909 -(poss bore name earlier-1900), Torp Boat DD and Res Drl Sh Malta, sold 19.06.1913 at Malta

ORPHEUS (1959) Ports, Hbr TS
SM, Hbr TS at DOLPHIN v FINWHALE 10.1987-93 - sold 1994

OSBORNE Osborne, Isle of Wight, RN College
Cd 01.04.1916 - closed 20.05.1921
College opened 04.08.1903.
Ex BETA, steam lch - Nom DS 1921 and tx to BRITANNIA(qv) as Nom DS 1922, listed as carrying Captain of RN College - was to have been RACER (qv).

OSBORNE Cowes, Isle of Wight, Base
Cd 01.1942, PO 08.06.42 - merged with TORMENTOR II to form VECTIS (qv)

OSBORNE Ryde, Isle of Wight, Base
Cd 01.10.1942, PO 15.08.45
Parent ship for all estabs on Isle of Wight from 01.10.42, acs Depot ex MEDINA
Nom DS: BETSY JANE 10.42-08.45

OSEA Osea Is, Clacton-on-Sea, Coastal MB Base
Cd 19.06.1918 - 19..04.21 - task to Haslar - see HORNET
23.01.19 Dover Coastal MB Base reduced to Sub Base of OSEA
Nom DS: CMB 40 19.06.18-11.08.18
Steam Lch 229 11.08.18-15.03.19
MB 1600 HERBERT SMITH 15.03.19-

OSIRIS (1898)/OSIRIS II Mudros, Aegean, A/P DS
Hired as AMC 08.1914, used as Fleet messenger 10.14. Cd 11.04.1915 at Malta, became DS for Tlrs and Drifters v BLENHEIM 07.15, Net Tlrs ex EGMONT 10.15. Renamed OSIRIS II 12.15 - 04.18 rb VALHALLA II, PO 12.05.18 and returned to Fleet Messenger Duty

OSIRIS Fayid, Suez Canal Zone, HQ Middle East
02.1949-12.54 - FO Middle East to APHRODITE 01.12.54
Tender to STAG to 30.04.59, then to ST NGELO
Nom DS: Barge of SNOME(conv Eureka LC) 1949
NSB 352 (ex Eureka LC 4849) 52-54 (poss same as above)
25ft MB 42505 08.54 - (PO 10.06.55)

OSPREY Portland, Base
Cd as A/S TE 01.04.1924 - 02.41 (A/ S Tng to NIMROD (qv) 06.40). Tx to Dunoon 15.01.41 - 31.10.46 (see next entry), Experimental Department to Fairlie 28.01.40 - see HARBINGER. Re-Cd 01.01.46 - became Base 01.01.48 when BOSCAWEN (qv) PO. Base closed 31.03.95 (handed over 29.03.95).
Helicopter sta (was under DAEDALUS then became part of OSPREY) opened 24.04.59 - closed to flying 12.02.99. Became tender to HERON 01.04.99 and site to DEO for disposal 01.11.99
Nom DS: ICEWHALE (Z12) (1915) 01.04.24-27 (sold 10.28)
Steam Lch 248 29.11.27-15.09.41 (became Nom DS ATTACK)
Steam Lch 248 01.01.46-22.03.46
HL(D) 42706 23.03.46-11.51
also 53-11.10.56 (and in NL 01.58)
HL(D) 42473 50-52
HL(D) 42585 10.12.56-62

OSPREY Dunoon/Belfast, A/S TE
Tx at 0001 on 15.01.1941 - 31.01.46
Originally to be known as SAREPTA -
Also a small A/S TE at Pollock Dock, Belfast established 10.43 as ancillary
Nom DS: MB ARACHNE 15.01.41-19.10.41
Pilot Cutter FANCY 20.10.41-01.11.422
36 ft HL 42524 cancelled
MFV HEKTOR FRAANZ 02.11.42-09.09.45
MFV ACRASIA (1931) ex MOED EN WERK 10.9.45-31.12.45

OTTER (1805) Milford, Qtn Sh
Slop, Qtn Sh 1814 - sold 1828

OTTER Sheerness, Coal Hulk
Ex GPO Vessel, tx 1837, gun vessel 1854, tug 1865, coal hulk Sheerness 1878 - sold 1893

OTWAY (1966) Sydney, RAN Hbr TS
SM, PO 17.02.1994, became Hbr TS at PLATYPUS, BU 01.96 at Garden Is. 07.06.97 top half of SM opened as memorial at Holbrook,NSW, Australia (named after Holbrook WWI SM VC)

OUR ALLIES (1915) Taranto, ML Parent
Drifter, hired 1915-19, parent ship Gallipoli and parent MLs 01.04.1918 v CATANIA - 03.19

OURAGAN (1924) Ports, DS/ Accom Sh

Fr DD, seized 07.1940, Polish manned to 04.41, taken over by Free Fr as DS Ports 30.04.41 and used as accom sh 06.41. laid up West Hartlepool 1944, returned to Fr 06.05.44

OUTLAW (1914) Ports, Accom Sh
HEPATICA, Yt (qv), hired as accom sh 21.08.1940, renamed OUTLAW 04.41, to War Department 1942

OVENS (1967) Cockburn Sound/Pt
Adelaide/Fremantle, RAN TS - SM Memorial SM, alongside TS STIRLING 1995-97, to Adelaide SM Memorial Park 1997 - to Fremantle, Western Australian Maritime Museum 1999.

OWEN GLENDOWER (1808) Gib, Prison/Rx Ship
5th Rate, prison ship 10.1842 - Rx Sh 1880 - sold 1884

OWL Fearn, Ross-shire/Evanton, RNAS
Tx from RAF 19.07.1942 and Cd 01.08.1942. PO 02.07.46 to C & M under FIELDFARE 02.07.46 - 53 Evanton, on loan from 09.44. Used as res storage 1944 - see FIELDFARE.
Nom DS: NAB EXPERT 08.42 - and 47-53
NAB ENDEAVOUR 09.44-03.45
NAB SUTOR - 06.45 (revert to GOOD-CHEER)
Steam Lch 225 10.07.45-06.49 (revert to No 396)

P

PACINOTTI (1922) Maddelena, SM DS
12.1944-12.1945
Italian ship under Allied control

PACTOLUS (1896) Lamlash/ Ardrossan, SM DS, A/P Parent
Cr, conv to SM DS 09.1912, Lamlash Flot 24.09.1912-14, 9 SM Ardrossan 12.14 - 7 SM 1916-18, also A/P Parent Ship Clyde 12.14-06.19. DS A/S Tng Ardrossan 1919, at Shandon in C & M 09.19, allocated RNR Clyde. Old 1921

PADLOPING ISLAND Padloping Is, North West Territories, RCN Radio Sta
10.09.1953 - 08.55 - to DOT

PADSTOW BAY (1945) Dev, RF Accom Sh
FF, accom sh 24.01.49 v HOUND -12.50 (at least), BU 08.59

PAKEHA (1910) DS
09.1939 take up for service as DS, refit Belfast, used as dummy BB REVENGE 09.39-06.41

PALATINA Poole, Accom Sh
Yt, 08.1942 - acquired 12.02.43, laid up/DST 06.45, C & M 07.45

PALATINE Hartington Rd, Preston, Lancs, Communications Tng Centre
Formed 1948, moved to Hartington Rd 1968, Cd 01.10.1984, ceremony 05.10.84, PO 31.01.92

PALLAS (1816) Plym, Coal Hulk
5th Rate, coal hulk 09.1836, sold 11.01.1862

PALLAS (1865) Kingstown, CG
Corvette, CG Kingstown 01.01.1870 - 10.1870, sold 20.04.1886

PAMPAM Okha, India
One ref in 1973

PANDION Loop Repair Ship, RAN
Cd 22.08.1944-

PANDORA (1902) Harwich/ Rosyth/ Ports, SM DS
Ex SETI, purch 1913, renamed PANDORA 19.11.14, SM DS 9 SM Harwich 1915-19, 1 SM Rosyth 08.19-05.22, Pembroke 03.21, Chat by 04.22, Ports SM Sch - used as hulk, not Cd 1923, renamed DOLPHIN (qv) at Gosport 03.10.24, sunk 23.12.39

PANDORA (1915) Littlehampton, Accom Sh
Yt, accom sh Air Sea Rescue Base Littlehampton 05.1942, resto 1945

PANGKOR (later PANG KOR) (1929) Bombay, Base// Accom Sh
Hired as A/P vessel 25.09.1939, allocated as Base Ship Eastern Fleet 21.10.43. lent RIN 1944-45 (at Bombay, PO Circular 22.03.44). Used as Base/Accom Sh Bombay 07.44 - 05.45, C & M Bombay 08.12.45, to be released/to Ministry War Transport 11.12.45, resto 1946

PANGLIMA RMNVR TE
09.1948 - 12.1949
Nom DS: MFV 1541 Tx and named 02.09.48-

PANTALOON Fixed A/S Defences & NP 874
Codeword for Naples in Op Avalanche - Salerno 09.1943. Fixed A/S Defences used name - arrived Malta 06.11.43.

PARAGON Hartlepool, M/S Base
Cd 27.10.1939 - apps from 25.08.39, PO 30.11.45, acs to SCARBOROUGH - FO Commanding RF W Hartlepool
Name sel for Base at comml pt Hartlepool 01.09.39 - NOIC ordered 23.08.39 - arrived by 29.08.39.
Base Supply Officer at Albert Rd, Middlesbrough 02.45
Nom DS: Pilot Cutter T H TILLY 27.09.39 (allocated but not used)
NAB DEIRA 09.08.43 (backdated to 39)-04.06.45
NAY TRICIA -11.45

PARAGON Finkle St, Stockton/ Middlesbrough, Communications Tng Centre
Cd 01.10.1984 - PO 31.01.1992
Moved to Linthorpe Rd, Middlesbrough 1989-90

PARIS (1912) Plym, Base
Fr BB, seized 03.07.1940 at Plym. Cd 12.07.40 under DRAKE - to be DS Polish personnel Tyne 07.40 but cancelled. Extension of DEFIANCE - accom sh Cd 12.09.40. A/P DS for Tlrs and Aux vessels v CENTURION at Plym Cd 09.06.41 - independent command - PO 30.06.45 rb COLOMBO. Returned to Fr Navy 14.07.45

PARKES (1943) Fremantle, RAN SO RF
M/S, SO RF Fremantle 31.12.1946-56, sold 02.05.57

PASCO Glenbranter Camp (Loch Fyne), Glenbranter, Strachur, LC Signal Sch
Cd 14.12.1942 - ex Prisoner of War Camp, listed to 10.45
Nom DS: 10ft dinghy 14.12.42-

PATENGA Chittagong, Bangladesh Naval Academy
1996-extant 1999

PATENGI Chittagong, Bangladesh Naval Estab
Extant 1999

PATRICIAN (1916) Esquimalt, British Columbia, RCN Drl Sh
DD, RCN 09.1920, Drl Sh autumn 1922-27, BU 1929

PATRIOT (1916) Halifax, Nova Scotia, RCN Drl Sh
DD, RCN 09.1920, Drl Sh Atlantic Coast autumn 1922 - 27, BU 1929

PATRIOT Cameron St North, Hamilton, Ontario, RCN FO Naval Divs
28.03.1953 in STAR, named 1955, Cd 01.02.56-66

PATROL (1904) Kingstown, ML and Hydrophone Flot DS
Cr, DS by 11.1918-01.1919 (at least). Was to be rb GLENMAY 11.18 but cancelled. Sold 04.1920

PATROL Lyness, Scapa Flow, Base
09.1939
Name sel for comml pt Lyness 01.09.39 - NOIC ordered 27.08.39
Appears in some lists but unclear whether used.
Yt PATHFINDER (1884) was renamed PATROL 03.1942 (poss to released name for new DD) - and lost 21.10.44 in storm in Clyde area - no known connection

PATUNGA Chittagong, RIN Local Naval Defence Base/Advanced CF Base
Listed 22.11.1943 - closed 08.03.46 - see BAKHTYER

PAULINE Yarmouth, Isle of Wight/Poole, NOIC & CF Base/Accom Sh
08.1942 - 10.12.42 acquired, 03.43 no longer required by BESSIER at Weymouth, re-allocated to MANATEE (Yarmouth). Cd 07.43 at Lymington as CO Base, PO 43. 07.43 Yarmouth, 03.44 Poole, 07.44 repairs Soton. 20.08.44 no longer required, laid up Lymington, 09.44 for disposal, 10.44 resto

PEACE Chichester, Accom Sh
Barge, 08.1942 - acquired 15.01.43 - 07.43 (at least)

PECCARY Bari, Fixed A/S Defences & NP 878
09.1943 - codeword for Bari - OpShingle - Anzio 01.1944

PEEWIT East Haven, Angus, RNAS
Cd 01.05.1943 - originally acs CONDOR, then Cd 01.03.44 independent command, own acs, PO 15.08.46
In 01.43 ref to being extended to 3 sqns - poss planning statement
Was to have been named DOTTEREL (qv)
Nom DS: DG tender BOY DAVID 01.05.43-
HL(D) 3960 - 08.46 (became Nom DS DRAKE)

PEGASUS (1917) Archangel, DS
Seaplane carrier, DS & Repair Ship for seaplanes & Coastal MBs, to leave UK by 14.04.1919 for Archangel, sold 08.31

PEGASUS (1914) Dev/Belfast, DS - Accom Sh
ARK ROYAL, seaplane carrier, temp SO RF Dev 1929-30, later DS renamed PEGASUS 21.12.34. catapult ship 04.41, accom sh Belfast for CO personnel 01.44 (name not used - under CAROLINE). Accom Sh Lisahally for SM crews - tender to CAROLINE 12.45, sold 18.10.46

PEGASUS Christchurch, New Zealand, RNZN Res Div
1948 - extant 1999
Nom DS; SDML 3563 1957-64

PEKIN (1907) Grimsby, A/P Base
09.1914 v LEANDER - PO 17.12.1919 - men to books PEMBROKE VII
1) Tlr No 24 PEKIN PO 28.02.1919
2) Tlr JOHN DUNKIN (1915) 28.02.19 - (sold 1921)
3) Tlr FESTING GRINDALL (1917) -PO 27.11.19

PEKIN Chat, Accom Sh
Ex TS ARETHUSA, hired as accom sh Chat 09.1940 v CORNWALL and renamed whilst so employed. Resto 07.1945

PELANDOK Spore, RMN Base
Cd 13.10.1939, tender to TERROR II. 01.01.40 tender to SULAN II - 02.42
TE and Depot for Malay Ratings

PELANDOK Woodlands, Spore/Lumut, Malaysia, Malaysian Naval TE
Poss from 1947 when RMN formed. Name in use to 01.01.51 - became MALAYA (qv) - name retained - tx to LCG(L) 450
Woodlands 1970, to Lumut 1981 - extant 1999
Nom DS: LCT(E) 341 Cd 08.04.49-
LCG(L) 450 01.01.51-

PELICAN Walvis Bay, Simonstown, SAN Base
1944

PELLEW Sidwell St/ Dryden Rd, Exeter, Communications Tng Centre
Cd 01.10.1984 - PO 29.07.94
Moved 1989/90

PELORUS (1896) Gib/ Suda Bay, Crete, DS
Cr, Tlr DS Gib 10..1915. DS Suda Bay 1916-19 - Base W/T Ship E Med 20.05.1916. Sold 05.20

PEMBROKE Forth/Harwich/ Chat, CG - RN Barracks
Cd at Chat 01.04.1873 (afloat). Cd ashore 30.04.1903 - first messes taken over 26.03.1902, ready for occupation 01.04.1903 - PO 1983
In 1914-1915 Royal Flying Corps Naval Wing personnel at RNAS were on books of PEMBROKE (Eastchurch, Isle of Grain, Calshot, Felixstowe, Gt Yarmouth, Dundee, Ft George, Ft Grange, Farnborough & Kingsnorth)
Included Naval Base Humber 1922 - see PEMBROKE II etc
RN Supply Sch was at PEMBROKE 01.04.58 ex CERES to 1983 (to RALEIGH)
Hydrographic Tng unit from Chat to Dev August/Sept 1959
Ships bearing the name:
1) PEMBROKE (1812), 3rd Rate, CG Forth 03.12.1856-01.03.1858, Harwich 01.03.1858 - 12.06.1869, Flag C-in-C Nore - Sheerness 12.06.1869 - 01.04.1873, Flag as Admiral Superintendent Chat 01.04.1873 - 1890, renamed FORTE (Rx Sh), sold 1905
2) .DUNCAN (1859), 1st Rate, renamed 1890 as Flag Admiral Superintendent Chat, Cd as general depot 01.08.1891, renamed TENEDOS II (qv) 09.1905, sold 11.10.1910
3) Subsequent vessels effectively Nom DS - TRENT (1877), gunboat, renamed 09.1905, renamed GANNET (qv) 01.06.1917, sold 21.02.32
4) NYMPHE (1888) Sloop, renamed WILDFIRE (qv) 12.1906, renamed GANNET (qv) 1916, renamed PEMBROKE 01.06.1917, sold 10.02.20
5) ACHILLES (1863) Iron Screw Ship, renamed HIBERNIA (qv) 1902, renamed EGMONT (qv) 03.1904, renamed EGREMONT (qv) 06.1916, renamed PEMBROKE 06.1919, sold 26.01.23
6) PRINCE RUPERT (1915) monitor ex M10, renamed PEMBROKE 24.04.22, reverted to PRINCE RUPERT 01.09.22, sold 05.23
7) DANIEL FEARALL,(1917) Tlr, renamed STOUR 1920, renamed PEMBROKE 01.09.22, reverted to STOUR 1939, sold 07.46
8) HL(D) 3827 Cd 23.01.1940 - 1961

PEMBROKE I Chat, Accounting Base
By 25.02.1940-1960
Officers, Seamen & WRNS of RN Barracks

PEMBROKE II Eastchurch, Sheppey, RNAS
06.1913 - 01.04.1918 to RAF

PEMBROKE II Chat, Accounting Base
By 25.02.1940 - 1957
Engine Room & Miscellaneous/Kite Balloon ratings to AEOLUS 12.1942/Retard Party ROBERTSON 08.46? RF 1947/ & CICERO 19.04.48

PEMBROKE III London, WRNS Accounting Base
By 31.03.1942 - (PRESIDENT III and PEMBROKE III merge into PRESIDENT I 01.07.46)-1952
Also various outstations where WRNS were borne including Westfield College; Wesley College, Leeds (see HEADINGLEY); Burghfield (see DAUNTLESS); London - Mill Hill, Southmead, Chelsea Court, Golden Square (Soho), Barkeston Gardens, Earls Ct, Crosby Hall (Highgate); Woodford Green; New College (Oxford))

PEMBROKE IV Chat, Accounting Base
1919-1920 - acs Gt Yarmouth - including Medical Staff Royal Hosp Gt Yarmouth - 1928
05.09.1939 RF Nore - remained in commission with acs DD ex RF Nore
04.40 - 15 DF acs
PO 30.06.46 - acs to PEMBROKE II
By 1952 - 30.09.60 (Tenders), closed 02.61
Base Supply Organisation - also NOIC London - became YEOMAN (qv) 07.41 and TOWER (qv) 01.41 and NOIC Southend (LEIGH 10.41) - retained Southend acs when London acs to WILDFIRE II 11.39. CO base Tilbury (ST CLEMENT) 1943.
Moved from RN Barracks to Gordon House, Star Hill, Rochester 03.44. Sub office at Chelsea Court closed 20.03.46

PEMBROKE V Dover/London
31.10.1919 ex ATTENTIVE II - 1923 - Naval Base Dover
1941-42, Secret Base ex Station X (Bletchley Park). By 03.45 - 09.03.46 - WRNS Units in London - Stanmore, Eastcote, Woburn Abbey, Stockgrove Pk, Wavedon House, Wavedon Pk Farm, Crawley Garage, RNSQ Crawley, Walton Hall, Walton Rectory, Gayhurst Manor, Steeple Claydon

PEMBROKE VI Chat, Accounting Section
28.11.1919 ex TYNE-
For Lerwick Mine Clearance

PEMBROKE VII Grimsby, A/P DS
17.12.1919 - Grimsby men from books PEKIN - to 1921

PEMBROKE VIII Humber, Base
01.01.1920 ex WALLINGTON - 1921 (at least) - Naval Base Humber

PEMBROKE X Sparrow's Nest, Lowestoft, RN Patrol Service HQ
Cd 21.12.1939 - 14.03.40 - became EUROPA (qv)
First men arrived 24.08.39, White Ensign aloft 29.08.39

PENELOPE (1867) Harwich/Cape, CG/ Guard Ship
Corvette, CG Harwich 12.06.1869 - 21.05.1887, Guard Ship at Cape 02.1889 v FLORA (qv) - 1896.

Prison Hulk 01.1897, sold 12.07.1912 at the Cape, BU 1914

PENGUIN/ PENGUIN II (1876) Sydney, New South Wales, RAN DS
Sloop, survey ship 1890, Rx Sh & DS at Sydney Cd 01.01.1909, to RAN 18.03.1913, Re-Cd at Sydney 01.07.1913 - mid 1923, became PENGUIN II, sold 1924, became coal hulk, burnt 1960

PENGUIN (1902) Sydney, New South Wales, RAN DS
ENCOUNTER, Cr, tx to RAN 05.12.1919, Rx Sh Sydney, renamed PENGUIN 05.23, SM DS Garden Is. 1923-29, hull scuttled off Sydney Heads 08.09.1932

PENGUIN (1916) PENGUIN II Sydney, New South Wales, RAN DS
PLATYPUS, DS, renamed PENGUIN 16.08.1929, SM DS Sydney - 26.02.41. renamed PLATYPUS 03.41 - Base ashore at Balmoral Barracks/Garden Is retained name as PENGUIN II Cd 14.07.42 - 31.12.42, then Base task to KUTTABUL 01.01.43 - sold 20.02.58

PENGUIN Balmoral, Sydney, New South Wales, RAN Barracks
01.01.43 - extant 1999
4 SM (RN) there to 17.08.1967, then 4 SM (RAN) - see PLATYPUS
Nom DS: Aux Schooner ROOANA 1943-

PENGUIN IV Brisbane, RAN Res Depot
Named BRISBANE (qv) 08.1940
Included Pt Moresby & Thursday Is

PENGUIN V Darwin, RAN Res Depot
Named MELVILLE (qv) 03.1942

PEPYS Pacific, Intermediate Base
Planned 02.1945 under codeword FOXEARTH, project abandoned

PEPYS Manus, Admiralty Is, Base
Cd 01.09.1945 (Senior RNO app 17.02.45 - prob follow on from previous entry) - PO 06.03.46
One ref to its becoming SEEADLER (qv)

PEREGRINE Ford, Sussex, RNAS
Cd 24.05.1939 ex RAF. PO 30.09.1940. To RAF but RN used it as lodger and at 1 month's notice for return.
01.08.45 ex RAF, Cd 15.08.45 - self accounting 01.10.45. C & M (rebuild) 30.06.48 under DAEDALUS (qv). ReCd 01.02.50. Closed to flying 21.09.58, PO 13.11.58 and closed 15.12.58
RN Sch of Photography to ARIEL 02.01.61
Nom DS: Hbr serv Lch 1854 24.05.39-
ML 1639 15.08.45 - (laid up 10.12.45)
TRSB 43774 By 04.48-54
ASL 14 1954-58

PEREGRINE Halifax, Nova Scotia, RCN Drafting Depot
01.10.1944 ex STADACONA II - 29.03.46

PERLIN Lpool, Qtn Sh
5th Rate, capt 1807, qtn sh 1813, sold 1846

PERSEPHONE Mobile Accom Sh for SNO PLUTO
1) Cable carrier - ex Dockyard Hopper W24, conv to cable ship, renamed PERSEPHONE 04.1943-06.06.45
2) IOLAIRE (1902), Yt, req 1941, accom sh 1941, renamed PERSEPHONE 07.06.45-allocated to Pluto organisation - PO 06.02.1946, resto 1946

PERSEUS (1812) Off the Tower, London, Rx Sh
6th Rate, Rx Sh 05.1818, BU 09.1850

PERSEUS (1861) Dev, Hbr Serv
Sloop, hbr serv attached DEFIANCE at Dev 1886, DEFIANCE II (qv) 1904, sold 26.06.1931

PERSEUS (1944) Rosyth, Maint Carrier
Ex EDGAR, aircraft carrier, completed as maint carrier, Cd 03.08.1945, Spore 12.45, Res Rosyth 12.46 - (living ship 48-50) - Cd 01.04.50 under FOCRF & brought forward for catapult trials USA 51-52. Ferry duties 52-54, under SO RF Clyde 23.01.55, proposed for conv to SM DS 04.55, but cancelled 03.57 and tx from Belfast to Gareloch, BU 06.05.58

PERSEVERANCE (1781) Ports, Rx Sh
5th Rate, Rx Sh 1819 - BU 1823

PERTHSHIRE (1893) RFA
Pt Depot Northern Base, Fleet Coaling Officer & Paravane Organisation WWI - sold 1934

PET (1865) Ports, Coal Hulk
Gunboat, hulked 1865, coal hulk 1870-1900. Known as C17 from 1900, sold 12.04.1904

PETEREL (1794) Plym, Rx Sh
Sloop, Rx Sh 1817 - sold 1827

PETEREL (1860) Dev, Coal Hulk
Sloop, coal hulk 1885 - sold 1901

PETULANT -
ex PELICAN WWI - Ment in a list

PHAETON (1883) Dev, TS
Cr, TS for stokers & seamen 1910, sold 1913 as TS INDEFATIGABLE (qv) - see also CARRICK II, BU 1947

PHAETON (1914) Dev, Accom Sh
Cr, accom sh for Torp Boat DDs 1922 - PO 31.05.22, sold 01.23

PHAROS Rosyth, Accom Sh
Allocated 02.1916 ex Special Service Sqn

PHAROS Alexandria, Torp Sch
Cd 01.06.1942, independent command, acs NILE, PO 30.06.42
Torp Sch at ASSEGAI (qv) 01.44
Nom DS: Steam Picket Boat 733 01.06.42-30.06.42

PHILOCTETES (1922) Freetown/Dev/. DS/Repair

Ship
Purch 08.1940, conv to DS at Belfast, Cd 29.11.41, allocated as DD DS Freetown and sailed 20.01.42. All acs to PHILOCTETES II by 03.44 and became Repair Ship. For release 09.45, C & M 12.45, PO Dev 31.01.46 - remained C & M and for use as accom sh Dev. Re Cd for passage to Harwich and PO 28.06.46, sold for BU 22.01.48
Known as "Flock of Fleas"
SM Accom Sh MERCATOR, tender to PHILOCTETES 05.01.43-15.02.43 for passage to Freetown, then became part of PHILOCTETES

PHILOCTETES II Freetown, Accounting Base
03.1944-04.46
Carried acs of Tlrs, MLs and CF Freetown 03.44. By 04.44 carried all acs. Tenders acs to ELAND 07.45

PHILOCTETES III Freetown, Accounting Base
03.1944
Acs of DDs, sloops, FFs, corvettes and A/S Vessels - all tx to PHILOCTETES II 04.44

PHILOMEL (1890) Auckland, RNZN Depot
Cr, Cd 15.07.1914 at Wellington as first representative of NZ Div of RN. Cd 20.04.1917 at Auckland. Cd 01.03.21 as TS & DS at Auckland, sold 17.01.47, hull scuttled 06.08.49 off E Coast New Zealand. Name tx to Depot at Auckland - extant 1999
Nom DS: ML 3565 01.58
ML 3571 59

PHILOMEL II Wellington, New Zealand, RNZN Navy Offices
1944 (at least) - 01.01.54 - became WAKEFIELD (qv)

PHOEBE (1939) Harwich, SO RF
Cr, RF 01.07.1951 - 11.51, BU 04.56

PHOENICIA Manoel Is, Malta GC, Base
Cd 14.06.1943, independent command, acs ST ANGELO, closed 20.07.64. PO 31.03.65
Initially a LC Base, later used by M/S (absorbed task from FAREHAM 16.12.46) and then by escorts (Main Accounting Base Malta 11.49).
Nom DS: Diesel Lch 3822 14.06.43-01.51 (at least)
FMB 41385 57-60

PHOENIX Fayid, Egypt, RN Aircraft Repair Yard
Ex RAF, name allocated 18.12.19940, Cd 15.05.41, independent command, acs GREBE, PO to C & M, acs STAG, 28.02.46. To RAF 04.06.46
Storage for up to 130 aircraft
Nom DS: 50.5ft ML No 18 15.05.41-

PHOENIX Londonderry, Joint A/S Sch
03.1947 - name sel to replace FERRET, but SEA EAGLE used instead.

PHOENIX Stamshaw, Ports, TE
Formed 1946 - ex Damage Control Sch for Officers, Colet Gdns W14 - independent command. 03.10.42 - and Anti-gas Sch Tipner. RN Sch of Chemical Warfare from Tipner to Stamshaw 09.05.49. Cd 01.09.49 - 01.57 - RN Defence Sch became Naval ABCD(Atomic, Bacteriological, Chemical and Damage Control) Sch, tender to EXCELLENT, and in 1964 was Naval Nuclear, Bacteriological, Chemical and Damage Control Sch
Nom DS: MFV 93 01.09.49-57

PHOENIX Tipner, Ports, TE
Same location as previous PHOENIX. Cd 01.03.1967 - (01.01.71 took on Seamanship Tng ex DRYAD) PO 02.09.1974 - renamed PHOENIX NBCD Sch under EXCELLENT, tx to control of NELSON 29.03.85. Closed 23.07.93. Re-opened as NBCD Sch Phoenix, Whale Is. 31.08.93 see EXCELLENT.

PICADOR Nom DS for Ferry Personnel (NP 1659)
Cd 06.05.1944, PO 25.08.44
NP 1659 in UK to 29.05.44, embarked in SS THYSVILLE (qv) 30.05.44 and crossed to France. Arrived Arromanches 08.06.44, left beaches 31.07.44, returned Cardiff for survey 01.08.44, to Newport for repairs and NP disembarked

PIETERMARITZBURG (1943) Simonstown, SAN
Accom Sh for M/S Base
M/S ex PELORUS, accom sh 17.06.1968-1991, laid up 1992, scuttled 11.1994

PIGMY Dev/Gosport, SM DS
Ex SIR LOTHIAN NICHOLSON, War Department vessel, tx 1905, 3 SM Dev 1910-14, attached DOLPHIN 16.02.1916-20, 5 SM (Res Half Flot) Gosport 1921-34, BU 1938

PIGMY Gib, SM Base
Cd 30.12.1940, PO 31.03.1941. Cd 23.11.42, PO 13.03.45.
Ex Polish TS ISKRA, renamed PIGMY 31.12.40 and 8 SM DS Gib - rb MAIDSTONE. Renamed ISKRA 31.03,41 as accom sh
Detail of second period unknown (was SO SM 8 SM 11.43)

PIKE (1872) Soton, BD
Gunboat, BD 1908 at Soton - sold 27.03.1920

PILGRIM Thames, Powder Hulk/ Accom Sh
23.03.1945, powder hulk became accom sh

PINCHER (1943) Pt Edgar, Accom Sh
M/S, accom sh 09.1949, BU 03.62

PING WO (1922) Pt Stephens, NSW, RAN TS/Repair Ship
Hired 1941, to Ministry of War Transport 04.42. Cd 22.05.1942 as RAN Fleet Tender. 1944 Pt Stephens as TS for CO. Repair Ship 1946. Resto 06.1946

PINTAIL Nutts Corner, Crumlin, Co Antrim, RNAS
To from RAF 09.07.1945. Cd 11.07.1945, inde-

pendent command, own acs, PO 31.03.46 - to RAF Transport Command 01.04.46

PIONEER (1899) Sydney, New South Wales, Accom Sh
Cr, PO by 07.1919, accom sh Sydney by 1921, sold 1926, hull scuttled 19.02.31

PIONEER Fairlie, Experimental Vessel
Paddle Steamer, allocated A/S Estab Fairlie as moored experimental tender (floating laboratory) 04.1944 - 09.44 (at least)

PIONEER (1944) Rosyth, Maint Carrier
Ex MARS, Ex ETHALION, ex aircraft carrier, completed as maint carrier Cd 05.01.1945, Broad Pennant Cdre Air Train British Pacific Fleet 16.06.45. res Rosyth by 12.46 - BU 05.54

PIQUE (1834) Dev, Rx/ Hosp Sh
5th Rate, Rx Sh 1872, Hosp Sh by 1880, lent Plym Pt Sanitary Authority 30.03.1882 - 1905, sold 12.07.1910

PITT (1816) Ports/Portland, Coal Hulk
3rd Rate, coal hulk Ports 1853-60, Portland by 1865 - BU 1877

PITT (1820) Ports, Coal Hulk
TRAFALGAR, 1st Rate, renamed CAMPERDOWN 1825, coal hulk 1857, renamed PITT 29.08.1882, coal hulk till sold 15.05.1906

PLANCIUS Ceylon, SM Accom Sh
Appears in one list

PLATYPUS (1916) RAN Fleet Repair Ship/ SM DS
DS, completed 23.12.1916, lent RN at Buncrana 2 SM 1917. Campbeltown 12.1917-11.1918, Pembroke Dock 12.1918, Rosyth 1919, Chat 01.03.19, PO 10.03.19. Cd RAN 11.03.19 and ReCd as SM DS 25.02.19, Geelong 04.22, DD DS 1922-28, Fleet Repair Ship, renamed PENGUIN (qv) 16.08.1929. SM DS 09.30. Base Sydney 1930-41. Reverted to PLATYPUS & Cd at Darwin 26.02.41. (PO at Darwin 13.01.43 -Post Office Circular). Fleet Repair & Maint Ship 1943-46, Cairns 11.43-07.44 (at least), HQ ship/accom sh Res Sydney 14.05.46 - 01.11.56, sold 20.02.58

PLATYPUS Neutral Bay, Sydney, New South Wales, RAN SM Base & TE
Cd 18.081967 (RAN SM1) - extant 1999 but ann to close by 2001 - SM to Western Australia, last O Class SM PO 12.99

PLATYPUS II (1868) Geelong, RAN SM DS
CERBERUS (qv), Australian Turret ship, renamed PLATYPUS II as SM DS Geelong 15.06.1921, sold 23.04.24, hull sunk 07.26 as breakwater

PLEIADES Scapa Flow, Drifter Pool
Cd 01.07.1943, independent command, acs PROSERPINE, PO as separate command 30.06.45 - task to PROSERPINE
Nom DS: NAB TAURUS 01.07.43-03.45
MFV MANX FAIRY (1937) 03.45-45

PLINLIMMON (1895) London, Accom Sh
Ex CAMBRIA, paddle steamer, hired 09.1939 as M/S, AA Ship 07.42, accom sh - allocated Ft William 09.43 but BOURNEMOUTH QUEEN (qv) sent instead. 01.44-11.46 at London - to DST 13.11.46

PLOVER (1870) Gib, BD
Gunboat, BD Gib 1905, renamed BANTERER 06.1915, sold 1928

PLUTO (1944) Barrow/Birkenhead, Accom Sh
M/S, accom sh Barrow 1959-69 for HERMES and SM under construction. SO Res Ships Barrow v BALLINDERRY 10.10.60— retained as temp office accom Barrow 07.66 - 06.67. 14.07.67 to Cammell Laird, Birkenhead as temp offices - 1968. Barrow 1969-72, sold 09.72

PLYM (1943) Belfast, Res Drl Sh
FF, allocated as Drl Sh v SPEY 02.1948 but not required (05.49). Expended 03.10.1952 in Monte Bello Test

PLYMOUTH (1959) Plym/Glasgow/ Lpool, Museum Sh
FF, PO 40.1988, Museum ship Plym 07.88-10.89, Glasgow 1990, Birkenhead 1992 - extant 1999

PLYMOUTH TRADER (1916) Plym, DS for Cable Ships
Aux Barge, hired 27.08.1939, Cd 07.12.40 as Cable DS Plym. Laid up 07.42-45 but listed as Cable Ship DS 29.10.44-05.45. To DST 05.46

POICTIERS (1809) Chat, DS
3rd Rate, DS Chat 1849-50, BU 03.1857

POLAR BEAR Thorshavn, Faroes, Base
Cd 26.03.1943 ex NORTHMAN (qv). PO 21.06.45
Nom DS: 16ft lifeboat EEH205 26.03.43-

POLE STAR Faroes, Base
Name originally sel for Base 02.1941, but Cd as NORTHMAN (qv) 01.04.41 - later POLAR BEAR (qv)

POLITA (1920) Soton, Accom Sh
Aux barge, hired as barrage balloon vessel 12.1939, accom sh 1942-11.45

POLYPHEMUS (1782) Chat, Powder hulk
3rd Rate, powder hulk 1813 - 1831 (at least)

POMONA Crockness, Scapa Flow, BD Depot
Cd 01.10.1943, independent command, own acs, absorbed PROSERPINE 01.11.45, 01.10.46 acs to COCHRANE, PO 29.03.57
CO was NOIC Orkney 31.03.46. Included Crockness Camp
Nom DS: Hbr Lch 256 01.10.43-
MFV 1163 01.10.49-11.54 (lost by grounding)
MFV 1258 13.06.56 - (listed to 59)

POMONE (1897) Dartmouth, TS

Cr, tng hulk Cd 05.01.1910 at Dartmouth. PO 01.08.1914. Sold 25.10.22
Captain & Officers of College borne on her books - see BRITANNIA

PONGOL Malaya
In a list

PORCUPINE (1943) Ports, LC - M/S Base
DD, damaged 09.12.1942 in Med, towed to UK, fore part became LC Base Stokes Bay, Ports, Cd 14.01.44. PO 01.03.46. Cd for Cdr M/S v MARSHAL SOULT 01.04.46 - tender to VICTORY III - PO 31.08.46 - approved to BU when no longer required as accom sh. Listed as sold 06.05.46, BU 1947
Note: DD broke in two halves, fore part known as HMS PORK, after part as HMS PINE

PORCUPINE II Stokes Bay, Ports, Hart Party Sch/CO Base
Cd 29.01.1944 tender to VICTORY III. Sch closed but Base Cd 29.04.44 - independent command, acs VICTORY III - PO 30.04.46.
Comprised hards at Stokes Bay & Ft Gillicker, loading point South Parade Pier

PORCUPINE (STOKES BAY) Alverstoke, CO Base
03.1945 - PO 30.04.46 - C & M Party to remain
Organisation for storage of minor LC on shore in C & M, attached PORCUPINE

PORT A Aultbea
09.1939-20.03.40 - see also HELICON
Title used when Port location was secret - NOIC appointed 20.09.39 - became NOIC Aultbea 1940, tender to FLORA. Clyde to be main Fleet Base and use of Pt A discontinued - tlrs from Pt A to Greenock 10.1939. Loch Ewe to be Fleet Base alternative to Scapa Flow/ alternative to Oban as convoy assembly anchorage/transit anchorage 01.41.

PORT B Kyle of Lochalsh
01.1940 - 15.05.40 renamed Port ZA - 06.40 - renamed TRELAWNEY (qv)

PORT CV Fixed A/S defences there WWII

PORT D Loch Erisort, Lewis
01.07.1942 - also referred to as Port ZD

PORT HHX Rothesay
1943-44

PORT HHY Pt Bannatyne?. W Scotland
1943-44

PORT HHZ Loch Cairnbawn, W Scotland
1942

PORT MAHON (1798) River Thames, Police Ship
Brig, capt 1798, Police Ship 1817, sold 1837

PORT Q Addu Atoll
To 05.1940, then became Port ZQ

PORT QUEBEC (1939) Component Repair Ship
Hired as M/L 1940, PO to C & M Lamlash 02.11.43. Conv to FAA Component Repair Ship on Clyde 11.43, Cd 28.09.44, renamed DEER SOUND (qv) 01.01.45

PORT REX East London, S Africa, SAN ACF Base
01.11.1954 - listed to 1961

PORT SAID Red Sea
In a list-prob ref to location

PORT T Addu Atoll
Work started 09.1941, operational 03.01.42 - name lapsed 07.02.42 - though used to 1945

PORT W Nancowry
08.12.1941 (in C-in-C's war Diary)

PORT Y Sullum Voe, Shetlands
11.1939 - extant 05.40

Code letters for interdepartmental designation of secret ports to be prefixed by "Z" from 05.1940

PORT ZA Kyle of Lochalsh
Ex Port B, retitled 05.1940, renamed TRELAWNEY (qv) 06.40, but term Port ZA still continued in use

PORT ZB
1944 - under ANCXF - Normandy ops

PORT ZC Normandy Coast
1944

PORT ZD Loch Erisort
A/S Defence Trials & Chariots 07.1942-08.1942

PORT ZH Loch Eribol

PORT ZQ Addu Atoll
Ex Port Q

PORTIA (1903) Milford Haven, A/P DS
Yt, hired A/P 08.10.1914-01.04.1919. Poss DS 1914-15 rb SABRINA (qv) - though acs state SABRINA relieved VIVID. Poss local Senior Officer's craft till arrival SABRINA.

PORTLAND BILL (1945) Maint & Repair Ship
Cd 02.11.1945, Res Gareloch 03.01.47 - 12.48, living ship RF Harwich 12.49-05.50. To MOWT 17.07.50, sold 01.51

POSEIDON Alexandria
In a List

POWERFUL (1895) Australia/Dev, Flag/Boys' TS
Cr, Australian Sta Flag 1905-1911 (and DS for personnel ashore), Cd 23.09.1913 as TS Dev, renamed IMPREGNABLE (qv) 01.12.1919, sold 31.08.1929
Cr ESSEX (qv)accom sh 11.1918

POWERFUL II (1897) Dev, Boys' TS
ANDROMEDA, Cr, renamed POWERFUL II 23.09.1913 as Boys' TS Dev, renamed IMPREGNABLE II (qv) 01.12.1919, renamed DEFIANCE (qv) 20.01.1931, BU 14.08.56

POWERFUL III (1882) Dev, Boys' TS
CAROLINE, renamed GANGES (qv) 04.1908, renamed POWERFUL III 23.09.1913, renamed IMPREGNABLE IV (qv) 01.12.1919, sold 31.08.1929

PRESERVER (1941) Halifax, Nova Scotia/ Newfoundland, RCN Fairmile DS/ Base Supply Ship
Cd 11.07.1942, Newfoundland - Botwood to 12.42, St John's 12.42-07.43, Red Bay 07.43-11.43, St John's 11.43-06.44, Red Bay 06.44-09.44, Nova Scotia - Sydney 09.44-45, refit Halifax, then St John's, then Shelburne 06.45 - PO 06.11.45, sold to Peru 04.01.46, BU 1961

PRESERVER (1969) Canadian Supply Ship
Cd 30.07.1970, Atlantic 89, extant 99

PRESIDENT London, HQs and Res Drl Sh
1) PRESIDENT (1829) 4th Rate, RNR Drl Sh West India Docks 01.04.1862 (and RN Artillery Volunteers 1872-) - became OLD PRESIDENT 25.03.1903 - sold 07.07.1903
2) GANNET (1878), sloop, renamed PRESIDENT as Res Drl Sh 16.05.1903, PO as Drl Sh 31.03.1911, lent as TS MERCURY 10.13, renamed GANNET 1971 - for preservation 1987
3) BUZZARD (1887)(qv) sloop, Drl Sh 1904 - at Blackfriars from 19.05.1904 - renamed PRESIDENT 01.04.1911, lent Marine Society 23.01.1918 (see WARSPITE), sold 06.09.1921
4) MARJORAM (1917) sloop, was to have been PRESIDENT 1921 but wrecked on passage to fit out
5) SAXIFRAGE (1918), sloop, renamed PRESIDENT 09.04.1921 - King's Reach from 19.06.1922. used for DEMS Tng 1939, by 04.40 Res Divs had closed. Res re-formed in PRESIDENT by 10.46. For preservation 1986, sold 1987 - on Thames still 1999 - Note - Flower called London Pride is Saxifrage
6) Notes: PRESIDENT ledgers 1914 - A and B - AA and MB Reserves, by 1916 - A-F - extant 1917. PRESIDENT also acted as the accounting base for Admiralty based personnel, later apps were to CENTURION. RN Section of PRESIDENT tx to ST VINCENT 15.09.83. Various addresses in London over the years: Royal Victoria Yard, Deptford (1918-21.04.1958), CO PRESIDENT was at Shrewsbury (1944-47), PLA Building (11.46-73), Furze House (21.04.58-76), Thomas More St (1970s), E Smithfield (78-79), Lavington St (79-82), St Katherine's Way (01.02.88 - Cd 04.88 - extant 1999)

PRESIDENT I London/Shrewsbury, Accounting Base
1918-1928 (at least) - Admiralty - acs ex Stornoway (IOLAIRE) 19.05.1919
1939 - at Royal Victoria Yard, Deptford, moved to 18 Mardol, Shrewsbury 09.40. 06.07.45 to Chelsea Ct, SW3. Took some NP acs ex ODYSSEY 31.01.46. Extant 1947-57
PRESIDENT III and PEMBROKE III merged under PRESIDENT I 01.07.46

PRESIDENT II Chat/London/ Shrewsbury, Accounting Base
1916 - included RNAS Dunkerque, Calais & Hendon - extant 12.1917
1939 - postal address RN Bks Chat (Naval Reserves)
1940 - postal address Lower Regent St W1 (Naval Res & CG from 28.05.40)
1941-47 - RN Shore Signal & Wireless
1944 - postal address Queen Anne's Mansions SW1 - also Shrewsbury

PRESIDENT III Bristol/Windsor/ London, Accounting Base
1916 - active service RFR, RNVR & RNR and Demobilisation - extant 12.17
1918 - Defensively Armed Merchant Ships - acs tx to VIVID 01.10.19
08.35 - acs of MNBDO
Estab 28.08.39 at Clark's College, 15 Whiteladies Rd, Bristol, HQs for all naval personnel allocated for service in Defensively Equipped Merchant Ships. Tx to addresses at Dedworth Manor, Windsor from 01.05.41-45, also Hodgson House, Eton College and in 1947 to Chelsea Ct, SW3.(By 31.05.44 held 30,500 acs) Ledger closed 31.07.46, remained an independent command, acs PRESIDENT III 01.07.46 as DEMS acs - merger of PRESIDENT III and PEMBROKE III under PRESIDENT I.

PRESIDENT IV London, Accounting Base
1918-26 (at least) Admiral Commanding CG and Reserves

PRESIDENT V London, Accounting Base
1918 - PO 30.09.1919 - at 54a Parliament St, SW1 - acs to PEMBROKE
Anti-aircraft duties, also RNR ratings at Admiralty & RNVR and some Prisoners of War, Armoured Car Sqn 20, Stratford Experimental Sta, Officers & men lent to the AF
Cd 01.11.1941 Highgate Sch, N6, TE for Accountant Branch Ratings - closed 14.07.44 - moved to Wetherby -see DEMETRIUS

PRESIDENT VI London, Accounting Base
1918-26 - Transport Services, Base for Murmansk tugs 02.1919, acs Officers in North Russia to LOBSTER (qv) 07.1919

PRESIDENT STEYN (1961) SAN Accom Sh
FF, accom sh 08.1980-81, sunk as target 29.04.91

PRESIDENT THEODORE TISSIER (1933) Ports, Free Fr TS
Fr survey ship, seized 03.07.1940 at Falmouth, TS at Ports 08.40, tender to COURBET - 06.42 (at least), Cd 11.10.43 with Fr crew as seagoing TS, to Fr Navy 1945

PRESIDENT WARFIELD (1928) Appledore, Accom Sh
US vessel under lease lend 07.1942. To Appledore v HANTONIA 01.43, released to US Navy 24.07.43, and Cd as part of USN Amphibious Tng Base 29.07.43 - 44. Returned to War Shipping of America 05.44. (at Normandy 06.44)

PRETORIA (1954) Hout Bay, South Africa, Museum Ship
M/S, Ex DUNKERTON, Museum Ship 05.12.1987 - extant 1992, Fishing vessel by 1999

PREVOST London, Ontario, RCN Base & Res Div
01.09.1939 - Cd 01.11.41 - 01.09.42 (tender to STADACONA)
01.09.42-30.11.62 - independent command - PO 30.11.64(?) - listed to 1971, reported extant 1992

PRINCE (1788) Ports, Rx Sh
2nd Rate, Hbr Serv 1819, Rx Sh 1835 - BU 1837

PRINCE Cromarty, Accom Sh for Dockyard Artisans
Ex German Prize PRINZ ADALBERT, allocated as accom sh. and Cd 17.12.1914 - renamed - see PRINCETOWN

PRINCE EDWARD Clyde, Accom Sh
Hired as accom sh RIN Ratings standing by sloops SUTLEJ (Cd 07.03.41)/JUMNA (Cd 05.05.41) building at Denny's, Dumbarton 03.1941

PRINCE GEORGE (1772) Ports, Sheer Hulk
2nd Rate, sheer hulk 1832, BU 1839

PRINCE GEORGE (1895) Chat, Hosp Sh/ DS
BB, hosp sh 1916, then storeship. Accom Sh Chat 03.1918-05.18, renamed VICTORIOUS II (qv) 1918, Cd 01.10.1918 temp for passage to Scapa Flow, returned to Chat as overflow ship 1919, renamed PRINCE GEORGE Cd as DD DS Chat 01.03.1919 - PO to C & M 21.10.1919, sold 01.1921

PRINCE GEORGE Clyde, Accom Sh
Hired for RIN Ratings standing by ships building - see PRINCE EDWARD

PRINCE HENRY (1930) Newfoundland/ Ports/Falmouth, DS - Accom Sh
RCN AMC 1940-43, DS Newfoundland Force St John's 1941-01.42, LS 1944-45, to RN 15.04.45, Cd 07.12.45, accom sh Ports/Falmouth 05.45-05.46, PO to MOWT 09.07.46

PRINCE OF ORANGE (1734) Chat, Powder Hulk
3rd Rate, sheer hulk 1772, sold 1810 but was powder hulk Chat 1819-20

PRINCE OF WALES (1902) Ports, Accom Sh
BB, accom sh 05.04.1917-06.19 (Cd 01.01.1918 to regularise duties as accom sh - allocated to Portland 19.01.18, but cancelled). Allocated for gunnery experiments 09.1919, sold 12.04.20

PRINCE RUPERT (1915) Chat, Base Ship
Ex M10, monitor. To be conv to DS 7 SM 07.1919 at Dev, but cancelled. To Humber in C & M 11.09.1919. Chat 1921-22 (accom for boats' crews & police) v CHALLENGER & HELENA. Renamed PEMBROKE (qv) 24.02.22 as Base Ship. Renamed PRINCE RUPERT 01.09.22, sold 05.23

PRINCESS ALICE Eckernforde, Germany, Pt Party - NP 1755
Cd 11.05.1945, arrived Eckernforde 11.05.45. PO 04.09.46 - NP 12.44-to 12.46
Nom DS: Ex German craft ATLAS (ex BERTHA DOWNS) 11.05.45-

PRINCESS AMELIA Europe, Pt Party
Name approved for use on the Continent 05.04.1945 - prob not used

PRINCESS AUGUSTA Hamburg, Germany, German M/S Administration Base - NP 1811
Cd 22.10.1945 - 48. NP 06.45-02.48
Nom DS: Ex German TRV SOPHIE 22.10.45-06.01.46
Lch TF23 06.01.46-

PRINCESS CHARLOTTE (1825) HK, Rx Sh
1st Rate, Rx Sh 1857 - sold 1875, rb VICTOR EMANUEL (qv)

PRINCESS ELIZABETH (1927) Alexandria, DS
Paddle steamer, hired as M/S 22.09.1939, AA ship 06.42, Cd 09.11.44 as DS for ZZ craft (ex Nom DS SAUNDERS(qv)). Renamed NADIA 12.44

PRINCESS IRENE Berlin, Germany, NP 1813
Cd 10.08.1945, PO 15.07.46 (NP 1813 08.45-02.56)
Name allocated to British Naval HQ, Berlin 08.45
Nom DS: M/L SUSIE 01.08.45-

PRINCESS JOSEPHINE CHARLOTTE (1930) Falmouth, DS
DS for Army Cdo for St Nazaire Operation 03.1942. refit 11.43, PO and to DST 10.10.45

PRINCESS LOUISA Brunsbuttel, Germany, Base (NP 1767 ex NP 1730X)
Cd 08.11.45, PO 24.05.46 (NP 11.44-08.46)
Nom DS: Ex German ML URSULA 08.11.45-

PRINCESS LOUISE Port Edgar, Accom Sh
Ex SS PRINCESS ROYAL taken up as Aux DS for WOOLWICH (Rosyth) 03.1915-1917 - resto 11.17 when shore estab instituted at Pt Edgar

PRINCESS MARIA JOSE (1922) Iceland, Accom Sh
Belgian, hired 17.09.1940 as A/S TS, known as TRAINING II - renamed SOUTHERN ISLES 01.11.40 - allocated Dunoon. Renamed NEMESIS (qv) 03.41, renamed BALDUR (qv) 06.10.43, reverted to NEMESIS 04.06.45, resto at Antwerp 12.07.45

PRINCESS MAY (1892) Scapa Flow Accom Sh
Paddle steamer, purch as accom Sh 1914, sold 26.01.20

PRINCESS MAY Clyde, Accom Sh
Hired to accom RIN ratings standing by ships building (see PRINCE EDWARD)

PRINCESS SOPHIA Pt Party
Name approved for use on Continent 05.04.1945 - prob not used

PRINCETOWN (1902) Invergordon, Repair Ship
German prize PRINZ ADALBERT, renamed HMS PRINCE (qv) as accom sh dockyard artisans Cormarty, Cd 17.12.1914 as repair ship, rb MARS 01.09.16 & PO 20.10.16. Sold 23.12.16

PROCRIS (1856) Dev, Cookery Depot
Gunboat, hbr serv 1869, cookery depot 1880 till sold 31.05.1893

PRODUCT (1941) Repair Ship
PORT JACKSON, Tlr, Cd 15.04.1943 as A/S and M/S repair and support ship PRODUCT. Naples 04.44-07.44, Malta GC 04.45-05.45. PO 29.07.46. Tx to Greek Navy

PROMETHEUS (1807) Ports, Qtn/Rx Sh
Fire ship, qtn sh 1807, Rx Sh by 1831, renamed VETERAN (qv) 1839, BU 1852

PROMETHEUS Alexandria/ Famagusta, A/P Base
Cd 01.0-7.1942 acs NILE. Alexandria 10.43 - local patrols Famagusta 04.44-07.44 (Naval Base Famagusta closed 01.12.45), Alexandria 05.45, PO 46

PROSERPINE (1896) Aden
Cr, acs of Aden and Suez WWI, sold 11.1919, BU 1923

PROSERPINE Soton
Name sel for comml pt 01.09.39, NOIC ordered 27.08.39, in post by 29.08.39 - name prob never used - note next entry

PROSERPINE Lyness, Scapa Flow, M/S & A/S Base
Cd 09.09.1939 (apps from 25.08.39) - was to have been DUNLUCE CASTLE (qv) (renamed). 06.45 took over tasks of Base Mail & Accom Sh from DUNLUCE CASTLE and 30.06.45 drifters from PLEIADES. PO 31.10.45 - task to(absorbed by) POMONA 01.11.45.
Known as "Proper Swine".
Nom DS; ML 1949 09.09.39-12.43
Lch controlled by KHM 12.43-

PROSERPINE II Scapa Flow
Name allocated to DUNLUCE CSTLE 1939, but she retained her own name as DS (qv)

PROTECTEUR (1968) Canadian Supply Ship
Cd 30.08.1969, Atlantic 1989-, extant 1999

PROTECTOR (1884) Australia, RAN SM DS
Cr, DS for RAN SM 1914, renamed CERBERUS 04.21, reverted to PROTECTOR 1924, sold 09.24

PROTECTOR Sydney, Nova Scotia, RCN Base/NOIC
09.1939 - NOIC 09.1939 - used RCMP vessel PROTECTOR - Naval Base 22.07.40 - 27.03.46. Became RCN SCC TE 1953-55. Became ACADIA (qv)

PROTECTOR II Prince Edward Is, Nova Scotia, RCN Base
15.03.1943 - 10.43 - became part of PROTECTOR
Site used as Naval Base from 05.09.1915 and post WW II

PROTECTOR (1936) Forth, SO RF
Netlayer, SO RF v QUEENSFERRY 01.12.1948-50 (at least). RF closed 31.05.1950 - see also NEPTUNE, DONALD, COCHRANE. Conv to Ice Patrol Ship 1955, BU 02.70

PROTECTOR RAN, SM Support vessel
1990

PROVIDENCE Ramsgate, A/P Base
Cd 06.06.1940. PO 1944
Nom DS: COB 12

PROVIDER (1942) Bermuda/Halifax Nova Scotia, RCN Fairmile DS
Cd 01.12.1942 - Halifax 12.42 - Trinidad 02.43 - Key West 03.43 - Halifax 04.43 - Gaspe 05.43 - Sept Isles 29.06.43-11.43 - Halifax 11.43 - Bermuda 11.43-07.44 - Halifax 31.07.44 - 09.44 - Bermuda 09.44 - 05.45 - Halifax 05.45-PO 22.03.46. Sold to Peru 1946, BU 1961

PROVIDER (1962) Canadian Supply Ship
Cd 28.09.63. Pacific 1989, PO 01.07.1998

PSYCHE (1899) Sydney, New South Wales, RAN DS
Cr, RAN 07.1915, at Sydney, PO by 07.1919 - used as DS. For sale 12.21, sold 07.22 at Sydney

PUNGENT
In a list. Drifter TYRIE (1908) was renamed PUNGENT 1943 - Examination and General Service Lossiemouth. No longer required 02.45

PURBECK Royal Hotel, Weymouth, LC Base/HQ
Opened 01.03.1944, PO 1500, 28.04.44 - personnel to BOSCAWEN, Royal Hotel to USN 29.04.44
Note: Force G for Op Neptune at PURBECK 21.03.44

PURBECK Studland Bay, Dorset, Range Clearance Estab
Cd 01.02.1946 independent command, acs DRAKE. PO 14.11.47
Nom DS: FMB 441397 01.02.46-05.46 (at least)(in MB list 01.1951)

PURSUIVANT Pt Stanley, Falkland Is, Base
Name sel 20.05.1940, Cd 05.03.41, PO and Base closed 26.05.48 W/T Sta to preservation, then NOIC and retard party to withdraw. NOIC withdrew 06.06.48, retard party left 06.07.48
Nom DS: 25ft FMB 36165 (left by EXETER) 05.03.41-

PURSUIVANT Falkland Is. Floating Hotel
Named 12.07.1983

PYRAMUS (1810) Halifax, Nova Scotia, Rx Sh
5th Rate, Rx Sh 1832 - BU 11.1879

PYRAMUS (1897) Mudros, DS
Cr, DS Mudros 1915 - PO in Med (Mudros) for use as hulk 03.18. PO 10.01.1919, used as overflow to EUROPA 03.19, Dev C & M 07.19, sold 04.20

PYRAMUS Orkney, M/S & A/S Base
Cd 06.09.1939, PO 31.07.45
Name sel for comml pt Kirkwall 01.09.39, NOIC ordered 27.08.39, in post 29.08.39
Nom DS: ST MAGNUS 09.1939 - cancelled
Motor drifter PILOT US 06.09.39-

PYRAMUS II Kirkwall, Orkney, Northern Patrol Tlr Parent
Cd 29.01.19400(apps from 08.11.39), PO 06.42
Nom DS: Drifter ROSEBAY 29.01.40 - 06.42
Actually Cd 06.06.41 through oversight

PYRRHUS (1945) Dev, Power Supply Ship
M/S, power supply ship for DEFIANCE 1949-02.55. To Res 23.03.55, BU 09.56

Q

QASIM Manora, Karachi, PN Coastal Battery
1955-57

QUADRA Como Spit, Comox, British Columbia, RCN SCC TE
Summer Camp 1956-87 (at least) ex NADEN II

QUARNEROLA (19—) August, SM DS
12.1944-12. 1945
Italian repair ship under Allied control, poss same as QUARNARO (1924)

QUEBEC Inveraray, Comb Tng Centre
Opened 01.09.1940, name approved 04.09.40. Cd 15.10.1940 independent command - was to have been tender to GLENGYLE but cancelled. PO 01.07.1946
CO boat tng to Dartmouth 01.43
Nom DS: LASSIE MAIN (1910) drifter 15.10.40-01.43
Unnamed dinghy 01.43-

QUEBEC II Hollywood Hotel, Largs, CO Centre
Cd 12.09.1941 as additional Base Ship, independent command. PO 31.03.42 (MONCK Cd at Largs 01.04.42 - qv)
HQ of Joint Air, Military Naval Staff. Flag struck Hotel had been HQ Rear Admiral Commanding Northern Patrol from 02.09.40 (ex Kirkwall). Flag struck 10.06.41, and later had been allocated as a Naval Hospital. Flag of Commandant CTC, Inveraray (QUEBEC) tx to QUEBEC II 10.03.42 as Vice Admiral Comb Tng
Nom DS: MB T26 (ex MOJA) 12.09.41-

QUEBEC Farnham, Quebec, RCN SCC Summer Camp
1982

QUEBEC Trois Rivieres, Quebec, RCN SCC Summer Camp
1983-86 (at least)

QUEEN (1902) Taranto, Italy/ Chat, Base Ship/ Accom Sh
BB, Base Ship Taranto 05.1915 - 03.1919 (Yts and MLs 10.16, Tlrs & Drifters v ADMIRABLE 01.03.17-06.18). Left Taranto 01.04.19, PO at Chat 19.05.19. Accom Sh 30.06.19 v HINDUSTAN & HIBERNIA, PO 21.11.19, sold 04.09.20

QUEEN II Taranto, Parent Ship RNAS Southern Italy
12.1917 - 03.1918
03.1918 parent of RNAS Southern Italy at Pizzone, Nr Taranto

QUEEN Regina, Saskatchewan, RCN Base & Res Div
01.09.1939 - Cd 01.11.41 - 01.09.42 - tender to NADEN. 01.09.42-30.11.64 - independent command. ReCd 28.09.75 - 1987 (at least)
Note: There was an HMS QUEEN, escort carrier 1943-10.46

QUEEN CHARLOTTE (1810) Ports, TS
1st Rate, renamed EXCELLENT (qv) 31.12.1859, sold 12.01.1892

QUEEN CHARLOTTE (1810) Ports, TS
BOYNE, 2nd Rate, renamed EXCELLENT(qv) 01.12.1834, renamed QUEEN CHARLOTTE 22.11.1859, BU by 06.1861

QUEEN CHARLOTTE Ainsdale-on-Sea, Southport, Lancs, AA Range
Cd 15.11.1941 - 31.01.46 then C & M party under EXCELLENT
Nom DS: AA boat DIRECTEUR GENERAL AME 15.11.41-
HL(D) 3819 11.45 - (still in MB List 01.51)

QUEEN CHARLOTTE Charlottetown, Prince Edward Is. RCN Base & Res Div
01.09.1939 - Cd 01.11.1941 - 01.09.1942 (tender), 01.09.42 - PO 15.12.1964

QUEEN ELIZABETH (1913) Portland/ Ports, TS/ Accom Sh
BB, Hbr TS Portland 12.1945 - rb HOWE 02.46 and to res. Living Ship RF Ports 03.46-02.48, BU 06.48

QUEEN OF KENT (1916) Accom Sh
Paddle steamer, hired as M/S 12.09.1939, accom sh Granton by 03.44. retained as accom sh 24.04.44 for service with ANCXF. Mulberry Accom & Despatch Control Isle of Wight & Dungeness. Granton 06.44. For defence of Scheldt Estuary 01.45 v GLENMORE . No longer required, to C & M 05.45, to DST Chat 05.06.45, resto 12.07.46

QUEEN OF THANET (1916) Accom Sh
Paddle steamer, hired as M/S 12.09.1939. accom

sh 01.44 with ANCXF 05.44. Mulberry Despatch ship Isle of Wight 06.44. Allocated for salvage HQ Ship ANCXF 09.44-06.46, though to C & M 30.05.45 and for release 19.10.45

QUEENSFERRY Rosyth, RF Forth Area Parent Ship
Cd 19.12.1945 v EMERALD - 01.08.47 RF offices in building in COCHRANE, but name retained to 01.10.48. RF Parent to PROTECTOR as SO RF 01.12.48. RF closed 31.05.50
Nom DS: FMB 441235 19.12.45-02.47
MFV 184 02.47-48

QUIBERON (1942) Melbourne, RAN Accom Sh
DD, FF 1957, accom sh Williamstown Naval Dockyard 06.64 - sold 02.72

QUORRA Apapa, Nigeria, Nigerian Base
1989 - extant 1999

R

RACEHORSE (1830) Dev, Coal Hulk
Sloop, coal hulk 1860 - sold 1901

RACER (1884) Osborne, TS
1) Gunvessel, rated sloop 1885, was tender to BRITANNIA at Dartmouth, tx to River Medina 1903 - Osborne College opened 04.08.1903, Captain & Officers of College borne on books of RACER - see also OSBORNE. Became a salvage vessel 1917
2) Yt BETA Cd 01.04.1916 as Nom DS and to be renamed RACER - still in lists as Nom DS College 1919 but named OSBORNE. College closed 20.05.21. Yt poss tx to Dartmouth College as Nom DS. Sold 11.1928

RACER Larne, Co Antrim, M/S and A/S Base
Cd 04.09.1939 (apps from 25.08.39), PO 30.06.45
Name sel for base at comml pt Larne 01.09.39, NOIC ordered 27.08.39, in post by 29.09.39.
Nom DS: ML QUEEN ELIZABETH 04.09.39-

RACER II Larne, Co Antrim, CF Base Larne
Named 27.05.41 ex CAROLINE II. Cd 01.08.1941, PO 27.07.42
Nom DS: MB from Yt TARANSAY(1930) 01.08.41-42

RACOON (1808) Ports, Convict Hosp Sh
Sloop, convict hosp sh 1819, sold 1835

RAGEA Alexandria, CF Base
Aux Schooner, used by RN then released 23.03.1942. Cd 27.04.1943 as tender to MOSQUITO, DS 12.04.44, PO 14.03.45 - became merchant manned. Resto 05.46. Spelt RAJEA in some lists

RAINBOW (1856) London, RN Artillery Volunteers Drl Sh
Gunboat, survey ship 1857, TS by Somerset House 1873 till sold 11.1888, rb FROLIC (qv)

RAINBOW (1891) Esquimalt, British Columbia, RCN DS
Cr, tx to RCN 04.08.1910. PO 08.05.1917. DS 05.07.1917 - PO 01.06.20 rb NADEN. Sold 1920 as freighter.
Esquimalt replaced Valparaiso as RN Base 29.07.1856, but was closed by Fisher. First used as a RCN Base 08.11.1910 on RAINBOW's arrival

RAJALI Arakan, India, Long Range Maritime Patrol Hbr TE
1993

RAJALIYA Puttalam, Ceylon, RNAS
Cd 01.02.1943, independent command, acs UKUSSA. 01.01.44 own acs, PO 31.10.1945. Tx to local civil authority 12.12.45
Used from 11.42 under LANKA (qv) - see also UKUSSA
Nom DS: Naval Aircraft Salvage Unit Lch PAT 01.02.43-

RAJAWALI Morib, Malaya, RNAS
Name ann 09.09.1941. Cd 01.1942, PO 01.42 (lost)

RAJEA see RAGEA

RALEIGH Torpoint, Cornwall, TE
Cd 09.01.1940 independent command - extant 1999
TE for RN Special Reservists, construction started 24.08.1939. Administered by DRAKE until Cd. First trainees arrived 17.01.40. Lent to Army 01.04.44 - 07.44 then used as overflow for DRAKE on C & M basis. Became Stokers' TE 10.47 when IMPERIEUSE (qv) closed. Undertook New Entry TE 1958, Supply Sch (ex PEMBROKE) 1983 & SM Sch (ex DOLPHIN) 17.09.97.
Nom DS: Drifter GLITTER(1918) 1939-46
Ex German Yt SCHWALBE II 46-47
Motor Cutter 45688 47
MFV 174 03.48-02.52(later DLIGENCE)
MSPB 41333 12.52-13.04.56
MSPB 5440 13.04.56-64
MSPB 5505 1965

RAMDAS (1935) Bombay, A/S TS
Coaster, hired 09.1939, A/S TS by 16.05.45-06.46

RAME HEAD (1944) Maint Ship
Completed & Cd 18.8.1945, to British Pacific Fleet, Brisbane then HK, also Japan. SO Ship HK 13.02.46-Captain Escort Forces British Pacific Fleet 13.02.46-left Far East 01.09.46. RF accom Sh Dev 12.46-10.56 rb EURYALUS, Dev 01.05.57-03.60, modernised Chat 1960-05.62, Cd 23.03.62. RF Chat 62-63, SO RF Ports 10.63-71, accom sh RF 1971-72. Accom sh Londonderry 1973-76. Ports, Static TS for RM attached EXCELLENT v ULSTER 1976-84. Rosyth FF support 12.84-87, Ports 03.87-, Dev to 12.88, RM TS Ports 12.88-12.90, Portland 12.90-14.02.96, Ports 15.02.96 - extant 99

RAMESES Rameses House, Grangemouth, DS for vessels under Rear Admiral (Minelaying)/Barracks
Cd 01.01.1918, Parent Rear Admiral (M) estab 24.01.18, Flag to ANGORA 20.02.19. PO 03.03.19
Nom DS: Drifter 27460 WILLIAM II 01.01.18-
Drifter BOY WILLIE (1904) 12.17-19 (Resto 11.06.19)

RAMILLIES (1785) Standgate Creek, Qtn Sh
3rd Rate, Qtn Sh 06.1831, BU 02.1850

RAMILLIES (1916) Ports, Accom Sh/ TS
BB, accom sh Ports 15.05.1945, with MALAYA (qv) was regarded as one estab VERNON (RAMILLIES), later called VERNON II (qv). TS at Ports 1946-47 v IMPLACABLE & FOUDROYANT, sold 20.02.48

RAND Johannesburg, S Africa, ACF Base
01.11.1954 - listed to 1961

RAND Transvaal, SAN Citizen Force Unit

RANEN (1918) Leith, Norwegian DS
07.1943-

RANGALLA Colombo, Ceylon, TE/Base
1952, PO 02.1964 (in Pink List 1958-02.64)
01.09.65 listed to 1979 (but as RENGALLA 1974-76) (HQ v GEMUNU 1974)
1950s-64 listed as Dyatalawa (Dijatalawa) Tng Base - reported as de-Cd 02.64. Not in NL 1965 but in 1966 appears as Naval Base Colombo

RANGER (1835) Kingstown, Dublin, Church Ship
Brig, hulk 1860, Church Ship 1865, sold 1867

RANGER (1880) Ammo Hulk
Gunvessel, sold 24.09.1892 as salvage vessel, hired 11.1914-19 as ammo hulk, BU 1947

RANGER Middlesborough, Base
Name sel for base at comml pt Middlesborough 01.09.39. NOIC ordered 27.08.39. Name reported not used

RANPURA (1924) Repair Ship
AMC 1939-43, to be conv to DD DS 03.42, purch 12.44, conv to Repair Ship 20.06.44-46. To Malta GC 30.05.46-47 (was to go to HK to set up dockyard there but diverted enroute). To Res on return UK 02.10.47 - Apprentices TS Rosyth 1947-48. Res Gareloch 48-52 (living ship 48). Cd 15.01.53 as Repair Ship Malta GC v TYNE - 58 (SO Res Ships 56-10.58 rb AUSONIA) Sail Malta 13.11.58 - Res Dev 23.11.58-09.05.61. BU 25.05.61

RAPAX Hiswa, Aden, RNAS
12.1944 - 06.45
RNAS at RAF Sta

RAPID (1883) Gib, Accom Sh/ SM DS
Corvette, accom sh 1902-, hulk 1906, coal hulk C7 1912, SM DS 1914, renamed HART (qv) 09.06.1915, sold 1948

RAPID (1942) Rosyth, TS
DD/FF, Cd as tender to CALEDONIA, day running 01.1967-08.73 rb EASTBOURNE. 8.73 target Aberporth. Sunk as target 09.81

RATANABON Rangoon, Burma, Burmese Naval Estab
Cd 01.12.1945 - 48 (57?)
Burma RNVR formed 06.1940, tx to RN operational control 05.07.44, ceased 04.01.48 on independence
Pt Party NP 2478 was a tender to CHINTHE/ RATANABON
Note: CHINTHE (qv) PO 30.11.45

RATTLER (1886) Clyde/Ports, TS/Hbr Serv
Gunboat, hbr serv 1910, attached ARIADNE at Ports as TS for stokers 1918. Then repair ship for Tlrs. Renamed DRYAD 09.19 as Navigational Sch Ship, sold 10.24
When lent to Clyde RNVR in 1904 (?) was first ship to be fully officered and manned by RNVR

RATTRAY Crimond, RNAS
1945 ex MERGANSER(qv) - 01.09.46
Appears in one list - though other lists show MERGANSER retained as the name

RATTRAY HEAD (1945) Maint Ship
Completed as merchant ship but appears in NL 10.1945

RAVEN (1829) Humber/Mizner Creek, Qtn Sh/ CG
Cutter, qtn sh Humber 01.1848, CG Mizner creek 1850 - sold 28.10.1859

RAVEN Eastleigh, Soton, RNAS
Cd 01.07.1939, PO 30.04.47
RN Air Sch of Medicine, also included lodger facilities at RAF Christchurch

RAYMONT (1916) Plym/ Normandy/ Chat, M/S DS
Tlr, hired 08.1940. M/S Store Carrier 04.44-03.46, Normandy 06.44, re-allocated to ANCXF Cdre Belge v STAR OF FREEDOM & GEORGE D. IRVINE 02.45, Chat repairs 05.45, to Belgian authorities 10.45

RAZORBILL Algiers, CF Base,W. Med
Cd 07.01.1943 acs HANNIBAL, closing down 09.43, PO 24.10.44
Also covered Bone
Nom DS: NAB BELINDA 07.01.43-44

RED DRAGON Dev, Store Hulk
Ex Y D'DRAIG GOCH, purch as store hulk WWI, at Dev 1918-47 (at least), BU 06.58

RED JACKET Bombay, RN Nom DS
01.01.1948 - 1959
Nom DS: Yard Craft BARQ ex MMS 154 01.01.48-

RED SANDS Thames Fort
1942 - Army manned, not RN

REDBREAST (1805) Lpool, Lazaretto
Brig, lazaretto 1815 - sold 1850

REDOUBTABLE (1892) Ports, Accom Sh
BB, REVENGE, renamed 1915. Overflow ship 01.1916-Cd 01.01.18 (to regularise) - PO 01.09.1919, sold 11.19

REDOUBTABLE Normandy, FOBAA & NP 1570
Cd 24.06.1944, PO 01.01.45 (NP 1570 04.44 - 02.45)
FOBAA, Flag ashore from SOUTHERN PRINCE 0800, 25.06.44 at Courseilles. HQ closed 0800, 15.09.44 and re-opened in ex German Naval HQ Clinque Tombereau, Mont St Aignan, Rouen 10.44. Task tx to SNO British Operational Port Forces 12.44.
Nom DS: Yt CLARINDA 24.06.44-09.44
HL(P) 43616 11.44-01.01.45

REDPOLE (1943) Harwich, Accom Sh
Sloop, accom sh 02.48, BU 11.60

REINDEER (1829) Gib, Hbr Serv
Brig, hbr serv 05.1841, sold 1847

REINDEER (1883) Dev, BD
Sloop, BD vessels 1904, at Dev 1910-14, salvage vessel 1917, sold as such 1924

RELENTLESS (1942) Queenborough/ Chat, Accom Sh
DD, alloc accom sh for M/S Queenborough 11.45 but replaced by ESKIMO, and for Chat 11.46. FF 1951, sold 04.71

RELIABLE Falmouth, LC Servicing
09.1943-, Quay Punt vessel

RELIANCE (1910) Dardanelles, Repair Ship
Ex KNIGHT COMPANION, purch 14.11.1912, repair ship 1913-18. Ports v FISGARD & FISGARD II when they went to Scapa Flow 08.1914. To Scapa to replace FISGARD II 10.1914. Dardanelles 1915, Mudros 1918-02.19. RFA Stores support 1916-02.19, then Dev. Sold 17.12.1919

REMNANT Ports, Accom Sh
Ex ML, 08.1942 - acquired 09.03.43, laid up Hamble/DST 08.44. no longer required, for disposal 09.44

RENARD London, Base
Name sel for base at comml pt of London 01.09.1939 - NOIC ordered 27.08.1939 - name prob not used.

RENGALLA see RANGALA

RENOWN (1895) Ports, TS
BB, Hbr TS for Stokers v NELSON 1909. Sold 04.1914

RENOWN (1916) Dev, Turret Drl Sh
BCr, turret drl sh 26.11.1945 v IMPERIEUSE (qv), res 12.46, sold 03.48 (PO 01.06.48)

REPULSE (1868) Leith/ Hull, CG
Ironclad 1868, CG Leith 01.03.1870 - 29.09.1872, CG Hull 15.04.1881 - 27.08.1885, sold 02.1889

RESEARCH (1888) Portland, A/P DS
Survey vessel, DS Portland 01.10.1915 v VICTORY/VICTORY VII - 04.20 (Portland became VICTORY XI). Sold 29.07.1920
A/P Office Portland closed 29.08.1919

RESISTANCE (1861) Lpool, CG
FF, CG Mersey 01.07.1869 - 73 and 17.05.1877 - 15.06.1880, sold 1898

RESOLUTE (1805)) Bermuda, Diving bell Vessel
Brig, diving bell vessel 1816 - BU 1852

RESOLUTION (1892) Lpool, CG
BB, CG 17.11.1901-09.04.1903, sold 1914

RESOLUTION (1915) Soton/Gareloch/Dev, Stokers' TS
BB, PO 03.11.1943, with REVENGE became TS at Soton (see SHRAPNEL II). Cd 27.04.44 and steamed to Gareloch where both ships PO & Re-Cd 12.05.44 as IMPERIEUSE II (qv). Towed to Dev under her own name, arrived and Cd 11.12.44 as IMPERIEUSE with REVENGE again as TE, which closed 1948. Sold 05.05.1948

RESOLUTION Christmas Is., Pacific, Base (NP 2512 & NP 5555)
Cd 24.12.1957 - 01.05.1960 (to Air Ministry)
For Op Grapple - H Bomb Trials
Nom DS: MFV 630 24.12.57-60

RESOURCE (1928) Repair Ship
Med 1930-37, res in Med 1937-39, Med 1939-40. Freetown 29.01.40 - 04.04.40, Med 1940-42, refit Durban 12.42-02.43, Eastern Fleet 1943-45 including spells at Manus & HK 1945. Ports 31.12.45, SO RF Ports v GREENWICH and RF parent v VICTORY III 01.04.46 - 50 (attached Mechanical TE). Res Clyde 11.53 - Handed over for BU 01.02.54

RESOURCE II (1865) Soton, DS
Yt, hired as DS and Cd 01.10.1915, lost by fire 12.11.15
Ex Admiralty Yt ENCHANTRESS, renamed RESOURCE, Cd as RESOURCE II (replaced by RESOURCEFUL, then by HERMIONE (qv))

RESOURCEFUL Soton, Static MB DS
12.11.1915 - 11.01.1916
MB 107 - temp DS after RESOURCE II lost 12.11.15 - renamed RESOURCE, then RESOURCEFUL, until HERMIONE arrived

RESTELVA Soton, Accom Sh
08.1942, acquired 29.01.43, to C & M Lymington/DST 07.44

RETRIBUTION (1779) Sheerrness, Convict Hulk
EDGAR, 3rd Rate, renamed 1814 as convict hulk - BU 1835

RETURN Tokyo, Base - NP 2503
Cd 01.01.1946 - 15.05.46, acs to GLENEARN, then to COMMONWEALTH
In Old Embassy, Tokyo

Nom DS: 25ft Yawl 01.01.46-

REVENGE (1859) Pembroke Dock/ Queenstown, CG/ Base
2nd Rate, CG Pembroke Dock 01.09.1865 - 1869, Base Ship Queenstown 16.08.1872 - 04.02.1890, renamed EMPRESS (qv) 03.1890, sold 31.12.1923

REVENGE (1892) Weymouth, CG
BB, CG 18.04.1901 - 03, renamed REDOUBTABLE (qv) 1915, sold 1919

REVENGE (1915) Soton/ Gareloch/ Dev, TS
BB, with RESOLUTION formed SHRAPNEL II (qv) Stokers and Engine Room Ratings' TS at Soton - Cd 15.11.1943. To C & M 24.11.43. ReCd in own name 27.04.44 for passage to Gareloch where, with RESOLUTION, PO and became IMPERIEUSE II Cd 12.05.44. Reverted to own name for tow to Dev, arrived 11.12.44 to re-form as Stokers' TE with RESOLUTION as IMPERIEUSE (qv) till PO 1948. BU 05.09.48

REVIVE (1922) Accom Sh
Yt, hired as BD Vessel 07.1940, accom sh 02.45, sold 03.46

REVLIS Cairn Dhu House &Arden Caple Castle, Helensburgh, Degaussing Estab
Cd 22.06.1942 independent command, acs ORLANDO, PO 02.47
Nom DS: Motor Yt REVLIS - req for serv in VERNON DG Helensburgh 22.06.42-

RHIN Standgate Creek, Qtn Sh
5th Rate, capt 27.07.1806, qtn sh 1838 - lent Thames River Authority 1875 till sold 26.05.1884

RICASOLI Ft Ricasoli, Malta GC, Barracks
Cd 01.09.1947-independent command, acs ST ANGELO - PO 21.07.58
Nom DS: MFV 26 01.09.47-foundered 22.10.53
27 ft whaler 2557/42 1957

RIFLEMAN (1943) Barrow-in-Furness, Accom Sh
M/S, accom sh 1966 - 72 (offices for contractors and overseers), sold 09.72

RIGOROUS Grimsby, Base
Name sel for basse at comml pt Grimsby 01.09.39, NOIC to arrive 23.08.39 - prob name not used

RINALDO Barry, Glamorgan, Base
Name sel for base at comml pt Barry 01.09.39, appears as Cd from 08.09.1939-23.09.39 in some lists. NOIC ordered 27.08.39 - NOIC lapsed 01.01.45 then came under FOIC Cardiff - Barry Naval Base closed
18.06.45

RINGTAIL Burscough, Nr Ormskirk, Lancs, RNAS
Cd 01.09.1943, independent command, part complement, PO 15.06.1946 - to C & M under BLACKCAP
Was under NIGHTJAR at one time.
Nom DS: RAVENSWOOD(1891) Paddle steamer 01.09.43 -18.04.44
PV BEDOUIN (ex TRIPHIBIAN) 18.04.44 - 11.05.45
Lch ROUNDELAY 05.45 - 12.45
MFV 1574 12.45-02.46

RINGTAIL II Woodvale, Formby, Lancs, RNAS
Cd 07.04.45 ex RAF on indefinite loan acs RINGTAIL - 28.01.46 (to RAF)
Had been used on lodger basis from 1942. RNAS at Speke tx to Woodvale 07.04.45

RIO GRANDE Soton, Accom Sh
07.1942 - acquired 02.02.43, - 10.44 (at least)

RISASI Kilindini, Kenya
1946

ROBBENILAND Robben Is, Capetown, S African New Entry TE/ Base
1957 - Listed to 1961

ROBERTS (1941) Dev, Accom Sh
Monitor, overflow accom sh Dev 01.1947 - Res Cat C 24.01.50, RF dev till sold 06.65

ROBERTSON Kitchener Camp, Richborough, Kent, CO Base
Name ann 01.12.42, Cd 23.06.43, PO 31.08.46 - retard party to 12.10.46 acs PEMBROKE II
Hutted accom encampment as holding base for RM LC personnel (Guns' crews) and minor LC Base
Nom DS: ML PROVIDENCE 23.06.43-13.12.45
Hbr Lch 44824 14.12.45 - 31.08.46

ROBERTSON Reading, Fleet Mail Office
Appears in a list - poss as ref to mails for CO personnel sent via GPO Reading late WWII

ROBIN (1934) HK, BD DS
Gunboat, BD DS 1941, lost 25.12.41 at HK

ROBIN Grimsetter, Kirkwall, Orkneys, RNAS
06.07.1943 ex RAF, Cd 15.08.1943 tender to SPARROWHAWK. Cd 01.03.44 independent command, acs SPARROWHAWK, PO 31.07.45 - to RAF - personnel to TERN II
Nom DS: Safety Boat 43781 1944 - 31.07.45 (became WAXWING)

ROCHESTER (1931), Drl Sh
Sloop, allocated as RNVR Drl Sh 08.1946, but not required 07.49, to res 10.49, BU 01.51

ROCKCLIFFE (1943) Esquimalt, British Columbia, RCN DS
M/S, DS and accom sh Pacific Coast Command RF Esquimalt 28.02.1947 v SCOTIAN - 52 (at least), BU 1960

RODENT Coldhayes, Liss, Hants, Special Boat Unit HQ
Cd 30.10.1943, independent command, acs VICTORY III, PO 17.02.44
Controlled RN Boom Commando, RMBPDs, CO

Pilotage Parties & Special Boat Sections

RODNEY (1884) Queensferry, CG
BB, CG Queensferry 22.09.1897 - 01.03.1901, sold 11.05.1901

ROMNEY (1815) Bermuda/ Havannah, Hosp Sh/ Rx Sh
4th Rate, Hosp Sh Bermuda 1820, Rx Sh Havannah 1837 - sold 1845

ROMOLA Lowestoft, M/S Base
Cd 07.11.1939, PO 14.03.1940
Name sel for base at comml pt of Lowestoft 01.09.1939 - NOIC ordered 27.08.39
Name used for DS Lowestoft, but discontinued at same time as EUROPA (qv) taken into use as name for RN Patrol Service Depot
Nom DS: ML CHUMS 07.11.39-

ROMULUS Rosyth, Base
Name sel for base Rosyth 1913, but COLUMBINE (qv) used instead

ROOKE Rosyth, BD Central depot
Cd 09.04.1940, acs closed 31.05.46 but remained independent command, PO 30.06.46 - renamed SAFEGUARD (qv)
Nom DS: Hbr Lch 241 09.04.40-06.41
Hbr Lch 39462 06.41 - 01.07.46

ROOKE Gib, Base
Cd 01.07.1946 ex CORMORANT (qv) - 01.10.1990 became Joint Service Base - not listed as HMS - PO 10.07.96 (new RN HQ at Devil's Tower Camp)
Nom DS: CORMORANT (1877) sloop 01.07.46-BU 1949
Hbr Lch 3977 01.07.51 - 11.76

ROSALIND (1941) Kenya and Zanzibar, RNVR
Tlr, RNVR Cd 06.08.1946 - 1962 replaced by BASSINGHAM, BU 04.63
Kenya VR absorbed by East African Naval Force 01.07.50

ROSARIO (1898) HK, SM DS
Sloop, SM DS HK 1910 - PO 19.10.19 - to C & M. Was Flag C-in-C in WWI. Sold 1921 at HK

ROSARIO (1943) Pt Edgar, Accom Sh
M/S, accom sh 05.1948. To Belgium 01.1953

ROSEMARY Ports, Accom Sh
Ex ML, 08.1942, but unsatisfactory survey - not used

ROSENEATH Rosneath, Dunbartonshire, CO Base
Cd 03.08.1942 ex LOUISBURG (qv) - PO 03.10.1942
Lent USN as US Base Two 29.09.42 - 12.01.43 (US Records show 24.08.42 - 01.43).
Cd 12.01.43 - PO 19.08.43 - ICE Sch and Fire Fighting Sch retained under MONCK.
Returned to USN as US Base Two 20.08.43 - (closed 05.05.45) (de Cd13.06.45) - to RN 15.06.45
Cd 13.06.45 - tender to MONCK - 29.10.45 became main holding base in UK for CO personnel v WESTCLIFF - 07.48
Name appears as ROSNEATH in some refs in 1945 & in NL 46 - CAFO et al spell it ROSENEATH
Nom DS: LCP(L)22 03.08.42-

ROSMARKIE Fortrose, Ross & Cromarty, LC Base
Cd 01.12.1943 acs MONSTER, PO 25.04.44
Nom DS: NAB MODERN GIRL 01.12.43 - 25.04.44

ROSS (1919) Ports, SM DS
M/S, ex RAMSEY, SM DS Gosport 12.08.1919 v SAINFOIN, Cd 28.08.19 for Experimental Half Flot 5 SM -1934, sold 13.03.47

ROUGHS FORT Off Harwich, Thames Fort (TESD No 1)
Cd 08.02.1942, to C & M 14.06.45, still in NL 1948. Listed as ROUGHS TOWER in some acs (later used for Radio Essex and declared 'The Independent Principality of Sealand' 02.09.67)

ROULA/ROULIA Shoreham, Accom Sh
07.1942, to DST for disposal at Shoreham 05.44, sold to former owners 12.44
Spelling varies

ROYAL ADELAIDE (1928) Dev/ Chat, DS/ Rx Sh
1st Rate, Flag & Depot at Dev 1860-31.12.1889, Rx Sh Dev 1891, by 1895 Rx Sh Chat till sold 04.04.1905

ROYAL ADELAIDE Tonning, Sylt, Germany, Pt Party - NP 1744
Cd 18.05.1945, PO 31.10.1945 - NOIC Sylt lapsed 11.46
Nom DS: Ex German vessel FLB 586 18.05.45-

ROYAL ALBERT London/Berlin/ Hamburg/Cuxhaven, Base - NP 1749
Opened 01.01.1945 as Base for Berlin at Princess Gardens SW7, Cd 01.04.45 - at Princess Gdns. Pay offices closed 30.09.45 - acs to various NPs. At Minden 06.45 to AM 15.09.46 to Hamburg - Flag in ROYAL ALBERT and 02.52 to Benkhausen. 01.03.51 ROYAL ALBERT to Cuxhaven (Elbe Sqn) PO 16.07.57 - FO Germany to ROYAL CHARLOTTE 15.10.57
Nom DS: Steamboat BREIRANBACH 01.04.45-WARNOW to 03.10.45
Diesel Lch COLUMBUS II 03.10.45-
P6030 ex German ML 1952

ROYAL ALEXANDRA Flensburg, Germany, NOIC-NP 1743
Arrive Flensburg 10.05.45, Cd 14.05.45, PO 31.10.45
At German police HQ, then at ex German Signal Sch
Nom DS: Ex German TRV No 8 14.05.45-31.07.45
U Boat DS OTTO WUNSCHE 31.07.45-31.10.45 (became GADFLY)

ROYAL ALFRED Travemunde,/ Kiel, Germany, FO

Desig Kiel, NP 1734
Cd 05.05.45, PO 16.04.46 at Plon
Flag hoisted at Travemunde 05.05.45. Used Flagship Hamburg-Amerika Liner MILWAUKEE, then to ROYAL HAROLD - 07.45 moved to site 15 south of Kiel (Plon) - FO Kiel became FO Schleswig-Holstein (FOSH) .
Nom DS: Ex German 45 ft Cabin Cr No 124 05.05.45-

ROYAL ANNE Arromanches, Mulberry, Pt Party - NP 1500
Cd 06.06.1944, PO 25.01.45
HQ of NOIC Arromanches established at noon Saturday 24.06.44 in Villa Arromanches. NOIC Mulberry B became new NOIC Arromanches 07.44
Nom DS: NAB AKELA III 06.06.44 - 11.44
Blockship EMPRIRE BITTERN (1902) 11.44 - 25.01.45

ROYAL ARTHUR (1891) Scapa Flow/ Rosyth, Guard Ship/ SM DS
Cr, Guard Ship Scapa Flow (Longhope) 1915 - 22.03.1918, DS 12 SM Grand Fleet 03.1918-1919, 1 SM Rosyth 1919-20, sold 1921

ROYAL ARTHUR Skegness, TE
Cd 22.09.1939, PO 1946
Ex Butlin's Holiday camp. Central Reception Depot for most naval entries 02.44 when RALEIGH (qv) tx to Army
Nom DS: 32ft cutter Ports No 6146 22.09.39-
HL(Steam) 309 04.46-

ROYAL ARTHUR Corsham, Wilts, POs'/ Leadership TE
Lypiatt Camp Cd 02.01.1947 (New Entry TE) - closed 15.03.50 (last trainees arrived 31.10.49) - PO 01.04.50 but name tx to PO Camp Kingsmoor from 16.03.50. last trainees left 11.12.1992, rear party to 05.03.93
Nom DS: Motor Cutter 431112 by 03.48 - 03.50
MFV 24 By 07.50-62 (sold 11.63)

ROYAL ATHELSTAN Antwerp, Pt Party - NP 1501
Cd 18.12.1944 - (Antwerp liberated 05.09.44), PO 01.12.45
Nom DS: Enemy MB 32819 18.12.44 - (sold 01.46)

ROYAL CAROLINE Lubeck, Germany, NOIC - NP 1741
Cd 06.05.45, PO 12.46
Nom DS: Ex German Hbr Lch No FTL202 06.05.45-

ROYAL CHARLES Le Havre/ Calais, NOIC - NP 1747
Cd 04.11.1944, PO 07.08.1945
Originally allocated to le Havre, but that port became US responsibility - so used at Calais instead. Administration at Calais from RN to Fr 01.08.45
Nom DS: Ex German Lch HANNIBAL No MB3 04.11.44-

ROYAL CHARLES Krefield, Motor Yt & HQ Ship 11.1951 - 53
Ex German KAREN II

ROYAL CHARLOTTE Cuxhaven, Base - NOIC - NP 1739
Cd 08.05.1945, PO 01.02.48
Nom DS: Ex German ship HELIGOLAND 08.05.45 - 24.07.45
Hbr Lch LOUISE 25.07.45-14.08.47
Ex Kriegsmarine Lch FLB 5001 15.08.47-

ROYAL CHARLOTTE Kiel, RN HQ Cologne, Wireless Sta
Cd 01.09.1955, FO Germany to 08.05.58 - Flag down. PO 28.11.58 - retard party for 3 months
Nom DS: ML 6028 01.09.55 - 04.02.57
HL(D) 5534 1957-

ROYAL CHARTER Grimsby, A/P Base
Cd 04.06.1940, PO 18.08.1941-acs to BEAVER/COLONSAY
PO on amalgamation of Humber M/S and A/P Forces
MFV ROYAL CHARTER was Nom DS for TRIPHIBIAN II (qv) 10.43 - 02.44 and was renamed BEAVER (qv) as Nom DS Humber, while BEAVER was renamed ROYAL CHARTER. BEAVER (ex ROYAL CHARTER) Resto 08.45
Nom DS: BEAVER (ex ENERGY) MVF/Drifter 04.06.40-retained name as duty boat Grimsby

ROYAL CLARENCE Rotterdam, Pt Party - NP 1732
Cd 17.05.45, PO 07.11.45
Nom DS: Yt HR4 15.05.45-
MB 10296 18.09.45-

ROYAL EAGLE (1932) Accom Sh
Paddle steamer, hired as accom sh 23.10.1939, Special service Vessel Chat 04.40, AA ship 04.40 - 16.05.46

ROYAL EDGAR Hamburg, Pt Party - NP 1730
Cd 1945 (NP at Hamburg by 22.05.45), 01.10.45 own acs, PO PM 15.09.46, NDCO lapsed 15.09.46 - ROYAL ALBERT to Hamburg in lieu
Nom DS: TWIEZIENFLETH to 03.10.45
Diesel Lch PREUSSIAN 03.10.45-

ROYAL EDMUND Ostend, Pt Party - NP 1763 - later also NP 1531
Cd 17.1.1944, PO 01.06.46 - revert to NP 1763
Nom DS; Ex Enemy Fishing Vessel OE1 17.12.44 - 28.09.45
MFV 99 28.09.45 - 05.46

ROYAL EDMUND II Ostend, RN Section Belge Depot
Cd 08.11.45, tender to ODYSSSEY,PO 01.02.46
Holding Depot for Section Belge Ratings

ROYAL EDWARD Dieppe, Pt Party - NP 1686
Cd 01.09.1944, 22.10.44 reduced to RNO status, PO 03.01.1945 - NP remain as BNLO

Nom DS: Dinghy 4 01.09.44-

ROYAL ELEANOR Minden, Pt Party
Name approved for Base on Continent though not allocated 09.12.1944.
Cd 21.06.1945, PO PM 14.09.46 when ROYAL ALBERT left Minden
Nom DS: MB LENNE 21.06.45-

ROYAL GEORGE (1817) Ports, Rx Sh
Yt, hbr serv 1843, Rx Sh 1865 till BU 09.1905

ROYAL GEORGE (1827) Kingstown, CG
1st Rate, ex NEPTUNE, CG 01.04.1864 - 31.12.1869, sold 23.01.1875

ROYAL HAROLD Kiel, NOIC Kiel - NP 1742
Cd 07.05.1945, Own acs 01.10.45, PO 29.02.48 - NP 1742 continued under ROYAL ALBERT
Allocated as Base name for Bremerhaven 11.44.
Co-located with ROYAL ALFRED (FOIC Kiel) (NP 1734) (qv) at one time. 01.46 - included NP 1566
Nom DS: German 25ft Cabin Lch No 1081 07.05.45-08.45
Ex German vessel HERMAN VON WISSMAN 08.45-
(Target vessel for E-boats - a photo shows her as NP HQ dated 05.45)

ROYAL HENRIETTA Heligoland, Pt Party NP 1746
Cd 16.05.1945, PO 30.09.1945
Nom DS: No 56(2) MAKRELE 16.05.45-

ROYAL HENRY Ft Southwick/ Port En Bessin - Granville - Chateau St Germain, France/ Minden Germany, HQ Allied Naval Cdr Expeditionary Force/FO Germany
Cd 17.08.1944 - - ceased 07.45
Name originally (07.44) allocated to Pt En Bessin - (NP 1502A) but appropriated to HQ ANCXF. HQ closed at Southwick Park - Ports - 0900 10.09.44, to Granville (Main) & St Germain (Advance), Flag to ADVENTURE (qv). All to St Germain 26.09.44. At Minden by 06.45
Nom DS: NAB MUSKEETA 17.08.44-11.44
Blockship PARKHAVEN 11.44-

ROYAL JAMES Rouen/ Boulogne, Pt Party - NP 1503
Cd 19.09.44 - PO 22.01.45 - NP to BNLO status
Originally allocated to Rouen 02.44, but that became US responsibility and name appropriated for Boulogne 10.44
Nom DS: Diesel Lch 4318 19.09.44-

ROYAL KATHERINE Wilhelmshaven, Pt Party/Base - NP 1738
Cd 08.05.1945, 01.10.45 own acs, PO 17.04.46 - FO Western Germany ceased 10.04.46
At RN Barracks Sengwarden Nr Wilhelsmhaven 01.07.45. To Buxtehude 10.07.45 (FO West Germany ex FO Wilhelmshaven)
Nom DS: Yt TAMMO 08.05.45-

ROYAL MAURICE Pt Party
Name approved for Base on Continent 09.12.1944 - prob not used

ROYAL OAK (1809) Ports/ Bermuda, Hbr Serv/ Rx Sh
3rd Rate, Hbr Serv Ports 1819, Rx Sh Bermuda 12.1825 - BU 1850

ROYAL PHILLIPPA Bremen/ Copenhagen, Pt Party - NP 1737
01.09.1945-10.46 Copenhagen
Allocated as Base name for Bremen 11.44, but by 10.45 was SBNO Denmark - Copenhagen - FO Denmark
(arrived Copenhagen 05.05.45)

ROYAL PRINCE Emdem, Pt Party - NP 1745
Cd 08.05.1945, PO 21.02.46

ROYAL PRINCE Krefeld, RN Parent Ship Germany - NP 1817
Cd 15.10.1949, PO 08.01.58 (Flotilla)/31.03.58 (Base)
Included Rhine Flot (NP 1817) 1949-58 (Base Krefeld). FO Germany to 1957 and Cdr Allied Naval Forces Central Europe. NP 1820 - Minden 1951-52.
Nom DS: ML 6028 1958

ROYAL RICHARD Mulberry A, Normandy, Pt Party
Allocated 07.1944, but Mulberry A abolished 07.07.44 (in Omaha - US Section)

ROYAL RICHARD Ghent, Pt Party - NP 1762
Cd 03.05.1945, PO 15.10.45 & NB Ghent closed
Nom DS: NEMO III 03.05.45-15.10.45

ROYAL ROADS Esquimalt, British Columbia, RCN College
Purch 11.1940, RCNVR Officers TE Colwood BC 13.12.40-02.42, RCN College Colwood BC 21.10.42-29.07.48. HMCS ROYAL ROADS RCN/RCAF) 1947-48. Royal Military College 1948 - but White Ensign to 1965. Still referred to as ROYAL ROADS till closed. 21.05.95 - final parade, PO 27.05.95

ROYAL RUPERT Wilhelmshaven, NOIC - NP 1735
Cd 06.05.1945, acs ROYAL ALBERT (from 01.04.45). 01.10.45 own acs, PO 21.06.50
Nom DS; Ex German U Boat DS WEICHEL ex MS SYRA (1923) 06.45-47
(Photo shows NP using Ex U Boat DS LOHZ 05.45)

ROYAL SOVEREIGN (1915) Rosyth, BB
BB, allocated Nom de Plume of HOPETOUN II (qv) 08.11.1943 whilst at Rosyth prior to tx to Russian Navy 30.05.44

ROYAL WILLIAM (1833) Dev, Guardship
1st Rate, guardship 1857, renamed CLARENCE (qv) 1885, TS, burnt by accident Mersey 07.1899

ROYAL WILLIAM Cherbourg, British Naval Liaison Party - NP 1713
Cd 18.09.1944, PO 30.12.1944 - revert to NP 1713

- BNLS
Nom DS: PL(D) 431223 18.09.44 30.12.44

ROYALIST London, Police Ship
Brig MARY GORDON, purch 1841, lent Thames Police as hulk off Somerset House 07.1856, sold 14.02.1895 - still listed 1900

ROYALIST (1883) Haulbowline, Asccom Sh
Corvette, hbr serv 02.1900 as hulk to receive crews of ships at Haubowline, renamed COLLEEN (qv) 01.12.1913, tx to Irish Government 19.02.23

ROYALIST (1942) Ports, TS
Cr, part of VERNON II 1947 and tender to VERNON to 12.49. RF living ship 1950-, RNZN 04.56, BU 11.67

RUBY (1876) Ports, Coal Hulk
Corvette, coal hulk 1904, renamed C10, sold 02.1921

RUHUNA Tangalle, Sri Lanka (Ceylon), Base
By 18.12.1971 - listed to 1979

RUPERT (1872) Hull/Pembroke/ Gib/ Bermuda, CG/ Guard Ship
Turret ship, CG Hull 27.08.1885 - 01.04.90, Guard Ship Pembroke 05.07.1893 - 09.05.95, Gib 12.1895 - 05.1902, Bermuda 05.1904 - 1907, sold 10.07.1907 at Bermuda

RUSHCUTTER Edgecliff, Sydney, New South Wales, RAN A/S TE & Res Depot
01.08.1940 - in use as depot for Base Staff Sydney, RANVR Depot Sydney including Pt Kembla. Named 13.02.42. PO 30.04.1956 - 01.07.57. listed to 29.07.1968
Nom DS: MB 168 1943
HDML 1321 1953-68

RUSSELL (1822) Falmouth, CG
3rd Rate, CG Falmouth 01.02.1858 - 03.05.1864, BU 1865

RUSSELL (1954) Ports, Hbr TS
FF, attached SULTAN v BLACKWOOD 1974 -sold 07.1985

S

SABINE (1876) Dev, Diving Tender
SABRINA, gunboat, renamed SABINE 1916 as diving tender to VIVID, renamed VIVID(qv) 1920, sold 07.22

SABRINA/SABRINA II(1899) Milford Haven, A/P DS
26.02.15-Cd 24.03.1915 v VIVID - 16.08.1916 rb IDAHO (acs tx 14.08.16)
Yt hired 05.02.1915 - 25.03.1919 - renamed SABRINA II by 01.16

SACKVILLE (1941) Halifax, Nova Scotia, RCN DS RF/ Museum Ship
Corvette, DS RF 04.08.1950-(53), Museum ship 1982 - Maritime Museum of the Atlantic - Canadian Corvette Trust - National Naval Memorial 04.05.1985, open to public 1990 - extant 1999

SAEBOL Saebol, Iceland, Radar Sta
RDF Sta, camp & DF Beacon situated near Saebol collectively known as SAEBOL 10.1942 - prob not a 'ship' name

SAFEGUARD Southend, Base
Name sel for shore base at comml pt Southend 01.09.1939, NOIC ordered 27.08.39, in post 29.08.39 - name not used

SAFEGUARD Calmore, Soton, AA Guard Base/DEMS
Cd 01.07.1941. Opened as AA Guard Base, AA Guard Base abolished and estab merged into DEMS 01.12.42. Closed 07.07.45, PO 14.08.45
Nom DS: NAB ALUSIA 01.07.41 -11.41
NAB CORMORANT 11.41 -09.44 (damaged in collision)
MB 421262 09.44 -14.08.45

SAFEGUARD Rosyth, BD Depot
Cd 01.07.1946 ex ROOKE (qv) - PO 1969 task to COCHRANE
Nom DS: HLD 39462 01.07.46 -62

SAFETY Tortola, W Indies, Rx Sh
Ex ECLAIR, schooner, guard ship W Indies 1808, prison ship 1810, Rx Sh Tortola 1841 till BU 1879

SAGESSE Ports, Convict Sh
Fr 6th Rate, capt 1803, convict ship 1819 - sold 1821

SAGITTA (1908) Gt Yarmouth, Flag Admiral Commanding East Coast
12.1914 v ZAREFAH - Cd 22.01.15 independent command, -10.1916
Yt, hired 12.14 - PO 06.02.18, PNTO E Med 1918-19, & WWII

SAGUENAY (1930) Sydney, Nova Scotia, RCN TS
DD, rammed by freighter off Newfoundland 15.11.1942 - stern damaged by depth charges and became TS 10.1943 - PO 30.07.45 for CORNWALLIS (qv) at Sydney, sold 17.07.1948

ST ADRIAN (1927) Normandy
Yt, hired 09.1939, later purch, Ferry Control Normandy 06.06.1944, sold 09.11.45

ST ANDREW Oban, Base
Cd 01.03.1941 - 01.07.1943 - renamed CALEDONIA (qv)
In some lists as ST ANDREWS
Nom DS: MB TAI-WO 01.03.41 -10.12.411
NAB ECILA 10.12.41 - 01.07.43

ST ANGELO Malta GC, Base
Cd 01.07.1933 ex EGMONT (qv) - 31.03.1979

(final withdrawal of RN from Malta GC at midnight)
Ft St Angelo tx from War Department to Adty 08.12.1906 for use as a barracks - took name EGMONT.
RAF Airfield Takali under ST ANGELO (see GOLDFINCH)
SM1 under ST ANGELO 11.39
Nom DS: BULLFROG (1881) ex EGMONT 01.07.33-sold 33
FIDGET (ex War dept MINER 18) - ex ADELAIDE ex ADDA 12.33-06.37
Tug (1935) hired as aux M/S lost by mine off Malta 30.05.42
Diesel lch 3972 30.05.42-
FMB 41513 Pre 08.58-
MFV 72 (ex GOLDFINCH) 10.56 - (sold 04.67) - listed to 11.76

ST ANGELO II Malta GC, Accounting Base for Med DDs
1934 - 01.04.1938 (merged into ST ANGELO)

ST ANGELO II St Paul's Bay, Malta GC, M/S Base
1944-45
Nom DS: M/S FAREHAM (1918)

ST ANGELO III St Paul's Bay, Malta GC, M/S Base
Cd 26.09.1943 independent command, acs ST ANGELO, PO 12.02.45 rb FAREHAM (qv) 23.02.45
Nom DS: Steam Pinnace 156 26.09.43-12.02.45

ST ASAPH Chichester, Accom Sh
08.1942, acquired 01.01.43, laid up Lymington 05.45, no longer required, to DST 06.45

ST BARBARA Bognor Regis, AA Range
Cd 10.09.1943 - task to DINOSAUR 23.01.45, PO 14.06.45
Nom DS: 14ft Sailing Dinghy No 1382 01.09.43-

ST BEDES Eastbourne, TS
RN W/T Sch at St Bedes, Eastbourne under MERCURY 11.1943 - prob not a formal 'ship' name

ST CHRISTOPHER Ft William, CF TE
Cd 31.10.1940, PO 31.12.44 - tng tx to BEE (qv)
Nom DS: Speedboat BEN TRAVATO 31.10.40-22.06.44
HL(P) 42604 06.44-

ST CLAIR (1937) Reykjavik, Iceland, Accom Sh
Hired 07.1940, accom sh Iceland 09.40, Cd 12.09.40, renamed BALDUR as Base Ship 10.40, reverted to ST CLAIR as rescue ship 10.43., resto 08.45

ST CLAIR (1918) Halifax, Nova Scotia, RCN DS/ TS
DD, ex USS WILLIAMS, Cd in RCN 1940. 01.44 became SM DS at Halifax. 08.44 was static hulk for Damage Control Sch. Hulk there to 1950 at least

ST CLEMENT Coal House Fort, Tilbury, Essex, CO Base
Cd 07.09.1943 independent command, acs PEMBROKE IV, closed 20.01.1946
LC Base for Major LC, also listed as DG Sta. Spelt ST CLEMENTS in some list
Nom DS: Repair Vessel BRITANNIC 07.08.43 - 10.44 (at least)

ST CLEMENT I Perrys, Tilbury
Cd 01.05.1944-

ST CLEMENT II St Johns, Tilbury
06.05.1944 - 20.01.46
Also listed at St Parrys

ST CLEMENT III Coal House Fort, Tilbury, Holding Depot
06.05.1944 - 20.01.1946
For personnel tx to Germany (v COCKFOSTERS (qv))

ST COLUMBA (1912) Greenock, BD Depot
Cd 02.07.1941, acs ORLANDO, PO 1946
Hired as accom sh for BD personnel Greenock 05.1941, name given to Depot - to MOWT 15.04.46, Depot remained at Revlis 02.46 - vessel rb ALECTO / CARRICK II 10.45

ST CROIX (1956) Halifax, Nova Scotia, RCN Hbr TS
FF, alongside TS 15.11.1971 - 1991, BU 1991

ST CYRUS Ports, Signal Sch
In a list - prob a location rather than ship name

ST DAVID St David's, Pembrokeshire, RNAS
Relief airfield for Brawdy (see GOLDCREST) 1947-61. Listed as re-opened 01.04.63 - about this time name in use by seagoing tender S Wales Res Div - prob ref to location rather than ship name.

ST ELMO Uplands Cres, Swansea, Base Accountant's Office & Staff
01.04.1942-

ST FIORENZO Woolwich/ Standgate Creek, Qtn Sh
5th Rate, capt 1794, qtn sh Woolwich 1814, Standgate Creek by 1831 - BU 1837

ST FRANCIS (1919) Deep Brook, Nova Scotia, RCN TS
DD, ex USS BANCROFT, tx to RCN 09.1940, static TS to CORNWALLIS (qv) 02.1944 - 11.06.1945 - wrecked enroute breakers 14.07.1945

ST GEORGE (1840) Dev/ Falmouth, Guardship/ CG
1st Rate, guardship Dev 08.1850-, CG Falmouth 04.05.1864 - 01.07.1869, BU 1883

ST GEORGE (1892) DS
Cr, conv to DD DS 1909-1910, DS 3 DF Nore 1910-12, 9 DF Chat/ Firth of Forth 1913-14, A/P DS Tyne v ILLUSTRIOUS 08.14-11.14, (Humber as 7 DF Humber 12.11.14-01.04.15), Tyne 02.15 - rb SATELLITE 07.05.15, A/P DS Immingham 05.15-06.11.15 rb WALLINGTON, dock Hull 11.15, DS Mudros 24.12.15 - Stavros Beach Party 01.01.17 v EUROPA, Corfu Base A/P DS Salonika v

LATONA 07.18 - 07.07.1919 (01.07.19 - acs to EUROPA), PO Ports for refit to SM DS 07.08.19, allocated 2 SM Rosyth 05.19 but to SM Sch Ports 09.19, sold 01.07.20

ST GEORGE Douglas, Isle of Man, TE
Cd 09.09.1939, PO 31.12.45
Boys' TE opened for boys evacuated from ST VINCENT & CALEDONIA - Cunningham Camp taken over 05.09.1939.
Nom DS: Yt 10.11.39-
MB RENOWN (ex lifeboat) 11.05.40-
MB 40146 05.42 -27.05.42
NAB ST MARJORIE 27.05.42 -31.12.45

ST GEORGE II/ST GEORGE Gosport, Hants, Barracks for Tng Short Serviice Ratings
Cd as ST GEORGE II 01.12.1945, Cd as ST GEORGE 01.01.46 - when tng at Isle of Man ceased - see previous entry. Barracks (built 1941) taken over from Army. New Entry Tng to RALEIGH (qv) 1948 and barracks returned to War Office
Nom DS: MSPB 44318 03.46-48

ST GEORGE Fraser Gunnery Range, Eastney, Ports, Officer Candidates' TE
Named Fraser Battery ex Experimental AA Battery 09.41. TE opened 16.09.1963 as part of EXCELLENT, Cd 01.08.1968 - 1973-task to DARTMOUTH - though estab listed at Eastney till 06.76

ST HELIER (1925) Dartmouth/ Fowey, CO Base
Base Ship CO Base Dartmouth 09.02.1941 - 01.42 - (acs QUEBEC since 13.10.40), tx to Fowey, Accountant Officer from BELFORT 10.41. Cd 16.06.42 independent command, Conv to LSI(H) Clyde 07.1942, PO 14.08.45, to MOWT 12.10.45

ST HYACINTHE St Hyacinthe, Quebec, RCN Signal Sch
Cd 01.01.1941 - though established earlier (see STADACONA II) - 20.02.46

ST KATHERINE (1927) Gravesend, Accom Sh
28.12.1943 - 01.46 (Salvage Department)

ST LAWRENCE (1806) Sheerness, Rx Sh
5th Rate - ex SHANNON, Rx Sh 1832, renamed ST LAWRENCE 11.03.1844, BU 11.1859

ST MAGNUS (1924) Kirkwall, Accom Sh
Req 31.08.1939 as guardship Kirkwall Base - fit out Aberdeen 30.08.39. To be named PYRAMUS (qv) but cancelled. Accom sh Kirkwall for Examination Service. To Military for Norway 05.40, rb VANDYCK. PO 16.07.40. resto 07.08.40

ST MATHEW Burnham-on-Crouch, CO Tng Base
Initially under Harwich, by 10.40 independent command, acs PEMBROKE IV, Cd 08.11.43 acs LEIGH, own acs, PO 31.10.45 and closed 07.12.1945 - task to QUEBEC
Accom in Commando Camp, Creeksea, task from EFFINGHAM, Tng CO Personnel, later tng just officers, ratings tng to HELDER 1944
Nom DS: Barge House Boat HARRY 08.11.43 - (laid up 11.09.45)

ST MINVER (1919) Freetown, Sierra Leone, A/P Base
Cd 01.04.1941v EDINBURGH CASTLE - 01.10.41 rb MOIRA(qv)
Tlr JONATHON COLLINS, renamed ST MINVER when sold by Adty, hired 09.1939-46

ST PATRICK (1873) Haulbowline, Tank & Cooking Vessel
1917-23
Ex SHAMROCK, renamed 01.11.1917

ST SUNNIVA (1932) Kirkwall, Guardship/ Accom Sh
Hired 29.08.1939 as guardship Kirkwall Base 08.39 - fit out Aberdeen 30.08.39. Accom sh Kirkwall 05.40, rb VANDYCK and to Military for use in Norway 04.40. At Scapa Flow as accom sh rb EXMOUTH 07.42, PO at Hull 08.42, refit Hull as Rescue Ship 09.42, lost 22.01.43

ST TUDNO (1926) Sheerness/ Ijmuiden/ Amsterdam, M/S DS
Hired as Armed Boarding vessel 08.1939, accom sh Standgate Creek, Sheerness 05.09.39, to be released for Norway 05.40 but cancelled. M/S DS Sheerness Cd 01.07.1941 (see WILDFIRE II) (ST TUDNO & Queenborough Pier were one estab by 02.41). Evacuated from Sheerness to Holehaven 15.04.43. Reported at Sheerness 29.10.44, Ijmuiden 11.44, Amsterdam 12.44, and Shererness 05.45-, replaced as accom sh Queenborough by ESKIMO & GARTH 01.46. To MOWT 18.01.46
Nom DS: Lifeboat BRENTFORD II to 11.44 (to SCC Worcester)

ST VINCENT (1815) Ports, DS/ TS
1st Rate, Ports as Flag & DS from 10.1841, TS 01.01.1862, PO 04.01.1906, sold 17.05.1906

ST VINCENT (1908) Ports, Flag RF/ Drl Sh
BB, Flag RF Ports 02.1919 - 28.11.19 rb GLASGOW, Turret Drl Sh Ports by 02.19 - 12.19 rb COURAGEOUS. Res Rosyth - sold 12.21

ST VINCENT Forton Barracks, Gosport, Boys' TE
Cd 01.06.1927 - closing ceremony 08.12.1968 - Ensign down & closed 02.04.1969. To Land Agent 03.04.69
Boys evacuated to Isle of Man - merged with CALEDONIA to be ST GEORGE (qv) 1939. Became Air Branch Officers' TE, overflow for RN Barracks, also a Signal Sch. Torp Tng Section opened there 22.07.1940. reverted to Boys' TE 01.12.45.
Nom DS: Steam Lch 288 01.06.27 - 39
45ft PL(D) 44201 by 03.48
PL(D) 4201 (poss renumbering of prev vessel) 1948-(listed to 62)
HL(D) 3947 by 05.52-Listed to 1960 (sold 19.02.59)

ST VINCENT Queen's Gate Tce, London, WRNS Accom
15.09.1983 - Cd 1985, PO 31.03.92
Building purch 1954 as WRNS Accom, RN Section PRESIDENT named ST VINCENT 15.08.83

ST VINCENT Whitehall, Communications Centre
Cd 01.04.1992 - PO 31.03.1998 - became MARCOMM COMCEN (ST VINCENT)

SAINTES (1944) Rosyth, TS
DD, Hbr Ts for CALEDONIA v CONCORD & CHEVIOT 07.1962 - 1972 rb DUNCAN, sold 26.06.72

SAKER Dartmouth, Nova Scotia, RNAS
Cd 01.10.1941 - ex SEABORN, PO 01.08.1942 - see CANADA
One account states SAKER II PO & rb CANADA

SAKER New York/ Washington/ Virginia, USA, Base
Cd 01.11.1942 ex SAKER II - extant 1990 (NL 1991 shows NP 1964 at Norfolk Va)
1943-45 Lewiston, Maine - USN Base used as part of SAKER. Also included Air Sta at Squantum (from 09.43-07.44), and Air Sta at Brunswick, Maine (from 08.43-08.45). 10.45 in New York City - 03.46 to 37 Wall St, New York, 12.46 combined with British Adty Delegation (BAD). 01.01.47 - 76 SAKER to Washington, then to Virginia. Naval Staff in District of Columbia and Crystal City, all to DC when SAKER closed.
Nom DS: MB 626(SAKER II) to 17.09.45
MB 42431 18.09.45-57
MSPB 5518 15.05.57-62

SAKER I Dartmouth, Nova Scotia (Prob Main part SAKER when SAKER II & III extant)
In PO Circular 13.01.1943 and 22.03.44

SAKER II Connecticut Ave, Washington, USA, Accounting Base
Cd 01.12.1941, became SAKER (qv) 01.11.42
For personnel standing by ships under construction and refit and other unattached personnel in USA
Nom DS: MB 626 01.12.41-

SAKER II Asbury Park, Accom Barracks
Extension of SAKER II Cd as ASBURY (qv) 01.10.1942

SAKER II Quonsett Point, Rhode Is, New York, Originally ASBURY (qv), but became SAKER II 31.03.1944

SAKER II Washington, USA, B.A.D.
1946

SAKER III Washington, USA

SALCOMBE Salcombe Hotel, Salcombe/ Imperial Hotel, Exmouth, CO Base
Cd 17.07.1943, PO 0900, 10.01.44 - renamed TENNYSON (qv)
Named at Salcombe and tx to Exmouth between 15 and 20.11.43
Nom DS: SHEILA II 17.07.43-10.01.44 - became TENNYSON

SALCOMBE II Exmouth
20.11.1943 - 10.11.45
In a list - poss a confusion through the tx of SALCOMBE to Exmouth - poss initiated during turnover period

SALDANHA Saldanha, S Africa, SAN Gymnasium
By 09.1957 - listed to 1961

SALDANHA Saldanha Bay, SAN TE
New TE 1976

SALENTINE Brindisi
Name sel for base at pt Brindisi for Disciplinary (Courts Martial) purposes 01.05.1944 - but not Cd

SALFORD (1919) Ports, SM DS
Ex SHOREHAM, M/S, DS 3 SM Ports 1920, sold 10.20

SALFORD Blackfriars St/ Bexley Sq, Salford, Communications Tng Centre
Cd 01.10.1984, to Bexley Sq 1991, PO 12.08.1994

SALISBURY Salisbury Is, Durban, SAN Estab
01.11.1955 - 59
HQ SANF from Salisbury Is to Simonstown 02.04.57
There was a Repair Base Salisbury Is - approved to close 09.1945

SALISBURY (1953) Dev, Hbr TS
FF, Hbr TS v ULSTER 1980-83 rb AJAX, sunk 09.85

SALSETTE Woolwich/ Sheerness, Rx Sh
5th Rate, Rx Sh Woolwich 1831-65, Sheerness by 1870

SALSETTE Bombay, CO Base
Cd 01.01.1943 tender to BRAGANZA, 01.07.43 independent command, acs BRAGANZA (pending arrival own staff), PO 01.04.1944 merged with BRAGANZA (qv)
Poss estab existed by 11.42 but Cd 1943. In NL 10.45
Nom DS: 32ft MB

SALSETTE I Bombay, CO Depot
Details as SALSETTE above - prob a name for main estab to distinguish from SALSETTE II and III

SALSETTE II Bombay, SO Assault Craft - including COSMO
01.01.1943 - PO 01.04.44 - became BRAGANZA II (qv)

SALSETTE III Bombay, Signal Centre, Bandra
Cd 01.01.1944, - 01.04.44 - became BRAGANZA III (qv)
TE comprised Comb Signal Centre, Bandra; Comb Aircraft Recognition Sch Juhu &

Navigational Aid Estab Bombay

SALTASH (1918) Alexandria, Accounting Base
M/S carried acs of Res M/S at Alexandria from 01.07.1938, though actual office was in Pt Said

SAMARANG (1822) Gib, Guardship & DS
6th Rate, at Gib 1847-1883, sold 10.1883

SAMBRO Halifax, Nova Scotia, RCN DD and Escort DS
Estab 28.07.1941, Cd 01.10.1941 ex SEABORN(Capt D Halifax) - PO 01.05.42, task to STADACONA on commissioning. Became VENTURE II 06.03.42

SAMBUR Plaisance, Mauritius, Base
Cd 01.04.1943, PO 01.08.46
RNAS planned for Choisy area 05.42, then altered to Plaisance, damaged in cyclone. Building 09.1942 - handed over to RAF 12.1944 when completed
Nom DS: Hbr Lch 421162 01.04.43-

SAMPSON (1781) Woolwich, Sheer Hulk
3rd Rate, sheer hulk 1802 - BU 1832

SAN ANTONIO Ports, Prison/ Powder Hulk
Fr ST ANTOINE, 3rd Rate, capt 1807, prison ship 1809, powder hulk by 1814, sold 1828

SAN GORGIO Alexandria/ Piraeus, Greek A/S Repair & DS
Cd 15.03.1944, tender to ST ANGELO, at Alexandria 04.1945, at Piraeus by 16.05.45, De - req & PO 16.06.45

SAN JOSEF Dev, Gunnery Sch
2nd Rate, prize 1797,Gunnery Sch 1837-49, BU 05.1849

SANDERLING Abbotsinch, RNAS
Used on lodger basis from 1939. Tx from RAF 09.08.1943, Cd 20.09.43 independent command. Closed for rebuilding 30.11.50-52, Airfield closed 14.09.63, tender to CONDOR 01.10.63, PO 31.10.53 - to Ministry of Aviation.
Was parent to NUTHATCH in C & M 31.03.58, also to BLACKCAP 31.12.58
Nom DS: FMB 40211 20.09.43 -12.07.46
RN Air Lighter No 13B 12.07.46-54
RN Air Lighter 3F 1954 - 30.11.56
MB 43780 (listed in MB Book 1955)
MFV 666 01.12.56-62

SANDERLING II Machrihanish, RNAS
In two lists -
LANDRAIL PO 16.04.1946 and ReCd as tender to SANDERLING, and also when in C & M 01.12.52.
(In 1943/44 SANDERLING II was a fireboat)

SANDFLY Peterhead, CF Base
Cd 05.05.1941 acs BACCHANTE, PO 25.10.43
Nom DS: M/S tender EINNAN 05.05.41 - 03.43
Norge MFV SVALEN 03.43-

SANDHURST (1905) DD DS
Ex MANIPUR, purch 1915, was dummy BB INDOMITABLE 1915. Fit out as DD DS 01.16 and Cd as DS 15 DF 20.08.16 - 19, also Fleet Repair Ship Scapa Flow 1916-18. 2 DF 01.03.19-, To Copenhagen v GREENWICH (2 DF Baltic) 09.09.19-, 3 DF Atlantic Fleet 1919-23, From E Med to UK 01.05.23. Med 10.25-35, Dev for survey 35-36, Nore DS then Mechanical TE 38-39. To complete at Chat & Cd 07.10.39 as Repair Ship & Accom Sh Dover. PO repairs 08.40 - C & M 04.09.40. Londonderry Cd 30.01.41 - immobile DS 02.42. Loch Ryan 05.45, Pt duties for U-boats Loch Ryan 20.01.46. To Rosyth 01.46 - PO 08.04.46, BU 04.46

SANDOWN (1934) France/ Ternezen, Holland, Accom Sh
Paddle steamer hired as M/S 10.1939, AA ship 07.42. Mulberry Control Ship Normandy 06.44, accom sh Terneuzen v ORIOLE Cd 07.04.45 - Base & Accom Sh to 10.45 - to DST 23.10.45

SANGDRAGON Seychelles, Base
Cd 22.03.1943. PO 19.02.46

SANDRINGHAM Swarbacks Minn, Shetlands, A/P DS
Cd 24.02.1918 v GIBRALTAR - 02.19 (Base PO 28.02.19)
BD Tlr, hired to 1919

SANGOLA Eaton College, Chester
Instructional boat at RN College 10.44 - 05.45 (at least)

SANJIVANI Cochin, IN hospital
1967 - listed to 1976

SANS PAREIL Plym, Sheer hulk
3rd Rate, capt 1794, sheer hulk 1810, BU 1842

SANS PAREIL (1887) Sheerness/ Weymouth, Pt Guard Ship/CG
BB, Pt Guard Ship Sheerness 18.04.1895 (Cd as Flag 11.05.1898) - 1903. CG Weymouth 1903 - 07.1903, sold 09.04.1907

SANTA MARGARITA Pembroke/ Lpool, Qtn Sh
Spanish 5th Rate, capt 1779, qtn sh Pembroke 1817, Lpool by 1831 - sold 1836

SAON (1933) Azores, A/S DS
Tlr, A/S Tlr 09.1939, conv Lpool to mobile A/S maint vessel 09.43-10.43, Horta 26.11.43, Punta Del Garda 11.43-, Plym 23.12.44, Milford Haven 25.12.44, refit Newport 01.45, C & M 02.45, Cd 23.04.45 - Tobermory 29.05.45, Lpool 30.05.45-03.07.45, PO 25.07.45, sold 1945

SAPPER
Was to have been Holyhead A/P Parent - see AMETHYST III

SAPPHIRE (1827) Trinco, Rx Sh
6th Rate, Rx Sh 1850 - sold 11.1864

SAPPHIRE II (1883) Portland, DS
Cr, IMPERIEUSE (qv), renamed 02.1905 - poss was SAPPHIRE but became SAPPHIRE II when new Cr Cd 1905. DS for TBD at Portland, reverted to IMPERIEUSE 06.1909, sold 24.09.1913 (listed as at Portland to 01.1915)

SAPPHO (1891) Firth of Forth/ Hamble, Res Drl Sh/ Accom Sh
Cr, seagoing Drl Sh Forth RNR 13.06.1903 -1905, accom sh Hamble River 1918, sold 03.1921

SAPPHO (1935) Guardship
Yt, hired as guardship 11.1939, Contraband Control Service, Plym 02.40, sunk 29.09.1940 off Falmouth

SARDO Maddelena, Corsica, Base
Name sel for base for convening Courts Martial 01.05.1944 - but ann not to be Cd 11.05.44

SAREPTA Portland, Experimental Hydrophone Estab & Parent for Hydrophone Craft/ Listening Sch
Cd 01.03.1918 - nominal parent, estab to be known as SAREPTA - repair Pool 06.1918, rb GIBRALTAR 01.11.1919.
ONYX (qv) attached 05.1919.
Nom DS: Drifter SAREPTA (1906) hired 01.1915 - 01.03.18-01.07.18-renamed WELCOME FRIEND
Drifter WELCOME FRIEND (1914) 01.07.1918-1919

SAREPTA Dunoon, TE
Name sel for A/S TE Dunoon when OSPREY was to be tx from Portland 01.1941, but name not used

SASEBO
In a list - poss ref to place in Japan - see LADYBIRD

SATELLITE (1881) North Shields/ South Shields, Res Drl Sh
Cr, Res Drl Sh N Shields 02.11.1903 - WWI. A/P Base ship Cd 06.05.1915 v ST GEORGE - PO 15.01.20 - M/S Base Milldown & S Shields closed 15.04.19, A/P Base Northumberland Dock closed 31.05.19. To RNR on completion of records 10.19- . RNVR N Shields between wars. DEMS & TS and Base Ship S Shields 09.1939 - 46. RNR re-constituted in SATELLITE at S Shields 01.10.46, sold 21.10.47

SATELLITE Tyne, Res HQ ship
1) MELITA (1942), M/S, renamed 04.1947 - 10.09.51 - to breakers 24.02.59
2) BRAVE (1943) M/S renamed & Cd 11.09.51 - BU 25.11.58

SATURN (1786) Milford, Qtn Sh
3rd Rate, qtn sh 09.1825, guardship 06.1854, also housed QHM by 1862. BU 01.02.1868 (see also NANKIN)

SATYAVAHANA Vishakapatnam, IN SM Sch
1984 - extant 1999

SATYR Sunderland, Base
Name sel for shore base at comml pt Sunderland 01.09.1939 - records actually read 'STAYR' - typing error? - NOIC ordered 27.08.39, in post by 29.08.39 - name prob not used. Naval Base closed 15.09.45

SAULT STE MARIE (1942) Esquimalt, British Columbia, DS/ Accom Sh
M/S THE SOO, renamed 1944, DS/ Accom Sh for MALAHAT 07.05.1949 - (no Res Div ashore 05.53 - 01.55) - PO 01.10.58. BU 05.60

SAUNDERS Kabret, Egypt, Comb Tng Centre Middle East
Cd 22.01.1942 ex STAG Div K (qv) independent command acs STAG. PO 16.07.1946 - tx to Army Main body to Gailes Camp, DUNDONALD (qv) 04.45
Nom DS: MV PRINCESS ELIZABETH 22.01.42-

SAUNDERS II Kabret, Egypt, CO Tng Centre
Cd 01.07.1945 - still listed to 10.47
In 08.45 was used for tx of CO Forces from UK to the Eastern theatre (crews of APPIAN (qv) craft & administration base of APPIAN craft)

SAUNDERS III Kabret, Egypt, CO Tng Centre
To 08.1945 - Listed under East Indies 02.46

SAVAGE (1830) Malta GC, Mooring Lighter
Sloop, Dockyard Chain Lighter 1853, BU 1866

SAVAGE (1942) Chat, Accom Sh
DD, living ship for ships refitting 1948-49, fender ship 1958 - tow to BU 10.04.62

SAXIFRAGE (1941) Dartmouth, Accom Sh
Corvette, accom sh 01.1947, weather ship 08.47

SCARAB (1915) Burma, Base Ship
Gunboat, Chartered to Burmese Government as Base Ship for LC Assault 05.1946, rb FAL/MAYU mid 1947, BU Spore 05.48

SCARBOROUGH (1812) Standgate Creek, Qtn Sh
3rd Rate, qtn sh 1835, sold 1836

SCARBOROUGH (1930) W Hartlepool, Flag RF
Sloop, 01.10.1944 RF v DOUGLAS - FO Commanding RF to KENT 21.10.45 - acs retained in SCARBOROUGH. Acs of PARAGON 30.11.45. PO 15.02.46 - acs to CUILLIN SOUND. Allocated as RNVR Drl Sh 05.46 but not used. Left for BU 01.07.49

SCAWFELL (1937) Normandy/ Portland, Control Vessel/ Accom Sh
M/S 1939, AA Ship 1941-45, Mulberry Control Vessel Normandy 06.44, accom sh Portland 07.44. To ANCXF for defence Scheldt 11.44, PO 24.05.45

SCIPIO Oran, Algeria, Tlr Base
Cd 02.1943 - PO 15.11.1943
Name sel 05.01.43 - ann as Base for Oran & Arzen 13.03.43. On closure staff remained at Oran on books HANNIBAL until CF Base Mers - El-Kabir

closed
Nom DS: MB 18946

SCORPION (1832) Blackwall, R Thames, Police Ship
Sloop, lent Thames Police 03.03.1858 until BU 17.10.1874

SCORPION (1863) Bermuda, Guardship
Ex Turkish (Egyptian-Confederate?) EL TOUSSON, purch 10.1863, guardship from 10.1869 until used as target 1901. Sold at Bermuda 02.1903

SCORPION Salisbury Is., S Africa, SAN HQ Strike Craft Flot
Cd 07.07.1980-

SCOTIA Doonfoot, Ayr/ Lowton St Mary's, Warrington, Signals TE
Named 19.05.1941, Cd 06.01.42. On 29.11.46 at lowton St Mary's - see CABBALA). Tng ceased 20.12.47, PO 19.01.48
Doonfoot built for 1500 visual and W/T trainees
Nom DS: 50ft MVF 815 12.46-01.48

SCOTIA Pitreavie/ Rosyth, Dunfermline, HQ Unit RNR
Cd 11.02.1959. Moved to RN Support Estab CALEDONIA 04.1996 on closure Pitreavie, still under name SCOTIA extant 1999

SCOTIAN Halifax, Nova Scotia, RCN Base & Res Div
01.06.1944 - Cdre Superintendent - PO 28.02.1947 - acs to ROCKCLIFFE (Pacific) and IROQUOIS (Atlantic).
23.04.1947 - 1987 (at least) Res Div - see also HALGONIAN

SCOTSTOUN (1916) Mesopotamia, DS for Gunboats
Stern wheel river steamer re-erected in Abadan, DS River Tigris 03.1918. To Military 05.1918, sold 04.1920

SCYLLA (1891) Harwich, Res Drl Sh
Cr, res Drl Sh Harwich v ANDROMACHE 12.1904 - 1905. Sold 04.1914

SEA BIRD Binga Bay, Nr Kawar, IN Air Sta
Under construction 1989, listed at Kawar 1992

SEA EAGLE Londonderry, Joint A/S Sch
Cd 21.06.1947 ex FERRET (qv) - was to have been renamed PHOENIX (qv) - PO 24.06.70-tx to Army RNAS Eglinton - ex GANNET (qv) 1959-63 and Ballykelly, came under SEA EAGLE - see also SEALION
Nom DS: MB 3629 -ex FERRET 06.47 - 09.47 (at least)
MB 441338 1947-30.07.55
RML 498 30.07.55 - 06.56
ML 2593 06.56 - 26.07.58
ML 5629 27.07.58 - 62

SEA SERPENT Bracklesham Bay & Birdham, Chichester, LC Base
Cd 20.10.1942, PO 30.06.1945 - leaving SEA SERPENT (Birdham)(Minor LC Base Birdham) as tender to VICTORY III - PO 30.11.45
Was a CO Suspense Base prior to being Cd. Used Sussex Ideal Holiday Camp & Gibson's Camp, Bracklesham Bay, Bracklesham Bay Hotel and various properties at Birdham including Birdham Pool & Maint Base
Nom DS: Houseboat ML 237(qv) 20.10.42 - 30.11.45

SEABELLE (1927) Persian Gulf/ Bombay, Base
1939 - (Bombay - PO Circular 07.07.1943 - 09.05.45) - 04.46
SEABELLE II hired as A/P Yt 09.1939, renamed SEABELLE Base Ship (Persian Gulf) v SHOREHAM 1941 (though Cd 16.09.1939). RIN A/S Yt 10.44-19.05.46. Resto Straits Settlement Government 04.46

SEABORN Halifax, Nova Scotia, Accounting Base for 3rd Battle Sqn
Used from 07.12.1939. FO 3rd Battle Sqn from ROYAL SOVEREIGN 27.01.40. Cd 01.05.40, PO 30.09.41 replaced by SAKER/ 3rd Battle Sqn lapsed. To C & M till RCN 31.10.41. Became HMCS SAMBRO (qv)
1) Ferry ex CHARLES A DUNNING, ex SEABORN
2) Drifter SEABORN (1939) hired 12.1939 - Nom DS 11.40 - renamed VENTURE II(qv) 09.41
Poss same vessel as SEABORNE below

SEABORN II Halifax, Nova Scotia, Base
Cd 07.09.1940 - PO 31.12.1940
For personnel & Base Staff of USN DDs tx to RN

SEABORN Dartmouth, Halifax, Nova Scotia, RNAS
From 14.09.1939 - Cd 07.12.39 acs CANADA. Closed 08.11.45, PO 28.01.46 - tx to RCN - see SHEARWATER.
Pre-war RCAF Sta, used by RN 1940 - see under SAKER and CANADA.
Also included Yarmouth RNAS (PO 30.03.45)
Nom DS: RN ir Lighter 12B 07.12.43-

SEABORN II Dartmouth, Nova Scotia
01.1944
In a list - could poss ref to RNAS Yarmouth when operating with RNAS Dartmouth - see SEABORN above

SEABORNE Halifax, Nova Scotia, SM Accom Sh
Yt, req 12.1939 as tender to RESOLUTION - 08.12.39 - poss same vessel as drifter SEABORN Nom DS above. Some reports say this was Yt SEABORN used as accom sh and which change her name to VENTURE 13.05.43 (qv)

SEABREEZE (1918) Orkney & Shetlands, Flag
Flag Orkney & Shetlands 20.07.1940
Drifter, sold 1946

SEAFLOWER (1873) Ports, Workshop
Brig, Workshop 01.1904, sold 07.04.1908

SEAGULL Sydney, Cape Breton, Nova Scotia, RCN

Patrol DS
01.05.1918 ex STADACONA II - PO 10.12.1920 at Halifax
Tug CD 74 ex LANIOLETTE

SEAGULL (1937) Leith, Res Drl Sh
Sloop, survey vessel 1945, Res Drl Sh Leith 1955, BU 05.56

SEAHAWK Ardrishaig, CF Base - A/S Tng Base
Cd 01.01.1941, PO 04.11.1944
Nom DS: No 1 Pinnace at Campbeltown 01.01.41 -03.43
NAB JOAN 03.43 -11.44

SEAHAWK Culdrose, Nr Helston, Cornwall, RNAS
Cd 17.04.1947 - extant 1999
Was to have been named CHOUGH
Nom DS: MFV 1004 17.04.1947 - 62

SEAHORSE (1847) Dev, Coal Hulk
5th Rate, coal hulk by 1865, renamed LAVINIA (qv) 05.05.1870, sold 1902

SEALION Ballykelly, RNAS
Quoted as SEALION by two authorities as the base for RNAS Ballykelly - but this was SEA EAGLE (qv). SEALION (1959) was a SM.

SEEADLER Manus, Admiralty Is., RAN Base
Cd 01.01.1950 replaced TARANGAU (qv) at Dredger Is - 01.04.50 - renamed TARANGAU
Quoted as at Lambrom, Los Negros Is, Papua New Guinea in one ref

SELSEY BILL (1945) Repair Ship
Cancelled

SERIRAMIS (1808) Plym, DS
5th Rate, DS 1835, BU 1844

SENESCHAL (1945) Ports, Hbr TS
SM, attached DOLPHIN as visitor/tng boat v TUDOR 10.1959, rb TELEMACHUS 01.60, BU 23.08.60

SENTINEL (1945) Ports, Hbr TS
Cr, Mechanical TE 1920-22, sold 01.23

SENTINEL Methil, Fife, Base
Name sel for shore base at comml pt Methil 01.09.39. NOIC ordered 27.08.39. Name does not appear to be used. DEMS Base Methil closed by 04.07.45. Torp defence tubes to be removed 07.45. To NOIC Status 11.45. From NOIC to RNO status 15.11.45

SERAPIS (1782) Jamaica, Hosp Sh
5th Rate, Hosp Sh 1819 - sold 1825

SERINGAPATAM (1819) Cape, S Africa, Rx Sh/ Coal Ship
5th Rate, Rx Sh 07.1847, coal ship 1850 till BU 06.1873

SERUWA Ratmalama, Ceylon, RN Aircraft Yard/Transit Camp
Cd 01.05.1945 independent command, acs BHERUNDA - acs to UKUSSA 01.11.45, PO 25.09.46
Nom DS: TRV 44 01.05.45-

SETON Newhaven, CF Base
In a list - though CF Newhaven was FORWARD II/AGGRESSIVE
SETON was Yt - Greenwich Pool 05.42, to DST 09.45

SEVEN BELLS Ports, Accom Sh
08.1942, but found unfit 09.42

SEVERN (1885) Harwich, CG
Cr, CG Harwich 27.05.1898 - 11.02.1903 rb MERSEY, sold 04.1905

SHAH (1873) Bermuda, Rx Sh. Coal Hulk
FF, ex BLONDE, renamed 1873, Rx Sh 1895, coal hulk (C470) by 1900, sold 09.1919

SHAHEED MOAZZAM Kaptari, Chittagong Hill Tracts, Bangladeshi Base
1984 - extant 1999

SHANNON (1806) Sheerness, Rx Sh
5th Rate, Rx Sh 1832, renamed ST LAWRENCE (qv) 11.03.1844, BU 11.1859

SHANNON (1875) Clyde/ Bantry Bay, CG
FF, CG Greenock 01.06.1883 - 05.08.1885, then Bantry 06.08.1885 - 03.05.1893, sold 1899

SHANNON (1906) Sheerness, Accom Sh
Cr, accom sh to ACTAEON Torp Sch (qv) 1919-22, sold 12.22

SHARPSHOOTER (1888) TS
Torp Gunboat, hbr serv 1904, renamed NORTHAMPTON (qv) 1912, lent to Lord Northampton, sold 27.03.1922

SHEARWATER (1900) Esquimalt, British Columbia/ Halifax, Nova Scotia, RCN SM DS
Sloop, at Esquimalt as RN SM DS 08.09.1914, PO as static Rx Sh - Cd in RCN 01.10.1914, tx to Halifax 1917, PO 13.06.19, sold at Ottawa 05.22

SHEARWATER II Esquimalt, British Columbia, RCN DS
09.08.1914 - 01.17 (at least)

SHEARWATER Dartmouth, Nova Scotia, RCN Air Sta
Cd 01.12.1948 - 01.04.1966 - became CFS SHEARWATER - listed to 1976 - extant 1986
Had been named SEABORN (qv) - became RCN Air Sta Dartmouth 11.45 on tx to RCN

SHEATHBILL Pt San Carlos, Falklands Is, RNAS
06.1982
Unofficial name for Forward Operating Base

SHEBA Aden, Base
Cd 01.04.1940 ex GLOUCESTER III (qv), to C & M 01.06.46, to PO 31.12.46 but cancelled, PO 29.11.67

RNAS at RAF Miswa, Aden, under construction 11.44. FAA used RAF Khormaksar on a lodger basis under SHEBA.
Nom DS: MB 1501 01.04.40-
ML 42615 26.09.56 - listed to 1960 (but sold 23.11.57)

SHEFFIELD (1936) Ports, RF HQ
Cr, RF HQ and living ship v VANGUARD 08.06.1960 - FO Commanding RF closed 29.08.60 - became SO RF - 07.64 rb BERRY HEAD - and Cdre Res Ships to 23/24.05.66 rb BELFAST. BU 09.67

SHEILING Soton, Accom Sh
09.1942 - acquired 17..12.42 - laid up Lymington/ C & M/ DST 01.45

SHELBURNE Shelburne, Nova Scotia, Base
12.1941 (NOIC) - Base 01.05.42 - 31.01.46
Joint RCN/ USN Oceanographic Sta 01.04.55 - 10.08.67 - became CFS SHELBURNE

SHERBROOKE Sherbrooke House, Glasgow, Radar TE
Cd 15.01.1946, independent command, acs ORLANDO - 18.02.46 - renamed MARRYAT
Adty Signal Estab Extension
Nom DS: MFV 1177

SHERWOOD Nottingham, Communications Tng Centre/ Res Tng Centre
Cd 01.10.1984 - extant 1999
At Carrington St to 1986, then Chalfont Drive

SHIHEEN Basra, Dumb Accom Barge
Dumb Barge, in use 12.1942

SHIKARI/ SHIKARI II (1914) Swansea, A/P Base Bristol Channel
Cd 16.02.1917 v LONGSET - renamed SHIKARI II 11.02.1918 - PO 01.02.1919 - personnel to IDAHO
Tlr, hired 1915

SHIPMATE Codeword
02.1945 - codeword for designated Supreme HQ Allied Expeditionary Force - Forward HQ. Opened at Rheims 20.02.1945. SHAEF Main closed at Versailles 15.06.45, opened at Frankfurt/ at same time SHAEF Forward then became SHAEF (Main). SHAEF (Rear) in London 06.45

SHIVAJI Lonavla, Bombay, RIN/ IN Mechanical TE
Cd 19.01.1944 - completed 31.12.44, Cd 08.01.45 (formal ceremony 15.01.45) - listed to 1976

SHIVERING SANDS Thames Fort
Army Fort WW II

SHOREHAM (1930) Persian Gulf, Accounting Base
Sloop, personnel in Gulf borne on her books 1939-41 - (replaced by SEABELLE). Sold 04.10.46

SHOTLEY Ports
In two lists - but no other data - GANGES (qv) was at Shotley Gate, Nr Ipswich - perhaps a name used for GANGES parallel estab ST VINCENT (qv)?

SHRAPNEL Soton, Base
Cd 09.06.1942 ex VICTORY V (qv) - independent command, accounting Base Soton. Closed & PO 03.09.1946
Included Government Tng Centre Letchworth 08.42, and carried acs of SQUID (qv) 09.42. SQUID merged into SHRAPNEL 01.02.46.
Nom DS: Fr Tug STIFF (seized 1940) 09.06.42 - 03.45
MFV 617 1945?
FMB 39129 03.45 - C & M 12.01.46

SHRAPNEL II Soton, Stokers' TE
Cd 05.11.1943 - 27.04.44
Collective name for REVENGE and RESOLUTION (qv) while acting as TE for Stokers and other Engine Room ratings. The ships reverted to their original names 27.04.44 when steamed to Gareloch to become IMPERIEUSE II (qv)

SHRIKE Maydown, Co Down, N Ireland, RNAS
Ex RAF tx 01.05.1943, Cd 15.05.43 as tender to GANNET. Re-Cd 01.03.44 independent command, own acs. PO 30.09.45 - became GANNET II (qv)
Nom DS: NAB ONORA 15.05.43 - 31.03.44
MFV CORNISHMAN 31.03.44-

SIDI IFNI (1892) Algiers/ Maddelena, Accom Sh
Ex German Yt, taken as prize 20.02.1943, Cd 20.02.43 as accom sh NID/ DDOD(I) Flot - African Coastal Flot. Condemned by Prize Court 07.43. Algiers to 17.12.43, then to Maddelena, Sardinia - PO 19.03.45. To MOWT 22.03.45. Store carrier in Naval service 06.45.

SIDONIA Southport, DEMS Depot
Name earmarked for Depot 06.1955

SILVA (1924) Lpool, Net Defence DS
Whaler, hired 05.1940, Hbr Serv 1942, DS by 09.44, sold 1946

SIMBA Kilindini, Kenya, Dockyard/ Barracks
Cd 06.03.1945 - PO 01.11.1945, Re-Cd as tender to TANA, PO 22.01.46
Originally named in error as KIMBO
Nom DS: Hbr Lch 421140 06.03.45-

SIMBANG Sembawang, Spore, RNAS
Cd 15.12.1945 ex NABROCK (qv), PO 31.12.1947 - to C & M. To RAF 15.01.48 (Nom DS TRV tx to RMNVR 06.06.48). C & M 09.49. Lent RAF 10.49 - 15.01.50 (also RMNVR Tng 12.49 and used by RNAS). Cd 16.01.50 and also 01.07.53 - PO to C & M 01.04.57 - Commando accom 1960 (advance party 01.60, full Cdo & NAS 06.60) - Cd 04.09.62 (3 Cdo Brigade) - by 1966 Fleet Amphibious Force Base - PO 30.09.71 - Tx administration to ANZAC Force 01.09.71
Originally Bukit Sembawang Rubber Estate, purch by RAF 1936. Opened 1937/8, to Adty 1939, to

RAAF 1940, evacuated 01.1942.
Nom DS: MFV 15.12.45-
MFV 224 04.46 (but cancelled)
MFV 755 15.12.46-
TRV 421029 (ex BAMBARA) 11.46 - 1949
FMB 44431 01.50 -52
MRC 1100 1957 -62

SIMBRA Kilindini, Barracks
Appears in a list as such, and NL has a SIMBRA (Whaler) with a Capt in Command - believe SIMBA (qv) is correct spelling of Barracks name

SIMONSBURG SAN TE
Cd 07.1963 - 1980s

SIMONSTOWN SAN Estab
Cd 07.1963-

SIMOOM (1868) Simon's Bay, S Africa, DS
MONARCH, had been guardship Simon's Bay 1897 - 1902, renamed SIMOOM as DS 03.1904, sold 04.04.1905

SINGAPURA Spore, RMNVR HQ
Ex LABURNAN (qv) 22.09.1963 - 1966 (at least)

SIR BEVIS (1918) Sheerness, TS
Sloop, TS at Sheerness 1922-23, renamed IRWELL (qv) 09.1923 - Drl Sh, renamed EAGLET (qv) 1926, BU 1971

SIR HUGO (1918) Hamble, DS
Sloop, DS for MLs in Hamble 03.1920, sold 25.06.30

SIRIUS (1940) Ports, Accom Sh
Cr, accom sh 03.1949 - 03.51 (at least). Then Flagship group (not living ship) 03.51 - 07.52, BU 10.56

SISKIN Dounreay, Caithness, RNAS
Name allocated when RNAS (ex RAF Sta) Building 1944. Sta tx to RN 04.44 but name used for RNAS Gosport, which was to have been WOODPECKER. Dounreay little used - see TERN II

SISKIN Gosport, RNAS
Cd 01.08.1945,independent command, acs DAEDALUS PO 31.05.56 - became SULTAN (qv)
Was to have been named WOODPECKER. Lent by RAF 01.08.45 (originally to 10.46). Tx to RN 10.48
Nom DS: MB 427 01.08.45 - 05.46 (at least)
HL(D) 37283 by 04.1948 - 56

SISTER ANNE (1929) Fowey/ Inveraray, Accom Sh
Yt, hired as accom sh 09.1940 - Falmouth with CF. Purch 05.41. Fowey 03.41 - 08.41, Oban 08.41 - 11.41, Inveraray 08.11.41 - 12.41, Clyde 01.42 - 06.42, Ports 06.42, Clyde 07.42 - 03.44, Inveraray 03.44 - 04.44, Clyde 04.44 - 05.44, as accom sh. Re-allocated ANCXF 06.44, Normandy 06.44 - 07.44, Ports 08.44 (to MONCK to de-equip 08.44), Clyde 09.44 - 10.44, Allocated Traffic Control duties Lpool 02.45, laid up 12.45 and to DST 20.02.46

SITA Colombo, Ceylon, RIN Comb A/S Sch
03.1944 - 16.05.44 (at least)
Cd as Holding Depot and Rest Camp Moratuwa, Nr Colombo

SKIDDAW (1896) Isle of Wight, HQ Ship
Hired as M/S and AA ship, HQ ship 14-24.06.1944. To ANCXF for defence of Scheldt 11.44. No longer required 05.45, PO 21.06.45

SKIDEGATE (1927) W Coast Canada, RCN TS
ML, Fishermen's Res TS WWII. Cd 25.07.1938 - PO 18.02.42 -see GIVENCHY II, sold 1946 - included in a list of shore estabs

SKIOLD Ports, Rx Sh
Danish 3rd Rate, capt 1807, Rx Sh 1808 - BU 1825

SKIPJACK (1855) Dev, Cooking Depot
Gunboat, cooking depot 1874 - BU 02.1879

SKIPPER (1904) Scapa Flow, BD
1918
In a list of shore estabs as a shore base. Was a coaster hired as Ammo Carrier 09.1914 - 1919 - could have been a Nom DS

SKIRMISHER Milford Haven, Base
Cd 12.09.1939, PO 31.08.45 acs to LUCIFER 01.09.45
Name sel for base at comml pt 01.09.39 - NOIC ordered 27.08.39. FOIC Milford Haven Flag down 14.08.45
Nom DS: Tlr GEORGE BAKER ON 157616 12.09.39 -24.01.44
Drifter SILVER PRINCE (1913) 24.01.44 - 19.07.45
ML EAST MORA 19.07.45 - 31.08.45

SKIRMISHER II Pembroke Dock, CF Base
Cd 01.05.1941, to C & M 11.43, To be closed 11.11.44
Nom DS: ML DIPLOMAT (ex MARGARET) 05.41 - 44

SLANEY (1813) Bermuda, Rx Sh
6th Rate, Rx Sh 1832, BU 1838

SLANEY (1877) Sheerness
Gunboat, diving tender 1906, reported sold 1919 but listed to 1921

SLUYS (1945) Dev, Hbr TS
DD, attached RALEIGH 05.1955, sold to Iran 07.1966

SNAPPER (1854) Ports, Coal Hulk
Gunboat, coal hulk 1865 till sold 1906

SOBER ISLAND Sober Is., Trinco, Ceylon, Camp
Cd 01.11.1944 -tender to WAYLAND - PO 30.06.1946
Nom DS: MFV ST43/558 01.11.44 - -
HL(P) 43588 01.11.44 - 30.06.46

SOBO (1899) Cromarty, Torp Sub DS
Purch 10.1914, DS Cromarty 02.1915 - PO

10.1919, sold 12.02.20

SOKOTO (1899) Scapa Flow, Torp Sub DS
Purch 10.1914, DS Scapa Flow 12.1914 - PO 24.06.1919 - task to Lyness 07.06.19. Sold 09.08.1919
Also used as Grand Fleet W/T Sch from 03.1915

SOKOTO ISLAND DS
WWI - In a list - poss ref to SOKOTO above which could have had a shore element (Lyness?)

SOLEBAY (1873) Deptford, TS
IRIS, 5th Rate, lent to Trinity House 10.1803 - renamed SOLEBAY 18.11.1809. Lent to Marine Society 1814 - 1833 (second ship - see WARSPITE). BU 10.1833

SOLEBAY (1944) Ports, Hbr TS
DD, attached SULTAN as Hbr TS 1962 v VIGO - 66 rb CROSSBOW. BU 08.67

SOLWAY FIRTH (1944) Maint Ship for Hull Repairs
Allocated Home Waters (prob not completed). Approved to BU 15.03.46 - sold 46

SOMERS ISLES St George's Bay, Bermuda, Work Up Base
Construction approved 06.1942. Cd (RN) 01.1943 - tender to MALABAR . PO 04.43 - amalgamated into one base MALABAR.
Cd 01.08.44 (RCN) - 16.10.1945

SONA (1922) Poole, Accom Sh
Purch as A/S Yt 09.1939. Cd 03.10.39 as accom sh. Cd 17.08.40 and sunk in air attack Poole 07.06.42 - PO 07.06.42

SONNEBLOM SAN Naval Command West HQ
23.09.1986-

SOUND FISHER Inveraray, Accom Sh
04.07.1943

SOUTHAMPTON (1820) Harwich/ Hull, CG/ TS
4th Rate, CG Harwich 01.01.1857 - 28.02.1858, lent to Hull Committee as TS 18.06.1867 till sold 26.06.1912

SOUTHAMPTON II Ceylon, Base
1921 - ex JUMNA (qv) - 1923, became CHATHAM II (qv)
Cr SOUTHAMPTON (1912) Flag E Indies 1921-23

SOUTHERN ISLES (1922) Iceland, Accom Sh/ Base
Belgian PRINCESS MARIE JOSE, hired 17.09.40 as A/S TS SOUTHERN ISLES (renamed 01.11.40) & Cd 18.02.41. Renamed NEMESIS 10.03.41, renamed BALDUR (qv) Base Ship 10.43 - reverted to NEMESIS 1945, Resto 08.1945

SOUTHERN PRINCE (1929) Normandy/ Southend, Temp HQ/ Accom Sh
M/L 1940, HQ FOBAA 25.05.44 - at JUNO, Normandy, by 10.06.44 - FOBAA ashore 25.06.44 - accom sh JUNO - no longer required 31.07.44. Accom Sh Southend PO 10.44 - to convert to Dockyard Labour Accom Ship (Red Ensign) Rosyth 11.44. Cd for passage 06.11.44 for conv in Canada - arrive Canada & PO 02.12.44. For British Pacific Fleet v CITY OF PARIS on completion - estimated 07.45. To be manned by 150 RN personnel and Red Ensign crew on completion of conv 17.10.45. Due Spore 01.46. No longer required, to DST 10.46. Sold 01.04.47

SOUTHLAND (1908) Inverary, Accom Sh
01.1943 - 06.44
American, lease lend to RN 03.42, returned US Authorities 06.44

SOUTHMEAD
Appears in a list - could ref to location - see PEMBROKE III

SOUTHWESTER Harwich, Accom Sh
Yt, for Capt M/S Harwich 06.1943, and renamed EPPING as Nom DS (qv)

SOUTHWICK Ft Southwick, Fareham, HQ Unit RNR
Opened 13.05.1958, Cd 11.06.58 - PO 31.03.1994
Name allocated 10.04.1959

SPANKER Pt Edgar, Accom Sh
M/S, accom sh 05.1948, to Belgium 02.53

SPARROW (1946) Tyne, Accom Sh
Sloop, RF Office accom sh 07.1956-, allocated as poss Res Drl Sh but no longer required 08.57. BU 05.58

SPARROWHAWK Hatston, Orkney, RNAS
Cd 02.10.1939, PO 01.08.1945 - became TERN II(qv)
Officer appointed to IRON DUKE as CO Hatston, FAA War Base 30.08.39. Satellite airfield at Skaebrae 03.40 -45, then under RN (qv). Further satellite at Sullum Voe 07.40 -41. RNAS Twatt Cd 01.01.41 as Satellite, became independent as TERN (qv) 01.01.42. RAF Grimsetter tx to RN 06.07.43 as tender to SPARROWHAWK, became ROBIN (qv).
Nom DS: Drifter LINNET 02.10.39 - (allocated but not used)
MV SANDRA 02.10.39-

SPARROWHAWK Halesworth, RNAS
Cd 05.08.1945 - C & M 28.02.46, PO 15.03.46 - and to RAF
Tx on loan from RAF 01.08.45 - 10.46

SPARTAN (1891) Holyhead/ Dev, Res Drl Sh/ TS
Cr, seagoing Res Drl Sh Holyhead 18.10.1903 - 1905. Tender to DEFIANCE 1907, renamed DEFIANCE II (qv) 1921, sold 1931

SPARTIATE Dev, Sheer hulk
3rd Rate, Fr, capt 1798, sheer hulk 08.1842 - BU 1857

SPARTIATE (1898) Ports, TS
Cr, stokers' TS 1913-, renamed FISGARD (qv)

17.07.1915, sold 07.1932

SPARTIATE Glasgow, Base DS
Cd 03.09.1939, 15.01.46 ledgers closed - independent command, acs ORLANDO till PO 31.03.46
Name sel for comml pt Clyde 01.09.39, NOIC ordered 27.08.39, in post 29.08.39. FOIC Glasgow lapsed 15.01.46
Nom DS: Motor Yt SEAWAY 03.09.39 -01.41
Yt BLUEBIRD (1911 01.41-12.44
MFV 1038 15.01.46 - 31.03.46

SPARTIATE II Tullichewan, WRNS TE
Cd 29.05.1943, PO 06.12.1944 (prob ref to Nom DS only) - in NL to 01.46 (not listed 04.46)
Nom DS: Patrol Craft TARKA II 29.05.43-06.12.44

SPEEDWELL (1935) Nore, SO RF
M/S, SO RF 1939, sold 05.12.46

SPENSER (1917) Nore, SO RF
DD Leader, SO RF v CASTOR 10.10.1927 - 12.27 rb CALLIOPE, BU 09.36

SPEY (1941) Belfast/ Dartmouth/ Dev, RNVR Drl Sh/ Accom Sh
FF, allocated Belfast RNVR v DELHI 05.47 but not used. PLYM allocated in lieu 12.47. Living ship RF Dartmouth 04.46-10.46. Living Ship RF Dev 10.46 - 04.47. Sold to Egypt 11.48

SPHINX Alexandria, Accom Camp
Was to have been named ABOUKIR. Cd 20.04.1941 acs NILE. PO 01.05.46
Nom DS: MB 904 20.04.41-

SPICA Polyarnoe, N Russia, Nom DS
Cd 01.07.1944 - 20.10.45
For SBNO, N Russia - NP 100 - see also BELLATRIX. SBNO appointed Murmansk 10.41, NP there by 08.41, acs PRESIDENT I - return UK 20.10.45
Nom DS: Steam Pinnace 746 01.07.44-

SPITEFUL (1799) Ports, Convict/ Hosp Sh
Brig, convict hosp sh 1818 - BU 1823

SPITFIRE II Poole, Accom Sh
Motor Yt, 08.1942, acquired 03.02.43 - laid up C & M 07.08.45

SPRINGS Springs, S Africa, SAN TE (ACF Res)
1956 - 60

SPRINGTIDE (1937) Base Ship
Purch as M/S 1940. Minedestructor 02.08.40 - deperming vessel 1941-47. Listed as Base Ship in one list - poss in East Indies (was in India & Kilindini 07.41 - 11.44)

SPURN POINT (1945) Maint Ship for LC
Home Waters, Cd 22.12.45 Esquimalt -sail 01.46, Clyde 02.46 - declared surplus 04.46 - PO 31.07.46 - sold 07.1947

SPURWING Hastings, Sierra Leone, RNAS
Tx from RAF 16.03.1943. Cd 22.03.43 independent command, acs ELAND. 15/.07.43 own acs. Being developed plus Class A Repair Yard 10.43. PO to C & M 31.12.44
Nom DS: NAB CORSAIR 22.03.43 -31.12.44

SQUID Soton, CO Base
Cd 01.09.1942 - PO 01.02.1946 merged into SHRAPNEL (qv)
Tank LC Repair Base established at Messrs Harland & Wolff, B Works, Soton. Flot Base at H & W & Redbridge - later Elmfield Court, Oakville Mansions, Devonshire Buildings & Southern Railway Depot used for SQUID
Capt GJ2 in SQUID 02.44
Nom DS: NAB CRISIS 01.09.42 - 08.43
Hbr Lch 42865 08.43 - C & M 12.01.46

SQUID II Westcliffe Hall Hotel, Hythe, LC Sqn Staff
Cd 26.02.1944. To C & M 19.04.45

SRI KLANG Kuala Lumpar, Selangar Div, Malaysian Res
1966 - listed to 1978

SRI LABUAN Labuan, Sabah, Malayasian Naval Base
1963 - extant 1994 (see SRI TAWAU)

SRI MEDINA Johore Bahru, Malaysian Res Div
1969 - listed to 1978

SRI PINANG Penang, Malaysian Res Div
1966 - listed to 1978

SRI REJANG Sibu, Sarawak, Malaysian Naval Base
1969 - extant 1994 - see SRI SANDAKAN

SRI SANDAKAN Labuan, Malaysian Naval Base
1998 - extant 1999 (ex _ REJANG)

SRI TAWAU Tawau, Sabah, Malaysian Naval Base
1969 - extant 1994 and 1999 (ex LABUAN)

STADACONA Halifax, Nova Scotia, RCN Depot/ Barracks/ TE
21.03.1918 - 01.05.1918 - A/P Depot Halifax, including Ottawa - became GUELPH
01.07.1923 ex GUELPH(ex CD 43) - 01.04.66 - became CFS HALIFAX
Flag Halifax post WWI. RCN barracks to 1942. TE Cd 01.05.42 v SAMBRO. From 01.06.42 was Advancement & Drafting for all RCN personnel
Nom DS: US Yt COLUMBIA (1899) Cd 13.05.1915-PO 31.03.20

STADACONA I Halifax, Nova Scotia, TE
WWII - was TE inside Dockyard

STADACONA II Sydney, Nova Scotia, RCN A/P Depot
21.03.1918 - 01.05.1918 - became SEAGULL

STADACONA II Halifax, Nova Scotia, RCN Barracks & Signal Sch
01.08.1940 - 30.08.1941 - moved and became ST HYACINTHE
01.1944 - 01.10.1944 - became PEREGRINE

(Drafting Depot)

STADACONA IIII Halifax, Nova Scotia, Officers' TE
Became KINGS 1941

STAG Pt Said, Base
Cd 08.01.1940 - ex FERMOY II - known as STAG (PORT SAID) from 01.08.1941. PO 31.05.1949
Included Haifa 1941-44, Ismailia 1941, Pt Said 1941
Nom DS: 25ft Adty MB 38205 08.02.1940 -08.41

STAG (A) Coast Near Adabya, S of W Shore Suez Bay, CO Estab
Cd 01.04.1943 - PO 30.09.1943
The (A) ref to location - manned by 2 Pt Parties & for Force G - in Suez Bay for Op Husky

STAG (DIVISION K) Kabrit, camp
Independent cammand 08.1941 - poss by 03.41. 21.01.42 renamed SAUNDERS
Nom DS: MV PRINCESS ELIZABETH 08.41-22.01.42

STAG (ISMAILIA) Ismailia, Estab
Independent command 08.41-in PO Circular 24.06.42
Nom DS: NAB HOULE 01.08.1941-

STAG (N) Geneiffa, Suez Canal Area, Camp
Cd 09.10.1941 - independent command
The 'N' stood for 'Nets' - used to cover the Canal at night to detect laying of mines
Nom DS: Houseboat 338 (Suez Canal Co) 09.10.1941-

STAG (PORT SAID) Pt Said, Base
Independent Command, renamed from STAG when series of independent 'STAG' estabs formed and ment 09.43. STAG (PT SAID) and STAG (HAIFA) mentioned 02.1948
Nom DS: 25ft FMB 38205

STAG (PORT TEWFIK) Pt Tewfik, BaseIndependent command 08.1941
Nom DS: NAB RAMSES II 01.08.1941 - 17.09.1943

STALKER (1944) Londonderry/ Rosyth, Support Craft
LST 3515, Cd 06.1945, named STALKER 1947. Support craft SM Londonderry 02.48 - 03.70. Rosyth refit ship 03.71 - for nuclear SM Rosyth by 1982, sold 1991, but extant at Rosyth 1999

STANDARD Keilder Camp, Hexham, Northumberland, Naval Labour Corps Camp
Cd 15.01.1942 acs CALLIOPE, PO 13.07.1945
Camp for neurotics. 08.1943 listed as for tng of 'CQ' ratings
Nom DS: Hbr Lch No 1 15.01.1942-

STAR (1835) Sheerness, CG vessel
Brig, CG vessel 1857, renamed WV11 1863, BU circa 1899

STAR Hamilton, Ontario, RCN TE & Res Div
01.09.1939 - Cd 01.11.41 - 01.09.42 - tender to STADACONA
01.09.1942 - 1987 (at least) - independent command - see also PATRIOT

STAR II Hamilton, Ontario
In a list 1946

STAR OF FREEDOM (1917) Solent/ Normandy, Tlr M/S DS
Tlr, store carrier, Solent to 24.06.1944, then Normandy (Utah) - took stores from Ports to AMBITIOUS. Allocated Cdre Belge 12.44 rb RAYMONT and allocated Dover M/S Force 02.45 - at Dover 05.45, temporarily Ostend M/S Force 07.45

STAR OF INDIA (1888) Ardrishaig, Accom Sh
Hired as A/S Yt 0-7.1940. Accom sh Ardrishaig 03.43 - had been allocated Kilindini but found unsuitable for service abroad - laid up 12.44, resto 1946
NAB STAR OF INDIA renamed INDIAN 03.44 - Colledge says SIOUX (Tug) renamed INDIAN 1944 - connection unknown

STATIONS were Fixed A/S Defences sent to locations to operate - not ship names - normally 'station' followed by 'letter'. RAN used Station followed by number for such things as Pt War signal Stations/ Controlled Mining Stations/ RDF Sch/ BD organisations etc
Some RN examples of Fixed A/S Defences and others are as follows:

STATION A - Fixed A/S Defences for MNBDO - joined 13.01.1941 E Med, arrive Alexandria 06.41 - Iskanderum (Alexandretta) Turkey

STATION B Fixed A/S Defences - for MNBDO - joined 13.01.41 in E Med, arrived Pt Said 06.05.41

STATION C - Fixed A/S Defences - Iskanderun, Turkey 10.1942

STATION D and E - Fixed A/S Defences for Greece - cancelled

STATION F Fixed A/S Defences - E Med - to Alexandria 31.05.1941

STATION H Fixed A/S Defences - Hvalfjorder, Iceland, under BALDUR - left UK 17.05.1942, arrived 21.05.42 - operated to 05.06.44

STATIONS J and K - Fixed A/S Defences for Greece - cancelled

STATIONS L and M - Fixed A/S Defences for MNBDO II - loaded by 31.01.1942 - left UK 12.08.1943 - became BULLFROG Party 30 and 31 (East Indies) respectively

STATION N Fixed A/S Defences - Iceland - Seydisforder - under BALDUR. Left UK 21.09.1941 - ceased operating 11.05.44

STATIONS O and P Packed in readiness for Shannon - not set up - returned to store

STATION Q Fixed A/S Defences for Trinco - under HIGHFLYER - RN Sta Elephant Ridge - left UK 29.11.1941, arrived 04.02.42 - operated to 10.45

STATION R - Fixed A./S Defences for Trinco - under HIGHFLYER - ready, left Clyde 20.12.1941, arrived Colombo 12.03.42 destination Sunda Strait, retained Columbo, then to Kilindini 05.42. early 1944 Ft St Joseph to C & M, party returned UK

STATION S Fixed A/S Defences - for Russia, left UK 11.1941, arrived Archangel 20.11.41

STATION T - Fixed A/S Defences for East Indies - left UK 06.01.1942, arrived Colombo 09.03.42 - for use in Trinco, then Kilindini

STATION U Fixed A/S Defences E Med - arrived Alexandria 18.05.1942, arrived Suez 17.04.42, for Mersin (Turkey), Smyrna 06.42 - to Turks

STATION V Fixed A/S Defences - E Med, arrived Alexandria 09.05.1942 - for Mersin (Turkey)

STATION X Not Fixed A/S Defences - was Bletchley Park Codebreaking organisation prior to becoming GCHQ

STAYR - see SATYR

STEPHEN FURNESS (1910) Invergordon, A/P DS (Cromarty & Peterhead)
18.01.1915 v COLUMBINE and EILEEN, - 09.03.1916 rb THALIA
Became store carrier, then armed boarding steamer, lost 12.1917

STICKLEBACK (1954) Duxford, Museum SM
Midget SM X51, named 1955. To Sweden as SPIGGEN 15.07.1958, to Imperial War Museum, Duxford 1977 - extant 1999

STIRLING Garden Is., Cockburn Sound, Western Australia, RAN Base
Cd 28.07.1978 - extant 1999
Work began at Woodman Pt 1911, stopped 1914. Started at Garden is 1971

STIRLING CASTLE (1811) Plym/ Ports, Convict Ship
3rd Rate, convict ship Plym 04.1839, Ports by 1845 - BU 1861

STOCKHEATH
In a list - poss ref to location

STONE FRIGATE Esquimalt, British Columbia, RCN Barracks
In 1938 a building in the dockyard, was known as 'Stone Frigate' - never Cd. Used as Barracks for NADEN 1922-24

STONE FRIGATE Kingston, Ontario, RCNVR Officers' TE
01.08.1940 - 27.06.40
At Royal Military College - named after dormitory which had originally been a storehouse for RN in 19th Century

STOPFORD Bo'ness, West Lothian, Tank LC Base
Cd 18.04.1942, Administration to Rosyth 01.09.1943 acs LOCHINVAR. PO 15.09.45
Major LC base used LNER Docks Bo'ness with Bo'ness Hosiery for ratings;' accom. Rosyth House extended for WRNS
Nom DS: Steam Picket Boat 659 18.04.1942 -04.43
Steam Pinnace 762 04.43-

STORK (1855) Ports, Coal Hulk
Gunboat, coal hulk 1874 till sold 1884

STORK (1882) Hammersmith, TS
Gunboat, survey ship 1887, lent as TS for boys to Kensington Branch of Navy League at Hammersmith 03.1913. BU 1950 in Kent - hull used as wharf

STRANGER HEAD Lyness, Orkney - in a list - was a signal sta - prob location not ship name

STRATHBLANE (1901) Scapa Flow, BD Accom Sh
Hired 1915 - 1919

STRATHDERRY (1911) Scapa Flow, Officers' Accom Sh
07.1917 - 09.1918 (at least)
Tlr, hired as M/S 1914. BD vessel 1917-18 & WW II

STRATHERBRIE (1914) Sierra Leone, A/P DS
Cd 01.04.1917 - PO at Gib 12.1918 - but listed 03.1919 (and in NL 12.1919)
Tlr, hired as BD Vessel 1914 - Base Ship 04.17-12.18 - mooring party Sierra Leone continued under CORMORANT

STRATHLEVEN (1910) Scapa Flow, Officers' Accom Sh
07.1917 - 09.1918 (at least)
Tlr, BD vessel WWI

STRIKER (1945) Malta GC, RF Living Ship
LST 3516, named 1947, living ship RF Malta GC 09.1950-05.51, to RF Gib 05.51, Res Chat 12.59-, Amphibious Warfare Sqn 1961 - PO 1966, waiting disposal Ports 1967-68, sold 02.70

STUART (1918) Dev, SM DS
DD Leader, listed v ADAMANT 2 SM Dev Spring 1932.-. To RAN 10.1933, sold 02.1947

STUYVESANT Holyhead, Dutch DS
17.06.1940 - rb ORANJE NASSAU 08.41 - to Netherlands Shipping Co 09.41

SUCCESS (1825) Ports, Rx Sh
6th Rate, Rx Sh 1832 - BU 1849

SUDAN Pt Sudan, Base
Cd 22.04.1943 independent command, acs STAG. PO 30.09.43 (in Red List 07.44 as PO and in NL 10.45)

SUI WO (1896) Spore, Accom Sh/ Hosp Sh
Req for examination Service Spore 06.1941. Hired as BD accom sh Changi 18.11.1941. Conv to Hosp Sh, sailed Spore 09.02.42, lost by bombing 13.02.42

SULPHUR (1826) Woolwich, Convict Ship/ TS
Bob vessel, survey ship 1835, convict ship 1843-, TS for Engineers 1843 - 46, BU 11.1857

SULTAN (1870) Ports, TS/ DS
BB, renamed FISGARD IV 01.01.1906, reverted to SULTAN 1932 as tng hulk (Mechanical TS). DS for M/S 1940-45, sold 13.08.1946

SULTAN Spore, Base
Cd 01.01.1940 and Cdre ic Spore - ex TERROR II (qv). Abandoned 11.02.1942 - PO 28.02.42. TERROR II acs renamed SULTAN as TERROR (ship) required elsewhere under own name
Nom DS: Dockyard lch 3706 01.01.1940 -

SULTAN II Spore, Accounting Base - Seagoing Tenders
Cd 01.01.1940, independent command - ex TERROR II. PO 01.04.1941 to become separate pay account of SULTAN - retained in NL to 1945

SULTAN III Penang, Accounting Base - for all services at Penang
Cd 01.01.1940 - 16.12.41 -personnel tx to SULTAN Retained in NL to 1946

SULTAN IV Spore, Accounting Base
10.12.1941 - 11.02.42
Acs of survivors of PRINCE OF WALES and REPULSE retained for duty in the Spore area

SULTAN Spore, Accounting Base for personnel at Keppel Harbour
Cd 15.09.1945 - PO 31.03.1947 - supply duties to TERROR
By 1946 included Staff of FO Malaya etc. At Balakng Mate Is 06.06.1946. Became British Pacific Fleet Drafting Authority v GOULD 12.09.46
Nom DS: Hbr Craft TANDJONG-BALEI 15.09.45-(Pre)02.46
MFV 1140 Pre 02.46(poss 10.45) - (sold 09.47)

SULTAN II Spore, Accounting Base for Personnel at Naval Base
Cd 08.10.1945 independent command, acs SULTAN, PO 15.05.46 - renamed TERROR (qv)
Nom DS: HL(D) 3706 08.10.1945 - 15.05.46

SULTAN Gosport, Hants, Marine Engineering TE & Sch of Aircraft Handling
Cd 01.06.1956 ex SISKIN - extant 1999
Tng element of Mechanical Tng & Repair Estab Flathouse Rd - part of RN Barracks - tx to Gosport
Nom DS: HL(D) 3819 01.06.1956 - 06.01.59
LST 3031 06.01.59 till sold 12.70 (dockyard fender ship 1961 onwards)

SUMAS Sumas, British Columbia, RCN Transmitting Sta
12.1942 - 1959 - became MATSQUI

SUNBEAM II (1929) Falmouth/ Helford, Base & Accom Sh
Yt, conv at Soton 06.1943 for service as Base & Accom Sh Helford. Cd 01.07.1943 - Inshore Patrol Flot - tender to FORTE, PO 16.03.1945. To C & M 14.05.45 - to DST 05.07.45

SUNHILL (1895) Ports/ Rosyth, Accom Sh
Hired as accom sh 23.09.1915-06.1920. Fitted out at Royal Victoria Dockyard 10.1915 - for Rosyth 11.1915. To Ports 05.1916 and Cd there 15.06.16 v SYRIA as Nom DS for mercantile ratings in RN Barracks - 1920.

SUNHILL II Ports/Soton/ Grimsby, Accounting Section for Officers & Ratings in SUNHILL
07.1916 from Ports to Soton. 11.16 to Grimsby. 01.17-12.18 at Immingham - separate ledger for Officers and Men serving in SUNHILL (qv). 06.1919 allocated to Baltic Passenger Service - acs to GREENWICH 01.10.19

SUNKHEAD FORT Thames - off Harwich, Thames Estuary Defence Unit No 2
Cd 01.05.1942. To C & M 14.06.1945

SUPERB (1875) Clyde, CG
BB, CG 14.04.1891 - 23.05.1894, sold 1906

SUPERB (1907) Nore, RF Parent
BB, RF Parent Gp 4 v BOADICEA 25.05.1919 - 1920. Sold 12.1922

SURF (1902) Dover, DS Rear Admiral Controlled Minefields
Base 05.1918 - independent command, Nom Parent Dover. PO 24.03.1919 - Flag to ATTENTIVE II
Yt - hired as A/P 02.1915 - 04.19 and WW II (lost)

SURF II
SS VICTORIA was to be taken up as DS Controlled Minefields, Dover under SURF 10.1918 and to be Cd 25.11.18, but cancelled

SURPRISE (1812) Cork, Convict ship
5th Rate, convict ship 1822, for sale 1837, still listed 1845

SURPRISE (1896) Downs, Guardship
Yt, hired WWI and 12.1939. To Downs as guardship v HOLDFAST. Cd 07.05.1940. For service abroad 07.40. Purch 08.41. Burnt and capsized Lagos 28.02.42

SUSSEX Maxwell's Wharf, Hove, Res HQ
1949 - Cd 28.04.1951. PO 31.03.1994
Naval Reserve Battery Sussex 1909 onwards - at 5 Victoria Tce 1922-28 (at least) - became KING ALFRED in WWII. CO appointed 10.01.46, Div reconstituted 01.10.46 in RNVR Battery Kingsway. New HQ opened 06.07.1968

Nom DS: Motor Whaleboat 45958 1952

SUTLEJ (1899) Dev/ Rosyth/, TS/ Accom Sh
Cr, stokers' TS Dev under IMPREGNABLE 07.07.1915. C & M 06.08.15. Overflow ship Rosyth 04.05.1917 - name SUTLEJ discontinued 06.17 - 1918 (see CRESCENT). Sold 05.21

SUTOR Cromarty, LC Base
Cd 15.12.1943, acs MONSTER. PO 14.04.44 - to C & M
Nom DS: NAB GOODCHEER 15.12.43 - 14.04.44(later OWL)

SUVLA (1945) Chat, Accom Sh
LST 3518, named 1947. RF Chat 11.01.1952. Cd 10.08.56. RF living ship Chat 10.01.57 - 59, sold 09.08.1960

SWAN (1811) Thames, Church Ship
Cutter, lent Church Missionary Society 05.1844. Thames till BU 07.12.1874

SWAN (1856) Ports, Coal Hulk
Gunboat, coal hulk 1869 at Ports till sold 1906

SWANWICK Accom Sh
09.1942 - but found unsuitable 03.43

SWIFT (1835) Cape, S Africa, Mooring vessel
Brig, mooring vessel at Cape 1861. Renamed YC3, sold 1866

SWIFTSURE (1804) Ports, Rx Sh
3rd Rate, Rx Sh 1819, sold 1845

SWIFTSURE (1903) Chat, Accom Sh
BB, Cd 15.06.1917 as accom sh - 10.1918. Conv to blockship Chat 1918 but not used. Sold 06.1920

SWINGER (1872) Dev, Stores Ship
Gunboat, hulked 1895, attached IMPREGNABLE by 1922 - sold 06.1924

SWORD Normandy, Beach Sub Area - NP 1569
Cd 06.06.1944 - NP to UK by 19.07.1944

SYLVANA (1907) Normandy/Ostend, M/S DS - HQ Ship
Yt, hired as danlayer 12.1939. DS 1944 - allocated ANCXF 08.44 as HQ ship. Left Dev for Brest 09.44. Ref to her at Ostend 01.45-02.45. Nore 06.45, Methil 07.45, allocated FO Denmark as M/S HQ Ship 06.45 - but cancelled - though movements show her Denmark 07.45-, at Rosyth for disposal 09.45, PO to C & M 06.11.45 and sold 1945

SYVERN (1937) Crete, CF DS
DS 05.1941, lost 27.05.41

SYLVIA (1944) Malta GC, RF Living Ship
M/S, living ship 13.03.1950 - 01.1951 (at least), sold 09.58

T

TABARD (1945) Ports, Hbr Tng SM
SM, Hbr TS for DOLPHIN v TACITURN 12.1968 - 11.73 rb ALLIANCE, sold 01.74

TABARIN Falkland Is Dependencies Expedition
09.1944 - 45 codename, not used after 08.1945 - became Falkland Is Dependency Survey

TACITURN (1944) Ports, Hbr Tng SM
SM, Hbr TS for DOLPHIN v TALENT 04.1967 - 12.68 rb TABARD, BU 23.07.71

TADPOLE Sydenham's Yard, Poole, CF Base
Cd 24.05.1944 tender to ATTACK, PO 30.11.1944 - absorbed into TURTLE (qv)
Also premises on the Royal Motor Yt Club, Sandbanks.
Nom DS: FMB 1647 24.05.44-

TAEPING (1937) Dundee, Base
10.05.1942 - 06.05.45
MFV hired as tender 11.39 - 02.46 - was Naval Base General Duties vessel

TAGARIN Freetown, Sierra Leone, BD Depot & Naval Base
Cd 10.10.1949 ex BARBROOK II - PO 31.10.1961 - acs to AFRIKANDER
BD Depot closed 08.08.59 but TAGARIN continued
Nom DS: HL(D) 5233 1957-61

TAIMUR (1945) Karachi, PN RF HQ Ship
DD, ex CHIVALROUS, PN 1954, RF HQ 1959, BU 01.60

TAIN - in a list, prob ref to location of RNAS - see Gazetteer

TALBOT (1824) Woolwich, Powder Hulk
6th Rate, powder hulk 02.1855 at Woolwich till sold 03.1896

TALBOT (1895) Dev, DS
Cr, temp DS 7 DF Home (Dev) 1913 - 1914, sold 1921

TALBOT Malta GC, SM DS
Cd 01.09.1941 - 10 SM - 31.03.1944, name tx to Sardinia (see next entry). SM10 absorbed in to SM1 in MEDWAY II 09.44. SM1 left Malta for a period and TALBOT was just a 'residual name'
Monitor M29, renamed MEDUSA (M/L) 01.12.1925, renamed TALBOT 01.09.41 - renamed MEDWAY II (qv) 02.44, renamed MEDUSA 01.04.45, sold 09.09.46

TALBOT Maddelena, Sardinia, Base
Cd 01.04.1944 - PO 21.09.44 when 10 SM absorbed into 1 SM in MEDWAY II

TALENT (1945) Ports, Hbr Tng SM
SM, Hbr Tng SM at DOLPHIN v TALLY HO 02.67 - 03.67 rb TACITURN, BU 01.70

TALLY HO (1942) Ports, Hbr Tng SM
SM, Hr Tng SM at DOLPHIN v TELEMACHUS 29.01.1960 - 04.65 rb TIRELESS, BU 10.02.67

TALWAR Nicol Rd, Bombay, RIN Signal Sch
Cd 01.04.1941, PO 08.46
RIN Signal Sch & A/S Sch combined - see MACHLIMAR

TALYBONT (1942) Harwich/ Rosyth, Living Ship/ Hbr TS
DD, RF living ship Harwich by 12.1950-11.51, attached CALEDONIA as Hbr TS 1956 - 1960 rb CHEVIOT, BU 17.02.1961

TAMAKI Motuihe Is, Auckland, New Zealand, RNZN TE
Cd 20.01.1941 as 'HMS', Cd 01.10.1941 as 'HMNZS' - extant 1999
1943 - 45 listed as Ex ONEWA (poss ref to Nom DS). Tx to Narrowneck Creek, North Shore 23.09.1963. 1995 to be reduced and grouped with Dev Base
Nom DS: ML 3553 1958-64

TAMAR (1814) Plym, Coal Hulk
6th Rate, coal hulk 1831, sold 1837

TAMAR (1863) HK, Base
Cd 01.10.1897 - 12.12.1941 (scuttled)
Iron Screw Troopship - temp relieved as Base in 28.08.1913 by TRIUMPH (qv) when refitting. After refit berthed alongside. Included RNO Spore 1923

TAMAR HK, Base (NP 2501)
Cd 07.09.1945 (apps from 01.08.45) - PO 10.04.1997
Included Kai Tak Airfield - see NABCATCHER. Acs escorts & M/S British Pacific Fleet in excess of TYNE by 12.45. Wellington Barracks - new Prince of Wales Barracks 1979 - to Stonecutters' Is 18.05.1993.
Nom DS: Small Hbr Lch 07.09.45-
AIRE (FF) 14.03.46 - 20.11.46
MSPB 44315 21.11.46 -56
MSPB 44313 1957-76

TAMAR II HK, Accounting Base
10.1926 - 21.10.39 - acs to MAIDSTONE II (qv)
Also in NL 1940-41 and 1945-47

TAMAR III HK, Accounting Base
1932 - 1934
Acs for Spore till TERROR Cd. Also listed 1945-46

TAMY No 1 – see NABSFORD

TAMY No 2 – Projected but not assembled

TANA Kilindini, Kenya, Base
Cd 01.05.1942 - PO 31.12.46. Base replaced by MVITA 01.07.1950
Acs of all personnel ashore (not FAA) in E Africa. Included RNAS at Mackinnon Rd, Pt Reitz, Voi & Tanga (see KIPANGA II and KILELE). Also SIMBA (qv) was a tender from 01.11.45
Nom DS: NAB MIREMBEMBE 01.05.42-14.03.43
NAB BALEIKA (also spelt BALARA) 14.03.43-15.11.43
MFV 13 16.11.43-03.46

TANA II English Point, Kilindini, Kenya, Transit Camp for Far Eastern Drafting Pool
Cd 01.10.1942 independent command - in PO Circular 02.06.43

TARA Stranraer, Supply Base for North Channel Patrol
02.1915 - 30.09.1915
Armed Boarding Steamer ex HIBERNIA(1900) - hired 08.1914 - sunk in Med 05.11.1915

TARANGAU Dredger Harbour, New Guinea, RAN Base
07.02.1946 - 01.01.1950 replaced by SEEADLER (qv)

TARANGAU Manus, Admiralty Is, RAN Base
01.04.1950 ex SEEADLER - PO 14.11.74 - to Papua New Guinea Defence Force
Also reported as located Lombrom, Los Negros, Papua New Guinea

TARANGAU II Pt Moresby, Papua New Guinea
16.11.1972 - 14.11.1974

TARANSAY (1930) Larne/ Dover, M/S DS
Yt, hired as danlayer 10.1939, Examination Service. To Larne ex Gt Yarmouth 11.40. She, or her boat, was Nom DS RACER II (qv) 01.08.1941 - 27.07.42. To ANCXF 04.44. M/S DS at Dover 01.45 - 07.46. PO and Laid up 23.11.46

TARANTULA (1915) Colombo, Ceylon, DS/ Accom Sh
Gunboat, Escort Base Ship 1941 - PO 01.07.44. Flag British Pacific Fleet 22.12.44 -04.12.44 . One ref states she was earmarked as target 1944. Used as Barracks 02.45-02.46 - for salvage teams working on AFD 23 that sank in raid 04.42. Still DS Colombo 04.45 - 05.45. Dismantled 1946 and hull sunk as target off Ceylon 01.05.46.

TARBAT NESS (1945) Repair Ship
Cancelled

TARLAIR (1908) Hawkscraig, Aberdour, Fife, Hydrophone Tng & Experimental Base
Cd 01.07.1917 - personnel previously under GUNNER - 06.08.1919 acs to CRESCENT - 15.10.19
Drifter, hired 01.1915 - 1919

TARTAR (1814) Chat, Rx Sh
5th Rate, Rx Sh 03.1830 – BU 09.1859

TARTAR (1854) Sheerness, Rx Sh
1865 - ex Russian corvette WOJN

TARTAR (1937) Dev, SO RF
DD, SO RF v UNICORN and RF acs v DRAKE IV 23.12.1946 - 11.09.47 rb NEWFOUNDLAND, sold 1948

TASAJERA (1938) Normandy, DS
Oiler conv to LST 05.1941 - 07.46. Rhino DS Normandy 08.06.1944, grounded in gale 19.06.44.

TASMAN Lyttleton, New Zealand, RNZN A/S TE
Cd 20.01.1944 – to C & M 1953, closed by 09.57
Nom DS: WAIRANGI 20.01.44 -
SDML 3563 1958

TAURUS Chichester, Accom Sh
Yt, accom sh 08.1942 - renamed ZOBAL 04.43 but still listed as TAURUS 07.44

TAWE Swansea, A/P Base
Cd 03.07.1940 – 10.1941 (at least) (not listed 05.42)
Nom DS: An Open Boat 03.07.1940-

TEAL (1955) Hobart, Tasmania, RAN Museum Ship
M/S ex JACKTON, Museum Ship 1977-79 - sold 1979

TEAZER (1943) Dev, Accom Sh
DD, accom sh 02.1948, conv to FF 1952, BU 08.65

TECUMSEH Calgary, Alberta, RCN Base & Res Div
01.09.1939 - Cd 01.11.1941 - listed to 1976 - extant 1987
In No 2 Police Sta, then (01.1940) leased office and garage 7th Ave/3rd St SW - 01.45 new building complete 17 Ave/ 24 St SW

TEES (1817) Lpool, Church Ship
6th Rate, lent 10.1826 as Church Ship - sold 28.06.1872

TELEMACHUS (1943) Ports, Hbr Tng SM
SM, Hbr Tng SM Ports attached DOLPHIN v SENESCHAL 01.1960 - 02.1960 rb TALLY HO, BU 08.1961

TEMERAIRE (1798) Plym/ Sheerness, Rx Sh/ Victualling DS
2nd Rate, Rx Sh Plym 1813, to Sheerness Rx Sh 1820, Victualling DS 1831 - BU 1838

TEMERAIRE (1876) Dev, Fleet Res DS
BB, Fleet Res DS allocated 1903, renamed INDUS II (qv) 1910

TEMERAIRE Pt Edgar, Upper Yardsmen TE
Cd 01.05.1955 ex HAWKE at Dartmouth (qv) - 19.08.1960 - name to a Div a Dartmouth
Nom DS: MSPB 4160 1955 - 60

TEMERAIRE Ports, Sch of Physical Tng
Opened at Ports 22.09.1910, Cd at TEMERAIRE 11.06.1971 - extant 1999
Was at Flathouse Rd, in 1988 to Burnaby Rd

TENEDOS (1812) Bermuda, Rx Sh
5th Rate, convict hulk 04.1843, then Rx Sh 1865 – BU 20.03.1875

TENEDOS (1870) Dev, DS for TBDs
04.1904 - 1905 - tx to Chat as TE (see next entry)
Ex TRIUMPH - had been DS in own name (qv) till 04.1904.

TENEDOS (1870) Chat, TS for Boy Artificers
Cd 01.01.1906 - 1910
Vessels of TENEDOS tx to INDUS (qv) by 10.1910 as basin at Chat required for other ships.
Ex TRIUMPH - DS in own name & as TENEDOS (see previous entry), then to Chat as TS - became INDUS IV at Dev, ALGIERS (qv) 01.1915 and sold 07.01.1921

TENEDOS II (1859) Chat , TE
Cd 01.01.1906 – 10.1910
Ex DUNCAN (qv) - renamed PEMBROKE (qv) 1890, renamed TENEDOS II 09.1905. Sold 11.10.1910

TENEDOS III (1821) Chat, TE
21.06.1906 - 1910
Ex GANGES (qv), renamed TENEDOS III 21.06.1906, renamed INDUS V (qv) 13.08.1910, renamed IMPREGNABLE III (qv) 12.10.22, sold 31.08.29

TENGRA Mandapam, India, CO Base
Cd 15.09.1944 independent command, acs BRAGANZA, 31.01.1946
Originally listed as name for Vizagapatam Base 08.1944, but Cd at Mandapam – see AMZARI.
Nom DS: Lch BURONG No XXXV 15.09.44 - (still listed 1951)

TENGRA II Mandapam, M/S Base
Cd 01.02.1946 independent command, acs HIGHFLYER, - PO 30.06.46 (lapsed 15.07.46)

TENNYSON Imperial Hotel, Exmouth, Landing Barge Base
Cd 0900, 10.01.1944 ex SALCOMBE, PO 24.07.1945 - personnel to DRAGONFLY
Nom DS: SHEILA II 10.01.44-
NAB DAVRIL - 03.45
NAB NISUS 03.45 – 24.07.45

TERMINIST (1912) Brightlingsea, Accom Sh
Yt, hired as accom sh 04.1941 - to C & M/ DST 23.07.45, sold 02.46

TERN Twatt, Orkney, RNAS
Ann to be developed v Skeabrae 06.1940 - in use 01.04.1941 as satellite to SPARROWHAWK (qv). Cd as TERN 01.01.1942 independent command, acs SPARROWHAWK - PO 20.10.45 (some acs report 30.09.46 - in NL 01.46 with apps, in 04.46 no apps). To C & M under FULMAR (qv) 04.48 - 01.57 - listed to 12.59 (but reported as no longer RN by 01.04.55)
Nom DS: HFV HOPEFUL (1929) 31.03.42 – 09.43

TERN II Skeabrae, Dounreay & Hatston, Orkney, RNAS
Dounreay - was to have been SISKIN (qv), built for Air Ministry 04.1940 - to RAF. RN to have Twatt in lieu 06.40. Tx to Adty 15.05.44 as TERN

II, in C & M by 07.46 when lent War Department for accom to 01.03.1947 - then lent on at 6 monthly intervals. To Air Ministry 01.10.54 but listed to 12.59
Skeabrae - satellite of SPARROWHAWK 1940 - post war TERN II - when in C & M under FULMAR (by 03.48). Reported as no longer RN 01.04.1955
Hatston - ex SPARROWHAWK (qv) became TERN II as satellite 01.08.1945 - 15.09.1945 (to C & M) - acs to OWL

TERPSICHORE (1785) Chat, Rx Sh
5th Rate, Rx Sh 1818 – BU 1830

TERRIBLE (1785) Sheerness, Victualling DS
3rd Rate, Rx Sh 1823, Victualling DS 1831 - BU 1836

TERRIBLE (1895) Ports, Accom Sh
Cr, accom sh 1915 - 1920 – allocated VERNON II 03.1916, accom sh for VICTORY 28.01.18, allocated FISGARD workshop 04.1919. PO to C & M 01.09.1919. To FISGARD 25.11.1919 - renamed FISGARD III 08.1920, sold 07.32

TERROR Bermuda, Base/ Rx Sh
1857 - 1914
TERROR, floating battery (1856) - Base Ship 1857-1901, sold 1902
MALABAR (1866) Troopship, Rx Sh 1897 (qv), renamed TERROR as Base Ship 01.05.1901 - for sale 1914, sold 01.1918

TERROR (1916) Ports/ Dev/ Spore, TS/ Base
Monitor, Gunnery Sch Ports v MARSHAL SOULT Cd 01.02.1919 - PO 15.07.21. Was to replace GLORIOUS at Dev, but cancelled, remained Ports. Gunnery trials 1922. Turret Drl Sh Ports v TIGER Cd 02.09.1924 - 33. To Dev 05.33. Cd 12.09.33 for passage and as Base Spore - 31.12.39. Sailed from Spore 29.01.40, sunk in Med 24.02.41

TERROR II Spore, Accounting Base
Cd 01.09.1934 – 31.12.39 - Cdre ic Spore renamed SULTAN 01.01.40 and seagoing tenders became SULTAN II
Nom DS: Steam Lch 290 01.09.34 - 31.12.39

TERROR III Penang, Base
10.1939 - name approved by C-in-C China – 31.12.39 - became SULTAN III

TERROR Spore, Base
Cd 15.05.1946 ex SULTAN II - RN Barracks tx to Australian Army 09.10.1971, not listed 06.1972
Fleet Accom Centre & Acs for tenders and Pt Parties 06.46, Fleet shore accom and Dockyard 09.1946. RN Barracks 02.49. Was extant 1972 but by 1976 replacement by RAN/RNZN Base (Woodlands Garrison/ Terror Barracks) was closing.
1991 RNLO Spore was NP 1022
Nom DS: HL(D) 3706 15.05.46 - 31.07.47
MSPB 2631 01.08.47 - 1952
MSPB 43924 11.1954 - 1962 (FO Malaya's Barge)

TEST (1942) Spore, Accom Sh
FF, lent RIN 05.1946 - 04.47, RF Spore 28.10.47-, accom sh for Malayan Naval Force 01.49-, RF living ship Spore to 20.04.51, BU 02.55

THAIS Ports, Accom Sh
08.1942, but found unfit 09.1942

THALIA (1830) Ports, RC Chapel
5th Rate, Chapel Ship 12.1855 – BU 11.1867

THALIA (1869) Cromarty Firth/ Peterhead, A/P Parent
Ex Troopship, storage hulk Cromarty 1891, Base ship Cormarty & Peterhead v STEPHEN FURNESS Cd 09.03.1916 - PO & Cromarty closed 31.05.1919 – retard party to MARS. Sold 16.09.1920
rb NAIRN at Peterhead by 03.1918, at Inverness by LAVATERA 01.06.1917.

THAMES (1823) Bermuda, Convict Ship
5th Rate, convict ship 1841 – sunk 1863

THAMES (1885) DS/ TS
Cr, SM DS Ports Cd 20.07.1903 - 1907, 5 SM Sheerness 1907-17 (Home Fleet 1909, Harwich 1914, 4 SM 06.1916 - , under MAIDSTONE 01.10.1917). 9 SM to 02.18. 6 SM SM Sch Ports 02.18, Periscope Sch Portland & to Campbeltown Cd 08.10.1918-09.19 rb VULCAN. PO Chat 23.12.19, sold 13.11.1920
Renamed GENERAL BOTHA (qv) as TS Simonstown, became known locally as THAMES in 1944 to avoid confusion with S African TE GENERAL BOTHA - became Nom DS of AFRIKANDER 09.44 and sunk in False Bay 13.05.1947

THAMES QUEEN (1898) Soton, Accom Sh
Hired 14.09.1939 as AA ship, conv to AA 02.42-05.42, Soton 1942(?) - 1947 (at Harwich 1942 – 43, Antwerp 1944), resto 02.47

THESEUS (1892) Aegean/ Black Sea, DS
Cr, DS for Tlrs Aegean 1918 and v MANTIS in Caspian Sea 31.12.1918/ Black Sea 1918-19. Sold 01.1921

THESEUS II Baku, DS Caspian Sea Force/ RNO Baku
Opened 01.1919 v MANTIS II, closed 02.09.1919
For all personnel Caspian Sea and Baku Base

THESEUS III Caspian Sea/ Baku, CF DS - for Coastal MBs
Cd 01.03.1919-
Coastal MB carrier personnel borne in THESEUS II

THETIS (1890) Lough Larne, A/P DS
Cr, DS Cd 18.12.1915(temp) & 01.01.1916 v HERMIONE - 05.01.18 rb VIGOROUS. PO 22.01.1918. Sunk as blockship Zeebrugge

23.01.1918

THISBE (1824) Dev/ Cardiff, DS/ Church Ship
5th Rate, DS Dev 1845 - 63, lent as Church ship 13.08.1863 – sold 11.08.1892

THISTLE Kyle of Lochalsh, Torp range
Name reported as sel in 1980s, but not used

THOMA II London, Accom Sh
Barge req and chartered to Pt of London Authority as accom sh during salvage operations 08.1942-

THORN (1779) Deptford, TS
Sloop, lent 1799 - 1814 as TS to Marine Society (see WARSPITE). Sold 28.08.1816

THORNBOROUGH (1943) Hartlepool, Living Ship
FF, RF Living ship by 23.09.1946 - 30.01.47 when handed over to purchasers

THUNDERBOLT (1856) Chat, Nom DS
Floating battery, temp pier at Chat 1873. Cd 25.12.1915 as DAEDALUS - Nom DS for RNAS 1915-19. BU 1949

THUNDERER (1872) Sheerness/ Pembroke Dock, Guard Ship
Turret ship, Pt Guard ship Sheerness 1892 – 18.04.1895, Pembroke Dock 09.05.1895 – 12.12. 1900, sold 13.09.1909

THUNDERER (1911) Dev, RF Parent & TS
BB, RF Parent v GLORIOUS & TS for Cadets 1921 - PO 31.08.1926 rb EREBUS. Sold 12.1926

THUNDERER Keyham & Manadon, Plym, RN Engineering College
Cd 01.12.1946 – PO 15.09.1995
First founded at Keyham 01.07.1880, was closed 31.07.1910 - 31.03.1914. First land at Manadon purch 1936, opened at Manadon 07.05.1940, Keyham closed 09.05.1958
Nom DS: Steam Picket Boat No 691 01.12.46 -
FMB 44467 1947 – 62 (but allocated SCC 07.60)

THYSVILLE (1922) Normandy, DS
Merchant ship assigned DS duties Normandy - Gold 06.1944 - see PICADOR - NP 1659

TIERCEL (1913) Ft William, Accom Sh
Yt, req 1941, accom sh RN Patrol Service Ft William 10.41, to C & M 24.01.42, re-allocated to BEE as torp target & recovery vessel 10.44, to DST at Cowes 27.08.45, for disposal 05.46

TIGER'S WHELP The Brunds, Alsager, New Entry Seaman Pt 1 TE
Cd 16.11.1942 - but renamed EXCALIBUR (qv) 22.12.42 restrospectively
Nom DS: 52.5ft HL(D) 3944 16.11.44 - 22.12.44

TILLICUM North Bay, Ontario, RCN SCC Summer Camp
1986

TIMBERTOWN Groningen, Holland, PoW Camp
1914-18 - Unofficial name for camp used by RN Div internees

TIRELESS (1943) Ports, Hbr Tng SM
SM, Hbr Tng SM for DOLPHIN 08.64 v TALLY HO – 06.65 rb TALENT, BU 09.68

TISSA Trinco, R Ceylon N/ Sri Lankan Base
1956 - listed to 1979

TITAN (1935) Ipswich, Accom Sh
Yt, hired as temp officers' accom 09.1939, PO 20.01.1943 & allocated Ipswich, rb EMPEROR OF INDIA 06.43, resto 1945

TITANIA (1915) SM DS
Purch 1915, DS 11 SM Cd 16.11.1915, Blyth - 01.19. 5 SM Blyth 01.03.19 - 06.19. At Ports (SM Sch) PO 30.09.19. 4 SM China v BONAVENTURE Cd 01.10.19 - 10.29 (Med temp 1920). 6 SM Portland 1930-34, Atlantic Fleet Gib with 5SM & 6 SM 1935 (6 SM to ALECTO), 3 SM Gib temp 10.09.35 - 36, 6 SM Portland 1936 - 39, Blyth 06.39 - 12.39 rb ELFIN, PO 22.12.39. C & M 23.12.39. To Portland as DS after refit Cd 06.07.40 - Londonderry Base 09.40, 3SM Rosyth 08.10.40 rb MAIDSTONE & to be 8 SM 01.41. 3 SM to FORTH, then mobile DS 7 SM acs CYCLOPS 12.41. DS for tng Loch Erisort (Hebrides) 05.42, detached 7 SM, independent command 06.42, Oban 03.43. From 12 SM to 3 SM 03.44, Ports 1945, PO 14.09.45 At DOLPHIN as hulk 1946-47, BU 1948

TITUMIR Khulna, Bangladeshi Naval Base
1984 - extant 1999

TONGUE SAND FORT Thames Estuary Defence Unit No 3
Cd 17.06.1942 acs BADGER, 01.08.42 acs WILD-FIRE, 06.45 to C & M, 01.48 evacuated
Sank E boat S 199 23.01.45 - only enemy warship sunk by fort guns during WW II

TOPAZE Ports, Rx Sh
5th Rate, capt 1814, Rx Sh 1823, BU 1851

TOPAZE (1858) Kingstown, CG
FF, CG 17.07.1877 – 02.07.1878, sold 1884

TORCH Holyhead, M/S & CF Base
Name sel for comml pt Holyhead 01.09.1939, NOIC ordered 27.08.39
Cd 11.09.1939. At 2359 17.10.43 became BEE (qv) - but in NL 1945 with no apps as parent Holyhead
Nom DS: BOY ROY 11.09.39 - 08.41
Hbr Lch 3980 08.41 –

TORCH II Holyhead, CF Base
Named 30.04.41, Cd 01.07.1941 - 30.06.43 amalgamated with TORCH
Nom DS: NAB WORCESTER CASTLE 01.07.41 - 01.42
NAB JANO 01.42 - 30.06.43

TOREADOR Clyde/ Tyne/ London/ Normandy Areas, RN Ferry Personnel - NP 1660
Cd 06.06.1944, PO 18.09.44
RN Ferry Personnel in Merchant Ship CAP TOURANE (qv), Clyde area to 17.05.44, Tyne area to 21.05.44, London area to 31.05.44, to Gravesend 01.06.44, to France 07.06.44 - Sword - arrive 08.06.44, to Gold 29.06.44, to Soton 10.07.44, to beaches 20.07.44 - end 08.44

TORMENTOR Hamble, Soton, CO Base
Cd 12.08.1940, PO 31.03.46 - small retard party remained
Established in Ex Household Brigade Yt Club as base for small craft ex MELISANDE (qv). Raiding Flot under ADOD(CO) 29.09.40, RC Tng Centre & CO tng for Southern Command 04.42, LC Base & Maint Base 08.45.
Nom DS; MV JAMIE 12.08.40 - 11.42 (became JUDITH)
NAB ALANNA II 11.42 –

TORMENTOR II Cowes, Isle of Wight, Tng Camp
05.1942 – 08.06.42 - amalgamated with OSBORNE (qv) to form VECTIS (qv)

TOROA Dunedin, New Zealand Res Div
1948 – extant 1999
Nom DS: SDML 3564 1957-64

TORRENS Adelaide, S Australia, RAN Depot
01.08.1940 ex CERBERUS IV – 01.03.1965, became ENCOUNTER (qv) to release name for new ship
Nom DS: MB 310 1943-

TORTOISE Milford/ Chat/ Ascension Is, Storeship
Ex SIR EDWARD HUGHES, 5th Rate, presented 1806, renamed TORTOISE 28.11.1807 as store-ship. Coal hulk Milford 1824, stores hulk Chat 1840, Ascension Is 1849 till BU there 10.1859

TORTOISE Durban, S Africa
10.1942 – 12.44
In a list/also in PO circulars 13.01.43/02.06.43

TOURMALINE (1875) Chat, Coal Hulk
Corvette, coal hulk 1899, renamed C115 12.1904, sold 11.1920

TOWER (1809) Deptford, Police Ship
Tender, lent Thames Police 1817 – sold 1825

TOWER London, A/P Base
Cd 10.01.1941 (acs ex PEMBROKE IV), PO 31.07.1945
Nom DS: Barge Yt HILDA (1885) 01.01.41 - 08.45

TRACKER (1945) Dev/ Ports, Accom Sh/Store
LST 3522, named 1947, Monte Bello 1952, Flood Relief 1953, RF 1953, accom sh Dev (EAGLE refit) 1954, accom sh Ports (VICTORIOUS refit) 01.1957 - 58, accom sh Ports 1960, lay apart store Ports 1961 - 62, lay apart store Dev 1964 - 70, sold 12.70

TRAFALGAR (1859) Leith/ Lough Swilly, CG
1st Rate, CG – Leith 01.03.1864 - 16.06.1867, Lough Swilly 13.11.1867 – 69. Seagoing TS for Cadets 1870, renamed BOSCAWEN (qv) 1873, sold 10.07.1906

TRAFALGAR (1887) Ports/ Chat, Pt Guard/ Parent Ship
BB, Pt Guard 10.1897 – 08.1902, parent special service vessels Chat 1909 - 1911, sold 1911

TRAFALGAR (1944) Ports, RF Living Ship
DD, RF living ship 11.1951, Flag of RF Group Cd 10.1951 - Spring 1952 - summer 1953. BU 06.70

TRAINING II – see PRINCESS MARIA JOSE

TRAINING III - see BATAVIA IV

TRATA Bombay, IN Estab - Coastal Batteries
12.12.1964 – listed to 1976

TREEKRONER Ports, Rx Sh
Danish 3rd Rate, capt 1807, Rx Sh 1809 – sold 1825

TRELAWNEY Lochalsh, Base
Cd 11.06.1940 – 16.07.45
Secret base for M/L operations, originally known as Port B (01.1940) and by 07.40 as Port ZA.
Nom DS: 35ft Motor Cr (MB 4015) 11.06.40 - 11.43
NAB NORESSIAN 11.43 – 16.07.45

TREMADOC BAY (1945) Dev, Accom Sh
FF, accom sh 05.1948 - 03.50, BU 09.59

TRENT (1796) Cork, Flag/ Rx Sh
5th Rate, Flag 1814, Rx Sh 1818 – BU 1823

TRENTONIAN (1943) Normandy
Appears in a list - HMCS TRENTONIAN was a corvette that operated off Normandy and was lost 22.02.1945

TREVOSE HEAD (1945) CF Maint Ship – see MULL OF OA

TRIAD (1909) Persian Gulf, SNO Ship
Yt, hired 01.1915, purch 06.1915, used as HQ Ship, served in Dardanelles WWI. SNO Persian Gulf 1920 – sold 05.1933

TRIAL S America, Coal Hulk
1843 – sold 1848

TRIDENT (1768) Malta GC, Rx Sh
3rd Rate, reported sold 1816, but listed 1820 as Rx Sh

TRINCOMALEE (1817) W Hartlepool/ Soton, Res Drl Sh
5th Rate, Res Drl Sh W Hartlepool 01.1861, Sunderland 01.04.1862 – 63, at W Hartlepool from at least 01.04.1868. Drl Sh Soton Water 01.01.1873 – sold 19.05.1897 - became TS FOUDROYANT (qv)

TRINITY Halifax, Nova Scotia, RCN Consolidated (Undersea) Sound Surveillance System Facility
Open 08.1994 - Cd 05.05.1995 –

TRIPHIBIAN Squires Gate Camp, Lytham St Annes, Lancs, TE
Cd 01.11.1943 independent command, own acs, PO 22.02.1944 - to Military
War Office Camp on loan for new entry procedures
Nom DS: Patrol Vessel BEDOUIN 01.11.43 - 22.02.44 (later NDS RINGTAIL)

TRIPHIBIAN II Uniacke Barracks, Harrogate, TE
Cd 08.11.1943 independent command, acs TRIPHIBIAN, 02.44 acs CABOT, PO 29.02.44 – to Army 01.03.44
Camp lent by War Office for Pt I Tng
Nom DS: MFV ROYAL CHARTER 08.11.43 - 29.02.44

TRITON (1882) Gravesend, TS
Survey vessel, hbr serv 1914, lent Gravesend Sea Sch 24.09.1919 till BU 10.1961

TRIUMPH (1764) Milford, Qtn Sh
3rd Rate, Qtn Sh 10.1813, Bu 06.1850

TRIUMPH (1870) Queenstown/ Falmouth/ Plym, Flag/ DS
Armoured ship, Flag Queenstown 04.02.1890 – 28.09.1893, conv to Base Ship 1900 – Falmouth 05.1900 (though some acs state Plym). TBD DS Plym 1903, renamed TENEDOS (qv) 04.1904, INDUS V (qv) 1912 & ALGIERS (qv) 01.1915, sold 01.1921

TRIUMPH (1903) HK, Base Ship
BB, relieved TAMAR at HK whilst TAMAR refitted 28.08.1913 – 01.15. Lost 25.05.1915 at Dardanelles

TRIUMPH (1944) Spore, Escort DS
Light Fleet Carrier, was Cadets' TS 09.1953 - 12.55. Conv to DS 12.64. Cd 07.01.65 - to Spore, arrived 26.02.65 v HARTLAND POINT – 1971. Arrived UK 01.72, to Chat 16.03.72, then in Res Chat till BU 12.1981

TROUBADOUR (1924) Lamlash, CO Craft C & M Base & Accom Sh
By 15.01.1946 when NOIC lapse, tender to FULLARTON, 18.04.46 tender to DUNDONALD – base closed & PO 12.09.46,
Ex WARRIOR, Yt, A/S Yt for service abroad 07.1940. req 1942. Mobile accom sh LCT personnel from 1942 - reduced complement for day passage only 03.42. Cd 11.05.1942, to Troon. Base ship Lamlash (dates above). To Greenock 15.09.46. Sold 1947

TROUBRIDGE (1942) Chat, Accom Sh
DD, accom sh 05.1948 – 11.51, conv to FF 1957, BU 02.1970

TUDOR (1942) Ports, Hbr Tng SM
SM, allocated as Hbr Tng SM for DOLPHIN 19.07.1958, replaced by SENESCHAL 10.59 and by TELEMACHUS 01.60, BU 07.63

TULA Black Sea, DS
1919 under THESEUS II

TULLICHEWAN Tullichewan Castle Camp, Ballock, Holding Base for CO Personnel
Cd 10.03.1945, PO 10.06.46 - retard party in MONCK
Camp used by WRNS 1942 - 44 for Tng – see SPARTIATE II.
Nom DS: Coble GEORGE AND MARGARET 10.03.45 –

TUNSBERG Lpool, Norwegian Naval Depot
Cd 18.12.1941 –

TURNSTONE Watford/ Fulham, TE
Cd 01.01.1944, independent command, acs DAEDALUS, PO 18.08.1945
Watford for Air Fitters' preliminary tng, Fulham Comb Independent Command closed down 23.06.44
Nom DS: MB SILVER FOAM 01.01.44 – 06.44
NAB LOTUS II 06.44 – 18.08.45

TURTLE Poole, CO TE/ Assault Gunnery Sch & LC Base
Cd 07.10.1942 independent command, PO 01.03.46, small retard party remained
Used Shaftesbury Homes Poole, Lake Camp Hamworthy, Round Is, LCT Hard Hamworthy. Closed 08.05.44, but absorbed TADPOLE (qv) 11.44. Minor LC Maint & Base Sandbanks to close 01.05.45. RM Amphibious Sch ex Eastney on site 01.12.1954
Nom DS: TURTLE 07.10.1942 - 12.42
Hbr Patrol, vessel CENTAURUS 12.42 - 03.43
NAB JULIETTA 03.43 - (laid up 10.45)
LCF 26 10.45 -

TUSCAN (1942) Ports, Accom Sh
DD, accom sh 02.1948 – 12.50 (at least), conv to FF 1953, BU 05.66

TYNE (1856) Dev, Storeship
6th Rate, storeship 1848, sold 1862

TYNE (1845) Sunderland, Drl Sh
ACTIVE, 5th Rate (qv), Drl Sh Sunderland, renamed TYNE 30.07.1867, renamed DURHAM (qv) 18.11.1867, sold 12.05.1908

TYNE (1878) Storeship/ DS
Storeship Med 1895, at Malta as storeship and DS for TBD Cd 01.03.1904. Assist SAPPHIRE (TBD DS) Portland 1907. DS 5 DF 1910, 8 DF Chat 1912 - 14, Cromarty 8 DF 01.16 - 17, 8 DF Leith 11.17 - 1919. A/P DS Stord (Lervick) Cd 23.04.1919 – at Stord 05.1919 (Mine clearance), PO at Nore 28.11.1919 – acs to PEMBROKE VI. Foundered 15.11.20

TYNE (1940) DD DS
Cd 17.02.1941, Home Fleet Scapa Flow v MAIDSTONE 12.41 – 44. Solent 06.1944 - 07.44, Scapa Flow 26.07.44 -, British Pacific Fleet 11.44 - 45 (Trinco, Fremantle, Manus, Leyte, Sydney). Res Harwich 10.12.1946 – 48 (SO RF v DUNCANSBY HEAD 21.01.47), refit Dev 28.02.49 – 26.10.50, RF living ship & DD DS & SO RF Malta GC V FORTH 10.50 - 02.53 rb RANPURA, Korea v LADYBIRD 11.04.1953 - 12.53, then HK, Spore. Home Fleet 10.54 - 08.56 rb MAIDSTONE, - 27.03.61 (Med 56 - 57 for Suez, 2 SM 1958-60), Ports accom sh 1961, SO RF Dev v WOOLWICH 15.08.61 – 64, accom sh Dev 1965 - 72 (RF to CO TYNE when ORION closed 31.12.66) (2 SM Dev 28.03.69 - 72), BU 25.07.72

TYNWALD Douglas, Isle of Man, Camp
08.1943 - Central Camp to be Cd as TYNWALD but was named VALKERIE II (qv)

TYRIAN (1826) Motherbank/Ports, Qtn/ Rx Sh
Brig sloop, qtn sh Motherbank, Spithead 1847 – Rx Sh Ports 1865 – sold 11.08.1892 (short break in 1870 as CG)

TYRIAN (1942) Harwich, Accom Sh
DD, accom sh 02.1948-, conv to FF 1953, BU 03.1965

U

UBIQUITY 114, Trinity Rd, Edinburgh, Cable Ship Depot for Tng & Drafting
Cd 05.12.1941, PO 29.06.46 - tx to Plym - see next entry
Nom DS: MB of CLAVERHOUSE 05.12.1941 –

UBIQUITY Turnchapel, Plym, Cable Ship Depot
Cd 29.06.1946 from Edinburgh - see previous entry, - closed 22.09.1947 - re-opened next day as civil estab HM Cable Ship Depot
Nom DS: 20ft MB 42192 1946-

UIDDEN – appears in a list 1941-43

UKUSSA Katukurunda, Ceylon, RNAS
Cd 15.10.1942, independent command, acs LANKA, PO 27.09.1946
RN Aircraft Repair Yd & Storage Unit, included RN Aircraft Repair Depot (Rowlands Garage), Colombo; RN Shipping Salvage Unit, Colombo; and, from 01.02.43, RNAS Puttalam (see RAJALIYA)
Nom DS: Lch 1498 (Colombo Hbr) 15.10.42-

ULKA Cox's Bazaar, Chittagong, Bangladeshi Naval Dkyd
1996 - extant 1999

ULSTER (1942) Ports/ Dev, Hbr TS
DD conv to FF, attached EXCELLENT as non seagoing tender 1973 v RAME HEAD - 1977 rb RAME HEAD; and then to RALEIGH as Hbr TS 1977 - 1980 rb SALISBURY, sold 04.08.1980

ULYSSES (1943) Dev, Accom Sh
DD, RF living ship 1948 - 50, conv to FF, BU 11.69

UNDAUNTED (1943) Dev, Accom Sh
DD, accom sh 02.1948 - 12.50 (at least), conv to FF 1954, sunk as target 11.1978

UNDINE Sheerness, Base Ship
Ex WILDFIRE, ex HIAWATHA, Yt, purch 1888, Base ship as WILDFIRE (qv) 1889, renamed UNDINE 01.1907, Flag C-in-C Nore, sold 09.07.1912

UNDINE (1943) Sheerness, Living Ship
DD, living ship 12.1950, conv to FF 1952-54, BU 11.1965

UNICORN (1824) Woolwich/ Dundee, Powder Hulk/ Res Drl Sh
5th Rate, powder hulk Woolwich 1855 - 62 (lent War Department), Res Sheerness, Res Drl Sh Dundee 05.11.1873, Cd 01.06.1874, crew ex BRILLIANT (qv), lent RNVR 1906, HQ SNO Dundee 23.11.1916 - used in WWI & reverted to RNVR 10.1919. Renamed UNICORN II (qv) (name required for new carrier) 02.1939. Renamed CRESSY 01.01.1942 - 14.07.1959. Re - Cd as UNICORN 14.07.1959 - 1968 (shifted berth 1962 as new bridge built - first move in 89 years). Shore HQ named CAMPERDOWN 08.1969. Ship to preservation 29.09.1968

UNICORN (1941) Dev, Aircraft Supply & Repair Ship/ SO RF
Completed 03.1943. Far East 1945 - 01.46 then to Res. SO RF Dev v DRAKE IV (and at 4 weeks notice as part of IMPERIEUSE Group from 09.46) 01.07.46 - 22.12.46 rb TARTAR and then again SO RF 10.03.48 v NEWFOUNDLAND - 17.05.49 (rb HOWE). Korea 1952, to Res 1954 BU 06.1959

UNICORN Saskatoon, Saskatchewan, RCN Base & Res Div
Cd 01.11.1941 – 01.09.42 - tender to NADEN & 01.09.1942 - 1987 (at least)

UNICORN II (1824) Dundee, Res Drl Sh/Base
5th Rate, UNICORN (qv), renamed 02.1939 - Res Drl Sh Dundee. Cd 07.09.1939 as Base at comml pt Dundee – NOIC ordered 27.08.39. Res Div closed by 04.40. Renamed CRESSY (qv) 01.01.42

UNITE Chat/Woolwich, DS/Convict Ship
5th Rate, Fr IMPERIEUSE, capt 1793, renamed UNITE 1803, DS Chat 1832, convict ship Woolwich by 1840 – BU 01.1858

UNITIE Duncan Docks, Capetown, S African Base & Res TE
01.1944 – SAN 01.11.1954 – listed to 1961

UNITY Simonstown, S Africa, TE

RN Court Martial Instructional Base – poss associated with previous entry

UPOLA (1891) RAN SM DS
Hired 08.1914, PO 20.11.1914 at Sydney
For RAN SM AE1 and AE2 in Australian waters

URANIA (1944) Dev, Accom Sh
DD, RF living ship 1949, conv to FF, BU 02.1971

URGENT (1855) Jamaica, DS
Ex ASSAYE, Troopship, DS 1876, Cd 21.07.1877 – till sold 06.1903 (naval estab moved ashore)

URLEY Ronaldsway, Isle of Man, RNAS
Ex Civil Airport, Cd 21.06.1944, acs VALKYRIE. Flying started 15.07.44. PO 14.01.46 to C & M under BLACKCAP
Nom DS: 32ft cutter XXII (1937) 21.06.44 –

UTKROSH Uchipuli, Pt Blair, IN Air Sta
1989 – extant 1994

UVA Diyatalawa, Ceylon, RN Rest Camp
Cd 01.12.1945, independent command, acs LANKA – 1957. To Air Ministry 30.09.58
Reported as built as PoW Camp for Boer War 1900 and used as RN Aux Hosp WW II
Nom DS; SPL 431224 01.12.45 - 08.50
HL(P) 441614 08.50 - (in MB List 01.51)
HL(P) 431224 1950 – 54
HL(D) 441614 1955 – 03.57
ML 4749 03.57-

V

VAIRI Sullur (Sular/ Sollur), Nr Coinbatore, India, RNAS
Tx from RAF 06.1944, Cd 01.02.1945, acs GARUDA, PO 01.04.1946
RN Aircraft Storage Depot for 500 aircraft.
Nom DS: MB EUREKA J993 01.02.45 –

VAISURA – see VALSURA

VALHALLA Shoreham, Accom Sh
House Boat – for Air Sea rescue boats' crews 12.1940 – req 09.01.41 – acquired 07.11.1942 - sold /DST 02.45

VALHALLA/ VALHALLA II (1892) Mudros, Parent Ship
Cd 17.07.1916 at Ports and Cd 01.09.1916 independent command. 17.02.1917 renamed VALHALA II tender to OSIRIS II. 04.1918 v OSIRIS II, 01.08.1918 at Mudros, tender to EUROPA, Densheros Cove 12.1918 - 03.19. To Cowes 30.08.1919
Yt fitted out as repair ship and mobile workshop for MLs at Ports 07.1916

VALIANT/ VALIANT (OLD)/ VALIANT III (1863) Limerick & R Shannon/ Bantry/ Plym, CG/ DS/ Oil Hulk
VALIANT, CG Limerick, Foynes , R Shannon, Tabert, Bantry Bay 09.1868 - 05.08.1885. DS Plym 1895, was INDUS (qv) 1898, TBD DS Dev 1900 and renamed INDUS IV (qv) 1904 - still TBD DS Plym. Lay apart store for 7 DF and renamed VALIANT (OLD) 1916. Tx to Kite Balloon Vessel and renamed VALIANT III 03.01.1918 - still lay apart store 7 DF. In 1918 was accom sh for RAS Merifield (Wilcove, Plym). Lay apart store 1922, oil hulk Dev 1923, BU 12.1956

VALIANT (1914) Plym, TS
BB, part of IMPERIEUSE (qv) at Dev Cd as accom sh 21.06.1946 – 08.47 (to Res), BU 11.48

VALIANT II (1893) Larne, A/P DS
Yt hired 11.1914. A/P DS Cd 12.03.1915, sail from Lpool 22.04.1915, A/P Belfast and Larne v COLLEEN. 01.06.1915 rb HERMIONE, resto 02.1919

VALKYRIE Regent Camp, Douglas, Isle of Man, Radar TE
Cd 21.07.1941, PO 31.12.46
Nom DS: NINA 21.07.1941 (poss cancelled)
Lifeboat conv to SM Target 23.10.41

VALKYRIE II Central Camp, Douglas, Isle of Man, TE
10.1943 – 11.01.44 independent command – PO 26.03.1945
Was to have been named TYNWALD (qv)
Nom DS: Skiff allocated Staff Officer (Ops) Isle of Man 07.44 –

VALKYRIE IV Central Camp, Douglas, Isle of Man, TE
10.1943 – PO 26.03.45

VALLURU Tambaran, Madras, India, RNAS & Class B Aircraft Repair Yd
Cd 01.07.1944 (ex RAF), PO 01.12.45 (to RAF as Transit Camp)
Nom DS: TRV 4192 01.07.44 –

VALOROUS (1917) Clyde, RNVR TS
DD, allocated Clyde RNVR 14.04.1939 as TS, Cd 20.06.39 as TS, mobilised 23.08.39, BU 03.47

VALSURA (also spelt VAISURA 1974-76), Bombay/ Rozi - 3 miles from Jamnagar, RIN/ IN Electrical Sch
Cd 12.1942 – listed to 1976
Original Sch at Bombay Dy 06.1942 - moved to Rozi Is 12.1942 - also listed as Torp sch

VAMPIRE (1956) RAN Museum Ship
DD, PO 13.08.1986, to National Maritime Museum, Sydney - lent 1990 - 1997, tx as gift 1997 - extant 1999

VANDYCK (1921) Kirkwall, Accom Sh
05.1940 v ST SUNNIVA & ST MAGNUS, rb ST SUNNIVA, but sunk 10.06.1940

VANCOUVER (1918) Esquimalt, RCNVR TS

DD, TOREADOR, renamed by RCN 01.03.1928, TS 01.05.28 – PO 25.11.36, sold 1937

VANESSA (1899) Loch Ewe & Stornaway, Temp A/P DS
12.1914 v ILLUSTRIOUS – 01.01.1915 rb MANCO
Yt, hired 10.1914 – 05.03.1919

VANESSA II (1899) Holyhead, A/P DS
22.05.1917 v MERSE, 18.02.1919 left Holyhead, PO 22.02.1919
Yt VANESSA hired A/P 15.10.1914, renamed VANESSA II 02.1917 - 05.03.1919

VANGUARD (1870) Kingstown, CG
BB, CG 06.07.1871 – 09.1875, lost by collision 01.09.1875

VANGUARD (1944) Ports, RF HQ
BB, FO Tng Sqn v ANSON 10.11.1949, Res 29.10.56, SO RF v BOXER 06.11.56, FO Commanding RF v CLEOPATRA 28.11.56 – 29.08.60 (Res Ships task to SHEFFIELD, SO RF to MULL OF GALLOWAY 08.06.60), BU 08.60

VANSITTART (1919) - Swansea/ Avonmouth, Accom Sh/ Base Ship
DD, res Pt Talbot 05.1944 - 08.44, Swansea 01.08.44 - 26.01.45, accom sh Swansea 29.01.45 - 09.02.45, accom sh Avonmouth 14.02.45 - 13.08.45. Base Ship Avonmouth 17.08.45 - 07.01.46, sold 25.02.46, BU 05.46

VANUATU Vita, New Hebrides, Base
To 1989

VARBEL Pt Bannatyne, Midget SM Base
Cd 11.09.1942 independent command, acs CYCLOPS, 01.03.43 own acs, PO 15.05.1945 (12 SM disbanded)
Believed named after Cdrs C H Varley DSC & T I S Bell involved in the midget SM concept. Started at Kames Bay, Isle of Bute
Nom DS: PRESENT HELP (1911) Drifter 09.1942 – 10.09.42
25 ft MB 3518 11.09.42 – (44 at least)

VARBEL II Loch Striven, Midget SM (Advance) Base
Cd 21.11.1942 tender to VARBEL, acs CYCLOPS, - PO 28.02.45
Nom DS: Motor Dinghy SYLVIA II 21.11.42 –

VECTIS Royal Yt Sqn, Seaview, Isle of Wight, Base/ HQ
Cd 08.06.1942 ex OSBORNE and TORMENTOR II (qv). HQ Force J 12.10.1942, Capt GJ3 in VECTIS 02.44, 30.09.44 no longer LC Base, under C-in-C Ports, PO 20.05.45
Nom DS: NAB GELYSHE 12.08.42 – 11.43

VECTOR Sheerness, Radar Sch
11.1946 (name appropriated) – 04.11.1947 merged into WILDFIRE (qv)

VECTOR, Kete
Name proposed for Kete, but HARRIER chosen 1948

VEERBAHU – see VIRBAHU

VEGA (1917) Soton, Res Div TS
DD, allocated Solent Res Div 14.04.1939 and due to commission 3rd week Sept 1939, but mobilised beforehand (not Wair conv till 11.1939), BU 03.48

VELDA Fowey, Accom Sh for MA/SB
09.1940

VENDURUTHI (also spelt VENDURUTHY)
Willingdon Is, Cochin, RIN TE
Listed 11.1943 - extant 1999
Name given to Local Naval Defence and CF Base, later became Comb TE - also listed as Naval Air Sta 1991

VENDURUTHI II Cochin, Naval Air Sta
Listed 1952 - 53 (see also GARUDA)

VENERABLE (1899) Taranto/ Kirkaldy/ Portland, DS
DD, DS Taranto 1915 – 12.1916. PPO 1917 at Ports, accom sh - Cd 01.01.18 (regularisation). Cd for passage Ports to Portland 02.18 then became tender to RESEARCH. DS Southern Patrol Force & Hydrophone Tlrs Portland 27.03.18. Northern Patrol DS to 07.18, Southern Patrol 08.18, to Falmouth 09.18, to Kirkaldy 29.10.18, to Portland 01.12.18. To Res 01.04.19, PO to C & M 20.05.1919, sold 04.06.20

VENETIA Scapa Flow, DS for Northern Flot of Tlrs
10.1914 – 11.1914
Fleet Messenger No 1

VENGEANCE (1824) Dev, Rx Sh
2nd Rate, Rx Sh 1861 till BU 10.05.1897

VENGEANCE (1899) Dev, Ordnance Hulk
BB, ordnance hulk 1918 – 1921, sold 12.1921

VENGEUR (1810) Sheerness, Rx Sh
3rd Rate, Rx Sh 1824 – BU 08.1843

VENTURE (1937) Halifax, Nova Scotia, RCN Accom Sh
Schooner, TS, accom sh for 3rd Battle Sqn 01.09.1939 – 11.1941 (included Cdr in Command Naval Estabs Halifax by 10.1940). Then guardship Tuft's Cove, Dartmouth, Nova Scotia. Name tx to SEABORN (qv) Yt, as Nom DS (see VENTURE II below) – 13.05.41. became Hbr Craft 190, sold 10.12.45

VENTURE Halifax, Nova Scotia, RCN Base
01.02.1941 – PO 01.05.1942 task to STADACONA/ CORNWALLIS (qv)

VENTURE Halifax, Nova Scotia, RCN base for Mls
Cd 06.05.1943 ex VENTURE II, acs STADACONA, still listed as VENTURE II 1945. PO 12.02.44 (30 06.45?) and then tender to SCOTIAN 01.07.45 - 14.01.46

Was to have been named GANNET (qv)
ex VENTURE II ex SAMBRO, ex SEABORN, ex VENTURE II, ex CHARLES A DUNNING, ex SEABORN

VENTURE Esquimalt, British Columbia, RCN New Entry Junior Officers' TE & Base
Cd 01.08.1954 – 01.09.1966 - continued as Joint Estab, name in use to 1970 (at least) - extant 1995

VENTURE Suva, Fiji, RNZN Base
Cd 01.01.1941 – 1947 (at least)

VENTURE I Falmouth, Servicing vessel
09.1943 – Quay Punt Vessel for serving LC

VENTURE II Halifax, Nova Scotia, DS for MLs
09.1941 – poss to 30.06.1945
DS for MLs 06.03.1942 ex SAMBRO – PO 04.42, continued as Non Cd VENTURE II to 12.05.43, when Cd as VENTURE (qv)
Nom DS: Ferry CHARLES A DUNNING – req 09.1939, to RN as SEABORN
Tlr (Yt) SEABORN 09.1941 - see VENTURE (1937) above - became VENTURE II 06.03.42

VENUS (1820) Woolwich, TS
5th Rate, lent Marine Soc 1848 - 1862 as TS (see WARSPITE), sold 07.10.1864

VENUS (1895) Newhaven/ Pembroke/ Ports, CG/ DS
Cr, CG Newhaven v AUSTRALIA 07.02.1903 - mid 1903, Temp DS Home Fleet 7 DF 1911, 1 DF 1912, 3rd Fleet Pembroke 1913 - 14, Ports 1914, sold 09.1921

VENUS (1943) Dev, Accom Sh
DD, accom sh 05.1948 – 03.1950, conv to FF 1952, BU 11.1972

VERA Poole, Accom Sh
07.1942 – 10.44 (at least)

VERNON Ports/ Brighton/ Pt Edgar, TE
26.04.1876 – estab as Torp sch, independent command, though had been instructing since 1872 in Fountain Lake as tender to EXCELLENT (qv). Moved to Portchester Creek 23.04.1895. A/P DS Ports WWI. Estab ashore in Old Gunwharf Ports, 01.10.1923. included Coastal MB Base 01.1922 - 06.23. PO 31.03.1986 - became NELSON (VERNON site), then NELSON (Gunwharf) 1987. Closed by 31.03.1991 - site in use to 01.04.96 when closed.
Was at Roedean Sch, Brighton 03.05.41 - 11.06.45
Other sections: - part at Pt Edgar Cd 01.10.1940 - 31.12.45: Mining Section at W Leigh Ho, Havant 05.41, Electrical Dept at W Leigh Cottage 05.41 - to W Leigh House 30.05.41: Controlled Mining at Hillside House , Purbrook 05.41: Whitehead Section at Argyll Works 28.02.41 - Alexandria, Dumbartonshire: BP at Rycroft, Ropley, Nr Alton 05.41; Acs to Mowden Sch, Droveway, Hove 05.41: Main Store to Mowden Sch 14.07.41: DG dept to Arden Caple Castle, Helensburgh 09.40 - see REVLIS: M/S Dept to Kimmerghame House, Fettes Cottage, Nr Edinburgh 21.04.41 - then also to Pt Edgar by 05.44 - ex Barracks HOPETOUN - 02.46: Part at Innellan closed 13.12.45: Electrical Trial & Equipment Sect - Eastleigh House, Havant, closed 18.07.46 - to COLLINGWOOD: Mining Centre Estab at FOIC Holland's HQ, The Hague 05.45.
Ships/Nom DS:
1) VERNON (1832) 26.04.1876 – 18.05.1925 (sold)
DONEGAL (1858) - 14.01.1886 – 18.05.1925 (sold)
STRATHCOE (1916) Tlr 01.1924 - 11.1938
SKYLARK (1932) 09.12.1938 – 01.10.1940 (renamed VESUVIUS)
Mining Lch No 9 (Steam Lch 292) 09.1940-
MSPB 4163 by 03.48 - 1965

VERNON II Ports, TS
MARLBOROUGH (1855), TS 1878, renamed VERNON II 03.1904. 03.16 TERRIBLE allocated as replacement, sold 10.1924

VERNON II Ports, Tlr Base
Estab as MINERVA (qv) 12.1939 - but by 26.03.1940 known as VERNON II – comprised MINERVA & IOLAIRE (qv). 10.12.1940 replaced by MARSHAL SOULT (qv)

VERNON II Ports, Torp Sch/ Accom Sh
23.05.1945 – PO 12.01.1948 – absorbed into VERNON (TAS)
BBs RAMILLIES & MALAYA as one estab, included Cr ROYALIST 01.1947 - 12.47 and sloop MODESTE 1947-

VERNON II Stokes Bay, Alverstoke, Accom Camp
1947 – 60 (listed in Pink List 1957 – 61)
Also refs to VERNON II as M/ S Base Falmouth (1940) and Pt Edgar (1940 - 45)

VERNON III Ports, TS
WARRIOR (1860), renamed VERNON III Cd 01.04.1904, PO 31.03.1924 to hulk WARRIOR - preserved ship at Ports extant 1999

VERNON (D) Dartmouth/ Brixham, Base
Cd 27.10.1944 – in ex CF Base which PO then - absorbed FIREWORK (qv) - tender to DARTMOUTH. 01.10.45 acs to VERNON, PO 30.11.45 - task to VERNON at Ports 01.10.45
Base for P Parties (NP 1571 - 1575 & 3006)

VERNON (M) West Leigh Cottage, Havant, Mining Base
1946 – 47 – see VERNON

VERNON (M/S) – see HOPETOUN
From Kimmerghame House & Fettes Cottage,Edinburgh to Pt Edgar 15.03.1946

VERNON (RAMILLIES) Ports, Accom Sh
15.05.1945 – 23.05.1945 - became VERNON II

(qv)
BB RAMILLIES and MALAYA as one ship

VERSOVA North of Bombay, CO Base
LC Base 02.1944

VESTFART Scapa Flow, TS
06.1943
MFV allocated as Mobile A/S Tng Unit

VETERAN (1807) Ports, Rx Sh
Fireship, PROMETHEUS (qv), Rx Sh 1819, renamed VETERAN 02.05.1839, BU 08.1852

VICTOR EMMANUEL (1855) HK, Rx Sh
REPULSE, 2nd Rate, renamed VICTOR EMMANUEL 07.1855, Rx Sh 1860 v PRINCESS CHARLOTTE (qv), at HK till rb TAMAR (qv) 01.10.1897. BU 1899

VICTORIA AND ALBERT (1899) Ports, Accom Sh
Royal Yt, approved for use as accom sh for EXCELLENT 30.04.1942 - 1945 - and continued in use as accom sh 1946 on, BU 06.12.1954

VICTORIOUS (1808) Ports, Rx Sh
3rd Rate, Rx Sh 05.1826, BU 01.1862

VICTORIOUS (1895) Humber/ Scapa Flow/ Repair Ship
BB, DS Humber 28.08.1914 (SNO Humber 24.08.1914) – 10.14, PO 04.02.1915 at Newcastle. 08.15 planned to be lent Tyne as canteen but cancelled 10.1915. Repair Ship Scapa Flow Cd 22.02.1916 (for passage) – DS & Accom Sh for Armed Boarding Steamers Scapa – (crew under MFA rules). Arrived Longhope 05.03.1916. 28.11.18 Flag to VICTORIOUS ex VICTORIOUS II. By 03.1919 all M/S at Kirkwall under VICTORIOUS. 21.07.19 duties of IMPERIEUSE to VICTORIOUS. Due to depart 09.1919 when Adty vessel (IMPERIEUSE) to be named VICTORIOUS as Nom DS - but still there 11.19 and to remain. 24.03.20 to Dev under own steam for INDUS. PO 14.04.1920. Renamed INDUS II (qv) 04.1920, sold 19.12.22

VICTORIOUS (1869) Scapa Flow, Rx Sh
AUDACIOUS, renamed FISGARD (qv) 1902, renamed IMPERIEUSE (qv) Rx Sh Scapa Flow 1914 - was to be renamed VICTORIOUS 10.1919 - poss became VICTORIOUS III (qv). Rx Sh 1919 poss at Rosyth, sold 1927

VICTORIOUS I Kirkwall, A/P DS
04.06.1919 – 27.08.1919
Section I of VICTORIOUS ledger - prob main ship account to distinguish from VICTORIOUS II

VICTORIOUS II (1895) Chat/ Longhope, DS
PRINCE GEORGE, BB, renamed VICTORIOUS II 29.07.1918, Cd 01.10.18 for passage, arrived Scapa Flow 20.10.1918, Re - Cd 24.10.1918 – overflow for VICTORIOUS - 10.18 Flag ex CYCLOPS - 28.11.18 Flag to VICTORIOUS -returned Chat as overflow ship 01.12.1918 - reverted to PRINCE GEORGE 02.1919 - later DD DS, sold 29.01.21

VICTORIOUS II Kirkwall, M/S Craft DS
Ex CYCLOPS II 01.04.1919 – 27.08.1919
M/S acs from ZARIA 01.03.1918. 01.05.1919 acs BD vessels ex CINCERIA. (Section II of ledger)

VICTORIOUS III DS
NL 1920 - erroneous allocation ex CYCLOPS II 02.1919 - name adjusted to VICTORIOUS II (qv) 01.04.1919

VICTORY (1765) Ports, Flag/ DS
1st Rated, Flag C-in-C Ports by 1840 v EXCELLENT (1825 in some acs). Moved into Dk 12.01.1922 and bore name of Barracks (opened 1903) until 01.08.1974 when Barracks became NELSON (qv)
A/P DS WWI (including Portland 08.1914 - 10.15 - then Portland became RESEARCH)
Still wears Flag (Second Sea Lord/ C-in-C Naval Home Command -1999). During WWII various accounting sections moved elsewhere(see entries below)
Overflow camp estab Leigh Park camp 21.04.1941 - known as Stock Heath Camp

VICTORY I Goodings, Nr Newbury/ Ports, Accounting Base
Tx to Goodings 04.09.1940 – 09.44 (at least) – Newbury at 46 Commercial Rd Ports by 12.44, absorbed VICTORY IV 01.04.47, and at RN Barracks 1952 - 61.

VICTORY II Crystal Palace/Sydenham, Tng Depot for RN Divs
1914 – PO 21.03.1919
Called HMS CRYSTAL PALACE

VICTORY II Newbury/ Ports, Accounting Section
To Goodings, Newbury 04.09.1940, at Ports (Commercial Chambers) 12.44 - 03.47, then to RN Barracks. Absorbed VICTORY III 01.04.47 - extant 07.1951

VICTORY III Ports/ Wantage, Accounting Section
RNR Battalion 21.08.1914 – 1917. 10.1915 for vessels at Portland.
Opened 01.10.39 for acs local BD vessels, Hbr Defence & Contraband Control, Exam Service etc. VICTORY IV merged with VICTORY III 27.10.39. To Woolley Park, Wantage Berks 16.10.40 – 45, returned Ports (Commercial Chambers) by 12.44. RF from VICTORY III to RESOURCE 01.04.46. PO 31.03.47 - task absorbed by VICTORY II

VICTORY IV London/Ports/ Petersfield, Accounting Section
RNR Battalion 28.08.1914 - 1917. At Crystal Palace 1918

VICTORY IV Ports, Accounting Section
Merged into VICTORY III 27.10.1939. Re-formed at Leydene House, Nr Petersfield 06.11.1941 - 45,

at Commercial Chambers, Ports by 18.12.44 - 09.46, PO 30.09.47 - acs to VICTORY I 01.04.47

VICTORY IV Ports, Accounting Section
1952 - 1961 – for tenders at Ports

VICTORY V South Western Hotel, Soton, Base
05.1941 ex COLLINGWOOD II – acs opened 05.04.41 - acs of staff and trainees at Government Tng Centres Redbridge, Wallsend-on-Tyne, Hounslow, Springburn (Glasgow) & Gas Light & Coke Co's shop Fulham. Renamed SHRAPNEL (qv) 09.06.42

VICTORY V Ports, Comb HQ
Cd 30.06.1944, independent command, acs VICTORY
Nom DS: Diesel lch 3505 30.06.44 –

VICTORY VI Crystal Palace, Depot for RN & RNR Divs
1914 – PO 21.03.1919 - see VICTORY II and CRYSTAL PALACE
10.9.1914 - 1916 - RNR Battalions - By 1916 Maint Unit & Signal Section & Seamen Unit

VICTORY VII Portland, A/P DS
08.1915 – 30.09.1915 – rb RESEARCH

VICTORY IX
1915 - 1916 – Reserves

VICTORY X Ports, Accounting Section
09.1917 - extant 04.1919

VICTORY X Ports, Accounting Section/ Demobilisation Centre
06.05.1946 – acs of RN personnel in Newfoundland
09.1946 - RN Camp Stamshaw
22.01.1947 – 1950 Commercial Chambers, Ports

VICTORY XI Portland Naval Depot
1920 - 01.07.1932 – became BOSCAWEN (qv)

VIENNA (1894) Accom Sh
Hired 29.08.1914 as accom sh to 12.14, later as Armed Boarding Steamer and as decoy ship

VIENNA (1929) CF DS
Hired 06.1941 - fitted out Green & Silley Weir, Royal Albert Dk, Blackwall, PO to C & M for conv 15.07.41. Acquired 22.08.1941. CF DS Cd 15.06.42, Med (Gib 1942, Algiers, Tunis, Oran, Bizerta 05.43, Bari 43 - 44 – hit by aircraft 02.12.43, Brindisi as store ship 25.09.43 -1944, Taranto 04.44-09.44), no longer required 09.44, PO 31.10.44, resto 10.44

VIGILANT (1904) Campbeltown, Accom Sh
Ex Scottish Fisheries Vessel 08.1941 – accom sh for Rescue Tug Base, Campbeltown, renamed IXION (qv) 15.04.43

VIGO (1810) Dev, Rx Sh
3rd Rate, Rx Sh 1827 – BU 08.1865

VIGO (1817) Dev, Rx Sh
AGINCOURT (qv), 3rd Rate, Hbr Serv 03.1948 , Rx Sh Dev, renamed VIGO 04.1865 – sold 10.1884

VIGO (1945) Chat/ Ports, Accom Sh/ Hbr TS
DD, RF living ship Chat 02.1948 – 12.48, Hbr TS attached SULTAN v LST 3031 18.01.1961 – 01.62 rb SOLEBAY, BU 12.64

VIGOROUS (1913) Larne, A/P DS
DS Cd 05.01.1918 v THETIS – 04.06.1919
Drifter, hired 1914 – 1919

VIJAYA (1944), Ceylon, R Ceylon N VR Drl Sh
M/S ex TILSONBURG, ex FLYING FISH, lent 07.10.1949 – 24.05.67, then sold to R Ceylon N VR (renamed VIJAYA), BU 04.75

VIJAYA Kalpitiya, Sri Lanka, Sri Lankan Base
1973 – listed to 1979

VIKING Clyde, Accom Sh
04.1943 accom sh for AFD IV v MECKLENBURG – 07.43 (at least)

VILLE DE PARIS (1795) Milford, Qtn Sh
1st Rate, qtn sh 1825 – BU 1845

VINDICTIVE (1813) Fernando Po / Jellah Coffee, Bread & Coal Hulk
3rd Rate, storeship at Fernado Po 1862, then Jellah Coffee, Bight of Benin 1865 -, to Fernando Po where wrecked 24.11.1871

VINDICTIVE (1897) Archangel. A/P DS White Sea
Cr, Cd 27.09.1916 for White Sea v IPHEGENIA. Murmansk 14.10.16, Yukanske 20.10.16, White Sea acs to 09.01.1917. Arrive Lpool to PO 12.1917. Cd 01.01.18 for trials, sunk as blockship Ostend 10.05.18

VINDICTIVE (1918) Freetown/ Malta GC/ Scapa Flow, Repair Ship
Cr, ex CAVENDISH, Baltic 02.07.19 -, TS 1937, Repair Ship 1940, Freetown 07.40 – 11.42, N Africa 1943, left Malta GC 15.10.44, Sheerness 22.10.44, Scapa Flow 07.11.44 – 18.06.45, to res Sheerness 20.06.45 - 15.02.46 – (07.45 - plans to be conv to dockyard labour accom ship Clyde), Blyth 16.02.46, PO 21.02.46 and handed over for BU

VINDICTIVE II Scapa Flow, Base
Extant 11.44 -PO 03.09.1945 – acs to PROSERPINE (qv)
Home Fleet DDs acs to manning ports 01.8.1945 - prob accounting section of VINDICTIVE (see previous entry)

VIOLET (1904) Scapa Flow, Officers' Accom Sh
03.1916 – 9.1918 (at least)
Drifter - BD accom sh 05.1915 – 1919

VIPER (1865) Bermuda , Tank vessel
Gunvessel, hbr serv 1890, tank vessel 1901 – sold 1908

VIRBAHU Vishakapatnam, IN SM Base

1972 – extant 1999
Spelt VEERBAHU in Pink List 1975 - 76

VIRGINIA Bermuda, Coal Hulk
Ex barque, purch 22.01.1862 as coal hulk, BU 03.1866

VIRGINIE Plym, Rx Sh
Fr 5th Rate, capt 1796, Rx Sh 1817 – Bu 1827

VITI Fiji, RNZN – Fiji RNVR Res Drl Sh
Cd 21.10.1955 – listed to 1961
Nom DS: SDML 3555 1958 - 59

VITI Togaleva, Fiji, Fijian Base
Cd 25.07.1985 – extant 1993
Name had been used by SDML 3555 when with Fiji Naval Vol Res 1958

VIVA – in a list
VIVA was RAF Rescue Serv Littlehampton 09.1940 /VIVA II A/S Yt Poole 09.40
VITA Naval Hosp sh PO 20.07.1946

VIVID Dev, RN Barracks
Cd 01.01.1890 ex ROYAL ADELAIDE (when task afloat) - Tng task PO 01.08.1914 and Re Cd 13.08.1914, - renamed DRAKE (qv) 01.01.1934
Barracks first occupied 04.06.1889 – was the first shore barracks, even before EXCELLENT
A/P DS WWI – included Falmouth to 01.10.15 (then became DREEL CASTLE)
VIVID (1883) Yt, tender to ROYAL ADELAIDE, Flag C-in-C Plymouth from 01.01.1890 v ROYAL ADELAIDE
VIVID ex CAPERCAILZIE (1891)
01.01.1892 – 20.11.1912 (sold) - Flag to 1900
CUCKOO (1873) Gunboat 1911 – 22.1.1919 became VIVID (OLD), sold 1958
SABINE (ex SABRINA) (1876) Gunboat 22.12.1919-sold 07.22
CAMBRIAN (1893) Cr - see also HARLECH 09.1921 – 21.02.23 (sold)
MARSHAL NEY (1915) Monitor 06.1922 – 01.01.34 (Flag v EREBUS 19.12.31-)

VIVID Mount Wise, Plym, Res HQ Unit
Cd 1957 – (name allocated 10.04.1959) – extant 1999
In 1996 moved from underground HQ to old Staff Officers' Mess

VIVID II Dev, Accounting Base
1914 – 1915

VIVID III Dev, Accounting Section
09.1917 – 12.18 (at least)

VIVID IV Falmouth, Accounting Base
Ex DREEL CASTLE (qv) – acs to VIVID IV 16.09.1919

VIVID IV Ireland, Accounting Base
15.03.1922 when COLLEEN & COLLEEN II PO – acs of Queenstown, Buncrana, Berehaven, Lpool - to 1923

VIVID V Milford Haven, Accounting Base
Ex IDAHO (qv) – acs to VIVID V 01.10.1919 – base closed 07.10.1921

VIVIEN (1918) Tyne, VR TS
DD, Wair conv allocated Tyne VR but not completed conv till 10.1939 so never used as TS, BU 08.1947

VOLAGE (1825) Chat , Powder Hulk
6th Rate, survey ship 04.1847, lent War Department as powder hulk Chat 19.01.1864, BU 12.1874

VOLAGE (1943) Ports, Hbr TS
DD, conv to FF, Hbr TS for RMs 1964 - 01.1971, then facilities ship Ports for DLG refits , sold 10.1972

VOLCANO (1836) Ports, Factory
Paddle sloop, floating factory 1862 – BU 11.1894

VOLCANO Holmbrook, Ravenglass, Cumberland, Bomb Disposal TE
Cd 31.01.1942 independent command, acs CLIO. To close by 17.09.1945, PO 10.45
Nom DS: NAB KYLE 31.10.42 –

VOLGA Black Sea, DS
1919

VOLONTAIRE (1923) Lpool, Fr DS
INGENIEUR CACHIN, Fr M/L, seized 03.07.1940, renamed VOLONTAIRE as Free Fr DS Lpool 16.10.1940, returned 1945

VOLTAIRE (1923) Scapa Flow, Accom Sh
Allocated to Scapa Flow as temp accom sh 08.39 - DUNLUCE CASTLE taken up to relieve her as accom sh - became AMC 1939 - 1941

VULCAN (1889) DS
Built as DS for Torp Boats. Med 1896 - 1905, SM DS Cd 05.01.1909, Home Fleet 1910. 7SM Leith 1914 – 06.1916 rb HEBE, 10 SM Humber v FORTH 06.1916 - , Berehaven 05.1917, Kingstown 03.1918 -, VULCAN SM Flot to be named 14 SM 01.10.1918 – at Blyth – 12.18, then Stornaway, 4 SM Blyth 01.03.1919 - 10.19 - remained for salvage H41, alloc Periscope Sch Portland 01.09.1919 v THAMES , there 10.19 - 1924. 6 SM Portland 1924 – 30 rb TITANIA, renamed DEFIANCE III (qv) 17.02.1931, BU 12.1955

VULCAN Malta GC/ Felixstowe/ Med, CF DS
Tlr ex MASCOT, ex ASTON VILLA, purch 1936 as CF DS. Cd 07.04.1937, Malta GC 17.07.37 – 16.11.39, Ports by 30.12.39, Felixstowe 01.40 – 12.40, Med 02.41 - 46 (Alexandria, Benghazi, Brindisi – 05.44 - 07.44, Taranto 07.44, Bari, Ancona 11.44/ 05.45/ 08.45, Trieste 05.45, Naples 07.45, Malta GC 08.11.45), Pembroke Dock 1946 – 02.47, sold 05.02.47

VULCAN Dounreay, TE
Work started 1957, reactor critical 1965. Cd

01.05.1970 - became VULCAN Naval Nuclear Propulsion Test Estab 13.05.1981, and then Nuclear Reactor Tng Estab 01.10.1984. Still listed as VULCAN Naval Nuclear Test Estab 1990, but not Cd. Extant 1999

VULCAN II (1892) Portland, SM DS
ONYX (qv) DS 1907 - renamed VULCAN II 06.1919, sold 1924

VULCAN II (1915) Portland, SM DS
LILY sloop, renamed VULCAN II 15.10.1923, attached 6 SM, renamed ADAMANT II (qv) 1930, sold 25.06.1930

VULTURE St Merryn, RNAS
Name ann 03.1940, Cd 10.08.1940. Renamed CURLEW (qv) 01.01.53
Nom DS: Hbr Lch 3506 10.08.1940 – 27.04.51
TRSB 43780 28.04.51 – 01.01.53

VULTURE II Treligga, Cornwall, Bombing & Gunnery Range
1939 – 1955

W

WAGTAIL Heathfield, Ayr, RNAS
Tx from RAF on loan 06.09.1944. Cd 06.09.1944, detached unit of SANDERLING, Cd 01.11.44 independent command, acs SANDERLING, 20.11.44, own acs, naval & air stores under SANDERLING, PO to C & M 10.03.46, acs SANDERLING.
Nom DS: TRV 4193 06.09.44 –

WAIMANA (1911) DS
Taken up for service as DS 09.1939, but used as dummy BB RESOLUTION, returned 02.1942

WAKEFIELD Wellington, New Zealand, RNZN Staff
01.01.1954 ex PHILOMEL II (qv) - extant 1999
If estab at Shelley Bay had opened it would have been named WAKEFIELD and Navy Office would have been WAKEFIELD II
Nom DS: ML 3554 1958
ML 3565 1959 – 64

WALLACE (1918) Lpool, Res TS
DD leader (Wair conv), allocated to EAGLET for AA tng 14.06.1939 - 08.39 - but Cd for post refit trials 22.05.39 - and 09.06.39, Re - Cd on mobilisation 26.08.39, BU 20.03.45

WALLAROO (1890) Dev/ Chat/ Immingham/ Brightlingsea, TS/ DS
Cr, ex PERSIAN, hbr serv 1906 attached INDUS at Dev, attached Mechanical TE Chat by 1910, re - armed as guardship Chat 1914. A/P DS Brightlingsea 05.1915 – PO 01.05.1916 rb WILDFIRE. Cd 17.03.1917 as overflow for RN Depot Immingham Dk. 31.01.18 tender to HEBE, 01.19 tender to WALLINGTON. Renamed WALLINGTON (qv) 05.03.1919, revert to WALLAROO 01.01.20, sold 27.02.20

WALLINGTON Immingham, A/P Base
Cd 06.11.1915 (v ST GEORGE 07.11.15) - also DS 7 DF. A/P Office closed 28.05.1919, PO 01.01.20 - acs to PEMBROKE VIII.
WALLINGTON (1911) Tlr, hired as BDV 1915 - 19, A/P DS 01.16 - 03.18 (renamed SHERATON), renamed ORIFLAMME 01.10.18, PO 05.19
Tlr SHERATON (1907), renamed WALLINGTON 01.03.1918, renamed SHERATON 01.10.18 (BDV 1915 - 19 & A/P 06.40-45)
ST GEORGE (1890) Yt, renamed ORIFLAMME 06.18, renamed WALLINGTON 01.10.18, reverted to ST GEORGE 05.03.19 and to Ports to resto
WALLAROO (1890) Cr (qv) 05.03.1919 – PO 01.01.20, reverted to WALLAROO, sold 27.02.20

WANDERLUST Chichester, Accom Sh
08.1942 – 10.44 (at least)

WAR WING (1915) Plym/ Normandy/ Ports/ Copenhagen/ Germany, M/S Store Carrier
Tlr, hired 12.1939. conv to M/S Store Carrier 03.44, at Plym/Normandy 06.44/Ports/Le Havre/Copenhagen/ Kiel/ Hamburg/Rosyth 12.45

WARA Komenda, Takoradi, Gold Coast, RNAS
To be developed 05.1942, Cd 10.10.1942 independent command, acs LEONIDAS, C & M 09.43, C & M – 3 mths notice 18.12.43
Nom DS: NAB GLENFRUIN 01.10.43-

WARATAH Washington/ Ottawa, RAN HQ
Cd 01.01.1966 ex CERBERUS III (qv) – listed to 1979

WARHORSE HQ Captain LC (Infantry)
Independent command, acs DINOSAUR - ann 15.02.1943 - but cancelled 10 days later

WARREN Largs, CO Base
Cd 12.10.1942, Flag of Rear Admiral CO. PO 31.12.46 retard party remained
Also HQ FO Commanding Overseas Assault Forces. Hollywood Hotel was part of the estab.
Aircraft Recognition Sch to DINOSAUR 02.06.45
Nom DS: HSL 3945 12.10.42 - 04.43
Hbr Lch (S) 301 04.43 –

WARRIOR (1781) Chat/ Woolwich, Rx/ Convict Sh
3rd Rate, Rx Sh Chat 1818, Rx h Woolwich by 1835, convict ship Woolwich 1840 – BU 1857

WARRIOR (1860)) Portland/ Clyde/ Pembroke Dk/ Ports, CG/ Fuelling Jetty/ DS/ Museum Sh
Iron armoured ship, CG Portland 01.04.1875 – 01.05.1881, CG Clyde 01.05.1881 – 01.06.1883, DD DS Ports 16.07.1902, renamed VERNON III (qv) 03.1904, hulk WARRIOR 1923, to Pembroke Dk as fuelling jetty 1929, renamed C77 27.08.42, for restoration & preservation 1979, Museum Sh Ports

16.06.1887 - extant 1999

WARRIOR (1944) Ports/ Plym, Accom Sh/ Hbr TS
Aircraft Carrier, lent RCN 01.1946 – 02.48, living ship RF Ports 03.50, allocated as Hbr TS for RALEIGH v NEWFOUNDLAND 01.07.50 – but used for trooping & OpGrapple, sold 07.58

WARRIOR Northwood, Middlesex, Fleet HQ
Name assumed 30.04.1963 - became Joint HQ 01.04.1996 - de Cd 31.03.99 became Joint Service Unit Northwood
Originally name of Admin Unit for RN personnel at HQ - became used as name for whole RN HQ (C-in-C ashore from 31.12.59)

WARSPITE (1807 et al) Woolwich, TS
Name used by three of ships lent to The Marine Society - whose ships were:
BEATTY, sloop, renamed THE MARINE SOCIETY 13.09.1786 – 1799 - Deptford
THORN (1799) lent 1799 – 1814 – Deptford
SOLEBAY ex IRIS (1783) lent 1814 – 1833 – Deptford
IPHEGENIA (1808) lent 1833 – 1848
VENUS (1820) lent 1848 – 1862 – Woolwich
WARSPITE (1807) lent 27.03.1862 - burnt by accident 03.01.1876
CLIO (1858) lent 1876 – 1877
WATERLOO(1833) renamed CONQUEROR 1862, renamed WARSPITE 11.08.1876 and lent, burnt 20.01.1918
PRESIDENT ex BUZZARD (1887), lent temp 30.01.1918 - Greenhithe
Ashore 1918 – 1922 – Tilbury Hotel
HERMIONE, Cr (1893) sold 18.12.1922 and renamed WARSPITE , sold 09.1940

WARSPITE (1884) Queenstown, Guard Ship
Armoured Cr, Pt Guard Ship Queenstown 28.09.1893 – 12.1896, sold 04.1905

WASP Lord Warden Hall, Dover, CF Base
Formed 26.08.1940, Cd 02.09.1940, PO 14.11.44
Nom DS: Hbr Lch 202 02.09.40 – 06.43
Steam Boat L673 06.43 – 14.11.44

WATCHFUL Gt Yarmouth, A/S – M/S Base
Name sel for comml pt Gt Yarmouth 01.09.1939, NOIC ordered 27.08.39, apps from 25.08.39. Cd 16.09.39, PO 31.07.45 - acs to MINOS
Nom DS: THE BRIT 16.09.39 – 31.07.45

WATCHWORD Padstow, Accom Sh (RN Patrol Service - under RNO)
03.01.1943 – 07.43 (at least)

WATERHEN Waverton, Sydney, New South Wales, RAN Minor Warships' Base
Cd 05.12.1962 on old BD Depot site - extant 1999

WATERLOO (1833) Sheerness, Flag
1st Rate, Flag Sheerness 1857, renamed CONQUEROR 02.1862, renamed WARSPITE (qv) 08.1876, TS, Burnt 01.1918

WATERRAIL Campbeltown, RNAS
In a list – name of RNAS Campbeltown was LANDRAIL – poss a pun for seaplane use?

WATERWITCH (1943) Barrow-in-Furness, Accom Sh
M/S, accom sh 1966 (contractors' & overseers' offices) - 1970, sold 10.1970

WATFORD I Watford, Herts, TE
Government Tng Centre, known as WATFORD I, became RN Aircraft TE, Hampstead Rd 09.06.1942 - not a ship name - see TURNSTONE

WATFORD II Watford, Herts, TE
Government Tng Centre, known as WATFORD II, became Air Fitters' TE 09.06.1942 – not a ship name - see TURNSTONE

WATSON South Head, Sydney, New South Wales, RAN TE
Cd 14.03.1945 ex Army Land, - extant 1999
Originally a Radar TE - became Surface Warfare TE
Nom DS: ML 536 1945 –

WAVE (1856) Ports, Coal Hulk
Gunboat, coal hulk 1869, renamed CLINKER (qv) 30.12.1882, sold 1890

WAVE Dartmouth, Moored tender
Purch 1882, at Dartmouth 1897, sold 1907

WAVENEY (1942) Normandy/ Gareloch, temp HQ Ship/ Accom Sh
FF, conv to HQ Ship Lpool 10.43 – 44, HQ ship Normandy 06.06.1944, Med 45, E Indies 04.45 – 01.46, to res 03.46, alloc as living ship Gareloch on completion refit 09.1952, Gareloch 1953 (not living ship), Lisahally 1955, sold for BU 08.11.1957

WAXWING Townhill, Dunfermline, Fife, RN Camp
Name ann 21.05.1942, Cd 01.07. 1942, independent command, acs MERLIN, PO 09.1946
Accom camp for Naval Air personnel waiting draft
Nom DS: 45ft Vosper Motor Cr 40211 01.07.42 – 01.44
NAB BENITA II 01.44 – 20.05.45
SB 43781 21.05.43 - (ex ROBIN)

WAYLAND (1921) Repair Ship
ANTONIA, req 1940, purch 1942, conv Ports, renamed and Cd 19.08.1942. Kilindini 05.43, Ferryville 12.43, Trinco 1944 – 26.10.45, refit Bombay – 07.02.46, arrive Gareloch 03.04.46, to Chat 26.05.46, PO 31.05.46, handed over to MOT 20.11.46, handed over for BU 22.01.48

WEAR (1942) Hartlepool, RF HQ
FF, CO RF 1954 – 09.56 rb LOCH TRALAIG, BU 10.57

WELLESLEY (No 1)(1815) Chat, Guard Ship/ TS
3rd Rate, Guardship Chat 1854 – 66 (last few years also a TS). Renamed CORNWALL (qv) 18.06.1868, sunk 24.09.1940 in air attack

WELLESLEY (1812) Newcastle-on-Tyne, TS
CORNWALL, 3rd Rate, renamed 18.06.1868, lent as TS, BU 18.01.1875

WELLESLEY (No 2) (1844) Newcastle-on-Tyne, TS
BOSCAWEN, 3rd Rate, renamed WELLESLEY 21.03.1874 and lent as TS. Damaged by fire 03.1914 and BU (still in lists 1921)

WELLESLEY Lpool, TE
Cd 08.05.1940, PO 31.01.1946
At Royal Southern Hospital – part destroyed 05.1941
DEMS TE?
Nom DS: MB KITIKAE 08.05.1940 – 02.41
ML of EAGLET 01.41 – 04.41
13.5ft skiff Dev 446 04.41 -

WELLINGTON (1816) Sheerness, DS
3rd Rate, ex HERO, renamed WELLINGTON 12.1816, renamed AKBAR (qv) TS 05.1862, sold 1908

WELLINGTON (1934) Embankment, London, HQ
Sloop, became HQ ship for the Worshipful Company of Master Mariners 06.02.1947. Arrived Embankment 12.1948 – extant 1999

WESER (WEZER) Malta GC, Distilling Ship
Gunboat, ex Prussian SALAMANDER, acquired 1855, distilling ship 1866, sold 10.1873

WESSEX Soton, Res Drl Sh
Formed 21.10.1938. Due to be Cd third week 09.1939 but overtaken by mobilisation (see VEGA). RNVR Solent closed 12.10.39. Re-opened 06.46 in temp HQ South Western Hotel, later Old Royal Southern Yt Club. Name allocated 1951. PO 31.03.1994
1) ZETLAND (1942) DD (qv)
10.12.1946 – 04.47
DERG (1943) FF - Soton 1947, renamed WESSEX 1951 – 04.52 - became CAMBRIA (qv)
ERNE (1940) sloop, allocated 02.1947 - Soton by 1949, Cd as WESSEX 04.06.52 – BU 27.10.65
HQ at No 14 berth, then 08.63 at 50 berth, Eastern Dks - first shore huts 12.1951. PO 31.03.1994

WESTCLIFF Southend, CO Base
Cd 17.11.1942 – tng from EFFINGHAM 12.43 when College tx to USN. Admin tx from Cdre Southend to C-in-C Nore 15.10.45. Task of UK main holding base for CO personnel to Roseneath 29.10.45, PO 21.01.1946, closed 06.03.46

WESTCLIFF II Southend, CO Holding Base
WW II - For RM LC personnel

WESTCLIFF III Burnham-on-Crouch, LC Base
WW II

WESTERN ISLES Tobermory, Work Up Base
Originally approved for Sea Tng Organisation Fr Atlantic Coast 09.04.1940, but cancelled as Germans advanced. Allocated Tobermory 25.06.1940, Cd 17.07.1940. Flag Cdre struck 31.08.45, approved to close 07.10.45, closed 03.11.45 - A/S work up to Portland
Satellite at Loch Na Lith Aich, Mull 06.43, tx to Stornaway 09.43 – under MENTOR, not WESTERN ISLES
Nom DS:
1) WESTERN ISLES (1891) Yt - ex MS TYNWALD, hired as TS 04.40 - renamed EASTERN ISLES 22.04.41
2) BATAVIER IV (1903) Dutch, hired 05.40, renamed EASTERN ISLES 11.40, Cd under Cdre Stephenson 18.04.41, renamed WESTERN ISLES 22.04.41 – PO and to DST 21.02.46

WESTERN LAND (1918) Repair Ship
Ex REGINA, purch 1942, arrived London 10.1942 for conv to DD DS, conv stopped 09.44, and to Sea Transport Officer 07.45, released 12.45

WESTWARD Poole, Accom Sh
05.1944 ex Accom Sh ZEPHYR/ ZEPHER (qv), laid up in C & M 07.45

WESTWARD HO! (1894) Dartmouth, Base/ Accom Sh
Req 1944, ex AA ship, ex M/S, accom sh for CF v KILORAN, refitted Rochester 07.43, Cd 01.01.44, tender to DARTMOUTH – to DST 15.03.46

WEYMOUTH Deptford/ Bermuda, Storeship/ Convict Sh/ Rx Sh
Ex Indiaman WELLESLEY, 5th Rate, purch 1804, storeship Deptford 1820 – 27,convict ship Bermuda 10.1828, Rx Sh at Bermuda by 1835 – sold 03.1865

WEYMOUTH (1910) Brindisi/Nore/ Dev/ Ports, SNO/ FO RF
Cr, SNO Brindisi 20.11.1918 – 28.03.1919 (Base closed), RF 1921 – 28, SO RF Nore 09.1922 - 12.25 (trooping toChina 01.25 and 12.25), RF Dev 01.26 – 04.26, Greenwich temp 06.04.26 – 30.04.26, FO RF Ports v CENTURION 30.04.26 – 01.04.27 rb DARTMOUTH, Ports for disposal, sold 10.28

WEZER – see WESER

WHANG PU (1920) Madang, New Guinea, Repair Ship
Hired 1941 as SM DS Malaya. Req 13.12.41 as SM DS. To RAN 20.04.42, accom sh Fremantle 07.42, repair ship 1944 - 46 (Madang 05.45 - 12.45), resto 04.46

WHITE EAR (1914) Gt Yarmouth, Parent Ship
Tlr, hired 1914. Parent ship v CAIRO 11.1914 - 11.04.15 rb MOIRA, resto 21.06.1919

WHITE OAK (1913) Poole, DS Net Drifters
Drifter, hired 1914 – 19, Parent ship Cd 26.01.1915 (Captain in Charge app 17.01.15) – PO 12.02.1919 - retard party another 14 days

WHITE OWL Chichester, Accom Sh
10.1942, acquired 12.42, laid up Lymington 05.45, to ST 06.45, for disposal 05.46

WHITE STAR Chichester, Accom Sh
House boat, 08.1942 - , acquired 26.02.43, to C & M, DST on Hamble 07.44, no longer required 10.44

WHITEHEAD (1880) Aegean, Tlr DS
Hired as stores carrier 08.1914, nominated as DS, sunk 15.10.1917, replaced by CHALKIS

WHYALLA (1941) Whyalla, RAN Museum Ship
M/S, RAN, Museum Ship Whyalla 1984, ashore there as exhibition 1987 – extant 1999

WIGTOWN BAY (1945) Dev, Accom Sh
FF, accom sh 05.1948, BU 04.1959

WILDFIRE Sheerness/Brightlingsea, Base
01.04.1889 – 03.1933. Re-opened 16.02.1937 – acs to PEMBROKE II 01.10.47 - PO 01.04.1950
Amalgamated with VECTOR (qv) 04.11.1947 and became Radar Plotter Tng Sch - cease as TE 30.09.49 – tng to DRYAD & HARRIER, and became tender to PEMBROKE.
Nom DS:
1) WILDFIRE ex HIAWATHA, Yt, purch 1888, became Base ship Sheerness 01.04.1889 v DUNCAN (qv), renamed UNDINE (qv) 01.1907, sold 07.1912
NYMPHE (1888), renamed WILDFIRE 12.1906, renamed GANNET (qv) 11.02.1916, renamed PEMBROKE (qv) 07.1917, sold 10.02.1920. Also acted as Parent Ship A/P Brightlingsea v WALLAROO by 10.1916 – 01.1917 rb CITY OF PERTH
CORNWALLIS (1813) jetty at Sheerness 1865, renamed WILDFIRE 01.04.1916, BU 1957
ML 1724 16.02.1937 – 12.41
Diesel lch 3949 12.41 –
ML 1724 10.45 – 1948
36ft FMB 3845 04.11.47 – 12.48

WILDFIRE Khyber Rd, Chat, Communications Tng Centre/ Res HQ Unit
Cd 10.09.1964 and under name 01.10.1984 – PO 02.09.1994
Was Chat HQ Unit RNR to 30.09.83, then Communications Tng Centre

WILDFIRE II Sheerness, Accounting Base for Aux M/S
Cd 01.10.1939 – abolished 29.02.40 – absorbed into WILDFIRE (Became ST TUDNO (qv) by some acs)
Also used for Examination Service & Pt and Hbr Defence

WILDFIRE II CO Base
07.12.1942 – 06.06.45
In a list - poss an error for WILDFIRE III(qv) - no mention in NL

WILDFIRE III Sheerness, Accounting Base
Abolished 29.02.1940 – absorbed into WLDFIRE

WILDFIRE III Sheerness, CO Base
Cd 07.12.1942 - tender to WILDFIRE – 03.44 (LC Base Queenborough), 10.44 CF Queenborough, 05.45 temp CF Base, 06.06.45 tx to Captain M/S Sheerness, 11.06.45 CF ceased, CF Base PO 15.10.46
Nom DS: Hbr Lch 3953 04.43

WILLOUGHBY FORT Bridgetown, Barbados, Barbadian Base
1982 – extant 1999

WILTON (1941) Cardiff, HQ Ship RF
DD, HQ Ship RF 1956 – 01.04.1959 rb DERG, BU 11.1959

WINCHESTER (1832) Aberdeen, Res Drl Sh
6th Rate, ex CONWAY, renamed 28.08.1861, Drl Sh Aberdeen 01.07.1862 – BU 06.1871

WINDSOR CASTLE (1790) Plym, DS
2nd Rate, DS 1835, BU 1839

WINGFIELD Wingfield, S Africa, SAN Base
1957 – listed to 1961

WIVERN (1863) Hull/ HK, Guardship/ Hbr Serv
Ex Turkish MONASSIR, purch 10.1863, CG Hull 01.1870 - 13.10.1870, guardship at HK 1880, then became distilling ship and steam reserve for DD workshop, sold 1922

WOLF (1826) Kingstown/ Queenstown, Coal Hulk
Sloop, coal hulk Kingstown 1848 – 50, lent Board of Works Dublin 1851 – 56, Queenstown 1865 (at least) – BU 08.1878

WOLFE (1920) SM DS
Ex MONTCALM, ex AMC, conv to SM DS at Baltimore 05.1942 – 01.1943. Re Cd 01.02.1943 – 3 SM Clyde 03.43, to Eastern Fleet/ refit Hebburn 08.04.44, 2 SM Trinco 09.44 – 07.11.45, Malta GC long refit 01.46, then Malta GC 1 SM 01.03.46 – sail for UK 20.10.47. Gareloch 1947, res Forth 1948, to MOT for disposal 22.08.50, BU 24.10.52

WOODBRIDGE HAVEN (1945) DS
FF, Ex LOCH TORRIDON, Cd 11.10.1945 as SM DS. To Res 21.12.45, used as target for SM Rothesay v HASTINGS 1946 – 12.53 (from 5 SM to 3 SM 25.09.47). Res Chat 15.12.53 – 55. To Med, Cd 06.08.55 – 06.59, Spore 23.10.59 - 07.63. Laid up Ports 07.63, BU 08.65

WOODCOCK (1942) Chat, Accom Sh
Sloop, accom sh 05.1948 - 12.50 (at least), BU 11.55

WOODPECKER Gosport, RNAS
Name proposed for Gosport RNAS 1945, but SISKIN (qv) used instead

WOODVALE
In NL 1946 – could ref to place – see RINGTAIL II

WOOLLOOMOOLOO Sydney, New South Wales, RN Repair Base
Cd 01.07.1945 ex GOLDEN HIND II (qv). PO 04.46
Nom DS: Tug TANAC 153 01.07.45 –

WOOLSTON (1918) Dundee, RNVR TS
DD, Wair conv, allocated Dundee as TS 14.04.39, but not conv till 09.39 so not used as TS, BU 02.47

WOOLVERSTONE Ipswich, LC Base & TE
Cd 01.01.1943, to C & M 09.07.43, ReCd 15.10.43, PO 20.02.46, resto 03.06.46
Originally 'suspense station' accom at Cat House Landing, later Harwich Yt Club and grounds of Woolverstone Hall. Harwich (Parkestone Quay) came under WOOLVERSTONE later in War.
Nom DS: NAB ROYAL PRINCESS 01.01.43 – 04.45
EMPEROR OF INDIA (ex BUNTING) 04.45 – 02.46

WOOLWICH (1912) DD DS
Cd 12.12.1913, 1 DF Home Fleet Harwich 1914, Rosyth 1915 – (1 DF and 13 DF), 13 DF Atlantic Fleet 1917 – 07.1918, 3 DF 07.1918 – 01.03.1919. Tender to TYNE at Lervick Stord (mine clearance) 27.06.1919 -(left UK 20.06.19) – 09.19, to Rosyth, acs to COLUMBINE 01.12.19. 1920 with Atlantic Fleet, RF Dev 03.02.1920 – PO 18.01.26, sold 13.07.26

WOOLWICH (1934) DD DS
Cd 28.06.1935 – to Med, Flag Rear Admiral Base Defences Med 01.1936. Red Sea 06.42 -, Arakan Coast 02.45 - 04.45, Trinco 01.45 - 05.46, Malta GC refit 06.46 - 05.47, Med 23.07.46 – 01.48 rb FORTH. SO RF Harwich 05.48 – 52 (living ship 05.48 – 12.50) (SORF v TYNE 1949 – 06.51). To Sheerness 06.51 – 26.09.51. To Rosyth refit 12.51 – 07.54. Harland & Wolff Govan 09.54. Laid up Gareloch 01.55 (HQ RF) – 04.57 (SM3 Clyde 12.56 - 06.04.57). Rosyth refit 04.57 - 08.57. SO RF Dev 23.09.57 v EURYALUS – 15.08.61 rb TYNE. Sail for BU 15.10.61

WOOLWORTH Freetown, Provisioning Hulk for Escort Forces
Ex ALFROESSA (qv) 02.1944

WORCESTER (1843) Greenhithe, Thames, TS
4th Rate, lent as TS Thames 1862 rb FREDERICK WILLIAM as WORCESTER (qv) 1876, BU 08.1885

WORCESTER (1860) Greenhithe, Thames, TS
2nd Rate, ex FREDERICK WILLLIAM, ex ROYAL FREDERICK, renamed WORCESTER 19.10.1876 - TS Greenhithe, HQ of Greenhithe section of London A/P and Administrative Centre for minewatching barges 15.07.1941 – released 11.05.45. Approved for disposal, and to be rb EXMOUTH (qv) 10.45, sold 09.07.1948, foundered 08.48, raised and BU 1953

WORCESTER (1905) Greenhithe, Thames, TS
Ex EXMOUTH, TS - req as DS 1939 – 45 (qv), renamed WORCESTER 1945, arrived Greenhithe 1946
For the period 1939 - 46 this tng was carried out ashore at Foot Cray Place, all TS on Thames being evacuated

WORCESTER (1919) Thames, Accom Sh
DD, mined 23.12.1943. Accom Sh 19.04.44, renamed YEOMAN 025.6.45 (qv), PO 31.07.1946, sold 17.09.46, handed over to BU 25.09.46

WUCHANG (1914) Spore/ Colombo/ Trinco, DS/ Accom Sh
Req as SM DS Spore 13.12.1941, escaped from Spore 02.1942. SM DS Colombo Cd 05.42, PO as independent command and Cd 29.10.42 as accom sh for LUCIA. SM 4 embarked ex ADAMANT Cd 29.05.43. Trinco 12.43 – 45. To be released 15.10.45, to DST 03.04.46

WYE (1814) Chat/Woolwich, Convict Ship
6th Rate, convict ship Chat 1828, Woolwich by 1850 – for BU 1852

WYVERN Chichester, Accom Sh
09.1942, acquired 01.01.43, laid up on Hamble/DST 08.44, no longer required, to DST for disposal 09.44, resto 01.45

X

X24 (1944) Ports, Museum SM
Midget SM, allocated DOLPHIN for Museum 05.1945 - unofficial name EXPEDITIOUS

XE8 (1943) Duxford/ Chat, Museum SM
Midget SM, bottom target to 05.1973, then Imperial War Museum at Duxford for preservation, at Chat DY 11.1995 -

YARMOUTH (1911) Falmouth, Flag
Cr, Flag Rear Admiral SM 1928, sold 1929

YEOMAN Thames, Base Ship London
Cd 19.07.1941, acs PEMBROKE IV – 31.07.1946
A/P Thames under TOWER (qv) from 01.1941
Nom DS: NAB JOSEPHINE FORD 19.07.41 – 06.45
WORCESTER (1919)DD 25.06.45 – (for BU 09.46)

YING CHOW (1905) Trinco/ Palk Strait/ Colombo, Ceylon, RIN Base
Req LC tng Ship 05.12.1942, Base ship Trinco 03.44, Base ship for Palk Strait Scheme Cd

15.01.1945 - tender to LANKA. At Trinco 05.1945, Colombo 08.45-11.45, sail for Bombay 04.11.45, PO 30.11.45, to DST 01.12.45, resto 1946

YOANJO Poole, Accom Sh
08.1942 – laid up Lymington/DST 08.44, no longer required, to DST 09.44, for disposal 05.46

YOLANDE (1894) Ports, Accom Sh
Yt, hired 1941. Balloon Supply Support Dartmouth 04.1941. Accom Sh Ports 07.42, C & M Dartmouth 07.43 - sold by DST 09.43 – but still listed as accom sh Ports 07.43 & 07.44, laid up Lymington 03.45, no longer required 06.45
Prob ref to two separate ships, one at Ports, one at Dartmouth

YORK (1807) Ports,Convict Ship
3rd Rate, convict ship 11.1819 – BU 03.1854

YORK Toronto, Ontario, Canada, RCN Base and Res Div
01.09.1939 – Cd 01.11.1941 – 01.09.1942 (as tender). 01.09.1942 – 1986 (at least) (buildings still there 1995)

YORKTOWN (1928) Base Ship
Hired 11.07.1942 for conv to Base Ship but lost 26.09.1942 before conv

YSELSTEIN Simons Town, S Africa, SAN Citizen Force Unit
Extant 09.1977

Z

ZAMA Italy, Base
One of six names allocated for bases in Italy 23.12.1943 and considered for Taranto, but not sel

ZAREFAH (1905) Gt Yarmouth, DS
Yt, Adty East Coast M/S DS by 12.1914 - 22.02.1915, rb SAGITTA, purch 05.1916, mined 08.05.1917

ZARIA (1904) Longhope, Orkney, A/P Base Orkney & Shetlands/ also Norway
Hired as RFA store carrier 11.1914. Cd 10.12.1914, completed 07.01.1915. Became A/P DS v CYCLOPS 25.01.1915 – 01.11.15 (Lerwick task to BRILLIANT), A/P DS Norway to 31.12.1915 and A/P Scapa Flow v ROYAL ARTHUR 22.03.1918 - and at Orkney as A/P DS 08.1918 (11.1918 to be rb JUPITER but cancelled) - 15.02.1919 rb VICTORIOUS. PO Lpool 05.05.1919

ZAZA (1905) Pembroke Dk/ Soton, Base/ Accom Sh
Yt, hired WI and purch 09.1939 as A/S Yt. Became accom sh Pembroke Dk for 764 Sqn 08.1941. Re - allocated as accom sh Milford Haven 10.43, laid up there pending re-allocation 03.44. Accom sh for Salvage Department 05.44. At Soton for Milford Haven 07.44. Milford Haven 09.44, Soton 10.44, sold 1948

ZEALAND Hbr Serv
3rd Rate, Dutch, seized 1796, hbr serv 05.1803, renamed JUSTITIA (qv) 19.08.1812, sold 02.11.1830

ZEALOUS (1864) Soton, CG
Ironclad, temp CG 1874 while HECTOR undergoing repairs, sold 1886

ZEALOUS (1944) Dev, Accom Sh
DD, accom sh 02.1948 – 11.1951, to Israel 07.1955

ZEBRA (1944) Harwich, Accom Sh
DD, accom sh 11.1951, BU 02.1959

ZEEBRUGGE (1945) Dev, Accom Sh
LST 3532, named 1947, Monte Bello 1952, accom sh Dev 1954 – 1960 (refits OCEAN & EAGLE), RF accom sh 1961 -, res Dev 1962 - 66, dockyard use 1967 -, sold 16.12.1974, BU 01.1975

ZENITH (1944) Chat, RF
DD, FO Commanding RF 17.09.1947 rb AUSONIA, RF living ship Chat 12.1948 - 1950, Harwich 11.1951, BU 05.1955

ZEPHYR (ZEPHER) Ports/Poole, Accom Sh
Motor Yt, accom sh Ports 08.1942, acquired 27.01.1943, at Poole by 07.43, renamed WESTWARD (qv) 05.44

ZETLAND (1942) Soton, Accom Sh
DD, HQ Ship for Solent RNVR 10.12.1946 – 09.04.47 rb DERG (see WESSEX), to R No N 09.1954, BU 1965

ZITA (1894) Iceland, Accom Sh
Yt, hired 1941, accom sh 03.1941 – 06.44, mooring hulk 1944 – 07.46
Used by RAF Coastal Command as accom sh Reydarfjordur, Iceland to 09.45 (at least)

ZOBAL Chichester, Accom Sh
Ex TAURUS 04.1943 –

ZUIDERKRUIS Colombo/ Addu Atoll, DS
Dutch – Colombo 28.11.1943-, Addu Atoll 01.44-

ZZ 23 Levant, Accom Sh for M/S Flot 251 – 1st Part
Cd 14.12.1944 – PO 30.11.45 in Trieste

ZZ 24 Levant, Accom Sh for M/S Flot 251 – 2nd Part
Cd 30.01.1945 – Disposed of 08.1946

ZZ 25 Levant, Accom Sh for M/S Flot 252 – 3rd Part
12.1944 -Not Cd – 08.1946 at Pt Said awaiting disposal

ZZ 26 Levant, Accom Sh for M/S Flot 252 – 4th Part
12.1944 – not Cd – 08.1946 at Pt Said awaiting disposal

Gazetter

Places are listed in alphabetical order, with places 'abroad' listed by country. Where two ships of the same name were located in the same area, only one entry is included. For convenience the following 'conurbations' have been included:

Forth	Bo'ness, Edinburgh, Grangemouth, Granton, Leith, Pt Edgar, Rosyth, N and S Queensferry
Greenock	Glasgow and Greenock areas
Harwich	Mouths of Stour and Orwell
Humber	Hull, Immingham
Medway	Chatham, Gillingham, Rochester, Sheerness
Mersey	Birkenhead, Liverpool, Rock Ferry
Pembroke Dk	Milford, Milford Haven, Pembroke
Plymouth	Devonport, Mt Edgcumbe, Manadon, Newton Ferrers, Noss Mayo, Plymouth, St Budeaux, Saltash, Stonehouse, Tamerton, Torpoint, Wembury
Portland	Portland & Weymouth
Portsmouth	Eastney, Fareham, Gosport, Havant, Hayling, Lee-on-Solent, Northney, Portsmouth, Southsea, Southwick
Scapa Flow	All the Orkney Area
Tyne	Hebburn, Newcastle-upon-Tyne, N & S Shields, Tynemouth

A

Abbotsinch – SANDERLING

Aberdeen – BACHANTE, CLYDE, CRESCENT II, NAIRN, WINCHESTER;

RNAS 01.1916 -; Medical Demob Centre closed 20.12.1919; Radio Sta 09.1928; RNTU at Gordon's College (closed 31.07.1946)/ Aberdeen Wireless College/ Wood St, Torry to CO RN Tng Centre by 07.1944; DEMS Tng Sch closed by 04.07.1945

Aberdour (Fife) – Operational HQ Rear Admiral (SM) established Corriemar 09.1939 – to Northway, London 03.1940

Acharacle (Argyll) – DORLIN

ADDU ATOLL – GLEN FORBES, HAITAN, HIGHFLYER, MARAGA, MATIANNA, PORT Q, PORT T, PORT ZQ, ZUIDERKRUIS

ADEN – British Colony 1937, Independent 29.11.1967 – CHEERFUL, DORIS, DUFFERIN, DULLISK COVE, EURYALUS, GLOUCESTER III, HOLM SOUND, LAOMEDON, LUCIA, NORFOLK III, PROSERPINE, RAPAX, SHEBA;

Naval Base 1839. Radio Sta to be built 12.1914; RNO closed 16.10.1919; RNAS to remain under C-in-C E Indies 12.1941 – to Kilindini 03.42.

ADMIRALTY ISLANDS – 10.1884 New Guinea British Protectorate, 16.09.1975 Independent – DEER SOUND, NABARON, PEPYS, RESOURCE, SEEADLER, TARANGAU

AEGEAN – BACCHUS, BLENHEIM, CHALKIS, CORDELA, PELORUS, ST GEORGE, THESEUS, WHITEHEAD;

RNAS Imbros , Kassandra (Mudros), Mitylene (Mudros), Stavros & Thasos 03.1918 Milo to be abandoned 12.1918; all but Lemnos closed 04.1919; Naval Base Syra closed 01.10.1919

Ainsdale-on-Sea (Southport) – QUEEN CHARLOTTE

Aldeburgh – RNAS 03.1916-03.1918

Alexandria (Dunbartonshire) – VERNON – RN Torp Depot closed 04.01.1971

Almondbank (Perth) – RN Aircraft Workshop post WW II - extant 1992

ALGERIA – BYRSA, CANNAE, CORIOLANUS, CYCLOPS, ELISSA, GEORGE II, HAMILCAR, HANNIBAL & II, MAIDSTONE, RAZORBILL, SCIPIO, SIDI IFNI, VIENNA:

Also RNAS at Tafar Oui WW II(see COR-

MORANT II). CF Base closed 25.08.1944; Algiers NAD closed 26.05.1945

Alsager (Stoke on Trent) – EXCALIBUR, TIGER'S WHELP

Alton – MNBDO II

Angle (Pembs) – GOLDCREST

Anglesey – CONWAY, RNAS WWI (03.1916)

ANTARCTICA Base A established Pt Locroy, Graham Land 02.1944 – Op Tabarin

Anthorn (Cumberland) – NUTHATCH

Antrim Bay – Lough Neagh, new torp range approved 02.1943

Appledore – APPLEDORE, HANTONIA, MARATHON, PRESIDENT WARFIELD:

USN Ampibious Tng Base Cd 29.07.1943 – PO 25.05.44

Arbroath – CONDOR

Ardglass Co Down, see Strangford

Ardrishaig – ORCA, SEAHAWK, STAR OF INDIA

Ardrossan – FORTITUDE & II, PACTOLUS

Arrochar – RN Torp Range 04.1912 – 19.12.1986

Arthog – MNBDO II

ASCENSION IS – ASCENSION, ATTENTION, CORMORANT, FLORA, INDEPENDENCIA, MAEANDER, TORPTOISE; -NOIC withdrawn 03.07.1945; Radio Sta closed 21.07.1945,

Ashford (Kent) – FERRET

Ashington (Northumberland) – RNAS WWI

Atwick (Yorks) – RNAS WWI

Auchengate – DUNDONALD & II

Auldbar (Angus) – RNAS WWI

Aultbea (Loch Ewe) – AMBITIOUS, CORONIA, FLORA, HELICON, ILLUSTRIOUS, IOLAIRE, JEANNE ET GENEVIEVE, PORT A, VANESSA; USN Port Office Loch Ewe De-Cd 30.11.1944

AUSTRALIA - Commonwealth established 1901 - RAN approved 10.07.1911, Fleet Status 01.01.1949 (see also New Guinea)

General – BANGALOW, ORLANDO, POWERFUL, PROTECTOR, UPOLU

Adelaide – CERBERUS IV, ENCOUNTER, OVENS, TORRENS

Bankstown - NABBERLEY

Brisbane – BRISBANE, DIAMANTINA, DULLISK COVE, FLAMBOROUGH HEAD, FURNEAUX & II, MILDURA, MORETON, NABSFORD, PENGUIN IV, RAME HEAD

Cairns – CAIRNS, KURANDA, PLATYPUS

Canberra – HARMAN

Darwin – COONAWARRA, DULLISK COVE, MELVILLE, PENGUIN V, PLATYPUS

Fremantle & Cockburn Sound – ADAMANT, CERBERUS V, DEER SOUND, HOLM SOUND, LEEUWIN, MAIDSTONE, OVENS, PARKES, STIRLING, WHANG PU: Henderson Naval Base – name allocated 1913 Woodman's Pt, Cockburn Sound – delayed by WW I and cancelled

Hobart – ANSON, CERBERUS VI, CURLEW, DERWENT, HUON, TEAL

Holmbrook (NSW) – OTWAY

Jervis Bay – CRESWEELL, FRANKLIN, NABSWICK

Launceston – NELSON

Maryborough – NABSTOCK

Meeandah (Queensland) - NABREEKIE

Melbourne – (including Geelong & Williamstown) – BEACONSFIELD, BURDEKIN, CASTLEMAINE, CERBERUS & III, DEER SOUND, KOOPA, LONSDALE & II, MALLOW, NELSON, ORARA, PLATYPUS II, QUIBERON

Newcastle – MAITLAND, ORARA

New Cape – HAROLD E HOLT

Nowra – ALBATROSS, NABBINGTON, NABSWICK

Pt Stephens – ASSAULT, PING WO

Scholfields – ALBATROSS II, NABSTOCK, NABTHORPE, NARIMBA, NIRIMBA,

Sydney – ALERT, CULGOA, DEER SOUND, DULLISK COVE, ENCOUNTER, GOLDEN HIND & I – III, GREAT BRITAIN, KARA KARA, KOOMPARTOO, KUTTABUL & II, MINDARI, NELSON, ONSLOW, OTWAY, PENGUIN & II, PIONEER, PLATYPUS, PSYCHE, RUSHCUTTER, VAMPIRE, WATERHEN, WATSON, WOOLLOOMOOLOO : Office of BRNO closed 30.06.1948

Thursday Island – BRISBANE, CARPENTARIA, PENGUIN IV

Torokina – LUSAIR

Townsville – MAGNETIC

Whyalla - WHYALLA

Woodside (Victoria) – Omega Navigation Sta acquired for low frequency communications by RAN 03.1998

Avonmouth – see Bristol

Ayr – WAGTAIL -USN CDB Heathfield closed 15.07.1945, vacated 18.07.1945

AZORES - ALACRITY, CHANTICLEER, HESPERIDES, LUSITANIA & II & III, SAON

B

Bacton – RNAS WWI (03.1916 - 03.1918-at least)

BAHAMAS – CORAL HARBOUR, MATTHEW TOWN INAGUA

Bahrein – see Persian Gulf

Baku – THESEUS II

Ballyhalbert – CORNCRAKE

Ballykelly – SEA EAGLE, SEALION

Ballyliffan (Co Donegal) – RNAS WWI

Banff – Lent to RNAS for bombing 1947

BANGLADESH – formed 03.1971 ex East Pakistan – BHATIARY, HAJI MOHSIN, HIRON POINT, ISSA KHAN, KAPTAI, MONGLA, NUMONGLA, PATENGA, SHAHEED MOAZZIN, TITUMIR, ULKA

Bangor (Caernarvonshire) – CLIO & RNAS WWI

Bantry – AURORA, COLLINGWOOD, DEVASTATION, DREADNOUGHT, SHANNON, VALIANT – see also Limerick

BARBADOS – Coast Guard 1973, Naval Arm of dfence Forces 1979 - WILLOUGHBY FORT

Barlow – Nr Selby, Yorks – RNAS WWI

Barmouth – MNBDO II

Barrow-in-Furness – BALINDERRY, CLIO, CYSNE II, DOVEY, FIREWORK, HAZARD, MINIDO, PLUTO, RIFLEMAN, WATERWITCH:

RNR Battery 1882;RNAS WWI (03.16 - 03.18 at least); RF ex Preston 31.08.1945 – to close 04.10.1947and also 1953 (for 21 ships, Hunt DD, River FF) - Devonshire Basin - see DOVEY - 24.01.1964

Barry – LUCIFER, RINALDO, RF 02.1954 – 29.08.1960

Basra – Navy House closed 10.05.1919; Naval estab closed down 01.1946

Beachy Head – RN Signal Sta 1923 – closed 31.08.1950

Beaulieu – MASTODON

Beccles – HORNBILL II

Bedhampton – see Portsmouth

Beith – RNAD – planned 07.1941, approved 11.1942

Belfast – ANTRIM, CAROLINE & II, DELHI, GADWALL, GANNET III, GIBRALTAR, GRAMPIAN, MAIDSTONE, NIOBE II, OSPREY, PEGASUS, PLYM, RAME HEAD, SPEY:

US Port Office closed 15.06.1945; FOIC Northern Ireland (Belfast Castle) Flag down 20.11.1945; RN Aircraft Yard ex RN Aircraft Maint Yd by 1952 – to RAF 02.07.1973.

BELGIUM – AMBITIOUS, CFMU I, LANDSEER, ROYAL ATHELSTAN, ROYAL EDMUND & II, ROYAL RICHARD: - Naval Base closed 07.10.1919 (Ostend & Zeebrugge)

Bembridge – BLAZER: RNAS WWI (Harbour & Foreland) (03.1916 - 03.1918 - at least)

Benbecula – RAF - Lodger Unit

Benson – RAF - Lodger post WWII

Berehaven – AMBROSE, VULCAN: -Separate A/P Base 05.07.1917; Kite Balloon Sta allocated to Air Ministry 14.02.1919 but not required; WWI Base closed 19.04.1919

Bere Island – Radio Sta 1901 –

BERMUDA – 1684 Crown Government, 06.1968 Self Government. ANTELOPE, BERMUDA, CASSIUS, COROMANDEL, DESPATCH, DOTTEREL, DROMEDARY, FORWARD, HOTSPUR, IRRESISTIBLE, MALABAR & II & III, MEDWAY, MINSTREL, MUTINE, PROVIDER, RESOLUTE, ROMNEY, ROYAL OAK, RUPERT, SCORPION, SHAH, SLANEY, SOMERS ISLES, TENEDOS, TERROR, THAMES, VIPER, VIRGINIA, WEYMOUTH: - ' Y' Sta closed 31.05.1949, Radio Sta equipment removed, Sta remained dormant 06.1950

Berwick – DF Sta 1923 – 24

Bircham Newton – RAF – Lodger unit

Birkenhead – see Mersey

Birmingham – FORWARD

BLACK SEA – AQUARIUS, CAESAR, GRAFTON, THESEUS, TULA, VOLGA

Blacksod – A/P Base moved to Kellybegs 06.1915

Bletchley Park – STATION X

Blyth – ELFIN & II, NETTLE, TITANIA; Naval Base closed 22.12.1919

Bodfford – Nr Llangefni, Anglesey, RNAS WWI

Bognor Regis – ST BARBARA

Bo'ness – see Forth

Bootle Station – Cumberland – MACAW

Boston (Lincs) – ARBELLA

Bournemouth – EXCELLENT II

British Pacific Fleet – NIGER

Braintree – CICERO: RN Barracks disposed of 07.1956

Bramcote (Nuneaton) – GAMECOCK, GODWIT

Bratton – GODWIT

Brawdy – GOLDCREST & II, ST DAVID

BRAZIL – CRESCENT, EGMONT, MADAGASCAR

Bridlington – RNO at 'The Gainsboro', 2 Fort Tce 03.1941

Bridport – RNAS WWI (to 03.1918)

Brightlingsea – AEROLITE, CITY OF PERTH, DUCHESS OF ROTHESAY, HELDER, HELENE, NEMO, TERMINIST, WALLAROO, WILDFIRE: -

Gunfleet Naval Base abolished - to be called Naval Base Brightlinngsea 10.1915; Coastal Flot Base 20.12.1940 (no name) under NEMO; Office of ML Chat to the Manor House 03.1941.

Brighton – BRIGHTON, CAVALIER, VERNON: -RNR Battery 1877 – 1906; Royal Sussex Hotel was req as rest home for Polish Naval Ratings 03.1942.

Bristol – BRISTOL, BRITANNIA IV, CABOT, CADMUS, DAEDALUS, FLYING FOX, FORMIDABLE, LOCUST, LUCIFER, PRESIDENT III, VANSITTART: -RNAS 03.1918 (AA position)

Brixham – VERNON (D): -Capt ML at Rockvilla 03.1941; ML/CF Base WWII 07.1943 - 09.44; CF Base to be closed soon after 09.1944; ML equipping Base closed 03.10.1944; DEMS closed by 07.1945

Brooklands - AA Position 03.1918

Brox Fare (Notts) – Tented Camp under CABBALA 07.1942

Bude – RNAS WWI

Bugle – US Ammo Depot 02.1944 - closed and vacated 15.07.1945

Buncrana – BERYL, HECLA & II, IMPLACABLE, PLATYPUS, VULCAN: -Kite Balloon Sta to Air Ministry 14.02.1919

Bungay – EUROPA II, HORNBILL II

Burford – (Oxford) - RN Sch of Music 1948 – 30.09.1949 (see Deal)

Burgh Castle – (Norfolk) - RNAS WWI to 03.1918

Burghfield – DAUNTLESS, PEMBROKE III

BURMA – From India 1937, Independent 04.01.1948

BARRACUDA, CHINTHE, FT14, GOMBROON, HEINRICH JESSEN, RATANABON, WOOLWICH; CF Bases Teknaaf (Advanced Base 02.1944 - 10.44) and Rangoon (by 05.45); Burma RNVR to RN operational control 05.07.1944, RNO Arakan lapse and bases at Akyab Kyanpyu & Jaffna closed 11.1945

Burnbeg – Radio Sta 1921 - 22

Burnham-on-Crouch – ALASTOR, ST MATHEW, WESTCLIFF III: -RNAS WWI; CG and Radio Sta 1920-22

Burscough – NIGHTJAR, RINGTAIL

Bursledon – see Soton

Bush Barn – KESTREL

Bute – See Pt Bannatyne

Butley (Suffolk) – RNAS WWI

Butt of Lewis – Signal Sta 01.01.1909 –

C

Caldale – (Orkneys) – see Scapa Flow

Calmore – BD Depot, Loperwood Manor vacated 31.08.1950

Calshot – RNAS 29.03.1913 – 04.1918 (to RAF) - between wars; LC Base (CO Naval Unit – CONU) 10.1942 – 01.1945 when reduced to RN Unit in RAF Calshot; RN Signal Sta only by 03.1945

Campbeltown – FERMOY, LANDRAIL & II, MAJESTA, MERLIN, MINONA, NIMROD, PLATYPUS, THAMES, VIGILANT, WATERRAIL

CAMEROONS – ASTRAEA

CANADA – Dominion created 1867, RCN established 04.05.1910. Unified Defence Force 01.02.1968

Alberta NONSUCH, TECUMSEH

British Columbia – ALGERINE, BURRARD, CAPE BRETON, CHARLOTTETOWN, CHATHAM, CHAUDIERE, DISCOVERY, ESQUIMALT, GIVENCHY & II, MALAHAT, MASSET, MATSQUI, MONTREAL CIRCLE, NADEN & II & III, PATRICIAN, QUADRA, RAINBOW, ROCKCLIFFE, ROYAL ROADS, SAULTE STE MARIE, SHEARWATER & II, SKIDEGATE, SPURN POINT, STONE FRIGATE, SUMAS, VANCOUVER, VENTURE: Esquimalt Base ('Squibbly') 29.07.1856 v Valparaiso – 1904 (reduced to cadre) - re-open 1911 (stores ex Chile). RCN College from Halifax to Kingston 1917 and to Esquimalt 1918, closed 1921

Cape Breton – Convoy office Sydney closed 30.11.1918

Manitoba – CHIPPAWA, CHURCHILL, GIMLI

New Brunswick – BRUNSWICKER, CAPTOR & II, COVERDALE. Depot for servicing vessels equipped with Adty net defences established 11.1943

Newfoundland – AVELON & II-IV, BRITON, CABOT, CALYPSO, CARIBOU, FORTH, GANDER, GREENWICH, PRESERVER. Radio Sta to be built St John's 25.12.1914

Nova Scotia – ACACIA, ALBRO LAKE, ALDERGROVE, AMBROSE, ANNAPOLIS, ASSINIBOINE, BLANDFORD, BRATFORD, BUXTON, CANADA, CAPE BRETON, CAPE SCOTT, CHAMPLAIN, CHARNY, CHICOUTIMI, COLUMBIA, CORNWALLIS, DIANA, FORTH, FRASER, GANNET, GRANBY, GUELPH, HAIDA, HALIFAX, HALIGONIAN, HALO, HAMILTON, HOWARD, INFLEXIBLE, IROQUOIS, KINGS, LA HULLOISE, LANSDOWNE, MILLCOVE, MULGRAVE, NEWPORT CORNER, NIAGARA, NIOBE, OLYMPUS, PATRIOT, PEREGRINE, PRESERVER, PROTEC-

TOR & II, PROVIDER, PYRAMUS, SACKVILLE, SAGUENAY, ST CLAIR, ST CROIX, ST FRANCIS, SAKER & II, SAMBRO, SCOTIAN, SEABORN & II, SEABORNE, SEAGULL, SHEARWATER, SHELBURNE,, STADACONA & I – III, TRINITY, VENTURE & II: Halifax Dockyard reduced to cadre 1904 – re-opened 1910. RCN College opened Halifax 10.1910, closed 1917 (due to explosion in port) - to Kingston 1918 then to Esquimalt. Halifax called 'Slackers' WW II.

North West Territories – AKLAVIT, INUVIK, PADLOPING ISLAND

Ontario – BYTOWN & II, CARLETON, CATARAQUI, CONESTOGA, FALKLANDS, FRASER, GLOUCESTER, GRIFFON, HAIDA, HOWARD, HUNTER, ONTARIO, PATRIOT, PREVOST, STAR & II, STONE FRIGATE, TILLICUM, WARATAH, YORK

Prince Edward Island – QUEEN CHARLOTTE

Quebec – CARTIER, CHALEUR & I & II, D'IBERVILLE, DONNACONA & II, FORT RAMSAY, HOCHELAGA & II, MONTCALM, MONTREAL & II, QUEBEC, ST HYACINTHE

Saskatchewan – QUEEN, UNICORN

Capel (Kent) Nr Folkestone - RNAS WWI - small airship sta 05.1915

Cape Wrath – RN Shore Signal Sta 1923 – 28

Cardiff – ALGERINE, CAMBRIA, CURACOA, DERG, HAMADRYAD, HAVANNAH, LUCIFER, THISBE, WILTON: - Base closed 12.02.1920 & 15.01.1946. FOIC Cardiff closed 09.11.1945, Flag down 23.11.45,became NOIC -NOIC lapse 31.01.1946. RF 1952 (20 ships increased to 28 1953) – 29.08.1960. CO RF S Wales in Imperial Building, Mt Stewart Sq, Cardiff 15.09.1956.

Cardington – RNAS WWI

Carnarvon – RNR Battery 1880 – 1909

CASPIAN SEA – CAESAR, MANTIS & II, THESEUS II & III

Castle Toward – Argyll – ARARAT, BRONTOSAURUS

Castletownbere – CG & Radio Sta 1921 - 22

Catfirth – Zetland – RNAS WWI to 03.1918

Cattewater – see Plymouth

CEYLON - Colony 1802. VR from RN 01.06.1946. Dominion 04.02.1948. R Ceylon Navy formed 09.12.1950, changed from White Ensign 09.12.1955. Ceylon became Sri Lanka 22.05.1972

ADAMANT, AIKLAM, ANDERSON, AORANGI, ARROGANT, BAMBARA, BARRACUDA, BHERUNDA, BULLFROG, CARADOC, CHATHAM II, CITY OF LONDON, DEER SOUND, DULLISK COVE, EFFINGHAM II, ELARA, ESAMBARA, FLAMBOROUGH HEAD, GAMANU, GAMUNU, GANUM, GANUNU, GEMUNU, GLOUCESTER II, GOULD, HATHI, HAWKINS II, HIGHFLYER, HOLM SOUND, JUMNA, KEDAH, LANDGUARD, LANDSWELL, LANKA & I – III, LUCIA, MAIDSTONE, MAYINA, MONARA, MULLION COVE, NORFOLK II, ORLANDO, PLANCIUS, RAJALIYA, RANGALA, RENGALLA, RUHUNA, SAPPHIRE, SERUWA, SITA, SOBER ISLAND, SOUTHAMPTON II, STATIONS Q & T, TARANTULA, TISSA, UKUSSA, UVA, VIJAYA, WOLFE, WOOLWICH, WUCHANG, YING CHOW, ZUIDERKRUIS:

Dockyard reduced to cadre 1904. Civil airport Ratmalana used 06.1941 (by RAF 06.42). RN Lodgers in China Bay 01.1940. FRU at Minneriya Air Sta 01.44 – 03.44, then China Bay 03.44 – 12.47 – to RN - RNAS Trinco 15.11.44 - RNAS Kantali developed and suspended 12.44, returned to RAF 11.1950. Radio Sta to be built 25.12.1914. Radio Sta Colombo & Trinco to be ready by autumn 1943. Radio Sta Perkar to 1957 and Kortugoola to 1962. RM Depot from Colombo to Trinco 16.05.45

CHANNEL IS – KESTREL: -Base on Guernsey closed 20.09.1919. RNO closed 30.01.1946

Charlesfield RNAD to close 1959

Charlton Horethorne – HERON & II

Chatham – see Medway

Chathill (Northumberland) – RNAS WWI

Chelmsford – RNAS WWI (10.1915)

Chichester – BLACK EMELLE, CELTIC, ELSIE, LADY GAY, PEACE, ST ASAPH, SEA SERPENT,

TAURUS, WANDERLUST, WHITE OWL, WHITE STAR, WYVERN, ZOBAL

Chickerell – Dorset – RNAS WWI and between wars

Chicksands – Beds – FERRET

CHILE – LIFFEY, NAIAD, NEREUS: - Valparaiso rb Esquimalt as RN Base 29.07.1856. Dockyard stores to Esquimalt 1903

CHINA – AMBROSE, BEE, MEDWAY, PORT W, TITANIA: -Naval Base at Wei Hei Wei 1898

Chingford – RNAS 1913 – 03.1918

Christchurch – RAVEN

CHRISTMAS ISLAND – Pacific – RESOLUTION

Cleethorpes – CG Signal Sta 1909, Radio Sta to 1921

Clifdon – CO Galway – Radio Sta 1908 -

Cloughey – Ireland – Radio Sta 02.1916

Cluntoe – GANNET

Clyde – AJAX, AL RAWDAH, AURORA, BALMORAL, BEN NEVIS, BLACK PRINCE, CASERNE BIROT, CUMBERLAND, DRAKE, DWARF, EMPRESS, HARTLAND POINT, HECLA, HOGUE,

IOLAIRE, LION, LORNA DOONE, MALAYA, MECKLENBURG, MINERVA, MULL OF GALLOWAY, NARCISSUS, NETTLE, PRINCE EDWARD, PRINCE GEORGE, PRINCESS MARY, RATTLER, SPURN POINT, TOREADOR, VALOROUS, VIKING, VULCAN, WOLFE, WARRIOR, WOOLWICH:

Main Fleet Base 10.1939. Glenarbuck Camp, Bowling, RIN personnel (see PRINCE EDWARD & PRINCE GEORGE) – to Polish Naval Camp 10.1943. SO RF in Clyde by 01.1945

Cobham – TE for Fairmile ML Engine Room ratings WWII (05.1940-)

COCOS IS – BROWN, JAMES, HOLM SOUND: -Base & RAF Sta established 21.04.1945 - naval estab closed 20.05.1946

Coleraine – Base closed 03.09.1940, MLs & MA/SBs to Londonderry

CORFU – AQUARIUS, BACCHUS, LATONA: -Kite & Balloon Sta closed 12.1918, Naval Base closed 03.02.1919 - hosp remained – last British personnel (RM Contingent) out 28.06.1919. Temp CF Base WWII

Cork – ACTAEON, CROCODILE, SURPRISE, TRENT

Corpach – Invernesshire, DD Repair Base 12.1941 – to be reduced by 08.1945

Corsham – Wilts – ROYAL ARTHUR

CORSICA – SARDO: -CF Advanced Base Bastia 11.1943 - , Calvi by 05.44 – both closed by 09.44

Coverhithe – Suffolk – RNAS 03.1916 – 03.1918

Coventry – MERCIA

Cowdray Park – Midhurst – DAEDALUS

Cowes – CHASSEUR 106, DILIGENTE, LOTUS, OSBORNE, TORMENTOR II

Crail – Fife – BRUCE, JACKDAW

Cramlington – RNAS WWI (not completed)

Cranwell – Lincs – RNAS TE – Cd 10.12.1915 independent command - 03.18

CRETE – MNBDO I, PELORUS, SYVERN

Crimond – See Rattray

Cromarty Firth – COLUMBINE, EILEEN, EVENING STAR, PRINCE, SOBO, SUTOR, THALIA, TYNE

RNAS (1912 –) and Radio Sta (closed 12.1919)

Culcheth – see Warrington

Culdrose – CHOUGH, SEAHAWK

Culham – HORNBILL

Culmhead – Church Stanton – RAF – Lodger

Culver Cliff – Isle of Wight – Radio Sta 1909 – 28

Cuper – Fife – Radio Sta redundant 02.1964

CYPRUS – Crown Colony 1925, Independent 16.08.1960 (2 Sovereign Bases)

APHRODITE & II, CORDELA, NILE, PROMETHEUS: -Naval Base 1878. Famagusta Naval Base closed 30.04.1919. CF Base Kyrenia mid 1941. Famagusta established as a defended port 07.1941, Naval Base closed 01.12.1945.

CYRENAICA – MOSQUITO III: -Beghazi to minor port status 10.1944

D

Dakar – BACCHANTE

Dale – GOLDCREST: -RNAD sub depot close 1964/65

DANUBE - GLOWWORM

DARDANELLES – ADAMANT, BELNHEIM, RELIANCE

Darley – FOREST MOOR

Dartmouth – ABERDONIAN, BELFORT, BOADICEA, BRITANNIA & II & III, BRYONY, CICALA, COMPTON CASTLE, DARTMOUTH & II & III, EFFINGHAM, ESPIEGLE, FARADAY, FIREWORK, HAWKE, HIGHFLYER, HINDOSTAN, ILTON CASTLE, KILORAN, KINGSWEAR CASTLE, POMONE, ST HELIER, SAXIFRAGE, SPEY, VERNON(D), WAVE, WESTWARD HO!

Raiding Sqn Base projected 23.09.1940. USNAAB Cd 24.12.1943 - final de-Cd 15.05.1945

Dawlish – CG Sta 1921

Deal – RN Sch of Music by 1922 – 01.06.1940 (to RMB Plym) and 30.09.1949 ex Burford – became RM Sch of Music 01.09.1950 – 29.03.1996 (tx to NELSON)

Defford – DAEDALUS, RAF – Lodger 01.06.1944-

DEMERERA – Radio Sta to be built 15.12.1914 – closed 1922

DENMARK - ANHOLT, CFMU 2, ROYAL PHILLIPPA, WAR WING

Deptford – BACCHANTE, BRAZEN, BREVDRAGEREN, DASHER, DEDAIGNEUSE, DISCOVERY, DOVER, DRIVER, GRAMPUS, HEROINE, HYAENA, MONMOUTH, PRESIDENT, SOLEBAY, THORN, TOWER, WEYMOUTH: -Royal Victoria Yd 1742 – 30.06.1961. RN Store Depot to close 1985

Detling - RNAS 03.1916 – to Military 03.04.1917. RAF Lodger 1940-41

Devil's Point – Radio Sta 1928

Diego Suarez - BNO lapse 07.03.1946

Doagh Island – Co Donegal – RNAS WWI

Docking – RAF Lodger 1942 – 44

Donibristle – COCHRANE II, MERLIN & II & III: - RNAS WWI - airfield. RN Aircraft Repair Yd – see MERLIN

Doonfoot – Ayr – SCOTIA

Dounreay – Caithness – SISKIN, TERN II, VULCAN

Dover – ARROGANT, ATTENTIVE & II & III, HAZARD, LYNX & II, PEMBROKE V, SANDHURST, STAR OF FREEDOM, SURF, TARANSAY, WASP: - RN Shore Signal Sta Dover Pier 1909-28. RNAS WWI – 2 (increase to 3 03.1916) - Gustan Rd 12.1914 – 03.1918, Marine Parade 11.1914-. Experimental Base closed 01.1919. Coastal MB Base WWI to be sub base OSEA 23.01.1919 - 03.21A/P Base closed 31.03.1919. Naval Base closed 15.10.1919. Dockyard closed 31.03.1920.

DOWNS – HOLDFAST, SURPRISE

Drem – MERLIN, NIGHTHAWK

Droxford – Soberton Towers – TE for Telegraphists, tender to VICTORY 10.1941. WRNS TE 1943 under VICTORY III/MERCURY

Dublin – MERMAID: - RNAS WWI. Naval Base closed 16.05.1919

Dundee – ACQUISITION, AMBROSE, BRILLIANT, CAMPERDOWN, CIRCE, CONDOR & II, CRESSY, FORTH, JEWEL, MARS, TAEPING, UNICORN & II, WOOLSTON: -RNAS 1912 - 03.1918

Dunfermline - SCOTIA

Dungeness – RN Shore Signal Sta 1924 – 24.03.51 - revert to War Office 1956

Dunino – Fife – JACKDAW II, MERLIN III: -RNAS WWI

Dunnet Head – RN Shore Signal Sta 1923 – 03.06.1951. AES 6 (Air Ministry) 07.1944

Dunoon – ARARAT, BRONTOSAURUS, CURLEW, NIMROD, OSPREY, PRINCESS MARIA JOSE, SAREPTA

Dunstaffnage – Nr Oban – DD Repair Base 12.1941 – to be reduced 08.1945, removed by end 1956

Duxford – HERON, STICKLEBACK, XE 8

E

Eaglescliffe – Spare Parts Distribution Centre closed 31.03.1997

East Fortune – E Lothian – RNAS 03.1916 – 03.1918

East Haven – Angus – CONDOR & II, DOTTEREL, PEEWIT

EAST INDIES – Station closed 07.09.1958 -ARTIFEX, ATREUS, AUSONIA, BEACHY HEAD, CORBRAE, DERBY HAVEN, HIGHFLYER, LUCIA, MANCHESTER CITY, MULL OF GALLOWAY, NIGER, SPRINGTIDE, WAVENEY.

East Meon – Nr Petersfield – MERCURY

Eastbourne – MARLBOROUGH, ST BEDES: - RNAS 03.1915 – 03.1918. RNVR Sub Unit closed 1931

Eastchurch – ACTAEON, PEMBROKE II: -RNAS WWI – 03.1918

Eastcote – RNAS WWI

Eastleigh – see Soton

Eastney – see Ports

Eaton – Chester – BRITANNIA, SANGOLA

Eccleshall – see Millmeece

Edinburgh – See Forth

Eglinton – GANNET, SEA EAGLE

EGYPT – 1914 British Protectorate, 1922 Independent, 1952 King Farouk deposed, 1953 declared Republic, 24.03.1956 British removed – last British troops out 13.06.1956

ABOUKIR, ARIADNE, BACOS, CEASAR, CANOPUS & II, CARLISLE, CORDELA, DUKE, DUMANA, ENDEAVOUR, ERIDGE, EURYALUS, FERMOY II, FOINAVON, FORTH, GRAFTON, GREBE, HANNIBAL, HIFAISTOS, IONIA, KATE LEWIS, MAIDSTONE II, MARTIAL, MEDWAY, MNBDO I, MOSQUITO & II, NADIA, NAPIER, NILE & II, OSIRIS, PHAROS, PHOENIX, PORT SAID, POSEIDON, PRINCESS ELIZABETH, PROMETHEUS, RAGEA, RAJEA, SALTASH, SAN GORGIO, SAUNDERS & II & III, SPHINX, STAG (Various), VULAN. ZZ 25, ZZ 26.

M/S at RN Depot Pt Said ex HANNIBAL 12.1917 tx to DUKE 01.07.1918. Alexandria & Pt Said Kite Balloon Sta being closed 04.1919. Port convoy office Alexandria closed 15.09.1919. Net Defences Depot Adabiah Bay & Net Defence Service Sta at BD Depot Alexandria approved 04.1943.

Emsworth – CASERN BIR HACHEIM

ERITREA – BULL

Essington – for Spurn Point – RN Shore Signal Sta 1901 – ceased 28.01.1950 (to CG)

Evanton – Ross & Cromarty – FIELDFARE, MERLIN, OWL: - RNAS lodger between wars

Exbury – Nr Soton – HAWKE, KING ALFRED & II, MASTODON

Exeter – PELLEW: -USN Advance Amphibious Supply Base Cd 03.02.1944 – 01.06.45

Exmouth – ALVISTA, SALCOMBE & II, TENNYSON

F

Fairlie – Ayrshire – HARBINGER, NIMROD, PIONEER

Fairlop – RNAS 03.1918

Falfield – Glos. – CABBALA

FALKLAND IS – DILIGENCE, PURSUIVANT, SHEATHBILL, TABARIN.

Radio Sta to be built 25.12.1914 - to preservation,

NOIC & Retard Party withdrawn 03.1948

Falmouth – AMBROSE, AURORA, DIXI, DREEL CASTLE, EAGLE, FORTE & 1 & IV, GANGES, GWEN MARG, IMPLACABLE, INSPECTOR GENERAL TWENT, MARGARET, MINIDO, PRINCE HENRY, PRINCESS JOSEPHINE CHARLOTTE, RELIABLE, RUSSELL, ST GEORGE, SUNBEAM II, TRIUMPH, VENTURE I, VIVID IV, YARMOUTH.

Port convoy office closed 31.12.1918. Dutch Naval College – Enys House 02.1941 – tx to Holland 04.46, vacated 05.46. Type 287 Radar Sta closed 03.44. USN Advance Amphibious Base to 31.07.1945. Title of SO RF lapse 06.49. RNO close 12.05.1950.

Coast Guard – (EAGLE 1931?), RUSSELL 01.02.1858 – 03.05.1864, ST GEORGE 04.05.1868 – 68 – to merge with Portland 1865

Farnborough – RNAS (Arnold House) 1912 – WWI

FAROES – NORTHMAN, POLAR BEAR, POLE STAR

Faslane – see Gareloch – pre invasion port to Metal Industries 15.08.1946 as breakers' yard

Fearn – MERLIN, OWL

Felixstowe – see Harwich. RNAS pre WWI and to 03.1918 Radio Sta 1920 – 27. BD closed 10.1957. Base for Res craft admin to SO RF Hythe 01.10.1955 and closed 01.08.1958 - tx to RAF.

Felpham – CG Sta 1919 – 22

FERNANDO PO – VINDICTIVE

FIJI – 12.06.1975 Naval Division formed. 10.10.1987 Republic

VENTURE, VITI: -Naval Base 1874. Radio Sta to be built 25.12.1914

Fishguard – EMERALD STAR: - RNAS 05.1917 – 03.1918

Flamborough – DF and Radio Sta 1919 - 27. RN Shore Signal Sta 1925 – 18.05.1951 – to CG

Fleetlands – see Ports. RN Aircraft Yard 05.1940 – 10.1988

Fleetwood – Sub Base WWI – closed 15.11.1919. DEMS Sch – closed by 04.07.1945

Flixton – see Bungay

Flowerdown – nr Winchester - FLOWERDOWN

Folkestone – ALLENBY, BLUEBIRD III: -RNAS 1915 – 03.1918 and Naval Base WWI – closed 15.09.1919

Ford – Sussex – DAEDALUS, PEREGRINE

Ft George – RNAS (Cromarty) 1912 – to close 05.1915 but listed 03.1916

Ft Grange - RNAS WWI

Ft William – ABERDONIAN, BOURNEMOUTH QUEEN, ORIOLE, ST CHRISTOPHER, TIERCEL

Forth - 'Conurbation' - ALONZO, AMBITIOUS, AMBROSE, ANSON, AQUARIUS, ARO, ARTIFEX, ATMAH, BLACKWOOD, BRAMBLE, BRUCE, CALEDONIA, CAMPANIA, CHEVIOT, CHEVRON, CLAVERHOUSE & II, CLYDE, COCHRANE & I-V, COLUMBINE, CONCORD, COURAGEOUS, CRESCENT, DARTMOUTH, DEER SOUND, DEVASTATION, DIDO, DODMAN POINT, DULLISK COVE, DUNCAN, DUNCANSBY HEAD, DUNDONALD, DURHAM, EASTON, EDINBURGH, EMERALD, FAVORITE, FEARLESS, FORTH, GALATEA, GIRDLE NESS, GOLDEN HIND, GREENWICH, GUNNER, HEBE, HEIMDAL, HERCULES, HOLM SOUND, HONNINGSVAAG, HOPETOUN & II, IMPERIEUSE, IRON DUKE, ITHURIEL, JULES VERNE, KENYA, KILLARNEY, KINGSCLIFF, LEANDER, LION, LOCHINVAR & II, LOFOTEN, LORD WARDEN, MAGNIFICENT, MAIDSTONE, MEDWAY QUEEN, MILNE, MULL OF KINTYRE, NARVIK, NEW ZEALAND, NEPTUNE, NIGERIA, NIGHTSWICK, PANDORA, PEMBROKE, PERSEUS, PHAROS, PINCHER, PIONEER, PLATYPUS, PRINCESS LOUISE, PROTECTOR, QUEEN OF KENT, QUEEN OF THANET, QUEENSFERRY, RAME HEAD, RAMESES, RANEN, RANPURA, RAPID, REPULSE, RODNEY, ROMULUS, ROOKE, ROSARIO, ROYAL ARTHUR, ROYAL SOVEREIGN, SAFEGUARD, ST GEORGE, SAINTES, SAPPHO, SEAGULL, SPANKER, STALKER, STOPFORD, SUNHILL, SUTLEJ, TALYBONT, TEMERAIRE, TRAFALGAR, UBIQUITY, VERNON, VULCAN, WOOLWICH.

Pt Edgar estab organised as naval establishment 11.1917. Several RNAS – Firth of Forth (to 03.1918), N Queensferry (to 03.1918), Rosyth (Seaplane – 03.1918). SM Base at Inverkeithing under construction 10.1918. DEMS Office Leith closed 24.06.1919. Naval Base Granton closed 30.11.1919. Naval Base Leith closed mid 01.1920. Rosyth Dockyard closed 07.1925 – re-opened 07.12.1938. RN Radio Sta 1923 - 28. US Port Office Leith closed 11.09.1944. A/S Fixed Defence Sta May Is closed 03.10.1945. Norwegian Naval Estab Edinburgh closed 31.05.46. RN Hospital Pt Edgar closed 31.05.1950. BD Sub Unit Grangemouth closed 10.07.1964. Pt Edgar Cdre Minor War Vessels, Mine Warfare & Diving 1992 – 07.11.95. Flag of C-in-C down 05.03.1996 (Cdre then at Faslane). Base handed over to Rosyth 2000 Ltd 31.03.1996. Pitraevie Castle to RAF 31.07.1996.

Coastguard: PEMBROKE 03.12.1856 -, EDINBURGH 01.03.1858 -, TRAFLAGAR 01.03.1864 -, DUNCAN 16.06.1867-, REPULSE 01.03.1870 -, FAVORITE 29.09.1872 -, LORD WARDEN 21.02.1876 -, DEVASTATION 07.09.1885 -, IRON DUKE 09.05.1890-, GALATEA 03.05.1893 –

12.1894 (exchange with EDINBURGH at Hull), EDINBURGH 12.1894 -, RODNEY 22.09.1897 -, ANSON 01.01.1901 - 07.1903 (re-organisation). CG Signal Sta 1909 -

Fortrose – Nr Inverness – MONSTER, ROSMARKIE

Fowey – BELFORT, ST HELIER, SISTER ANNE, VELDA: - RNR Battery 1882. DEMS Base closed by 04.07.1945. USN Advance Amphibious Tng Sub Base closed 14.06.1945

Framewood Manor – Nr Slough – accom for WRNS trainee boatwrights 1943

FRANCE ADVENTURE, ALBATROSS, ALBRIGHTON, AMBITIOUS, AETON, ASCANIUS, BACHAQUERO, BEN TABERT, CAP TOURAINE, CERES, CFMU I, CONIDAW, DACRES, DANAE, DESPATCH, DUIKER, DURBAN, FRATTON, FROBISHER, GEORGE D IRVIN, GOATHLAND, GOLD, HASLEMERE, HAWKINS, ISLE OF THANET, JUNO, KINGSMILL, KOSMOS, LAWFORD, LOCUST, MATADOR, MISOA, NITH, NYCTEA, ORIOLE, PICADOR, PORT ZB/ ZC/ ZF, RAYMONT, REDOUBTABLE, ROYAL ANNE, ROYAL CHARLES, ROYAL EDWARD, ROYAL HENRY, ROYAL JAMES, ROYAL RICHARD, ROYAL WILLIAM, ST ADRIAN, SANDOWN, SCAWFELL, SOUTHERN PRINCE, STAR OF FREEDOM, SWORD, SYLVANA, TASAJERO, THYSVILLE, TOREADOR, TRENTONIAN, WAR WING, WAVENEY.

RNAS WWI (Marquise 07.1915 -) (Boulogne) (Cherbourg 07.1917 – 03.1918)(St Pol 1917)(Dunkirk (03.1916 – 03.1918). RNAS WWII (Hyeres, Toulon – TSR Deck Landing 01.05.1940-)

Naval Base Dunkirk closed 15.04.1919, Bordeaux closed 22.04.1919.

CF Base Dunkirk WWI. CF Mobile Base Bastia (15.10.1943 - 29.06.44) (see Med).

USN Advanced Base Le Havre Cd 18.10.1944. RNO Brest left 06.09.1945. BNLO Le Havre withdrawn 18.11.45.

Fraserburgh – RAF - Lodger

Fremington – N Devon – CO Estab – Sch of CO (Beach & Boat Section) – 06.1949 – see APPLEDORE

Frinton – see Brightlingsea

Fulham – TURNSTONE

G

Galloway – CG Sta 1920-22

Galway – to be reduced 12.1918

GAMBIA – 1843 – Independent British Colony. 1965 Independent Member of Commonwealth

DUMANA, MELAMPUS: -Radio Sta Bathurst (to be built 25.12.1914) - 15.07.1921

Gare Loch – includes Faslane. ADAMANT, ALAUNIA, ARTIFEX, ATTACKER, AUSONIA, BEN LOMOND, BUCHAN NESS, CAPE WRATH, IMPERIEUSE & II, JUPITER, KENT, MAIDSTONE, MESSINA, NARVIK, NEPTUNE, PORTLAND BILL, REVENGE, RESOLUTION, REVLIS, VERNON, WAVENEY, WOLFE: - A/S Experimental Sta WWI

GERMANY - ADVENTURE, CFMU 1-3, GADFLY, ML 291, PRINCESS ALICE, PRINCESS AUGUSTA, PRINCESS IRENE, PRINCESS LOUISA, ROYAL ADELAIDE, ROYAL ALBERT, ROYAL ALEXANDRA, ROYAL ALFRED, ROYAL CAROLINE, ROYAL CHARLOTTE, ROYAL EDGAR, ROYAL ELEANOR, ROYAL HAROLD, ROYAL HENRIETTA, ROYAL HENRY, ROYAL KATHERINE, ROYAL PHILLIPPA, ROYAL PRINCE, ROYAL RUPERT, WAR WING

GIBRALTAR – ANDROMACHE, ARIGUANI, BLACK DRAGON, BORDE, CALCUTTA, CALPE, CHILDERS, CORMORANT & II, DEVASTATION, EURYALUS, GIBEL DERSA, GOSHAWK, HART, HERCULES, ISKRA, ITHURIEL, MAIDSTONE, OWEN GLENDOWER, PELORUS, PIGMY, PLOVER, RAPID, REINDEER, ROOKE, RUPERT, SAMARANG, STRIKER, TITANIA, VIENNA,

Radio Sta 1908 – . Port Convoy Office closed 15.09.1919. RN Hospital closed 15.12.1922 - reopened later.

RNAS 1915 – 04.1918 (to RAF). Kite Balloon Sta being evacuated 04.1919

RF of 12 FF (SO in ROOKE) 07.1953-. Dockyard closed 1984.

Glasgow – see Greenock

Glenarbuck – PRINCE EDWARD, PRINCE GEORGE - camps then used by Polish personnel 10.1943 –

Glen Caladh – JAMES COOK

Glenbranter – PASCO

Glenfinnart – ARMADILLO

Godmersham Park – Kent – RNAS WWI

GOLD COAST – British West Africa – 1874 British Crown Colony, 1960 fully Independent Republic in Commonwealth, renamed Ghana.

LEONIDAS, WARA

Gosport – See Portsmouth

Grain – Isle of – RNAS 10.1912, Cd 01.01.1913 (First RNAS? - First Flying Sch was Eastchurch) – 03.1918

Grangemouth – See Forth

Granton – see Forth

Gravesend – FLAMER, GENERAL GORDON, GORDON, ST KATHERINE, TRITON

Grays – Essex - GOLIATH

Great Baddow – Essex – LEIGH

Great Malvern – Worcs – DUKE

Great Yarmouth – ALECTO, CAIRO, FREEWILL, KINGFISHER, KOOLUNGA, MAHELAH, MIDGE & II, MIRANDA, MIURA, MYLODON, OMEGA, PEMBROKE IV, SAGITTA, WATCHFUL, WHITE EAR, ZARIFAH

RNR Battery 1906. Naval Base closed 29.01.1919. RNAS 1911 – 03.1918. RN Hospital to Lancaster early WW II, returned Gt Yarmouth 07.03.46. FOIC flag down 31.07.1945

GREECE – see also Aegean & Corfu – COREOPSIS, DELAMARE, EUROPA & II, HINDU KUSH, HIFAISTOS, JOHN BOWLER, OSIRIS II, PYRAMUS, ST GEORGE, VALHALLA II

Naval Base Salonika closed 21.08.1919, Piraeus closed 14.03.1919, Suda Bay closed 03.09.1919. RN Barracks Phaeleron closed 05.1946.

CF Bases Casteloriso (E of Rhodes) by 10.1943; Chios /Khios by 09.44; Kehia; Lecos (Leros?) & Kithera 16.09.44 -.

RNAS WWII (Eleusis, Maleme (Crete))

Greenhithe – ARETHUSA, FLAMER, PRESIDENT (ex BUZZARD), WORCESTER

Greenland Top – Lincs – RNAS WWI

Greenock – ALCA, ALECTO, BENBOW, BLUEBIRD, CARRICK & II, CASERNE BIROT, DALRIADA, FARAWAY, GRAHAM, HERCULES, HUNTER, INDEFATIGABLE, IOLAIRE, IXION, LEDSHAM, MARRYAT, MONCK & II, MULLION COVE, NIOBE, ORLANDO, PLYMOUTH, ST COLUMBA, SHANNON, SHERBROOKE, SPARTIATE, SUPERB

RNR Battery 1906. NOIC at Navy House, Clarence St 12.1939. Naval Dockyard – approved for construction of berths for DDs and DD DS in Greenock 01.1941 and additional building 12.1941 - closed 31.07.1946. RIN Depot at Bishopton to Stamshaw Camp, Ports 20.01.1943. Captain(D) Greenock lapse 31.07.1945. FOIC Greenock to NOIC 15.02.1946

RF Glasgow closed 17.04.1951. RF for 16 LST (CORF Greenock ashore) 07.1953 -, Refit Office RF Glasgow closed 17.04.1957

Greenwich – CALEDONIA, DREADNOUGHT: -Also RN College 01.02.1873 – closed 06.06.1998 – to Greenwich Foundation – White Ensign down 21.10.1998

Grimsby – BEAVER I, COLONSAY, COQUETTE, PEKIN, PEMBROKE VII & VIII, RIGOROUS, ROYAL CHARTER: -BD Depot closed 26.07.1957

Grimsetter - see Scapa Flow

Grove Point – RN Shore Signal Sta 1924 – 28

Grutness – AES 1 (tx to Air Ministry 07.1944)

GUAM – USA - LACHLAN

Guernsey – see Channel Islands

H

Haldon – Devon – HERON & II

Halesworth – Suffolk – HORNBILL II, SPARROWHAWK

Hamble – Nr Soton – LOTUS, MELISANDE, NAUTILUS, SIR HUGO, SAPPHO, TORMENTOR

Harrogate – TRIPHIBIAN II

Harrowbeer – RAF – Lodger 1944

Hartlepool – CAROLINE, DOUGLAS, FOUDROYANT, LOCH ARKAIG, LOCH TRALAIG, PARAGON, SCARBOROUGH, THORNBOROUGH, TRINCOMALEE, WEAR

RNR Battery 1882. RF Base closed & SO RF Tyne lapse 31.01.1947 – last ship THORBOROUGH. Re-open for 28 ships – CO RF in LOCH ARKAIG - 22.09.1952 – CO RF Tyne close & under Hartlepool 30.08.1955 – close 29.06.62

Harwich – 'Conurbation' – ADAMANT, ALECTO, ANDROMACHE, BADGER, BEEHIVE & II, BLAKE, BLENHEIM, BONAVENTURE, BOURNEMOUTH QUEEN, BUNTING, CAMPERDOWN, CAROLINE, CARRON, CAVENDISH, CFMU 1 & 2, CHASER, CUILLIN SOUND, CYCLOPS, DIDO, DODMAN POINT, DUNCANSBY HEAD, EPPING, ETHALION, FERRY PRINCE, FORTH, GANGES & II, GRUNO, HEBE, HERCULES, HOTSPUR, HYDROGRAAF, JULES VERNE, LOCUST, MAIDSTONE, MARS, MELAMPUS, MERSEY, MILNE, MINONA, MULL OF GALLOWAY, MULL OF KINTYRE, NIZAM, PANDORA, PEMBROKE, PENELOPE, PHOEBE, REDPOLE, SCYLLA, SEVERN, SOUTHAMPTON, SOUTHWESTER, TALYBONT, THAMES QUEEN, TYNE, TYRIAN, VULCAN, WOOLVERSTONE, WOOLWICH, ZEBRA, ZENITH

RNAS (Felixstowe 1912 – WWI, Shotley WWI – Kite Balloon not required by Air Ministry 06.1919)

Parkestone Quay Naval Stores closed 09.1919

SM Base 11.1939(CYCLOPS) – closed 15.11.1940

RF (pay office ex Parkestone Quay to TYNE 10.12.1946) -closed 31.01.1947. RN Base Hosp to close 03.1957

Coast Guard – SOUTHAMPTON 01.01.1857 -, PEMBROKE 01.02.1858 -, PENELOPE 12.06.1869 -, HOTSPUR 21.05.1887 -, MERSEY 09.05.1893 -, SEVERN 22.05.1898 -, MERSEY 11.02.1903 –

07.1903 (re-organisation)

Haslar – see Portsmouth

Haslemere – CENTURION, KESTREL, MERCURY II

Hastings – RNR Battery 1877 – 1909

Hatston – see Scapa Flow

Haulbowline – see Queenstown

HAVANNAH – ROMNEY

Hawkscraig – Fife – TARLAIR: -Naval Experimental Sta closed 15.10.1919. RNAS pre and during WWI

Headingley – HEADINGLEY

Heathfield – see Ayr

Heath Row – Fairey Aviation – Lodger 1944 – 45

Hebburn – see Tyne

Helensburgh – see Gare Loch

Helford – SUNBEAM II

Hendon – RNAS 03.1916

Henstridge – DIPPER, HERON & II: - CF Store Depot closed 01.10.1951

Heston – DAEDALUS

Hexham & Keilder – STANDARD

Hickling Broad – Norfolk – RNAS WWI

Highnam Court - Gloucester – CABBALA, GANGES

Hinstock (ex Ollerton) - Shropshire – BLACKCAP, GODWIT

Holehaven – Essex – LEIGH

HOLLAND – AMBITIOUS, CFMU 1, GLEN USK, GLENMORE, GOATFELL, LOCUST, ORIOLE, ROYAL CLARENCE, ST TUDNO, SANDOWN, TIMBERTOWN: - Ostend capt 09.09.1944. Terneuzen to RNLN 01.10.1945. BNLO Rotterdam closed 21.12.45. M/S Base Ijmuiden closed 07.09.1946

Holmbrook – Cumberland – VOLCANO

Holt – Norfolk – RNAS 03.1916 – 03.1918

Holton Heath – Cordite factory for disposal 12.1957

Holy Loch – EMPIRE COMFORT, EMPIRE SHELTER, FORTH, MONTCLARE, TITANIA

Holyhead – AMETHYST III, BEE, BELFORT, BOADICEA, BOUCLIER, COLOSSUS, COUCY, DEFENCE, EDGAR, HOTSPUR, ILEX, NEPTUNE, ORANJE NASSAU, SAPPER, SPARTAN, TORCH & II, VANESSA II: -2 RNAS WWI (1915)

HONG KONG – 1842 Treaty of Nanking and Naval Base, 1997 to China

ALLIGATOR, AORANGI, CHUNHSING, CLOWN, CORNFLOWER, DEER SOUND, FLAMBOROUGH HEAD, FLAMER, FLYCATCHER, HERCULES, KELANTAN, MAIDSTONE, MARAZION, MEDWAY, MEEANEE, MELVILLE, MIDGE, MINDEN, NABCATCHER, OPOSSUM, PRINCESS CHARLOTTE, RAME HEAD, RESOURCE, ROBIN, ROSARIO, TAMAR & II & III, TRIUMPH, VICTOR EMANUEL, WIVERN,

Radio Sta to be built 25.12.1914. Signal Tng Centre to Kranji 10.1951. Dockyard closed 30.01.1959

Honnington – RAF – Lodger 1972-78

Hornsea Mere – Yorks – RNAS WWI – to close 01.1919 - tx to Killingholme 02.1919

Horsea – CG Sta 1909 –

Houton Bay – see Scapa Flow

Hove – KING ALFRED, SUSSEX, VERNON

Howden – Yorks RNAS 12.1915 – 03.1918

Hull – see Humber

Humber – 'Conurbation'

AMBITIOUS, AUDACIOUS, BEAVER & II & III, BONAVENTURE, CALCUTTA, COCKATRICE, CORNWALLIS, DAUNTLESS, DIDO, DUNLUCE CASTLE, EDINBURGH, ENDYMION, ELFIN. FORTH, GALATEA, HEBE, ILLUSTRIOUS, INVINCIBLE, IRON DUKE, LEANDER, NEWCASTLE, NIMBLE, ORIFLAMME, PEMBROKE VIII, RAVEN, REPULSE, RUPERT, ST GEORGE, SOUTHAMPTON, SUNHILL II, VICTORIOUS, VULCAN, WALLAROO, WALLINGTON, WIVERN

RNAS – Immingham to 03.1918 - Kite Balloon Immingham to close 03.1919. Port Convoy Office closed 31.12.1918. DAMS Office Hull closed 30.09.1919.

Rear Admiral AA Ships to County Hotel, Immingham ex RN Barracks Chat 25.04.1940 - post lapsed 11.10.1940

US Port office Hull De-Cd 11.09.1944, FOIC Humber post reduced to NOIC 30.09.1945. Hull Naval Base closed 15.01.46, NOIC post lapsed 12.03.46

Coastguard: CORNWALLIS 01.01.1857 -, DAUNTLESS 01.04.1864 - , WIVERN 01.1870 -, INVINCIBLE 13.10.1870 -, AUDACIOUS 07.1871-, IRON DUKE 07.1875-, ENDYMION 01.10.1875 - AUDACIOUS 01.08.1879, REPULSE 15.04.1881-, RUPERT 27.08.1885-, AUDACIOUS 01.04.1890 -, EDINBURGH 07.02.1894 -, GALATEA 12.1894 -, DIDO 11.02.1903 – mid 1903 (re-organisation)

Hythe – DILIGENCE, SQUID II

I

ICELAND – ADALVIK, AMBITIOUS, ARON, BALDUR & II & III, BLENHEIM, FORCE PROFIT, GREENWICH, MANELA, MNBDO, NEMESIS, PRINCESS MARIA JOSE, SAEBOL, ST CLAIR, SOUTHERN ISLES, STATIONS H & N, ZITA: - AES 7 in W II

Ilfracombe – APPLEDORE II, ODYSSEY

Immingham – see Humber

Inchinnan – RNAS WWI

Inchkeith – RN Radio Sta 1920 – 24. RN Shore Signal Sta 1925 - 28. RN Estab Inchkeith (XDO Forth) closed 03.09.1945

INDIA – also includes places later part of Pakistan/ Bangladesh. Dominion 1947 – separation 14.08.1947

Bombay Marine became Indian Marine 01.05.1830. Indian Marine became Indian Navy 30.04.1863. RIN became IN 26.02.1950

Ahmednagar – JAHANARA

Arakonam – RAJALI

Bay of Benin – VINDICTIVE

Bengal – MAID MARION

Binga Bay – Nr Goa – SEA BIRD

Bombay – AGNIBAHU, AKBAR, ALBATROSS, ANGRE & II, ASVINI, BALFURA, BARPETA, BARRACUDA, BLINJOE, BLUEJACKET, BOMBAY, BRAGANZA & II & III, CHEETAH, CHEMBUR, CLIVE, DALHOUSIE & II, DILWARRA, DORIS, DUFFERIN, EL HIND, FALSETTE, FEROZE, HAITAN, HAMLA, & II, HAMLAWAR, JALA PADMA, JUMNA, KHANJAR, MACHLIMAR, MADRAS, MARVE, MOTI, PANGKOR, RAMDAS, REDJACKET, SALSETTE & II & III, SEABELLE, SHIVAJI, TALWAR, VALSURA, VERSOVA

Calcutta – BARRACUDA, CHILWA, HAITAN, HEINRICH JESSEN, HOOGHLY, NALIN, NETAJ, SUBHAS – RNLO and RN Barracks closed 31.03.1946

Chittagong – BARRACUDA, FT 14, KEDAH, PATUNGA: SO Arabian CF set up HQ in Chittagong 01.10.1944

Cochin – CHINKARA, DRONACHARYA, GARUDA, KALUGU, LANDSWELL, VENDURUTHI & II

Coimbatore – AGRANI, GARUDA

Cocanada – JEHANGIR

Delhi – HATHI: Radio Sta to be established Delhi/Simla 03.1941

E Zhimala – JAWARHALAL NEHRU

Goa – GOHANTAK, GOMANTAK, HANSA, JEEVANTI, MANDOVI

Jamnagar – VALSURA (VAISURA)

Karachi (and Manora) – BAHADUR, BALDAHUR, CHAMAK, DALHOUSIE, DILAWAR, HIMALAYA & II, IQBAL, KARSAZ, MONGE/MONZE, QASIM, TAIMUR

Madh – MADH

Madras – ADVAR/ADYAR, BARRACUDA, VALLURU

Mandapam – AIK LAM, BURONG, HILSA, TENGRA & II

New Delhi – INDIA

Okha – DWARKA, KATHIAWAR, PAMPAM

Poona – CO Base -Kharakvasla 02.1944

Pt Blair – JAWARA, KARDIP, UTKROSH

Sular – VAIRI

Vishakapatnam (Vizagapatam) – AMZARI, CHILKA, CIRCARS, DEGA, KALYANI, SATYAVAHANA, VEERBAHU, VIRBAHU

Inskip – INSKIP, NIGHTJAR

Inverailort – LOCHAILORT

Inveraray – ELTRICH, NORTHLAND, QUEBEC, SISTER ANNE, SOUND FISHER, SOUTHLAND

Invergordon – AKBAR, ALGIERS, CRESCENT V, ESA 194, FLORA & II, MARS, PRINCE, PRINCETOWN, STATION P, STEPHEN FURNESS: Contraband Control Office closed 24.04.1940

Inverness – BRILLIANT, BRITON, INVERNESS, LAVATERA, NETLEY: CG Sta 1909 -; RN Radio Sta 1919 - 28. US Base 18 PO 17.09.1919

Ipswich ALISDAIR, BUNTING, EMPEROR OF INDIA, FREELANCE, FREEWILL, GERBERDINE JOHANNA, HELENA, TITAN, WOOLVERSTONE

Irvine – Ayrshire – DINOSAUR II, FULLARTON

Isle of Man – INDUSTRY, ST GEORGE, TYNWALD, URLEY, VALKYRIE & II & III : RNR Battery 1882; RNAS WWI (Ramsay & Ronaldsway); Junior Section of RN Sch of Music to Howstrake Camp 17.07.1941 when camp ceased to provide emergency accom for junior terms Dartmouth College

Isleworth – Middx – TE at Frazer Nash Sch 1942

ISRAEL – see PALESTINE

ITALY – ADAMANT, ADMIRABLE, ADRIATICO, AEGUSA, AGRIPPA, ARCHAIS, BYRSA, CATANIA, ECONOMUS, ELISSA, ESTON, FABIUS, FUSTIAN, GALLIPOLI, GELO, GLUTTON, GUISCARD, GUNMETAL, HAMILCAR & II, HANNIBAL, HASDRUBAL, HIFAISTOS, INCISOR, KAI, LADBROKE, MANZANITA, MARCO POLO, METALLUS, MIRAGLIA, MYLAE, OUR ALLIES, PANTALOON, PECCARY, PRODUCT, QUARNEROLA, QUEEN & II, SALENTINE, VENERABLE, VIENNA, VULCAN, WEYMOUTH, ZAMA, ZZ 23:

AES 14 (Radar Sta) Mt Gibele, Pantellaria – arrived 06.1943 - operating 06.07.1943.

Otranto Kite Balloon Sta by 03.1918 -evacuated 03.1919. Bizerta & Brindisi Kite Balloon Sta evacuated 04.1919. Naval Base Brindisi closed 26.03.1919, Naval Base Gallipoli closed 05.12.1918, and Tricase 02.12.18. Leuca Hydrophone Sta closed 30.11.1918. Pt Convoy Office Taranto closed 06.1919.

Temp CF Bases WWII – (Advance/Mobile) see Med – covered Ancona (RNO closed 17.09.45), Augusta, Bari (VIENNA), Brindisi (09.43-, MIRAGLIA 03.44-), Ischia (by 16.09.43 - 03.46), La Maddelena, La Spezia, Leghorn, Manfredonia (12.43), Syracuse, Trieste (03.46)

Naval Base Messina closed 13.04.46 (see HAMILCAR). NOIC Taranto withdrawn 31.01.46

J

JAMAICA – 1670 Treaty of Madrid, 06.08.1962 Independent

ABOUKIR, BUZZARD, CAGWAY, GALATEA, IMAUM, KINGSTON, MAGNIFICENT, MALABAR & III, MARIANNE, MOGA, MORGAN, MUTINE, SERAPIS, URGENT: Dockyard reduced to cadre 1904. Aproved to close RNAD 05.1945

JAPAN – ALERT, COMMONWEALTH, LADYBIRD, MANILLA, MULL OF KINTYRE, RETURN

JAVA – ANKING

JERSEY – KESTREL

K

Kenley – A Position 03.1918

KENYA – 1885 British control, 1895 E African Protectorate. East African Naval Force in effect 01.07.1950 – absorbed Kenya VR. 1963 Full Independence.

ADAMANT, ANTONIA, KARONGO, KORONGO, KATHIWAR, KIPANGA, MTONGWE, MVITA, RISASI, ROSALIND, SIMBA, SIMBRA, TANA & II, WAYLAND: Naval Radio Sta Mtwapa, Mombasa in S African Government 31.05.1963

Kete – Pembs – HARRIER, VECTOR

Kildonan – RN Shore Signal Sta 1923-24

Killeagh – CO Cork – RNAS WWI

Killingholme Haven – Lincs – RNAS 09.1914 - to USN 20.07.1918 - vacated by USN 1200 -06.01.1919.

Killybeg – A/P Base ex Blacksod 06.1915 – Base closed 21.02.1919.

Killylarne – Co Londonderry – Radio Sta (not RN) to remain USN 12.1946. Radio Sta 1961 -76

Kings Lynn – ARBELLA

Kings Moor – Nr Yeovilton – Dummy Airfield WW II

Kingseat – RN Aux Hosp - admissions cease 01.12.1945

Kingsnorth – Kent – RNAS pre and during WWI

Kingstown – Co Dublin – AJAX, AUDACIOUS, BELLEISLE, BOADICEA II, EAGLE, ESSEX, GLENMAY, ILEX, IRON DUKE, LATONA, MELAMPUS, PALLAS, PATROL, RANGER, ROYAL GEORGE, TOPAZE, VANGUARD, WOLF:

Coastguard – AJAX 01.02.1858 -, ROYAL GEORGE 01.04.1864 - , PALLAS 01.01.1870 -, AUDACIOUS 10.1870 -, VANGUARD 06.07.1871 – Sunk 01.09.1875, IRON DUKE 01.10.1875 -, TOPAZE 17.07.1877 -, BELLEISLE 02.07.1878 -, MELAMPUS 01.05.1893 – 07.1903 (re - organisation)

Kingswear – see Dartmouth

Kirkham – RN Air Section at RAF Sta, closed 17.04.1947

Kirkistown – Co Down – CORNCRAKE II

Kirkleatham – Yorks – RNAS WWI

KOREA – War 25.06.1950 – 27.07.53. TYNE

Kyle of Lochalsh – Wester Ross – THISTLE, TRELAWNEY, PORTS B & ZA: - Naval Base closed 19.02.1919

L

Laira – see Plymouth

Lamlash – Isle of Arran – BOURNEMOUTH QUEEN, CORONIA, PACTOLUS, TROUBADOUR: - Pt Convoy Office closed 31.12.1918. CO craft C & M Base closed 12.09.1946.

Lancaster RN Hosp ex Gt Yarmouth early in WW II - returned Gt Yarmouth 07.03.46

Landguard Point – Radio Sta 1901

Lands End - RNAS (Temp) 1940 near St Just

Langham – RAF Lodger 1942 – 44

Largs – COPRA, MONCK, QUEBEC II, WARREN

Larne – Antrim – HERMIONE, RACER & II, TARANSAY, THETIS, VALIANT II, VIGOROUS: - RNAS 01.1916 – 03.1918, Radio Sta 02.1916

Launceston – US Store Depot closed 25.06.1945

Lawrenny Ferry – Pembs – DAEDALUS II

LEBANON – MEDWAY II, MOSQUITO II, NICHOLAS: Naval Base Beirut closed 27.04.1919 and Tripoli closed 28.04.1919. DEMS Base closed by 04.07.1945.

Lee-on-Solent – see Portsmouth

Leeds – HEADINGLEY, PEMBROKE III: WRNS Central TE 1944. RNTU 05.1944 - closure approved 05.1945.

Leith – see Forth

Lerwick – see Shetlands

Letchworth – TE for Wiremen 15.08.1942 – under SHRAPNEL

Leuchars – Fife – RNAS WWI - then to RAF & Lodger 1935-38 & 1972 - 29.09.78

LEVANT – ZZ 23 – 26

Leydene (House) – SCU tender to MERCURY, then DRYAD 1995, then independent estab 1995 – see Petersfield

LIBYA – NILE: Radio Sta closed 12.1943. Tobruk a minor port 01.01.1944.

Limavady – RAF Lodger 1944 – 45 - tx to Adty 01.12.45 but not used – for disposal 06.1958

Limerick – DEFENCE, FREDERICK WILLIAM, STATIONS O & P, VALIANT – see also Bantry

Coastguard: FORT WILLIAM (from Queenstown) 31.01.1866-, VALIANT 09.1868 - (? DEFENCE 1874 temp whilst VALIANT refitting), SHANNON 06.08.1885 -, AURORA 03.05.1893, DREADNOUGHT 30.03.1895 - , COLLINGWOOD 09.03.1897 – (DEVASTATION temp 01.04.1898 – 09.1898 as tender to COLLINGWOOD) - 07.1903 (Re-organisation)

Lincoln – AA Position 03.1918

Lisahally – U boats 05.1945 – 01.46. RF (16 FF under SEA EAGLE) 04.1953 – 24.01.64.

Liss – Hants -RODENT

Littelhampton – PANDORA

Littlestone – Kent - CG Sta 1919-22

Liverpool – see Mersey

Lizard – RNAS 03.1916 – see Mullion. RN DF Sta 1921 -28

Llanegryn – MNBDO II

Llanelly – RF of 20 LCT (No HQ) - 23.06.1953 – close 07.11.1956

Llanfair PG – CONWAY

Llangenech – RN Store Depot closed 30.11.1989

Llwyngwril – MNBDO II

Loch Cairnbawn – PORT HHZ

Loch Eriboll – PORT ZH

Loch Erisort – PORT D & ZD, TITANIA

Loch Ewe – see Aultbea

Loch Na Lith Aich – Work-Up Base for M/S Tlrs – WESTERN ISLES 06.1943

Loch Ryan -SANDHURST

Loch Striven – BONAVENTURE, VARBEL II

Loch Tarbert – Kintyre – CARMELA

Lochboisdale – Radio Sta tx to GPO 17.04.1919

London – and Thames – AUSONIA, BELFAST, BUZZARD, CARINA, CARPENTARIA, CASERNE SURCOUF, CERBERUS II, CHICHESTER, CHRYSANTHEMUM & II, COCKFOSTERS, COOK, COPRA, CYSTAL PALACE, DISCOVERY, DOROTHY, EVOLUTION, EXCELLENT II, EXMOUTH, FENTONIAN, FIREWORK, FROLIC, GIPSY/GYPSY, GOLDEN EAGLE, HILDA, INVESTIGATOR, LEVEN, MAORI, MONARCH, NIOBE, NORTHAMPTON, ODYSSEY, ORANGE NASSAU, PEMBROKE III & V, PERSEUS, PILGRIM, PLINLIMMON, PORT MAHON, PRESIDENT & I-VI, RAINBOW, RENARD, RHIN, ROYAL ALBERT, ROYALIST, ST VINCENT, SCORPION, STORK, SWAN, THOMA II, TOREADOR, TOWER, VICTORY II & IV & VI, WELLINGTON, YEOMAN:

RNAS WWI – Wormwood Scrubbs (03.1915), Chingford (1913-03.1918), Hendon (AA Position 10.1915-03.1918), Crystal Palace (03.1918), Roehampton (03.1918)

Pt Convoy Office closed 31.12.1918. RN W/T Whitehall 1921 – extant 1995

WRNS - Westfield College 1941-. Comb Tng & Drafting Depot Mill Hill 06.1942 – ex Nat Inst of Med Research. Cannons Corner, Stanmore by 11.1942

Vice Admiral (SM) Northways, Swiss Cottage - ex Aberdour & DOLPHIN 03.1940 - tx to DOLPHIN 26.09.1945. CF HQ Wendover Ct, Golders Green 1941 – . FO Commanding RF Vintry Ho E4 10.1945. FOIC London lapse 01.04.1946.

Experimental Sta Queen Mary Reservoir, Staines & Premises of United Dairy Wembley taken over 01.04.1944. Polish HQ, 28 Wimpole St W1 09.1945. MOLCAB Assembly Depot, B Shed, W India Dks 08.1945

See also Thames Forts/ Fulham/ Greenwich

Londonderry – FERRET & II-IV, FOXGLOVE, HARTLAND POINT, NIOBE, PHOENIX, RAME HEAD, SANDHURST, SEA EAGLE, STALKER, TITANIA: Approved to set up DEMS Sub Base 11.1941. US Op Base established 05.02.1942. Radio Sta – see Killylarne

Long Kesh – RAF – Lodger 1944 – 45

Longside – Aberdeen – RNAS early 1915 – 03.1918

Lossiemouth – Morayshire – FULMAR: - RNAS WW I

Lough Foyle – BATAVIA II, EAGLE: - RNAS WW I – used by rN to 06.1919 - not by RN. Kite Balloon Sta (ex US) not retained 20.05.1919

Lough Larne – see Larne

Lough Neogh – RNAS WW I - not completed

Lough Swilly – CAMPERDOWN, HAWK, HAWKE, TRAFALGAR

Coastguard: TRAFALGAR 13.11.1867 – 69. Not a CG area 1900. CAMPERDOWN 05.07.1900-, HAWKE 06.05.1903 – 07.1903 (re-organisation)

Lowestoft – Suffolk - EUROPA, HALCYON & II, MANTIS, MARTELLO, MINOS & II, MYLODON, PEMBROKE X, ROMOLA: - WWI Base amalgamated with Gt Yarmouth 20.09.1919 and closed 30.11.1919. RNAS 10.1915 - 03.1918

Lowton – Lancs – see Warrington

Lowthorpe – Yorks – RNAS WWI

Luce Bay – Wigtownshire – RNAS 03.1916 – 03.1918

Ludgershall – USN Inspection Depot Tidworth (Hedge end) 10.1943 – closed 22.05.45

Ludham - Norfolk – FLYCATCHER & II & III, NABARON, NABBERLEY, NABBINGTON, NABSFORD, NABSWICK, NABTHORPE

Lulworth – RN Shore Signal Sta 1924 – 27

Lundy Island – RN Shore Signal Sta 1924 – 28

Lymington – Hants – PAULINE: CF Material Supply Depot Pylewell closed 31.03.1951

Lympne – Kent – BUZZARD, DAEDALUS II & III: - RNAS WW I – 03.1918

Lynmouth – CG Sta 1921 – 22

Lynn – RNR Battery 1873

Lytham St Annes – Lancs – TRIPHIBIAN

M

Machrihanish - Argyllshire – LANDRAIL, SANDERLING II: - RNAS WW I

MacMerry – E Lothian – NIGHTHAWK

MADAGASCAR – AFRIKANDER V, IRONCLAD

Maidstone – Kent – RNAS WWI

Malahide – Co Dublin – RNAS WW I

MALAYA – including Malaysia & Spore – Naval Base 1819, Federation 1948, RMN formed 1952, Independent 08.1957.

ANKING, AQUARIUS, ASSISTANCE, BEAULY FIRTH, CANNA, DERBY HAVEN, DULLISK COVE, ENDEAVOUR, FLAMBOROUGH HEAD, FORTH, GLOCAR, HAWKINS, KEDAH, KUDAT, KUTCHING BASE, LABUAN, LABURNAM, LANDLOCK, LANDSWELL, MALAYA, MANXMAN, MEDWAY, MICHAEL, MULL OF KINTYRE, NABROCK, NASAR, PANGLIMA, PELANDOK, PERSEUS, PONGOL, RAJAWALI, SIMBANG, SINGAPURA, SRI KLANG, SRI LABUAN, SRI MEDINI, SRI PINANG, SRI REJANG, SRI SANDAKAN, SRI TAWAU, SUI WO, SULTAN & II-IV, TAMAR III, TERROR & II & III, TEST, TRIUMPH, WOODBRIDGE HAVEN, WUCHANG:

RNAS Morib, Selangor & Sembawang and RN Aircraft Repair Yard Khatib, Sembawang 08.1941. RN Aircraft Holding Unit Seletar 1959-70. Naval Aircraft Support Unit Tengah 1960 – 65 - to Changi 1965 – 05.69. RNAS temp Kutching 10.1963 – 12.12.63.

Radio Sta to be built Spore 25.12.1914. Woodlands Radio Sta conv to barracks for Malayan Naval Forces – re-opened 16.11.1949. Signal Tng Centre from HK to Kranji 10.1951

SO RF Spore title lapse 01.05.1951

Malay RNVR at Penang & Selangar (KL) post WW II.

C-in-C Eastern Sta from Phoenix Pt to Naval Base 10.03.1958

New Tng Base under construction 1996 – Tanjong Pengelish

Malin Head – RN Radio Sta 1921 – 22

MALTA GC – 1814 British Crown Colony, 12.1974 Republic:

ADAMANT, ALECTO, AUSONIA, BASTIG, CEYLON, CHILDERS, CORINTHIA, CRUISER, DIEPPE, DILIGENCE, EGMONT & II, EUROCLYDON, FALCON, FAREHAM, FERMOY, FORTH, GOLDFINCH, GREGALE, HIBERNIA, LATONA, LOFOTEN, LOYAL, LUCIA, MEDWAY II, & III, MIRAGLIA, ORION, ORONTES, PHOENICIA, PRODUCT, RANPURA, RICASOLI, ST ANGELO & II & III, SAVAGE, STRIKER, SYLVIA, TALBOT, TRIDENT, TYNE, VINDICTIVE, VULCAN, WESER, WOLFE, WOOLWICH:

RNAS Calafrana - work started 01.1916 – open 07.1916, to RAF 01.04.1918 – 12.36. Kalafrana 12.36. Tx to RN 30.06.1946, to Air Ministry 1965. Kite & Balloon Sta being maintained 04.1919.

Radio Sta 1908 – . Pt Convoy Office closed 15.09.1919. RN Barracks Camarata (Valletta) WW II.

Dockyard tx 30.03.1959

Manchester – BRONNINGTON, IRWELL

Manston – DAEDALUS: - RNAS 05.1917 – 03.1918

MARTINIQUE – DIAMOND ROCK, FORT DIAMOND

Martlesham Heath – RFC Sta 03.1918

Maryport – RNR Battery 1873

MAURITIUS – Ceded to Gt Britain 1814. Independent Sovereign State 1968

MAURITIUS, SAMBUR: Radio Sta to be built 25.12.1914 - closed 15.07.1921. RN Hosp from Army 15.06.1960 - closed 13.02.1976

Maydown – GANNET & II, SHRIKE

MEDITERRANEAN – ALECTO, ANNA CAPANA, AQUARIUS, B11, BLAIRESK, CHALKIS, CYCLOPS, FIERCE, GREENWICH, H 2, HUMBER, LEANDER, MAIDSTONE, MEDWAY, MINNA, NARVIK, NSB 51, RESOURCE, ST GEORGE, SANDHURST, STATIONS A, B, F, U & V, TYNE, VIENNA, WAVENEY, VULCAN,

WOODBRIDGE HAVEN, WOOLWICH:

C-in-C from Naples to Malta 17.02.1946

CF Mobile Base Med - formed Alexandria 09.1942, to Mersa Matruh 11.42, Tobruk 11.42, Ras Helat (Nr Benghazi) 11.42, Bone 02.43, Syracuse 12.07.43 -, to August 15.07.43, to Maddelena (09.43 - closed 29.09.44), to Bastia (15.11.43 – 29.09.44), To Leghorn 29.09.44 -.

Also CF Mobile Base formed Alexandria 03.1944 (Ras - el-Tin) - mainly personnel ex CANOPUS, accom 10 miles from Alexandria in tented camp. Embark EMPIRE STAR/LCT 05.44, to Taranto, to Bari, to Manfredonia, to Guiliano, to Porte San Georgio, to Ancona (29.07.44 -)

Also CF Advance Bases at Manfredonia (10.1943 - 08.44) - moved to Ancona mod 06.44 – established 08.08.44

MEDWAY – 'Conurbation' – ABERCROMBIE, ABOUKIR, ACHERON, ACHILLES, ACTAEON, ACTUA, AGINCOURT, AIGLE, AISNE, AJAX, ALECTO, ALGIERS, AMBITIOUS, ANEMONE, ANSON, AQUARIUS, ARETHUSA, ARGUS, AUDACIOUS, ARK ROYAL, AUSONIA, BACCHANTE, BELLEISLE, BELLEROPHON, BEN LOMOND, BENBOW, BERRY HEAD, BIRMINGHAM, BLAKE, BLANKNEY, BLENHEIM, BLOSSOM, BOSCAWEN, BUFFALO, BRILLIANT, BRUNSWICK, CALEDON, CALLIOPE, CAMBRIAN, CAMILLA, CANADA, CANOPUS, CARDIFF, CARRON, CASSANDRA, CASTOR, CHALLENGER, CHAMPION, CHARGER, CHASSEUR, CHATHAM, CHRISTIAN VII, CLEOPATRA, COLUMBINE, CORNWALLIS, COURAGEUX, CUMBERLAND, CYCLOPS, DAEDALUS, DERBY HAVEN, DIADEM, DIANA, DIDO, DILIGENCE, DODMAN POINT, DOMINION, DORDRECHT, DUKE, DUNCAN, DINCANSBY HEAD, EGREMONT, EMERALD, EREBUS, ERIN, ESKIMO, EURYALUS, FLAMBOROUGH HEAD, FORMIDABLE, FORTE, FORTH, FORTITUDE, GANNET, GARTH, GEORGE D IRVIN, GLOUCESTER, HANDY, HAYDON, HEBE, HECLA, HELENA, HERMES, HEROINE, HIBERNIA, HINDUSTAN, HOOD, HOPE, HUSSAR, ILLUSTRIOUS,, IMPERIEUSE, INDOMITABLE, INFLEXIBLE, JUMNA, JUTLAND, KEMPENFELT, KENT, LEANDER, LEONIDAS, LEVEN, LION, LONDON, MAIDSTONE, MANXMAN, MARSHAL NEY, MARSHAL SOULT, MELAMPUS, MENELAUS, MERCURY, MINERVA, MINOTAUR, NAMUR, NEWCASTLE, NORTHAMPTON, NORTHUMBERLAND, NYMPH, NYMPHE, OCEAN, OCELOT, OTTER, PEKIN, PEMBROKE & I & II & IV, POICTIERS, POLYTHEMUS, PORTLAND BILL, PRESIDENT II, PRINCE GEORGE, PRINCE OF ORANGE, PRINCE RUPERT, QUEEN, RAME HEAD, RAMILLIES, RAYMONT, RELENTLESS, RETRIBUTION, RHIN, ROYAL ADELAIDE, ROYAL EAGLE, ST FIORENZA, ST GEORGE, ST LAWRENCE, ST TUDNO, SALSETTE, SANDHURST, SANS PAREIL, SAVAGE, SCARBOROUGH, SENTINEL, SHANNON, SIR BEVIS, SLANEY, SPEEDWELL, SPENSER, STAR, SUPERB, SUVLA, SWIFTSURE, TARTAR, TEEMERAIRE, TENDEDOS & II & III, TERPSICHORE, TERRIBLE, THAMES, THUNDERBOLT, THUNDERER, TORTOISE, TOURMALINE, TRAFALGAR, TROUBRIDGE, TYNE, UNDINE, UNITE, VECTOR, VENGEUR, VICTORIOUS II, VIGO, VOLAGE, WALLAROO, WARRIOR, WATERLOO, WELLESLEY, WELLINGTON, WEYMOUTH, WILDFIRE & II & III, WOODBRIDGE HAVEN, WOODCOCK, WOOLWICH, WYE, XE 8, ZENITH

RNAS (Isle of Grain 1911 -)(Sheerness - not required by Air Ministry 06.1919), (Kite Balloon Sta Sheerness closed 05.1919)

Hydrophone TE Queenborough Pier closed 31.01.1919

Sheerness Radio Sta 1921-28. Signal Sta Garrison Pt closed 01.10.1960

RN used St Mary's Military Barracks & Borstal Camp 02.1940 - Borstal portion returned 07.1942 - rest to Home Office 31.10.1942.

Westfield House, Rochester req as WRNS Hostel - renamed Cunningham House to avoid confusion with Westfield College 01.1942.

US Naval Advance Amphibious Base Nore Cd 10.04.1944 – de-Cd 1100 – 01.09.1944, vacant 10.09.44

RM Barracks Chat closed 31.08.1950. Sheerness Boom Salvage Depot closed 30.03.1960. RF closed 11.05.1960. Sheerness Dockyard sold 26.06.1959, closed 31.03.1960 (after 295 years). Mechanical TE Chat to SULTAN 09.1960. RN Depot Chat (Deptford) closed 01.12.1960. Nore closed 31.03.1961 - Flag became FO Medway. Chat Dockyard closed 31.03.1984.

Merifield – Cornwall – RNAS 1918 - at Wilcove with detachment at Torquay

Merryfield (also spelt Merrifield) – Somerset - HERON

MERSEY – 'Conurbation' – ACHILLES, AKBAR, ARETHUSA, BACCHUS, CALEDONIA, CLARENCE, COLLEEN II, CONWAY, DANAE, DEFENCE, DEFENDER, DRUID, EAGLE, EAGLET & II & III, EASTERN ISLES, ETOILE POLAIRE, EXPERIEMENT, HASTINGS, INDEFATIGABBLE, INGENIEUR CACHIN, IRWELL, LAVINIA, MAJESTIC, MERSEY, NEWCASTLE, ONSET, ONYX, PERLIN, PLUTO, PLYMOUTH, REDBREAST, RESISTANCE, RESOLUTION, SANTA MARGARITA, SILVA, TEES, TUNSBERG, VIVID IV, VOLONTAIRE, WALLACE, WELLESLEY:

Pt Convoy Office closed 31.12.1918

'Greenhay' and 'Westralia', Blundels req for RNoN personnel 01.1942

FOIC Lpool flag down 31.01.1946. RF refit offices closed 01.08.1958

Coastguard: - HASTINGS 03.04.1857 -, MAJESTIC 01.02.1860 -, DONEGAL 01.09.1864 -, RESISTANCE 01.07.1869 – 04.1874, CALEDONIA 10.1874 (poss temp 01.1873) -, ACHILLES 01.04.1875 - , RESISTANCE 17.05.1877 -, DEFENCE 15.06.1880, HOTSPUR 08.08.1885, NEPTUNE 21.05.1887 -, COLOSSUS 16.11.1893 - , RESOLUTION 17.11.1901 -, EDGAR 09.04.1903 - 07.1903 (re-organisation)

Merston – used by FAA 1945-46

MESOPOTAMIA – SCOTSTOUN

Methil – Fife – AMBITIOUS, SENTINEL

Middle Wallop – Hants – FLYCATCHER, NABCATCHER, NABHURST, NABREEKIE, NABROCK, NABSTOCK

Middlesbrough – Cleveland – PARAGON, RANGER: - DEMS Tng Sch closed by 04.07.1945

Milford/Milford Haven – see Pembroke Dock

Millmeece – Eccleshall – Staffs – CABBALA, FLEDGLING

Milltown – Morayshire – FULMAR II

Mizner Creek - RAVEN

Moreton – Dorset – RNAS WWI – not completed

Mortenhoe – Radio Sta closed 10.06.1943

Motherbank – off Ryde – AEOLUS, EDGAR, MENELAUS, TYRIAN

Mount Batten – see Plymouth

Mullaghmore – RAF – Lodger 1944 – 45

Mullion – Cornwall – RNAS 10.1915 – 04.1918 (to RAF). First known as Lizard Airship Sta

N

Narborough – RNAS to War Office 28.03.1916

Needles – RN Shore Signal Sta 1924 – to CG 01.02.1950

Nells Point – RN Shore Signal Sta 1923 -28

Neston – Chesshire – MERSEY

Netheravon – RAF – Lodger 1931 – 34

NETHERLANDS EAST INDIES – ANKING, GILOLO, HARMONY

NEW GUINEA – BASILISK, BRISBANE, FAIRFAX, LADAVA, MADANG, PENGUIN IV, TARANGAU & II, WHANG PU

New Haggerton – Northumberland – RNAS WW I

NEW HEBRIDES – VANUATU

NEW ZEALAND – 1907 Dominion, NZ Division formed 14.03.1921, RNZN formed 25.02.1942, 1947 complete autonomy : - AVALON, COOK & II & III, IRIRANGI, KUPARU, LACHLAN, MOA, NGAPONA, OLPHERT, PEGASUS, PHILOMEL & II, TAMAKI. TASMAN, TOROA, WAKEFIELD: Calliope Dock opened at Devonport 16.02.1888

Newbury – Berks – VICTORY I & II

Newcastle-upon-Tyne – see Tyne

Newcastle - under Lyme – DAEDALUS II: - RNAS WW I

Newhaven – AGGRESSIVE, ARROGANT, AUSTRALIA, DAUNTLESS, FORWARD & II, HYPERION, IRRESISTIBLE, MELAMPUS, NEWT, NORTHAMPTON, SETON, VENUS: - RNAS to 03.1918. Examination Service taken over by RN 12.1917. A/P to close 12.1918. From NOIC to RNO 07.07.1945

Coast Guard – also covered Soton – MELAMPUS 01.01.1857-, ARROGANT 01.03.1858 -, DAUNTLESS 28.08.1859 -, IRRESISTIBLE 01.04.1864 -, HECTOR 01.05.1868 -, (ZEALOUS temp – 1874 while HECTOR in refit), NORTHAMPTON 22.04.1886 -, INVINCIBLE 23.08.1886 -, AUSTRALIA 08.06.1893 -, VENUS 07.02.1903 – 07.1903 (re-organisation)

Newlyn – RNAS Lands End 1917 – 04.1918 - to RAF

Newport – Mon – DAHLIA, ITHURIEL, LUCIFER, MUTINE

Newquay - Cornwall – CG Sta 1918 – 22

NIGERIA – 1861 Lagos Colony and Naval Base, 1906 Nigeria Colony, 01.10.1960 Independent Sovereign State: - ANANSA, ASAKO, ASTRAEA, BEECROFT, MUNSHI, QUORRA

NORTH AFRICA – BORDE, HANNO, HIMERA, MAGO

North Coates – Lincs – RNAS WWI, RAF Lodger 1940-41

North Queensferry – see Forth

North Shields – see Tyne

Northwood – Middx – NORTHWOOD, WARRIOR

NORWAY – KING ARTHUR, KING BORS, KING MARK, KING MELIODAS, KING PELLINORE, MASHOBRA, MNBDO I, TYNE, WOOLWICH

Norwich – AA Position 03.1918

Nottingham – SHERWOOD

Novar – see Evanton

Nutts Corner – Antrim - PINTAIL

NYASA – Naval vessels PO 31.03.1919

O

Oban – CALEDOINIA, CELTIC, COEL MARA II, CRESCENT, ENTERPRISE, LORD LANSDOWNE, NESMAR II, ST ANDREW, TITANIA: A/P sub Base established 05.1917. Naval Base books to CRESCENT 09.05.1919, closed 11.11.1919

Okehampton – BALTYK

Ollerton – see Hinstock

Orkneys – see Scapa Flow

Osborne – Isle of Wight – ALEXANDRIA, OSBORNE, RACER

Osea Island – OSEA

Oulton Broad – Accom for 'suspense sta' 09.1942

Owthorne – Yorks – RNAS WWI

P

Padstow – WATCHWORD: - RNAS Trevose Head 03.1918-04.1918(to RAF). USN Advance Amphibious Sub Base closed 14.06.1945

PAKISTAN – see also India/Bangladesh. Separation 14.08.1947: AKRAM, ATTOCK, BAKHTYAR, BHAWALPUR, CHTTAGONG, HAIDER, IQBAL, JAHANGER, JAHANGIR, JINNA, MEHRAN: - Karachi Dockyard founded 22.09.1952.

PALESTINE – MNBDO I, MORETA, MOSQUITO I, STAG(HAIFA): - Naval Base Haifa closed 12.03.1919

Pantellaria – GUNMETAL

Peebles – RN Aux Hosp closed 01.11.1919

Pembroke Dock – 'Conurbation' - AKBAR, ALARM, AMPHRITITE, ANDROMACHE, BELLEROPHON, BLENHEIM, CARMELA, CELEBRITY, COLLEEN III, DRAGON, DRAKE X, EAGLE, ELENA, FAME, GIBRALTAR, HANNIBAL, HOOD, HOPE, IDAHO, LAPWING, MULGRAVE, MILFORD, NANKIN, OTTER, PLATYPUS, PORTIA, REVENGE, RUPERT, SABRINA & II, SANTA MARGARITA, SATURN, SKIRMISHER & II, THUNDERER, TORPIOISE, TRIUMPH, VENUS, VILLE DE PARIS, VIVID V, VULCAN, WARRIOR, ZAZA:

Dockyard first apps 26.04.1810-(Officer-in-Charge 31.10.1815) - closed 31.05.1926 - 12.03.1941. Small Repair Base established 01.04.1941.

RNAS 01.1916-, Kite Balloon Sta, Castle Hill, Milford Haven 06.1917. RN Radio Sta 1921 – 28

In WW II 17,000 convoys , aggregate 63 million tons. USN Advance Ampibious Base Milford Haven closed 17.10.1944

Title SO RF lapse 06.1949. RNO closed 31.08.1950 - re-open 29.05.1956

Coast Guard: - EAGLE 01.01.1857 -, AMPHRITIE 05.03.1857-, BLENHEIM 12.06.1860-, REVENGE 01.09.1865 -, CG Signal Sta 1909.

Port Guard: - BELLEROPHON 30.04.1892 -, RUPERT 05.07.1893 -, THUNDERER 09.05.1895-, HOOD 12.12.1900 – 01.1901.

Penarth – S Glam – CAMBRIA, DERG: - RN Shore Signal Sta 1923 - 28. USN Advance Amphibious Maint Sub Base PO 16.07.1944. RF opened (12 ships) 09.1952 – closed 29.08.1960

Penzance – RNR Battery 1906. A/P Base to close 12.1918. Naval Base closed 15.03.1919. DEMS Base closed by 04.07.1945. USN Advance Amphibious Sub Base closed 14.06.45

Peplow – Shrops – GODWIT & II

Perranporth – RAF Lodger 1944

PERSIAN GULF – ADRIA, ALERT, DALHOUSIE, EUPHRATES, GOMBROON, HELIOPOLIS, HERALD, HORMURG, HORMUZ, JUFAIR, MELCHICK TREVIS/MELCHIOR TREUB, MRC 1097, OMAN, SEABELLE, SHIHEEN, SHOREHAM, TRIAD: - Naval Base Basra to be closed and handed over to Military 03.1918. Naval Base Baghdad closed 18.03.1919. Naval Base Khor Kuwait to Pt War Signal Sta 11.04.45 and tx to RAF 01.09.1945. Naval Base Basra closed 01.1946. Bahrein Radio Sta closed 11.07.1946. HQ SNO Persian Gulf to Bahrein 01.04.45 -to be afloat in WILD GOOSE 11.07.1946. Small Aircraft Holding Unit at Muharrag, Bahrein 07.1964.

Perth – RN Aircraft Workshop 1979 – 89

PERU – NAIAD

Peterhead – COLUMBINE, CRESCENT II, FT 7, MEDEA, NAIRN, SANDFLY, THALIA: - RNR Battery 1876, RNAS WW I

Petersfield – MERCURY, VICTORY IV

PHILIPPINES – MAIDSTONE

Pin Mill – Nr Ipswich – MONARCH

Plymouth – 'Conurabation' – Dev known as 'Guz'

ACTIVE, ADAMANT, ADVENTURE, AGINCOURT, AJAX, ALAMEIN, ALAUNIA & II, ALBATROSS, ALBEMARLE, ALBION, ALECTO, ALEXANDER, ANDROMEDA, ANSON, APOLLO, ARGO, ARIADNE, AURORA, BELFAST, BELLEROPHON, BELLONA, BERRY HEAD, BLACK BAT, BOUCLIER, BRADFORD, CAESAR, CALCUTTA, CALEDON, CALLIOPE, CAMBRIAN, CAMBRIDGE, CAMPERDOWN, CANOPUS, CAPETOWN, CAPRICE, CAPTAIN, CAPTIVITY, CARYSFORT, CAVENDISH, CENTAUR, CENTURION, CERES, CIRCE, CLEOPATRA, COLLINGWOOD, COLOMBO, COLOSSUS, COMET, COMUS, CONQUESTADOR, CORDELIA, DAPPER, DEFIANCE & II – V, DERWENT, DEVASTA-

TION, DIADEM, DIEPPE, DILIGENCE, DIOMEDE, DODMAN POINT, DOMINION, DRAKE & I & II & IV & V & X, DREADNOUGHT, DUBLIN, ECLIPSE, EDEN, EGERIA, EMERALD, ENDYMION, EREBUS, ESSEX, EURYALUS, EXMOUTH, FALCON, FALMOUTH, FAVOURITE, FISGARD, FLAMINGO, FLY, FOLIOT I-IV, FORTH, FOUDROYANT, GATESHEAD, GENOA, GLORIOUS, GOLDEN FLEECE, GREYHOUND, HARLECH, HARLEQUIN, HASTINGS, HEROINE, HIMALAYA, HOTSPUR, HOUND, HOWE, IMPERIEUSE & II, IMPLACABLE, IMPREGNABLE & II-IV, INCONSTANT, INDUS & II – V, INDUSTRY, INTREPID, INVINCIBLE, JACKDAW, JUPITER, KENT, KING GEORGE V, KINGFISHER, LAVINIA, LEANDER, LEDA, LION, LIVELY, LOCH GORM, LONDON, LUCIA, MADAGASCAR, MAGNIFICENT, MAIDSTONE, MALTA, MARSHAL NEY, MARSHAL SOULT, MATAPAN, MEDWAY, MESSINA, MILFORD, MONMOUTH, MOUNT EDGCUMBE, NEPAL, NEWCASTLE, NEWFOUNDLAND, NIGERIA, NILE, NIMROD, NIOBE, ODIN, ONYX, ORCADIA, ORION, PADSTOW BAY, PALLAS, PARIS, PEGASUS,, PERESUS, PETEREL, PHAETON, PHILOCTETES, PIGMY, PIQUE, PLYMOUTH, PLYMOUTH TRADER, POWERFUL & II-III, PROCRIS, PYRRHUS, RALEIGH, RAME HEAD, RANPURA, PAYMONT, RED DRAGON, REINDEER, RENOWN, RESOLUTTION, REVENGE, ROBERTS, ROYAL ADELAIDE, ROYAL WILLIAM, SABINE, SALISBURY,SAN JOSEF, SANS PAREIL, SAPPHO, SEAHORSE, SEMIRAMIS, SKIPJACK, SLUYS, SPARTAN, SPARTIATE, SPEY, STIRLING CASTLE, STUART, SUTLEJ, SWINGER, TALBOT, TAMAR, TARTAR, TEAZER, TEMERAIRE, TENEDOS, TERROR, THISBE, THUNDERER, TRACKER, TREMADOC BAY, TRIUMPH, TYNE, UBIQUITY, ULSTER, ULYSSES, UNDAUNTED, UNICORN, URANIA, VALIANT & IIII & OLD, VENGEANCE, VENUS, VIGO, VIRGINIE, VIVID & II - V, WALLAROO, WAR WING, WARRIOR, WEYMOUTH, WIGTOWN BAY, WINDSOR CASTLE, WOOLWICH, ZEALOUS, ZEEBRUGGE:

RNAS WWI – Cattewater Laira (Saltram Pk) – Cd 05.1918 - /Mt Batten 13.03.1917 - 04.18 to RAF/ - used by RN between wars/ Merifield Kite Balloon Sta as TS 06.1919/ RNAS Tregantle Ft 11.1917.

RN Hosp Stonehouse open 13.03.1762 – 03.1995

Pt Convoy Office closed 31.12.1918. RN to use camps at Lyneham, Glenholt, Beechwood, Blarrick (Ft Tregantle - closed 04.1956) & Kings Tamerton Sch 07.1941.

RNoN Depot – Wingfield Nursing Home, Molesworth Rd, Stoke Cd 01.07.1941

Vicarage Rd Camp, St Budeaux closed 04.1956 - WRNS at St Budeaux to DRAKE 06.1967

USN Advance Amphibious Base Cd 08.11.1943 – de-Cd 31.08.1945. USN Aux Rx Base Vicarage Gdns, St Budeaux closed 25.09.1945

Pointe Noire – Fr Equitorial Africa – BNLO closed 26.06.1945

Polegate – Sussex – RNAS 03.1916 – 03.1918 tx from Dover to Ports command 23.07.1917

Pontefract – RN Tng Unit 1944

Poole – BRIES, DAEDALUS II, DAWN, DAYSPRING, FIREFLY, FLINDERS, FLORINDA, GONDOLA QUEEN, ISLA, OP HOOP VAN ZEGERN, LADAS, MAH JONG, MTB 685, MURAENA, PALATINA, PAULINE, SONA, SPITFIRE II, TADPOLE, TURTLE, VERA, WESTWARD, WHITE OAK, YOANJO, ZEPHYR: - RNR Battery 1873. USN Advance Amphibious Base Cd 11.05.1944 – PO 07.08.1944

Pt Bannatyne – VARBEL

Pt Edgar – see Forth

Pt Ellen – RAF – Lodger 1943

Pt Talbot – DEMS Base WW II – closed by 04.07.1945

Portishead – ANTELOPE, HUSSAR

Portland – 'Conurbation' – ACHILLES, AGINCOURT, ALECTO, ALEXANDRA, ANSON, ATTACK, ATTENTIVE, BEE, BESSIER, BLACKHAWK, BLENHEIM, BOSCAWEN & II & III, BRITANNIA, CHASER, COLLINGWOOD, COLOSSUS, CYCLOPS, DAEDALUS, EREBUS, EXWEY, FERMOY, FLORINDA, FREDERICK WILLIAM, GIBRALTAR, GRASSHOPPER, HARBINGER, HAREBELL, HEATHER, HERCULES, HOLDFAST, IMPERIEUSE, KING GEORGE V, KREDEMNON, LOFOTEN, LONDON, MAEANDER, MAIDSTONE, MINOTAUR, NELSON, NETTLE, NORTHUMBERLAND, ORION, OSPREY, PITT, PURBECK, QUEEN ELIZABETH, RAME HEAD, RESEARCH, SANS PAREIL, SAPPHIRE II, SAREPTA, SCAWFELL, THAMES, TITANIA, VENERABLE, VICTORY VII & XI, VULCAN & II, WARRIOR:

RNAS by 09.1916 – 04.1918 to RAF. Seaplane base closed 18.06.1919

CF Base ann to close 26.11.1918. A/P closed 29.08.1919.

RN Radio Sta 1901 – 28. FOIC to lapse 31.07.1945

USN Advance Amphibious Base 04.1944 - De-Cd 18.06.1945

Dockyard closed 07.1959, Base closed 29.03.1996

Coast Guard: - MAEANDER 01.01.1857 -, BLENHEIM 01.02.1858-, COLOSSUS 11.06.1860 -, FREDERICK WILLIAM 01.07.1864 -, ST GEORGE 04.05.1864 (at Falmouth - Falmouth & Weymouth merge 1865), ACHILLES 01.07.1869, WARRIOR 01.04.1875, HERCULES 01.05.1881 -, NORTHUMBERLAND 13.05.1890 -, ALEXAN-

DRA 08.03.1891 -, REVENGE 18.04.1901 - 1903, SANS PAREIL 1903 – 07.1903 (re-organisation)

Portmadoc – RNO acs from EAGLET to TORCH 01.03.1942

Portsmouth ('Pompey') – 'Conurbation': - ABERFOYLE, ACCRINGTON, ACHILLES,, ACTAEON, AEOLUS, AFRICA, ALBATROSS, ALBION, ALECTO, ALEXANDRA, ALLIANCE, ALONZO, AMIABLE, AMPHITRITE, ANTELOPE, AORANGI, ARGONAUT, ARIADNE, ARIEL, ARROGANT, ASHANTI, ASIA, ATLAS, BARROSA, BELFAST, BELLEROPHON, BELLONA, BELVIDERA, BERRY HEAD, BITER, BLACK EMELLE, BLACKWOOD, BLAKE, BLANCHE, BLENHEIM, BLONDE, BRECON, BRISTOL, BRITANNIA, BRITON, CALCUTTA, CALYPSO, CAMPERDOWN, CARNACTIC, CARYSFORT, CENTAUR, CWENTURION, CERES, CFMU 1 & 3, CHAPLET, CLEOPATRA, CLINKER, CODFORD, COLLINGWOOD, CONQUEROR, CONSTANCE, CORUNNA, COUCY, COURAGEOUS, COURBET, CROSSBOW, DAEDALUS & III, DARTMOUTH, DAYDREAM, DEFENCE, DESPATCH, DEVASTATION, DIADEM, DIAMOND, DIDO, DOLPHIN & II & III, DONEGAL, DRAGONFLY, DRYDGE, DRYAD, DUKE OF WELLINGTON, DUKE OF YORK, DWARF, EDINBURGH, EFFINGHAM, ELFIN, EMELLE, EMPRESS OF RUSSIA, ENCHANTRESS, EPINAL, EREBUS, EVOLUTION, EXCELLENT & II, FALMOUTH, FIRE QUEEN, FISGARD & II-IV, FOINAVON, FORESTER, FORTE, FORTH, FOUDROYANT, FRANCES, FROBISHER, FURIOUS, GEORGE D IRVIN, GLASGOW, GRAMPUS, GRIFFIN/GRIFFON, HANNIBAL, HARDY, HAZARD, HELENA, HEPATICA, HORNET, HYACINTH, ILLUSTRIOUS, IMPLACABLE, IMMORTALITE, INFLEXIBLE, INGENIEUR MINARD, INTREPID, IOLAIRE, IRON DUKE, JAMAICA, JUNO, KELANTAN, KENT, KING GEORGE V, LANDSEER, LEDA, LEVIATHAN, LILY, LIVERPOOL, LONDONDERRY, LUCIA, LUPIN, MAGNIFICENT, MAGPIE, MAIDSTONE, MALABAR, MALAYA,, MARINER, MARLBOROUGH, MARS, MARSHAL NEY, MARSHAL SOULT, MARY, MAURITIUS, MECKLENBURG, MEDEA, MEDINA, MELAMPUS, MELISSA, MENACE, MENAI, MERCURY & II, MERLIN, MERSEY, MGB 16, MINERVA, ML, MNBDO I & II, MODESTE, MONARCH, MULL OF GALLOWAY, MURAENA, MYRTLE, NELSON, NORTHNEY & I -IV, ORESTES, ORONTES, ORPHEUS, OURAGAN, ORION, OUTLAW, PANDORA, PERSEVERANCE, PET, PHOENIX, PIGMY,PITT, PORCUPINE & II & (Stokes Bay), PRESIDENT THEODORE TISSIER, PROMETHEUS, QUEEN CHARLOTTE, QUEEN ELIZABETH, RACOON, RAME HEAD, RAMILLIES, RATTLER, REDOUBTABLE, REMNANT, RENOWN, RESOURCE, ROSEMARY, ROSS, ROYAL GEORGE, ROYALIST, RUBY, RUSSELL,, SAN ANTONIO, SEAFLOWER, SENESCHAL, SEVEN BELLS, SHEFFIELD, SHOTLEY, SIRIUS, SISKIN, SKIDDAW, SKIOLD, SNAPPER,, SOLEBAY, SOUTHWICK, SPARTIATE, SPITEFUL, STAR OF FREEDOM, STIRLING CASTLE, STORK, SUCCESS, SULTAN, SUNHILL & II, SWAN, SWIFTSURE, TABARD, TACITURN, TALENT, TALLY HO, TELEMACHUS, TEMERAIRE, TERRIBLE, TERROR, THAIS, THALIA, THAMES, TIRELESS, TITANIA, TOPAZE, TRACKER, TRAFALGAR, TREEKRONEN, TUDOR, TUSCAN, TYNE, TYRIAN, ULSTER, VANGUARD, VENERABLE, VENUS, VERNON & II & III & (M) & (RAMILLIES), VETERAN, VICTORIA AND ALBERT, VICTORIOUS, VICTORY & I-V & IX & X,VIGO, VOLAGE, VOLCANO, WAR WING, WARRIOR, WAVE, WEYMOUTH, WOODPECKER, YORK, ZEPHYR:

RNAS WWI – Gosport to 03.1918, Lee-on-Solent to 03.1918, Tipner to 03.1918 - closed 05.1919 and not required by Air Ministry 06.1919. RN Aircraft Yd Fleetlands 05.1940 – extant 1995

CF Base WWI

Camps at Stockheath (07.1941), Widley Farm(Purbrook) – unsuitable 11.1941 - & Belmont Pk (Cd 27.12.1941 as overflow RN Barracks). COPP Depot Haylinng Is closed 30.09.1945

RN Regulating Sch from Sparkwell to Ft Wallington 31.08.1946 - then to Braintree 15.09.1947

RM Gunnery Sch Eastney closed 30.006.1958

RN Hosp Haslar became Royal Hosp Haslar (Tri-Service) 1996

Prawle Point – Devon – RNAS 04.1917 – 03.1918. RN Shore Signal Sta 1923 – to CG 2359 – 01.06.1951

Predannack – RNAS from 15.12.1958 – extant 1990

Preston – Lancs – PALATINE : - RF closed 31.08.1945 – to Barrow

Prestwick - Ayr – GANNET

Puckpool – Isle of Wight – MEDINA

Pulham – Norfolk – RNAS 03.1916 - 03.1918

Purbrook – VERNON

Pwllheli – GLENDOWER

Queensferry – see Forth

Queenstown – AEOLUS, ALARM, BLACK PRINCE, BONAVENTURE, COLLEEN, EMERALD, EMPRESS OF INDIA, ENDYMION, FREDERICK WILLIAM, HAWK, HAWKE, HOOD, HOWE,

MEDUSA, MERSEY, REVENGE, ROYALIST, ST PATRICK, TRIUMPH, VIVID IV, VULCAN, WARSPITE, WOLF: - Naval estab 1806 – 02.06.1921. RNAS WW I (used by USN – not returned 05.1919). Dockyard closed 06.1921.

Coast Guard: - HAWKE 01.01.1857 -, FREDERICK WILLIAM 06.03.1865 -(to Lerwick by 31.01.1866).

Flagships: - BLACK PRINCE 1867-68, TRIUMPH 02.1890-09.1892,

Guard ships: - WARSPITE 08.1893 -, HOWE 12.1896-10.1901

Rx Sh: - HOOD 07.1910 - 03.1911

R

Rame Head – RN Radio Sta 1901-28

Ramsay – see Isle of Man

Ramsgate – CETO, FERVENT & II, HARRIER, PROVIDENCE: - RNAS 12.1914-. Office of Downs Boarding Flot in Clock Tower, Ramsgate 08.1914

Rathmullan – Donegal – RNAS to 03.1918. CG Sta 1920-22

Rattray – Aberdeenshire – MEGANSER, RATTRAY: - RNAS WW I

Reading – ROBERTSON

Redcar – CO Durham – RNAS 03.1916 – 03.1918

RED SEA – WOOLWICH

Richborough – Kent – ROBERTSON

Richmond Park – Surrey – RNAS WW I

Risley – see Warrington

Rochester – Airport – lodger 1950 – 62

Rochford – RNAS WW I - tx to War Office 03.1916

Ronaldsway – see Isle of Man

Rosneath – Dumbartonshire – LOUISBURG, MONCK, ROSENEATH: NATO POL Depot withdrawn (ann 03.1982)

Rosslare – RNR Battery 1906. Naval Base closed 28.02.1919

Rostellan – Seaplane Sta 02.1918

Rosyth – see Forth

Rothesay – ADAMANT, AL RAWDAH, ALECTO, BREDA, CYCLOPS, MONTCLARE, PORT HHX, WOODBRIDGE HAVEN: - Shore estab & berthing for 7 SM approved 11.1940 - but cancelled 03.1941

Roxborough – RNAS tx to Air Ministry 01.05.1942

RUSSIA – ALDEBARAN, ARCHANGEL, BELLATRIX, BORODINO, CYCLOPS II, FOX, GLORY & I-IV, INTREPID, IPHEGENIA, LOBSTER, PEGASUS, SPICA, STATION S, VINDICTIVE : - Murmansk Base closed 11.1919. Russian Armoured Car Sqn and Sqn 20 (Tank) tx RNAS to RM 21.11.1917. There were also Radio Sta at Archangel & Polyarnoe/ British Naval Mission at Archangel/ SBNO at Murmansk

Ryde – LAGUNA BELLE, OSBORNE – see also Motherbank

Rye – Sussex – HAIG

S

St Abb's Head – RN Shore Signal Sta 1923 - 2359 - 03.06.1951

St Anne's Head – RN Shore Signal Sta 1901-28

St Catherine's Point - RN Shore Signal Sta 1924 – 2359 - 03.06.1951

St David's Head – Pembs – GOLDCREST II: - Radio Sta closed 03.06.1943

St Eval – RAF Lodger 1940-44

ST HELENA – RM there 1920 – replaced by Military 17/18.10.1939

St Ives – RM Cliff Cdo Assault Wing to Bickleigh Nr Plym 01.02.1949

St Margaret's Bay – RN Radio Sta 1919-22

St Mawes - USN Advance Amphibious Sub Base PO 20.05.1944

St Mawgan – Cornwall – RAF - Lodger 1954-56

St Merryn – Cornwall – CURLEW, VULTURE

St Osyth – see Brightlingsea

Salcombe – IVERNIA, SALCOMBE:-_ USN Adance Ampibious Sub Base Cd 25.11.1943 - De-Cd by 15.06.1945

Salford – SALFORD

Sandbanks – Dorset -see Poole

Sandbanks – Argyll – ML Base started closing 30.10.1945 - completed 20.11.1945

SARDINIA – MADDELENA, PACINOTTI, SIDI IFNI, TALBOT: - CF Mobile Base ex Messina at Maddelena 09.43 (see 'Med')

Scapa Flow – 'Conurbation' – ALGOMA, AMBITIOUS, ASSISTANCE, BORODINO, CAMPANIA, CANNING, CHANCELLOR, CINCERIA, CITY OF YORK, CRESCENT, CYCLOPS & II, DEMETER, DILIGENCE, DUNLUCE CASTLE, EXMOUTH, FAVOUR, FULMAR, GANNET, GOURKO/GHURKO, GREENWICH, HANNIBAL, HARMONY, ICARUS, IMPERIEUSE, IMPLACABLE, IRMA, IRON DUKE, LEANDER, MAGIC CIRCLE, MAIDSTONE, MANORBIER CASTLE, MARGARET WEATHERLEY, MNBDO 1, OCEAN FISHER, PATROL, PERTHSHIRE,

PLEIADES, POMONA, PRINCESS MAY, PROSERPINE & II, PYRAMUS & II, ROBIN, ROYAL ARTHUR, ST MAGNUS, ST SUNNIVA, SANDHURST, SEABREEZE, SKIPPER, SOKOTO, SPARROWHAWK, STRANGER HEAD, STRATHDERRY, STRATHLEVEN, TERN & II, TYNE, VANDYCK, VENERABLE, VENETIA, VESTFART, VICTORIOUS & II, VINDICTIVE & II, VIOLET, VOLTAIRE, ZARIA: - AES 5 – controlled Mining, Ward Hill, S Ronaldsay, Orkney 04.1944.

RNAS WW I - Caldale (airship then Kite Balloon), Houton Bay (2 - Seaplane & Kite Balloon), Scapa Bay. Smoogroo (airfield), Stenness, Swarbacks Minn (closed 28.02.1919). RAF Barrage Balloon Camp St Mary's Holm to RN 25.04.1944.

BD Depot closed 31.10.1919. Naval Base to peace status 15.02.1920 - to be Fleet Exercise Base not war anchorage 26.07.1920 - to be Main Fleet Base 01.03.1940 - Repair Base Lyness to be reduced by 08.1945. FO Orkney became FOIC Orkney 01.11.1945. FOIC & Admiral Superintendent Orkney lapse 31.03.1946. Ann to close 08.1956

Approved to close AA TE Hoy 01.1940. Kirkwall Contraband Control ordered to close 25.01.1942.

Approved to construct TLC accom Crockness, Hoy for 384 – 06.1942.

Scarborough – RNAS 11.1915 - 03.1916 (at least). RN Radio Sta 1920-28

Scilly – RN Radio Sta 1901 -. St Mary's RNAS 05.1917 – 03.1918. A/P Sub Base established 03.1915 -Naval Base closed 06.03.1919

Seahouses – Northumberland – RNAS WWI

Seaton Carew – Co Durham - RNAS WW I

Seaview – Isle of Wight – VECTIS

Sedgeford – RNAS by 03.1916 – to RFC 05.04.1917

Selsey – CG Sta 1918 – 22

SENEGAL – FANN MELAMPUS II

Sennon Cove – CG Sta 1910-

SEYCHELLES – SANGDRAGON: - Radio Sta to be built 25.12.1914 - closed 15.07.1921

Shandon – Dunbartonshire – CRESCENT III

Shannon – see Limerick

Sheerness – see Medway

Sheffield – HALLAM

Shepton Mallet – CF Overhaul Base 08.1941 - closure approved 04.45

Shetlands – AMBITIOUS & II, AMBROSE II, BRILLIANT, CFMU 2, CYCLOPS, FOX & II, GIBRALTAR, IMPLACABLE, MINNA, PORT Y, VENERABLE : - RNR Battery Lerwick 1876 – 1906. Base Lerwick closed 13.12.1919. RNAS to RAF 04.1918. Advance Base Lerwick/Scalloway for coastal craft approved 07.1942. NOIC withdrawn 30.09.1945. AES Unst established 23.08.1957

Shoeburyness - Essex - ESSEX: - RN Shore Signal Sta 1923

Shoreham – AMENARTUS, ASTREIOD, AVEREST, EMMA, LIZARD, ROULA/ROULIA, VALHALLA

Shotley – see Harwich

Shrewsbury - Shropshire – PRESIDENT & I-II

SIERRA LEONE – Colony 1808, Independent 1961: - AFRIKANDER V, ALBATROSS, ALCA, ALFROESSA, BARBROOK & II, EDINBURGH CASTLE & II, ELAND & II, ISIS, JAMES CHAPMAN, KISSY, MAIDSTONE, MERCATOR, MOIRA, PHILOCTETES & II & III, RESOURCE, ST MINVER, SPURWING, STRATHERBRIE, TAGARIN, VINDICTIVE, WOOLWORTH: - Naval Base Freetown closed 08.11.1919 - BD party remain under Commanding Officer JAMES CHAPMAN

Sigwells – Nr Sherborne – HERON

SINGAPORE – Naval Base fell 15.02.1942 - re - entered 03.09.1945 – see MALAYA

Skeabrae - see Scapa Flow

Skegness – ROYAL ARTHUR

Skerries – CO Dublin – Radio Sta 02.1916

Skitten – RAF – Lodger 1940-41

Slindon – Sussex – RNAS WW I

Slough – Framewood Manor, accom for WRNS trainee boatwrights 07.1943

Smoogroo – see Scapa Flow

SOLOMON ISLANDS – KAHU

Somerford – KESTREL

SOUTH AFRICA - Union of S Africa 1910, SA Div RNVR formed 1913 ex Natal Naval Volunteers & Cape Naval Volunteers, S African Naval Service 01.04.1922 - separate 04.11.1932. Sovereign State 1931, SDF formed 09.10.1939, SAN Force ex RNVR(SA) and SDF 01.08.1942, SANF part of S African Defence Forces 01.05.1946. SAN formed 01.01.1951. Independence 31.05.1961.

AFRIKANDER & II-IV, ASSEGAI, BIRMINGHAM, BLOEMFONTEIN, BLUFF, BONAVENTURE, BUFFALO, CASTOR, CHAPMAN, CONGELLA, DONDIN, DONKIN, DROMMEDARIS, DURBAN, FIELD MARSHAL SMUTS, FLAMINGO, FLORA, GADFLY, GANNET, GENERAL BOTHA, GNU, GOOD HOPE, HUGO BIERMANN, HYACINTH, IMMORTELLE, INDUSTRY, INKONKOWI, KEMPENFELT, KONGONI & II, LOWESTOFT, MALAGAS, MONARCH, NUBIAN, PELICAN, PENELOPE, PIETERMARTIZBURG, PORT REX, PRESIDENT STEYN, PRETORIA, RAND, ROBBEN EILAND, SALDANA, SALISBURY, SCORPION, SERINGAPATAM, SIMONSBURG, SIMONSTOWN,

SIMOOM, SPRINGS, SWIFT, THAMES, TORPOISE, UNITIE, UNITY, WINGFIELD, YSELSTEIN:

Naval Base Cape of Good Hope 1815. Simonstown Dockyard Act 1898, complete 1910 – 02.04.1957.

Radio Sta to be built Walfish Bay, Durban 25.12.1914.

Saldanha Bay from RN to SANF 06.1944. HQ SAN Pretoria to Simonstown 06.03.1957

S Queensferry – see Forth

S Shields – see Tyne

Southampton – ALEXANDRA, ANONYMA, APOLLO, AUSTRALIA, BOADICEA, BOSCAWEN, BRILLIANT, CARMENITA, CAVALIER, COLLINGWOOD II, CRICKET, DERG, DILIGENCE, DORITA, DOROTHY, EAGLE, ELIZABETHVILLE, ENCHANTRESS, ERNE, FAIR LADY II, FORTUNA, HAPPY LASS, HECTOR, HERMIONE, INDUSTRY, INGENIEUR CACHIN, INVINCIBLE, LAGUNA BELLE, LOWENA, MAGPIE, MARYLOU, MAYFLY, MEDEA, MINERVA, NONSUCH, OLIVIA, PIKE, POLITA, PROSERPINE, RAVEN, RESOLUTION, RESOURCE II, RESOURCEFUL, RESTELVA, REVENGE, RIO GRANDE, SAFEGUARD, SHEILING, SHRAPNEL & II, SQUID, SUNHILL II, THAMES QUEEN, TRINCOMALEE, VEGA, VICTORY V, WESSEX, ZAZA, ZEALOUS, ZETLAND: - For Coastguard see Newhaven

USN Advance Amphibious Base Cd 11.05.1944 - De -Cd/vacated 12.07.1945

Southend – and Westcliff – see also Thames (Naval Control) -AMBITIOUS, COPRA, LEIGH & II, SAFEGUARD, SOUTHERN PRINCE, WESTCLIFF: - RN Shore Signal Sta 1925 – to CG 28.02.1951.

Southmead – PEMBROKE III

Southport – SIDONIA: - RN Artillery Volunteers 1880

Southwold – FORAL

Sparkwell – S Devon – RN Regulating Sch at Beechwood to 31.08.1946, then to Fareham

Speke – BLACKCAP

Spurn Point – see Essington

Stenness – see Scapa Flow

Stockton – Cleveland – PARAGON: - RN Radio Sta 1923-25

Stoke-on-Trent - see Alsager

Stonehenge – RNAS 03.1918

Stornoway – FLIRT, IOLAIRE, MANCO, MENTOR & II, VANESSA: - RNR Battery 1906

Strabane – see Machrihanish

Strangford – CO Down – RNO also known as RNO Ardglass 04.1941

Stranraer – FIREBRAND, TARA: NOIC lapse - Captain SM in charge of pt 31.07.1945

Stratford – Late RNAS to be Adty Estab – RN Experimental Factory 1918 - under PRESIDENT V

Strathbeg – Aberdeenshire – RNAS to 03.1918

Stretton – Chesshire – BLACKCAP

Studland Bay – Dorset – PURBECK

SUDAN – SUDAN: - Radio Sta closed 30.09.1919 - tx to Sudan Government

Sullum Voe – SPARROWHAWK

Sumburgh – RAF – Lodger 1941-42

Sunderland – ACTIVE, DURHAM, SATYR/STAYR, TRINCOMALEE, TYNE: DEMS Tng closed by 04.07.1945

Swansea – DRAGON, GIPSY, LONGSET, LUCIFIER, OMBRA, ST ELMO, SHIKARI & II, TAWE, VANSITTART: - A/P Closed 01.02.1919

Sydenham – see Belfast

SYRIA – RNO Tripoli withdrawn, Naval Base closed 03.1946

T

Tabert – see Limerick

Tain – RAF - Lodger 1942-44

TANGANYIKA – Protectorate 1890, Independence 1961: KILELE

Tangmere – DAEDALUS, HERON

Tarbert – Kintyre – ORCA

Tavistock - Devon – DRAKE V

Tees – LUCIA: SM base under construction 10.1918

Teignmouth – Devon – MOUNT STEWART: - RNAS ment 08.1940. RNO at Royal Hotel 02.1941

USN Advance Amphibious Base 10.1943 - 04.44 (to Weymouth).

Telscombe Cliffs – Sussex – RNAS WWI

Ternhill – RAF - Lodger to 03.04.1946

THAILAND – Port Party Bangkok withdrawn 15.10.1946

Thames – Forts – KNOCK JOHN FORT, ROUGHS FORT, SUNK HEAD FORT, TONGUE SAND FORT (Red Sands, Great Nore & Shivering Sands were Army). Forts from 12.1941 - built Gravesend and towed out by tugs – operated from Spring 1942 -. Thames Naval Control from Palace Hotel Southend to Royal Terrace 01.03.1940. A/P HQ at Tower Pier 06.1940.

Thorney Island – DAEDALUS, KESTREL

Tilbury – Essex – ABASTOR, CORNWALL, LAWSON, ST CLEMENT & I - III: - DEMS Tng Sch closed by 04.07.1945

Tipner – see Portsmouth

Tiree – DF Sta closed 10.02.1945

Tiverton – USN Stores depot 05.09.1943 – closed 12.07.1945, vacated 15.07.1945

Tobermory – Mull - BATAVIA IV, LADY BLANCHE, WESTERN ISLES

Toller – Dorset – RNAS WW I

Tollesbury – CG Sta 1920-22. Type 287 Radar Sta PO 16.12.1943

Toome – N Ireland – GANNET

Torbay – ONYX: - Naval Base closed 24.04.1919

Torquay – RNAS 03.1918 (hut and South and Haldon Piers – floatplanes) and balloon detachment from Merifield. To RAF 04.1918

Totland – CG Signal Sta 1910 –

Townhill Camp – Dunfermline – WAXWING

Townsend – Kent – Signal Sta revert to War Office 11.1956

Trecwn – RN Armament Depot opened 01.05.1940 - closed 31.07.1995

Tregantle & Withnoe – Depot RNAS 03.1918

Treligga – VULTURE II

Tresco – RNAS Nr New Grimsby 26.02.1917 – 04.1918 - tx to RAF

Trevose Head – see Padstow

Tring – AEOLUS

TRINIDAD AND TOBAGO – 1802 ceded to Britain. 31.08.1962 Independent Member of Commonwealth. 01.08.1976 Republic: - BENBOW, CORTICELLI, EILEEN II, MALABAR II, PROVIDER: - Naval Base closed 06.1919. DEMS Base closed 22.06.1945. RNVR demobilised by 05.1947

TRISTAN DA CUNHA – Annexed 1816: - ATLANTIC ISLE

Troon – Ayrshire – ALICE, DINOSAUR, TROUBADOUR: Naval Base closed 17.02.1919

Tullichewan – Dunbartonshire – SPARTIATE II, TULLICHEWAN

TUNISIA – HASDRUBAL, LARGS, VIENNA: Kite Balloon Sta Bizerta evacuated 03.1919

TURKEY – see also AEGEAN – JULIUS

Turnhouse – Midlothian – RNAS 03.1918. RAF Lodger 1942-44

Twatt – see Scapa Flow

TYNE – 'Conurbation' - ANDROMACHE, BONAVENTURE, BRILLIANT, CASTOR, CALLIOPE, CAVALIER, ELFIN, FALMOUTH, HEBE, HELICON, ILLUSTRIOUS, ISLAND PRINCE, JOSEPH STRAKER, MEDUSA, NAIAD, NORTHUMBRIA, ST GEORGE, SATELLITE, SPARROW, TOREADOR, VIVIEN, WELLESLEY & (No2): RNAS S Shields 03.1918. RNAS to be constructed 05.1942. Pt Convoy Office closed 31.12.1918. Net Defence Depot approved Hebburn 02.1943.

RF (28 ships in Northumberland Dock & 4 DD/FF Albert Edward Dock) - HQ in LST 3033 17.05.54; CO RF Tyne close, RF under Hartlepool 30.08.1955; refit office RF Tyne closed 22.03.57

US Port office De-Cd 11.09.1944

U

Upavon – RAF – Lodger 1934-35

Upper Cove – RNR Battery 1906

Upton – Dorset – RNAS WW I

USA – ASBURY, CERBERUS II & III, NIAGARA, PROVIDER, SAKER & II & III, WARATAH

US Forces in UK (& France) – Some WW I DS mentioned in text. Also USN Advance Amphibious Bases in WW II at Dartmouth, Falmouth, Milford Haven, Nore, Poole, Portland (Cd 01.05.44 - see GRASSHOPPER), Plymouth, Rosneath (see ROSENEATH), Soton, Weymouth. USN Advance Tng Bases at Appledore, with Sub Bases at Calstock, Fowey, Padstow, Penzance, St Mawes, Salcombe, Saltash, Teign,mouth. USN Advance Amphibious Maint Sub Bases at Nore & Penarth. USN Operating Base Lisahally 05.02.1942-02.09.44. USN Port offices Belfast, Hull, Leith, Loch Ewe & Newcastle-upon-Tyne. There was an Ammo Depot at Bugle. Stores Depots were at Exeter, Launceston, Ludgershall & Tiverton. Also Advance Bases Cd at Cherbourg (Cd 15.07.1944-PO 01.07.45), and on UTAH (Cd 12.07.1944) and OMAHA Beaches and at Le Havre. – see also under individual locations in Gazetteer.

Also USS ADONIS (ARL) – arrived Milford Haven 01.02.1944/ Plym 03.02.44/ France 08.06.44:

USS ATLAS (ARL) arrive Falmouth 29.03.44/ Plym 28.05.44/ France 07.06.44:

USS MELVILLE arrive Rosneath 23.03.44/ Portland 18.04.44 (see main section entry)

V

Valentia – RN Radio Sta 1921-22

Vendome – RNAS Sch 03.1918

W

Walmer – Kent - RNAS to 03.1918

Wantage – Berks – VICTORY III

Warminster – see Zeals

Warrington – Lancs – ARIEL, & II, BLACKCAP, CABBALA, GOSLING, SCOTIA

Watford – TURNSTONE, WATFORD I & II

Wellbank – Cumberland – see Bootle Station

West Ayton – Yorks – RNAS WW I

West Freugh – RAF – Lodger 1940 -43

West Hartlepool – see Hartlepool

West Howe – Underwater Launching Estab to UK Atomic Energy Authority 01.07.1959

WEST INDIES – EILEEN, LEVIATHAN, SAFETY

West Mersea - CG Sta 1919-22

West Mersham – Kent – RNAS WWI

West Raynham – RAF – Lodger 1945-46

Westhampnett – RAF – Lodger 1945

Westgate – Kent – RNAS 03.1916

Weston Park – Shropshire – GODWIT & II

Weston-Super-Mare – BIRNBECK: - RNR Div disbanded 1909

Westward Ho! – RNAS WW I

Wetherby – Yorks – CABOT, CERES, DEMETRIUS

Wexford – RNAS (Seaplanes) WW I (used by USN). Radio Sta 02.1916

Weybridge – CF Depot closed 30.09.1952

Weymss Bay HDA Sta to close 10.1944

Weymouth – see Portland

Whiddy Island – RNAS (Seaplanes) WW I – used by USN

WHITE SEA – BOMBARDIER, VINDICTIIVE

Whitehaven – DEMS Base closed 07.1945

Whitley Bay – RNAS 03.1916

Wick – RNR Battery 1906 -, CG Sta 1910 -, Naval Base closed 24.02.1919. RAF Lodger 1939-40

Windsor – PRESIDENT III: - RN Artillery Volunteers 1879

Wittering – HERON

Wittersham – Kent – RNAS WW I

Woodvale – Lancs – RINGTAIL II

Wooley Park – see Wantage

Woolston – ABATOS: - RN Store Depot to 1984

Woolwich – AIGLE, ALONZO, BATAVIER, CHARGER, DASHER, DEFENCE, DISCOVERY, FISGARD, GANYMEDE, HEBE, IPHEGENIA, JUSTITIA, LEVEN, MERCURY, MESSENGER, MONMOUTH, NARCISSUS, NYMPHE, ST FIORENZO, SALSETTE, SAMPSON, SULPHUR, TALBOT, UNICORN, VENUS, WARRIOR, WARSPITE, WYE: - RN Armament Depot to close 1959

Workington – DEMS Tng Centre closed 04.07.1945

Wormwood Scrubbs - RNAS WW I & Repair Depot 08.1917

Worthy Down – ARIEL & II, KESTREL

Wrabness – Essex – Mining Depot Manningtree 10.1918 & 1940 - close by 31.03.1965

Wraxhall – Nr Bristol – RN Aux Hosp Wraxhall Ct closed 08.05.1946

Wroughton – Aircraft Repair Yd 05.04.1972 ex RAF – closed 09.1992

Wroxham – Norfolk – Naval Base 02.1942

Y

Yarmouth – Isle of Wight – MAGPIE, MANATEE, PAULINE

Yeadon – Leeds – CERES

Yeovilton – Somerset - HERON

Ynys Y Maengwyn – MNBO II

YUGOSLAVIA – COLOMBO: -Temp CF Bases – Hvar 10.1943; Komiza (Viz) 16.10.1943-(LCH 282 to Ist 20.10.44) – 11.44; Zara 02.44

Z

ZANZIBAR – LONDON: Naval Base 1890 in exchange for Heligoland. Closed 30.09.1919. RNAS to 03.1918.

Zeals – HUMMING BIRD: - RNAS WW I